24 Jan 92: PJK told me that Irvin Ehrenpreis
read the TS. of this book for Virginia & refused
as absolutely unacceptable papers that had been
commissioned from Henry Snyder & George Rousseau.
Rousseau's, on coronations, has since been
published in BJECS, he thought,

USC paid Virginia $11,000 to publish this book.

GREENE
CENTENNIAL
STUDIES

A group of members of the first Executive Board of the American Society for Eighteenth-Century Studies, meeting at Rockford College, Illinois, in 1970. *From left to right:* Donald Greene (secretary), Louis Gottschalk (second president of the Society), James L. Clifford (third president), Peter J. Stanlis (treasurer) Charles R. Ritcheson, A. Owen Aldridge.

GREENE
CENTENNIAL
STUDIES

Essays Presented to

Donald Greene

in the Centennial Year of

the University of

Southern California

Edited by Paul J. Korshin and Robert R. Allen

UNIVERSITY PRESS OF VIRGINIA
CHARLOTTESVILLE

THE UNIVERSITY PRESS OF VIRGINIA
Copyright © 1984 by the Rector and Visitors
of the University of Virginia

First published 1984

Library of Congress Cataloging in Publication Data
Main entry under title:

Greene centennial studies.

Includes index.
1. English literature—18th century—History and
criticism—Addresses, essays, lectures. 2. Johnson,
Samuel, 1709–1784—Criticism and interpretation—
Addresses, essays, lectures. 3. Greene, Donald Johnson.
I. Greene, Donald Johnson. II. Korshin, Paul J.,
1939–   . III. Allen, Robert R., 1933–   .
PR442.G7 1984   820'.9'005   84–33519
ISBN 0–8139–1030–7

Printed in the United States of America

Contents

CONTENTS

Contents

Acknowledgments

In the long preparation of this volume, the editors have received much assistance and support from many people connected with it, commencing with that of the late James L. Clifford of Columbia University, who enthusiastically urged us forward as soon as he heard our original plans in November 1977 and whose intention to contribute to it was eclipsed by his death the following April. Generous financial support for publication has come from various parts of the University of Southern California. In particular, we are grateful for the aid of Max Schulz, formerly Chairman of the Department of English; David Malone, who was Dean of the Division of Humanities, College of Letters, Arts, and Sciences when work on *Greene Centennial Studies* began and who was later interim Dean; the late David S. Wiesen, his successor as Dean of the Division of the Humanities; and Irwin C. Lieb, Vice-President and Dean of the University's College of Letters, Arts, and Sciences. The President's Circle at the University of Southern California is one of the principal sources of funds for the volume. Finally, the staff of the University Press of Virginia merits our thanks for its considerate handling of a complicated and lengthy manuscript.

THE EDITORS

Donald Greene

Two Views

1. An Informal Sketch

Few of the contributors to this volume know very much about Donald Greene's early years, so it is best to let Don, who has long been an admirer of autobiography, speak for himself. In the last article of this festschrift, he talks of his writings in the years before he received his M.A. degree from University College of the University of London. "Like others who came to academia late—thanks, in my case, to the Great Depression and drought of the 1930s, and then World War II—I did a fair amount of pre- and nonacademic writing, chiefly in the hope of earning a few much-needed bucks." That writing, of which there is a good deal (still uncollected), related to Don's boyhood in Saskatchewan and, later, to his first career as an elementary schoolteacher in the country schools of western Canada. The fact that this career lasted for five years, from 1934 to 1939, or as long as an average graduate school training or the tenure of an assistant professor these days, shows how much he must have loved—and needed—the job, which involved teaching a mixed group of Canadian and Indian children and, afterward, high school students. Don still maintains that small children are the most rewarding to instruct and holds strong views about the need to teach basic skills to children at the earliest levels. A hint of his teaching on the Canadian prairies comes through in one of his early scholarly publications. This is a long chapter entitled "Comment and Criticism," in Hilda Neatby's critique of Canadian public education, *So Little for the Mind* (1953), where Don eloquently recalls a great many of the concerns that must have filled his hours in the mid and late thirties.

Don started college by correspondence, finally beginning his university career at the University of Saskatchewan in 1939. He took his first, general, B.A. in 1941 and his honors B.A. in 1946, but interrupted his student years for more than four years of service with the Canadian army, serving first with the Royal Canadian Artillery and later, for a time, with the paratroopers. After the war, Don completed college in just a year and, with a two-year Graduate Overseas Fellowship from the I. O. D. E.—the Imperial Order, Daughters of the Empire, the patriotic Canadian women's organization—set forth for London. Don is sentimental about the University of London and eagerly shows off its neoclassical facade and the remains of Jeremy Bentham (on days when the famous box is open). Mainly, though, University College allowed Don to read freely, widely, and independently, and to set his own standards (which were dauntingly high). He had little money and lived in modest student digs where one paid for the electricity—and the heat—by dropping shillings into a meter. Just as Don had walked to school in rural Canada, now he started to walk around London, not only the London of the West End, the museums, and the City, but the neighborhoods as well which, just after the war, still retained some of their earlier character as villages.

I remember being surprised when, living for a summer in a flat far from central London, I discovered that Don had walked through most of my neighborhood more than twenty years earlier and knew the *voisinage* intimately. Don's travels around London included virtually every place with any sort of eighteenth-century interest—the City, Twickenham, Marble Hill, Kenwood, Strawberry Hill—so that, when he came to write *The Age of Exuberance* several decades later, he had *seen* a great many of the artifacts whose importance he now undertook to describe. In the summer of 1974, this time with Jim and Virginia Clifford and Bert and Ruth Davis, Don repeated his classic eighteenth-century jaunt along the Thames west of London, from Chiswick to Strawberry Hill, with Jim Clifford, then in his early seventies, leaving the younger walkers behind in his enthusiasm for the scenery. And, of course, Don visited many of the great country houses, on whose role in history he remains something of an authority. Nor did he forget where he had been and what he had seen. Once, revisiting Strawberry Hill in 1976, Don encountered a British schoolmaster who fulminated against rich "Americans" who plundered England's artistic heritage (no doubt the man had W. S. Lewis's rescuing of Horace Walpole in mind). The man then maliciously gave Don and his guest wrong directions back to Twickenham. Don, for some reason, did not bother to lecture the helpful fellow on what *North* Americans had done to restore that very heritage and, of course, ignored the misleading directions.

When Don took his M.A. in July 1948, he did not go on at once with further graduate studies as so many scholars like him have done. He returned, instead, to his alma mater, Saskatchewan, for four years as an instructor and then a lecturer in English. His first articles, notes, and reviews are all signed from the University of Saskatchewan. Don's early scholarly writing is mostly, but not exclusively, on Johnson. One of the exceptions among those early essays, " 'Logical Structure' in Eighteenth-Century Poetry," in the 1952 volume of *Philological Quarterly,* showed (not for the first time) Don's unique ability to challenge long-accepted assumptions about eighteenth-century studies. When some enterprising publisher gathers and reprints Don's uncollected scholarly writings, this famous essay will surely occupy the first position. Don left Saskatchewan in 1952 to continue his graduate education at Columbia, just touching the period of Dwight Eisenhower's presidency of that university. Eisenhower's presence at the university had not been major, but it had its significant moments, and Don still recalls with admiration his farewell address, late in 1952, to the Columbia student body. The students, Don remembers, had been about ninety-five percent for Stevenson, and Eisenhower's speech, apparently extemporaneous, was a fine piece of irony which most of the students doubtless missed. Indeed, Don's high regard for Eisenhower long foreshadowed the by now favorable reassessment of his years in the White House.

Don's teachers at Columbia included many members of that great faculty, but those whose thought and work undoubtedly affected him the most were Allen T. Hazen, Marjorie Nicolson, and James L. Clifford. After Don's doctoral defense in the spring of 1954, as Sidney Burrell recalls, the examiners walked together across the campus from Philosophy Hall, pausing for a farewell chat before the statue of Alma Mater. Jim Clifford turned to the others and announced that he expected Don to become a significant literary scholar. It was a prophecy whose fulfillment Jim always thoroughly enjoyed. Contemporaries from that period at Columbia recall how much Don contributed to Jim's *Young Sam Johnson* (1955). Jim, in turn, helped draw Don into some of the urbane scholarly gatherings that are so numerous in the East, and Don duly became a member of The Johnsonians and, later, joined the editorial board of the Yale Edition of the Works of Samuel Johnson. Only after Jim's death, in 1978, did he resign from The Johnsonians and the editorial board, but his association with Jim's interests continued, for he compiled the index to *Dictionary Johnson* (1979), and even now continues Jim's studies, in a way, with his work on Johnson's biography after 1763. Jim was the first person to agree to contribute to this volume; he was delighted with the idea when I first mentioned it to him in November 1977. The following March, I met Jim in New York and he told me with his customary excitement that he had decided on the subject of his essay. It was to deal with Johnson's life from 16 May 1763 (the day of the advent, as it were, of Boswell) to Boswell's departure for Holland in August, for Jim had come to realize that the beginning of Boswell's personal acquaintance with Johnson did not at all mean that the "obscure middle years" had ended. It is a view that Don has long held, so perhaps it is fitting that the opening chapters of his biography of Johnson's "Boswell years" will cover the very topic that his teacher had planned to present in this festschrift.

From 1954 to 1968 Don taught at five different universities (at one of them—the University of California, Riverside—twice, from 1954 to 1958 and 1966 to 1967). These were Brandeis (1958–60), the University of New Mexico (1960–62), the University of Toronto (1962–66), and the University of Wisconsin (1967–68). Don received his first Guggenheim Fellowship in this period, a few years after leaving Columbia (1957–58); it led to his publishing *The Politics of Samuel Johnson* (1960). A second Guggenheim, in 1979–80, helped Don get started on his biography of Johnson after 1763. By the time *The Politics* appeared, Don was already acknowledged as a leading authority on Johnson and the thought and literature of his age, and ever since he has been a frequent defender of Johnson against the opinion—still sometimes heard—that sees him as a rigid political conservative. Don's scholarly eminence led to his being a contributor to almost every important collection of studies on eighteenth-century literature in the 1960s. But his scholarly travels did more—they introduced him to a network of colleagues around North America and the English-speaking world. Don's academic positions and many visiting lectures made him acquainted with numerous people working in the eighteenth-century vineyard, scholars of all ages. The younger scholars found him a ready encourager of their work (provided it was up to his standards), while the senior people found him a demanding but generous contemporary.

One of Don's trips in the sixties took him to the Second International Congress on the Enlightenment at St. Andrews, in 1967. After this conference, with the assistance of some of the leaders in the field, the late Theodore Besterman organized the beginnings of the International Society for Eighteenth-Century Studies. Don took an active part in these arrangements and, early in 1968, convinced his North American colleagues that the time had come to establish a national organization for eighteenth-century studies in North America. In the next two years, with the help of many of the scholars he had met in the previous decade and a half, he started the American Society for Eighteenth-Century Studies. Many people assisted—among them Lester Crocker, then of Case Western Reserve University, and Jim Clifford—but Don himself was responsible for the principal organizing tasks. As provisional secretary, he attended the 1968 MLA Convention in New York and personally handed out brochures to hundreds of prospective members of the infant society. And, in the young organization's first years, it was Don who had most of the ideas for making the still small group nationally significant and distinguished. Don had helped to found *Eighteenth-Century Studies* during his second term at Riverside, in 1966–67; now he persuaded its editors to make it the official journal of the society. He persuaded the editors of the annual bibliography of eighteenth-century literature that had appeared in *Philological Quarterly* since 1926 to expand the work's coverage to the entire field of eighteenth-century studies, not just English. He saw the need for a strong annual meeting and for an annual volume that would print its proceedings. He wanted a periodical newsletter, a prize for the best essay of the year in eighteenth-century studies, and many other

[xiii]

good things that go into making a learned society an important body for the advancement of scholarship. When I succeeded him in 1973 as secretary (the title was changed a few months later to executive secretary), I learned from the files that Don passed on to me that he had already thought of almost everything that I was to do in the next five years. But Don, with his usual modesty, stepped aside and let me run the organization as best I could, never failing to offer praise for accomplishments (or to criticize me and the organization when we did something that he thought careless or insensitive).

At the end of the 1960s, Don had moved again—as it happened—for the last time, becoming Leo S. Bing Professor at the University of Southern California. The generosity of Don's resources for research and other support there and the willingness of the university's central administration to listen to and approve of his proposals meant that the American Society for Eighteenth-Century Studies had a generous patron in its early years. Don, in a manner that seemed almost effortless, found it possible to run the society's office, co-sponsor meetings, support publications (including the book review section of *Eighteenth-Century Studies*, which he started and whose first editor he was), and generally to fulfill many aspirations for himself and his field of study that he had nurtured for several decades. He now had greater freedom to travel to conferences in North America and abroad, always—on whatever continent he landed—with the advancement of eighteenth-century studies in mind. In Australia, to take one example, he helped the organizers of the excellent David Nichol Smith Memorial Seminars get started, and took part in the second of these, in 1970. At this gathering, almost incidentally, he advised his Australian and New Zealand friends on starting their own society for eighteenth-century studies. Although his secretaryship of the ASECS made him an administrator of a sort, his scholarship continued with little abatement. To the late sixties and early seventies belong the revision of the bibliography of Johnsonian studies that he did with Jim Clifford, the influential *Age of Exuberance* for Random House, and his overview of Johnson's life and work in one short volume for the Twayne series. After he left the ASECS secretaryship, he finished his edition of Johnson's *Political Writings* for the Yale Edition of the Works (where it appeared, in 1977, as

Volume X). And the travels and contributions to journals and volumes of essays have continued to the present day and, no doubt, will flow on for many more years.

A scholar's chief debts usually appear in his footnotes, not his acknowledgments; thus it follows that the list of one's published writings reveals most about a person's interests. In Don's case, however, this rule is true only part of the time. His writings reveal his abiding interest in and love for Jane Austen and Evelyn Waugh, in eighteenth-century music and twentieth-century British poetry. Nor are these the efforts of a dilettante. Don's knowledge of twentieth-century poetry, for instance, is rich in discernment and instructive criticism, for he has always seen eighteenth-century poetry as immediately relevant to the practising poet today in that it offers a range of genres and styles which the force of Romanticism conspires to obscure. When he published Donald Davie's poem "Trevenen" in *Eighteenth-Century Studies* (Spring 1973), he added a note that implied this conviction very clearly. But Don's bibliography somehow fails to reveal his astounding knowledge of British culture—a knowledge that permits him to complete the *Times* crossword with the skill of a Londoner—or his pride in being a Canadian citizen. And not all of Don's scholarly contributions have appeared in print. He just never got around to preparing some of his lectures and professional papers, he told me once in the mid seventies, and so some excellent pieces have enlightened only those who happened to be in the audience at the time.

One of these pieces—an important continuation of his 1952 *Philological Quarterly* essay—was a lecture entitled "On the Continuity of English Poetry in the Eighteenth Century" which he read at the old English VIII meeting at the Modern Language Association's 1967 Convention at the Palmer House. This was one of those drowsy meetings that started at 8:30 in the morning and the MLA, in those days still an association of scholars and not yet a disorganized grab bag of pressure groups, even had coffee available outside the Monroe Room. But one of the speakers who followed Don on the program must have ignored the coffee, for she fell asleep, while smoking, during Don's paper. Suddenly she awoke with a start, her paper in flames ("It must have been highly flammable stuff," someone observed afterwards), and flung the burning paper to the floor of the stage. Don hastened over from the lectern and stamped the fire out, and all was well. But much of the paper was burned, and during her reading of what remained, the later speaker murmured, "The rest is silence." Later Don, a heavy smoker himself, did not condemn the woman's falling asleep while smoking. All he said was, "It's always best to speak first on a program."

Donald Greene's career has had many more ramifications and excellences than a short sketch like this one can possibly note. So, too, his character has many qualities that an unprofessional memoirist cannot bring out in a few pages. Perhaps Don's love of autobiography will some day lead him to write a more accurate memoir.

PAUL J. KORSHIN

2. His Intellectual Achievement

Donald Greene begins his "Augustinianism and Empiricism" with "Toward a Demythologizing." This phrase summarizes what Greene has been up to since the time of his earliest publications. It is entirely appropriate that Greene's major area of specialization has been Samuel Johnson, a man, like Greene himself, quick to question received wisdom, vigorously devoted to the destruction of apriorisms and easy generalities. Even before he began his doctoral studies at Columbia in 1952, Greene had begun his assault on the scholarly and critical fictions that were burdening eighteenth-century studies. The same year that he entered Columbia, Greene published " 'Logical Structure' in Eighteenth-Century Poetry," an exuberant demonstration that the poetry of Pope and his contemporaries is poetry at its most moving and lively, much more than versified syllogisms. This early piece was a signpost not only for our profession but also for Greene's career. A recent work, a study of Johnson's use of the term *conceit*, still expresses the same desire to discard the commonly accepted belief and to look again at the source.

Samuel Johnson's description of the aims and methods of a proper empirical approach could stand also as a description of Donald Greene's methodology. "The studies of mankind . . . are perpetually tending to error and confusion. Of the great principles of truth . . .

[xvi]

the simplicity is embarrassed by ambitious additions, or the evidence obscured by inaccurate argumentation." As much as any other scholar of our time, Greene has exposed and denounced the results of inaccurate argumentation in a wide variety of fields. And, although he has been a kind and helpful supporter of younger scholars, he has also achieved some notability for his willingness to expose those established ideas perpetuated by ambition and carelessness.

It was once said of Donald Greene that he thinks if he could correct eighteenth-century studies, he could save the world. The witticism is not far-fetched. "The systems of learning . . . must be sometimes reviewed, complications analysed into principles, and knowledge disentangled from opinion." That close inspection which "reveals the genuine shoots of consequential reasoning," that freedom and freshness which topple "the accidental prescriptions of authority," that intellectual rigor which denounces abstract speculation, broadens narrow principles and breaks the fetters of prescriptive criticism describes Greene's technique in eighteenth-century studies, and indeed, as Johnson himself would point out, indicates the way of honesty, evidence, and caution without which the world would in fact be lost.

Greene's recovery of the radical postulates of the eighteenth century and its literature has taken place in such varied fields as political, cultural, and intellectual history, biography, bibliography, and criticism. And he has illuminated our vision of Johnson, Swift, Pope, and Jane Austen, among others. It seems unnecessary to mention here the titles of his many books, articles, and reviews. How many of these have in fact radically and we suspect permanently changed our thinking about many of the most fundamental subjects: the dramatic texture of Pope's poetry, the imagistic richness of Johnson's poetry and prose, the devastating sanity of Swift's scatalogical poems. Will the Boswell industry recover from his spirited indictment of Boswell's accuracy as a biographer? His two books on Johnson's politics redefine for our century what the eighteenth century meant by Whig and Tory. Nor has Greene shrunk from the "dull duties of an editor": besides his contribution to the Yale Edition of the Works of Samuel Johnson, he has given us, with James L. Clifford, the definitive bibliography of Johnson studies.

Although Greene's work in the eighteenth century constitutes his great contribution, he has not limited his publications solely to his area of specialization. Probably few of his colleagues know that in 1951 he was awarded second prize in the "Atlantic Firsts" for "The Adjutant," a short story about the Second World War. Born in Moose Jaw, Saskatchewan, he has kept a strong interest in Canada, especially its western provinces, having written on Canadian public education, and "With Sinclair Lewis in Darkest Saskatchewan"; he has also edited Claude Lewis's journal of the Lewis trip to Manitoba and Saskatchewan. His passionate and varied interests in literature are reflected in his work on such Victorian and modern writers as Thackeray, Waugh, and Donald Davie. A "perpetual moralist," his interest in literature is one facet of a larger interest in all the humanistic disciplines, and he has manifested this with his concern for theology and psychotherapy in such articles as "The Sin of Pride" and "From Accidie to Neurosis." Indeed, Greene is neither afraid to address the common reader nor is he too solipsistic to write for the nonspecialist. But he is no mere popularizer: the clarity and approachability of works like *The Age of Exuberance* and *Samuel Johnson* never encroach on their scholarly integrity.

HARVEY D. GOLDSTEIN
JAMES W. HOWALD

GREENE
CENTENNIAL
STUDIES

Shaping the Augustan Myth

John Dryden and
the Politics of
Restoration Augustanism

MAXIMILLIAN E. NOVAK

RECENTLY, DONALD GREENE ROSE DURING A SEMINAR AT THE Clark Memorial Library to question the purpose of an upcoming meeting at the English Institute on "Augustanism." Should there not be a preliminary discussion, he asked, devoted to the question: Is there any Augustanism about which a seminar ought to be held? Such a response might be expected from a critic who has argued that the period in question was more Augustinian than Augustan and, elsewhere, that for all the logic in the arguments for calling the period from 1660 to 1800 Augustan, we might just as well use the more euphonic and equally valid term "Mesopotamian."[1] Behind Professor Greene's objections and those of Howard Weinbrot, who has spent years working on "Anti-Augustanism" during this period, is an insistence upon seeing literature in its historical contexts. If E. P. Thompson's remark on the politics of England under Walpole possessing "something of the sick quality" and configuration of a "banana republic" has any application for the rest of our period, analogies with Rome under Augustus seem patently absurd.[2]

Yet Thompson notes in passing that one of the worst rascals of the eighteenth century, Sir Francis Page, had a funeral monument placed in his church depicting himself and his wife in the form of

[1]See his review of Pat Rogers's *The Augustan Vision*, *Eighteenth-Century Studies*, 9 (1975), 128–33.

[2]*Whigs and Hunters* (New York, 1975), p. 197.

Romans reclining at a banquet. We know that such gestures were symptomatic. And if we are to understand the period, we have to examine both the myth and the reality. Even such an un-Augustan figure as Daniel Defoe will produce an *Augusta Triumphans* toward the end of his life. We have to pay attention to certain attitudes and aspirations of the period which aimed at concepts that English writers in the Restoration and eighteenth century continued to associate with ancient Rome. Perhaps the Brutan Age would be a more accurate appellation, since appeals to English liberty might call on both the Brutus who invented Roman liberty and the Brutus who was the last to defend it, but when they wanted to praise a monarch for establishing peace at home or abroad, poets writing after Dryden were likely to reach for the easiest analogy. And that was almost invariably Rome in the time of Augustus.[3] If Pope and Swift sometimes treated such comparisons ironically, we should recall Johnson's warning about the folly of judging the age through the Scriblerian view of things.

But I don't want to argue for the retention of the term *Augustan*. Inaccurate labels are as likely to produce bad results in literary history just as they do in cooking or medicine. What I want to do is to speak mainly of John Dryden as one writer during this period who, up to a point, is not merely comfortable with the notion of a new Augustan Age but who consciously attempted to develop an Augustan myth. The most important aspect of Dryden's argument lies in the pronouncement that the new age ushered in by the Restoration of Charles II will be utopian in bringing an improvement in English art and society along with a new greatness in its relations with other nations. Although one might think such an idea unoriginal enough, at the Restoration, only John Evelyn and a few others seemed willing to follow Dryden into an analogy that

---

[3] Howard Erskine-Hill argues that criticisms of various aspects of Augustus' reign did not mean that the term had entirely bad connotations. *The Craftsman*, for example, attacked Augustus for his restrictions on freedom of the press but praised him for permitting Horace to write satires. See Hill, "Augustans on Augustanism: England, 1655–1759," *Renaissance & Modern Studies* (U. of Nottingham), 2 (1967), 79–80; *The Craftsman* (London, 1731), II, 126; III, 238; V, 231; VII, 35–36. See also James Johnson, "The Meaning of Augustan," *Journal of the History of Ideas*, 19 (1958), 522, for a somewhat different viewpoint.

implied an end to English liberty. To quote Dryden's translation of Tacitus' *Annals*, "They who found their account in the Change of Government, were more willing to embrace the Present Slavery, with an assur'd prospect of Ease and Quiet, than to run the Hazard of new Dangers for the recovery of their Ancient Freedom."[4] Now it is true that, for the most part, H. T. Swedenberg and Edward Hooker were correct in arguing that from reading the poems published on the occasion of Charles II's return to England "one might conclude that all drew from a common pool of ideas."[5] After all, the limited human imagination working on such intractable subject matter is likely to produce similar imagery. But Dryden's *Astraea Redux* was the only poem that was completely consistent in suggesting that the occasion might be compared with the era established by Octavian after his victory over Marc Antony at Actium.

Other comparisons seemed to leap to poetic minds more often. Thomas Higgons, for example, thought of a different bit of Roman history:

> And when Domitian's hated Government
> The distrest World had thrown into despair,
> Trajan by Heaven was in Mercy sent,
> The Ruines of the Empire to repair.[6]

Higgons associated Augustus with Trajan as an afterthought, but that might well be lost in his comparisons of Charles to the sun, to Aeneas giving laws to Rome, and to some kind of mythic, kingly figure who was to reward merit wherever it might be found and restore the bond that ought to exist between Englishmen. Lluelyn Martin compared Charles to Camillus coming just in time to rescue Rome.[7] Sir Robert Howard thought Charles was more like Julius Caesar and compared him to the sun as did Edmund Elis, Richard Flecknoe, and Edmund Waller.[8]

[4] *The Annals and History*, trans. John Dryden et al. (London, 1697), I, 78.

[5] John Dryden, *Works*, ed. Edward Niles Hooker, H. T. Swedenberg, et al. (Berkeley, 1956—), I, 214.

[6] *A Panegyrick to the King* (London, 1660), p. 5.

[7] *To the King's Most Excellent Majesty* (London, 1660), p. 5.

[8] Howard, *A Panegyrick to the King* (London, 1660), p. 7; Elis, *Anglia Rediva*, p. 3; Flecknoe, *Heroic Portraits*, sig. B1ᵛ; Waller, *To the King upon His Majesties Happy Return* (London, [1660]), p. 1.

[3]

Charles's opportunity to become England's Sun King was enhanced by the star that had been visible at his birth, and Cowley took the opportunity to distinguish true lights from the false:

> The *foolish Lights* which *Travailers* beguile,
>   End the same night when they begin;
> No Art so far can upon *Nature* win
> As e're to *put out Stars*, or long keep *Meteors in.*
> Where's now that *Ignis Fatuus*, which erewhile
>   Misled our *wandring Isle?*
>   Where's the *Impostor Cromwell* gon?
>   Where's now that *Falling Star* his Son?
>   . . . . .
> When in the midst of this confused Night,
> *Loe*, the blest *Spirit* mov'd, and *there was Light.*[9]

Cowley, like another poet, Alexander Brome, saw in the Restoration a return of English liberty and freedom, which had been suppressed by the various governments under the Commonwealth and a return to respect for English laws.[10]

And then there were the usual typological interpretations. Charles was pictured as a new David. Sermons by Simon Ford and Francis Gregory developed this at length, and a sermon of 1650 by Edward Parry, *David Restored,* was reprinted in the year of Charles's return. Waller described Charles as Job-like in his patience, Christ-like in his forgiveness.[11] Again the star at his birth was often used to buttress this image, though it might also be used to refer to the star of Julius Caesar that was adopted by Augustus. Undoubtedly the oddest comparison was to the weapon salve that could cure wounds at a distance. The hope was that Charles II would prove a healer of England's woes, a combination of master physician and witch doctor.[12]

[9]Abraham Cowley, *Ode upon the Blessed Restoration and Returne of His Sacred Majesty, Charles the Second* (London, 1660), p. 10.

[10]Brome, *A Congratulatory Poem on the Miraculous and Glorious Return of that Unparallel'd King Charles II* (London, 1660), pp. 8, 15–17; Cowley, p. 4.

[11]Edmund Waller, *To the King upon His Majesties Happy Return* (London, [1660]), p. 7.

[12]Robert Wild, *Iter Boreale*, in *Poems on Affairs of State*, ed. George de F. Lord et al. (New Haven, 1963–75), I, 6.

When Charles died in 1685, it should have been obvious that he had fulfilled none of the prophecies made in 1660, but this fact did not prevent Dryden from writing his *Threnodia Augustalis,* extending the association between Charles and Augustus. Few followed him. Crowne praised Charles for being above the cares of politics:

> He laugh'd at Fortune, Glory, Pomp and Fame,
> And scorn'd to hunt after such Childish game:
> Who toyles for Glory, shews his Spirit low,
> For Honours only from inferiors flow.[13]

Not much in the way of Augustan greatness here. If Charles brought peace to anyone it was to himself, as Crowne suggests in a turgid image:

> A deep pacifique Ocean was thy mind,
> Where never tempest cou'd a harbour find.[14]

Durfey returned to the sun images of the early poems, describing how Charles "gave Light to every place."[15] A Sir F. F. compared Charles to Solomon in his wisdom,[16] and Edmund Arwaker praised him as the defender of the faith.[17] It should not be surprising that these last two poems were dream visions. One can only think that J. Knap's poem announcing Charles as a person almost "free from sin" ought also to have been cast in this form.[18] Compared to the poems written at the time of the Restoration, and as was suitable for elegies, there was less imagery and allusion.

Two conclusions, I think, are obvious from the positive and negative evidence in the poetry as well as from the image of Augustus in the drama: no one used the analogy between Charles and Augustus without a full awareness of the political implications of such a comparison; and, perhaps as a consequence of such political

[13]John Crowne, *A Poem on the Lamented Death of Our Late Gracious Sovereign, King Charles the II* (London, 1685), p. 8.

[14]Ibid., p. 13.

[15]Thomas Durfey, *An Elegy upon the Late Blessed Monarch King Charles II* (London, 1685), p. 2.

[16]*A Pindarick Ode on the Sacred Memory of Our Late Gracious Sovereign, King Charles II* (London, 1685), p. 2.

[17]*The Vision* (London, 1685), p. 3.

[18]*England's Sorrow for the Death of His Late Majesty King Charles* (London, 1685).

implications, there was no clear pattern suggesting that Charles might be viewed as England's Augustus. A few poems, like those of Rachel Jevon and Henry Bold, conceived of Charles's star strictly in terms of the deified Roman emperor, and the author of "Ireland's Tears" might conclude a poem by daringly declaring Charles "August."[19] But in the outpouring of poetry in praise of Charles's Restoration and in grief over his death, it remained a relatively unusual comparison. Charles was clearly a difficult man around whom myths could be shaped. He was surely no Solomon, no Moses, no Aeneas, and despite Dryden's witty effort at identifying him with David in matters of politics and sex in *Absalom and Achitophel*, Charles was plainly no David. Only Dryden in poetry and, to a lesser extent, Evelyn in prose succeeded in shaping a fairly effective and consistent image of Charles as a new Augustus.

Behind Dryden's Augustan mythologizing is a historical sense of Augustus' contribution to Roman civilization, his remaking a crude culture deeply embroiled in politics and, by taking all real power to himself, reducing it to a condition in which the arts could flourish. The implication has to be that of a progress from barbarianism to culture, from the life of the forest to that of the city. Its sources might be found in Lucretius, Vitruvius, or Hobbes, and Panofsky has shown how artists like Piero di Cosimo depicted it in visual terms.[20] Transferred to the conditions of England in the Restoration, the new age of Charles II had to shine out as superior to the past in almost every way, for in the process of finding peace the citizen must abandon his brutal freedom. The horrors of the past had been made the justification for the end of the Roman Republic, and in England they could be used to justify the prerogative of the king to dispense with laws.

[19]Jevon, *Exultationis Carmen to the Kings Most Excellent Majesty upon His Most Desired Return* (London, 1660), pp. 2–5; Bold, *Aniversary to the King* (London, 1661), p. 3; and "Ireland's Tears," *A Collection of Loyal Poems*, ed. Nathaniel Thompson (London, 1685), p. 358.

[20]See Erwin Panofsky, "The History of Man in Two Cycles of Paintings by Piero di Cosimo," *Studies in Iconology* (New York, 1962), pp. 33–67. The negative aspect of this myth may be found in Dryden's satires against the mob as those who would return to a life of savagery. For a brief discussion of this theme, see Sanford Budick, *Poetry of Civilization* (New Haven, 1974), p. 101.

In his *Panegyrick* on Charles II, John Evelyn reminded his readers of what life was like before Charles returned:

> Let us then call to mind (and yet for ever cursed be the memory of it) those dismal clouds, which lately orespread us, when we served the lusts of those immane Usurpers, greedy of power, that themselves might be under none; Cruel, that they might murther the Innocent without cause; Rich, with the publick poverty; strong, by putting the sword into the hands of furies, and prosperous by unheard of perfidie. Armies, Battails, Impeaching, Imprisonment, Arraining, Condemning, Proscribing, Plundring, Gibbets and Executions were the eloquent expressions of our miseries: There was no language then heard but of Perjury, Delusion, Hypocrisie, Heresie, Taxes, Excises, Sequestration, Decimation, and a thousand like barbarities: In summe, the solitudes were filled with noble Exiles, the Cities with rapacious Thieves, the Temples with Sacrilegious Villains; They had the spoils of Provinces, the robbing of Churches, the goods of the slain, the Stock of Pupils, the plunder of Loyal Subjects; no Testament, no State secure, and nothing escaped their cruelty and insatiable avarice.[21]

One feels like saying, "Now it couldn't have been that bad." But Evelyn needs this picture to present Charles as the returning hero, the new Jason, or Moses, the new phoenix. As Montesquieu noted on Augustus' termination of the republic, "In a free state in which sovereignty has just been usurped, whatever can establish the unlimited authority of one man is called good order, and whatever can maintain the honest liberty of the subjects is called commotion, dissension, or bad government."[22] Augustus does not make his appearance here in Evelyn's *Panegyrick*, but in his translation of Roland Freart's *A Parallel of Architecture both Ancient and Modern*, Evelyn compared his dedication of that work to Charles with Vitruvius' dedication of his work on architecture to Augustus, arguing that London was an "*Imperial* City," that the control of the seas made his empire as universal as that of the Roman emperor, and that, like Augustus, Charles would bring civilization to England:

[21]London, 1661, p. 4.
[22]*Considerations on the Causes of the Greatness of the Romans and Their Decline*, trans. David Lowenthal (New York, 1965), p. 121.

"*If such were those glorious* Hero's *of old, who first brought* Men *out* of Wildernesses *into Walled and well built* Cities, *that chased* Barbarity, *introduced* Civility, *gave Laws to* Republiques, *and to whose rare* Examples and Industry *we are accomptable for all that we posess of* useful *in the* Arts, *and that we enjoy of* benefit *to the* Publique; *how much cause have we in these* Nations *to rejoyce, that whilest Your* Majesty *pursues these Laudable* Undertakings, *that* Race *of* Demy-Gods *is not altogether extinct!*"[23] The note struck is right out of Vitruvius' dedication to Augustus. Evelyn also seemed to believe that by reforming the architecture of England, it might be possible to reform the barbaric English personality:

> It is from the asymetrie of our Buildings, want of *decorum* and proportion in our *Houses*, that the irregularity of our *humours* and *affections* may be shrewdly discern'd: But it is from His *Majesties* great *Genius*, and the choice he has made of such an *Instrument*, that we may hope to see it all reform'd; it being in so worthy an imitation of that magnificent Emperor, that touch'd with the like indignation at the *Encroachments* and *Deformities* of the publick *Edifices* and *Waies*, caused a like reformation also; so as we may now affirm of London as the *Poet* once of *Rome*,
>
> Nunc Roma est, nuper magna taberna fuit.
> [Now Rome exists, of late it was a huge shop.][24]

The central notion is that of reforming the outside, the environment, and hoping that it would eventually reform the inner character of the English, an architectural concept that later had its ethical counterpart in the public moral projects of Swift and Defoe. A facade of polite manners might disguise and perhaps gradually reform the irregularity within. Politically speaking, it was an announcement that the rough days of republican virtue were over and a time of genuine monarchy had arrived.[25]

[23]London, 1664, sig. a4.

[24]*A Parallel*, sig. B1[v]. Sir William Davenant expressed the hope that Charles would refine England's *"Civilities"* in such a way that both manners and politics would assume a new decorum. See *Poem upon his Sacred Majesties Most Happy Return to His Dominions* (London, 1660).

[25]Commenting on the reign of Augustus, Saint-Evremond remarked, "There was no more a sufficient Vertue to sustain Liberty" (*Miscellaneous Essays* [London, 1692], p. 104).

John Dryden projected a similar image, acting out, in his position as poet laureate and historiographer royal, the roles of Augustus' great propagandists, Virgil and Horace. If Pope could say that Virgil's *Aeneid* was as much a "party piece" as Dryden's *Absalom and Achitophel*, it was because he was accurately gauging the way both poets responded to the will of their masters. There was nothing unconscious in Dryden's assumption of this role. *Astraea Redux* is modeled on Virgil's fourth Eclogue with its Sibylline prophecy of a new golden age, of conquests abroad and peace at home:

> At home the hateful names of Parties cease
> And factious souls are weary'd into peace.
>   . . . . .
> The discontented now are only they
> Whose Crimes before did your Just Cause betray:
> Of those your Edicts some reclaim from sins,
> But most your Life and Blest Example wins.
> Oh happy Prince whom Heav'n hath taught the way
> By paying Vows, to have more Vows to pay!
> Oh Happy Age! Oh times like these alone
> By Fate reserv'd for great *Augustus* Throne!
> When the joint growth of Armes and Arts foreshew
> The World a Monarch, and that Monarch *You*.[26]

In *Threnodia Augustalis*, Dryden continued the theme of the Restoration as a new Augustan Age. Charles is praised for his "peaceful triumphs" even though England was shaken by domestic turmoil and foreign wars throughout his twenty-five-year reign. There was, then, a "Peace of the Augustans," to use Saintsbury's phrase, but it was all the creation of a few writers, an imaginative and utopian construct.[27]

On the other hand, the feeling that progress was being made toward civilizing England was probably real enough. By the end of the seventeenth century few men of letters could contemplate

[26]John Dryden, *Poems*, ed. James Kinsley (Oxford, 1958), I, 24.
[27]George Saintsbury, *The Peace of the Augustans* (London, 1916). The subtitle, "A Survey of Eighteenth Century Literature as a Place of Rest and Refreshment," says much about his approach as does his praise of the period's "massive common sense" (p. 379).

English society before 1660 without genuine embarrassment. In 1693 John Dennis, comparing Lord Dorset to Maecenas, the patron of Virgil and Horace, congratulated his lordship on his good fortune that "in your Lordship's time England had more good Poets, than it could boast from the Conquest to You before."[28] We should not underestimate the tremendous confidence that Dryden and other Englishmen felt in their age. In the presence of French greatness in art, war, and culture, John Dryden proclaimed the superiority of contemporary English art over that of the French, from whom he borrowed shamelessly, and over the art of England's past. He was attacked for it at the start, but by the end of the century his arguments had prevailed. And with his translations from the great Augustans in the 1680s and 1690s, which served, as Nietzsche maintained of French translations of this period, as a form of "conquest" of Rome, he passed on a living body of English Augustan literature. Dr. Johnson's famous phrase about Dryden's contribution to English poetry, "He found it brick and left it marble," was, of course, Vitruvius' praise of Augustus.[29]

The progress of English art is clearly outlined in Dryden's "To my Dear Friend Mr. Congreve," though the most famous line from that poem is Dryden's comment on "the giant race, before the flood." Ian Watt, in his discussion of Augustanism, merely points to this line to indicate the sense of inferiority felt by the poets of the Restoration.[30] But we have to be aware how, in constructing his compliment to Congreve, Dryden subtly undercuts the writers of the past while modestly underrating himself and the poets of his own generation. Given the fairy tales of our youth, our notion of giants may not be wholly favorable, but in Dryden's time they would have been associated with wickedness and impiety. In appearance they were either rough or monstrous, "men of huge stature and of fierce, wicked, cruel dispositions, such as afterwards would scale heaven if they could," as Dryden's contemporary George

---

[28]*Miscellanies in Verse and Prose* (London, 1693), sig. A4.

[29]Samuel Johnson, *Lives of the Poets*, ed. G. Birkbeck Hill (Oxford, 1905), I, 469. Cf. Vitruvius, *On Architecture*, trans. Frank Granger, Loeb Classical Library (London, 1962), p. 3.

[30]"Two Historical Aspects of the Augustan Tradition," *Studies in the Eighteenth Century*, ed. R. F. Brissenden (Canberra, 1968), p. 70.

Hughes called them.[31] Hughes also made the customary association between the giants of Genesis and those of classical mythology. In short, they were beings of great strength but formless. It is an image that may be transferred easily over to art, and Dryden proceeds after that line to establish the opposition between natural power and art:

> And thus, when *Charles* Return'd, our Empire stood.
> Like *Janus* he the stubborn soil manur'd,
> With Rules of Husbandry the rankness cur'd:
> Tam'd us to manners, when the Stage was rude;
> And boistrous *English* Wit, with Art indu'd.[32]

If the builders of the Restoration were "with want of Genius, curst," there is no indication in the poem that they were inferior craftsmen. Dryden had begun by announcing:

> WELL then; the promis'd hour is come at last;
> The present Age of Wit obscures the past.

He is stating that the proper progress of society toward greater refinement in art has finally been fulfilled. The giants who were overthrown by the Gods might still rumble underneath the earth, but their monstrous and formless strength is, for the most part, safely buried. For force and strength are insufficient for great art.

Some of the same ambiguity enters into Dryden's line "The second Temple was not like the first." Smaller and less ornamented than its predecessors, the second Temple nevertheless had a beauty of its own.[33] Speaking of the greatest gothic cathedrals of Europe, to which Solomon's first temple was sometimes compared, Evelyn criticized them as "mountains of stone, vast and gigantic buildings

---

[31]*An Analytical Exposition of the Whole First Book of Moses* (N.p., 1672), p. 22. See also Matthew Poole, *Synopsis Criticorum Aliumque S. Scripturae Interpretum* (London, 1669), I, cols. 79–80.

[32]*Poems*, II, 852.

[33]See Thomas Fuller, *A Pisgah-sight of Palestine* (London, 1650), pp. 412–18, and Samuel Lee, *The Temple of Solomon* (London, 1659), p. 368. Christian writers maintained that through its direct association with Christ, the second Temple might be regarded as spiritually superior to the first in spite of the absence of the holy relics lodged in the earlier building.

indeed, but not worthy the name of Architecture."[34] He concluded his attack on what he considered vast and shapeless structures by arguing that their strength and durability did not entitle them to real respect: " 'Tis not we see enough to build for strength alone (for so these Gothic piles we find stand their ground, and the Pyramids of *Ægypt* have outlasted all that art and labour have to shew), or indeed for bare accommodations only, without due proportion, order and beauty, and those other agreements and genuine characters of a perfect and consumate building."[35] Of course strength is necessary in a building, but it should be placed at the foundation. In Dryden's poem the artful corinthian columns are placed at the top:

> Firm *Dorique* Pillars found Your solid Base:
> The Fair Corinthian Crowns the higher Space:
> Thus all below is Strength, and all above is Grace.

Congreve's arrival on the literary scene is announced as the joining of natural strength with the artistry of the new age. In him are combined all the best qualities of his predecessors. From the "Last Age" Congreve has Jonson's "Judgment," Fletcher's "ease," and Shakespeare's genius. From the playwrights of the Restoration, Congreve inherits all that England's most brilliant age of social comedy could give him:

> In Him all Beauties of this Age we see;
> *Etherege* his Courtship, *Southern*'s Purity;
> The Satire, Wit, and Strength of Manly *Witcherly*.

Walter Jackson Bate has remarked of this, "The gentle irony, in so large a claim, is as obvious as the obsession of the period with the achievement of the past."[36] I confess to find no irony here. Certainly contemporaries saw none. One remarked:

> In Congreve Dryden's ours, to Him we owe
> The tuneful Notes which from Alexis flow:
> He chose out Congreve, and inspir'd his Flame;

---

[34]*An Account of Architecture*, in *Miscellaneous Writings* (London, 1825), p. 367.
[35]Ibid., p. 368.
[36]*The Burden of the Past* (London, 1971), p. 26.

Congreve, his best belov'd, and next in Fame:
Whose Beams the unexpecting World surprise,
As when unseen the Sun in Clouds does rise,
Then breaking through at once attracts our Eyes.
Unlike in this, no Night succeeds his Day,
But still shines with one continued Ray.
When in full Glory *Congreve* first appear'd,
We saw, we wonder'd and confest the Bard:
Dryden by thee all own these Wonders done,
Thou taught'st this Eagle to approach the Sun.[37]

In the context of the Restoration, for Congreve to have surpassed the greatness of English poets amounted to his having surpassed Dryden.

The brilliance of Dryden's poem depends in large part on its assured sense of history. Its frame of reference moves from the prehistory of the giants and early cultivation to a survey of modern playwriting. Then it switches to a discussion of the friendship among men of true ability and the concept of succession with all its contemporary political overtones of a reversal of the order of excellence in the light of the past in which the painter Romano might yield to a Raphael as in Rome a Fabius might rejoice in the success of Scipio. But in spite of the rule of Thomas Shadwell and Thomas Rymer, Dryden, assuming a prophetic role, predicts Congreve's eventual assumption of his rightful place "High on the throne of wit."

Allowing for the usual exaggeration of such compliments, that, I think, was precisely what Dryden thought at the time. Congreve's comedies embodied all that the period treasured in literary art—wit, sophistication, subtlety, and a sense of dramatic history. We can construct a Dryden who was a profound admirer of Shakespeare from the many statements he made over his lifetime, but his contemporaries considered him a detractor of the great Elizabethans. In fact he always admired their genius and force just as he was always contemptuous of their artistry. In the prologue to his revision of *Troilus and Cressida,* Dryden has Shakespeare appear as a ghost

---

[37]*The Mourning Poets* (London, 1695), p. 4. For another comparison of Congreve with Shakespeare, see Trajano Bocalini, *Secretario di Apollo: or, Letters from Apollo* (London, 1704), pp. 160–61.

whose bays are forever green and from whose being such power emerges as revives all those poets who came into contact with it:

> Untaught, unpractis'd, in a barbarous Age,
> I found not, but created first the Stage.
> And, if I drain'd no *Greek* or *Latin* store,
> 'Twas, that my own abundance gave me more.
> On foreign trade I needed not rely,
> Like fruitfull *Britain,* rich without supply.
> In this my rough-drawn Play, you shall behold
> Some Master-strokes, so manly and so bold,
> That he, who meant to alter, found 'em such,
> He shook; and thought it Sacrilege to touch.[38]

Shakespeare is holy, magical, and comparable to a force of nature. It is a splendid compliment, yet Dryden says nothing for him as a craftsman. Dryden used much the same compliment in the prologue to *The Tempest,* where he compared him first to a magnificent fruit tree nurturing other poets:

> He monarch-like gave those his subjects law;
> And is that Nature which they paint and draw.

And then to a magician:

> But Shakespeare's Magick could not copy'd be;
> Within that Circle none durst walk but he.[39]

The point about all these compliments is that they omit the question of artistry and craft. Ascribing Shakespeare's errors to his times may seem adequate enough, but in the "Dedication to the Aeneis" Dryden distinguished between two kinds of literary "Pleasures": "One conduces to the Poet's aim, the compleating of his Work; which is driving on, labouring and hast'ning in every Line: The other slackens his pace, diverts him from his Way, and locks him up like a Knight Errant in an Enchanted Castle, when he should

---

[38]*Dramatic Works,* ed. Montague Summers (London, 1932), V, 28.
[39]*Works,* X, 6.

[14]

be pursuing his first Adventure."[40] Now Dryden may not have thought the introduction of diverting "novels" into poetry, of which he is speaking here, the same as Shakespeare's magic, but the language of enchantment and of magical imagination are much the same. The distinction is between the illusions of the magician and the solid craft of the artist. Dryden thought, in fact, that the excessive use of metaphor in Shakespeare created effects that once were acceptable but no longer worked. Thus the modern artist would find that if he tried to keep the demonic critics off the way Shakespeare did, by staying within the protected magic circle of metaphor, he would be torn apart. The pose is genuinely Augustan to the extent that Horace followed the warnings of the Alexandrians and turned to artistic effects rather than to Homer's broad epic sweep.

Dryden's half compliments to Shakespeare must be compared to the full praise of Congreve as England's "best Vitruvius," with its suggestion of increasing craft and skill as the way of creating civilization. In addition, Dryden's analogy with architecture places a high value on technical skill as a necessary base for genius. And by way of analogy with the poets of Augustan Rome, perhaps Dryden is praising Congreve for incorporating the materials of his predecessors into his own work. If, as one critic has argued, the Roman's experience of reading Virgil and Horace would have to be compared to our listening to Prokofiev's *Classical Symphony*, so attending a Congreve play must have been a similar type of experience for the audience of the 1690s.[41] And this explains why his most derivative play, *The Old Batchelor*, was everyone's favorite. As one contemporary noted:

> For the Old Batchelor, without a Plot,
> Will Live, when the poor *Mourning Bride*'s forgot.[42]

[40]*Poems*, III, 1003. Dryden's stress on achievement and labor makes his concept of an Augustan Age quite distinct from a primitive ideal. For a blurring of the two "myths," see Thomas Fujimura, "John Dryden and the Myth of the Golden Age," *Papers on Language and Literature*, 11 (1975), 149–67.

[41]See J. K. Newman, *Augustus and the New Poetry*, Collection Latomus (Brussels-Berchem, 1967), LXXVIII, 306.

[42]*The Town Display'd* (London, 1701), p. 15.

Shakespeare provided little in the way of this use of learning. And while Dryden's attempt to dismiss the Elizabethans on the basis of faulty grammar and anachronism may seem unconvincing, few in the audience at the performance of the second part of the *Conquest of Granada* would have dissented from the compliment he paid his own age:

> If Love and Honour now are higher rais'd,
> Tis not the Poet, but the Age is prais'd.
> Wit's new arriv'd to a more high degree;
> Our native Language more refin'd and free.
> Our Ladies and our men now speak more wit
> In conversation, than those Poets writ.[43]

Of course, there is nothing unusual in the poets of one period thinking of themselves as superior to their predecessors. Arnold's prose writers of the indispensible eighteenth century who erred in believing they were writing poetry is evidence enough of this belief. But Dryden's remarks are a distinct echo of Horace's criticism of Ennius and Accius in the *Ars Poetica* and of Lucilius in the tenth satire of book one. In the *Defense of the Epilogue*, Dryden refers directly to this passage, in arguing that "one Age learning from another, the last (if we can suppose an equality of wit in the writers) has the advantage of knowing more, and better than the former."[44] It was to such attitudes that Swift was to address himself in *A Tale of a Tub*. But afterwards it was Pope who remarked to Spence that "it was mighty simple in Rowe to write a play now, professedly in Shakespeare's style, that is professedly in the style of a bad age."[45]

The epilogue to the second part of *The Conquest of Granada* was unusual for Dryden in its daring, to use one of Dryden's favorite words, and it brought down a barrage of objections. Dryden's usual method in prose and verse was that of disguise in which meanings might be concealed under statements that seem more ambiguous the more they are read. This is the way I have read his poem to

---

[43] *Dramatic Works*, III, 164.

[44] Ibid., p. 166.

[45] Joseph Spence, *Observations, Anecdotes and Characters of Books and Men*, ed. James M. Osborn (Oxford, 1966), I, 183.

Congreve, and while it is obvious that he indulged much more in such techniques after the Glorious Revolution, their presence raises questions about the nature of disguise in all of Dryden's poetry and of the audience that was supposed to understand his meaning. Was Dryden simply indulging in a kind of private play? In "The Dedication of the Georgics," he wrote of Virgil: "I must confess the Criticks make it one of Virgil's Beauties, that having said what he thought convenient, he always left somewhat for the imagination of his Readers to supply: That they might gratifie their fancies, by finding more in what he had written, than at first they cou'd; and think they had added to his thought, when it was all there beforehand, and he only sav'd himself the expence of words."[46] Even in his early years, when Dryden seems to have adapted what Michael McKeon calls Charles II's "court ideology" and functioned as a court propagandist, his enemies were suspicious of his sincerity in politics as they were later to question it in matters of religion. Certainly dangerous times encourage a degree of ambiguity, and having to defend the court in his role as laureate and royal historian may have left him feeling overexposed. At any rate, plays like *Troilus and Cressida* and *The Spanish Friar* are not at all clear in their political direction. Small wonder that some thought Dryden to be "the best of Rhimers and the worst of Men."[47]

In his poetry he moved in the direction of work that contained hidden meanings under relatively plain surfaces. Hence his fascination with the fable on one hand and a poetry of allusions and half echoes on the other. Although Dr. Johnson thought that Dryden's attempt to defend various lines in his plays as echoes of Virgil and Horace an example of Dryden's unwillingness to acknowledge his mistakes, the likelihood is that Dryden was indeed echoing the Roman poets; not merely in those obvious passages pointed to by Reuben Brower but in his very choice of words and rhythms.[48] What Ralph Cohen has recently argued about Pope's poetry, then,

[46] *Poems*, II, 914.
[47] British Library, Harleian MS. 2947, fol. 233.
[48] See Reuben Brower's excellent study of Dryden's use of Virgil, "Dryden's Epic Manner and Virgil," in *Essential Articles for the Study of John Dryden*, ed. H. T. Swedenberg (Hamden, Conn., 1966), pp. 466–92.

was also true of Dryden's.[49] Both wrote a poetry of disguise, though how private the audience for allusions and hidden message was to be remains a puzzle.

The answer may lie in Dryden's praise of the conversation of his time, with all the implications in the word of social intercourse and community. In the "Epistle Dedicatory" to *The Assignation*, Dryden praised the poets of Augustus' time for having an ideal community among themselves and with those leaders of the country who were part-time poets:

> Certainly the Poets of that Age enjoy'd much Happiness in the Conversation and Friendship of one another. They imitated the best way of Living, which was to pursue an innocent and inoffensive Pleasure; that which one of the Ancients called *Eruditam voluptatem*. We have, like them, our Genial Nights; where our Discourse is neither too serious, nor too light; but alwayes pleasant, and, for the most part, instructive: the raillery neither too sharp upon the present, nor too censorious on the absent; and the Cups onely such as will raise the Conversation of the Night, without disturbing the business of the Morrow.[50]

Dryden was eventually to exclude the libertine wits, like Rochester and Buckingham, from his ideal community, and they, in turn, mocked his praise of Mulgrave and a "private Virtue . . . removed from the Notion of Pomp and Vanity confin'd to a Contemplation of itself and centering on itself,"[51] but Dryden continued to support the ideal of a small social group that would form the basis of a polished literary society.

Such a concept might lead to a number of things: the Kit-Cats playing out the roles of Virgil and Horace to the Whig Junto, Pope and Burlington acting out ideals of Horatian retirement at

---

[49]"Pope's Meaning and the Strategies of Interrelation," *English Literature in the Age of Disguise*, ed. Maximillian E. Novak (Berkeley, 1977), pp. 101–30.

[50]*Dramatic Works*, III, 276. See also the anonymous author of *A Commentary upon the Present Condition of the Kingdom and Its Melioration* (N.p., 1677), p. 3, who wrote of the way time had improved England: "And farther it differently influences the nature of Mankind, that those of our generation are quite of another disposition than in former ages; The civil Conversation we now cultivate, within Four or Five hundred years, was a Military Discipline and Feats of Arms."

[51]*Dramatic Works*, IV, 83; *Poems on Affairs of State*, I, 345–47.

Chiswick; or, as the concept of conversation diffused itself through society, its praise as "the brightest and most beautiful part of life," which occurs in *Serious Reflections of Robinson Crusoe.*[52] Dryden praised the conversation not only of his small coterie but of the court and town as one of the elements that distinguished Restoration England from the past, and in this there was a general sense of self-congratulation. "If we compare them now, to what they formerly were," wrote one observer in 1683, "we shall have reason to wonder how so great a change to the better could happen in so short a time."[53] It was not only the art of the time that had improved; the audience had either followed after or brought the art along with it.

In the 1690s Dryden moved toward a different myth, idealizing the life of the private gentleman and retirement. Seeing the monarchy under William as a corruption of history rather than its providential fulfillment, he turned to praising the retreat from political life of his cousin John Driden of Chesterton, Philip Earl of Chesterfield, and Hugh Lord Clifford. Perhaps Cowley, the "English Horace," had been over such ground before, but the secret message was often quite different. In the dedication to his translation of Virgil's *Pastorals,* he refuses to compare what he calls "our miserable Age with that of Virgil."[54] The poems and plays of these years skirt outright Jacobite statements only through ambiguity, but the "politics of Nostalgia," to use Kramnick's phrase, comes through clearly enough.[55] If Pope did not need Dryden to provide him with his "terrorist" view of a public world sliding toward decay, he nevertheless had an available model in the last works of the former laureate. As his poem to Congreve demonstrates, he could still strike the optimistic tone of his early years, but, unrewarded by William III's government, he seldom had the opportunity.

I have been trying to argue that some of Dryden's attitudes were indeed consciously Augustan, whether he was trying to impose a new ideology and mythology based on the ideals of the court, advocating a civilization perfected through conversation, or writing a

[52]Daniel Defoe, *Narratives,* ed. George Aitken (London, 1895), III, 66.

[53]*The Whole Art of Converse* (London, 1683), p. 116.

[54]*Poems,* II, 871.

[55]Isaac Kramnick, *Bolingbroke and His Circle* (Cambridge, Mass., 1968), pp. 205–35.

poetry of hidden allusions and meanings. In treating the economic realities of England's sordid war with the Dutch, he consciously imposed a mythology of English unity, destiny, and greatness. One may treat the realities of the period along with the art as Ian Watt does in establishing a homology between the popularity of Virgil's *Georgics* and their English imitations and the power of the great Whig landowners.[56] I, for one, am convinced that there is such a connection. But too many other things were happening in society and literature to confine its name to one of its dullest interests. Besides, that too was a form of mythologizing.

Throughout this paper I have treated Augustanism as one of many disguises in an Age of Disguise. Dryden's position as poet laureate gave official sanction to his image of Charles as the new Augustus, although the poems I quoted at the start constitute a body of competing mythologies. Yet from Dryden to Fielding the more encompassing image for the time has to involve deception and disguise, and the realization that, at a time when masquerades were so popular, the most effective disguise was the face and costume of daily life. As one playwright told his audience,

> of your real Shapes you're all afraid
> And the whole World is one Great Masquerade.[57]

Augustanism should be considered an important disguise for the time, as well as a serious form of play, engaging some of the best minds of the period. In arguing this particular position, I am in some disagreement with Howard Weinbrot's very able demolition of Augustanism as a descriptive term for life and letters in the Restoration and early eighteenth century. Demonstrating that almost every facet of Rome's Augustan Age came under attack during the seventeenth and eighteenth centuries, he has rightly shown that there was no thoughtless acceptance of parallels with a period signifying the end of the Republic.[58] Nevertheless the statue of Charles

---

[56] *Two Historical Aspects*, p. 86.

[57] Charles Johnson, *The Masquerade* (London, 1719), p. [xii].

[58] *Augustus Caesar in "Augustan" England* (Princeton, 1978), especially pp. 3–80. Weinbrot argues that although Augustus was "infinitely adaptable" as a symbol, for all but those entirely committed to the monarchy, "to be politically Augustan was to be politically bad."

II at Windsor looks very Augustan, and in spite of some sneering references to the subservience of poets in the court of Augustus, Dryden was capable of striking an Augustan pose whenever he found it useful.[59]

For if Augustanism could be a masquerade, it might also be a conscious program. Just as Augustus had taken all power to himself under the pretense of being a mere consul, so Charles II had gradually expanded his power under a disguise of negligence. A new London rose from the ashes of the medieval city, and a new type of poetry under Dryden. If writers of the mid eighteenth century— Hume, Warton, Goldsmith—refused to recognize in the libertinism of life and art under Charles II the refinement of taste they associated with Augustanism, it was, in part, because the program of reforming English poetry and civilization had been so thoroughly successful.

[59]Weinbrot points to Dryden's criticism of Augustus and his court poets in his "Preface to Ovid's Epistles" and in *A Discourse concerning the Original and Progress of Satire*, but the first was written in 1680, a time when Dryden was somewhat uncomfortable with his identification with the court, and the second in 1693, when Dryden was a critic of the reign of William III. See Weinbrot, pp. 63–64, 75; and Dryden, *Of Dramatic Poesy and other Critical Essays*, ed. George Watson (London, 1962), I, 263–67, II, 134–35.

Barrow, Stillingfleet, and Tillotson on the Truth of Scripture

GERARD REEDY, S.J.

1

IN THE SECOND HALF OF THE SEVENTEENTH CENTURY IN ENG-
land, certain epistemological questions were being posed systematically for the first time concerning the truth of Scripture. How
do we know that Scripture is the word of God? Is such knowledge
true "knowledge," in conformity with the use and end of reason as
known in natural philosophy? Or is this a question of "faith" or
"belief," subjective acts that can be made because we trust in the
authority of the scriptural authors? How can such belief be called
"rational"? Is Christianity, based on Scripture alone, a rational
religion, or must we divorce it from all other codes of human learning because it builds on entirely different epistemological premises
from theirs?

In *Leviathan* (1651) Thomas Hobbes enunciated at least one state
of the question. For Hobbes, the difficulty in ascertaining the truth
of Scripture occurs because men have improperly named their acts
of religion:

> It is a question much disputed between the divers sects of Christian
> Religion, *From whence the Scriptures derive their Authority;* which question
> is also propounded sometimes in other terms, as *How wee know them
> to be the Word of God, or, Why wee beleeve them to be so:* And the difficulty
> of resolving it, ariseth chiefly from the impropernesse of the words

The research and writing of this essay have been greatly helped by the access I
was generously afforded to the collections of The Union Theological Seminary of
New York.

[22]

wherein the question it self is couched. For it is beleeved on all hands, that the first and original *Authour* of them all is God; and consequently the question disputed, is not that. Again, it is manifest, that none can know they are Gods Word, (though all true Christians believe it,) but those to whom God himself hath revealed it supernaturally; and therefore the question is not rightly moved, of our *Knowledge* of it. Lastly, when the question is propounded of our *Beleefe*; because some are moved to beleeve for one, and for others for other reasons, there can be rendred no one general answer for them all.[1]

We cannot know the Scripture is God's word; we can only believe it. Whereas knowledge and truth in *Leviathan* are the products of Hobbes's rather narrow, mathematical view of reason as "reckoning," belief is only the result of "trust" in a scriptural author's veracity.[2] Belief looks to the source of a scriptural statement, reason to its contents.

Using Hobbes's categories as a base, chronologically the earliest I will treat in this essay, we may see that thought on the truth of Scripture moved in at least two directions in the second half of the seventeenth century. The first direction we may accurately call "rationalism," because of the stringent rational analysis to which it subjected the contents of Scripture. Thus in Spinoza's *Tractatus theologico-politicus*, translated into English in 1689 from the Latin work of 1670, a strikingly inductive method of reading Scripture was proposed. With Richard Simon, the French Oratorian and his contemporary, Spinoza was the father of modern biblical criticism. Spinoza wanted to read Scripture on its own terms, not as the illustration of some preconceived set of dogmas. For him "the method of interpreting Scripture does not widely differ from the method of interpreting nature—in fact, it is almost the same."[3] Spinoza generally subordinated doctrine in Scripture to its morality. He wrote

---

[1]*Leviathan*, ed. C. B. MacPherson (Baltimore, 1968), p. 425.

[2]Ibid., pp. 111, 132–33. It was apparently common in the seventeenth century to distinguish between faith in a person, or testimony, and faith in statements. Hobbes writes that the former is at stake in scriptural faith; Barrow and Tillotson, as I shall show, accept the distinction between the two types of faith but argue that faith in Scripture involves the latter.

[3]*The Chief Works of Benedict de Spinoza: A Theologico-Political Treatise and A Political Treatise*, trans. R. H. M. Elwes (New York, 1951), p. 99.

that "faith does not demand that dogmas should be true as that they should be pious." Scripture "very often treats of matters which cannot be deduced from principles known to reason."[4] The end result of Spinoza's methodology was to make Scripture a historical curiosity, except for its moral teaching. Dogmas in Scripture suggested, to Spinoza, a lack of freedom of thought; religious persecution would inevitably follow, to ensure uniformity of doctrine.

Spinoza was revolutionary in suggesting that in ascertaining the truth of Scripture we should look first not at the authority with which it is written but at its contents. He differed from Hobbes in his stress on the knowledge we gain from looking at Scripture with an impartial eye. He resembled Hobbes in that he regarded the divine authority of Scripture as something not by itself open to human reason; that is, the excellence of the contents leads to our belief in the divinity of authorship. I call this option *rationalism* because in it the truth of Scripture only becomes apparent when it can be seen to concur with the truths of reason and experience.

In 1696, at the end of the period I deal with here, John Toland reiterated the rationalist position, toward which I presume many more thinking men were moving throughout the Restoration. In *Christianity Not Mysterious*, Toland wrote, against the practice of more orthodox theologians, that "the Order of Nature is in your Systems of Divinity quite inverted. They prove the Authority and Perfection, before they teach the Contents of Scripture; Whereas the first is in great measure known by the last."[5] To put the theory of Spinoza and Toland into Hobbesian terms: truth and knowledge are categories that can be verified in Scripture, but only in those places where its contents can be seen to conform with the findings of natural reason.

A second direction toward theories of how Scripture can be true was charted by a group we now call "Anglican rationalists," especially Isaac Barrow (1630–77), Edward Stillingfleet (1635–99), and John Tillotson (1630–94), three theologians who knew one another and profited from one another's work. I would like to show that these theologians reaffirmed the traditional view that the entirety

[4]Ibid., pp. 185, 100.
[5]*Christianity Not Mysterious* (London, 1696), p. xxvii.

of Scripture may be talked about in terms of knowledge and truth; that, for Stillingfleet, even the argument from authority was self-consciously stated in rational terms; and that Barrow and Tillotson, reiterating the rational argument from authority and testimony, also effected a compromise with fully rationalist critics by stressing the rationality even of the contents of Scripture.

To follow the thought of Anglican rationalism about the truth of Scripture, one should stress that their working methodology was fundamentally different from that proposed by Spinoza and Toland. Barrow, Stillingfleet, and Tillotson never asserted that the truth of Scripture is a function of the agreement of this or that scriptural doctrine with natural reason. The only scriptural doctrine that can and—Tillotson said—*must* be reached by reason unaided by revelation is the existence of God—and this for reasons clearly spelled out and applicable in this case only. The rest of scriptural truth rested, for these theologians, on a complex of evidences; to call Anglican rationalism a rationalism does not imply that its practitioners claimed to prove by reason each of the truths of Anglican Christianity. These theologians were rationalist only in their assertion that Christianity as a whole is reasonable. Individual doctrines are true because the foundations of Christianity are clear and reasonable; that is, they can be believed without compromise by an intelligent and well-meaning person.

The history of Anglican rationalism, a very great chapter in Anglican theology, remains to be written.[6] It has been too easy in the past for commentators to pull a passage extolling reason—especially from Tillotson—out of its context and to suggest that he and others believed reason to be a religious guide superior to revelation. On the contrary, these Anglican theologians were always and explicitly aware that the core contents of Christianity, the Trinity and the divinity of Jesus, are above the reach of reason. In the 1690s the unified opposition to the anti-Trinitarians of Stillingfleet and Tillotson made this position clear; but even earlier

[6]Secondary sources on Anglican rationalism include: Phillip Harth, *Swift and Anglican Rationalism* (Chicago, 1961), Ch. 2, and Irène Simon, *Three Restoration Divines* (Paris, 1967), pp. 75–148. H. R. McAdoo treats the same authors under the title "latitudinarian"; see *The Spirit of Anglicanism: A Survey of Anglican Theological Method in the Seventeenth Century* (London, 1965), Chs. 5–6.

writings showed evidence of their concern about carrying reason too far and usurping the function of revelation.

The Anglican rationalists argued the truth of Scripture both from the authority with which it is written and from its contents. In contrast to Hobbes, they considered both arguments sufficient to provide not only belief but true knowledge. Explicitly disagreeing with the Hobbesian split between faith and reason, Barrow and Tillotson insisted that faith is a cognitive act. Barrow, for example, wrote that "faith doth involve knowledge, knowledge of most worthy and important truths, knowledge peculiar and not otherwise attainable, knowledge in way of great evidence and assurance."[7] Both theologians stressed that faith is a persuasion and showed that it is part of a continuum of other persuasions, based on various types of different evidences. As Tillotson wrote, "Faith is a persuasion of the mind concerning anything; concerning the truth of any Proposition; concerning the existence, or futurition, or lawfulness, or convenience, or possibility, or goodness of anything, or the contrary; or concerning the credit of a person, or the contrary."[8]

Tillotson went on to list four causes for such persuasion: sense, experience, necessary or plausible reason, and authority or testimony. Religious faith may involve any of these four evidences. For example, seventeenth-century Anglicans denied the Roman Catholic doctrine of transubstantiation because they alleged that it violated the knowledge, from the senses, that bread remained bread; they believed in the existence of God because it could be proved necessary by reason. Although Barrow, Stillingfleet, and Tillotson agreed that the evidence of testimony is essential to the truth of Scripture, they also insisted that such evidence is rational, that is, comparable to the evidence in which we take many things to be true. It was essential to their project of a rational Christianity to underscore the continuity of the cognitive acts involved in perceiving both natural and supernatural realities.

---

[7] Isaac Barrow, *Theological Works,* ed. Alexander Napier (Cambridge, 1859), V, 39. Subsequent quotations of Barrow will be from this edition—hereafter referred to as *TW* and followed by volume and page numbers, in parentheses in the text.

[8] John Tillotson, *Works,* 2d ed., ed. Ralph Barker (London, 1717), II, 428. Unless otherwise noted, subsequent quotation will be from this edition—hereafter referred to as *W* and followed by volume and page numbers, in parentheses in the text.

In contrast to the Hobbesian premise that scriptural faith is personal trust, Barrow denied that the primary object of faith is personal: "The phrase believing a man, or a tree (taken properly, or excluding figures) is altogether insignificant and unintelligible: indeed to believe, πιστευειν, is the effect του πεπεισθαι, of a persuasive argument, and the result of ratiocination" (*TW*, V, 115–16). The faith that justifies a believer "doth relate only to propositions revealed by God" (*TW*, V, 131), not to the person of God. Barrow conceived of only two intellectual operations in this context: simple apprehension (perceiving single objects) and persuasion (being convinced of something by demonstration). To make faith a simple apprehension somehow denigrated it for Barrow. To make it a persuasion heightened its value for him because religious faith then takes its place at the side of knowledge we gain from reasoned conclusions about historical, social, physical, and moral nature— even though he maintained always, as did Stillingfleet and Tillotson, that faith involves only moral certitude. Barrow's insistence that a person cannot be the primary object of faith may seem strange today; it goes against the grain of the personalist philosophy that grounds much contemporary theology. Barrow was not of course writing against some protopersonalism; he wanted to cope with the Hobbesian premise that faith, as trust, is an inferior form of knowledge.

2

In *Origines Sacrae* (1662), the first major work of theology in the English Restoration, Edward Stillingfleet announced his opposition to those who maintain "the inconsistency of the belief of the Scriptures with the principles of reason."[9] The book was written inside the context of belief-as-knowledge that had been negatively defined by Hobbes and, presumably, other mid-century speculative thinkers on religious questions. Stillingfleet discussed at great length in *Origines Sacrae* the rationality of the argument from authority as to the truth of Scripture (Book II) and of the argument from at least

[9]*Origines Sacrae*, 3d ed. (London, 1666), sig. b2ᵛ. All references to *Origines Sacrae*, unless otherwise noted, will be to this edition; page references will be given in parentheses in the text.

some of the contents of the histories and doctrines of Scripture. *Origines Sacrae* was written when its author was thirty years old; though showy in its display of lore and too sure of itself, the book did set the direction of rational theology that would dominate theological inquiry in the Restoration.

Stillingfleet devoted much of Book II of *Origines Sacrae* to Moses, who is proved to be the author of the Pentateuch and to be writing with divine authority—that is, truthfully. With no knowledge of the critical method a scientific scholar like Richard Simon would later develop to prove Moses' authorship, Stillingfleet relied on the universal consent of judicious men and the fact that a commonwealth had been founded on Moses' writings to prove his authorship (pp. 113–18). An intermediate argument showed that Moses, because of his Egyptian education, possessed enough learning to deal with the many fields of human knowledge discussed in the Pentateuch (pp. 119–34).

For Stillingfleet, "the *rational evidence* of that *divine authority* whereby *Moses* acted" is given in "that *divine power* which appeared in *his actions*," that is, in his miracles (p. 139). To God alone belongs the power to change the course of nature; if a man possesses this power, he shows himself accredited by God and therefore is to be believed when he writes or speaks. Stillingfleet set up various rational checks on this model of doctrine proved by miracles: we are only to expect miracles, for example, when the agent of them has some extraordinary service to perform or when the content of his message repeals some previous law held to be of divine origin (p. 142). Stillingfleet wrote: "What convictions there can be to any sober mind concerning the *Divine authority* in any person without such a *power* of *miracles* going along with him, when he is to deliver some *new Doctrine* to the world to be believed, I confess I cannot understand" (p. 143).

Herein we find the standard Restoration argument from authority for the truth of Scripture. God always speaks the truth; a human author—Moses, the prophets, or the apostles—proves that he speaks the truth when he shows that he is from God; the preeminent way of his showing this authenticity is by miracles performed. We should note that in this argument, surely the most frequently relied upon in Restoration theology to prove Scripture true, no mention was

[28]

made of content. The argument does not work from the wisdom, justice, or rationality of scriptural sayings. It only seeks rationally to undergird scriptural authors. Throughout, Stillingfleet proceeded by way of "common sense";[10] he says that the proofs for matters like Moses' authorship and authority provide the same sort of certainty that we possess, for example, for the existence of Archimedes and Euclid's authorship of the geometry attributed to him (p. 111).

Using Tillotson's categories, we may understand the faith or persuasion of the truth of Moses' authorship to be based on the evidence of reason and experience, the sort of evidence rational men usually accept in historical matters. The proof for the truth of the Pentateuch, that its author worked miracles, is much more of a problem. Stillingfleet probably assumed that it rests also on reason and experience. Yet the proof seems hopelessly circular. Moses is dependable because of his miracles, which men traditionally accept as proof of divine authority; yet the occurrence of the miracles—their very historicity—is accepted because Moses says that they occurred. Moses' authority is both the proof and what is to be proved. I have been unable to find a rigorous critique of this argument—though Barrow and Tillotson come close to one—in any of the Anglican theology of the period.

The third book of *Origines Sacrae* doubles back over ground already covered. There Stillingfleet proves the truth of Moses' writings from rational and historical evidence pertaining not to their authorship but their contents. Stillingfleet first sets out to prove from reason the existence of God—which Moses had assumed—"for those whose *minds* are so *coy* and *squeamish* as to any thing of *Divine Revelation*" (p. 367). The Cartesian and other arguments used for deducing the existence of God and the immortality of the soul and the historical, philological, and geological data assembled concerning Adam and Eve, the deluge, and the multiplication of the nations—the validity of these arguments need not concern us. Liberal theologians of every

[10]For an analysis of this aspect of Stillingfleet's thought, see Robert Todd Carroll, *The Common-Sense Philosophy of Religion of Bishop Edward Stillingfleet, 1635–1699* (The Hague, 1975). Carroll has a brief, helpful description of "reasonable faith" in Stillingfleet (pp. 67–70).

generation use what they can of contemporary science and philosophy in their arguments; succeeding ages invariably find them, as we find Stillingfleet, credulous and uncritical.[11]

What is important is the relationship Stillingfleet sets up between Books II and III of *Origines Sacrae,* between the arguments about authorship and content. First, as I have quoted him, he clearly considers the latter as icing on the cake; the truth of Moses' writing as a whole he has already proved in Book II, but arguments about content are added for the coy and squeamish. Second, in both books Stillingfleet prepares the way for specifically Christian "revelation," used in a technical sense, as matters "such as it had been impossible for the *minds* of *men* to reach, had they not been immediately discovered by *God* himself" (p. 600).

The proof for these matters seems to be twofold. The writers of the New Testament, having performed miracles, are thereby trustworthy. Also, Stillingfleet considers the existence of God and the immortality of the soul—matters assumed by Moses—as the basis of all future revelation: "from the general *principles* of the *existence* of *God* and *immortality* of the *soul,* we have deduced by clear and evident *reason* the *necessity* of some particular *Divine Revelation,* as the *Standard* and *measure* of *Religion*" (p. 362). If God exists and man is immortal, that is, destined for him, man must know something more of his goal and how to get there. There is a kind of rational necessity for the Scriptures, which give us the story of man's attempts—sin and repentance—and God's standard—the law of Moses and the gospel of Jesus. In the last chapter, "The Excellence of the Scriptures," Stillingfleet shows how they are the "fullest *Instrument*" (p. 609) of the present and future state of the soul. This rational argument, that the Scriptures are a necessary consequence of first principles, becomes a standard topos in Restoration theology. We already know the Scriptures are true from the authority of its authors; reason also shows us how they are necessary.

In its interweaving of arguments from authority and contents, *Origines Sacrae* is difficult reading. In Book III especially, certain

[11]Stillingfleet himself, in the last years of his life, revised *Origines Sacrae* and changed his mind about the value of a Cartesian proof for God's existence that he had used in the first *Origines Sacrae.* See Stillingfleet's *Works* (London, 1709), II, sigs. L3^v–M2^r (sep. pag., 80–85).

passages seem to strike a discord in the careful harmony between rational authority and contents that Stillingfleet intends. He argues at one point that "the greatest evidence we can have of the truth of a thing, is, a clear and distinct perception of it in our minds" (p. 396). This Cartesian dictum seems to slight the argument from authority. Yet Stillingfleet later writes that some doctrines "may be *unsearchable* to our *reason*, as to the particular manner of them" (p. 611). Do we not then possess them with the "greatest evidence"? To answer this, we must look to context: in the first instance the author refers to the existence of God, true because Moses assumed it and also susceptible to tightly rational proof. In the second instance the Trinity and the divinity of Jesus are discussed, doctrines that are believed solely on the authority of Scripture. In his excitement over applying philosophical norms to Scriptural truths, Stillingfleet did, admittedly, overstate. As is the case with any such rationalistic sentences in Restoration theology, we must read them in the context of a full work or a writer's full theology.

3

In their many sermons, Barrow and Tillotson reiterate the main arguments of *Origines Sacrae*; they are in full agreement with Stillingfleet, for example, on the priority of the argument from authority for the truth of Scripture. As Tillotson says, the "Miracles . . . which *Moses* and the *Prophets*, and the *Apostles* wrought, were Testimonies from Heaven, that they were Divine Persons, and that what they said was to be credited" (*W*, II, 448). When I stress the argument from content, in the following, in the writings of Barrow and Tillotson, I do not mean to say that Stillingfleet does not argue this way; in the last chapter of *Origines Sacrae* he does, and continues to do so in later works.

Still, the whole of Barrow's and Tillotson's writing, compared with the whole of Stillingfleet's, enunciates the rationality of content in a more programmatic way. Stillingfleet is in fact a theologian and historian of great variety; Barrow and Tillotson devoted themselves more narrowly to that greatest of Restoration topics, the rational grounds for the Christian religion. As Barrow writes, "We profess to be persuaded in our minds, concerning the truth of the propositions annexed [some of the first principles of Christianity], not implying our persuasion to be grounded upon only one kind of reason, that drawn from authority; but rather involving all reasons proper and effectual for the persuasion of all the points jointly, or of each singly taken" (*TW*, VII, 19). Again we find disagreement with the Hobbesian premise that only belief in authority can undergird the truths of religion in Scripture.

For Barrow and Tillotson, the only doctrine that rests solely on the evidence of reason, unaided by revelation, is the existence of God. Both theologians are aware that the argument from authority may be circular. Thus Barrow: "How can we believe that God doth this or that . . . before we believe that he is?" (*TW*, VII, 21). Tillotson also writes: "A Divine Revelation cannot possibly be an Argument inducing me to believe the Existence of a God; . . . before I can be persuaded that any Revelation is from God, I must be persuaded there is a God" (*W*, II, 433). In their sermons Barrow and Tillotson move at great length through the traditional rational arguments for God's existence and his concurrent truth and power. The various traditions of natural theology flow together easily in their writings; they are very careful to establish grounds for firm assent, even as we do not find originality in them on this point.[12]

Both theologians also provide traditional arguments for two other related principles of natural religion, the immortality of the soul and the certainty of a future state. Before he gives these arguments, however, Tillotson admits that they are not essential. Once a veracious God is proved to exist, one can easily accept the testimony and authority of God in Scripture as a proof for immortality and a future state (*W*, II, 433). Rational arguments on these points are, as for Stillingfleet on God's existence, icing on the cake of rational religion, helpful for those who psychologically need them but not essential.

The three foregoing doctrines of natural religion, while necessary to Christianity, do not yet make a man a Christian. What of specifically Christian doctrines? Can these be rationally proved from content, as we already have sufficient grounds to believe them

---

[12]See, for example, Barrow's sermons on "the being of God" proved from "the frame of the world," "the frame of human nature," "universal consent," and "supernatural effects" (*TW*, V, 181–289) and Tillotson's sermon on the "truth" of God" (*W*, I, 653–60).

from the testimony of the veracious God in Scripture? Tillotson establishes one rational guideline. No revelation can be true that contradicts our fundamental notions of God: that he is good, for example, or that he seeks our well-being. Thus, "if any thing should be offer'd to me as a Revelation from God, which plainly contradicts those natural Notions which I have of him, I must necessarily reject it, yea tho' it were back'd with a Miracle; because no Man can at the same time believe that there is a God of such and such Perfections, and entertain any thing as from him, which evidently contradicts those Perfections" (*W*, II, 526–27).

Because such a methodological directive seems to retreat from the use of miracles as a rational argument for the truth of revelation, some explanation is necessary. We may first note that when Tillotson writes this way he invariably gives as examples of what he is talking about the truths of natural religion, truths that lie much closer than many in revelation to first principles. He does not intend us to take the Trinity, for example, and compare it, to establish its truth, with our "natural Notions"; in the 1690s Tillotson in fact spent time and effort combatting those who would do precisely this.

Secondly, I have discussed the rational theology of the Restoration from the point of view of the Hobbesian and rationalist position on faith and belief which the Anglican theologians rebutted. There are at least two other contexts that may be involved when Tillotson warns us about new revelation: the left, of dissenting sects, and the right, of Roman Catholicism. When Tillotson uses the word *revelation*, he writes with an eye to the living, prophesying spirit of the sects and the potentiality of "new" doctrine in Roman Catholic claims of infallibility. Should the left or right produce new revelation, even confirmed by miracles, Tillotson discourages belief in it and them, unless the doctrines newly offered conform to what the human mind, informed by Scripture, already knows to be true. Unfortunately, it is difficult to date many Restoration sermons; we do not always know Tillotson's exact contexts. Denominational apologetics better explain his role about revelation contradicting "natural Notions" than does the generic context of revelation and reason that I have been delineating.

In their discussions of rational content in Scripture entailing specifically Christian doctrines, Barrow and Tillotson have one overriding guideline: that once "divine revelation" is proved—that there is a God and that he has revealed himself in Scripture—it is churlish to examine every doctrine in an impartial way. Tillotson writes: "Every man who believes the H. *Scriptures* to be a truly *Divine* Revelation, does implicitely believe a great part of the *Prophetical Books* of Scripture, and several obscure expressions in those Books, though he do not particularly understand the meaning of all the Predictions and expressions contained in them."[13] Anglican rationalism is primarily interested in proving the fundamentals of Christianity; although it frequently discusses the reasonableness of this or that particular doctrine, it refuses to consider itself bound to cover the whole field.[14]

Barrow is especially strong on this point. Drawing on his background in mathematics, he insists that theological methodology, in certain respects, does not greatly differ from that in science, even if the first principles of each may rest on different evidences:

> The principles of any science being either demonstrated out of some higher science, or evidenced by fit experiments to common sense; and being thence granted and received, it is afterward unlawful and absurd to challenge the conclusions collected from them; so if it have been proved and acknowledged, that our principles are true; (for instance, that God is perfectly veracious; and that Christian Religion hath his authority, or attestation to it) it will then be a part of absurd levity and inconsistency to question any particular proposition evidently contained therein. [*TW*, V, 399–400][15]

[13]*Sermon Concerning the Unity of the Divine Nature* (London, 1693), pp. 18–19.

[14]See, for example, Barrow's discussion of the individual doctrines of the Trinity (*TW*, IV, 492–523) and the Resurrection (*TW*, VI, 338–89), revealed doctrines in the technical sense, as above reason; by his discussion Barrow shows that they do not contradict it.

[15]Here as elsewhere Barrow likes to compare theology favorably with science. The difference seems to be that the first principles of science are proved by evidence of sense and reason, while those of theology by a less rigorous concept of reason and by testimony—but never by sense, God and the soul being spiritual. Barrow writes that God "hath not made the objects of faith conspicuous to sense, nor the propositions thereof demonstrable by reason, like theorems of geometry" (*TW*, V, 77). After the first principles of each are proved, there appears to be a congruence of method in secondary principles following from first. If the first principles of theology were necessary truths, like those of geometry, faith would lose its character as a free act.

An infidel is free to examine impartially, he concludes, but it is "vain and inconstant" for a Christian to do so. In fact, he thereby "renounces the whole, and subverts the foundation of his faith; at least ceases thereby to be a steady Christian" (*TW*, V, 400).

Thus though a Christian certainly has rational grounds for being so—this is the great theme of much of the writing of Barrow and Tillotson—he does not return to first principles when he tries to understand the individual doctrines of his religion. The authority of Scripture, which holds them, can be rationally proved; the general doctrine of divine revelation can also be shown to be reasonable. These generic proofs should suffice for firm rational assent to individual doctrines.

Nor does the Christian begin from a psychological zero. The strong point of Anglican rationalism does not lie in its theory of grace. Yet both Barrow and Tillotson assume a firm foundation of divine activity in their theories of the act of faith. They do not believe, as does Hobbes, that God must reveal things "supernaturally" to each believer. Rather, grace permeates the knowing subject in a more natural way. Tillotson writes an entire sermon on how the Holy Spirit "can raise and heighten our Faculties" (*W*, II, 455). He also writes that we experience true revelation as a "Foreign Impression" in our minds (*W*, II, 443). Revelation *feels* as if it comes from the outside, from God, and not as of our own invention.

Barrow discusses the difficulty of believing certain Christian doctrines because of our "carnal sense" and "profane mind." He gives as examples the poverty of Jesus, the general resurrection, and the demand that we each carry our crosses. He suggests that we can only believe such doctrines and counsels because of an innate orientation to God. "God our parent hath stamped on our nature some lineaments of himself, whereby we resemble him; he hath implanted in our soul some roots of piety toward him; into our frame he hath inserted some propensions to acknowledge him and to affect him" (*TW*, V, 56). These theologians do not delineate exactly how such orientations affect rational belief; the possibility is presented, the means left unexamined. Anglican rationalism is often said to have retained only the shell of the Cambridge Platonism that preceded it, while discarding its inner light. In their discussion of grace and reason, Barrow and Tillotson alleviate some of the rational coldness of much of their work.

We may glance at one final way in which Barrow and Tillotson find the contents of Scripture to be rational. It has been suggested that in their work we find a strain of what the next century in England will call "sensibility."[16] Sometimes the Christian religion is true because it feels true. Jesus' teachings, for example, warm the tenderhearted; the power of God exercises our faculty for wonder. This kind of argument, integrating reason and emotion, is as old as Christianity itself. We may cite one passage from Barrow that illustrates it. The first Christians, he writes, "relied partly upon principles of reason, taking in the assistance and attestation of sense. They that beheld the sincerity and innocency of our Saviour's conversation; the extraordinary wisdom and majesty of his discourses; the excellent goodness and holiness of his doctrine; the incomparably great and glorious power discovered in his miraculous works . . . were by these considerations persuaded, not merely by his own testimony" (*TW*, VII, 22). I choose this passage not only to show that the strain of sensibility latent in Anglican rationalism involves a kind of proof for the felt truth of Christianity. In its easy movement from reason to sense, from history to universality, the passage also shows how, for Barrow, the act of rational faith, for all its different bases of evidence, remains a smooth, psychological unity. In the preceding pages I have tended to separate various kinds of evidences—testimony and contents, for example—which Barrow assumes flow easily into one another in the world of real belief.

4

One great problem in the history of seventeenth-century English theology is categorization. In the last century historians like Mark

---

[16]The relationship between the theologians I have been discussing and "sensibility" has recently been questioned by Donald Greene in "Latitudinarianism and Sensibility: The Genealogy of the 'Man of Feeling' Reconsidered," *Modern Philology*, 75 (1977), 159–83. Greene is more intent on what he considers misrepresentations of these authors' moral thought than on their dogmatics, which I deal with here. Greene's insistence on the traditional orthodoxy ("Augustinianism") of the authors with whom I deal is a helpful corrective to much secondary material published on them.

Pattison and Leslie Stephen understood theologians like Barrow and Tillotson as part of the irreversible movement to deism.[17] A recent writer puts Tillotson among the "atheists" of his generation, theologians attacked by conservative churchmen for their liberal views.[18] Ought we to group thinkers like Barrow, Stillingfleet, and Tillotson with Hobbes, Spinoza, and Toland? Is Anglican rationalist opposition to these—which could be far more amply demonstrated than I have done—a smoke screen of incidental difference hiding essential similarity?

In the second half of the seventeenth century, a complex of new attitudes arose about Scripture and reason. On the one hand, the argument from authority was devalued to the level of "faith," or personal trust, an act of inferior epistemological value to reason as it worked in the sciences. On the other hand, there was also a drive to accept as scriptural revelation only what is rational—a new chapter in the ancient struggle to make the mind of God strictly accountable to man's. Baconian science had already begun to segregate those passages of Scripture that could not be held to teach scientific doctrine; this necessary movement carried with it the risk of dismissing also certain theological contents of Scripture that proved difficult to rationalize.

Against this doubly rationalist movement major Anglican divines of the later seventeenth century waged steady battle. The argument from authority, they insisted, is rational; also, the first principles of Christianity are clear enough to give us moral certitude about particular doctrines. In insisting on these truths, the Anglican

[17]See Pattison, "Tendencies in Religious Thought in England, 1688–1750," *Essays* (Oxford, 1889), I, 42–118, and Stephen, *History of English Thought in the Eighteenth Century*, 3d ed. (London, 1902), I, 76–77.

[18]John Redwood, *Reason, Ridicule, and Religion: The Age of Enlightenment in England, 1660–1750* (Cambridge, Mass., 1976), pp. 162–63, 170. A recent review of Donald Greene's article (see note 16), taking Redwood's approach, criticizes Greene for not considering that "Tillotson's contemporaries called him an apostate and an atheist" and that Tillotson "recommended dropping Athanasius's Creed for the gentler Apostles' Creed" (*The Scriblerian and the Kit-Cats*, 10 [1978], 114–15). This interpretation itself forgets the entirely orthodox theology of Tillotson's several hundred sermons; it prefers to rely on the evidence of his political enemies without adequately treating this context. See my own review of Redwood's study in *Eighteenth-Century Studies*, 11 (1977–78), 260–63, for fuller discussion.

[37]

rationalists divorced themselves very clearly from truly rationalist teaching on reason and Scripture, as exemplified by Hobbes, Spinoza, and Toland. However diligently intellectual historians have worked to characterize the late seventeenth century as an age a sure and steady growth, on many fronts, towards rationalism, Barrow, Stillingfleet, and Tillotson, in their teaching on Scriptural truth, do not fit the pattern.

These remarks may understandably by construed to miss the obvious. The Anglican rationalists may have disagreed with certain of their contemporaries on formulations of particular doctrines; did they not all agree, however, that a doctrine's excellence consists in its inherent reasonableness? In our own day we—believers or no—generally pay homage to intuitive, personal knowledge; in the later seventeenth century did not the Anglican rationalists surely place themselves firmly with all other rationalists of the time in their love for demonstration and in their valuing of what is rational?

Such questions, involving grand cultural categorizations, are very difficult to answer satisfactorily. One may note first, however, that the subject of this essay, Anglican rationalist teaching on the truth of Scripture, is by no means simply one particular doctrine among many. What a theologian understands as the relationship between written revelation and human reason will radically qualify the content of his theology. In his late arguments with Descartes and Locke, Stillingfleet acutely realized that the models for even natural theology must be analyzed with an eye to doctrines at the end of the theological process, such as the Trinity. Throughout their writings, Barrow, Stillingfleet, and Tillotson were careful never to set up rational norms that might conflict with Christian fundamentals.

Secondly, recent commentators on Anglican rationalism stress that its theological method was not innovative but traditional. If these Anglican theologians again and again praised the conformity of their religion with reason, it may be too simple merely to categorize them as a preamble to deism. There is a larger, much older tradition of Christian rationalism—evidenced principally by Saint Thomas Aquinas and, nearer to our subject, Richard Hooker—that may illuminate the work of Barrow, Stillingfleet, and Tillotson. This grander context has hardly been systematically explored.[19] Yet the radical discontinuity of Anglican rationalism with the secular rationalism around it—on the central question of scriptural truth—suggests we look outside its own day for an analogy helpful in understanding it.

[19]The Thomist context has been noted by Irène Simon, *Three Restoration Divines*, I, 90, and more fully by H. R. McAdoo, *The Spirit of Anglicanism*, pp. 180–82. Phillip Harth also discusses how Anglican rationalism differs from Aquinas and Hooker on faith and reason (*Swift and Anglican Rationalism*, pp. 42–44), though his research on this difference need not be interpreted as denying the general context Simon and McAdoo subsequently sketch.

Divine Causality

Newton, the Newtonians, and Hume

RICHARD H. POPKIN

THE USUAL PICTURE OF THE DEVELOPMENT OF CAUSAL THEORY in modern science is to portray the transformation from metaphysical to mechanistic explanations during the seventeenth century and to show that the mechanistic explanations did not account for why things happened but only constituted statements of regularities in nature. From Galileo to Hume occult qualities and necessary connections were removed from the study of nature. God as first cause dwindled in importance as Hume transformed Malebranche's denial of the efficacy of secondary causes into a commentary on the inefficacy of first causes—God's action. Father Nicolas Malebranche had shown very acutely that secondary agents cannot function as efficient causes. Malebranche derived this claim in part from his contention that God, the Omnipotent Being, is the sole and unique cause of everything. One kind of evidence that Malebranche offered to establish the inefficacy of secondary causes was that nothing is perceived in the alleged agent that could affect the recipient (as in the case of two billiard balls colliding).[1] Hume studied Malebranche carefully and used the French priest's ideas in his own famous analysis of the idea of necessary connection. But Hume then applied Malebranche's critique to the conception of divine causation. Hume contended that no connection is found

Some of the research for this paper was supported by grants from the National Endowment for the Humanities (No. RO-22932-75-596), and from the Memorial Foundation for Jewish Culture. I should like to thank both foundations for their kind assistance.

[1]See, for instance, Nicolas Malebranche, *Entretiens sur la Métaphysique et sur la Religion,* in *Oeuvres complètes,* Tome XII (Paris, 1965), Entretiens VI and VII, pp. 130–72.

between the idea of the Deity and any perceivable effect. He also contended that appealing to the relation of God to events added nothing to our understanding of how or why events occur as they do.[2] With Hume, we have often been told, theological and metaphysical notions of causality were exploded, clearing the way for a purely scientific theory of causality. This history of the transformation of the notion of causation to a purely scientific one may look plausible long after Hume, when most philosophers have come to adopt this view (as they only did when positivism became a major position).

However, to grasp the magnitude of the transformation that has occurred, I think that one has to appreciate fairly the views held by major scientists of the time. In this paper I shall try to show that three of the major scientists—Isaac Newton, David Hartley, and Joseph Priestley (and there were many more like them)—held a view about divine causality that overshadowed their views about natural causality and made their scientific achievements subordinate to their millenarian religious views. Natural history for these thinkers was going on within divine history and would last only as long as necessary to fulfill God's prophetic history.

I have not chosen these three because of the uniqueness of their views. Many other contemporaries of Newton and members of the Newtonian movement held the same kinds of views and often held them more blatantly (as in the case of Newton's chosen successor, William Whiston). Newton, Hartley, and Priestley were the leading figures in their fields of scientific endeavor, and in many ways their views were typical of the mainstream of intellectual activity of the time.

This sort of science seen within a religious framework continued into the nineteenth century with figures like Faraday, but the mainstream of scientists tended toward the deism, agnosticism, and atheism of the French Enlightenment, culminating in LaPlace's Newtonian cosmology without God that he presented to Napoleon.

Newton is often portrayed as the perfect empirical scientist because of his denial of hypotheses about why bodies gravitate, in favor of such a statement of the law of how gravitation goes on, and because

[2]David Hume, *A Treatise of Human Nature* (Oxford, 1951), Book I, Part III, sec. XIV, pp. 159–60.

of his rules of right reasoning, which appear to be rudimentary maxims for empirical induction. For fifty years or more a dispute has been going on among scholars as to whether Newton was such an empiricist or whether he was some kind of metaphysician believing in occult qualities and forces.[3] The vast Newtonian literature gives ammunition to both sides, but I think the evidence, especially from the Newton manuscripts, supports the contention of McGuire and Rattansi that Newton was in the Renaissance Hermetic tradition and that Newton believed in a *prisca theologia* going back to Moses and Hermes that contained all wisdom about the world.[4] Lord Keynes, who made a pretty exhaustive study of the Newton manuscripts (and saved many of them for Cambridge University before they were dispersed), claimed Newton was not the first to live in the age of reason but rather was the last of the magicians.[5] Keynes claimed that Newton "looked on the whole universe and all that is in it *as a riddle*, as a secret which could be read by applying pure thought to certain evidence, certain mystic clues that God had laid about the world to allow a sort of philosopher's treasure hunt to the esoteric brotherhood."[6] If Newton held to a magical metaphysical view as to how things happened in nature, he also had a theological view as to why (and how) they happened. It is this view that I want to trace in this paper.

Before examining Newton's theological causal theories, let me outline what I will try to cover. Newton was *the* dominant intellectual figure in the British scientific world of the early eighteenth century. Two major figures who tried to develop the Newtonian approach in other areas were David Hartley (in psychology) and

[3]See for instance, E. A. Burtt, *The Metaphysical Foundations of Modern Physical Science* (New York, 1925), pp. 280–93; E. W. Strong, "Newton and God," *Journal of the History of Ideas*, 13 (1952), 147–67; and Alexandre Koyré, *Newtonian Studies* (Cambridge, Mass., 1965), esp. Ch. i, "The Significance of the Newtonian Synthesis," pp. 16–24.

[4]J. E. McGuire and P. M. Rattansi, "Newton and the 'Pipes of Pan,' " *Notes and Records of the Royal Society of London*, 21 (1966), 108–43; and J. E. McGuire, "Force, Active Principles, and Newton's Invisible Realm," *Ambix*, 15 (1968), 154–208.

[5]John Maynard Keynes, "Newton, the Man" in *Essays in Biography* (London, 1961), p. 311.

[6]Ibid., p. 313.

Joseph Priestley (in electricity and in chemistry.) All three would have won the Nobel Prize if it had existed in their day. Hartley and Priestley both developed in more detail the kind of prophetic theology of Newton as the ultimate interpretation of what is going on in the world. They represented a theological tradition now ignored or forgotten, but one that was the mainstream view of the scientific community of their day. Priestley, who was the only one to live until Hume's supposed solution of the problem of the possibility of knowledge of scientific causality, sternly rebutted Hume's analysis and pointed out what he saw as its inadequacies.[7] This tradition of Newton, Hartley, and Priestley was central in eighteenth-century intellectual history. If we are to understand how we got where we are and what we have gained or lost, I believe we have to look honestly at our past and not try to ignore it or falsify it.

Having said this much, let us look at the data. Everyone knows Newton was religious. He offered a proof of the existence of God (by the argument from design) in the second edition of *Principia Mathematica*. He wrote on questions like the structure of the ancient Temple in Jerusalem. His last two published works were *The Chronology of Ancient Times*, justifying Biblical chronology, and the posthumous *Observations on the Prophecies of Daniel and the Book of Revelation* (1733). When Newton died, his followers tried to prevent the publication of the latter work, plus the voluminous religious writings, most of which are still unpublished.[8] Later explanations have claimed

[7]See Joseph Priestley, *Letters to a Philosophical Unbeliever, Part I. Containing an Examination of the Principal Objections to the Doctrines of Religion, and especially those contained in the Writings of Mr. Hume* (Bath, 1780). Priestley criticized Hume in many of his works, and especially in this work attacked Hume's causal analysis. See R. H. Popkin, "Joseph Priestley's Criticisms of David Hume's Philosophy," *Journal of the History of Philosophy*, 15 (1977), 437–47.

[8]On what happened to the manuscripts, see H. McLachlan, Introduction, *Sir Isaac Newton's Theological Manuscripts* (Liverpool, 1950). See also Keynes, p. 323. On the struggle about the *Observations on the Prophecies of Daniel and the Book of Revelation*, see Frank E. Manuel, *Isaac Newton Historian* (Cambridge, Mass., 1963), Ch. x. The greater part of Newton's theological papers are in the National Library of Israel, Jersusalem, forming Yahuda MSS Var.1. Out of this vast collection, only one item has been published, as an appendix to Frank Manuel's *The Religion of Isaac Newton* (Oxford, 1974). Professors B. J. Dobbs, Richard S. Westfall, and myself are preparing an edition of all of Newton's theological and alchemical papers, which Cambridge University Press will publish.

this suppression was (1) due to trying to save Newton's reputation as a scientist, and (2) to cover up the fruits of Newton's senility. As Frank Manuel has pointed out, however, the testimony of Newton's star disciple and later archenemy, William Whiston, shows that Newton was writing the religious material all of his life, including the period of his greatest scientific achievements.[9]

In fact, even the long delay on Newton's part in publishing his theory of gravitation seems to have been due to religious factors. In 1680 Henry More described how he and Newton were studying the Bible and "Apocalyptical Notions" together.[10] Newton drew from the passage in Daniel, which reads, "O Daniel, shut up the words and seal the book, *even* to the time of the end: Many shall run to and fro, and knowledge shall be increased," the interpretation that "tis therefore a part of this Prophecy, that it not be understood before the last age of the world; and therefore it makes for the credit of the Prophecy, that it is not yet understood. But if the last, the age of opening these things, be now approaching, as by the great successes of later interpreters it seems to be, we have more encouragement than ever to look into these things."[11] Newton believed that the text "In the time of the end the wise shall understand, but none of the wicked shall understand" applied to those of his time and that immediately following. Because of this belief, apparently, Newton told Robert Hooke that he, Newton, had "been endeavouring to bend myself from philosophy to other studies in so much that I have long grudged the time spent in that study unless it be perhaps at idle hours sometimes for a diversion."[12] Nonetheless, Newton was finally induced by Halley and others to work out and publish his *Principia Mathematica* in 1687.[13]

[9]Manuel, p. 171. Keynes states that Newton's writings on esoteric subjects and on theological matters "were nearly all composed during the same twenty-five years of his mathematical studies" (p. 316).

[10]Arthur Quinn, *The Confidence of British Philosophers, an Essay in Historical Narrative* (Leiden, 1977), p. 31, drawn from Henry More, *A Plain and Continued Exposition of the several Prophecies or Divine Visions of the Prophet Daniel* (London, 1681).

[11]Ibid., p. 32. Cited from Isaac Newton, *Observations upon the Prophecies of Daniel and the Apocalypse of St. John* (London, 1733).

[12]Quinn, pp. 32–33.

[13]Ibid., pp. 33–34.

The suppression of Newton's religious writings seems more likely due to the fact that Newton was a heterodox Christian. Like Whiston he was an Arian *and*, in early eighteenth-century terms, a Unitarian. Whiston proclaimed and published such views and got himself fired from Newton's chair at Cambridge and from the Royal Society. Newton, who led the fight against Whiston, was a closet heretic.[14] The publication of Newton's religious writings would have ruined his reputation with the positivist-agnostic scientists of the day. (A few documents have been published by H. McLachlan. Both he and Keynes contend that Newton was not even a Unitarian, but a "Judaic monotheist of the school of Maimonides.")[15]

(Recently I met an American mathematician. When he found out what I was working on, he asked me if it was really true that the great Isaac Newton held strange religious views. When I told him that I thought the answer was yes and that Newton believed stranger things than has been suspected, the mathematician was heartsick. How could it be possible that the discoverer of the calculus believed such nonsense?)

In Newton's theological view, God created and directs nature through intelligent design. God still intervenes in nature to keep the stars from colliding and to maintain the stability of the solar system.[16] Newton said in one of his theological papers that one should keep religion and science separate, "that religion and Philosophy are to be preserved distinct. We are not to introduce divine revelations into Philosophy nor philosophical opinions into religion."[17] However, Newton's views about the Bible would suggest this cannot be done. First, by vindicating biblical chronology, Newton made clear that he accepted Mosaic chronology *including* the creation story in Genesis 1. Frank Manuel, in his chapter "Israel Vindicated," in his *Isaac Newton, Historian,* shows that Newton was trying to deflate the claims to greater antiquity of the Greeks, the

[14]Cf. McLachlan, Ch. ii, "Newton's Theology," in *Newton's Theological Writings,* esp. pp. 12–16; Manuel, p. 143; and Keynes, pp. 316–18. James Force has done an excellent study of Whiston as a dissertation under my direction. He is presently preparing it for publication.

[15]McLachlan, p. 13, and Keynes, p. 316.

[16]Dudley Shapere, "Isaac Newton," in *Encyclopedia of Philosophy,* V, 490.

[17]Isaac Newton, "Seven Statements on Religion," in McLachlan, p. 58.

Romans, the Egyptians, the Chaldeans, the Persians, or the Chinese over the Jews. In his argument over ancient chronology Newton maintained that "the Bible [is] the most authentic history in the world."[18] Nature, therefore, starts when God commences history. Nature is part of the historical creation. In the *Observations on the Prophecies of Daniel and the Book of Revelation* Newton laid down a theory of interpreting prophetic passages that he took over principally from Joseph Mede's *Key to the Apocalypse.* Mede (1586–1638), who was professor at Cambridge early in the seventeenth century, said that he had become a complete skeptic after his university studies. He found no certainty in any of the sciences he had examined. Finally, he was saved from complete despair by discovering the key to the Apocalypse. He then became the theoretician for those trying to interpret the prophecies, especially in Daniel and Revelation. In fact, his system, with some alterations, is still being used, at least in Southern California. Mede's major work, *Clavis Apocalyptica,* became the source and model for a great many biblical interpreters, including Isaac Newton.[19]

In the theological paper "The Language of the Prophets," Newton claimed that to understand the prophets one has to understand their unique mystical language.[20] In the *Observations on the Prophecies of Daniel and the Book of Revelation* he contended that "the authority of the Prophets is divine, and comprehends the sum of religion."[21] The prophecies in Daniel and Revelation describe the development of the postbiblical world until the end of time (and of history and nature). Newton did not hold that one could foretell future events this way. Rather, as events took place, one could figure out that they had been foretold in the prophecies. These are part of the clues that God has put into creation for us to find. But the whole

---

[18]Manuel, Ch. vi. The quotation is on p. 89.

[19]On Joseph Mede, see "The Author's Life," in *The Works of the Pious and Profoundly Learned Joseph Mede, B.C.* (London 1672), pp. I–XXXIV; Ernest Tuveson, *Millennium and Utopia* (Gloucester, Mass., 1972), pp. 76–85; Quinn, pp. 11–12; and Peter Toon, *Puritans, the Millennium and the Future of Israel: Puritan Eschatology, 1600–1660* (Cambridge and London, 1970), pp. 56–65.

[20]McLachlan, pp. 119–20.

[21]Isaac Newton, *Observations upon the Prophecies of Daniel and the Apocalypse of St. John,* p. 14.

structure of human history had been foreordained in the prophecies.[22] Newton traced how Roman and medieval history is all the
fulfillment of the prophecies. However, he did not follow out further
history as Hartley and Priestley did to the immediate present and
the millennial future (including the end of physical creation).[23]

In the Newtonian picture God creates, directs, and has ordained
a plan for history that his prophets have set forth. This plan not
only involves the destruction of the mighty empires of the world
but, if one takes the Book of Revelation seriously, the world itself.
Newton's scientific contemporary John Ray gave a graphic picture
of how the physical world will end in a fire.[24] Whiston wrote on
this subject, too.[25] The result would be that Newtonian physics is
an explanation of a physical universe that will last about six thousand years; it is an explanation inside a prophetic reading of the
Bible. Without worrying about miracles and how they might fit in,
physical science is a uniformitarian picture of an aspect of the
historical creation that will be true until the prophecies about the
end of the world come true.[26]

Newton did not spell out this scheme as clearly as I have painted
it, though he came close to it in his *Observations on the Prophecies of
Daniel and the Book of Revelation*. David Hartley (1707–1757) made
the case crystal clear. Hartley, like Hume, claimed he was discovering the Newtonian laws about mental life.[27] His *Observations on*

[22]Ibid., p. 251.

[23]In the *Observations* Newton covered events in prophetic terms up to the fall
of Constantinople in 1453.

[24]John Ray (Fellow of the Royal Society), *Three Physio-Theological Discourses concerning, I. The Primitive Chaos, and Creation of the World. II. The General Deluge, its Causes
and Effects. III. The Dissolution of the World and Future Conflagration* (London, 1713).

[25]William Whiston, *A New Theory of the Earth from its Original, to the Consummation
of all Things, wherein the Creation of the World in six Days, The Universal Deluge, and the
Great Conflagration, as laid down in the Holy Scripture, are shown to be perfectly agreeable
to Reason and Philosophy With a Discourse concerning the Mosaick History of the Creation*
(London, 1696). This is the work of Whiston's that first brought him to Newton's
attention.

[26]There was some dispute about whether the natural world had proceeded by
uniform laws, or whether the Flood had altered the laws.

[27]In his opening chapter, Hartley indicated that both his methods and his
subject matter derived from Newton. David Hartley, *Observations on Man, his Fame,
his Duty and his Expectations* (London, 1749), facs. ed. (Gainesville, Fla., 1966),

Man (1749) was more successful than Hume's *Treatise of Human Nature* and is a more scientific and systematic presentation of a mechanistic psychology. Through his influence on Coleridge and on James Mill, Hartley became the founder of modern psychology.[28] Those who know about his theory of association of ideas seem unaware that there is a second and at least coequal part of his book, devoted to explaining natural and revealed religion.[29]

Hartley began by proving God's existence principally through the argument from design. He then turned to justifying acceptance of the biblical account of how God acts in the world. Basically, Hartley followed the commonsense argument that had been developed in seventeenth-century Anglican theology, principally by William Chillingworth, Bishop Edward Stillingfleet, and Archbishop John Tillotson; namely, that it is more reasonable to accept the Mosaic account than to deny it. It is implausible that Moses and the prophets would lie. It would fly in the face of common sense to deny an account of the world that fits the facts and has been accepted by so many eminent persons. Hartley also argued that "the Genuineness of the Scriptures proves the Truth of the Facts contained in them," as well as their divine authority, and that "the Prophecies delivered in the Scriptures prove their divine Authority."[30]

If it is reasonable to accept the Bible, then a crucial part of this acceptance is recognizing the role of prophecy. That biblical prophecy is a genuine way of foretelling events is first of all established by the fact that within the Bible prophecies are made about events to come in Jewish history, and these events happened, such as the fall of the first Temple, the Babylonian captivity, the return from

introd. by Theodore L. Huguelet. Hume, in the *Treatise*, claimed he was introducing the Newtonian method of reasoning into moral subjects (title page), and later on that he, Hume, had discovered the law of attraction for the mental world (Book I, Part I, section iv).

[28]Coleridge even named his son Hartley. T. L. Huguelet traces Hartley's influence in the development of psychology. See his introduction to the Scholars' Facsimile ed. of Hartley.

[29]One of the few studies of the relation of the two parts is Robert Marsh, "The Second Part of Hartley's System," *Journal of the History of Ideas*, 20 (1959), 264–73.

[30]Hartley, *Observations*, Part II, Chs. i and ii.

the exile, the fall of the second Temple. More important, prophecies principally in Isaiah foretell the coming of the Messiah. The Gospels show over and over again the way in which the arrival of Jesus of Nazareth is the fulfillment of those prophecies. Finally in Daniel, in certain lines in the Gospels, and especially in the Book of Revelation, prophecies about postbiblical history are made. Hartley claimed the same kind of success rate. The fall of the Roman Empire was predicted, and it fell. The dispersion of the Jews was predicted, and they are scattered to the four corners of the earth. And Hartley went on and on, with great detail.[31] Then he moved to the next state of things. The time for the fulfillment of the final prophecies was near. What he envisaged (though he wouldn't date when all of this would happen) was revolutions all over the world, the collapse of kingdoms, the reemergence of the Lost Tribes of Israel, the return of the Jews to Palestine, the rebuilding of the Temple, the second coming of Jesus, and the conversion of the Jews.[32] At this point developmental history would be over. Jesus would reign for one thousand years, the Millennium, and then the historical and natural world would disappear in the destruction of the world by fire (presumably a spiritual world would survive for all eternity).[33] So in Hartley's scheme prophetic history is the blueprint for what will happen in both natural and human history, and God brings about his plan through the fulfilling of prophecies in history. Hartley was more detailed than Newton (at least in his published writings). In adjoining his theological work to his psychological one, he obviously saw his scientific work as both compatible with his theology and to some extent explained by it. Hartley also made the fulfillment of the prophetic plan an immediate issue in that the specific program set forth in Revelation was about to take place though one could not tell exactly when.

[31]Ibid., Ch. ii.

[32]Ibid., Ch. iv, sec. ii, propositions 81–84. While making it appear that signs point to the rather imminent fulfillment of these prophecies, Hartley cautiously said, "How near the Dissolution of the present Governments, generally or particularly, may be, would be great Rashness to affirm" (p. 368).

[33]See proposition 85, *"It is not probable, that there will be any pure or complete Happiness, before the Destruction of this World by Fire,"* p. 380. Sect. iii, which follows this proposition, deals with *"Of a Future State after the Expiration of this Life."*

[49]

Joseph Priestley (1733–1804) brought this kind of scientific theology to a climax. Priestley, unlike Newton or Hartley, was a preacher by profession, albeit a heterodox one. He was extremely influenced by Hartley's writings and was always recommending them to people. He gave Benjamin Franklin a copy of Hartley to cure him of his deism.[34] He said over and over again that Hume would not have offered so many bad arguments and would not have come to so many wrong conclusions if he had read Hartley's *Observations*.[35] Priestley put out an edition of Hartley (making his explanation of sensory processes even more materialistic and Newtonian than it was in the original).[36] And when Priestley fled to America in 1794 (when he was driven out of England for his pro-French views), he read the Bible and Hartley's religious views on the ship for comfort and solace.

Priestley made fundamental contributions to modern science in his *History of Electricity* and his work on oxygen. He also wrote dozens and dozens of religious works. He held a position similar to that of Newton and Hartley about the evidence of God's existence from the argument from design and the authenticity of the Bible as world history. In his *Discourses Relating to The Evidences of Revealed Religion*, he held that prophecy was God's exclusive province which God gave to certain Hebrews and Apostles.[37] In his *Letters to The French Philosophers*, Priestley claimed it was evident that prophecy is true from the fact that Moses predicted the fate of the Israelites to the end of the world, and his prophecies have been accurate up to the present. Also, Jesus prophesied the destruction of the Temple in

[34]Joseph Priestley, *Observations on the Increase of Infidelity*, 3d ed. (Philadelphia, 1797), p. 110, and *The Memoires of Dr. Joseph Priestley*, ed. and abr. John T. Boyer (Washington, D.C., 1964), p. 77.

[35]Hartley was brought up throughout Priestley's answer to Hume in the *Letter to a Philosophical Unbeliever*. At one point Priestley declared, "Mr. Hume had not even a glimpse of what was at the same time executing by Dr. Hartley, who, in an immence work, of wonderful comprehension and accuracy, has demonstrated" (p. 20).

[36]Priestley's edition was entitled *Hartley's Theory of the Human Mind, on the Principle of the Association of Ideas; with Essays Relating to the Subject of It* (London, 1775).

[37]Joseph Priestley, *Discourses relating to the Evidences of Revealed Religion, Delivered in the Church of the Universalists at Philadelphia* (Philadelphia, 1796).

Jerusalem, and it happened.[38] Since many of the prophecies have come true, it appeared to Priestley that the ultimate ones were about to be realized. In view of the fact that many of these prophecies involve the Jews, Priestley began a campaign in 1787 to convince the Jews of their role in prophetic history and to urge them to act accordingly by becoming Christians. In 1787 Priestley rejoiced at the prospects for the Jews.[39] The French Revolution increased Priestley's conviction that the millennial prophecies were about to be fulfilled.[40] (Many English theologians saw prophetic implications in the French Revoluton and the Napoleonic era. There is some similar literature in France, mainly by Jansenists).[41] In his *Mémoires*

---

[38]Joseph Priestley, *Letters to the Philosophers and Politicians of France*, in *Theological and Miscellaneous Works* (London, 1817–32), XXI, 122.

[39]Joseph Priestley, *Letter to the Jews* (Birmingham, 1787) in *Theological and Miscellaneous Works*, XXI, 231.

[40]Priestley's strongest statement on the role of the French Revolution in fulfilling prophecies is his *The Present State of Europe Compared with Ancient Prophecies* (London, 1794). Newton is used as a source.

[41]Two leading English prophetic interpreters of the French events were the Reverend James Bicheno with his *The Signs of the Times; or the Overthrow of the Papal Tyranny in France, The Prelude of Destruction to Popery and Despotism* (London, 1793), and *The Restoration of the Jews, The Crisis of All Nations to which is now prefixed, A Brief History of the Jews from their first Dispersion to the Calling of their Grand Sanhedrin at Paris, October 6, 1806*, 2d ed. (London, 1807); and the Reverend George Stanley Faber, *A General and Connected View of the Prophecies relative to the Conversion, Restoration, Union, and Future Glory, of the Houses of Judah and Israel; The Progress and Final Overthrow of the Antichristian Confederacy in the Land Palestine*, 2 vols. (London, 1809).

For a survey of prophetic interpretations of French events from 1789 to Waterloo, see Leroy E. Froom, *The Prophetic Faith of our Fathers*, Vol. II (Washington, 1948), pp. 744–82, and Mayir Vereté, "The Restoration of the Jews in English Protestant Thought," *Middle Eastern Studies*, 8 (1972), 3–50.

There is a French Millenarian literature that has hardly been studied. There are works like *Dissertation sur l'époque du Rappel des Juifs, et sur l'heureuse révolution qu'il doit opérer dans l'Eglise* (Paris, 1779); and *Avis aux Catholiques sur le caractère et les signes du temps où nous vivons; ou de la Conversion des Juifs, de l'Avènement intermédiaire de Jesus-Christ et de son Règne visible sur la terre* (N.p., 1795). A small portion of French millennial thought is treated in R. H. Popkin, "La Peyrère, the Abbé Grégoire and the Jewish Question in the Eighteenth Century," *Studies in Eighteenth-Century Culture*, 4 (1975), 209–22. See also Clarke Garrett, *Respectable Folly* (Baltimore, 1975).

[51]

there is a note that in the early 1790s he told people that the second personal appearance of Christ was very near, and he placed it at no more than twenty years.[42]

The Jews rejected his advances. At least one Jewish writer, David Levi of London, denied in his answer to Priestley that biblical prophecies could be translated into current history.[43] Priestley, nonetheless, became more convinced by the course of events. From Philadelphia he declared in 1797 that on reading Scripture he was especially impressed by "the glorious prospects that are given us of the future state of things in the world, with respect to the great events which seem now to be approaching."[44] In 1799 Priestley tried to make clear to the Jews (and everyone else) that the great events had arrived. In *An Address to Jews on The Present State of the World and the Prophecies Relating to it*, Priestley said the Jews had been wise in not trying to fix a time of their redemption. But now "the state of the world at present is such as cannot fail to engage your particular attention."[45] The fall of various European powers and the capture of the pope indicate that several prophecies in Daniel about the deliverance of the Jews are about to be fulfilled. Priestley dated it all within fifty years, with the Turkish Empire falling first. He presented the French Revolution as the beginning of the whole process leading to the culmination of history.[46] (Priestley was such an enthusiast for the French Revolution that he was made an honorary French citizen and a member of the National Assembly. He never took his seat.) Priestley saw that the prophetic theory advanced by Newton and Hartley was becoming reality. And in this, he, unlike them, saw immediate events as the culmination of divine history. Since he died a few years before his date

---

[42]Priestley, *Memoires* (London, 1831–82) II, 119.

[43]David Levi, *Letters to Dr. Priestley in answer to his Letters to the Jews* (London, 1787).

[44]Priestley, *Observations on The Increase of Infidelity*, 3d ed. (Philadelphia, 1797), p. vi.

[45]Priestley, *An Address to the Jews on the Present State of The World and the Prophecies Relating to it* (Northumberland, 1799) in *Theological and Miscellaneous Works*, XX, 283.

[46]Ibid., pp. 286–89.

for the second coming, he never knew that history just went plodding on.

What does this brief survey show? Three of the greatest mechanistic scientists in the late seventeenth and eighteenth centuries held to a picture of the natural world functioning within the divine world. The divine world was not just a general design but a prophetic plan in which nature was created when divine history began and in which nature would last only as long as divine history. They held to the view that was stated by one of Newton's greatest admirers, his namesake, Bishop Thomas Newton, who held Sir Isaac's scientific and theological work in the highest esteem. In his *Dissertation on the Prophecies* (1758), Bishop Newton declared, "In any explication of the prophecies you cannot but observe the subserviency of human learning to the study of divinity. One thing is particularly requisite, a competent knowledge of history sacred and profane, ancient and modern. Prophecy is, as I may say, history anticipated and contracted; history is prophecy accomplished and dilated; and the prophecies of scripture contain, as you can see, the fate of the most considerable nations, and the substance of the most memorable transactions in the world from the earliest to the latest time."[47]

Ultimately, the cause of everything was God acting through his prophetic plan. This picture was held to not only by Newton, Hartley, and Priestley but by most of the scientists in the United Kingdom.

Hume was a misfit in his day because he did not believe in divine causality, Scripture, or prophecy and saw events as just parts of regular sequences. In his earliest work, the *Treatise*, Hume had said that "if no impression, either of sensation or reflection, implies any force or efficacy, 'tis equally impossible to discover or even imagine any such active principle in the deity. Since philosophers, therefore, have concluded, that matter cannot be endow'd with any efficacious principle, because 'tis impossible to discover in it such a principle; the same course of reasoning shou'd determine them to exclude it from the supreme being. Or if they esteem that opinion absurd and impious, as it really is, I shall tell them how they may avoid it; and that is, by concluding from the very first, that they have no

[47]Thomas Newton, *Dissertation on the Prophecies*, 2d ed. (London, 1760), III, 439.

adequate idea of power or efficacy in any object."[48] Thus divine causal power is unknown, as is any other kind of causal power.

In his later works Hume went on to question any meaningful role that divine causation was supposed to have. In the *Enquiry*, when Hume discussed miracles, a major alleged form of divine causality, he contended that the occurrence of miracles was always extremely improbable. Also, he maintained that it was always more probable that the testimony concerning the occurrence of a miracle was false than that the supposed miraculous event had occurred. Hume applied this analysis to the Pentateuch, and declared, "I desire any one to lay his hand on his heart, and after a serious consideration declare, whether he thinks that the falsehood of such a book, supported by such a testimony, would be more extraordinary and miraculous than all of the miracles it relates; which is, however, necessary to make it be received, according to the measures of probability above established."[49] Hume followed by saying that the same point can be made about prophecies, since prophecies are supposed miracles.[50] (If they were not, they would not count as proofs of revelation.) Because human beings are not able to foretell future events by using their natural capacities, prophecies are therefore supposed to go beyond what can be known by natural means. In the next chapter, entitled "Of a Particular Providence and of a Future State," Hume insisted that "all the philosophy, therefore, in the world, and all the religion, which is nothing but a species of philosophy, will never be able to carry us beyond the usual course of experience, or give us measures of conduct and behavior different from those which are furnished by reflections on common life. No new fact can ever be inferred from the religious hypothesis; no event foreseen or foretold; no reward or punishment expected or dreaded, beyond what is already known by practice and observation."[51]

[48]Hume, *Treatise*, p. 160.

[49]Hume, "Of Miracles," in *An Enquiry concerning Human Understanding*, ed. Selby-Bigge (Oxford, 1966), p. 130.

[50]Ibid., pp. 130–31.

[51]Hume, *Enquiry*, p. 146. See also R. H. Popkin, "Hume: Philosophical versus Prophetic Historian," in K. R. Merrill and R. W. Shahan, eds., *David Hume, Many-Sided Genius* (Norman, Okla., 1976), pp. 83–95.

Hume's empirical theology does not allow for such speculation about what may take place in the world. In the *Dialogues concerning Natural Religion* Hume's character, Philo, asserted that it was dangerous to speculate about the two eternities "before and after the present state of things" because we have no basis for making any meaningful judgments.[52] At the close of the *Dialogues* Hume had Philo say "that the cause or causes of order in the universe probably bear some remote analogy to human intelligence."[53] From this situation no further data could be inferred. Hume, thus, had constructed a view of the world in which no providential events are likely to take place and in which there could be no prophetic knowledge of them.

On the other hand, the prophetic scientists had made great discoveries in the sciences. But their days of glory came to an end in the early nineteenth century. Two factors seem to have played a part in changing the role of the scientist from interpreter of prophecy to predicter of regularities. One is the translation of prophetic historian to interpreter of immediate events that came to a critical point in the failure of the French Revolution and the Napoleonic age to lead to the millennium. The continuation of the world after Waterloo made most see the world in secular terms. Those who continued the prophetic interpretation after 1815 (and there were and are plenty of them) were mainly outside the scientific community and became the founders of fundamentalism.[54]

The other major development was the emergence of a new scientific mentality as expressed by Pierre-Simon de La Place (1749–1827). He, unlike Newton, Hartley, or Priestley, could conceive of a Newtonian world without God. As a product of the French Enlightenment, he had been divorced from the religious and theological traditions so strongly rooted in England. During the chaos of the French Revolutionary and Napoleonic periods, La Place worked out a modernized and polished version of the Newtonian world system. He believed that everything in the world could be

[52]Hume, *Dialogues concerning Natural Religion*, ed. Norman Kemp Smith (London, 1947), pp. 134–35.

[53]Ibid., p. 227.

[54]Ernest R. Sandeen, *The Roots of Fundamentalism, British and American Millenarianism, 1800–1930* (Chicago, 1970).

explained by this system and that all future observations would confirm it. Unlike Newton, La Place was sure that such a perfect and beautiful system required no divine maintenance. When he explained the system to his former student, the emperor Napoleon Bonaparte, the latter asked him, according to the story, "Where does God fit in your system?" La Place is supposed to have replied, "I have no need for such an hypothesis."[55]

One reason for making such a claim was that La Place was certain that our knowledge of future events came only from our scientific knowledge of causes and effects. He said, "Being assured that nothing will interfere between these causes and their effects, we venture to extend our views into futurity, and contemplate the series of events which time alone can develop."[56] Here we have the complete separation of scientific thought from any prophetic religious view. There is no possibility in this view of prophesying the future. It can only be revealed in terms of the continuation of scientifically established causal laws. And, as a consequence of what La Place is supposed to have told Napoleon, there is no longer any need for the hypothesis that there can be prophetic clues about the future.

The failure of prophecy and the separation of science from religion created our modern scientific mentality. To appreciate what that is and what it has become, one must remember what it emerged from. And to understand the heroes of previous ages, like Newton, Hartley, and Priestley, one has to be willing to appreciate them for what they really were like, rather than what we might wish them to have been. In so doing, perhaps we will gain a richer appreciation of some of the conflicting currents of ideas that have gone into the making of our intellectual world.

[55]R. Harre, "Pierre Simon de LaPlace," *Encyclopedia of Philosophy*, IV, 291–92.
[56]Ibid., p. 393.

Swift and the Senses

ROBERT H. HOPKINS

Nihil in intellectu, quod non prius in sensu.

Thomas Aquinas

Sensual pleasure is the summum bonum. This is the great principle of morality.

George Berkeley

All thought dwells in its subsidiaries as if they were parts of our Body.

Michael Polanyi, *The Tacit Dimension*

MY CONCERN IN THIS ESSAY IS WITH THE DEFINITION OF A problem involving what I call "poetic epistemology." I believe that imaginative literature constitutes one way of coming to an accommodation with a world that we shall never fully understand. I believe that such literature must achieve this accommodation through an extraordinarily creative use of language. I believe also that although a great work of literature creates its own unique context, such a work must ultimately be evaluated by its empirical relation to the world as experienced by mankind through the senses. My concern in this paper, then, will be with empiricism and the eighteenth-century English poetic imagination. I shall focus on Jonathan Swift, for I believe that there are serious misconceptions about Swift's treatment of the senses in his poetry and imaginative fiction and that Swift's poetic empiricism is of the utmost importance to the world's body of poetry today.

One such misconception was that of Father Walter J. Ong who, in 1954, argued that Swift was unconsciously influenced by a kind of Newtonian world view that associated empirical reasoning with a mechanical and geometrical method of demonstration.[1] Father

---

[1] "Swift on the Mind," *Modern Language Quarterly*, 15 (1954), 208–21. Donald Ault has argued on the side of William Blake, attacking Newtonian concepts of space and time. Insofar as Newton obviously is a target of Blake's prophetic works,

Ong suggested that with Swift "the frame of thought in which the observations are set is often of more significance than the observations themselves" (p. 208) and that Swift often falls back on "mechanistically conceived imagery and conceptualizations" and often reduces "psychological operations and situations immediately into spatial or local-motion components" (p. 214). Ong concludes that Swift was "moving in the current of mechanistic thought so strong in his day" and that, like the "ideally isolated system of the Newtonian physicist," Swift's own poetic system was based on a myth of asepsis, of isolating a "field of some sort" from all "outside influence" and maintaining "the conditions of such a field by enforcement of various removal techniques" (pp. 218–19). Ultimately, according to Ong, Swift was so obsessed with a desire to "discern a unity in things" and so used to conceiving of "things in terms of ideally isolated systems," that his primary literary method may be defined as that of sterilization, the "universal elemental remedy of a mechanistically driven civilization" (p. 220). At no point in his essay, however, did Ong indicate that in the works from which he derived those metaphors revealing Swift's "frame of thought" (*A Tale of a Tub*, *A Discourse concerning the Mechanical Operation*, or *Gulliver's Travels*), we are dealing with fictive, dramatic works involving all of the complexities of fictitious narrators and speakers. At no point is there a hint that Swift may be satirizing the very frame of mind that Ong so arbitrarily identifies as Swift's own.

One would prefer to let Ong's essay die a natural death were it not that in his book on Swift (1969) Denis Donoghue resurrected it in support of his own thesis that Swift, fearing that "the image of God is dark, the political balance precarious, and the moral order merely figurative," constructed a "working model of life" that reduces "complex phenomena to extremely simple terms," "takes possession of a certain area of experience and fends off rival forces."[2] According

Ault's focus seems sound. I should not want to extend Blake's view of Newtonianism to one that the Restoration and eighteenth century as a whole held, or ought to have held, in literary criticism and poetry. See Ault's *Visionary Physics: Blake's Response to Newton* (Chicago, 1974).

[2] *Jonathan Swift: A Critical Introduction* (Cambridge, 1969), p. 36. I admire Ong's many writings, but the Ong-Donoghue model for Swift's poetic epistemology extended to the "Augustans" needs to be examined critically and refuted.

to Donoghue, the terms of this "model of life" are "quantitative, geometrical," "terms of position, size, and shape," and the "ideal analogue is the self-enclosed diagram in geometry, the triangle or the square, anything that exhibits a blocked-off unity of apprehension, no loose edges." After quoting from Locke to reveal Swift's essential state of mind, Donoghue identifies Swift's strategy with that of "Augustan literature" as a "series of strategic withdrawals, retreats in good order from positions deemed too metaphysical or Faustian to be held" (p. 38).

Behind this approach to Swift is, I believe, an assumed myth based on a false history of ideas. This myth postulates that as a result of Cartesian dualism, Newtonian science, and Lockean empiricism, which undermine the primacy of the senses by placing a higher truth value upon secondary qualities, Restoration and eighteenth-century English writers become victims of a dualistic, subject-object epistemology until the Romantics, spearheaded by German idealistic philosophy, restore unity through emphasis on the "poetic imagination." The falseness of this myth is based on what William Youngren has shown to be the fallacy of selecting passages from one universe of discourse (philosophy) to illustrate a thesis and then arbitrarily selecting passages from another universe of discourse (imaginative literature) to prove that the thesis holds true.[3] The myth ultimately assumes that Swift and his contemporaries were so affected by a mechanistic weltanschauung that their poetry suffers either from a distrust of direct immediate sense experience or that it shortchanges the poetic imagination and relies too much only on the five senses. Both of these assumptions, I believe, are false. Rather than equating the empirical poetic vision of Swift with a positivistic philosophy, we should take a new look at what we mean by empirical poetry and then see how it works in the context of some of Swift's imaginative writing.

One modern English poet who exemplifies such an empirical commitment and who, as Donald Davie notes in his provocative book on Thomas Hardy, has been scandalously neglected is Charles Tomlinson. When *The Necklace*, Tomlinson's first volume of poetry,

[3]"Generality, Science and Poetic Language in the Restoration," *ELH*, 35 (1968), 158–87; see esp. pp. 180–84 for misunderstandings about Restoration poetics that are created by projecting back onto the period assumptions from nineteenth-century positivistic views of science.

was published in 1955, Donald Davie wrote that the poems "appeal outside of themselves only to the world perpetually bodied against our senses" and that they "improved the world."[4] In his preface to the edition of 1966, Tomlinson saw himself as differing from Wallace Stevens's insistence on "the supreme fiction" in that he accords "objects their own existence" (p. vii). Tomlinson's Phi Beta Kappa address at Colgate University (1967), entitled "The Poem as Imitation," rejected poetry that substitutes a "rhetorical stance" for empirical observation and argued for a poetry that "looks for significance in what is at hand" and "salutes the world of phenomena because it is through them and with them that we take this grip on significance."[5] Tomlinson argues for a poetic consciousness, an active kinesthetic self, whose perception reaches for "alien phenomena" but avoids trying "merely to reduce objects to our own image," "respects their otherness," and tries to find a way into "contact with that otherness." Much of Tomlinson's poetry is an impressive achievement of a contemporary poetic imagination committed to a nonsolipsistic vision that is a counterweight to modern critical attitudes that dismiss all too cavalierly an empirical poetics.

Empiricism is not outmoded nor is a poetics grounded on such empiricism. Its most distinguished modern-day advocate, Rudolph Arnheim, has argued against the absurdity of the view that "words come before the experience" or that "our senses furnish nothing better or worse than the raw material of experience."[6] Because Arnheim's gestalt empiricism distrusts language as adequate to express experience, he has the greatest respect for language. He argues, for example, that the etymological study of root words shows that "every word originated in a perceptual experience" and that as a personal rule in writing, he tries to make a "conscious effort

[4]Donald Davie, Introduction to Tomlinson, *The Necklace* (New York, 1966), p. xii. For Davie's vigorous defence of Tomlinson, see "An Afterword for the American Reader," *Thomas Hardy and British Poetry* (New York, 1972), pp. 183–88.

[5]*The Poem as Imitation* (Hamilton, N.Y., 1967), p. 7.

[6]I shall quote Arnheim throughout this essay from a remarkable interview conducted by James R. Petersen, "Eyes Have They, But They See Not," *Psychology Today*, 6 (1972), 55. Nowhere else does Arnheim reflect so critically on the lack of sensitivity in our society and of the need of our educational institutions to cultivate such sensitivity in our citizenry.

to keep the words tied" to "experience" and not to become entrapped by "concepts which prevent one from returning to experience" (p. 56). Arnheim argues that his colleagues are wrong who "believe that in order to be able to reason" one has to "move away from the perceptual image": "The opposite is true. You have to move *into* what is given" (p. 57). For Arnheim true rationality is "one based on immediate experience rather than verbal processes" (p. 58). True originality in the arts for Arnheim does not mean "divergent thinking" but "getting back to the origin, to the roots of one's experience," to "go back to the object—the way it smells, the way it feels, the way it is" (p. 58). If, as I suspect, the supposed malaise of modern poetry claimed by Harold Bloom's *Anxiety of Influence* is the result of the impasse created by poets and literary critics who are entrapped by their own subjective visions, this malaise—if it really does exist—is only a temporary aberration. I refer specifically to Bloom's thesis that as "poetry has become more subjective, the shadow cast by the precursors has become more dominant."[7] There will always be truly original poets in Arnheim's sense, like Charles Tomlinson, who, inspired by the empirical poets of the past, will return to the "roots of experience" and find a fresh poetical language to match that experience. Poetic empiricism is not a negative defensive strategy; it affirms the very stuff of which poetry is made. I should like to argue here that Swift's empiricism is not dualistic but holistic, not mechanical or abstract but organic and sensitive. In that Swift is always directing us back to the roots of our sensitive experience before we conceptualize it to the point of abstraction, his poetry and imaginative fiction are truly phenomenological.

There is not enough space here to review the components of empiricism in seventeenth-century science, Church of England theology, philosophy, and literature; many critics have shown how important this sense-empiricism was to imaginative literature of the Restoration and eighteenth century.[8] Although it is assumed

---

[7] *The Anxiety of Influence* (New York, 1973), p. 11.

[8] Discussions of sense experience in Descartes, Hobbes, and Locke, and in Spenser, Marvell, Rochester, and Dryden are innumerable. John Yolton has argued persuasively against the thesis that Locke undermined "the reality of sensitive knowledge" by a doctrine of "representative perception" (*Locke and the Compass of Human Understanding* [Cambridge, 1970], pp. 40–43). Donald Greene has argued for the belief in the reality of sensitive knowledge as essential for poets (in "Smart,

that Lockean psychology is a cause of an increasing emphasis on the exactitude of poetic perceptions in eighteenth-century poetry, it is more accurate to see Lockean psychology as itself part of a growing commitment to empiricism throughout European culture. Illustrative of the shift in the arts from allegory to a more concrete, sense-directed empiricism is the treatment of the theme of the five senses by artists. The allegorical treatment of the pleasures of the five senses may be found in the twelfth-century Cluny tapestry of *The Virgin with the Unicorn,* in the episodes of the siege of the five gates of the Castle of Alma, or the pleasures of the Bower of Bliss of *The Faerie Queene,* or in Jan Brueghel, the Elder's (1567–1625) seven paintings in the Prado on the five senses. What is not generally known, however, is the continued treatment of the five senses in the concrete, particularized genre and still-life paintings of the seventeenth-century Dutch and Flemish painters. What remains to be done is a thorough study of the symbolic values that individual artists assign to each of the five senses.[9] Sight, for example, is given

Berkeley, the Scientists and the Poets: A Note on Eighteenth-Century Anti-Newtonianism," *Journal of the History of Ideas,* 14 [1953], 427–52). (Although this essay borders on the kind of fallacy later attacked by Youngren, in assuming that Newtonianism necessarily denies the reality of sensitive knowledge, it still offers a valuable insight into the relationship between belief in the senses and poetry.) An English translation of Johannes Kepler, under a page heading "The Authority of the Bible in Philosophical Controversies," argues that Copernican cosmology is not a threat to Scripture because so much of Scripture is poetical, and poetical language often describes valid illusions that are phenomenologically true while mathematically false. And if the "Psalmist knew that the Sun went forth of the Horizon, as out of its Tabernacle, and yet it seemeth to the Eye to do so," "neither is it to be adjudged false . . . *for the perception of the Eyes hath its verity*" (bound in a Bodleian Library volume entitled *Salisbury Mathematical Collections & Translations,* Tome 1. Part 1 [n.d.; my italics]).

For Swift see an important unpublished dissertation by Robert W. Uphaus, " 'The Narrow Path of Sense': A Study of Jonathan Swift's Poetry," *Dissertation Abstracts International,* 30 (1969), 2502A. In this essay I shall not discuss Swift's treatment of "sensationalism" in *A Tale of a Tub,* about which a great deal has already been written.

[9]See F. C. Legrand, *Les Peintres flamands de genre au XVII siècle* (Brussels, 1963), pp. 242–44. For an illuminating survey, scan under the heading "five-senses" the *Decimal Index of the Art of the Low Countries* (The Hague, 1968). For an excellent survey of the literary traditions of the five senses, see Louise Vinge, *The Five Senses: Studies in a Literary Tradition* (Lund, Sweden, 1975).

priority among the five senses for being the sense of education. In the allegorical paintings sight is represented by optical instruments: the microscope, which extends man's vision to the infinitesimal; the telescope, which extends man's vision to infinity. But sight may also signify a sense of eroticism. Hearing is, of course, also a sense of education usually represented by musical instruments. Taste is identified with food, often with gluttony. Smell in the allegorical works is associated either with exquisite fragrances or with repulsive odors from a rotten egg or human feces. Finally, touch is depicted as the most erotic sense by the embrace of a man and woman or conversely as the sense of pain depicted by a surgeon lancing a burgher's carbuncle or extracting a tooth. These variations in the painterly treatment of the senses invite study, by extension, of their treatment in poetry, and such a study would be particularly illuminating when applied to Swift.

Swift's "A Description of the Morning" (1709) not only is one of the great poems of English literature but is particularly rewarding to a close analysis of its sensitivity. The frame of the poem as denoted by its title is a painting or a pictorial representation, and as such displays an amazing visual acuity. But the poem is even more remarkable for what it does with sounds and the appeal to hearing.

> Now *Betty* from her Masters Bed had flown,
> And softly stole to discompose her own
> > [Lines 2–4]

or, later,

> The Smallcoal-Man was heard with Cadence deep,
> 'Till drown'd in Shriller Notes of Chimney-Sweep,
> Duns at his Lordships Gate began to meet,
> And Brickdust *Moll* had Scream'd through half the Street.
> > [Lines 11–14]

Beginning at dawn and in silence, the poem catalogues urban noises of increasing intensity by means of a remarkable acoustic play on *s* sounds: the voiceless *s* of "softly stole," then the choking texture of "*Sh*riller" and "*Ch*imney," and finally the brutal phrase "Brickdust *Moll* had *S*cream'd." Sounds are used to represent the temporal progression of the day until in the concluding couplet the poem shifts back to the spatial dimension represented by sight and to a freezing of the action.

> The watchful Bailiffs take their silent Stands,
> And School-Boys lag with Satchels in their Hands.
>
> [Lines 17–18]

The action of the poem is presented through a series of successive images and sounds within the mutability of time, but the poem's pictorial representation of the frame transcends the mutability. Sound represents mutability, sight simultaneity and permanence. Surely this kind of explanation approximates the enveloping pattern of the poem, which begins in silence and returns to the stunning phrase "silent Stands." The poem ends, as does temporal experience, but the image lingers on.

This kind of explication, however, does not exhaust the complexity of what Swift has done in this poem with the senses of sight and hearing. The philosopher J. O. Urmson in a brilliant British Academy lecture of 1968 coined the phrase "linguistic phenomenology of perception" for a fundamental kind of analysis of the properties of the five senses as they are expressed by ordinary language.[10] In his discussion of sounds, Urmson shows that sounds possess peculiar linguistic properties shared in common with physical objects: they are (1) individual, (2) may be counted, and (3) last for a finite time. F. W. Bateson has argued that Swift's poem is an implicit satire on "the laissez-faire individualism of urban capitalism" and that there is an underlying Christian thesis "that we are members of one another."[11] If Swift wished to depict a kind of

[10]"The Objects of the Five Senses," *Proceedings of the British Academy*, 54 (1968), 119. Although Urmson's analysis is of the Austin school and tends to occupy itself with whether or not one can frame a philosophical problem in ordinary language, Urmson does offer valuable insights into how assumed properties of sight and hearing are linguistic properties, surely of some importance for studying poetic sensitivity.

[11]*English Poetry: A Critical Introduction* (New York, 1950), p. 177. Laissez-faire capitalism, as is well known, was not implemented until the nineteenth century; perhaps *possessive individualism* would be a better term. See C. B. Macpherson, *The Political Theory of Possessive Individualism: Hobbes to Locke* (London, 1962), and Nathan Rosenberg, "Mandeville and Laissez-Faire," *Journal of the History of Ideas*, 24 (1963), 183–96.

naturalistic urban atomism, he could not have used a more apt
poetic technique than to rely on a series of sounds, given their
properties as described by Urmson. But Urmson in the same lecture
discusses the difference between sounds and the looks of things: "to
talk about sounds is primarily to talk about physical phenomena
caused and emitted by things; to talk about looks is to talk about
things in so far as they are objects of sight." As I understand
Urmson's distinction, sounds tend to be identified with external
phenomena, looks more with sight or the interior consciousness of
a perceiver. The isolated urban images and hypocrisies of "A
Description of the Morning" are unified by the painter of the
description, the poetic perceiver, and this act of unification shows
that London is a human community. By audacious verbal trickery,
Swift fuses the primacy of sense perception with the semantics of
his poem in the penultimate couplet:

> The Turnkey now his Flock returning *sees,*
> Duly let out a Nights to Steal for Fees.
>
> [Lines 15–16, my italics]

The reader visually unifies aurally disconnected phenomena. It is
not merely the Turnkey who *sees,* but we, who have read *Oedipus
Rex* and *King Lear* and Swift's poem. Swift urges us not merely to
look but that we—in E. M. Forster's phrase—"Only connect." Swift
forces us to perceive more keenly, so that "consciousness becomes
conscience."[12]

The same integration of sensing and poetic language is found in
"A Description of a City Shower" (1710), a poem that is remarkable
for its appeal to four senses. First, there is smell:

> Returning Home at Night, you'll find the Sink
> Strike your offended Sense with double Stink.
>
> [Lines 5–6]

Then the tactile:

[12]The phrase is E. San Juan, Jr.'s, "The Anti-Poetry of Jonathan Swift," *Philological Quarterly,* 44 (1965), 396. To call poetry anti-poetry seems questionable, as Robert Uphaus observes in "Swift's Poetry: The Making of Meaning," *Eighteenth-Century Studies,* 5 (1972), 569–86. For an inspirational account of sensitivity as intrinsic to great literature, see Maynard Mack, "To See It Feelingly," *PMLA,* 80 (1971), 363–73.

A coming Show'r your shooting Corns presage,
Old Aches throb, your hollow Tooth will rage.

[Lines 9–10]

Swift's visual acuity fuses with an exquisite sense of the tactile in the image of the needy poet whose "only Coat, where Dust confus'd with Rain, / *Roughen* the Nap, and leave a mingled Stain" (lines 29–30, my italics). The appeal to hearing is made particularly effective by means of an alliterative poetic texture:

Box'd in a Chair the Beau impatient sits,
While Spouts run clatt'ring o'er the Roof by Fits;
And ever and anon with frightful Din
The Leather sounds, he trembles from within.

[Lines 43–46]

It is marvelously apt that sounds frighten the Beau, the symbol of a corrupt aspect of an urban civilization that secludes itself by artifices from nature. (The targets of Swift's most corrosive satire are beings at odds with themselves because they have lost touch with their senses.) The great conclusion of this poem appeals to the senses of sight and smell to make an implied moral comment on civilization's hideous assault on nature:

Filth of all Hues and Odours seem to tell
What Street they sail'd from, by their Sight and Smell.
. . . . .
Sweepings from Butchers Stalls, Dung, Guts, and Blood,
Drown'd Puppies, stinking Sprats, all drench'd in Mud,
Dead Cats and Turnip-Tops come tumbling down the
        Flood.

[Lines 55–56, 61–63]

Swift's scatological and satirical poetry can be enormously disturbing, and many critics have extrapolated from Swift's treatment of smell a biographical profile of a disturbed genius alienated from nature, possibly suffering from an anal fixation. I should like briefly to outline here a theory as to how Swift uses the senses to attack various human types who are themselves alienated from the senses.

Erwin Straus, a pioneer in phenomenological psychology, has written a classic essay, "The Upright Posture," in which he discriminates between man's upright posture, unique to man, and the postures of animals with a lateral digestive axis. Straus argues that in the evolutionary development of man, smell, touch, and taste, the most bodily of senses, are replaced as dominant senses by seeing and hearing, what Straus terms the "senses of distance." Straus goes on to argue that the upright posture of man, encouraging the extension of man's senses, indicates that there is no basis for claiming "any kind of priority for the drives," that in fact the "rational" is biologically as "genuine a part of human nature as the 'animal.' " Ultimately, for Straus, sensing and reasoning should ideally be integrated in rational becoming.[13]

What is particularly illuminating in Straus's essay is the idea that man, through overemphasis on the "senses of distance," may become alienated from his bodily consciousness. Surely it becomes clear how Swift uses smell to satirize poetic characters who refuse to accept the empirical truth of bodily consciousness. But Swift also uses smell to satirize the hedonist who, obsessed by sensual pleasure, is unable to cope with stink and pain. It is this short-circuiting of pleasurable expectations that makes Swift's poetry so powerful.

For the rest of this essay, I should like to hint at just how fundamental sense experience is in *Gulliver's Travels*. The miraculous verisimilitude of Part I, which enables us to experience so readily the presence of Lemuel Gulliver in the land of the Lilliputians, is due in no small part to Swift's sensitivity. When Gulliver falls asleep after reaching the shore, he describes the grass as "very short and soft." When he awakes and finds himself bound he feels the heat of the sun. When he unties his left arm, the arrows shot into his hand "pricked" him "like so many needles" and Gulliver falls "a groaning with grief and pain." The tactile, Descartes noted, is "the most reliable of our senses." Swift reinforces the tactile with taste

---

[13]*Phenomenological Psychology*, tr. in part, Erling Eng (New York, 1966), pp. 137–65. Straus's thesis that sensitivity is a rational faculty seems strikingly similar to John Yolton's interpretation of Locke's conception of "perceptual consciousness." See his *Locke and the Compass of Human Understanding*, p. 41, n. 1. I am grateful to my colleague Thomas Hanzo for introducing me to Straus's writings.

when Gulliver finds a Lilliputian hogshead—equivalent to half a pint—to be "much more delicious" than a "small wine of Burgundy." When Gulliver once again thinks of breaking his bonds, he remembers "the smart" of the "arrows" upon his face and hands "which were all in blisters." When the Lilliputians apply an ointment to his face and hands to remove the smart, Gulliver observes that it is "very pleasant to the smell." Touch, taste, and smell, then, the primary senses of bodily consciousness, provide a mode for readers of *Gulliver's Travels* to enter into that world and experience it vicariously in a minimal amount of time. To use a painterly analogy, Swift lays a ground of sense experiences in Part I, upon which he will build. In Part I, Chapter 6, there is one key passage pertaining to sight that looks ahead to later books: "Nature hath adapted the eyes of the Lilliputians to all objects proper for their view: they see with great exactness, but at no great distance." Here, I believe, Swift presents one of his central themes, namely, that human consciousness is adapted to a particular human scale of ordinary living and that extension of this scale may be a threat to civilization.[14]

In Part II the tactile sense is used again to place us in Gulliver's world, this time the land of the giant Brobdingnagians. Picked up by the farmer, Gulliver groans and sheds tears to let him know "how cruelly" he is hurt "by the pressure of his thumb and finger." The sound of the farmer's voice pierces his ears like the noise of a windmill. Liquor from a two-gallon dram-cup is like a "small cider" and "not unpleasant." From here on, however, the senses of vision and smell are used to magnify those aspects of everyday experience that at an ordinary scale of perception would usually be ignored. If sight in some of the paintings on the five senses, and in Spenser, is a sense of eroticism, Swift reduces it to an illusion by using a

---

[14]Locke was concerned that the extension of man's observation through optics might be "disorienting for man" (John Yolton's phrase); see *Essay concerning Human Understanding: Problems and Perspectives*, ed. Yolton (London, 1969), p. 185. Andrew Marvell expresses a similar uneasiness in "Upon Appleton House," as has been brilliantly shown by the late Rosalie Colie, who uses the term *scalar disruption* to show the impact of new techniques of optics on perceptual consciousness. (*"My Ecchoing Song": Andrew Marvell's Poetry of Criticism* [Princeton 1970], pp. 191, 205–11).

disgusting magnification of women's breasts and bodies, and by a fusion of sight and smell. The Maids of Honour emit a "very offensive smell," but their "natural smell" is "much more supportable than when they used perfumes, under which [Gulliver] immediately swooned away." The "horror and disgust" which Gulliver feels, I submit, do not demonstrate Swift's misogyny but, just the opposite, satirize the stereotyped image of women as sex objects. (Recall that in Part I, Chapter Six, the young Lilliputian ladies are educated "much like the males" and "despise all personal ornaments beyond decency and cleanliness"; it is a maxim in Lilliput that a "wife should be always a reasonable and agreeable companion, because she cannot always be young.") The range of this magnification is used to emblematize the existential human condition: a cancer in a woman's breast, a wen in a beggar's neck, and the lice crawling on the beggar's clothes.

The senses are depicted in Part III as being perverted or abused. It is in the land of the Laputans that the scale of ordinary consciousness is disrupted by beings whose very environments are abstracted from sense experience. Contrary to Ong and Donoghue, it is not Swift but the Laputans whose "ideas are perpetually conversant in lines and figures," who describe the beauty of a woman by "Rhombs, Circles, Parallelograms, Ellipses, and other Geometrical Terms," and who are so "wrapped up in cogitation" and "taken up with intense Speculations," that they can neither "speak, nor attend to the Discourses of others, without being rouzed by some external Taction upon the Organs of Speech and Hearing" or upon the eyes when they are walking (III. 2). It is the Laputans, not Swift, who lack "any Relish for the common Pleasures or Amusements of Life." It is in the grand Academy of Lagado, and particularly in the school of political projectors, where the professors appear to Gulliver to be "wholly out of their Senses." Read in the context that I am discussing here, the phrase is no longer a dead metaphor. There is the projector, "the most ancient Student of the Academy," experimenting with an "Operation to reduce human Excrement to its original Food," who emitting "a horrible Stink" gives Gulliver "a very close Embrace," a compliment that Gulliver "could well have excused." There is the man born blind who teaches apprentices to mix colors for painters on the basis of feeling and smelling. Finally, there is the professor who advises "great States-men to examine into the Dyet of all suspected Persons," to take a "strict View of their Excrements, and from the Colour, the Odour, the Taste, the Consistence, the Crudeness or Maturity of Digestion, form a Judgment of their Thoughts and Designs." Surely, Swift is satirizing here a civilization which by abstracting the senses from qualitative values and constructing quantitative norms is truly out of its senses. (Compare the reference to the taste of human excre-ment here in Part III to the incident of the famished Gulliver in Part I tasting a delicious wine.) It is not without consummate purpose that Swift then deals with the ageless Struldbruggs who at ninety have "no Distinction of Taste" and eat and drink "what-ever they can get, without Relish or Appetite" (II.10).

Although Part III was supposed to have been written last, its position in the work is logical. For as we now know all too well, the future is here and we are it, and our continued survival depends on our moral nature. In Part IV Gulliver is forced to confront the paradox that he is a truly human creature, who, to the surprise of his Houyhnhnm master and unlike the Yahoos, has the "Affectation of walking continually" on his "two hinder Feet" (IV. 3), but who sees the ideal of the upright posture embodied in sitting horses while the bestial is embodied in the Yahoos. No wonder Gulliver is driven to the point of madness at the shock of recognition that he too is a Yahoo! The emphasis in this book is on touch and smell, and Gulliver is so conditioned by the repulsive smell of the Yahoos that on reentering his house back in England, when his wife embraces him, he, "having not been used to the Touch of that odious Animal for so many Years," fell in a swoon. The "very Smell" of his wife and children is so "intolerable" that he could not "suffer them to eat in the same Room" nor ever let them take him "by the Hand." This ending is certainly vexing, but it is also comic. The equilibrium of the senses, imagination, and reason has been replaced by the end of *Gulliver's Travels* with the split between body and soul, with Yahoo bestiality moving on all fours along the digestive, genital, and excrementary axis (see Blake's design of Nebuchadnezzar in *The Marriage of Heaven and Hell*), and the promise of the upright posture—Milton's Adam and Eve "God-erect"—being comically exemplified by the friendship and benevolence of the Houyhnhnms.

[70]

I have outlined here a thesis about genuine empiricism and the life of the senses being at the very heart of great imaginative literature. I have suggested how such a thesis might be developed in an interpretation of Swift. I do not see this empiricism as outmoded for the twentieth century but as being in fact far more phenomenological than some of the other modes of English literature to which this epithet has been applied. I see Swift as standing ultimately for the primacy of the senses as a corrective to a culture that tends to abstract us all from our sensitive experiences. Rudolph Arnheim has complained about how educational systems so often deprive us from sensitively experiencing the real world, about how we have come to "associate the senses with sex, which has been separated from love as fatefully as seeing has been separated from understanding," so that we "equate the senses only with sensuality" (p. 55). Arnheim has also complained about how our culture over the past decades has neglected its sense of significant form, an "invisible culture" which hides function so that a "transistor radio looks like an electric razor, and the razor looks like a car." In contrast Arnheim describes as an example of a visible culture his residence in Italy where one could still see "women with copper jars on their heads going to the well," where "there was a visible continuity of existence," where the "relation between man and nature was right on the surface." Arnheim speaks, as Swift and his contemporaries did before him, for a "perceptual experience of a life" in which "the basic facts of existence are still understandable to the senses" (p. 58).

Some Reflections on Defoe's *Moll Flanders* and the Romance Tradition

HENRY KNIGHT MILLER

D ANIEL DEFOE HAS, ON THE WHOLE, BEEN WELL TREATED IN recent years. From the time of Ian Watt's vigorous restatement, in 1957, of what one may call the Victorian-Edwardian intellectualist damn-the-middle-class view of Defoe, which has been seminal (indeed, remains so) in evoking or provoking answers and redefinitions, a thoroughly fresh picture of the man and of his works has emerged.[1] As usual, the contributions to this revaluation of a major writer have taken two well-marked paths: on the one hand, historical scholarship that asks for a consideration of Defoe's work (and life) in terms of his own context—religious, casuistical, and demonological, economic, social, legal, and even philosophical; on the other hand, contemporary criticism, whose major task is to assimilate works of the past to the shifting values and interests of the present day, has demonstrated through several changes of fashion that Defoe's work—once thought so elemental, if not indeed elementary—can serve as a focus for extraordinary critical ingenuity, and that it will not only submit to a modern critical vocabulary and modern critical passions, such as "the reader" or "the self,"[2] but can

[1] *The Rise of the Novel* (London, 1957), Chs. 3–4. A like view is found in Denis Donoghue, "The Values of *Moll Flanders*," *Sewanee Review*, 71 (1963), 287–303. Much cruder is Mark Schorer's "A Study in Defoe: Moral Vision and Structural Form," *Thought*, 25 (1950), 275–87, reprinted as the introduction to the Modern Library College Edition of *Moll Flanders* ("Defoe's announced purpose is probably a pious humbug, and he probably meant us to read the book as a series of scandalous events").

[2] The latter topic has even spawned several books; see also James Egan, "Crusoe's Monarchy and the Puritan Concept of the Self," *Studies in English Literature, 1500–1900*, 13 (1973), 451–60.

be discussed in terms that summon up the names of such as Kier-kegaard, Jung, Borges, Lévi-Strauss and Derrida. And *Moll Flanders* has been used (as an artifact that has persisted in time) for purposes so varied as a stick to beat capitalism or a document in the history of feminine oppression.

Defoe was thought a protean figure in his own time;[3] he has exhibited perhaps even more facets in our day. What I should like to do is to add a footnote to this kaleidoscopic revaluation—primarily on the historical rather than the critical side, which is to say that, although my argument is speculative, I am not here concerned to make Defoe palatable or current for that amiable tyrant the modern reader. Rather, I hope to pose some questions about the assumptions that lay behind his fiction and helped to shape its manner of treating human experience.

1

To speak of Defoe and the romance tradition may seem at first a bit odd; for Defoe, like most Puritans and Dissenters, had seldom a good word to say for "meer Romances." The general attitude of his age, in fact, toward such prose fiction was that which spawned the adjective "romantick," meaning extravagant, fantastical, and chimerical. The old chivalric romances had long since been reduced to penny chapbooks and were likely to be thought of as reading for boys or for the cits of the middling ranks, like Defoe himself;[4] and the female-oriented, aristocratic French romances of the seventeenth century had become (if the playwrights and essayists are correct) matter for serving maids and overimaginative young girls. So that the term *romance* was scarcely in good critical odor. But if it had such specific associations, *romance* was also, along with *history*, the most often used generic term for long prose fiction as a literary form. Thus, the Brother in *A New Family Instructor* (1727) argues with his sister about "the Reading or not Reading Romances, or fictitious Stories" (and goes on to contrast "a Fiction, or what they

[3]The best demonstration in brief is Maximillian E. Novak's paper "Defoe's Use of Irony," in *The Uses of Irony: Papers on Defoe and Swift* (Los Angeles, 1966), pp. 5–38.

[4]See Louis B. Wright, *Middle-Class Culture in Elizabethan England* (Ithaca, 1935), pp. 83–90, 393–94, et passim.

call'd a Romance" with a true history).[5] The terms *history* and *romance* overlap in actual use, of course; and I take *romance* as inclusive of histories and tales of any length, for I am less interested here in seeking to make generic distinctions that perhaps cannot be made than I am in the assumptions that lay behind most long prose fiction of Defoe's era and of earlier periods. And also in the challenges to those assumptions that came to a focus in the eighteenth century. The romance tradition in the Christian world had for centuries reflected the ideals of a feudal and then a merely aristocratic hierarchy; but its Christian vision long continued to shape modes of prose fiction even as the social and political hierarchies crumbled.

I have chosen *Moll Flanders* as a center for my comment, but *Robinson Crusoe* would have done as well. Defoe's other novels, including *The Fortunate Mistress,* are rather more problematic and less clearly structured; but much of what I have to say is, I think, with proper reservations applicable to them. For if Defoe, like his contemporaries, inherits values that go well back into Renaissance and even medieval times (like England's legal system), he brings to these values an individual and local comprehension and modus.

The first and most important fact for the historical scholar to absorb is that Defoe, in what was still very much a functioning Christian environment, is himself a serious and a practising Christian.[6] True, he is a Puritan; and, for the modern world, including

[5]London, 1727, pp. 51–52. Among other critics who have mentioned the persistence of romance motifs in Defoe's work is James Walton, "The Romance of Gentility: Defoe's Heroes and Heroines," *Literary Monographs 4,* ed. Eric Rothstein (Madison, Wis., 1971), pp. 89–135.

[6]The Term Catalogues, before they disappear after the first decade of the eighteenth century, testify beyond cavil that the vast majority of works coming from London presses had to do with some aspect of the Christian religion; there was no other topic, obviously, that so dominated the consciousness of early eighteenth-century readers—not even politics! The tendency of historians to choose selective evidence, after their own interests, has sadly obscured the actual interests of the period. For instance, Leslie Stephen, following his own skeptical bent, made the deists central to his discussion of religion in the age; and for incautious scholars it has remained central. But every deist pamphlet was immediately pounced on by a dozen answers from every variety of Christian thinker. (Anthony Collins's *Discourse of Freethinking,* in 1713, was dissected in the same year by Richard Bentley,

many historical scholars, that has been condemnation enough. I must not here go into the history of that modern revival of the term *Puritan* (complete with all the overtones of hypocrisy and mealy-mouthed piety that the seventeenth-century Anglicans had attached to it) for the purpose of attacking an entirely different phenomenon, the anti-intellectual, effeminate, and primly self-righteous Evangelical wing of the Anglican church that provided the dominant religious tone by the end of the nineteenth century.[7] But informed modern students of Puritanism have (perhaps futilely in the face of the myth) pointed out the vast differences between seventeenth-century Puritanism and the targets of modern attack: for, far from being anti-intellectual, Puritanism (especially the dominant Presbyterian version) held Reason in the highest regard and had a vested interest in a learned clergy—a fact to which the seminaries of Harvard, Yale, and Princeton owe their existence. And, far from being effeminate and primly self-righteous (though like other Christians and non-Christians they could be self-righteous enough), Puritans held to a tough-minded, independent and various, morally searching faith, centered in the Word of God.[8]

Francis Hare, Jonathan Swift, William Whiston, Benjamin Hoadly, Daniel Williams, Benjamin Ibbot, and George Berkeley, among others.) Deism was certainly a challenge; but it was far from central to religious thought, and to make it so is savagely to distort history. Supposedly secular books were scanned on religious principles (see Charles Gildon's observations on *Robinson Crusoe* cited in J. P. Hunter, *The Reluctant Pilgrim* [Baltimore, 1966], pp. 20–21). See also Clifford Johnson, "Defoe's Reaction to Enlightened Secularism: *A Journal of the Plague Year*," *Enlightenment Essays*, 3 (1972), 169–77. Donald Greene's "Augustinianism and Empiricism," *Eighteenth-Century Studies*, 1 (1967), 33–68, should be reread at least once a year by anyone writing on the eighteenth century.

[7]The same was true of other countries, e.g., the German-Scandinavian attack upon a moribund Lutheranism. The Weber-Tawney thesis of the connections between Protestantism and capitalism (rather thoroughly discredited by now) emerged from this milieu and added a further negative emotional charge to the intellectuals' antipathy for Christian moralism, meaning really, Evangelical moralism.

[8]Among other important studies may be cited William Haller, *The Rise of Puritanism* (New York, 1938); Perry Miller, *The New England Mind:* "The Seventeenth Century" and "From Colony to Province" (Cambridge, Mass., 1939–53); and Owen C. Watkins, *The Puritan Experience: Studies in Spiritual Autobiography* (New York, 1972).

If Defoe's Christian commitment is not taken into account, one can scarcely be said to speak historically of the whole man.[9] It is an inescapable fact of his existence; and the attitude of the modern reader toward Christian commitments of any kind is quite irrelevant (once again, speaking historically). Now, of course that personal commitment takes on different shades as one views Defoe the merchant, Defoe the political pamphleteer, Defoe the composer of prose fiction, and Defoe in his multitudinous other guises: but it remains a full commitment throughout, and it remains central to any historical reading of Defoe's fictional and nonfictional work. The works need not, obviously, be read as religious tracts (unless they *are* religious tracts); but they are all rooted in a Christian scheme of values and assumptions that affords them far profounder depth and reverberation than the old-fashioned realistic criticism could fathom. The many other intellectual currents to which Defoe's wide-ranging mind was open must necessarily be referred to the Christian consciousness that received them.

For my purposes, the peculiarities of seventeenth-century Puritanism[10] (and Defoe, of course, became a Puritan, or better, Dissenter, only by virtue of the fact that his parents' Anglican clergyman was a victim of the Act of Uniformity),[11] and, indeed,

[9]Maximillian Novak, although emphasizing the influence of the tradition of natural law, rightly observes, "We must never underestimate Defoe's religious beliefs" (*Defoe and the Nature of Man* [Oxford, 1963], p. 153).

[10]Among these peculiarities were its Bible-centered and preacher-centered nature; its emphasis upon the notion that every man is (in a sense) his own priest and need only look into his own heart to find the law of God written there; its conservative emphasis upon the calling, or fixed station in life; its fascination with Particular Providences in the everyday world and its demand that natural events be accorded a spiritual application; its insistence upon the necessity of bearing witness to operations of Grace in the heart; its concern with Old Testament rather than classical heroes, and with Christ the Warrior more than the infant Christ or Christ crucified (which are just the aspects that would be stressed by the Evangelicals of the later eighteenth century); and, finally, in England particularly, its general Arminian softening of Calvinistic doctrine. The diary (or the spiritual autobiography), it has been suggested, took the place of the confessional in the Roman church.

[11]John Robert Moore, *Daniel Defoe, Citizen of the Modern World* (Chicago, 1958), pp. 13 ff. "Defoe was always more Christian than Presbyterian, more lover of the Church of Christ than Dissenter" (p. 19). This is surely true, although Defoe does follow many of the patterns associated with seventeenth-century Puritanism; and he is looked upon as a typical enough Dissenter by many of his contemporaries.

of Protestantism in general are less important than certain assumptions common to Western Christendom. One of these, for instance, was that the world of human activity, pressing though it unquestionably was, represented merely a limited part of the cosmos; and that human beings were not only surrounded by multitudes of invisible spirits, good and evil,[12] but were spiritually located in a larger moral universe, ultimately hierarchical, orderly, and rational—a universe which the fallen world of man mirrored most imperfectly but from which ideals and images could be drawn that brought some degree of significance and order to the disorderly, passion-driven, meaningless earthly stew. Defoe's characters may sometimes lose sight of the Angelic Vision when most embroiled in vice and sin (which no one, Defoe least of all, would have denied to be *interesting* activities, though seldom viewed with the complacency that marks modern moral conceptions);[13] but this, of course, does not mean that the vision ceases to exist! Even the Lady Roxana is fully aware at the end of her story that she is damned—and why.

Hence, Christian emblems like that old rhythmical triad of the enemies of man, the World, the Flesh, and the Devil (doubtless about as evocative for *us* as Peanuts, Popcorn, and Cracker-Jack) had for Defoe a genuine and vibrant resonance that must be re-created imaginatively in reading his fiction. He knew very well the abiding attractions of the world and the flesh, and he assuredly believed in the existence of the devil—even if not in the tricked-up form of popular superstition.[14] For Defoe the omnipresent devil

[12]This general topic has been thoroughly canvassed by Rodney M. Baine, *Daniel Defoe and the Supernatural* (Athens, Ga., 1968), one of the few modern studies to treat historically and seriously of Defoe's most serious belief in the Devil.

[13]To be moral, in modern popular thought, would appear to involve either an intense concern with social leveling or a strained effort at psychological *Einfühlung*, but one finds little said about personal responsibility. Not surprisingly, some critics in their defense of Defoe as a significant novelist have taken for granted that he shares such a moral perspective—a somewhat dubious assumption about the author of *The Great Law of Subordination Considered*, despite his consciousness of imperfections in the social order and his genuine sympathy for the disinherited of the world. Defoe moves in a tradition that urged one to hate the sin but love the sinner, to identify crime as crime (not "self-expression") and yet pity the criminal (in particular, as Novak has observed, when he is driven by true necessity). The modern position would seem to be somewhat less discriminating, as well as less interesting.

[14]See Baine, p. 41.

worked rather more subtly, through dreams and hints and suggestions (or, less traditionally, through poverty and want) that appealed
to the imagination and the passions of a corrupt and fallen human
nature, providing "an evil Counsellor within."[15] It is important to
observe, since the modern world tends to be sensitive about determinism other than its own respectable social, economic, and psychological brands, that the prompting role of the devil is *not* viewed
deterministically: even fallen man has free will[16] and moral choice,
and the devil, who operates with God's permission, to test the
human soul, cannot compel the will. All that he can do as the
motivating agent to crime is work upon the weaknesses of the human
soul itself.

The structure of *Moll Flanders*, as has long since been observed,[17]
follows in essence the moral history of mankind as Calvinist (indeed,
Anglican) theology would have viewed it: birth in sin—the heritage
of post-Adamic man—but in possession still of a primal innocence
toward the world that can be lost through the temptations of the
world and the devil, recapitulating the fall of Adam (often in a
paradisical setting); the testing of the human soul on this earth;
and the soul's ultimate coming to awareness of its sin and seeking
reconciliation with God. A simpler and more obvious structural
pattern for Moll's checkered career, however, would be merely:
the World, the Flesh, and the Devil.[18] It is the devil who prompts
Moll in her original fall into the fleshly life, as she observes after
her "Vanity prevails over [her] Vertue": "But as the Devil is an

[15] *Moll Flanders*, ed. G. A. Starr, Oxford English Novels (Oxford, 1971), p. 193.
Subsequent references, given in the text, are to this edition.

[16] On the gradual modification by seventeenth-century Puritanism of Calvin's
strong stand against the freedom of the will (and the restatement of his position
by the Synod of Dort), see Haller et al.

[17] Jonathan Bishop, "Knowledge, Action, and Interpretation in Defoe's Novels,"
Journal of the History of Ideas, 13 (1952), 3–16.

[18] Most critics have shown some consciousness of the structural division of Moll's
criminal career into a sexual pattern and a thieving pattern, despite overlapping
elements, such as also attend the distinction between the Flesh and the World.
Moll does say, after her second act of theft, "Thus I enterpriz'd my second Sally
into the World" (p. 194), which by itself might seem odd, for she has actually
been in the world for some time. See also William Bowman Piper, "*Moll Flanders*
as a Structure of Topics," *Studies in English Literature*, 9 (1969), 485–502.

unwearied Tempter, so he never fails to find opportunity for that Wickedness he invites to" (p. 26); and the large first section of the narrative, after the opening that brings her to Colchester orphan school, concerns itself with the temptations of the flesh—not only lust, although that has always served as the most obvious emblem of submission to the flesh, but the appeal of vanity and the servile dependence upon those goods that nurture fleshly needs (a dependence that places one firmly within the orbit of mere fortune and subject to her whims, as the complete soul never is). For Defoe, Moll's "thorough Aversion to going to Service" (p. 10) is truly ironic: she is on the way toward creating for herself a servitude more total and profound.

Again, after Moll has run through five husbands and several lovers and subsisted by a life of whoredom, she is thrown upon the world, reduced to poverty and dire need; and the devil, finding this a likely situation, speaks once more: "This was the Bait; and the Devil who I said laid the Snare, as readily prompted me, as if he had spoke, for I remember, and shall never forget it, 'twas like a Voice spoken to me over my Shoulder, take the Bundle; be quick; do it this Moment" (p. 191). And thus Moll is led into her life of thievery, proceeding from a mere chance theft that fills her soul with horror, through a spiritual "hardening of heart,"[19] until, even when she has found through the old midwife some honest work, "the diligent Devil who resolv'd I should continue in his Service, continually prompted me to go out and take a Walk, that is to say, to see if any thing would offer in the old Way" (p. 199). Blindly obeying his summons, she comes off with a tankard that the old "Governess" melts down, with the pointed observation "there's no going back now" (p. 200). The governess becomes, in fact, an agent of Satan, the "new Tempter who prompted me every Day" (p. 209); and Moll is "enter'd a compleat Thief, harden'd to a Pitch above all the Reflections of Conscience or Modesty" (p. 202).

Entirely in the hands of fortune or fate (cf. p. 262), with no vision of Providence either to sustain or prohibit, Moll eventually comes

---

[19]See G. A. Starr, *Defoe and Spiritual Autobiography* (Princeton, 1965), pp. 141 ff. et passim. Starr points out that hardening of heart "is in fact a spiritual state, not merely a psychological one" (p. 141).

to the emblematic end for those who have served the World, the Flesh, and the Devil: capture, judgment, and immurement in that "Emblem of Hell itself" (p. 274), Newgate Prison, "whence I expected no Redemption, but by an infamous Death" (p. 273).[20] This brings Defoe to the climactic third part of his narrative, Moll's conversion and true repentance in Newgate, detailed with scrupulous care for authenticity in terms of the tradition of conversion experiences (which shows how significant and central Defoe felt it to be to his narrative);[21] followed by Moll's providential pardon and the departure for Virginia with Jemmy, "as new People in a new World" (p. 304)—the return to paradise or to the *locus amoenus*[22] that so often marked the concludings of the old heroic romances.

2

The overall macrostructure, then, is orderly and logical enough. Criticism has usually, however, been prompted by the microstructure, the episodic manner in which Moll's criminal careers of the flesh and of the world are presented by Defoe. And, although some ingenious (and often even reasonable) orderings of the events within these frames have been suggested,[23] the narrative stubbornly remains episodic in comparison to the more tightly woven "figure in the carpet" of the later art-novel. Of this, one can perhaps say little in modern critical terms—except to say that they are irrelevant to Defoe.

The kind of structure that we properly enough admire in the later novel was in large measure, perhaps, a response to crucial loss—namely, the loss of an external ordering principle that guaranteed, as it were, the ultimate structural significance of narrative. As has been often observed of the Romantic poets, deprived of a

[20]"Redemption," like "deliverance" in *Robinson Crusoe*, becomes, of course, a term with a double sense.

[21]See Starr, *Autobiography*, and Hunter, *Reluctant Pilgrim*.

[22]As my former student Albert Rivero reminds me, the typological analogue would be with the Israelites' departure from the fleshpots of Egypt to seek the Promised Land.

[23]For example, Terence Martin, "The Unity of *Moll Flanders*," *Modern Language Quarterly*, 22 (1961), 115–24; Piper; and J. A. Michie, "The Unity of *Moll Flanders*," in *Knaves and Swindlers: Essays on the Picaresque Novel in Europe*, ed. Christine J. Whitbourn (Oxford, 1974), pp. 75–92, which has the virtue of emphasizing Moll's personal moral responsibility.

Providence that had ensured the meaningfulness of the natural world, they turned to a projection of meaningfulness from within themselves. So, too, as novelists found no longer accessible the certainty of ultimate order in the providential frame, they made a virtue of necessity and framed their own order within the narrative—not now as a mirror of the ordered cosmos but as a projection of the artist's ordering mind. Clearly enough, such an ordering could not be simply assumed or taken for granted, as the external providential order had been by readers of romances; hence, much more scrupulous and thoughtful attention had to be devoted to the *internal* ordering principles of narrative than had ever been required before. For, as long as writers of prose fiction could *assume* beyond the frame of their own narrative an external and unquestionable order that gave any narrative significance by reference to that paradigmatic realm of eternal values and certain judgments, the purely internal narrative ordering of the fiction was free to reflect the interestingly disordered and disjointed nature of the world of fortune, the world of man, marked precisely by its episodic, unstructured, ever-changing, and necessarily finite qualities, in implicit contrast to the realm of significance, the rational, immutable, and eternal cosmos of Providence. Presumably this is one reason that the episodic narrative was commonly not felt to be in itself inartistic (even after the rediscovery of Aristotle's *Poetics*), although there was, in any case, a long tradition of praise for the episodic, because it offered the sine qua non of narrative—variety, which, in most cultures, has been honored above other artistic demands. Hence, in the end, there is small need to apologize for Defoe's episodic narratives. The only need is to educate readers in artistic principles not their own.[24]

So, too, with the treatment of character. The conception of a complex or rounded character has been shaped by new secular interests and concerns. The emphasis upon a gradual temporal

---

[24]As A. D. McKillop observed, in what is still one of the soundest essays on Defoe, "He does not share our interest in the isolation and exact analysis of narrative intent. His way is to cite detail in support of an argument or moral, and it is hard to say when the detail becomes feigned narrative" (*The Early Masters of English Fiction* [Lawrence, Kan., 1956], p. 8); so also: "We may derive Defoe's fiction from the fact, circumstance, or episode, interesting in its own right and connected with a larger end" (p. 12).

progress in human affairs in the later eighteenth century, which would ultimately make possible a theory of evolution in the nineteenth, contrasts sharply with earlier conceptions that saw time more often in terms of definite stages (the seven ages of the world or the climacterics of human life) that were ritually demarcated. Ultimate value resided, not in a gradual progress through finite time, but in a vertical reference to the abiding higher paradigms above man's temporal and temporary lot. Not surprisingly, therefore, earlier fiction, from classic times through the early eighteenth century, displays small interest in character development—for, after all, why should it? That was not where significance or value lay. Particular *stages* of man's existence did, however, vibrate with moral and ritual overtones; and, for the Puritan writer (as indeed, for all writers in the Christian tradition), that astonishing leap into a new life called conversion was among the most exciting and complex phenomena with which literature could concern itself. Samuel Richardson signaled a new era by disapproving of it.

All fiction, all literature, needs a paradigm of ultimate explanations. Our paradigms tend to be scientific and deterministic: if something can be referred to a scientific (meaning sociological, economic, psychological, as well as physicochemical) root or determination, then it has been explained finally and satisfactorily—there is small need to go further. Thus the modern novelist (and reader) could scarcely do without psychology, for it is our court of final appeal on the nature and behavior of the human animal. If we are to talk about character, we cannot really think of doing so without implying psychology, because for us they are one. But it has not been always so: many ages of the earth have been able to discuss human nature most effectively without any reference to psychology at all. To be sure, they had their equivalents for our psychology; but, when we employ the term *psychology* in speaking of the literature of the past, we are necessarily assimilating *their* equivalents to *our* measure. Earlier writers (Shakespeare, for one) knew not the word *psychology* and did not see human character in the terms that this modern, secular, and deterministic discipline implies.

What Christian literature *was* concerned with, always, was the state of the rational human soul, since it was this that made man

[82]

human, gave him superiority to the beasts, represented his tie to a realm of value beyond the material and the sensate, and, as the immortal principle within a merely temporal case of flesh, offered him a life beyond death. Small wonder, then, that literature should have focused upon the human soul as the most interesting, the most crucial, the most complex subject it could know.

In Defoe's time, psychology (or as the great Willis spelled it, "psyche-ology")[25] still meant the *logos* of the *psyche*, the state of the soul (although Willis himself would be instrumental in reshaping the term to mean the *logos* of that physical network we call mind);[26] and, although Defoe had his own equivalents for what we denominate psychology—shrewd observation from experience, conceptions of human nature framed from a multitude of written sources (including natural law and economics, moral treatises, criminal biographies, voyage literature, etc.), he was also, very obviously, concerned with the intricate problematics of the soul.

Much of the drama and the intensity of fiction that dealt with human "psyche-ology," the moral and spiritual condition of the human soul, lay in the fact that concern with the soul was an ultimate concern—*everything* was ventured, for in the final state of the soul rested one's hope for eternal felicity or fear of unending damnation. There is, of course, in the concept of deterministic psychology nothing remotely equivalent to this dramatic reach; and we may perhaps imaginatively forgive our ancestors the judgment they would surely have made upon our psychology as a mere scholasticism of the accidental and trivial, without any final reference, or any word of essence, or any link to a realm beyond the merely natural.

I am only too well aware that to speak of Defoe in such terms is to invoke the wrath of the committed secularist (I am, to be sure, myself a secularist, but uncommitted: history comes first), and the indignant charge that I am seeking to carry Defoe back to the

---

[25]Thomas Willis (1621–1675), the father of modern neurology. See Richard Hunter and Ida Macalpine, *Three Hundred Years of Psychiatry, 1535–1860* (London, 1963), p. 187 et passim.

[26]See the important essay by G. S. Rousseau, "Nerves, Spirits, and Fibres: Towards Defining the Origins of Sensibility," in *Studies in the Eighteenth Century III*, ed. R. F. Brissenden and J. C. Eade (Canberra, 1976), pp. 137–57.

Middle Ages. But one does not have to go that far to find this sort of language. One finds it *in* Defoe and all about him; for it is the language of his day.[27] To be sure, there were other languages (including some that we are pleased to call secular), and Defoe availed himself of them; but, despite his immersion in the world of business and affairs, he never really forgot for long that he was a created being with a soul to save. Nor did he forget it for his characters.

One more word, and then I shall return to *Moll Flanders*. We are given to supposing, doubtless because of the example of Victorian-Edwardian Christianity, that the secular and the religious denote inexorably separate islands of being. If we find in literature of the past an interest in everyday concerns, or a commitment to mercantile matters (especially!), or a sense of humor, or displays of irony, we presume that these cannot be part of a religious sensibility, because these things are *predefined* by the Victorian-Edwardian ethos as secular. So, too, if a work of the past does not carry specific allusions to the Trinity and exemplifications of Christian humility, then it cannot be Christian, for that has likewise been predefined—ergo, the work must be secular. But the Christianity of Boccaccio or Rabelais or Spenser or Herbert or Dryden or Swift (and they were all firm, albeit quite different, Christian writers) does not observe this trivializing demarcation of worlds: the religious and the secular go hand-in-hand. They may, for one purpose or another, be temporarily or juridically distinguished; but none of these writers

---

[27]One may choose at random from one's bookshelves. My hand unfortunately lights on *Essays upon Several Subjects*, by the much belabored city knight Sir Richard Blackmore (London, 1716). No matter: he is typical enough of contemporary (not merely bourgeois) thought on the subject: "Since after this Body is buried in the Grave, I shall still remain in Being, nor will my Existence be discontinued in any Period of Duration, it is of the highest Concern to know, whether I shall be Happy or Miserable in that Everlasting State. I am a Creature and a Subject of the Supream Ruler of the World, and by the rational Faculties with which I am endow'd, I can easily discern there are many natural Laws and moral Duties, which I am bound to obey; and that therefore I am an accomptable Being, and shall be rewarded or punish'd, according to my Observance or Contempt of those Divine Precepts and Rules of Life; and how terrible will be the Sentence, should I be condemn'd to endless Sufferings and Despair?" ("An Essay upon the Immortality of the Soul," *Essays*, pp. 297–98).

ever loses sight of the fact that the human soul represents the intersection of *both* realms. Nor do any of these writers, whatever secular elements they may introduce, ever forget that the *ultimate* aim of human existence is salvation. Of the rational soul.

3

The testing of Moll's soul is carried out, of course, in *this* world, as in all the romances and as in actual life, for, even when the romance narrative was allegorized or removed to some exotic and unknown latitude, it always carried an implicit reference (like beast fables, for that matter) to the world of the actual, the world of men, the stage upon which the soul conducted its battles and won or lost its struggle. Once again, a concentration upon the world of actuality need not at all suggest a secular consciousness: indeed, to have done with the thing, it is entirely doubtful that any such concept, in the modern sense of the term, existed, however much we populate the Renaissance and seventeenth century with "people like us." But, if the narrative action inevitably was located in the world of fortune, the *significance* of that action lay elsewhere. The values by which human action was judged were not presumed to be of merely human creation, as is the case today; rather, they lay in the great realms of divine and natural law, eternal, universal, and abiding. (Even the despised deists normally agreed with this proposition, made it in fact the basis of their own argument for universal religion.)

If the narrative behind the narrative is, then, the adventure of a human soul, Defoe's constant reflections upon evil and sin and the moral life are not at all the excrescences that an age peering anxiously about for any hint of psychological or realistic elements has supposed them to be: they are, in fact, the central matter of the central story, just as Defoe always insisted they were. Moll's reflections, like her actions, offer Defoe's reader cues to the state of her soul and of her spiritual existence (a truly compelling question for readers who were concerned for the state of their own souls), and this was not a matter of pious moralizing or conventional platitudes, but a life-and-death struggle, with the crucial addendum that it represented a stuggle for *eternal* life or death. It concerned forever. To quote Blackmore again, since I have chosen him at random (hundreds of other writers are saying the same thing at the same time, just as today thousands of writers are repeatedly and conventionally explaining human existence on psychological and sociological grounds): "So short is the Extent of our present Existence, if consider'd in an absolute Sense; but how momentary will it seem when compar'd with Ages that never end? What is this Span of Life, when we reflect upon interminable Duration? What is Time but a little Rill, or Drop, compar'd with the boundless Ocean of Eternity?"[28] What indeed? If the modern reader can enjoy an amiable frisson in contemplating the inconceivable notion of infinity, he may be able to summon up some historical appreciation of what the notion of eternity meant to ages that linked it inextricably with man's ultimate hopes and fears.

I shall not here trace at large the history of Moll's soul, which is the implicit narrative focus; but to trace it in detail would be to recover most nearly, I think, the book that Defoe's contemporaries read (which is not at all to say that even the most orthodox among them found no enjoyment in her worldly adventures; of course they did). If one tried the experiment of leafing through the various critical studies of *Moll Flanders* in this century, replacing all reference to psychology with "psyche-ology" or "the state of the Soul," and then added to this all the passages that have been dismissed as "mere conventional moralizing," one would have a pretty fair beginning for such a history. Born in sin, Moll displays very early her vanity and her refusal to accept her place in society (both of which we are likely to find admirable, but our opinion means nothing to the integrity of *Defoe's* tale).[29] As usual in the romances, childhood is given only the briefest sketch, primarily to establish traits that belong to the essence of a character; for, once again, the romances were not interested in character development—and neither was

---

[28]Ibid., p. 295.

[29]We are somewhat given to the circularity of projecting our attitudes into Defoe's characters, reading Defoe's own views from them, and then examining the characters in terms of "Defoe's" necessary attitudes. Moreover, Defoe's unquestioned skill at personation of alien individuals has led us into supposing a closer identification of Defoe with his various rascals than the evidence warrants. What *we* find sympathetic or appealing, we tend to assume that Defoe, too, like a sensible man, must have felt. The conclusion does not follow.

Defoe. What should have led him to be? He was not a nineteenth-
or early twentieth-century novelist. The narrative proper begins,
of course, with the snares of the older brother, which Moll is willing
enough to wander into. Though somewhat innocent of the world,
she has a "Head full of Pride" (p. 22), which was, after all, sufficient
to the original loss of paradise: "But as the Devil is an unwearied
Tempter, so he never fails to find opportunity for that Wickedness
he invites to: It was one Evening that I was in the Garden . . ."
(p. 26). After her fall, Moll repents only when the younger brother
proposes honorable marriage (p. 31); but, of course, the repentance
is not genuine and is "dissipated in worldly schemings." For Moll
is *in love with* her sin; and even after marriage she commits "Adultery
and Incest" in her heart by continuing to yearn after the older
brother (p. 59). Actual incest and adultery will follow this prophetic
heart-sin in the course of Moll's career. Through her string of
husbands, whenever Moll is left to her own devices, she displays
some new weakness of soul—from vanity and luxury through greed
and near-despair.

Approaching the structural center of Moll's criminal career, just
before the death of her last husband, we find her looking back and
observing: "I had a past life of a most wretched kind to account
for, some of it in this World as well as in another" (p. 187). But
as her funds decrease, following the husband's death, the busy Devil
appears again; and Moll responds like a sleepwalker: "But as the
Devil carried me out and laid his Bait for me, so he brought me to
be sure to the place, for I knew not whither I was going or what
I did" (p. 191). So, earlier, on occasions when an advisor is serving
as agent of the devil, Moll finds herself "Reason'd out of her Reason" (pp. 57, 173), which is to say, out of the faculty that can
identify and distinguish sin. So, as "the diligent Devil" prompts,
"I blindly obeyed his Summons" (p. 199): "Thus I that was once
in the Devil's Clutches, was held fast there as with a Charm, and
had no power to go without the Circle, till I was ingulph'd in
Labyrinths of Trouble too great to get out at all" (p. 203). It is
probable that Moll's observation on her lack of power to deny the
devil's summons has less to do with a narrator's attempt to palliate
her sins than it has with a striking exemplum of the moral impotence
that follows upon slavery to Satan: "Ye are of your father the devil,

[87]

and the lusts of your father ye will do" (John 8:44). By degrees her heart becomes hardened to reflection and she ceases to be a free moral agent: " 'Tis evident to me, that when once we are harden'd in Crime, no Fear can affect us, no Example give us any warning" (p. 221). Hopelessly a slave, genuinely "in service" now, Moll finds that "I could not forbear going Abroad again, *as I call'd it now*, any more than I could when my Extremity really drove me out for Bread" (p. 253). The final stage of degradation comes when Moll actually begins to take *pride* in her capacities as a thief: "I could fill up this whole Discourse with the variety of such Adventures which daily Invention directed to, and which I manag'd with the utmost Dexterity, and always with Success" (p. 241). If Moll, the narrator, is personating the soul's estate of young Moll the thief, we have here a recognizable voice: the mortal sin of presumption, which rises from despair of God's grace; and Moll the thief is at this point no different from the impudently merry inhabitants of Newgate: "But how Hell should become by degrees so natural, and not only tollerable, but even agreeable, is a thing Unintelligible, but by those who have Experienc'd it, as I have" (p. 276). And, in Newgate, Moll will explicitly despair of Grace: "I neither had a Heart to ask God's Mercy, or indeed to think of it, and in this I think I have given a brief Description of the compleatest Misery on Earth" (p. 279).

The stages of her final repentance in Newgate have been soundly outlined by Starr and need not here be recapitulated.[30] One may observe, however, that this phenomenon of repentance is not a psychological phenomenon, as we conceive psychology. It is, rather, "psyche-ological"—a working in the soul. And, since a character's essence—which is what the romance tradition was interested in—resides in the soul, not in the various inessential accidents that for a later tradition would create individuality and realism, a potent change in the soul is quite literally a change in the person's essence, a change in essential character. So that Moll is entirely correct when she declares, as she is awakened to true reflection: "In a word, I was perfectly chang'd, and become another Body" (p. 281). She will take on a new being with her conversion, a new character, reborn and "restor'd" to herself (p. 281):

[30]Starr, *Autobiography*, pp. 155–60.

I am not capable of reading Lectures of Instruction to any Body, but I relate this in the very manner in which things then appear'd to me, as far as I am able; but infinitely short of the lively Impressions which they made on my Soul at that time. . . . . It must be the Work of every sober Reader to make just Reflections on them, as their own Circumstances may direct; and without Question, this is what every one at sometime or other may feel something of; I mean a clearer Sight into things to come, than they had here, and a dark view of their own Concern in them. [pp. 287–88]

There are, of course, complexities that follow upon repentance and conversion. John Bunyan's *Grace Abounding to the Chief of Sinners*, which records a soul-wrestling rather more strenuous than Moll's, confronted honestly the problem of backsliding and weakening of resolve;[31] and Christian, in the moral romance of *Pilgrim's Progress*, found that his severest difficulties and the real test of his faith only *began with* his conversion. For God's grace is continually required (as the good minister in Newgate observes to Moll after the sentence of transportation, "*He said*, I must have more than ordinary secret Assistance from the Grace of God, if I did not turn as wicked again as ever," p. 293). And Defoe, as "editor," notes in the Preface that Moll upon her return to England "was not so extraordinary a Penitent, as she was at first" (p. 5). The point, despite the argument of the Synod of Dort,[32] is that conversion offers no automatic guarantee of continued Grace (nor does it lift man above the condition of the human, as some modern critics seem to expect; he remains a fallen creature). Thus Bunyan's Christian, at the last stage of his pilgrimage, observes Ignorance being thrust into a door in the side of the Hill: "Then I saw that there was a way to Hell even from the Gates of Heaven, as well as from the City of Destruction."[33]

4

The microcosmic narrative of the pilgrimage or testing of the human soul took place necessarily in the world of man, the world of the actual, which is where the race was run. But throughout the Christian era it was taken for granted (and not only by platonists) that another world, more perfect and more *real*, intersected the world

---

[31]Everyman's Library ed. (London, 1928), pp. 77 ff.
[32]The last of the "Five Points," the Perseverance of the Saints.
[33]Everyman's Library ed., rev. (London, 1954), p. 162.

of man precisely through the rational soul. Access to that higher reality was possible only by means of the instructed moral reason and God's good grace; but of its existence no one was in doubt. Even skeptics of the Renaissance and well through Defoe's time seldom doubted the *existence* of such a realm: their "error" lay in trying to reduce its definition to the terms of a different and alien mode of rationality, the mathematical, critical, and scientific. In the heyday of the chivalric romance, this higher world of ultimate value, by which were judged the actions of men in actual life (or those in fictive representations), was often simply assumed; and the romances had no great need to stress the matter, any more than the modern novelist need stress the assumed fact that each of his characters is possessed of an unconscious mind. But, by Defoe's time, the various challenges to religious assumptions of the past century, though still scattered and unfocused, had at least created an atmosphere in which the sure existence of a providential realm was felt in need of emphasis. (Such a feeling lay behind the defenses of poetic justice like that of John Dennis.)[34] Hence, whereas earlier audiences for the romance might take for granted the fact that characters of a fiction, though acting in a simulacrum of the actual world, were operating morally and spiritually under the sure-judging eye of Providence (and it was this certainty, as I have said, that provided the ultimate macrocosmic structure for romance narrative), Defoe seems to feel that he must make this still-believed principle explicit: "Really [says Moll] my Heart began to look up more seriously, than I think it ever did before, and to look with great Thankfulness to the Hand of Providence, which had done such wonders for me, who had been myself the greatest wonder of Wickedness, perhaps that had been suffered to live in the World" (pp. 336–37). And then she can return to "the fact" of her narrative, the microcosmic discourse.

[34]For instance, this, in the *Remarks upon Cato* (1713): " 'Tis certainly the Duty of every Tragick Poet, by an exact Distribution of a Poetical Justice, to imitate the Divine Dispensation, and to inculcate a particular Providence. 'Tis true indeed upon the Stage of the World the Wicked sometimes prosper, and the Guiltless suffer. But that is permitted by the Governour of the World, to shew from the Attribute of his infinite Justice that there is a Compensation in Futurity" (*The Critical Works of John Dennis*, ed. Edward N. Hooker [Baltimore, 1943], II, 49).

That Defoe was still presuming the structural and judgmental function of Providence in his narrative and expecting that his readers would feel it as an external ordering principle that made scrupulous and minute internal ordering unnecessary, seems to me likely. Narratives had been doing just this for hundreds of years and obviously their audiences had responded properly; there was little reason for Defoe to doubt that they would continue to do so; but he had, in any case, taken care explicitly to point out the providential frame—perhaps for those who might be uninstructed, but also perhaps because the Puritan tradition (like the Anglican, for that matter) simply took pleasure in recognizing the providential hand in the mere natural world.

The major assumption that lies behind my argument, as should be clear by now, is that we have too much tended in our portraits of the early eighteenth century to stress those elements that we should like to see there because they are comfortable (or exciting) to us. But this emphasis on relevance seems to me ultimately a very narrow box, one that does not ask the reader to stretch his imagination and enter into worlds of thought that do *not* provoke mere knee-jerk reactions of recognition and satisfaction. Certainly the historical scholar should not be concerned with what *we* find central, but with what the era under consideration found central. We have much overblown the skeptical currents, deism, secularism, and the impact of science (actually still under a form that has very properly been called by E. A. Burtt "metaphysical"), in the age, and ignored, for a variety of reasons, none of which serves the historical enterprise, the solidly Christian frame in which the greater part of the era's literature was produced.

Nevertheless, if this is admitted one can then agree that there *was* a difference from earlier Christian ages and that within the ruling Christian frame a multitude of tiny divagations was present—directions that before the century was out would be shaping a thoroughly different intellectual and spiritual world.[35] If it is

[35]I subjoin a note to assure those who may nurture a tendency toward willful misreading that I am quite conscious of the many and subtle modifications of the romance tradition that took place in Defoe's fiction (the specific localizations of place, the greater—if still casual—attention to chronology, the "ordinary" personages as central characters, the bourgeois emphases, the unvarnished style that

anachronistic to project the values of that brave new world back upon an earlier time when only its seeds were germinating, it is nevertheless not wrong to see that the seeds were there. Daniel Defoe's restless, inquiring mind led him to rake over many of those seeds (as modern scholarship has admirably documented), often without any prevision of what might burgeon forth from them. But it is my conviction that in his fictive narrations, as in his life, the microcosmic world of the insistent actual was brought within the judgmental and ordering macrocosmic configuration of Divine Providence.

often resembles contemporary court testimony, etc., etc.). But these topics have been a major concern of Defoe criticism for years past and need scarcely be recapitulated here, since they would merely obscure my central argument—which is, that much also remained in essence unchanged from the past.

Persius, the Opposition to Walpole, and Pope

HOWARD D. WEINBROT

PERSIUS HAS GENERALLY BEEN CONSIDERED FAR LESS ATTRAC-
tive than Horace or Juvenal, and thus far less important as a
contributor to the history of British satire. Indeed, the few modern
studies of Persius' relevance for the eighteenth century suggest an
advanced case of anorexia, a willful starvation and withdrawal of
nourishment rather than a healthy leanness.[1] Most earlier readers
also placed Persius beneath Horace and Juvenal, though still in
their qualitative group, and still of great interest and significance.
His dark, rough, grave poems were essential for the ongoing Renaissance view of what satire should be, and his other conventions
mingled well with those of Juvenal to create a satirist of immediate
utility for Pope and the opposition to Walpole—the biting, hostile,
somber, virtuous outcast who attacked a society rotting from the
top down.

This essay is adapted from Chapters 2, 4, and 8 of the author's *Alexander Pope and
the Traditions of Formal Verse Satire.* Copyright © 1982 by Princeton University Press.
Adapted by permission of Princeton University Press.

[1]The standard view has been stated by Raman Selden, who believes that
Lucilius and Persius "were not used directly as models by the English Augustan
satirists" (*English Verse Satire 1590–1765* [London, 1978], p. 11). For other views,
however, see William Frost, "English Persius: The Golden Age," *Eighteenth-Century
Studies,* 2 (1968), 77–101, and especially Cynthia Dessen's study of Benjamin
Loveling's *First Satire of Persius Imitated* (1740): "An Eighteenth-Century Imitation
of Persius, Satire I," *Texas Studies in Language and Literature,* 20 (1978), 433–56.
Some of Persius' apparently political qualities, and consequent utility for the
opposition to Walpole, are discussed in this useful essay as well. For more clas-
sically oriented studies, see Cynthia Dessen, *Iunctura Callidus Acri: A Study of Persius'
Satires,* Illinois Studies in Language and Literature, No. 59 (Urbana, 1968), and
J. C. Bramble, *Persius and the Programmatic Satire: A Study in Formal Imagery* (Cambridge, 1974).

Some of his attraction can be documented in the list of English translations from 1616 to 1817: Holyday (1616), Dryden (1693), Eelbeck (1719), Sheridan (1728), Senhouse (1730), Stirling (1736), Brewster (1733–42), Burton (1752), Madan (1789), Drummond (1797), anonymous (1806), Howes (1809), and Gifford (1817).[2] Oldham acknowledges his debt to Persius for the Prologue of his *Satyrs upon the Jesuits* (1679); F. A. imitates the third satire in 1685; Tom Brown tries his hand at the Prologue and part of the first satire in 1707; six different imitators emerge between 1730 and 1740; Thomas Neville imitates most of the satires in 1769; Edward Burnaby Greene follows suit in 1799; an unknown author applies the fourth satire to Pitt in 1784; William Gifford's *Baviad* (with its title-page motto from Juvenal I.1–4) massively expands the first satire in 1791; and George Daniel's *Modern Dunciad* performs a similar task in 1814.[3] Persius was of course commented upon in

[2]These are, respectively, Barten Holyday, *Aulus Persius Flaccus His Satires Translated into English* (Oxford, 1616; reprinted with his Juvenal in 1673); John Dryden et al., *The Satires of Decimus Junius Juvenalis. . . . Together with the Satires of Aulus Persius Flaccus* (London, 1693); Henry Eelbeck, *A Prosaic Translation of Aulus Persius Flaccus's Six Satyrs* (London, 1719); Thomas Sheridan, *The Satyrs of Persius* (Dublin, 1728); John Senhouse, *The Satires of Aulus Persius Flaccus, Translated into English Prose* (London, 1730); John Stirling, *A. Persii Flacci, Satirae: or, The Satires of A. Persius Flaccus. . . . For the Use of Schools* (London, 1736); Thomas Brewster, *The Satires of Persius* (London, 1741–42; printed individually from 1733); Edmund Burton, *The Satyrs of Persius* (London, 1752); Martin Madan, *A New and Literal Translation of Juvenal and Persius*, 2 vols. (London, 1789); Sir William Drummond, *The Satires of Persius* (London, 1797); *The Satires of Aulus Persius Flaccus; Translated into English Verse* (London, 1806); Francis Howes, *The Satires of A. Persius Flaccus* (London, 1809); William Gifford, *The Satires of Aulus Persius Flaccus* (London, 1817, in vol. 2 of his Juvenal). This list should be supplemented with the several editions of Holyday's Persius (5th ed., 1650), Dryden's Juvenal and Persius (7th ed., 1754), and Brewster's Persius (2d ed., 1751), which also was reprinted in *D. Junii Juvenalis et A. Persii Flacci Satirae Expurgatae: In Usum Scholarum* (London, 1784; also includes Johnson's *London* [1738] and *Vanity of Human Wishes* [1749]), and in Edward Owen's *The Satires of Juvenal. . . . Also Dr. Brewster's Persius* (London, 1785). William Gifford's Persius appeared in 1821 as well.

[3]For these, see Oldham, *Some New Pieces* (London, 1684), with its separate pagination and title page for *Satyrs upon the Jesuits*, 3d ed. (London, 1685), sig. A2r; F. A., *The Third Satyr of A. Persius, In Way of a Dialogue, or Dramatick Interlude* (London, 1685); Brown, *The Works of Mr. Thomas Brown, Serious and Comical*, 4 vols., 5th ed. (London, 1720), I, 56–59; the six different imitators are discussed in section 2,

numerous encyclopedias, manuals, discussions of Roman satire, and Latin editions of his works, and was often translated in France, where he again was regarded as the least exalted of the elevated three. No doubt this is a partial list, since the voluminous miscellanies and collected poems must harbor other individual efforts. One may say, erring on the side of conservatism, that from the earlier seventeenth to the earlier nineteenth centuries in Britain, Persius enjoyed a minimum of thirteen complete translations, two nearly complete groups of imitations, eleven imitations or translations of individual satires, and much commentary, controversy, and pedagogical application. Multiple English, Continental, and Latin editions, many known in Britain, would swell this list substantially. Reclamation of Persius' conventions and reputation suggests that his influence must have been virtually inevitable, and inevitably in the direction of Juvenal and Pope.

1. Perceptions of Persius

The eighteenth century's Persian inheritance probably begins in 1605, with Isaac Casaubon's *Prolegomena* and edition of the satires which—together with his revolutionary *De Satyrica Graecorum et Satira Romanorum*—became loci classici of the study of Persius and formal verse satire. To Casaubon goes the credit for permanently forcing Persius into the same circle as Horace and Juvenal, vigorously resisting Scaliger's attacks upon him, and establishing Persius' reputation as a dominantly political satirist. From Dacier and Dryden to Drummond and Howes, most roads lead to and from Casaubon.[4]

His *Prolegomena* insists that the three Roman satirists must be examined with respect for their different individual contributions

below; Thomas Neville, *Imitations of Juvenal and Persius* (London, 1769); [Edward Burnaby Greene], *The Satires of Persius Paraphrastically Imitated and Adapted to the Times* (London, 1799); *The Fourth Satire of Persius Imitated, and Much Enlarged, In Application to the Right Honourable William Pitt* (London, 1784); William Gifford, *The Baviad. A Paraphrastic Imitation of the First Satire of Persius* (London, 1791); George Daniel, *The Modern Dunciad. A Satire. With Notes Biographical and Critical* (London, 1814).

[4]André Dacier's edition and translation of Horace probably was the best known such version in the seventeenth and eighteenth centuries, and includes a "Préface sur les Satires d'Horace, Où l'on explique l'origine & le progrès de la Satire des Romains; & tous les changemens qui lui sont arrivez." Dacier quickly announced

and for their "nearly equal . . . diverse virtues," each of which he describes in familiar terms.[5] Casaubon's defense implies that he prefers Persius to his brother-satirists, but he nonetheless concludes modestly "that there is no one of these who was not superior to the rest by a certain virtue peculiar to himself; and, again, that there was no one who was not inferior to the rest for some reason" (p. 294).

Obscurity was one of the points on which Persius needed defense. Casaubon turns that apparent fault into an asset, and characterizes Persius as a courageous and clever satirist in the face of political intimidation: "In Persius what spirit? What ardor? What stimulus? For indeed his outspokenness was so great that he could not be induced even by fear of death to spare Nero" (p. 293). Since Persius was not foolhardy and did not court the separation of body from soul before its proper time, he intentionally wrote obscure verse "out of fear of that most cruel and bloodthirsty of tyrants against whom" his satires were written. The source of this wisdom was his tutor Cornutus, "who as an old man repeatedly whispered to him the words, 'be obscure.' Although Probus, or whoever is the writer of the life, does not say this explicitly, he nevertheless reports matters from which we ought to infer this much" (p. 296). These and comparable remarks would echo throughout the next two hundred years.

After 1605, in fact, nearly everyone agreed that Nero was Persius' main target in several of his six satires. In England translators from Holyday to Howes, from 1616 to 1809, tell British readers that, as Senhouse puts it, Persius "aims particularly at [Nero] in most of

---

his indebtedness to "le savant Casaubon." See *Œuvres d'Horace en Latin et en François, avec des Remarques,* 10 vols., 3d ed. (Paris, 1709), VI, 1 and passim. The third is the revised and preferred edition. For brief discussion of contemporary knowledge of Dacier, see Howard D. Weinbrot, *The Formal Strain: Studies in Augustan Imitation and Satire* (Chicago, 1969), pp. 60–68.

[5]As translated by Peter E. Medine, in "Isaac Casaubon's *Prolegomena* to the *Satires* of Persius: An Introduction, Text, and Translation," *English Literary Renaissance,* 6 (1976), 288. Subsequent quotations are given in text. Casaubon's distinction between satiric kinds already was becoming commonplace. "Description in Horace," for example, "is humbler, in Persius grander, in Juvenal often sublime" (p. 294).

his Satirs."[6] This opinion appears in France as well, and even though the formidable Pierre Bayle, later joined by the Abbé le Monnier in 1771, characteristically doubts that received truth, he admits that his is a minority opinion. "I should never have done," he says, "if I undertook to quote all the Authors who imagine that." Persius attacks Nero's unfortunate taste and poetry by citing four lines from his presumed, and bad, tragedy.[7] These commentators also tend to follow Casaubon in explaining Persius' obscurity. As Holyday says, difficulty in reading Persius proceeds in part "from the want of Libertie, which in his desperate times, was altogether lost."[8] Far later Senhouse confirms that "the Fear of his Safety under *Nero,* compell'd him to this Darkness in some Places" (sig. A4r). In 1736 John Stirling offers a similar commonplace to his schoolboy audience: though Persius aimed at Nero in nearly all of his satires, he was "prudent enough not to arraign him openly and plainly."[9]

For some critics, the veil of obscurity extended beyond the grave. According to M. Selis in 1776, Persius' satires appeared after his death because only in that way of self-censorship could he be secure in attacking Nero. He thus joined caution to courage. "Il eut la sagesse de retenir son Ouvrage, & il mourut dans son lit." Since Cornutus had comparable affection for his own life, he refused to edit the satires, surrendering them instead to Caesius Bassus. Salis is confident that Persius' consistent attacks upon Nero are clear enough so that haters of the tyrant would recognize them, and obscure enough so that the tyrant himself could not understand them. No courtier would dare to explicate such satire in order to

---

[6] *The Satires of . . . Persius* (n. 2, above), p. 1. Subsequent citations from Senhouse are given in text.

[7] *A General Dictionary, Historical and Critical,* tr. John Peter Bernard, Thomas Birch, John Lockman, et al., 10 vols. (London, 1734–41), VII, 327. Subsequent references are cited in text. See also the Abbé le Monnier, *Satires de Perse* (Paris, 1771), pp. xix-xxi. Le Monnier is aware of, and comments upon, Bayle in several places—pp. xvii-xviii, for example.

[8] *Aulus Persius Flaccus His Satires* (n. 2, above), sig. A3v. Subsequent citations from Holyday are given in text.

[9] *The Satires of A. Persius Flaccus* (n. 2, above), sig.[π]3r. Subsequent citations from Stirling are given in text.

illumine his master's darkness. Apparently, for courtiers as well as poets, "il falloit être obscur ici, sous peine de la vie."[10]

Nero was a target because of his own corrupt taste and character and their influence on his subservient aristocrats, for, as a bad poet, the emperor encouraged a perverse emulation of incompetence. According to Senhouse, in Satire One "*Persius* covertly strikes at *Nero*, some of whose Verses he recites with Scorn and Indignation. He also takes notice of the Noblemen and their abominable Poetry, who in the Luxury of their Fortune, set up for Wits and Judges" (p. 6). John Stirling adds that "as a Friend to true Learning," Persius sharply lashed "the corrupt and degenerate Taste both of the Poets and Orators of his Time" (sig. A3r), and especially the poetry of Nero. Persius thus appeared to Pope's ancestors and contemporaries as a poet concerned with the decay of letters and with the imperial cause of that decay. "Indignation breaks out more and more because they would make such base and affected Verse," Eelbeck observes of Satire One.[11]

These cultural and political poses evoked a variety of related satiric conventions, four of which are especially useful for our purposes: disguise, dialogue, the nature of the adversarius, and irony.

John Stirling discusses the consequence of Persius' politically enforced obscurity—disguise, or what we might call the use of a persona for the poet, and historical label or analogue for his victim. Persius, Stirling claims, "was oblig'd to strike at [Nero] under borrowed Names, the better to evade his cruel Resentment" (sig. A3r). Comparable remarks pervade the criticism of Persius throughout the seventeenth and eighteenth centuries. According to Dryden, such role-playing begins in the Prologue itself, which hoped to conceal its author's name and station. "He liv'd in the dangerous Times of the tyrant *Nero*; and aims particularly at him, in most of his Satyrs. For which Reason, though he was a *Roman* Knight, and of a plentiful Fortune, he wou'd appear in this Prologue, but a

---

[10]*Satires de Perse, Traduites en François, avec des Remarques* (Paris, 1776), pp. xxviii (sagesse) and 116 (peine de la vie).

[11]*A Prosaic Translation of Aulus Persius Flaccus's Six Satyrs* (1719; n. 1, above), p. 15, n*. Subsequent citations from Eelbeck are given in text.

Beggarly Poet, who Writes for Bread."[12] In 1728 Thomas Sheridan observes that in Satire One "it is very probable that *Persius* levels at *Nero* under this covert Name" of Polydamus. Sheridan also joins previous commentators and anticipates later ones in saying that in Satire Four Persius "levels at *Nero* under the name of *Alcibiades*, for presuming to undertake the Administration of publick Affairs, without sufficient Qualifications for so great an Undertaking."[13] Just two years thereafter John Senhouse offers virtually the same argument and traces its provenance to Casaubon, who "made it apparent, that the Sting of this Satir was particularly aim'd at *Nero*" (p. 97).

The many shifts of speaker were another reason for the apparent obscurity of Persius. According to Casaubon, because of satire's "affinity with the plots of drama, it is complicated by the shifts of personae" (*Prolegomena*, p. 297). De la Valterie dutifully concurs in 1680 and says that because satire is a species of comedy, there are frequent changes of voice in Persius' poems. "La première est toute de cette sorte. . . . C'est un Dialogue perpetuel."[14] These shifts were thought to have been largely sorted out by the eighteenth century, and so readers knew who was speaking to whom. The dialogue between them, however, is quite different from that of Horace and the Pope of *Fortescue* and *Arbuthnot*, where dialogue is an emblem of dialectic, of the thrust, counterthrust, and resolution of argument. Persius does not offer a sense of growth and interplay between speakers. Instead we have unchanging characters enunciating noble or ignoble set pieces, and, often, with general rather than particular targets. Edward Burnaby Greene observes something along these lines when, in 1779, he says that Horace portrays "*living* Characters" in action, whereas Persius is busy "'teaching the passions to move' in the higher circle of *Personification*" and that his dialogues were closer to "the spirit of Epic Poesy" than to the conflict between

---

[12]*The Works of John Dryden*, Vol. IV, *Poems, 1693–1696*, ed. A. B. Chambers, William Frost, Vinton A. Dearing (Berkeley and Los Angeles, 1974), p. 255.

[13]*The Satires of Persius*, 2d ed. (London, 1739), pp. 6, 60.

[14]Abbé de la Valterie, trans., *Les Satyres de Juvénal et de Perse*, 2 vols. (Paris, 1680), II, sig. Liiir. The translation of Persius is dedicated to Boileau.

"the human puppets of the *Horatian Drama*."[15] More than forty years later William Gifford would complain that Persius "drew his ideas of mankind from the lessons of his preceptor, and looked upon human actions in the abstract; not modified and controlled by conventional circumstances, but . . . independent of all extrinsick influence."[16]

I suspect that Burnaby Greene and Gifford have overstated the degree to which disembodied voices palaver in the thin air of Persius' poems; but there is a satirically and aesthetically sound reason for such relatively nonterrestrial conflicts; namely, the participants are so morally distant that they cannot hear or influence one another. Eighteenth-century readers knew that the Monitor who tried to dissuade Persius from writing shared the values of Nero's court and courtiers. When he warns Persius that the doors of the great may be closed to him and that he will be in danger if he continues to write, the Monitor is not trying to protect Persius, but the objects of Persius' satire (lines 107–10). In a comparable situation Horace was able to move Trebatius to his side, for the emperor and his aristocratic friends were Horace's allies (*Satires* II.1). Persius, on the other hand, has created an adversarius who is unchanging in his support for the corrupt values that a decent man would abandon. John Aden accurately points out that Persius is the only one of the three Roman satirists to use such a device.[17] Horace reforms, dismisses, or shares values with his adversaries; Juvenal's occasional real—rather than nonce—adversarius normally is on his side or is scarcely vocal enough to ruffle the poem's rhetorical monologue; Persius alone gives us a corrupt or uneducable foil to the morally triumphant but defeated satirist. Because the satirist cannot refute someone incapable of understanding his own folly, Persius invited his readers to see the adversarius discredit himself. Pope, I shall argue, was among those who recognized this device,

[15] *The Satires of Persius paraphrastically imitated* (n. 3, above), pp. xxvii–xxviii.

[16] *The Satires of Aulus Persius Flaccus* (n. 2, above), p. xvi. Subsequent citations from this edition are given in text.

[17] *Something like Horace: Studies in the Art and Allusion of Pope's Horatian Satires* (Nashville, Tenn., 1969), p. 6. Aden also observes that in this respect "Pope more nearly resembles [Persius] than he does either Horace, whom he ostensibly imitates, or Juvenal, with whom he has very little in common at all" (p. 7).

and saw, as Francis Howes remarks, that "the objector is represented as sliding imperceptibly into self-ridicule till he exposes his own cause."[18]

As a result of the impenetrable dullness before him, Persius sometimes must retreat behind the protection of both masked and revelatory irony. Henry Eelbeck observes that the fourth satire's apparent attack upon Alcibiades really is "an Ironical Oration, vehement and very sharp," that labels Nero an unprepared ruler "intirely ignorant, either to condemn the Guilty, or to defend the Innocent" (p. 43, n*). The sixth satire includes "A Satyrical Irony in the Person of some third Speaker" (p. 80, n*). In 1752 Edmund Burton praises the politics and political irony in Satire One, for the satirist could not openly attack his emperor as a bad poet. Indeed, most auditors praised Nero's verse, "it being his constant custom to bribe people into an approbation of his ridiculous writings."[19] Hence, Burton says, in a passage that illuminates Persius' use of political opposition, disguise, and irony, "The following five lines [from line 59] are beautifully couched under a strong irony, and the greater pains we take to discover their beauties, the greater will be the pleasure which results from a true knowledge of their meaning. By the word *Iane* [*Janus*] we are to understand *Nero*, as by the words *patricius sanguis* [*blue-blooded patricians*] following, is meant the *Roman* nobility. By this subtle irony *Persius* seems to be paying *Nero* a great compliment; whereas those three lines mean quite the reverse of what they seem to import" (p. 20).

Similarly, when the Monitor warns Persius not to be so critical, or he will be in professional and personal danger, Persius immediately plays the docile poet and says: "Well, well, have your way; I will paint everything white henceforth. Bravo! Bravo! You shall all be paragons of creation. Will that please you?" (lines 110–11).[20]

---

[18]*The Satires of A. Persius Flaccus* (n. 2, above), p. xvii. Subsequent references are cited in text.

[19]*The Satyrs of Persius* (n. 2, above), p. 19. Subsequent citations are given in text.

[20]The translation is from the Loeb Classical Library, *Juvenal and Persius*, trans. G. G. Ramsay (London and Cambridge, Mass., 1961), p. 327. Dryden's version is "All, all is admirably well for me" (*Poems, 1693–1696*, n. 12, above, p. 273). Sheridan is slightly more expansive and, perhaps unexpectedly, energetic: "Why

Whether it pleased the Monitor we cannot say, though the wit did please Burton: "This is an ironical concession. . . . This is said with a masterly sagacity, to appease the person he is speaking to here, who cautions him against writing too fully" (p. 30).

Commentators and readers also were interested in the man behind "Persius," and found that he was both like and unlike his satiric mask. Barten Holyday praises Persius' prudent bravery, political virtue, consequent anger at those without it, and the punishment he must therefore inflict. Such a reincarnation of Brutus and his now dead Roman virtues shall take his purer fire and burn out "th' envenom'd fogges of Vice" from their seat of infection.

> And then inflame
> Them, that they may be lights to their own shame;
> Which as a Comet, may affright the Earth
> With horror, at its own prodigious birth;
> And, with its darting tail threatening dread
> Vengeance, point-out to wrath each guilty Head.

F. A., in 1685, relates Persius' bravery to the poet's own virtue, which must overcome all. He thus has the tutor, thought to be a persona for Persius in the third satire, tell his student: "*Dare* to be good;—and *Vertue* be thy Guide; / No way to daring *Vertue* is deny'd."[21] Henry Eelbeck, on whose list of "Encouragers and Subscribers" Dr. Arbuthnot appears in 1719, characterizes Persius as scorning the vulgar opinion of his Monitor who discouraged his writing of satires. He would vigorously soldier on, "notwithstanding all the Vengeance that might befal him either from *Nero* the Emperor, or any Nobleman at *Rome*" (p. 3). And, as Senhouse insists, Persius, who "is of a free Spirit, breaks through all these Difficulties, and boldly arraigns the false Judgement of the Age in which he lives" (p. 7).

then, let their Geese be all Swans for me—I shall not dispute it—Every thing is fine—It is all admirable." *Persius* (n. 2, above), p. 23. Quotations from Persius' Latin are from *D. Junii Juvenalis, et A. Persii Flacci Satirae*, ed. Ludovicus Prateus, 7th ed. (London, 1736).

[21]For Holyday, see *Decimus Junius Juvenalis, and Aulus Persius Flaccus Translated and Illustrated* (Oxford, 1673), p. 341, "An Apostrophe of the Translator to his Authour Persius." For F. A., see *The Third Satyr of A. Persius* (n. 3, above), p. 3.

Prudent bravery, good taste, and animosity to bad taste clearly bring with them other important traits of personal and literary character. In the first satire Persius describes himself as a teller of harsh truths (lines 56–57, 120–23) and a man whose petulance and spleen ("sed sum petulanti splene," line 12) burst forth in response to miserable art, for he knows true passion and can be moved only by it (lines 90–91). This indignation easily can be, and was, praised as necessary for the opponent of imperial vice. It also could be seen as unpleasant. In his *Poetices* (1561) Julius Caesar Scaliger labels Persius "morosus." By 1674 René Rapin tells readers in France and England that Persius is grave, vehement, obscure, and "speaks not but with *sadness*, what by *Horace* is said with the greatest mirth imaginable, whom sometimes he wou'd imitate; his moroseness scarce ever leaves him . . . and he never sports, but after the most serious manner in the world." Boileau calls Persius "un Philosophe chagrin"; the Abbé Batteux regards him as grave, serious, and "ever melancholic"; the *Encyclopédie* thinks him "un peu triste," as indeed does Edward Burnaby Greene, who remarks Persius' "gloom of severity due to the collapse of learning and morals in his age."[22]

Persius' indignation and sadness could be matters for reasoned evaluation, one group arguing that outrage and unhappiness are the appropriate responses to vice, the other arguing that the speaker seems to enjoy being hurtful and gives no pleasure with his solemnity, especially since the generic source of satire is comedy, not tragedy. But there was no difference of opinion regarding the essential morality of Persius the man. Many of his editors were schoolmasters who naturally were moved by the admiring and respectful

---

[22]Scaliger, *Poetices Libri Septem* (Lyons, 1561), p. 323. ("Persii vero stilus, morosus"); Rapin, *Reflections on Aristotle's Treatise of Poesie* [trans. Thomas Rymer] (London, 1674), p. 139; Boileau, *Œuvres de M. Boileau Despréaux*, ed. M. de Saint-Marc, 4 vols. (Paris, 1747), I, 116; Batteux, Abbot Charles Batteux, *A Course of the Belles Lettres: or, the Principles of Literature. Translated from the French . . . by Mr. Miller*, 4 vols. (London, 1761), III, 155; *Encyclopédie, ou Dictionnaire raisonné*, 17 vols. (Neufchâtel, 1765), XIV, 701, "Satyre." The article is by the chevalier de Jaucourt, and includes the "Parallèle des satyriques romains & françois" by Batteux (see Miller's translation, III, 192–95, which substitutes Dryden and Young for the French satirists); Greene, *The Satires of Persius*, p. xxxiv.

relationship between the young satirist and Cornutus who, as John Stirling says, taught Persius to abhor the vices of Nero and the decline of learning. Stirling also admires the "unparallel'd Gratitude to his Master *Cornutus*" (sig. A3r). Moreover, Persius was exemplary in other ways as well, and morally superior to either Horace or Juvenal. Like other commentators, Pierre Bayle draws his kind words from Probus' life of Persius. "He was a Roman Knight, and related both by blood and marriage to persons of the highest rank. . . . He was a good friend, and a better son, brother and relation. He was perfectly chaste, though a very handsome man; he was sober, gentle as a lamb, and modest as a young virgin: so true it is, that we must not always judge of a man's morals from his writings, for Persius's *satyrs* are very licentious, and full of rancour and gall" (7, 324–25).

Such beneficence was praised throughout the seventeenth and eighteenth centuries. Bishop Gilbert Burnet frequently was cited as having recommended Persius' satires as excellent quasi-Christian sermons.[23] In 1705 Thomas Jaffray also notes that Persius' morality often was Christian, and one year later in France, Le Noble argues that Persius was a wiser and more accomplished philosopher than Horace or Juvenal, as his spiritually Christian fifth satire makes clear. Stirling thus is conventional when he observes that Persius "had a sincere Veneration for Religion, as may be discover'd by his Writings" (sig. A3r). Near mid-century "Sir" John Hill is aware of Persius' many weaknesses—including his insults rather than more pleasing laughter—but, he tells a noble lord no doubt interested in such matters, "he is worth the pains: his sense is worth the search. His virtue is a point in which he excels all the rest of the satyrists,

---

[23]As one important citation of Burnet's remark in his *Discourse of the Pastoral Care* (1692), pp. 162–63, see Dryden's "Discourse concerning the Original and Progress of Satire," prefatory to Juvenal and Persius of 1693, in *Poems, 1693–1696*, p. 56. Burnet singles out Persius' second satire. His judgment appears as late as 1789 in Martin Madan's Juvenal and Persius (n. 2, above), I, 4. Jaffray, *An Essay for Illustrating the Roman Poets for the Use of Schools* (Edinburgh, 1705), p. 11. Le Noble, *Satires de Perse traduites en vers François* (Amsterdam, 1706), sig. *5r. This is one of the three ways in which Persius is preferable to Horace or Juvenal. But all are "admirables dans leurs manières & exelens dans leurs genres" (sigs. *4v–5r).

and to me his eminence in this compensates for all and would compensate for more than all his faults."[24]

During the Restoration and eighteenth century, then, there was one nearly unchallenged view of Persius: he was the brave, prudent, serious satirist who attacked moral, political, and literary vice, especially as exemplified by the tasteless, wicked, bribing Nero and his court. Since open attack would have meant death, he resorted to masks, irony, a self-refuting, self-condemning, and uneducable adversarius, and the obscurity his friend and tutor urged upon him; he even refused to publish his satires until after his death, thus assuring that he could be reasonably satirical during his lifetime. The decay around him both angered and saddened him, but did not affect his personal ethics, family life, or religious views, all of which were excellent, in spite of the severity and occasional vulgarity in his poems. Though probably not so great a satirist as Horace or Juvenal, he was their moral superior, and certainly in their approximate qualitative rank.

With these traits and conventions before us, two remarks must be made. First, as many readers knew, in spite of Persius' use of some Horatian techniques, his satiric vision includes more of Juvenal's declining world than Horace's stable one, and thus includes more bitterness than equanimity. Late in the century William Boscawen was among those who had made the connection between Persius and Juvenal. Post-Horatian times

> Saw angry Satire, wak'd by daring crimes;
> When from the Stoic school grave Persius brought
> The rigid lore her ancient sages taught,
> And ardent virtue with sublimer rage
> Inspir'd fierce Juvenal's indignant page.[25]

[24]*Observations on the Greek and Roman Classics. In a Series of Letters to a Young Nobleman* (London, 1753), pp. 261–62. In the "Inspector," No. 136, Hill refers to Persius' "one continued insulting sneer" (*The Inspector*, 2 vols. [London, 1753], II, 254). See also Dryden's "Discourse," where Persius "rather insulted over Vice and Folly, than expos'd them, like *Juvenal* and *Horace*" (*Poems, 1693–1696*, p. 52).

[25]*The Progress of Satire* (London, 1798), p. 8. This poem is reprinted in Boscawen's *Poems* (London, 1801). The association of Persius and Juvenal—with full awareness of differences as well—was familiar. See, for example, [William Combe's?] *Belphegor. The Diabo-Lady. Or, A Match in Hell* (London, 1777). The author claims

The choice of satiric options thus was heavily weighted on the side of a satirist portraying himself as the outnumbered, brave, hostile enemy of daring crimes in the state, crimes commonly inspired by monarchic and aristocratic precedent. Second, Persius, like Juvenal himself, was therefore adaptable for the needs of Alexander Pope and his colleagues in the outraged, gloomy, disaffected, "patriot" opposition to Sir Robert Walpole.

2. Persius and Opposition

As early as 1685 an angry adapter of Persius struck what would become a familiar pose. The tutor, confident of the power of "daring *Vertue*," speaks to his student and hopes that the "Great *Sovereign* of the Skies" will vouchsafe "To scourge the Pride of Tyrants" by showing them the face of goodness and the felicity they have lost. So punished, they will *"turn pale*, and pine away, and dye."[26] Whether this satire was read in the 1730s is doubtful, and irrelevant, for it nevertheless shows Persius' lashing and contemplative mode and makes plain that he was known to poets as well as commentators for his dialogue, praise of virtue, insistence on close human relationships, and immediate involvement in the resistance to tyranny.

Several of these traits were blended with Persius' melancholic and, in this case, marginally political mode in John Lord Hervey's unsigned *A Satire in the Manner of Persius: In a Dialogue Between Atticus and Eugenio. By a Person of Quality*.[27] Atticus at first is indignant regarding man, and his young friend Eugenio is sadly disillusioned: "I thought Men worthless, now I've prov'd 'em so," he laments (p. 10). Since Atticus already has that knowledge and is aware of the "Senate's sinking Fame" and Britain's mere "Shew of Freedom dwindled to a Name," lashing the wicked age is appropriate (p. 6).

---

that he is Juvenalian (sig. A1v); the "editor," however, adds that "we are of opinion that he more resembles *Persius*; whose writings are both more severe and obscure" (sig. a3r).

[26]F. A., *The Third Satyr of A. Persius*, pp. 3, 4.

[27]Robert Halsband states that this poem was "composed by Hervey during the 1720s," and was published in 1730 and 1739. I have not seen the 1730 version, and quote from that of London, 1739. The "Christian stoic point of view," according to Halsband, "is not characteristic of his thinking" (*Lord Hervey, Eighteenth-Century Courtier* [New York, 1974], p. 325, n. 38).

After this Juvenalian outburst Atticus goes on to offer quasi-stoical advice and urges Eugenio to laugh at men's follies before he weeps at their faults. If the wicked prosper,

> submit, for Prudence lies
> In suffering well—'Tis equally unwise
> To see the Injuries we won't resent,
> And mourn the Evils which we can't prevent.
>
> [p. 8]

In spite of Eugenio's efforts, he cannot take this sound advice, and regretfully says that he is immune from disappointments, because immune from the vain hopes of joy: "Repuls'd, I strive; betray'd I trust no more" (p. 9). After several complaints, lashings, and reluctant acceptance of the world's miserable condition—"What Joy for Truth, what Commerce for the Just?" (p. 14)—Atticus praises his friend's early wisdom and refusal to be seduced by secular tinsel. He consoles us with a Christianized stoic vision and an orthodox answer to a familiar question regarding the existence of evil, for man's dim sight cannot see God's just plan:

> undeserv'd he ne'er inflicts a Woe,
> Nor is his Recompence unsure, tho' slow.
> Unpunish'd none transgress, deceiv'd none trust,
> His Rules are fix'd, and all his Ways are Just.
>
> [p. 17]

The manner of Persius is reflected in the stoical but also bitter personal and political tones of the educated and aristocratic speakers appropriate for the highest born and most academic of the three great Latin satirists.

Hervey's commitment to Walpole's government made it difficult for him to portray too corrupt a political world, for that would reflect upon those from whom he still hoped to gain rewards. Most of the poem thus is general and laments the human, not Walpolean, situation. But Walpole's literary enemies were quick to realize that the general could be made particular, Zeno could be altered to Cobham, the tyrants of the mind replaced by the tyrants of the court, and that Nero could evoke George II, Walpole, or both. Historical parallels were popular with the opposition in part because of the legal camouflage they supplied. In 1741 the anonymous author of *The Art of Poetry* (London) ironically tells his antiministerial readers that

> Old *Roman Names* your Characters suit best;
> Secure, as if in *Roman* Armour drest.
> Happy the Author whose Performance shines
> With living *Nero*'s, living *Catilines*!
>
> [p. 9]

At least five such occasional well-armored efforts suggest that, in varying degrees, the opposition was in league with Juvenal and Persius and generally found Horace irrelevant or antithetical for its purposes. Indeed, as the "progress" of these poems suggests, the imitations get harsher, more overtly political, more Juvenalian, and more indebted to Pope as the decade advances.

The first is a relatively muted anonymous adaptation of the fourth satire and its attack upon Nero. In *Advice to an Aspiring Young Gentleman of Fortune* (London, 1733) that unpleasant emperor has been replaced by his modern equivalent, the author's *"garter'd* Friend . . . / To whom an injur'd Nation Vengeance owes." The court is a place "of *well-invented* Lies" where the "Dangers of *Excise*" must be slurred over (p. 5), where the corrupt rich thrive, where purchased coronets abound, and where flattery, and not achievement, will "fit you for *Preferment* in a trice" (p. 10). It is best, the honest speaker urges, to leave the ticklish helm of government "to ——*y*'s saving Hand" (p. 10). That line surely supports replacement of Walpole with Pulteney, is hostile to the gartered knight, and commissions Persius as a Roman officer in the opposition's British army.

One year later the pseudonymous Griffith Morgan D'Anvers is less subtle than his predecessor. D'Anvers's *Persius Scaramouch: Or, a Critical and Moral Satire on the Orators, Scriblers, and Vices of the present Times* (London, 1734) imitates Persius' first satire and dedicates it to Pulteney, without benefit of nonobfuscating dashes. D'Anvers, in dialogue with Henley, immediately opposes the "ministerial Crew of profligate Scriblers" (p. iii) who try to defame Pulteney, aligns himself with Juvenal, who also had to say, "Semper ego auditor tantum nunquamne reponam?" (p. iii), and labels himself "a Man of a true old *British* Spirit and Integrity." D'Anvers also alludes to, and approves of, Pope's earlier and potential attacks on the administration. He himself offers his political and moral enemies "a little present and gentle Chastisement"; but he is assured that their miserable characters "will be transmitted to Posterity with all the Infamy they deserve, by a Person of as great a Genius as this, or perhaps any other Age hath produc'd" (p. iv).

For some the mask of Persius has a partially downturned tragic mouth; for many others it has bared teeth and satyr's horns by which the administration was not amused, and which it hoped its own writers could obviate. In *Persius Scaramouch*, for instance, Sir Robert is mocked as inviting hacks to "caper nimbly o'er [his] Stick," and to sing "Not to their own, but to his Honour's Notes" (p. 7). Similarly, the named "W—p—le's Gold and Coxcomb's Praise" have also allowed "worthless Scriblers" to usurp the laureateship (p. 13). Juvenalian qualities in the Persian poem, however, consist of more than opposition and attacks on the Robinocracy by a nonaristocratic speaker; they also include both personal bitterness of tone and a cultural theory of causation, each related to the political climate induced by Walpole. Hence the main speaker stresses his "*British* Mind" (p. 9), refusal to compromise with corruption (pp. 9, 11, 13 and passim), persecution because of his poverty and virtue (pp. 9, 17), and consequent anger, gall (p. 9), and spite (p. 19). This imitation could have as its motto the Juvenalian tag "Who cannot write satire in such an age?" One of the reasons he must write far transcends personal deprivation: Wherever he looks he sees decay. "How ripe for Ruin is the present Age!" the poem begins (p. 9), in a more than free rendering of Persius' "O Curas hominum! O quantum est in rebus inane!" to which D'Anvers's facing line refers. Commons, peers, courts of law, bishops, and most groups in society are corrupt in a world where "Who can be wickedest Men seem to strive" (p. 11). The reason for such ruin is made clear in the attack on the poet laureate appointed by the prime minister.

> Some *Cibber*'s Works peruse, and some rehearse
> Thy Flights *Blancoso* in *Miltonick* Verse.
> No wonder therefore, if the younger Fry,
> Unable to distinguish, read and try
> To write pert Nonsense, like the *London* Spy.
>
> [p. 15]

The British people, like British virtues, are banished, "since *French-men*, like a mighty Flood, / O're-spread the Land" and "belie our Father's Reins" (p. 17). Pope again must be the scourge who "roastedst well the Witlings of our Isle" (p. 19). D'Anvers, told by Henley that a surly Welshman like himself will never get past the great man's door, where only courtiers and Henleys prosper (p. 17), must retreat to the privacy of his close-stool for release from his spleen and spite. There he "Shall tear some Trifler's Works whene'er I sh—te" (p. 19).

By 1739 one Mr. Dudley, with better contol of his bowels, had also turned the *First Satire of Persius* (London) to opposition use. His translation is dedicated to the Society of Antient Free Catonians, since there is a "near Affinity . . . in the respective Characters and Principles of our Satirist" and Cato. Each man enjoyed an abstemious severity in the cause of virtue and freedom: "If *Cato* scorn'd and detested *Caesar* on Account of his Tyranny and Usurpation; *Persius*, animated with the same Godlike Spirit, disdain'd to be the Slave of *Nero*, and held that Monster of Impiety in a like Abhorrence" (p. iv). The Argument of the poem also indicates that Persius hated the bad taste of Nero and his nobles, and emphasizes that Nero was "the Patron of every mean Pretender" to wit (p. 9), a man, the reader might suspect, perhaps something like Sir Robert. This Persius is the Juvenalian-Popean noble adversary of the horde of bad, court-encouraged poets, even though his prudent friend urges him to "desist. Invidious Truths conceal" (p. 11). For Dudley's Persius, if "none dare their Follies to disclose," his own "warm indignant Zeal" shall act: "Be mine the Province," he claims as protector of poetic virtue. "What can I do? My Spleen is too severe, / Such sordid Scribblers urge the scornful Sneer" (p. 11). In so doing, he is consciously in the great tradition of Lucilius, who "lash'd the latent Vices of the State" (p. 25), and of "subtle *Horace*," who slyly and politely destroyed foibles. "Shall I be cow'd, / Nor dare to whisper what they spoke aloud?" (p. 27). Clearly not, though Dudley is threatened with hanging by his ungentle adversarius (p. 25).

Even fuller antiministerial suggestions in the first satire were not to wait long before being plucked from the politicized classics. In 1740 Benjamin Loveling published his *First Satire of Persius Imitated*

(London), the third known version in six years, and abandoned even the pretense of being deliberative, general, or stoic. He offers sheer opposition propaganda that clarifies the "Obscurity" of the poem by cleverly attacking the court and administration and praising Pope and the opposition. Loveling's Persius is a product of what the commentators long had taught. He ridicules "Bad Poets . . . Bad Orators, and . . . the depraved Taste of Rome, in admiring the wretched Performances of *Nero* and his *Nobles*" (sig. A1r). His modern counterpart implicitly compares the Neronian and Georgian dispensations, for he dislikes "what *Cibber* sings" and "*Grubstreet* Swans [who] delight the Ear of Kings" (p. 5). "Gazetteers" are the mere "Beings of a Day" (p. 9) and, though he purports to admire George II, he knows that he himself is the lone soldier fighting barbarism (p. 7), that his adversarius thinks it grand to be "By Kings rewarded, and by Nobles prais'd" (p. 9), and that he himself can be praised by such paragons of taste only if he writes a birthday ode, those "Songs by the Court and vulgar Great admir'd" (p. 11). Predictably, certain opposition leaders are exiles from such a world:

> *Stair* and *Cobham,* Names to *Britain* dear,
> Names which the Virtuous and the Wise revere,
> Sick of the Fool's and Parasite's Resort,
> Retire, illustrious Exiles from a Court!
>
> [p. 13]

The poem is punctuated with references to stage licensing, Fanny, poor Jenkins's lost ear, echoes of Pope's satires and celebration of that satirist as "sworn Foe to Knave and Fool" who assailed Timon, Chartres, Peter, Ward, and Balaam (p. 19). The imitation has plucked the fig leaf of obscurity from Persius' satire upon "Nero," and left itself covered only by the shadow of a column from Cobham's opposition seat at Stowe, a world far different from the one Loveling sees in Walpole's London, where Truth is anathema:

> Feign but a Senate where Corruption reigns,
> And leads her courtly Slaves in golden Chains,
> Where one directs three hundred venal Tongues,
> And owes his Grandeur to a People's Wrongs;
> To ———'s Favour can the Bard pretend?

No Hints he cries, the Minister's my Friend;
And for the *Sock* the Stage is never free,
For draw a Blockhead ———'s Death! the Dog means me!
[p. 15]

In contrast, "Tis Noise and Froth that *Young* or *Blackmore* sings, / Tho' both were favour'd with the Smiles of Kings" (p. 17). Not surprisingly, by now this modern Persius is unwilling even to pretend to keep his harsh satire in the secure privacy of his book. His heroes are not Lucilius and Horace but Dryden and the hostile Pope,[28] and his poetical enemies are all those including Boileau and Prior, who praise kings. By 1740 Loveling's Persius has eschewed even the transparent irony of earlier masks and insists on speaking out. His satirist will remain undaunted in the cause of virtue, and "Yes, I will sneer the Follies of Mankind" (p. 19).

This indignant opposition Persius is a close kinsman of Pope and Juvenal, as Paul Whitehead makes clear in his unsigned *The State of Rome, Under Nero and Domitian: A Satire. Containing, A List of Nobles, Senators, High Priests, Great Ministers of State, &c. &c. &c.* (London, 1739). This bitter poem pretends to be written "by Messrs. Juvenal and Persius" and imitates scattered sections of Persius, *Satires* 1 and 4, and Juvenal, 1, 3, 7, and 8, whose patchwork quilt of supporting Latin is reproduced at the foot of the page. The amalgamated satirist asks, "What Ribs of Iron can my Gall contain?" (p. 4), and proclaims that "Fierce Indignation boils within my Veins"

---

[28]Pope often was invoked by other satirists as the lonely warrior defending decency against its powerful enemies. The "patriot" author of *The Wrongheads. A Poem. Inscrib'd to Mr. Pope. By a Person of Quality* (London, 1733), for instance, asks and answers his own indignant question:

> Shall knaves and fools commend the world's applause,
> And censure 'scape, because they 'scape the laws?
> No—*Pope* forbids, and fir'd with honest rage,
> Resolves to mend, as well as charm the age;
> Nor fears the cause of virtue to defend,
> Nor blushes to confess himself her friend. (p. 3)

See also Paul Whitehead, *The State Dunces. Inscrib'd to Mr. Pope* (London, 1733), pp. 2–5, Thomas Gilbert, *A View of the Town* (London, 1735), p. 18, and Whitehead's (?) *State of Rome Under Nero and Domitian*, above. The attribution to Whitehead is questioned by David Foxon, in *English Verse, 1701–1750*, 2 vols. (Cambridge, 1975), II, 755.

(p. 5) at the political and consequent literary corruption around him. He thus turns to Pope for support in his Juvenalian-Persian poem and alludes to his satires as another natural ally in the resistance to corrupt government and a corrupt nation in which "No social Virtue meets one Friend at Court" (p. 7). Accordingly, in this emotive rhetorical monologue, Messrs. Juvenal and Persius virtually become Pope and proclaim with him, in lines stemming from *One Thousand Seven Hundred and Thirty Eight* and the *Epistle to Dr. Arbuthnot* (1735),

> Spread, Satire, spread thy Wings, and fearless fly
> To seize thy Prey, tho' lurking ne'er so high.
>   · · · · ·
> Here *Sporus* live—and once more feel my Rage,
> Once and again I drag thee on the Stage;
> *Male-Female* Thing, without one Virtue made,
> Fit only for the *Pathick*'s loathsome Trade.
>   [pp. 5, 9]

Walpole's "depending, gaping, servile Court," his manipulation of George II (p. 14), and the consequent degradation of Britain appear in uncomplimentary Roman dress. Britain is a land in which an absolute Nero refuses to accept advice (p. 16), and which, like an overlarge dead fish long out of water, stinks and rots just below its surface (p. 17).

Several important points should emerge from this review of Persius' role in what was largely a drama cast and directed by the opposition to Walpole. As is obvious, he is far closer to Juvenal than to Horace and shares many of his conventions and tones. The familiar Horatian device of dialogue is transmuted by this Juvenalian spirit of hostility to the dim adversarius who wishes only to gain official praise, even at the expense of truth and virtue. The imitations of Persius become more hostile to Walpole as the decade advances; along the way they also become more Juvenalian and allied with Pope, the frequent parent of their invective and one probable source for their own notion of how "Persius" should write. Horace, as perceived in the seventeenth and eighteenth centuries, was the only Roman satirist to support his government. By the mid 1730s, however, that government already was seen as the corrupt father of Nero's and Domitian's tyrannies against which Persius and Juvenal were forced to complain, just, indeed, as Pope was forced to complain about his own Augustan tyranny.[29]

3. Persius and Pope

Pope alludes to Persius' satires at several places throughout his career. The first seems to be in 1704, in his youthful pastoral "Summer." Thereafter, he and his commentators note two allusions to the Prologue, six to the first satire, and two to the third satire in Pope's other works.[30] He mentions Dryden's notes to Persius' sixth satire and quotes *Satires* V.41–44, in a letter to Cromwell on 12 October 1710; and he quotes the same Latin lines when writing to Broome on 24 April 1724. On 12 October 1728 he thanks Thomas Sheridan for the gift of his Persius; on 26 July 1734 he makes clear to Dr. Arbuthnot that he accepts the standard interpretation of Persius as an enemy of Nero and in the process associates his own age with Nero's and Persius with Juvenal. He also refers to Persius' description of Horace in Satire One, lines 116–17 in the summer of 1739 and again in April of 1742.[31] Pope thus both has a general knowledge of Persius' satires and at least two major translations of him; and he joins his eighteenth-century colleagues in reacting more

---

[29]For further discussion of Pope and Augustus, see Howard D. Weinbrot, *Augustus Caesar in "Augustan" England: The Decline of a Classical Norm* (Princeton, 1978), pp. 137–41, 182–217.

[30]All line references are from the Twickenham Edition of the Poems of Alexander Pope. To avoid excessively complex annotation, I have cited all of the allusions by means of the specific volume of the Twickenham edition (TW), where the source of the discovery may also be found. The pastoral "Summer" l. 75, alludes to Persius II.78 (TW, I, 77). Allusions to Persius' Prologue appear in the "Messiah" (1712), l. 4 (*Prol.* 2–3; TW, I, 112), and the *Dunciad* of 1743, I.304 (*Prol.* 6; TW, V, 291). Allusions to Satire 1, are in the *Essays on Criticism* (1711), l. 17 (Dryden's Persius, I.110; TW, I, 241) and l. 337 (I.63–66, TW, I, 276), "Essay on Homer" (I.4; TW, VII, 62), and the *Iliad*, IV.55 (I.4–5, 50–51; TW, VII, 223, where Pope also mentions the commentary of the old scholiast on Persius). Allusions to Satire 3 are in the *Dunciad* of 1743, IV.151 (III.56; TW, V, 356), and the *Iliad*, XIX.209 (III.105; TW, VIII, 381).

[31]For the remarks in letters, see *The Correspondence of Alexander Pope*, ed. George Sherburn, 5 vols. (Oxford, 1956), I, 99 (to Cromwell); II, 231 (to Broome); II, 523 (to Sheridan); and III, 420 (to Arbuthnot). For the remarks in 1739 and 1742, see Joseph Spence, *Observations, Anecdotes, and Characters of Books and Men*, ed. James M. Osborn, 2 vols. (Oxford, 1966), I, 228 (No. 540), and I, 150 (No. 336).

strongly and most frequently to Persius' first satire, the dialogue which shows outsider and insider in futile exchange and which laments the collapse of literature, national virtue, and political morality under Nero.

We may reasonably hypothesize that many of the general and presumed Horatian traits of Pope's satires also have roots in Persius. For instance, the contemplative, sometimes abstract qualities of the *Essay on Man* (1733–34) may adapt Persian gravity and religious thoughtfulness as well as Horatian ethics. Pope's warm adherence to Bolingbroke in that poem and elsewhere as a guide, philosopher, and friend at the very least parallels Persius' affection for Cornutus in Satire Five.[32] Similarly, the use of dialogue, so important in Pope's poems, has its primary source in Horace but includes as a supplementary and differentiating source Persius' hostile and uneducable adversarius. Pope's *One Thousand Seven Hundred and Thirty Eight* is "Something like" Persius as well as Horace. Pope's insistence upon his affectionate family relations, his essential goodness, his inner drive to write satire and speak out against the vicious also suggest models other than Horace and, in the latter case, Juvenal. Pope's concern with the world of letters often is closer to Persius than to Horace as well, for Pope is more concerned with the decline than the prosperity and continuity of thriving literary traditions. And in Persius, more than in either of his fellow Romans, one is aware of a persona who is consciously and obviously made as a foil to the satirist; someone who, as Persius says, he has made to speak as an adversarius, but who then takes on a fictive life of his own ("Quisquis es, o modo quem ex adverso dicere feci" [line 44]). The opponent exemplifies the values of the hated Nero, who provided one of the many unpleasant historical parallels and labels the opposition tacked on to George II and Walpole.[33]

These similarities in general effects also suggest similarities in specific settings and uses of conventions. In at least one case the

[32]Both William Gifford and G. G. Ramsay use Pope's words to describe Cornutus' relationship with his pupil. See Gifford's Persius of 1817 (n. 2, above), p. xv, and Ramsay's Juvenal and Persius (n. 20), p. xxiii.

[33]For examples of such practice, see the imitations of Persius and *The State of Rome Under Nero and Domitian*, discussed above. See also Maynard Mack's *The Garden and the City: Retirement and Politics in the Later Poetry of Pope, 1731–1743* (Toronto, 1969), pp. 166–67, 180 n. 4.

combination of these perhaps led the printer Bettenham and the bookseller Cooper to place Pope's name on the title page of Thomas Brewster's collected *Satires of Persius* in 1741. Indeed, Brewster's Argument to Persius' first satire could serve as a gloss for much of *Fortescue, Arbuthnot,* and even *One Thousand Seven Hundred and Thirty Eight,* and suggests how congenial Persius could be for Pope. The Argument points out uses of personae, dialogue, and conflict with the adversarius, an attempt to stifle satire, a divorce from the values of the debased and debasing court, the isolation of the satirist, and the collapse of modern freedoms as contrasted with the unshackled, thriving past: "We may suppose the Author to be just seated in his Study, and beginning to vent his Indignation in Satire. At this very Juncture, comes in an Acquaintance, who, upon hearing the first Line, dissuades him, by all Means, from an undertaking so perilous; advising him rather, if he needs must write, to accommodate his Vein to the Taste of the Times, and to write like other People." Brewster goes on to say that Persius would not seek fame or patronage under such shameful terms, that he in fact exposes the wretched literary taste of Roman nobles and their followers, and that he laments how "he dares not speak out with the Freedom allowable in former times, and practised by his Predecessors in Satire, *Lucilius* and *Horace.* He then concludes, expressing a generous Disdain for all worthless Blockheads whatever: The only Readers whose applause he covets, must be Men of Virtue, and Men of Sense."[34]

Brewster's gloss demands that we focus on the dramatic relationship between the moral satirist and his incorrigible opponent. That is one of Pope's characteristic devices, one, we recall, with scant parallel in Horace and none in Juvenal. Pope hints at such a dubious relationship in *Fortescue.* That lawyer offers darker implications than Horace's Trebatius, who agreed that any legal action against Horace would be quashed when once he affirmed his satiric virtues and, more important, aristocratic friends. Fortescue, however, says:

---

[34] *The Satires of Persius Translated into English Verse,* 2d ed. (London, 1751), pp. 5–6. Someone, perhaps an eighteenth-century reader, has tried to erase "By A. Pope" from the title page of the 1741 edition in the Princeton University Library.

> Alas young Man! your Days can ne'er be long,
> In Flow'r of Age you perish for a Song!
> Plums, and Directors, *Shylock* and his Wife,
> Will club their Testers, now, to take your Life!

Fortescue later reminds Pope that "in *Richard*'s Times / A Man was hang'd for very honest Rhymes."[35] Whether this grim interpretation of the court's possible decision was influenced by Persius' first satire is difficult to say. Pope was, after all, well aware of ministerial annoyance with dispraise and needed no classical precedent to learn of his own frailties. Nonetheless, as we have seen, Persius' adversarius in a comparable situation heard the growling guard dogs at the great man's gate, and Mr. Dudley in 1739, perhaps himself influenced by Pope, appreciated the administration's ability to intimidate those it could not buy. The Monitor in Dudley's imitation of Persius' first satire says:

> Yet the Resentments of the Great are strong,
> And if they snarl, they snap before 'tis long:
> Hold in your Hand, avert the pointed Sting,
> Or you may chance to starve, if not to swing.
>
> [p. 25]

Dudley's warning of the gibbet has no counterpart in Persius, just as Pope's has no counterpart in Horace: the modern satirists are closer to each other than to their sources, but each is closer to the perceived spirit of Persius' uncertain world than Horace's stable one. The adversarius is the unchanging voice of the government's values. He triumphs over the satirist in practical terms, for he is incapable of feeling the shame that might bring reform, and is quite capable of threatening him with physical force, loss of audience, and literary seclusion. As a result, Persius must retreat into irony, appear to praise what he despises, and to destroy his own satire.

---

[35] *The First Satire of the Second Book of Horace Imitated* (1733), in The Twickenham Edition of the Poems of Alexander Pope, Vol. IV, *Imitations of Horace*, ed. John Butt, 2d ed. corr. (London and New Haven, 1961), pp. 15 (ll. 101–4), 19 (ll. 145–46). Quotations from the *Epistle to Dr. Arbuthnot* (1735) and *One Thousand Seven Hundred and Thirty Eight* also are from this edition. For a comment on the association of "Richard" and George II, see Mack, *Garden and the City*, p. 140.

Pope's adversarii are more complex than Persius'. The Monitor hopes to silence Persius because his satire is vexing to Rome's delicate ears; he wishes to protect not Persius from the court but the court from Persius. Dr. Arbuthnot, on the other hand, is concerned with the vulnerable, hostage, body of his sick friend, and not with the court, which he too "could," and later will, satirize:

> No Names—be calm—learn Prudence of a Friend:
> I too could write, and I am twice as tall,
> But Foes like these!
>
> [Lines 102–4]

Pope's reply immediately acknowledges the doctor's scarcely hidden point: "It is the Slaver kills, and not the Bite" (line 106). By the end of the poem Arbuthnot agrees with Pope and seconds his apologia; but it is a tenuous victory, for the ominous external world may temporarily have been intimidated, but it has not been converted. The full-blown court disciple thus appears with frightening confidence in the two dialogues of *One Thousand Seven Hundred and Thirty Eight*, a poem that is Horatian in its familiar repartee, Juvenalian in its rage, and Persian in its dialogue with a deaf man and the satirist's consequent retreat. When the hostile "Friend" tells Pope to mute his satire and "charitably comfort Knave and Fool" (Dialogue 1, line 62), he is adapting the advice of Persius' Monitor in Satire One, and evokes a similar response, as Pope cries:

> Dear Sir, forgive the Prejudice of Youth:
> Adieu Distinction, Satire, Warmth, and Truth!
> Come harmless *Characters* that no one hit,
> Come *Henley*'s Oratory, *Osborn*'s Wit!
>   . . . . .
> So—Satire is no more—I feel it die—
> No *Gazeteer* more innocent than I!
> And let, a God's-name, ev'ry Fool and Knave
> Be grac'd thro' Life, and flatter'd in his Grave.[36]
>
> [Lines 63–66, 83–86]

[36]Compare Benjamin Loveling's passage from his *First Satire of Persius Imitated* of 1740:

> Well, well, I've done; my Muse correct thy Lays,
> All, all have Virtues, and let all have Praise:

The later outburst ("Not to be corrupted is the Shame," line 160) leaves Persius standing in his tracks, as Pope rushes to an apocalyptic Juvenalian conclusion in which "Nothing is Sacred now but Villany" (line 170). But it returns to the Persian dense adversarius in the second dialogue's first line, as the Friend complacently says, "Tis all a Libel—*Paxton* (Sir) will say." Yet more complacently, it ends with the same adversarius, morally torn asunder by Pope and his own lack of perception and principle, still muttering:

> Alas! alas! pray end what you began,
> And write next winter more *Essays on Man.*
> [Lines 254–55]

In several instances Pope's general tone (indignation against the government) and specific conventions (dialogue with a corrupt friend) have parallels in Persius' satires and, I suspect, draw their initial sustenance from fertile Persian lands. This is true as well in a particular passage in *Arbuthnot*, whose possible and richly allusive source is the accepted commentary on comparable lines in Persius' first satire. We recall that at least from 1605 the poem was regarded as an attack upon Nero, his tragedy, and his nobles for their collective abuse of poetry. Since such mockery could not go too far without an invitation to open veins in a warm bath, Cornutus prevailed upon Persius to change and soften a key line that drew upon the familiar story of Midas, the king of Phrygia who was granted the wish that everything he touched be turned to gold. More important here is Midas' poor taste in music, for he preferred the music of Pan to Apollo, who promptly punished Midas by giving him asses' ears. Midas hid his shame beneath his cap, but his barber discovered the ears, and was bursting with his knowledge. He thus dug a hole in the earth, told it, refilled the hole, and both relieved

> Sir *W—l—* in Senate shines for Freedom bold,
> *P—* has a strong Antipathy to Gold;
> *Horace* each Gift of Nature and of Art,
> And *R——d* Sense, and *G——ch* an honest Heart.
>   Peace, Peace, ye wicked Wits, imagine here
> A Messenger, a special Jury there;
> Let Sense and Goodness both attend on State,
> Nor charge one Vice or Folly on the Great. (p. 17)

his burden and kept the secret—he wrongly thought, for on that place a reed grew and whispered its secret to the world.[37]

Persius revitalizes the second part of the myth. At line 8 he cries, "Who is there in Rome who is not. . . ." He cannot yet say what demands to be said, and so waits until line 121, when he asks, "Who is there who has not the ears of an ass?"—"auriculas asini quis non habet?" According to the old scholiast, whose remark was broadly accepted by Pope's ancestors and contemporaries, this line originally was "Auriculas asini Mida rex habet"—King Midas has asses' ears, or, as Cornutus feared that everyone would understand it, Emperor Nero has asses' ears and thus has the taste, talent, and intelligence of the ass he resembles. For Romans the word *rex* also was a virtual synonym for tyrant, and so the line had to be generalized and made apparently unimperial in its attack. Students of Persius in Pope's generation probably would read the line about Midas' ears and recall both the Midas myth and Persius' putative original use of it as an attack upon Nero and bad poetry.[38] That being so, is it not probable that "Midas" in other satires hostile to a court would also evoke that same association? Is it not more likely still if that association is helped along by the word *king* and by a particular action that associates the modern king with an ass? Here is *Arbuthnot*'s conflation of Persius' Midas section:

> 'Tis sung, when *Midas*' Ears began to spring,
> (*Midas*, a sacred Person and a King)
> His very Minister who spy'd them first,
> (Some say his Queen) was forc'd to speak, or burst.
> [Lines 69–74]

[37]Pope himself glosses l. 72 of *Arbuthnot*: "The Story is told by some [*Ovid Met.* XI. 146 and Persius *Sat.* I.121] of his Barber, but by *Chaucer* of his Queen. See Wife of Bath's Tale in *Dryden*'s Fables [ll. 157–200]." The information in brackets is John Butt's. Dryden also clarifies the allusion in his own Persius, where we see that "by *Midas*, the Poet meant *Nero*" (*Poems, 1693–1696*, p. 279 n. 15). Dryden is following Casaubon, p. 664 n. 240. See also Prateus, *D. Junii Juvenalis, et A. Persii Flacci Satirae*, p. 324 n. 121, on *Auriculas asini, Mida rex habet*; Prateus adopts "Casaubonus, Lubinus & alii."

[38]Pope apparently assumes such recollection of the myth in the *Dunciad* of 1743 when he has Settle happily proclaim of Cibber: "See, see, our own true Phoebus wears the bays! / Our Midas sits Lord Chancellor of Plays" (III.323–24) (The Twickenham Edition of the Poems of Alexander Pope, Vol. V, *The Dunciad*, ed. James Sutherland, 3d ed. [London, and New Haven, 1963], p. 335).

Arbuthnot dismisses Pope's plight with "Tis nothing," and hears the outraged echo, "Nothing? if they bite and kick?" (line 78). He then blurts out the secret which Persius held for 111 more lines and which he would make even more overt in his imitation of Horace, *Epistles* I.1 (1737), where "a Minister's an Ass" (line 96):

> Out with it, *Dunciad!* let the secret pass,
> That Secret to each Fool, that he's an Ass:
> The truth once told, (and wherefore shou'd we lie?)
> The Queen of *Midas* slept, and so may I.
> [Lines 79–82]

Pope is casting Arbuthnot in the role of the dissuading, protective Cornutus, for as soon as Midas appears the worried Doctor urges Pope to forbear and not "name Queens, Ministers, or Kings" (line 76). As "Out with it" may suggest, Pope is bringing the scholiast's meaning from its limbo of censorship, telling his adversarius that he will not be a docile pupil and abandon satire, and asserting his bravery in labeling King Midas an ass during his own lifetime and not thereafter. Indeed, to carry the Cornutus-Arbuthnot analogy one step further, when Arbuthnot himself becomes a satirist and lashes Sporus as a "mere white Curd of Ass's milk" (line 306), Pope makes clear that in such a world even a friendly dissuader must become actively involved with the protection of virtue and battle against vice.

Moreover, as Maynard Mack has shown, the word *kick* connoted the fierce anger of George II and his "savage temper which could only be relieved by kicking somebody or something." Hence on 16 July 1737 *Fog's Weekly Journal* portrays Augustus Caesar *cum* George II kicking a football and then his flattering courtiers. This derogatory number "with its audacious parallel," as an eighteenth-century reader called it, goaded the government into arresting the printer.[39] Pope also incriminates Walpole (and Queen Caroline) by insisting that the first minister, and not a mere barber, sees the

---

[39]*The Garden and the City*, p. 130; see also p. 138, and "An Essay on Kicking" there mentioned. For the context of *Fog's Weekly Journal*, see Weinbrot, *Augustus Caesar in "Augustan" England*, pp. 111–12. The remark regarding the "audacious parallel" is written on the British Library's Burney Collection copy.

king's folly and no doubt shares it.[40] In fact, since Midas gained his asses' ears for offending the god of poetry, Walpole emerges as an accomplice, as the man who brought bad judgment in poetry— the selection of Cibber as poet laureate for example—to the king. At the same time, however, Pope adopts Persius' prudence in the face of powerful enemies by veiling much of this meaning and having the possible recourse of claiming Boileau's ninth satire (1667) as his innocent source, for Boileau there writes that "Midas, le roi Midas a des oreilles d'ane."[41] If Louis XIV took no umbrage, surely, one might argue, George II should not as well. Pope also adopts at least part of Persius' printed, uncensored version by generalizing onto the literary world: each London and Roman fool is an ass, for

[40]At one point Pope made his meaning behind l. 71—"His very Minister who spy'd them first"—even more overt. The Huntington Library owns Jonathan Richardson, Jr.'s, transcription of several of Pope's manuscript versions to his own set of Pope's 1735 *Works*. Page 61 of that *Arbuthnot* (HEH 6009) includes an illuminating annotation, in Richardson's hand: "Depressis scrobibus vitium regale *minister* / Credidit.' Auson. Paulino xx[v] iii. 18." Pope probably thought the citation too bold and dropped it.

[41]*Œuvres de Boileau*, Texte de l'édition Gidel, Notes and Preface by Georges Mongrédien (Paris, 1952), p. 64, 1. 224. Boileau is of course not attacking Louis XIV but Chapelain as king of his literary enemies. Pope may be looking at Boileau through English spectacles. Compare this section from the 1712 translation of Boileau's ninth satire, with Pope's Midas-section in *Arbuthnot*. This "Boileau" provides Midas, the choleric tone, and the ineffectual satirist, adopted at different places in *Fortescue, Arbuthnot,* and parts of *One Thousand Seven Hundred and Thirty Eight*:

> When his pretended Right [to high poetic praise] some Fools proclaim,
> My Choler with Disdain is in a Flame,
> And if I durst not vent my raging Spleen,
> Or tell the World my Grievance with my Pen,
> Like the fam'd Barber I shou'd dig a Hole,
> And there discharge the Burthen of my Soul.
> There whisper to the Reeds that *Midas* wears
> Beneath his Royal Crown an Asses Ears.
> What hurt has my impartial Satire done?
> Its talent is not baulkt, it labours on;
> *Folio*'s on *Folio*'s still are brought to light,
> And *L—s* Garret's groan beneath the Weight. (*The Works of Mons. Boileau. Made English from the last Paris Edition By Several Hands*, 2 vols., 2d ed. [London, 1736] I, 244–45).

in literary, moral, and asinine matters the principle of *ad exemplum regis* extends down the social scale. I believe that Pope bases his Midas passage on Persius' printed text and the commentary upon it, and in the process intensifies its impact by condensing, enriching, and making plain the theory of causation presumed implicit in Persius' "auriculas asini quis non habet?" Neither Persius nor Pope has such beastly organs, and they become progressively lonelier in their sadly normal states, and progressively more endangered. The asses "bite and kick" as well as taunt Pope by perking their ears in his face (lines 78, 74); unlike their antique royal paradigm, they lack even a sense of shame for their ears and the reason for their presence. The world is worse than worst, it seems under King Midas II. Pope's magnifying rage sees "a bursting World" (line 88) that demands satire, however ineffectual and dangerous it might be. In the process he becomes the informing barber, the speaking rushes, the Persian satirist, the tutor of Cornutus, and the British scholiast-hero undaunted by friendly or courtly pressures.

I cannot claim that contemporary readers recorded their awareness of the *Mida rex* analogue; but several eighteenth-century readers were aware of mingled and Persian qualities in Pope's satires, and in *Arbuthnot* in particular. In 1753 the Abbé Yart includes Pope's poem as part of his *Idée de la Poësie Angloise* (1749–56), and observes that *Arbuthnot* contains a great number of facts concerning Pope, his friends, and enemies. Over and above these facts, the poem offers "des morceaux admirables, écrits avec la force & la véhémence de Juvénal, la légèreté & la finesse d'Horace, la précision & la noblesse de Perse. M. Pope semble avoir affecté en quelques endroits de prendre non-seulement le ton & les Dialogues de ce dernier Poëte, mais encore son air mystérieux & son obscurité, pour dérober aux yeux de ses ennemis dangereux ou puissans, les traits qu'il leur lançoit." Yart goes on to say that when dealing with Pope one must remember that he was, among other things, "un Philosophe chagrin & sévère,"[42]—that is the term that Boileau had used to characterize Persius.

The humblest member of the triumvirate of classical satirists

---

[42]*Idée de la Poësie Angloise, ou Traduction des Meilleurs Poëtes Angloises,* 8 vols. (Paris), III, 96–97 (*Arbuthnot*), 239 (*To a Lady*).

deserves the praise that Pope himself surely would have offered, perhaps in words similar to those of Martin Madan in 1789: "However the comparative merit of *Persius* may be determined, his positive excellence can hardly escape the readers of his Satires."[43] The evidence suggests that at least some of these excellences escaped neither Pope nor the opposition to Walpole. He provided conventions that were borrowed and generously repaid—in part by associating Persius with the more vigorous Juvenal and the braver Pope, with the defense of Britain from its apparent Neronian threats, and with a resurrected Cornutus now willing to join him in battle. Persius, in short, was both useful in his own specific satires adapted by the literary opposition, among others, and for specific conventions that could be blended with the conventions of other satirists, as the Abbé Yart saw so clearly in the *Epistle to Dr. Arbuthnot*. Pope's shade could not have been surprised by Yart's comments. Nor, I think, should we.

---

[43]*A New and Literal Translation of Persius* (n. 2, above), II, 3 of the unnumbered Preface.

The Tragic Muse in Enlightened England

CALHOUN WINTON

S TAGE TRAGEDY OF THE EIGHTEENTH CENTURY IS TODAY A
perpetual embarrassment for literary critics and scholars. Other
artistic genres have received sympathetic attention: the eighteenth-
century novel, history painting, the oratorio, all of these, as examples, have benefited from the cumulative scholarship and criticism
of the twentieth century and are now available, as it were, for
aesthetic contemplation. History painting may still not be to everyone's taste but, after the work of Rosenblum, Prown, and others,
we now know what we are looking *at* and *for*, and for some of us
it has become a genre to be appreciated with acute pleasure.[1] Not
so, it is fair to say, with tragedy. It has not quite disappeared;
rather it remains embarrassingly present, an occasion for long pauses
in the lecture, for looking at the ceiling, for titters from the back
of the classroom.

And yet, and yet. It is indisputable that some of the writers
whose artistic standards we have come to appreciate and admire,
writers such as Alexander Pope, Voltaire, and Samuel Johnson,
read, saw acted, discussed, wrote, and even professed to enjoy this
very form, stage tragedy, which we find so distasteful. Voltaire's
marked preference, R. S. Ridgway has pointed out, "was for the
theatre, and particularly for tragedy."[2] It was indeed for his own
tragedies that Voltaire was principally esteemed by his contemporaries and those who followed him; Mme de Staël felt that Voltaire had positively gone wrong in writing *Candide* and abandoning
the tragic muse for satire. "Le plus grande poète du siècle, l'auteur

---

[1]See Robert Rosenblum, *Transformations in Late Eighteenth Century Art* (Princeton,
1967); and Jules David Prown, *John Singleton Copley* (Cambridge, Mass., 1966).
[2]R. S. Ridgway, *Voltaire and Sensibility* (Montreal, 1973), p. 163.

d'*Alzire*, de *Tancrède*, de *Mérope*, de *Zaïre*, et de *Brutus*, méconnut dans cet écrit [*Candide*] toutes les grandeurs morales qu'il avait si dignement."[3] *Candide* was unworthy of his genius, which should have been employed writing stage tragedies.

Samuel Johnson, Walter Jackson Bate has shown, invested great quantities of intellectual energy in writing his tragedy *Irene*, without receiving much praise from posterity for his efforts. Bate's own sympathies with the undertaking are limited. When one reads *Irene*, he writes, "the heart begins after a while to sink except in the most resolute Johnsonian, and sometimes even then."[4] Johnson, it is true, altered his own views on tragedy as his life went on. He "was to develop what amounted to nothing less than an obsession against the kind of play that he was writing now."[5] But the fact remains that the century's outstanding man of letters in the English language chose to open his formal literary career with an attempt to write stage tragedy.

Even after Malcom Goldstein's book there still remains much to be investigated on the subject of Alexander Pope's relationships with dramatic literature and the stage.[6] By the 1730s the texture of Pope's literary and political life had become so dense that it is difficult to sort out precisely what he felt about anyone or anything, particularly anyone or anything he somewhat disliked or distrusted. One might recall from an earlier period, however, that Pope once wrote a prologue for a play in which, avoiding the facetiousness common to the genre of prologues and speaking seriously, he called on the audience to value what they were to see:

> *Britons*, attend: Be worth like this approv'd,
> And show, you have the virtue to be mov'd.[7]

The play attracting the young poet's admiration was of course Addison's *Cato*, an admiration confirmed by, among other evidence,

[3] As quoted ibid., p. 265.

[4] *Samuel Johnson* (London, 1978), pp. 157–60, 168–69.

[5] Ibid., p. 158. See also R. D. Stock, *Samuel Johnson and Neoclassical Dramatic Theory* (Lincoln, Neb., 1973).

[6] *Pope and the Augustan Stage* (Stanford, 1958).

[7] Alexander Pope, *Minor Poems*, ed. Norman Ault and John Butt (London, 1964), p. 97.

six separate translations into Italian within five years of its initial production.[8]

Critical treatises, formal or less so, on stage tragedy were written; controversies over individual plays erupted in the periodicals; many of the principal British writers of the period tried their hand at tragedy, one time or another. There is no reason to believe that the eighteenth century thought it a dead or moribund genre. The concern of this essay is not, however, with tragic theory but with dramatic success; it will deal not with what critics approved but with what audiences demanded.

Interestingly enough, this genre of stage tragedy, which drew so much critical attention and acclaim, was on the whole not successful in production on the British stage. This was not for lack of effort by dramatic writers. A glance at the scores of titles in Carl Stratman's bibliography of English tragedy will convince the hardiest skeptic that the authors were trying.[9] But not succeeding. The freezing of the London repertory is one of the most puzzling aspects of the whole matter. Complaints resound on all sides from the disappointed authors, who often ascribe their lack of success to the rapacity of the theater managers—a charge perhaps not without substance—or the debasement of public taste. Aaron Hill, a dramatic author and careful student of the stage, expressed his frustration in a letter to the veteran actor Barton Booth: "Tho' Tragedy is what ought to please most—it is too provoking a truth, that it does not. . . . It is easier, to invent *ten taking Farces*, and Pantomimes, than plan the conduct of *one good Tragedy*."[10] The power of the audience's whim, alluded to in Johnson's famous "Prologue on the Opening of Drury Lane" ("For we, that live to please, must please to live"), was very real, as Leo Hughes has documented at length.[11] This being so, it seems of value to ascertain what that whim demanded, what the audiences were voting for by their attendance

[8]Hannibal S. Noce, "Early Italian Translations of Addison's *Cato*," in *Petrarch to Pirandello: Studies in Italian Literature in Honour of Beatrice Corrigan*, ed. Julius A. Molinaro (Toronto, 1973), pp. 111–30.

[9]Carl Joseph Stratman, *Bibliography of English Printed Tragedy* (Carbondale, 1966).

[10]*The Works of the Late Aaron Hill, Esq.* (London, 1753), I, 181 (letter of 25 December 1732).

[11]*The Drama's Patrons* (Austin, Tex., 1971).

or absence, whether or not the authors chose to listen to their suffrage.

Authors who did so listen would have found that the tragic repertory had stabilized to a remarkable degree during the first ten or fifteen years of the century and was to remain surprisingly static— Shakespeare excluded—until about the decade of the 1770s. The present discussion does not include Shakespeare except in passing, although the reception of Shakespeare is an interesting and important subject in itself, well worth treatment at book length. Shakespeare, being dead, was hardly in a position to profit from a study of audience taste. Living authors who heeded audience preferences, and there were some—most notably John Home—found that tragic plays which succeeded fell into one of two general categories.[12] The first, which I have elsewhere called the Roman play, presents a protagonist, usually but not invariably male, in a stressful situation from which he emerges as an *exemplum virtutis* by displaying the putative Roman virtues of courage, endurance, and self-sacrifice for the common good.[13] *Cato* was obviously one of these and so was Shakespeare's *Julius Caesar*. It is significant that whereas we read *Julius Caesar* in the context of Shakespeare's other plays—it would scarcely occur to us to do otherwise—eighteenth-century theatergoers saw it in relation to other Roman plays, with speeches added to and deleted from the version presented on the London stage to enhance the supposed Romanness of Brutus' actions. Thomas Killigrew, master of the revels, was concerned even so about the image of Brutus and suggested that he be given additional speeches. In Act III "after the rest have Sued in vain for Metellus' being recalled, Say thus," Killigrew advised: "Brut. Peace ye unworthy of the Name of Romans, how can you think on privat wrongs, whilst Romes in chains and murdred Liberty calls loud for Justice."[14]

[12]Home has not been sufficiently studied. Two important articles by James S. Malek are "The Ossianic Source of John Home's *The Fatal Discovery*," *English Language Notes*, 9 (1971), 39–42; and "John Home's *The Siege of Aquileia*: A Revaluation," *Studies in Scottish Literature*, 10 (1973), 232–40. See also the article by Susan Staves, n. 43.

[13]"The Roman Play in the Eighteenth Century," *Studies in the Literary Imagination*, 10 (1977), 77–90.

[14]Killigrew sets forth his notions in an undated letter apparently to Henrietta Howard, later Countess of Suffolk, in British Library, Add. MS. 22629, folios 238–39. As a guess, I would date it in the early 1720s.

Killigrew also wanted to delete "Et tu, Brute?" because the words "blacken Brutus with Ingrate" [*sic*].

The expression of Roman "sentiments" by a principal actor was regarded as the high point of a Roman play; if this misfired the play failed. Aaron Hill, who was trying to talk Garrick into acting the part of Julius Caesar in his *Roman Revenge*, complained of the manner in which actors were letting opportunities slip in the production of *Cato*: "Mr. *Booth*, at *Cato*'s first appearance, always raised from forty-eight to fifty thund'ring claps on *sentiments* which he made felt; but which are so composedly shed upon our present audiences, that *Cato*'s claps, I think, stretch now and then, to almost *half a dozen*."[15] If Garrick will play Caesar, Hill ensures him that happy days will be here again. He has reluctantly composed his character in accordance with public notions of Caesar (Hill thought that Brutus was guilty), "but he shall still preserve a *soul* and *dignity* . . . in his weight of *sentiments*, (not stoical, sour, preaching sentences but warm and generous irruptions from his heart) and I will forfeit all pretence to any thing like judgment, of a stage, or *you* should hold the house, throughout that part, in one continued uproar of applause—renew'd in more than one hundred places."[16]

The audience was of course expected to applaud the sentiments of the *exemplum virtutis* and deplore those of the *exemplum mali*, transferring Roman virtues to British contexts. Very often playwrights underlined the importance of this transference in the prologue, as Pope had done in his prologue to *Cato* ("Be worth like this approv'd, / And show, you have the virtue to be mov'd."). William Whitehead opened his successful play on the Horatii theme, *The Roman Father*, with a prologue that made the point for those in the audience too slow to pick it up:

> BRITONS, to-night in native pomp we come,
> True heroes all, from virtuous ancient Rome;
> In those far distant times when Romans knew
> The sweets of guarded liberty, like you;
> And, safe from ills which force or faction brings,
> Saw freedom reign beneath the smile of kings.[17]

[15]*The Works of the Late Aaron Hill, Esq.* (London, 1753), II, 155.
[16]Ibid., p. 156.
[17]*Poems on Several Occasions, with the Roman Father, a Tragedy* (London, 1754), p. [171].

Sometimes the transference was alluded to in the play itself. The playwright flirted with the ludicrous in doing this, but plenty of playwrights were content to take the risk. James Thomson, for example, sets his *Sophonisba* in the time of the Punic Wars (c. 200 B.C.) but still feels constrained to offer his audience guidance in the curtain lines of Laelius, who is speaking of the dead queen of Carthage, Sophonisba:

> She has a *Roman* soul; for every one
> Who loves, like her, his country is a *Roman*.
> . . . . .
> If parent-liberty the breast inflame,
> The gloomy *Libyan* then deserves that name:
> And, warm with freedom, under frozen skies,
> In farthest *Britain Romans* yet may rise.[18]

It is tempting but misleading to assign the Roman sentiments to a particular party orientation. Sometimes this can be done, but as a rule the sentiments are purest political commonplace; it is dignifying them unduly to term them Whig, Tory, or even Stoic. Most Britons, after all, of whatever political persuasion, would opt for freedom if polled. It is difficult, moreover, to identify self-confessed defenders of tyranny in eighteenth-century England, though accusations flew freely enough.

Someone familiar with Thomson's biography might represent his play as a bid for ministerial favor, but a clever playwright could present Roman sentiments that were acceptable to any party or to those who professed to bear no party allegiance. This is what Addison did with *Cato*; Whigs and Tories alike saw their supposed virtues reflected in the play and continued to do so right through the century. Self-sacrifice for the common good, the supreme virtue of the civic religion, is as I have noted elsewhere so generalized as to be almost universally applicable. *Cato* could be presented to George Washington at Valley Forge and to British general officers at Drury Lane in the same year without anyone's remarking on the oddity. Roman virtues were durable and highly adaptable.

These virtues were always Roman and usually identified as such, but they could be displayed on stage by *exempla virtutis* of either sex

[18]London, 1730, p. 75.

and of various ethnic origins. King Philip of Macedon's virtuous son, Demetrius, "benignly bright," is revealed to have received his education at Rome in Edward Young's *The Brothers* (1753): "Rome's manners won him, and his manners Rome."[19] His brother Perseus lacked his advantages and became an *exemplum mali*. Roman virtue might be under suspension, as it were, in Rome itself, as in the different Diocletian plays, Crowne's *Caligula* or Richard Glover's *Boadicia* (i.e., Boadicea), an ancient British Roman play. In this tragedy the Britons' Queen Boadicia and Dumnorix, chief of the Trinobantians, are rebelling against the cruelties of Roman rule. The Roman captives Aenobarbus and Flaminius are entirely willing to admit that matters are in a bad way back home, under Emperor Nero:

> Our ancestors, who liv'd, while *Rome* was free,
> Might well prefer a noble fate to chains;
> They lost a blessing we have never known;
> Born and inur'd to servitude at home,
> We only change one master for another,
> And Dumnorix is far beyond a Nero.[20]

Dumnorix, finally defeated, gives his wife poison and kills himself rather than accept captivity, thus displaying Roman virtue to the Romans who have lost their own. In like manner Lars Porsenna, the king of Tuscany in William Bond's *Tuscan Treaty*, has annexed the Roman virtues though he is an Etruscan and a foe of Rome. But Rome is groaning under the tyranny of Tarquinius Superbus (this is still another Lucius Junius Brutus play, without Brutus), and it is given to Lars Porsenna to conquer the last of the Tarquin kings in battle and send him packing into banishment because he has sacrificed Rome to his "mean unprincely Pleasures."[21]

---

[19]Text from *The New English Theatre in Eight* [twelve] *Volumes* (London, 1776–77), XII, 6.

[20]London, 1753, p. 17.

[21]The authorship of this play is in doubt. The title page of the first (and only separate) edition (London, 1733) carries the notation *Written by a Gentleman lately deceased, Revised and Altered by W. Bond, Esq.* Aaron Hill, Bond's sponsor, almost certainly had a hand in the alteration.

That curious subgenre the American Indian Roman play, such as John Dennis's *Liberty Asserted*, had its origins, I have learned since writing an earlier article, in the practice of the Jesuit explorers of North America, who customarily reported the speeches of the Indians as if they were classical orations.[22] The principal Indians are portrayed on the stage as possessing all the virtues of a Cato Uticensis or a Regulus. Col. Robert Rogers's *Ponteach* (i.e., Pontiac) has apparently never been produced. Most unfortunately, for the scene in Act III in which the assembled Indians sing their war song ("Let us with Courage then away / To hunt and seize the frighted Prey") to the tune of "Over the Hills and Far Away" would have provided a rare moment in the theater.

Roman plays, usually based on historical legends familiar to the audiences, lent themselves to scenes like tableaux in which the climactic sentiments would be expressed. Aaron Hill in *The Prompter*, No. 56, 23 May 1735, called for increased emphasis on visual, or even compositional, elements in the production of plays: "Upon occasion of some striking scene, we should, as in a finished history-piece, the work of a great master, behold the stage *one living group* of figures."[23] If theater managers were to look to history painting for guidance in arranging their actors on stage—and I am not aware of evidence that any of them literally did so—painters, Robert Rosenblum has demonstrated, increasingly *dramatized* their presentation of these well-worn stories, composing the subject matter as if it were being seen by an audience of playgoers.[24]

Interestingly and, I believe, historically significant as these Roman plays were, there can be no doubt that the second category of tragedies had as a group vastly more audience appeal in the eighteenth century. In these the action is dominated or controlled by

[22]John H. Kennedy, *Jesuit and Savage in New France* (New Haven, 1950), cited in Ridgway, p. 11.

[23]Hill and William Popple, *The Prompter*, ed. William W. Appleton and Kalman A. Burnim (New York, 1966), p. 68.

[24]Rosenblum points out that the use of two motifs from classical antiquity, the deathbed scene and the virtuous widow, were "so prevalent from the mid century on that examples may well run into the thousands" (p. 28). Readers of eighteenth-century tragedy will not need to be reminded that these were favorite motifs of the playwrights as well.

the presence of one or two female characters, at least one of whom is in a stressful situation involving marriage, existing or impending. However exotic the setting, however remote in time the action, these plays have in common the central importance of the marriage relationship. This concern they share with the comedies of the last decade of the seventeenth century and the first of the eighteenth, as Robert D. Hume and Shirley Strum Kenny have shown.[25] In most other respects they are different from the comedies: the tragedies are usually offset in time or setting or both; contemporary tragedies set in England are unusual. Comic scenes and comic dialogue are excluded, almost without exception, as they are from the Roman plays. But all involve marriage and its responsibilities.

Some of these plays are survivors of the seventeenth century, some were written in the early years of the eighteenth, and a handful entered the repertory after 1720. No writer of tragedies was able to establish himself as such by general critical acclaim after Nicholas Rowe, however. In 1776 and 1777 a group of the leading London booksellers published an elaborate collection of plays in twelve volumes with the title *The New English Theatre*. This handsome work had title pages and illustrations by leading painters and engravers then working in London: Angelica Kaufman, Isaac Taylor, and Benjamin West among them.[26] The collection was intended to present the accepted repertory of dramatic literature, excluding Shakespeare and all musical drama, or, as the subtitle put it, "the Most Valuable Plays which have been Acted on the London Stage." The muse of comedy is represented on the title page of the first volume, a buxom English country lass depicted sitting surrounded by volumes bearing their authors' names on the spines: Steele, Centlivre, Vanbrugh, Farquhar, Congreve, Gay. Volume II portrays Melpomene, a neurasthenic counterpart of her comic sister and with only two volumes at her feet: those of Otway and Rowe. Together the title pages illustrate the extreme conservatism of the London

[25]Hume, "Marital Discord in English Comedy from Dryden to Fielding," *Modern Philology*, 74 (1977), 248–72; and Kenny, "Elopements, Divorces, and the Devil Knows What: Love and Marriage in English Comedy, 1690–1720," *South Atlantic Quarterly*, 27 (1978), 84–106.

[26]See note 19 above for full data.

repertory at that time, three-quarters of the way through the century. Most of the authors represented had been dead fifty years or more; not a single volume by a living author was included.

Although John Banks was not a member of the tragic muse's exclusive pantheon, one of his plays was in the collection itself, in adapted form. *The Unhappy Favourite*, known in Henry Brooke's adaptation as *The Earl of Essex*, will serve as an introductory example of what eighteenth-century British audiences apparently were looking for in tragedies. Although published in 1682, its early stage history is uncertain due to the scarcity of records. By 1703 it was in the London repertory, however, and it stayed there for many years, with scores of performances in the first fifty years of the century. Brooke's adaptation of 1761 gave it a continuing stage life.[27]

Banks's play is based on an anonymous pamphlet of the 1650s, *The History of the most renowned Queen Elizabeth*, and, like the pamphlet, has only the most tenuous relationship to historical circumstances. The unhappy favorite of the title, the earl of Essex, reaps the tragic consequences of his rebellious nature and loses his head on the scaffold, but the dramatic focus is on Queen Elizabeth's illicit and impossible love for him. Essex, who is represented as being secretly married to the countess of Rutland, plays quite knowingly on the queen's love and manages to keep her in an emotional turmoil. She observes in a soliloquy:

> Love that does never cease to be Obey'd
> Love that has all my Power and strength betray'd,
> Love that swayes wholly like the Cause of things.
> Kings may Rule Subjects, but Love Reigns o're Kings.[28]

The countess of Nottingham, a past mistress of Essex, conspires with Ralegh to bring about his downfall and execution, which cannot in the end be prevented even by the token ring the queen has given to Essex.

---

[27]*The Unhappy Favourite: or The Earl of Essex* (London, 1682). This theme was used in several other plays on the Continent and was discussed by Lessing. For a full discussion see Helen Margaret Scurr, "Henry Brooke," Diss., Minnesota, 1922, pp. 74–77.

[28]*The Unhappy Favourite*, p. 47.

Of all Banks's plays this is the one that by popular mandate stayed in the repertory, decade after decade. Certain aspects of it merit comment. There are three substantial female roles (the two countesses and the queen), and each of these characters influences the action of the play directly. It is a truism to observe that the arrival of actresses on the English stage in 1660 brought about an increase in, and an increased importance for, female parts. *The Unhappy Favourite* surely allows full scope for the principal actresses of a theater company. These females, furthermore, are human size. In spite of the royal flummery, the pseudohistorical details (Queen Elizabeth's ring is of course pure romantic moonshine), and the talk about queenly responsibility, this is not heroic drama but a thoroughly domesticated play. The villainness, the countess of Nottingham, is no outsize noble personage but a petty schemer, a conniver, an Arabella Harlowe. *The Unhappy Favourite* is domestic drama, directed quite explicitly to the women in the audience, or as Banks phrases it in the epilogue, "To all the shining Sex this Play's addrest," going on to assure the shining sex,

> If you are pleas'd we will be bold to say,
> This modest Poem is the Ladies Play.

"The Ladies Play" in what respect? Banks means, one assumes, attractive to female audiences, but plays could not be produced for women only, obviously: theater managers could not afford to bring forward a play that would drive away the male customers. There are excellent roles in *The Unhappy Favourite* for Essex and Ralegh, but the female characters control and direct the action. It is a ladies' play, then, in that it is designed to attract female audiences, but it is also a ladies' play as it focuses on women, love, marriage, and the choices involved; topics apparently of interest to male audiences as well, to judge by the play's continuing stage life.

Nicholas Rowe, the premier writer of tragedies in eighteenth-century England, probably understood these matters as well as anyone of his time. His most successful plays are essentially domestic tragedies, with the exception of *Tamerlane*, which is the special case of a genuinely and specifically political play. *The Fair Penitent* and *Jane Shore* conform very well to the pattern described earlier: the female figure under stress, confronted by a problem involving betrothal or marriage. On one ill-chosen occasion Rowe referred to his plays as "she-tragedies," in an epilogue intended to be humorous.[29] This epithet was seized upon and has remained a term of derogation, the implication apparently being that she's are not permitted to have tragedies, the genre fit only for he's. They have also been called "pathetic" or "affective" tragedies, with the argument that their central figures are acted upon instead of acting, are passive rather than active, feminine rather than masculine.[30] There is an element of truth in this contention, and in Restoration drama proper the pathetic drama, so-called, perhaps makes for a useful contrast with the heroic. As applied to the eighteenth-century tragic repertory, where heroic drama scarcely exists, the term is misleading. The central figures of eighteenth-century tragedy are acted upon right enough and they are of course female, but they make crucial choices and are aware of the choices they make.

For example, Jane Shore, Rowe's heroine, is unarguably acted upon at various points in the tragedy bearing her name, but it is precisely her action, resisting the advances of Hastings, which, Douglas Canfield has contended, demonstrates her contrition and furthers the process of repentance for her earlier misdeeds. These are bringing her misfortune on earth but her contrition and penance for them will presumably reap salvation hereafter.[31] Jane Shore's misdeeds are clear: she has betrayed her husband while enjoying life as the king's mistress. She is guilty, and she understands and accepts the consequences of her guilt.

Even heroines who are innocent, however, may suffer for their acts, committed or omitted, as one sees in the example of Voltaire's Zaïre. Voltaire, I would argue, was much influenced by Rowe, whose plays had become standard pieces in the London repertory during the years Voltaire spent in England. Not much work has been done on Rowe's influence in Europe, Annibel Jenkins has

[29]The epilogue to *Jane Shore*. Humor was never Rowe's long suit.

[30]References to the various critical opinions are conveniently set forth in the introductory material of Cynthia Sutherland's article " 'Spectatress of the Mischief Which She Made': Tragic Woman Perceived and Perceiver," in *Studies in Eighteenth-Century Culture*, 6 (1977), 317–19.

[31]*Nicholas Rowe and Christian Tragedy* (Gainesville, Fla., 1977), p. 151.

noted, but it was probably considerable.[32] Zaïre, at any rate, has always seemed to me much more nearly related to Calista, the fair penitent, and to Jane Shore, than to Shakespeare's Desdemona. If this is true, an interesting reciprocal influence was at work across the Channel because Voltaire's tragedy, in the translation of Aaron Hill (*Zara*, 1736), became one of the most popular plays of the century, presented repeatedly on the London stage, in the provinces, and in the American colonies. (It was, it might be recalled, produced by a group of loyalist refugees in Florida during the American Revolution.)[33]

Zara was a drama of great appeal to English-speaking audiences, concerning as it does the dilemma of the Christian slave Zara, beloved by the sultan Osman. She must choose between marriage to him, whom she loves, and fidelity to her father, the Crusader Lusignan, and to their religion. "Am I a lover most? or most a Christian?" she asks herself.[34] In the end she chooses religion and dies for it, stabbed to death by the distraught Osman. Although this may resemble *Othello* in some particulars, as critics have contended, it is a very different play. Discussing the differences between Voltaire's Zaïre and Desdemona, Eva Jacobs makes the important point that "Zaïre herself is to some extent responsible for and aware of what is happening.[35] Her actions have been innocent; unlike Jane Shore she is not guilty. But like Rowe's heroine she knows what she is doing and what she has done. In these plays the female figures are self-aware.

If they were guilty they paid for their crimes even as they confessed them, and the mode of punishment was often the knife. Female characters are dispatched by dagger with quite startling frequency in eighteenth-century tragedy. The faithful wife in Aaron Hill's interesting domestic tragedy *The Fatal Extravagance* does, it is true, unknowingly take the poison prepared for her by her husband, but when it does not work *he* stabs himself, as if to compensate the

[32]*Nicholas Rowe* (New York, 1977), p. 145.

[33]See my essay "The Theater and Drama," in *American Literature, 1764–1789: The Revolutionary Years*, ed. Everett Emerson (Madison, Wis., 1977), p. 101.

[34]Text from *The New English Theatre*, X, 38.

[35]*Zaïre*, ed. Eva Jacobs (London, 1975), p. 36.

audience for what it has missed. Victims of cold steel abound in the plays that "took": Zara, Imoinda in Southerne's *Oroonoko*, Lavinia in Otway's *Caius Marius*, and so on. One presumes that a generation of scholar-critics brought up on a phallic interpretation of the penknife scene in *Clarissa* will need no guidance at this juncture.

And yet, without making too much of death by dagger in eighteenth-century tragedy, one feels called to make something of it. Cynthia Sutherland has termed the weapon the "phallic dagger of authority" and has drawn our attention to the rather overheated eroticism of some of these final scenes.[36] I believe that she is on the right track but would put the matter somewhat differently. On a basic level the female character's death represents a resolution of the stressful situation in which she has been placed, but what sort of resolution? It may be thought of as analogous to that resolution employed in successful comedies of the time, as Shirley Strum Kenny has demonstrated; that is, a concluding dance.[37] In other words, no resolution at all. No convincing dramatic resolution to these problems of betrothal and marriage was possible within the terms offered by eighteenth-century society. Just as there was no future for the romance of Archer and Mrs. Sullen beyond the last act of *The Beaux' Stratagem*, so there was no way out for the enslaved African royalty in *Oroonoko*, in a society that was not yet ready seriously to consider either divorce or emancipation.[38] In the comedy a dance, in the tragedy a ritual death, provided the resolution, such as it was.

On a more abstract level, death by violence may be taken as the price exacted by a male society for these dramatic representations of female jealousy, self-assertion, hate, and infidelity. It is as if the drama's laws stated that women might get away with these things but must pay for them. From time to time, though rarely, a female character is allowed to express some resentment at the double standard of behavior. Millwood, George Barnwell's debaucher in *The London Merchant*, does so with startling vehemence, speaking to her

[36]Sutherland, p. 322.

[37]Kenny, p. 101.

[38]For a good discussion of the ambiguities about slavery in *Oroonoko*, see the Introduction by Maxmillian Novak and David Rodes to their edition (Lincoln, Neb., 1976).

[138]

maid Lucy: "It's a general maxim among the knowing part of mankind that a woman without virtue, like a man without honor or honesty, is capable of any action, though never so vile. And yet, what pains will they not take, what arts not use, to seduce us from our innocence and make us contemptible and wicked."[39] Jane Shore voices a similar complaint to her friend Alicia, in pentameter verse:

> Mark by what partial Justice we are judg'd;
> Such is that Fate unhappy Women find,
> And such the Curse intail'd upon our kind,
> That Man, the lawless Libertine, may rove,
> Free and unquestion'd through the Wilds of Love;
> While Woman, Sense and Nature's easy Fool,
> If poor weak Woman swerve from Virtue's Rule,
> If strongly charm'd, she leave the thorny way,
> And in the softer Paths of Pleasure stray;
> Ruin ensues, Reproach and endless Shame,
> And one false Step entirely damns her Fame.[40]

Although Jane's sisters today might object to her characterization of woman as "Sense and Nature's easy Fool," within the context of eighteenth-century tragedy she undeniably scores a point: if woman makes one mistake, ruin ensues. Ordinarily the lovely woman in tragedy who has stooped to folly accepts her fate without complaint, as Goldsmith advised her to do:

> The only art her guilt to cover,
> To hide her shame from every eye,
> To give repentance to her lover.
> And wring his bosom—is to die.[41]

And die they did, even the innocent ones who had *not* stooped to folly. Monimia, for example, the famous orphan of Otway's play, is the victim of fraud. Polydore, one of her suitors, accuses her of having improper longings, like the rest of her sex: "And when your loose desires once get dominion, / No hungry Churle feeds coarser

---

[39] *The London Merchant*, ed. William H. McBurney (London, 1965), p. 16.

[40] Nicholas Rowe, *Three Plays*, ed. James R. Sutherland (London, 1929), pp. 267–68.

[41] *The Vicar of Wakefield*, ed. Arthur Friedman (London, 1974), p. 133.

at a Feast."[42] But Monimia as depicted by Otway gives no indication of loose desires. Later in the play Polydore slips into her bedchamber in the guise of Castalia, her secret husband. Monimia must die and she does, without complaint.

Isabella, heroine of Thomas Southerne's *The Fatal Marriage*, finds herself in a similar situation. First produced in 1694 and in both its original form and as adapted by Garrick a staple of the London repertory right through the eighteenth century, the play signals the marriage's fatality by its subtitle, *The Innocent Adultery*. Isabella has been left an impoverished widow with a small son by the death in battle of her husband Biron. Pressed by her poverty, she has in all innocence remarried when Biron turns up again, quite alive. In a long and tempestuous final act, Biron dies on stage and Isabella stabs herself, leaving the boy to her father-in-law's care. Innocent or not, Isabella has lost her virtue, in the very specific meaning of the term as understood in the eighteenth century: she has had sexual relations with a man not legally her husband. She dies, by the knife.

The presence of the child in *The Fatal Marriage* provided another element of stress for the central female figure which recurs in these tragedies: concern of parent for child. Isabella was played by Mrs. Siddons with her little son Henry on occasion in the child's role. This produced stress for Mrs. Siddons, the *London Morning Post* reported on 10 October 1782: "Yesterday, in the rehearsal of the 'Fatal Marriage,' [Henry], observing his mother in the agonies of the dying scene, took the fiction for reality, and burst into a flood of tears, a circumstance which struck the feelings of the company in a singular manner."[43]

In a most interesting essay Susan Staves uses Home's *Douglas* as the focal point of an investigation of the parent-child relationship in eighteenth-century tragedy.[44] She argues that Lady Randolph rather than the eponymous hero is the central figure of the play and draws on contemporary evidence to demonstrate that the scenes between Lady Randolph and her son were regarded as the high points of the drama. The focus on maternal sentiment Staves relates

[42] *The Works of Thomas Otway*, ed. J. C. Ghosh (Oxford, 1932), I, 18.

[43] As quoted in Susan Staves, "Douglas's Mother," unpublished paper delivered at the North East Modern Language Association meeting, 1980, p. 20. I am indebted to Professor Staves for lending me the typescript of this important essay.

[44] Ibid.

to a growing interest in the parent-child relationship: "In eighteenth-century England the development of new sentiment toward children and new tenderness in the relationship between mother and child is variously evidenced in books of advice to women, in the campaign to promote maternal breast-feeding, and in the establishment of the foundling hospital. . . . Somewhat similarly, it is possible to find in English advice literature of the eighteenth century a relatively novel stress on warmth of affect between parents and children."[45]

Another domestic relationship, that of the patient wife and the extravagant husband, is treated directly in Aaron Hill's *The Fatal Extravagance* (1721) and Edward Moore's *The Gamester* (1753), both of which had long lives in the repertory. The dramatic focus is necessarily on the wastrel husband in these plays, but the wife is left with the problem, so to speak. Beverly, the husband of Moore's play, is portrayed as a pathological gambler who has gone through his own and his wife's estates and is trying to get his sister Charlotte's so he can spend that, too. Charlotte urges Mrs. Beverly to take some action, but she refuses to do so, remaining throughout the play the patient Griselda. Eventually Beverly, stricken with remorse, takes poison and dies. His friend Lewson pronounces the curtain speech, telling "frailer Minds" that they should learn from this "that Want of Prudence is Want of Virtue."[46] Mrs. Beverly is presented as the picture of virtue from beginning to end but it is difficult not to sympathize with Charlotte's impatience with her and her feckless husband. Presumably Mrs. Beverly is not culpable—a wife is supposed to be unfailingly patient—but there is an interesting ambiguity here. Is Mrs. Beverly's inaction "Want of Prudence" and thus "Want of Virtue"? The question is not resolved.

The tragedies—Shakespeare aside—that stayed in the repertory, as I have attempted to demonstrate, were either Roman plays or those female-centered plays, essentially domestic tragedies, that dealt with the the problems of betrothal and marriage. These problems, even when set in exotic surroundings, were real problems or were believed to be real problems in the eighteenth century. What does a woman do who loves someone who is not, or who cannot be, her husband? What is the woman's responsibility when her

[45]Ibid., p. 15.
[46]London, 1753, p. 84.

husband or son or daughter is caught in some impossible political or moral dilemma? No adequate dramatic resolution was possible, one might argue, because there existed no adequate social resolution. Readers could feel that Clarissa had been victimized by Lovelace and sympathize with her plight, yet agree with her that life had no future after she had been deflowered. The wages of sin is death; Lovelace's sin and Clarissa's death.

The twentieth-century reader finds these plays implausible, but the eighteenth-century theatergoer evidently suspended his or her disbelief, returning again and again to see Mrs. Siddons as Lady Randolph in Home's *Douglas* or Garrick as Biron in *The Fatal Marriage*, discussing the players' interpretations of the roles, even writing pamphlets on the subject.[47] The issues treated were, they felt, live ones. And perhaps they were right. It is possible to see these dramatists obliquely approaching domestic problems that had not earlier been understood as problems at all. From a feminist viewpoint the plays might be regarded as footnotes to the still-unwritten history of the woman.

The Roman plays died with the demise of the century's classicism, sharing the fate of history painting, to which in some interesting ways they are related. Just why the female-centered domestic tragedies disappeared is a larger question than can be adequately treated here and is properly in the domain of nineteenth-century studies anyway. A few of them, of course, survived for a long time in repertory, especially those of Otway and Rowe. It has been asserted that most did not continue alive because their authors were inadequate dramatic craftsmen or that the patent theaters turned away the best literary talent. In any event, they did have offspring, these tortured females so threatened by dagger and poisoned cup. In some sense the eventual descendants of these women under stress were perhaps Ibsen's dynamic heroines; their immediate progeny, I would argue, are to be found in the novel and in grand opera: Clarissa and Lucia di Lammermoor.

---

[47]See, e.g., the anonymous pamphlet *The Beauties of Mrs. Siddons; Or, A Review of Her Performance of the Characters of Belvidera, Zara, Isabella, Margaret of Anjou, Jane Shore, and Lady Randolph; In Letters from a Lady of Distinction, to her Friend in the Country* (London, 1786). I owe this reference to Susan Staves.

Johnson and Chronology

PAUL K. ALKON

To understand why Johnson thought time especially obedient to the imagination, a conviction that accounts for much that is best in his writing, it is necessary to consider his relationship to chronology. Many of Johnson's ideas about time in literature and morality, as well as the words that he employs for discussing such ideas, show his awareness of that obscure branch of learning whose methods are now incorporated into history, archaeology, astronomy, and related fields. Despite Joseph Scaliger's brilliant achievement of a standard time scale, chronology as a separate study has vanished. It is seldom thought of by literary critics as referring to anything more than a list of dates. In this essay I wish to consider what chronology meant for Johnson and his readers, then to survey his knowledge of chronology, his attitude toward it, and its influence on his writing. I will also argue that by supporting eighteenth-century convictions that physical as well as psychological time is relative, chronologists provided a climate of opinion favoring Johnson's insistence that "time is, of all modes of existence, most obsequious to the imagination; a lapse of years is as easily conceived as a passage of hours."[1]

1

In the Preface to *The Preceptor* Johnson affirms that "the study of *Chronology* and *History* seems to be one of the most natural Delights of the Human Mind."[2] Like most others throughout the seventeenth and eighteenth centuries, Johnson assumed that chronology is not just a part of history. The difference is explained in the widely read

---

[1] Samuel Johnson, *Preface to Shakespeare*, 1765, *Johnson on Shakespeare*, ed. Arthur Sherbo with introduction by B. H. Bronson, Vols. VII and VIII of the Yale Edition of the Works of Samuel Johnson (New Haven, 1968), VII, 78.

[2] [Samuel Johnson] Preface to *The Preceptor* (London, 1748), I, xx.

Breviarium Chronologicum: "'Tis certain Chronology and History don't coincide; for Chronology explains time itself, and declares how it comes to be distinguished by such and such Characters. But History only reports things done in time."[3] This distinction is apparent in seventeenth-century iconology. In the title page engraved by William Marshall for Henry Isaacson's *Saturni Ephemerides* (London, 1633), the emblem of chronology is a female whose attributes are an eagle and a telescope (fig. 1). She sits by the left hand of time. At time's right is history (fig. 2). Richard Crashaw's poem "On the Frontisipiece of Isaacson's Chronology Explained" stresses the supremacy of chronology's role in discovering truth by observing history:

> If on TIMES right hand, sit faire HISTORIE . . .
> Let Her be
> Ne're so farre distant, yet CHRONOLOGIE
> (Sharpe sighted as the Eagles eye, that can
> Out-stare the broad-beam'd Dayes Meridian)
> Will have a PERSPICILL to finde her out,
> And through the Night of error and dark doubt,
> Discerne the DAWNE of Truth's eternall ray.[4]

There is nothing unusual in this claim for the priority of chronology over history. Nor was there much doubt that chronology is important. Some of Europe's most powerful minds were attracted to the topic. Isaac Newton worked for many years on *The Chronology of Ancient Kingdoms Amended* (London, 1728).[5]

Attempts like Newton's, to date historical events, were a major concern of chronologists. Another was the task of working out accurate computations together with a vocabulary for describing the various divisions of time: epochs, cycles, periods, days, months, years, hours, minutes, moments, and the like. Both concerns are glanced at in *The Preceptor* when Johnson states that every student of history needs "some knowldge of *Chronology*, the Science by which Events are ranged in their Order, and the Periods of Computation

---

[3][Aegidius Strauchius] *Breviarium Chronologicum* (London, 1699), p. 2.

[4]Richard Crashaw, "On The Frontispiece of Isaacson's Chronology Explained," in Henry Isaacson, *Saturni Ephemerides* (London, 1633), opposite title page.

[5]See Frank E. Manuel, *Isaac Newton Historian* (Cambridge, Mass., 1963).

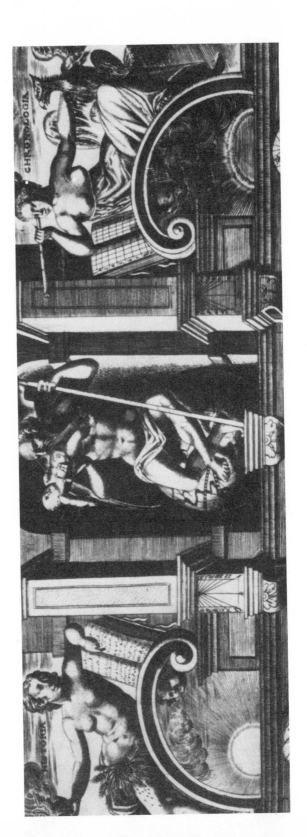

are settled." Of "the Technical Part of Chronology, or the Art of computing and adjusting Time," Johnson remarks that it "is very difficult" and therefore "is not of absolute Necessity, but should however be taught, so far as it can be learned without the Loss of those Hours which are required for Attainments of nearer Concern."[6] Johnson's ambivalence toward ruling out such instruction suggests his own fascination with "the Technical Part of Chronology." More than casual knowledge of it is implied by his awareness of its difficulty. Only the uninitiated could suppose it easy. Ephraim Chambers, for example, remarks in his *Cyclopaedia* that "there is more difficulty in Chronology than every one is aware of; it requires not only the knowledge of astronomy and geography, and consequently that of arithmetic, geometry, and trigonometry, both plain and spherical; but also a world of application to the antient monuments."[7] One can see its attraction for men like Isaac Newton. One can see, too, why Johnson's involvement with chronology has been neglected.[8]

Yet from the outset of his career to the end of his life Johnson was in touch with developments of chronology. By 1748 he was able to recommend that students of *The Preceptor* who wish additional instruction in "the Historical Part of *Chronology*" consult *"Helvicus's* and *Isaacson's* Tables." For those who are "desirous of attaining the Technical Part," Johnson recommends *"Holder's Account of Time, Hearne's Ductor Historicus, Strauchius,* the first Part of *Petavius's Rationarium Temporum*; and at length *Scaliger de Emendatione Temporum."*[9] In 1762 Johnson provided the dedication and last paragraph of John

[6]Johnson, Preface to *The Preceptor*, I, xxi.

[7]Ephraim Chambers, "Chronology," *Cyclopaedia*, 7th ed. (London, 1751).

[8]Johnson's interest in chronology is mentioned in James William Johnson, *The Formation of English Neo-Classical Thought* (Princeton, 1967), pp. 114, 115, 204. It is misleading, however, to cite an exchange between Johnson and Boswell, as recorded in Boswell's *Life of Samuel Johnson*, to suggest that there was not "much difference between history and chronology to the Neo-Classical mind" (p. 204). Johnson's remarks in the Preface to *The Preceptor* show that he accepted the usual seventeenth-century distinction between chronology and history. For an excellent account of the historical problems dealt with by early chronologists, see J. W. Johnson, "Chronological Writing: Its Concepts and Development," *History and Theory*, 2 (1962), 124–45.

[9]Johnson, Preface to *The Preceptor*, I, xxi–xxii.

Kennedy's *Complete System of Astronomical Chronology, Unfolding the Scriptures*. In 1762 Johnson also wrote the preface to Thomas Flloyd's translation of Nicolas Lenglet du Fresnoy's *Chronological Tables of Universal History*.[10] In that preface Johnson remarks of John Blair's *Chronology and History of the World* (London, 1754) that its method is "very clear and pleasing" although it suffers from an "inconvenience" that works of "Tabular Chronology" must "always" share: "the same, or nearly the same space upon paper being allotted to one year as to another, some barren years will have blank columns, and some years crouded with events, cannot be fully dilated and displayed."[11] This observation implies that Johnson had examined many such works. In his library at the time of his death were at least eight books on chronology, including Johnson's subscription copy of Samuel Musgrave's *Examination of Sir Isaac Newton's Chronology*, published in 1783.[12]

Johnson's interest in chronology is also evident in his praise of Scaliger as a man who "had unravelled with his intellect the vicissitudes of empire, the movements of the heavens, and the great cycle of the ages": "imperiique vices, coelique meatus, / Ingentemque animo seclorum voverat orbem."[13] In 1792 Arthur Murphy caught the fervor of Johnson's admiration for Scaliger's writing on chronology by rendering this passage from the 1771 Latin poem "Know Thyself" as a statement that Scaliger had soared aloft "on eagle wings . . . To fix the aeras of recorded time."[14] While the

---

[10]Allen T. Hazen, *Samuel Johnson's Prefaces and Dedications* (New Haven, 1937), pp. 74–77, 84–89.

[11]Nicolas Lenglet du Fresnoy, *Chronological Tables of Universal History*, trans. Thomas Flloyd (London, 1762), I, vii–viii.

[12]Donald Greene, *Samuel Johnson's Library: An Annotated Guide*, University of Victoria English Literary Studies, Monograph Series, No. 1 (Victoria, B.C., 1975). In addition to Musgrave, there were: Flloyd's translation of Lenglet du Fresnoy's *Chronological Tables*; John Kennedy's *Complete System of Astronomical Chronology* or his *New Method of Stating and Explaining the Scripture Chronology Upon Mosaic Principles*, or both; Eusebius's *Thesaurus temporum*; Benjamin Marshall's *Chronological Tables;* Isaac Newton's *The Chronology of Ancient Kingdoms Amended*; Dionysius Petavius's *Opus de doctrina temporum*; and Petavius's *Rationarium temporum*.

[13]*Samuel Johnson: The Complete English Poems*, ed. J. D. Fleeman (Harmondsworth, 1971), pp. 148, 146. The translation of Johnson's Latin is Fleeman's.

[14]Samuel Johnson, *Poems*, ed. E. L. McAdam, Jr., with George Milne, The Yale Edition of the Works of Samuel Johnson, Vol. VI (New Haven, 1964), 273.

imagery of Murphy's version is an addition, his statement of what Scaliger accomplished shows that an allusion to historical chronology was still clear to readers at the end of the eighteenth century. Although by then chronology was increasingly regarded as merely an aspect of history, the distinction was maintained not only by controversialists like Musgrave and works like those of Kennedy and Flloyd to which Johnson contributed a few paragraphs but by such popularizations as James E. Weeks's *Gentleman's Hourglass, or an Introduction to Chronology: Being a Plain and Compendious Analysis of Time, and its Divisions . . . Containing a Brief Account of the Flux of Time; the Value of Lives, and Explanation of Stiles, Epochs, Aera's, Periods, Revolutions, &c. For the Use of Schools and Universities* (Dublin, 1750). Whether or not this forty-seven-page outline was ever adopted in a school or university, its publication at mid-century is another measure of the persistent belief, which Johnson shared, that every student ought to know something about chronology.

Outside the academies chronology was also relevant to a century whose time systems were unstable. In *The Political History of the Devil*, for example, Defoe remarks that "*Satan*, who, no doubt, would make a very good Chronologist, could settle every Epocha, correct every Kalendar, and bring all our Accounts of Time to a general Agreement; as well as the *Grecian Olympiads*, the *Turkish Heghira*, the *Chinese* fictitious Account of the World's Duration, as our blind *Julian* and *Gregorian* Accounts, which have put the World, to this Day, into such Confusion, that we neither agree in our Holy-days or Working-days, Fasts or Feasts, nor keep the same Sabbaths in any Part of the same Globe."[15] Of course in suggesting that were Satan inclined to be helpful he might settle those disputes for which chronologists were notorious, Defoe is not branding chronology a satanic activity. He is only resorting to comedy as a way of expressing a discomfort that many shared when faced with the practical consequences of competing and often conflicting ways of measuring time. To the issue of calendar reform, Johnson also responded with laughter.

In *Rambler* 107 he provides a letter from Properantia, a young girl who, after being told the alteration from old to new style calendar refers to "the stated and established method of computing

---

[15][Daniel Defoe] *The Political History of the Devil*, 4th ed. (London, 1739), p. 12.

time," wonders "why we should be at so much trouble to count what we cannot keep." She finds it "strange, that with all the plots that have been laid against time, they could never kill it by act of parliament before." Hearing from the chronologists "Mr. Cycle and Mr. Starlight" that to put the calendar in order a "year of confusion" is necessary, Properantia is delighted: "Dear Mr. Rambler, did you ever hear of any thing so charming? a whole year of confusion!" Properantia understands this to mean "a whole year, of cards in one room, and dancing in another, here a feast, and there a masquerade, and plays, and coaches, and hurries, and messages, and milaners, and raps at the door, and visits, and frolicks, and new fashions." She therefore does "not care what they do with the rest of the time, nor whether they count it by the old stile or the new."[16] *Rambler* 107 thus establishes a comic parallel between 1752 and the year of Julius Caesar's calendar reform, which Macrobius labeled *annus confusionis*. Johnson's satire, which is hardly very barbed, is not so much aimed at chronology as at those who misunderstand its uses.

His reading list on chronology in *The Preceptor*, which reflects Johnson's more serious views on the topic, is intended to help students avoid such misunderstanding. In *Some Thoughts concerning Education* John Locke had established the pattern for Johnson's recommendations by devoting two sections to the necessity of teaching every "young Gentleman" the elements of chronology.[17] For that purpose Locke, like Johnson, suggests the historical tables of Helvicus (Christopher Helwig) and the English version of Strauchius (Giles Strauch), the *Breviarium Chronologicum*. These remained standard texts well into the eighteenth century; it was from the latter that Gibbon "imbibed the elements of chronology."[18] Locke states that without knowledge of "*Chronology* . . . History will be very ill retained, and very little useful; but be only a jumble of

[16]Samuel Johnson, *The Rambler*, ed. W. J. Bate and Albrecht B. Strauss, The Yale Edition of the Works of Samuel Johnson, Vols. III, IV, V (New Haven, 1969), IV, 204–7.

[17]John Locke, *Some Thoughts concerning Education*, 3d ed. (London, 1695), pp. 318–20.

[18]Edward Gibbon, *The Memoirs of the Life of Edward Gibbon*, ed. George Birkbeck Hill (London, 1900), p. 45.

Matters of Fact, confusedly heaped together without Order or Instruction.[19] Johnson also affirms that "*History* can only be made intelligible by some knowledge of *Chronology*." He then puts the case for chronology more forcefully by insisting that every young student should be warned that without grasping the elements of chronology "he will consume his Life in useless reading, and darken his Mind with a Croud of unconnected Events, his Memory will be perplexed with distant transactions resembling one another, and his Reflections be like a Dream in a Fever, busy and turbulent, but confused and indistinct."[20] This simile is among Johnson's most striking comparisons.

It achieves—*horresco referens*—an almost metaphysical power in suggesting how the opposite states of sleeping and waking may be yoked together if ignorance of chronology allows thoughts about history to take on the timeless confusion of feverish dreams. Johnson exaggerates the comparison to enforce a warning for young students, but the passage nevertheless reveals a craving for stable time relationships that is perhaps another impulse behind his endorsement of chronology. His approval remained general. Neither in *The Preceptor* nor elsewhere did Johnson affiliate himself with a particular school of chronologists. Because he never wrote a history, there was no need to take sides in what Frank Manuel calls the eighteenth-century "battle of dates" stirred up by Newton's *Chronology of Ancient Kingdoms Amended.*[21]

In a letter written to Edward Cave in 1743, however, Johnson did comment on the way to handle dates in their "Historical Design," an uncompleted project that Boswell identified as "an historical account of the British Parliament."[22] After taking the unusual step of calling the issue "wholly indifferent to me" and asking Cave to consider the comments as "my opinion only not my Resolution," Johnson proceeds: "I think the insertion of the exact dates of the most important events in the margin or of so many events as may

[19]Locke, *Thoughts*, pp. 318–19.
[20]Johnson, Preface to *The Preceptor*, I, xxi.
[21]For the controversy over dates, see Manuel, pp. 166–93.
[22]James Boswell, *The Life of Samuel Johnson, LL.D.*, ed. G. B. Hill, rev. L. F. Powell, 6 vols. (Oxford, 1934–64), I, 155.

enable the reader to regulate the order of facts with sufficient exactness the proper medium between a Journal which has regard only to time, and a history which ranges facts according to their dependence on each other, and postpones or anticipates according to the convenience of narration." Despite equivocation about whether to include the dates of all important events or only enough dates to allow readers to achieve a "sufficient" grasp of chronology, this remark also reveals Johnson's conviction that any student of history must have some way of ordering events with respect to time. By "sufficient exactness" Johnson seems to mean enough temporal precision so that readers can understand those causal relationships that it is the historian's chief task to explain: the "dependence on each other" of events. Johnson adds that "our work ought to partake of the Spirit of History which is contrary to minute exactness, and of the regularity of a Journal, which is inconsistent with spirit. For this Reason I neither admit numbers or dates nor reject them."[23] How dates can be neither admitted nor rejected is not clear. What stands out in the letter to Cave is Johnson's opinion that while chronology must always be taken into account, it is equally important for historians to avoid preoccupation with time as the only principle for ordering narrative sequence.

This opinion is reflected in *Rambler* 122 when Johnson laments that most histories are "of no other use than chronological memorials." So too in *Rambler* 60, Johnson observes of biographers that too often they "imagine themselves writing a life when they exhibit a chronological series of actions and preferments." In the *Preface to Shakespeare* Johnson remarks of history plays that in the Elizabethan period "history was a series of actions with no other than chronological succession, independent of each other, and without any tendency to introduce or regulate the conclusion."[24] Such comments reveal Johnson's abiding conviction that for the biographer and playwright no less than for the historian causal relationships are more significant than temporal ordering and deserve greater prominence. The distinction is a matter of priority—not mutual exclusion. It did not follow in Johnson's critical theories or narrative

[23] *The Letters of Samuel Johnson*, ed. R. W. Chapman, 3 vols. (Oxford, 1952), I, 20.

[24] Johnson, *The Rambler*, IV, 288, III, 322; *Preface to Shakespeare*, VII, 68.

practice that chronology was dismissed as irrelevant. Temporal sequence as an ordering principle is so conspicuous in *Rasselas* and the biographies as to become a major feature of Johnson's style. Early in his career Johnson seems to have assumed that his readers would expect such ordering. Thus when he departs from chronological sequence in the *Life of Savage*, Johnson is careful to explain both what he is doing and why as he introduces "an incident, which was omitted in the order of time, that it might be mentioned together with the purpose which it was made to serve."[25] Toward the end of his life Johnson betrayed equal sensitivity to the importance of chronology in historical narratives by remarking in "The Author's Advertisement" to the *Lives of the Poets* that "in this minute kind of History the succession of facts is not easily discovered, and I am not without suspicion that some of Dryden's works are placed in wrong years. . . . and if I shall hereafter obtain a more correct chronology will publish it."[26] It is in connection with journals, however, that Johnson is most insistent on the necessity of recording dates. In a letter to Mrs. Thrale in 1777 he advises her to keep at her Thraliana and offers advice: "Do not remit the practice of writing down occurrences as they arise, of whatever kind, and be very punctual in annexing the dates. Chronology you know is the eye of history."[27] The other eye was said to be geography.

In the *Breviaricum Chronologicum* Strauchius remarks that "History has two Eyes, *Chronology* and *Geography*."[28] In the *Ductor Historicus* Hearne quotes an earlier chronologist's assertion that "Chronology and Geography, were two inseparable Sisters, and the two Eyes of History, without which she must inevitably be either Blind or very Obscure."[29] Although Johnson thought well of geography and recommended it in *The Preceptor* as necessary for complete understanding of every "other Branch of Literature," his inclination was to associate chronology more closely with the study of history.[30] Johnson

---

[25] Samuel Johnson, *Lives of the English Poets*, ed. George Birkbeck Hill, 3 vols. (Oxford, 1905), II, 351.
[26] Ibid., I, xxvi.
[27] *Letters*, II, 201–2.
[28] Strauchius, *Breviarium Chronologicum*, p. 3.
[29] [Thomas Hearne] *Ductor Historicus* (London, 1698), p. 115.
[30] Johnson, Preface to *The Preceptor*, I, xix–xx.

had no quarrel with those chronologists who ranked their subject above geography, as Isaacson does in a definition that promotes one eye above the other; "The chief Light and Eye of *History* is *Chronology*, and the very *Load-Star*, which directeth a man out of the Sea of *History*, into the wished for *Haven* of his Reading."[31] Whatever their hyperbole or mixture of metaphors in such polemic aphorisms, chronologists agreed in their less figurative moments that both geography and chronology were essential preliminaries to the study of history. As it was explained in the anonymous chapter on history and chronology in *The Preceptor*, one field provided necessary acquaintance with "the various Distributions of the Earth" while the other provided "general Comprehension of the whole Current of Time."[32]

2

The image of time as a river is so familiar in eighteenth-century writing that it may create an impression that everyone thought of time as flowing in a single stream at a uniform rate not easily altered—even imaginatively in such plays as Johnson defends on the grounds that time is in fact most obsequious to the imagination. But if time had been regarded only in the absolute terms implied by the metaphor of a current, the premise of Johnson's argument against dramatic unity of time would hardly have been so effective in the way he presents it: as a self-evident statement for which no explanation is necessary. In that remark Johnson appeals to every reader's experience: we know that it *is* as easy to conceive a lapse of years as a passage of hours. Johnson also appeals, however, to our encounters with literature in which, whether critics approve or disapprove, the obedience of time to the imagination is undeniable. Shakespeare's plays are the examples that Johnson's *Preface* calls most immediately to mind, of course. They bear out the truth of his premise, leaving as matter for dispute only whether their treatment of time is to be applauded. It has not often been asked what other works Johnson's statement may have recalled to eighteenth-century readers. We can only speculate. I suggest chronology books:

---

[31]Henry Isaacson, "To the Reader," *Saturni Ephemerides* (London, 1633).
[32]*The Preceptor*, I, 242.

their tables of historical events illustrate how easily even the lapse of centuries may be envisaged. Whatever the associations evoked by Johnson's assertion, moreover, it is true that for readers introduced in school days to the elements of chronology, there could have been little doubt that time can be made to conform to a writer's fancy, and not only because the passage of centuries could be displayed on a page and taken in at a glance. Many chronologists also regarded time itself as relative.

We associate relativity with the twentieth century and absolute time with Newtonian physics. Where books like *Clarissa* and *Tristram Shandy* remind us that early writers were aware of how differently the same clock time might seem to pass within the minds of those experiencing it, we turn for explanation to Locke's account of duration. The variability of psychological time, critics usually assume, was explored by philosophers, novelists, and critics within a framework of comfortable assumptions about the stability of physical time. This assumption is reinforced by a notion that if all watches did not show the same time at any moment within the heyday of Newton's clockwork universe, the problem was merely technical: the art of watchmaking had not yet been perfected. References to clocks often encourage this impression, as Pope certainly does early in the *Essay on Criticism* when he remarks that " 'Tis with our *Judgments* as our *Watches*, none / Go just *alike*, yet each believes his own." There is also Johnson's remark that "Dictionaries are like watches, the worst is better than none, and the best cannot be expected to go quite true."[33] Such comments seem to imply that a sufficiently well made watch might tell the *one* true time. Anyone familiar with the brilliant achievement of John Harrison's marine chronometers might even credit the eighteenth century with coming very close to realizing the dream of a perfect timekeeper: Harrison's prize-winning fourth chronometer of 1759 had in an eighty-one day voyage to Jamaica lost only 5.1 seconds.[34]

The purpose of achieving accuracy in a chronometer, however, is to enable that comparison of times which tells where you are.

[33]*Letters*, III, 206.
[34]Humphrey Quill, *John Harrison: The Man Who Found Longitude* (London, 1966), p. 105.

Any traveler can determine his location by comparing two clocks that show different times provided they *both* show time correctly: "if one sets a watch at the local time of one's home port, then every four minutes by which that local time differs from say the local noon time at sea represents one degree of longitude east or west of the home port."[35] Within a Newtonian universe time varies according to location. Two clocks may, and unless they are in the same place *must*, show different times if both are accurate. And there is yet another way in which clocks must often vary from local time, as chronologists announced toward the end of the seventeenth century. The cause, which increasingly accurate watches made it possible to measure with great precision, is quarterly as well as daily variation in the length of solar days. In almanacs and elsewhere, tables showing such variations were given wide distribution, especially that drawn up by Flamsteed, England's first astronomer royal and the founder of the Greenwich Observatory.

In William Holder's *Discourse concerning Time*, which Johnson recommended as an introduction to the technical part of chronology, Flamsteed's table is introduced by an invitation to suppose "a Watch, or a Clock, to be made and set so exactly to correspond with the Day of the Middle Motion of the Sun, that it will continue to go truly according to that Motion of the Sun for a whole Year." There will be a problem with this completely accurate timekeeper because "the days if one be compared to another successively throughout the Year, are found not to be Equal, and will not justly correspond with any Artificial, or Mechanic Equal Measures of Time; as by Watch, Clock, &c." In January the watch will go "Too Fast," in May "Too Slow," in July "Too Fast," and in October "Too Slow." For anyone who looks at such tables, what stays in mind is the relativity of time as shown by what Holder calls "an Equal going Watch."[36] Here is a situation, familiar to many

---

[35]Samuel Macey, "The Early History of Chronometers: A Background Study Related to the Voyages of Cook, Bligh, and Vancouver," *BC Studies*, No. 38 (Summer 1978), pp. 14–23. See also Rupert T. Gould, *The Marine Chronometer: Its History and Development* (1923; rpt. London, 1971).

[36]William Holder, *A Discourse Concerning Time* (London, 1694; facs. rpt., New York, 1977), pp. 29–30, 64, 63. For another discussion of Flamsteed's table in a book recommended by Johnson in *The Preceptor*, see Strauchius, *Breviarium Chron-*

eighteenth-century readers including Johnson, in which a hypo-
thetically perfect timekeeper must, partly because it does realize
the dream of complete accuracy, run sometimes too fast and sometimes too slow. Such tables did not hammer home the idea that
time is absolute.

Of course, before Einstein a notion of absolute time was accepted
in a way that cannot now be maintained. I do not mean to deny
the differences between modern theories of relativity and the
assumptions about time in classical mechanics. Newton's idea of
relativity must not be confused with Einstein's. It is quite correct
to say that for eighteenth-century physics time itself is absolute.
The idea is expressed by Newton. It is echoed in philosophy by
Locke. It was spread by their popularizers. It was never denied by
chronologists, who for the most part avoided discussions about the
nature of time itself. But it did not follow that even in Newtonian
physics relativistic views of time played no significant part in eighteenth-century thought. Quite the contrary. Newton himself "distinguished absolute time from 'relative, apparent, and common
time' as measured by the apparent motions of fixed stars, as well
as by terrestrial clocks."[37] For him the notion of absolute time
simplified the laws of mechanics while also allowing acknowledgment of realms such as our planet where measurement of time is
relative.

Anyone who knows about twentieth-century physics is aware
that time most dramatically varies within unlikely situations involving travel near the speed of light somewhere in outer space, and
that such variation is only apparent to a hypothetical independent
observer or to the traveler who returns from what is still an impossible voyage. For those living on the earth's surface or traveling no
farther than its moon, time seems to flow along at a steady pace
measurable by atomic clocks accurate to within one part in ten

ologicum, pp. 26–27, where Flamsteed's figures are printed as "A Table of the
Equation of Days, by which may be found how much a good Pendulum Watch
ought to be faster or slower than a true Sun-Dial, every day in the Year." There
are columns marked "Watch too fast" and "Watch too slow."

[37] J[ohn] J[amieson] C[arswell] S[mart], "Early Modern and 19th-Century
Scientific Philosophies of Time," *Encyclopaedia Britannica,* 15th ed. (Chicago, 1977),
XVIII, 413.

[155]

billion.[38] The accuracy of our clocks together with the rationalization of our calendars encourages us to forget time's variability. For us time is relative in theory, but in practice relative somewhere else, stable at home. Anyone in the eighteenth century who knew its physics and its calendar problems would have been led—even if all watches were equally accurate—to think of *local* time as relative. For the English traveler before 1752, a visit to France was an eleven-day leap forward in time. Merchants and others who stayed in England often had to reconcile old and new style calendars. Differences of four or five years between the so-called true and vulgar Christian eras were mentioned. Time was in flux at home, theoretically stable elsewhere.

There was thus little to prevent writers from stressing time's relativity. From chronologists they had every encouragement to do so. *The Gentleman's Hourglass*, for example, starts its second chapter, which provides "A Short and Comprehensive View of Time, since the Creation of the World," by remarking that "time is divided by *Philosophers* into absolute and relative." This is correct according to Newtonian physics. *The Gentleman's Hourglass* goes on to explain that "absolute time is Duration itself, which flows equally, independant of any thing external; relative Time is that Portion of Duration, which is measured by external Accidents; such as the Motion of the celestial Bodies, or the Succession of our Ideas." This too is sound Newtonian doctrine. *The Gentleman's Hourglass* adds that in taking up the topics of chronology it is "of this last Species of Time, we are to treat."[39] From the viewpoint of classical physics, chronology in dealing as it did with all aspects of humanly recorded time was understood to be concerned *only* with "relative Time."

A corollary of such emphasis on relativity is awareness that time measurement in everyday life is arbitrary. Thus in his chapter "Of Measure in General," Holder observes that "we measure our Time by law, and not by Nature. . . . As . . . of Measures of Length, and of Capaciousness, and likewise of Weights: So here also, the Measures of Time, are (in their way) subjected more or less to Civil Sanction." The arbitrary aspects of time measurement are most conspicuous,

[38]Samuel A. Goudsmit, et al., *Time*, rev. ed. (New York, 1969), p. 107.
[39]James E. Weeks, *The Gentleman's Hourglass* (Dublin, 1750), p. 10.

however, because "we cannot keep by us settled and Permanent Material Standards for the Measures of Time, as we do of the other." Holder accordingly finds it necessary, as other chronologists also did, to distinguish between standard measures (as understood for weights and distances) and equivalent time measures that "are improperly called Standards, because . . . they cannot be made Standing Measures; for to be such does not compart with the Nature of Time." The correct term is "*Stated* Measures," which emphasizes the fact that such measures are determined legally and are "something different from Nature."[40] When in *Rambler* 107 Johnson has Properantia told that calendars are "the stated and established method of computing time," he shows that, unlike his amusing brainchild, *he* is familiar enough with the technical part of chronology accurately to employ its vocabulary.

One of Holder's illustrations of "how we measure our Time by Law, and not by Nature" is the solar month which, though highly variable, is "yet by Civil Sanction, and Constitution . . . made to us, the Chiefest Measure of the Year." Minutes, hours, and weeks are also "Arbitrarily, and Artificially deduced" from motions of the sun and moon which in turn are "only measured by an Act of the Mind."[41] One virtue of *A Discourse concerning Time*—and perhaps a reason why Johnson recommended it as the place to begin learning about the technical side of chronology—is that in it Holder stresses the ultimately subjective nature of all time measurement. Without denying the role of clocks and other mechanical devices, Holder keeps in sight the fact, increasingly obscured by advances in technology, that all methods of reckoning time are in the final analysis dependent upon "an Act of the Mind." No reader of Holder's book could avoid noticing that in this way time is subordinate to mental activity. Although Holder does not explicitly say that time is obsequious to the imagination, his comparison of time and space measurement would leave readers convinced that time, more than space, is amenable to mental manipulation.

So would other accounts of how time is measured. To start with the most familiar divisions: anyone who looks up *year* in Johnson's

---

[40]Holder, pp. 16–19.
[41]Ibid., pp. 20, 12, 16.

Dictionary will find that instead of providing one definition, or any definition of his own, Johnson prints a passage from Watts's *Logick* warning against confusion that may be created when people refer to the lunar year, solar year, or year of twelve months of thirty days as though all three kinds of years were the same.[42] Nathan Bailey's *Dictionarium Britannicum* (2d ed., London, 1736) explains differences between the natural or tropical year, the lunar year, and the sidereal year, giving the time of each. Bailey also stresses the relativity of calendar time when he explains that "*the Civil* YEAR is that which each nation has contrived to compute time by, and is very various, both as to its beginning and to its length; according as they follow either the course of the sun or moon, or both." Johnson's definition of *month* spells out the differences among lunar, solar, and calendar months, remarking that it is the last "by which we reckon time." Bailey is again more technical, defining the astronomical or synodical month, the calendar month, the lunar synodical month, lunar periodical month, lunar illuminative month, month of apparition, month of illumination, month of decretorial, month medical, month of consecution, month of progression, month of peragration, and month periodical. Here under *month*, too, Bailey calls attention to the cultural relativity of time measurement by defining *Civil Month* as "a month suited to the different customs of particular nations." Such definitions suggest that time was relative even for those who did not trouble their heads about metaphysical dissertations upon the subject of duration and its simple modes.

Nor was the relativity of time measurement only displayed in various ways of conceiving the lapse of months and years. The vocabulary for describing smaller intervals was changing. According to the *Brevarium Chronologicum*, "Ancient Chronologers divided the Hours into *Points, Moments, Uncias* and *Atomes*: so that the Point was the 4th part of an Hour, a Moment the 10th part of a Point, an Uncia the 12th part of a Moment, and an Atome the 47th part of an Uncia; so that a whole Hour contains 4 Points, 40 Moments, 480 Uncia's, 22,560 Atomes." Although Strauchius remarks that "this Division is now grown obsolete," his explanation of current

---

[42]Samuel Johnson, *A Dictionary of the English Language*, 4th ed. (London, 1773). Subsequent references are to this edition.

[158]

words denoting time includes one that would have seemed obsolete
to *his* readers after the first few years of the eighteenth century:
Chapter I of the *Breviarium Chronologicum* takes up "some terms in
Chronology and those the most common, *viz.* Minutes, Scruples,
and Moments." Two kinds of scruples are explained. One is "the
1080th part of an Hour, divided usually farther into Moments"
each of which is "the 76th part of a Scruple." The other kind of
scruple, "taken in the usual and Mathematical sense" is the 60th
part of an hour, known increasingly throughout the eighteenth
century as a minute.[43]

For Strauchius the terms are interchangeable: "A Minute is usually the least Part of time, which is commonly called a *Scruple.*"[44]
As late as 1736 Bailey defines *scruple* "with *Chronologers*" as "a small
part of time used by several eastern nations, among the *Chaldeans,*
a 1/1086th part of an hour." Johnson omits any definition of *scruple*
as a time word, giving in his *Dictionary* only its meaning when
referring to doubts ("generally about minute things"); to measures
of weight ("twenty grains; the third part of a dram"); and to any
"proverbially small quantity." As Johnson defines *moment* (without
any reference to scruples) only as "an indivisible particle of time."
As Johnson's omission of some obsolescent time words suggests, it
was possible to avoid thinking about such matters, just as for the
most part we get along without remembering that years are still
classified by astronomers as tropical, siderial, Bessalian, eclipse, or
Julian, and months divided by them into synodic, sidereal, anom-
alistic, draconic, and tropical. It is easier in the twentieth century,
however, to live without such knowledge.

In the eighteenth century the technical part of chronology was
more frequently encountered by students of the liberal arts. After
recommending it to every young scholar in *Some Thoughts concerning
Education,* Locke insisted that "a young Lad" should be given history
books to read only *after* "he is instructed in Chronology, and
acquainted with the several *Epochs* in use in this part of the World,
and can reduce them to the *Julian Period.*"[45] This reference is not

[43]Strauchius, *Breviarium Chronologicum,* pp. 8–9.
[44]Ibid., p. 8.
[45]Locke, *Thoughts,* pp. 318–20.

to the calendar introduced by Julius Caesar (and retained in England until 1752 as the last vestige of the Roman Empire) but to the time scale of 7,980 years devised by Scaliger. In *The Preceptor*, whoever wrote the section on chronology put with equal insistence the case for teaching all students the Julian period: "There is nothing more important in Chronology, than to have a distinct Comprehension of this Period, and see the Manner of its Application."[46] Agreement on this was almost universal. For those few who did not insist that every student of history must first learn how to translate time references to their place on the Julian scale, the problem was not that doing so is difficult but that it requires ability to imagine an impossible time interval. As Thomas Hearne explains in his *Ductor Historicus*, "We suppose, in *Chronology*, this Period to be 765 Years older than the World."[47]

For this reason Hearne omits consideration of the Julian period from his introductory textbook: "One can never be too careful in removing Difficulties from a Subject, which is so intricate of it self. For after all, if you tell young People, and even those that are come to Man's Estate, that the *Julian Period* begins 765 Years before the World, you'll amaze them to that degree, that tho' you tell them afterwards, That this is but a Supposition, you will have much ado to bring them back again to themselves."[48] I do not know whether Hearne wanted dramatists to observe the unity of time. Arguments in its favor were grounded on an assumptions like his that it is impossible or at best confusing to imagine a passage of years when in fact (or on stage) no years have elapsed. The majority of chronologists saw no such difficulty in the Julian period. They and their readers would have been disposed by familiarity with it to reject arguments, like those for the unity of time, based on the notion that it is hard to think about lengthy imaginary intervals.

Nothing, after all, could be more hypothetical than 765 years before the beginning. Nor was any imaginary period more familiar. Even Hearne had to explain the Julian period—and thus invite consideration of its imaginary interval—while telling his reasons

[46]*The Preceptor*, I, 255.
[47]Hearne, *Ductor Historicus*, p. 8.
[48]Ibid.

for avoiding extensive discussion of the topic. The utility of Scaliger's time scale obviously warranted its inclusion of an interval that could never have existed. The only question was when students should be introduced to it. Everyone who learned anything about history in a systematic way, which is to say just about every eighteenth-century reader educated in universities and schools as well as anyone who turned on his own to books like *The Gentleman's Hourglass*, eventually encountered discussions of the Julian period and was urged to appreciate the advantages of its fictional time before the beginning.

For such readers there was not likely to be much resistance to Johnson's arguments about time in the *Preface to Shakespeare*. His premise there, to be sure, is closer to Locke's explanation, in *An Essay concerning Human Understanding*, of how people may differently imagine the age of the world: "Some men imagine the duration of the world, from its first existence to this present year 1689, to have been 5639 years . . . and others a great deal more; as . . . the Chinese now, who account the world 3,269,000 years old, or more; which longer duration of the world . . . though I should not believe to be true, yet I can equally imagine it with them." In choosing this way of demonstrating that large intervals of time can be thought about as readily as smaller ones, Locke shows his familiarity with chronologists. He evidently thought such examples would be especially effective for an audience that could hardly have been attracted to his *Essay* without having been exposed somewhere along the way to books on chronology. Earlier sections of Locke's seminal chapter on duration and its simple modes refer to Julius Caesar's calendar reforms, to the Julian period, and to the fact that irregular solar motion "adds no small difficulty to chronology."[49] Locke assumes that such allusions will be understood by his readers sufficiently to further his arguments. Ideas from chronology are thus especially relevant to his discussion of how the mind handles time.

In the passage that refers that ability to the imagination, Locke continues with a statement that most closely parallels Johnson's use of *conceive* in "a lapse of years is as easily conceived as a passage

---

[49]John Locke, *An Essay concerning Human Understanding*, ed. A. C. Fraser, 2 vols. (1894; rpt. New York, 1959), I, 254, 248.

of hours": Locke observes that even if the world really is 5,639 years old, "it hinders not at all my imagining what others mean, when they make the world one thousand years older, since every one may with the same facility imagine (I do not say believe) the world to be 50,000 years old, as 5639; and may as well conceive the duration of 50,000 years as 5639."[50] Here the comparison is not between imagining years and imagining hours, but despite a difference in scale Locke's point is the same as Johnson's: it is as easy to conceive the passage of a very large interval as of a smaller one. This coincidence of thought and phraseology does not prove that in the *Preface to Shakespeare* Johnson borrows from Locke or even alludes to the *Essay concerning Human Understanding*. Rather, Locke's use in the *Essay* of so many examples from chronology to bolster an argument similar to Johnson's premise about how we experience duration points to a wider intellectual background for ideas about time that are most often associated exclusively with Locke.

3

In her excellent essay " 'A Succession of Amusements': The Moralization in *Rasselas* of Locke's Account of Time," Phyllis Gaba argues that Johnson's comments on time "are rooted in a coherent theory of time, whose central notions and terms come from Locke, and which underlies much of Johnson's work." After acknowledging the religious background of Johnson's exhortations to use time properly, she suggests that "both his vocabulary and the mechanisms which he assumes come from Locke's epistemological account." There can no longer be any doubt that Johnson's views on the psychology of time perception are Lockean. Nor can there be any question that in his periodical essays and other writings no less than in *Rasselas* Johnson, as Gaba suggests, "invests change with a moral value" partly by charging with ethical significance the terminology of Locke's chapter on duration.[51] Words like *succession, duration,* and *variation* are, as Gaba remarks, put to uses that distinguish the moral essayist from the philosopher. This genealogy

[50]Locke, *Essay*, I, 254–55.
[51]Phyllis Gaba, " 'A Succession of Amusements': The Moralization in *Rasselas* of Locke's Account of Time," *Eighteenth-Century Studies*, 10 (1977), 451–63.

of Johnson's vocabulary for time is correct although incomplete. While Johnson doubtless found in *An Essay concerning Human Understanding* several words and ideas referring to time, some of Locke's terms, like his examples, are in their turn borrowed from or at least shared with chronologists. In their books Johnson also encountered part of the vocabulary of time concepts that he moralizes. The chronologists, moreover, taking their cue from theologians, had already moralized the vocabulary of time.

Students of chronology were often reminded that the week was "instituted to perpetuate the Memory of the Creation."[52] This commonplace hardly depended for its currency upon chronologists. Their reiteration of it and related ideas, however, maintained a connection between religion and the technical part of chronology. In *A Discourse concerning Time*, for example, Holder includes a reminder that God acted on the fourth day to make measurement of time possible: "We read in *Moses, That God created Lights in the Firmament of Heaven, to divide the Day from the Night, and appointed them for Signs, and for Seasons, and for Days, and for Years.* Gen. 1.14." With the legitimacy of timekeeping thus set before his readers, Holder explains that however arbitrary the choice of a given time system by civil authorities may be, there is also inevitably at least some element of conformity to God's plan in *any* way of measuring time by recording celestial motions: "We therefore, following the Guidance and declared Design of the Almighty Providence, deduce our Measures of Time from the successive Motions of the Sun and Moon, and most from the Sun." Of the many purposes for perfecting methods of time measurement and applying them, chronologists like Holder stressed utility "to Ecclesiastical Computations." These depend upon such intervals as "the Lunar Month; which is Natural, and Periodical, and by which the Moveable Festivals of the Christian Church are regulated."[53] Secular uses of chronology are not rejected, but neither are they its main justification.

[52] *The Preceptor*, I, 246. Strauchius, *Breviarium Chronologicum*, p. 62, provides another typically elaborate explanation "the week is a System of 7 Days continually recurring; and to this end divinely ordained, that the Memory of Six Days Creation might be preserved, that the seventh might be kept holy, and that Man and Beast might rest."

[53] Holder, pp. 20–21.

Nor did chronologists encourage their readers to view history apart from its moral lesson. An advantage of chronological tables over narrative history was often said to be that relationships in time are spatialized and thus made visible in the tables for instantaneous apprehension. Isaacson argues that "by *Chronology* . . . many Histories of fore-passed *Ages* (or at the least the *Quintessence* and substance of them) are at once represented to us. . . . And surely in a *chronology* (of necessity) must be much more matter of Delight, Variety, and Ease, than in *Story*, because that by it at the first sight a man may behold the Originall, Encrease, Decrease, and Period of all the Monarchies, Kingdomes, and principall States of the World, whereas reading the several *Histories* of them, would require much time, and exact from the diligent Peruser, a *patience* as infinite, as his paynes."[54] In addition to the convenience of saving time and effort, taking in at a glance sequences of political or other events affords what to chronologists was the nice fringe benefit of avoiding any entanglement with story. To them if to no other class of critics the aesthetic virtues of "Delight, Variety, and Ease" are sacrificed or at least diminished by the very choice of a narrative mode for instruction. On this point, surely, Johnson and the chronologists parted company. What the tables also allow that is more significant from the viewpoint of many chronologists, however, and more in line with Johnson's critical outlook, is ready appreciation of moral patterns.

God's providential designs are made visible. Thus the author of the essay on chronology in *The Preceptor* observes that by using the Julian period to correlate events in Greece and Rome, it is possible to "gather, that at the very Time *Alexander* was establishing the *Macedonian* Greatness in the *East*, an Empire was rising in the *West*, reserved by Providence to crush the Tyranny he was forcing upon Nations, at the Expence of so much Blood and Treasure."[55] Although such lessons are sometimes enforced explicitly by chronologists, they more often encourage readers to do so for themselves. In the *Ductor Historicus* Hearne apparently assumes that readers will always grasp the moral implications of those historical cycles that

[54]Isaacson, *Saturni Ephemerides*, "To The Reader."
[55]*The Preceptor*, I, 269.

chronological tables present to the eye (and imagination) in a single moment: "As Maps, by representing to our Sight the Extent of Countries and the Distance and Situation of Towns, leave a clear and distinct Notion of them in the Imagination . . . just so do Chronological Tables figurate to us the Series and Concatenation of Times: we see there, at once, the Rise of Great Monarchies, the Progress they make by impetuous Conquests, and afterwards how they are canton'd and dismember'd, and finally dwindle away and disappear, to make Room for others that succeed 'em."[56] By describing expansion as "impetuous," Hearne inclines readers to see decline as a just consequence of imperial ambition rather than simply as a neutral phenomenon in the natural history of kingdoms. Such a view of empire building must have been congenial to Johnson.[57] More germane to the question of how books on chronology may have shaped or sustained his attitudes toward time is the fact that in remarks like the foregoing from *A Discourse concerning Time, Ductor Historicus*, and *The Preceptor*, every aspect of time-reckoning systems and their application to the dating of historical events is invested with moral significance.

So are words that would not otherwise have been associated with chronology's specialized vocabulary. *Succession*, for example, which, as Gaba remarks, is a key term in Locke's account of how the mind arrives at its ideas of duration, and a word often used by Johnson, is equally prominent in chronology. The title page of Isaacson's *Saturni Ephemerides* proclaims the book to contain "a chronological Series or Succession of the foure Monarchyes . . . As also a Succession of the Kings and Rulers over most Kingdoms and Estates of the World" together with "an Appendix of the . . . Encrease of Religion in . . . Britayne . . . with a Chronological Succession of Bpps there, & a Brief Relation of their Acts." In his preface Isaacson explains that even in the presentation of secular history, the "succession" of events will teach lessons in morality: "By the Prophane *History* we may be informed of the Succession of other *Kingdomes* and *Common-Wealths*, with Gods providence in ordering and disposing

---

[56]Hearne, *Ductor Historicus*, p. 35.
[57]See Donald J. Greene, "Samuel Johnson and the Great War for Empire," *English Writers of the Eighteenth Century*, ed. John H. Middendorf (New York, 1971), pp. 37–65.

of them." Isaacson also states that history shows "the *Series* and Succession of Generations." The title page of Hearne's *Ductor Historicus* announces that the book not only contains "Definitions and Explications of Terms used in History and Chronology" but (among other things) "a Compendious History of the most considerable Transactions in the World to the Time of our Saviour, In a Series of the Successions of the Ancient Monarchies and Governments of the World." Such usage, which is typical of books dealing with chronology, associates *succession* with both the contents and subjects of those books, and also with moral or religious lessons.

Even though *succession* is occasionally used as a synonym for *series* as in two of the quotations from Isaacson, the term most often stands out as a word referring to a central concept in chronology or to the science itself. *Succession,* not *series,* is the preferred term when chronology is defined. In *The Preceptor* students are told that to benefit from their study of history "it will be necessary to have some previous Knowledge of the Succession of Times, and of the several Nations and Kingdoms, where these Transactions took place." Geography provides the second kind of knowledge. The first kind is chronology: "the Succession of Times." Later in this part of *The Preceptor* students are told how application of the Julian period will be helpful in attaining "a distinct View of the Succession of Time."[58] The subject of chronology is succession. In referring to it Johnson is adapting to his purposes the vocabulary of chronology as well as echoing ideas about duration explained in Locke's *Essay.*

In a passage from *Idler* 43 that Gaba cites to illustrate moralization of Lockean words for time, Johnson remarks that seasonal changes enforce notice of "duration," whereas "if the parts of time were not variously coloured, we should never discern their departure or succession, but should live thoughtless of the past, and careless of the future, without will, and perhaps without power to compute the periods of life, or to compare the time which is already lost with that which may probably remain."[59] Here Johnson's attention to the role of change in arousing ideas of duration is indeed Lockean. Familiar terms from

[58] *The Preceptor,* I, 241, 273.
[59] Samuel Johnson, *The Idler and The Adventurer,* ed. W. J. Bate, John M. Bullitt, L. F. Powell, The Yale Edition of the Works of Samuel Johnson, Vol. II (New Haven, 1963), 135–36.

chronology, however, are also put to use when Johnson refers to the "succession" of "the parts of time" and to computing periods. This activity applied to historical epochs rather than individual lives was the main business of chronology, which Johnson defines in his *Dictionary* as "the science of computing and adjusting the periods of time; as the revolution of the sun and moon; and of computing time past, and referring each event to the proper year." Bailey, like Phillips, defines *chronology* with more emphasis on its historical concerns: "the Art of computing Time from the creation of the World for Historical Uses, and preserving an Account of remarkable Transactions, so as to date truly the Beginnings and Ends of the Reigns of Princes, the Revolutions of Kingdoms and Empires, signal Battels, &c."[60] Johnson's definition puts greater emphasis on the technical part of chronology.

There were various definitions of *period*, although its most general sense, which Johnson gives as its third meaning in his *Dictionary*, was "a stated number of years." This meaning is there illustrated by two quotations from Holder's *Discourse concerning Time*. Bailey defines *period* as "(in *Chronology*) an epocha or interval of time by which the years are accounted; or a series of years whereby in different nations, and on different occasions, time is measured." A chronologer, according to Johnson's *Dictionary*, is "he that studies or explains the science of computing past time, or of ranging past events according to their proper years." Thus when in *Idler* 43 Johnson insists on the moral importance of being able "to compute the periods" of our own lives, he is using the vocabulary of chronology metaphorically to suggest that for proper appreciation of mortality every man must become his own chronologer.

4

Boswell in his essay "On Time" remarks that study of chronology could "make those who apply to it have a slight notion of themselves; for what is the longest life of man compared with centuries and still larger portions of Time with which chronologists are versant." Neither in this essay nor elsewhere does Boswell adapt so conspicuously as Johnson does the vocabulary of chronology. To

[60]Bailey, *Dictionarium Britannicum*. See also Edward Phillips, *The New World of Words*, 3d ed. (London, 1671).

Boswell the most interesting potential use of chronological methods for other than historical purposes is not much related to morality: "To apply chronology to the lives of individuals, would be an entertaining, but .. a very humiliating experiment. Were an accurate table to be made out with various columns, in which upon a fair computation the portions of Time appropriated to eating, drinking, sleeping, conversation, study, business, amusements, in short, all the several modes of existence were to be marked, we should be surprised to see the short duration, the small quantity of any thing which has our love or our approbation."[61] What attracts Boswell is not the technical part of chronology, which intrigued Johnson, but the technique of presenting time relationships spatially in tables. Boswell did not find a way of emulating that method when writing biography. Nor did Johnson, although his attention to how biographees spent their time (the routine of their familiar day), like Boswell's concern with this matter, may reflect some measure of influence from the chronologists who presented tables showing how time was employed. Equally speculative but more significant is the possibility that awareness of chronology played some role in attracting Johnson and other poets to spatial renditions of time relationships.

Pat Rogers observes that "a common device of eighteenth-century poets is what might be called the shift in dimension" from spatial to temporal description—as when Johnson opens *The Vanity of Human Wishes* by inviting readers to "Survey Mankind from *China* to *Peru*" but then provides "an historical rather than a geographical survey" ranging "more freely over the past than the present world." In other poems such as *Windsor Forest*, Thomson's *Liberty*, and Goldsmith's *The Traveller* we are also "invited first to *look* . . . and then to *think back*" over a span of historical time.[62] There is no single explanation of this strategy. Among the traditions that may have encouraged poets to adopt it, however, is the attention given in chronological tables to what chronologists called synchronism. Hearne exlains that "as by a Map we may see the Whole Earth at

---

[61]James Boswell, "On Time," *The Hypochondriack*, ed. Margery Bailey, 2 vols. (Stanford, 1928), II, 251.

[62]Pat Rogers, "Time and Space in *Windsor Forest*," *The Art of Alexander Pope*, ed. Howard Erskine-Hill and Anne Smith (New York, 1979), p. 40.

once, and observe all the Countries that lie in this same Climate; so Chronological Tables give us a Prospect of a general *Synchronism*, that is, the History of what has happen'd, and the eminent Men that have liv'd in the same Age, in all the several Nations of the World."[63] The tables create a prospect, and thus like many prospect poems are an invitation to *see* imaginatively, although more directly than such poems, the tables invite observation of activities synchronous in time.

Because they provide an opportunity to observe parallel histories of eminent men who share an age, the tables show what might be called dynamic rather than static synchronism. That is, they do not freeze time by giving a cross section of simultaneous activities stopped for inspection as in a display of snapshots. The tables do not usually portray one moment or any short interval. An *age*, according to Johnson's *Dictionary*, is an indeterminate but long time: "Any period of time attributed to something as the whole, or part of its duration . . . a succession or generation of men . . . the time in which any particular man, or race of men, lived, or shall live, as the *age* of heroes . . . the space of a hundred years; a secular period; a century." What the tables thus show are many correlated and often protracted sequences.

In this way chronological tables are analogous in structure to poems like *The Vanity of Human Wishes*. Though it is not concerned with placing events in one age or correlating them with respect to calendar time, which is for Johnson's purposes only incidentally relevant morally and hardly at all important structurally, there is in *The Vanity of Human Wishes* a series of histories of eminent men which though necessarily presented to the reader sequentially are to be held in mind for simultaneous contemplation of the related lessons taught by each account. The reader is in effect invited to regard them in one prospect of time, or "extensive view" just as if looking at a page of chronological tables. As Hearne's analogy of the map suggests, surveying mankind from China to Peru has affinities to surveying mankind from past to present. For those eighteenth-century readers who, like Johnson, were familiar with tables affording such prospects, poems constructed like *The Vanity of Human*

[63]Hearne, *Ductor Historicus*, p. 35.

Wishes, its Juvenalian model, or other eighteenth-century works employing the dimensional shift that Rogers has identified, would be especially congenial. To this extent chronology may have contributed to the eighteenth-century preference for literary structures that we would call (in Joseph Frank's useful term) examples of spatial form.[64]

But I only suggest this as a possibility worth considering. Influence of one literary structure upon that of another genre cannot often be proved. Nor do I suppose it now demonstrated that concepts from chronology, especially those involving relativistic views of time, provided a climate of opinion *necessary* to the adoption and success of Johnson's strategy in building his case against dramatic unity of time upon the premise that time is especially obedient to the imagination. Causation is always multiple, and in cases like this hard to pin down because there is no way to know what might have happened in different circumstances. It is likely that Johnson would have proceeded as he did with equal persuasive force had there been no chronology books or had he and his readers not been so familiar with them. There is no ready way of saying exactly how much his knowledge of such books strengthened attitudes toward time derived from other sources as well, although available facts suggest that chronology did reinforce convictions shaped also by Locke's *Essay* and by Johnson's reading in theology.

What does appear certain on the basis of the evidence that I have outlined here is that Johnson was interested in chronology, that he knew a great deal about even its technical part, and that he adapted its vocabulary to his purposes as critic and moralist. Equally clear is that the most obvious examples of such use, as when he remarks that Shakespeare was "not the only violator of chronology" in the Elizabethan period, or that Milton's learning

---

[64]Joseph Frank, "Spatial Form: Some Further Reflections," *Critical Inquiry*, 5 (1978), 275–90, remarks that "the emergence of spatial form in twentieth-century narrative should no longer be regarded as a radical break with tradition" (p. 284). There is increasing recognition that spatial forms play a significant role in earlier literature. For discussion of related issues, see Joseph Frank, "Spatial Form: An Answer to Critics," ibid., 4, (1977), 231–52; Eric S. Rabkin, "Spatial Form and Plot," ibid., 4 (1977), 253–70; William Holtz, "Spatial Form in Modern Literature, a Reconsideration," ibid., 4 (1977), 271–84.

prevented him from "frequent outrages of . . . chronological propriety," are not Johnson's most significant adaptations of chronological concepts.[65] More important, because more characteristic of Johnson's prose, poetry, and criticism, are the ways in which chronology apparently played a role in shaping his view of time as an ordering principle for narration. And here there is a paradox that illustrates the variety of chronological methods as well as eighteenth-century generic distinctions. The popularity of historical tables may have encouraged Johnson when writing poetry to *eliminate* or minimize time as a structural device in favor of spatial forms that were nevertheless intended to invite consideration of the past. When writing or criticizing prose narratives, however, Johnson's awareness of chronology's concern with dates and the sequence of events surely worked to reinforce his conviction that although explanation of causation is more crucial than merely showing calendric relationships in history, biography, drama, and fiction—indeed in all narratives except journals—writers must nevertheless also adhere to and find ways of describing what in the *Life of Savage* Johnson calls "the order of time."

[65]Johnson, *Preface to Shakespeare*, VII, 72; *Rambler* 140, *The Rambler*, IV, 377.

Johnson as Patron

GAE HOLLADAY AND O M BRACK, JR.

JOHNSON'S DENUNCIATION OF LORD CHESTERFIELD'S BRAND OF patronage in the famous letter of 1755 and his definition of *patron* in the *Dictionary* as "commonly, a wretch who supports with insolence, and is paid with flattery" carry such authority that Johnson's distaste for the system of patronage long stood as part of that familiar figure, Boswell's Johnson. Thomas Carlyle referred to the Chesterfield letter as "that far-famed Blast of Doom, proclaiming . . . that Patronage should be no more!"[1] Recently, however, in a more sensitive probing of the Chesterfield affair, Johnson scholars have combed manuscripts, isolated issues, and defined terms in attempts to translate Johnson's attitude toward patronage from myth into reality.

The crucial issue surrounding Johnson's rejection of Lord Chesterfield's patronage seven years after he had accepted it appears to be just what "great professions" the patron made to the lexicographer.[2] One scholar presents evidence that Chesterfield made his "professions" and read Johnson's signed "Fair Copy" before the *Plan* of 1747 was published (contrary to Boswell's understanding that Chesterfield got a copy of the *Plan* accidentally), so that the *Plan* "seems to be an announcement by Johnson and the booksellers of Chesterfield's patronage, rather than his bid for it."[3] Furthermore, Jacob Leed suggests, Johnson probably interpreted Chesterfield's "professions" as intended financial support. Paul Korshin points out that "small gift" patronage was the most common variety in the 1740s and reasons that Chesterfield made his "small gift" of £10 to Johnson, intending afterwards only the "higher patronage"

[1]"Boswell's Life of Johnson," *Fraser's Magazine*, 5 (1832), 398.

[2]*Boswell's Life of Johnson*, ed. G. B. Hill, rev. L. F. Powell, 6 vols. (Oxford, 1934–64), I, 259. Hereafter cited as *Life*.

[3]Jacob Leed, "Johnson and Chesterfield: 1746–47," *Studies in Burke and His Time*, 11 (1970), 1685. See *Life*, I, 184–85.

of intellectual support and of what Browning labeled in reference to another vain aristocrat, the "gift of a nine-hundred-years-old name."[4]

Whichever Lord Chesterfield intended, "small gift" or "higher" patronage, Johnson remained certain that neither obligation was met and that "neither pride nor modesty" would permit his further attendance on the patron. Chesterfield, said Johnson, failed to offer the *Dictionary* "one act of assistance, one word of encouragement, or one smile of favour." By "assistance" Johnson means here financial aid.[5] Furthermore, the language in the first 1755 *Dictionary* entry (unchanged in the 1773 edition)—"one who supports with insolence, and is paid with flattery"—strongly suggests that money is the basic encouragement a patron should, but does not always, dispense.[6]

In keeping with Johnson's association of patronage with expected financial assistance for the *Dictionary*, the *Rambler*, written during the period of disillusionment with Chesterfield's promises, shows Johnson typically concerned with "the provision of economic security for the client—this is what the aspirants are seeking and what the patrons either dangle or deliver."[7] The predominant themes of the papers dealing with patronage are the "vicious flattery" the client's dependence forces him into and the neglect that follows a patron's false encouragement.

[4]"Johnson and Literary Patronage: A Comment on Jacob Leed's Article," *Studies in Burke and His Time*, 12 (1970–71), 1808. Leed responds that many writers could still expect "large gift" financial support even at mid-century, and that Johnson did not, after the *Plan* was published, need Chesterfield's name, "for he already had that" (ibid., 13 [1971], 2014).

[5]*Life*, I, 261–62. Boswell adds as a note to the 1755 letter the following clarification by Langton: "Dr. Johnson, when he gave me this copy of his letter, desired that I would annex to it his information to me, that whereas it is said in the letter that 'no assistance has been received,' he did once receive from Lord Chesterfield the sum of ten pounds; but as that was so inconsiderable a sum, he thought mention of it could not properly find place in a letter of the kind that this was."

[6]One of the illustrative quotations for *patron* continues the monetary strain: "Ne'er cease to mention the continu'd debt, / Which the great *patron* only would forget. *Prior*."

[7]Jacob Leed, "Patronage in the *Rambler*," *Studies in Burke and His Time*, 14 (1972), 6. See, for example, *Rambler* Nos. 104, 136, and 163.

Without financial independence, Johnson asserts, intellectual independence is merely an ideal. What cost, the Rambler asks repeatedly, patronage? Johnson's persona wears a very thin disguise in the final paper, which answers that even poverty is not reason enough to martyr truth: "I must remain accountable for all my faults, and submit, without subterfuge, to the censures of criticism, which, however, I shall not endeavour to soften by a formal deprecation, or to overbear by the influence of a patron. . . . Having hitherto attempted only the propagation of truth, I will not at last violate it by the confession of terrors which I do not feel: Having laboured to maintain the dignity of virtue, I will not now degrade it by the meanness of dedication."[8] Even before Johnson's biting response to Chesterfield's reviews of the *Dictionary* in the *World*, the Rambler had characterized the uncertainty of a patron's good will. In *Rambler* 153 a young man enjoys, then suffers from, his association with a wealthy uncle. Revising for the collected edition of 1752, Johnson presented the benefactor not as an uncle but as a patron.

The second definition of *patron* in the *Dictionary*, "a guardian Saint," and the fourth definition, "one who has donation of ecclesiastical preferment," carry extraliterary meanings. But the third definition must concern us here, for it names *patron* as "advocate; defender; vindicator." Johnson appears to have in mind here not a wealthy supporter of struggling literary men but the more abstract meaning of one who supports an idea, ideology, principle, or cause. His two examples support this interpretation: (1) "We are no *patrons* of those things; the best defence whereof is speedy redress and amendment." (2) "Whether the minds of men have naturally imprinted on them the ideas of extension and number, I leave to those who are the *patrons* of innate principles."

Neither of these illustrative quotations is burdened with the ambivalence of the one quotation illustrating the noun *Patronage* ("support; protection"):

Here's *patronage*, and here our art descries,

---

[8]The *Rambler*, ed. W. J. Bate and Albrecht B. Strauss, Vols. III, IV, and V of The Yale Edition of the Works of Samuel Johnson (New Haven, 1969), No. 208. Hereafter cited in the text as *Rambler*.

What breaks its bonds, what draws the closer ties,
Shows what rewards our services may gain,
And how too often we may court in vain.

This quotation would seem to indicate Chesterfield's neglect was very much on Johnson's mind during the making of the *Dictionary* and just afterward. The famous letter was dated 7 February 1755. In March, in Dodsley's *Collection of Poems*, appeared the revised lines of *The Vanity of Human Wishes* naming the ills of the scholar's life not "Toil, envy, want, the garret, and the jail" but "Toil, envy, want, the patron, and the jail." Then on 15 April the *Dictionary* was published, containing the definition of *patron* as a wretch paid with flattery.

Though after the *Dictionary* business Johnson was proud of never accepting the kind of patronage defined by a writer's gaining financial security from a wealthy individual, he did employ the benefits of subscription publication (*Shakespeare*), publication through booksellers' conger (*Dictionary* and *Lives of the Poets*), and a pension which at least in 1782 fell under the government's records of rewards to "Writers Political."[9] The abuses by the wealthy of individual patronage that resulted in a writer's servility, disillusionment, and dependence evidently did not extend for Johnson to other kinds of countenance, support, and protection considered in the eighteenth century, as they are now, to be patronage. The "shackles of patronage" Liberales suffers in *Rambler* 163—constraints that demand one to flatter vanity and sacrifice truth—are the shackles of direct economic dependency.

In fact, Johnson knew that not even all wealthy patrons deserved the scathing press the general class received in the 1755 letter. Many solicitors deserved the neglect (if not the false encouragement) they met. All-too-human, patrons were sometimes avaricious. But Johnson knew too that they were sometimes "cheated by credulity, or overpowered by resistless solicitation. They are sometimes too strongly influenced by honest prejudices of friendship, or the prevalence of virtuous compassion" (*Rambler* 160). Johnson, himself a patron, was subject to precisely these weaknesses.

[9]Paul J. Korshin, "Types of Eighteenth-Century Patronage," *Eighteenth-Century Studies*, 7 (1974), 470–71, n. 49.

Scant attention has been paid to Johnson *as* a patron of literature, even though little stretching is required to fit him into his own definitions of patron as one who countenances, supports, protects, advocates, defends, or vindicates persons, causes, or ideas. Within this generous view Johnson fulfilled the obligations of patron in all aspects except direct financial support—that aspect he saw as putting the most constraints upon the sincere but needy writer. His many remarks about the need to be paid for writing are reminders of the close relationship Johnson imagined between financial and intellectual liberty. Johnson could not support other writers financially, so he used every other available means to improve his clients' capabilities to earn money for themselves.

The discrepancy between Johnson's often-quoted definition of patron and his practice of assisting others in a variety of ways should not be troublesome. As John Wain comments in his biography, Johnson's viewpoints in matters professional, political, and social not infrequently occupied "an interesting middle position": "The broad comprehensiveness of his views prevented his taking a clear-cut stance on anything except the great questions of religion and morality. On any topic that arose out of the fertile tangle of human life his attitude was pragmatic, which means that it took account of the contours of experience."[10] Just as Johnson's remarks about women preachers and "female Amazons of the Pen" conflict boldly with his practice of assisting, indeed patronizing, women writers, so his attitude toward patronage must be balanced between theory and practice.

Flattery and Caprice, offspring of Patronage and Pride in the allegory comprising *Rambler* 91, hold captive the Sciences cruelly thrust from the Hall of Expectation, where Johnson had once waited, until they "were led at last to the cottage of Independence, the daughter of Fortitude; where they were taught by Prudence and Parsimony to support themselves in dignity and quiet." While writers and other artists in the eighteenth century were learning the truth of Johnson's remark, in another context, that "the world has always a right to be regarded,"[11] they, too, gradually supported

[10]*Samuel Johnson* (New York, 1974), p. 179.
[11]*The Letters of Samuel Johnson*, ed. R. W. Chapman, 3 vols. (Oxford, 1952), I, 160. Hereafter cited as *Letters*.

themselves by exercising prudence and parsimony. In the eighteenth century independence became an increasingly workable alternative to royal and aristocratic patronage. Late in the seventeenth century, for example, John Bannister attempted to relieve the musicians' dependence upon the court by presenting in 1672 the first concerts for which the public paid a fee.[12] Opera and incidental music for theaters gave composers a chance at a livelihood; and the market for journalists improved with increasing periodical publications. Even the graphic arts discovered a market in the growing publishing enterprises that began to flourish in the eighteenth century.

Scholars have had difficulty precisely reconstructing the bridge between a private system of patronage and a public commercial market.[13] Whatever the reasons for the transition, Johnson, knowledgeable and influential in the booktrade, helped many writers complete the crossover. His efforts as a patron of literature were primarily invested in (1) writing reviews, (2) signing subscription lists, (3) influencing booksellers, (4) contributing to others' works, (5) revising others' works, and (6) writing prefaces and dedications. An extensive list of examples of Johnson's work in each of these categories might be compiled from existing Johnsoniana and scholarship. The present study of Johnson as patron, however, focuses

---

[12]Michael Foss, *The Age of Patronage: The Arts in England, 1660–1750* (Ithaca, 1972), p. 77.

[13]In his early study *Authorship in the Days of Johnson* (London, 1927), A. E. Collins notes the decline by mid-century of the kind of friendship and disinterested patronage extended by Burlington, Oxford, Peterborough, Chandos, and the Queensberrys, to Pope, Swift, and Arbuthnot. Because of the abuses of the time-honored system of patronage, and the failure of wit to be any longer associated with wealth, the literary calling, he theorizes, "was disentangling itself from peers and dependence, passing towards the middle class and independence" (p. 191). In his recent study, *The Age of Patronage*, Foss presents the shift as philosophical and political: "The fall of absolutism and the rise of parliamentary government, the collapse of royal patronage and the growth (in power and wealth) of political lords, the discovery of a rational world by the arts, science, philosophy, and the appearance of a numerous, vocal and expectant public—all silently conspired to make the arts obedient to social and political ends." Later in the century, he seems to agree with Collins, "the cheerful state of the London market now encouraged the arts to abandon some of the old forms of private patronage, and put their works at the mercy of the general public" (p. 177).

on Johnson's dealings with particular clients. All six varieties of patronage, for example, Johnson exercised on behalf of Charlotte Lennox. Drawing the main details from their professional relationship, then adding illustrations of others he patronized in similar ways, we should make clear the impact of Johnson's continual support of writers.

Among the first women to earn her living by her pen, Charlotte Lennox over her long troubled career gained a reputation for literary merit and for winning Johnson's patronage. Challenging every limitation imposed by unfortunate circumstances and a competitive profession, Mrs. Lennox exploited all possibilities for patronage in many forms, including the advice and assistance of Johnson, Richardson, Goldsmith, Garrick, and the earl of Orrery, to maintain a meager subsistence. No dilettante, Mrs. Lennox wrote for money. Johnson respected her efforts to live independently and often assisted her in her struggle, as he assisted the struggles of many others who attempted to live by their pens. The first record of Johnson's attention to Charlotte Lennox is Sir John Hawkins's account of the Ivy Lane Club's celebration of her "first literary child," her novel *Harriot Stuart* (1750).[14] Johnson's promise in a letter to her to "speak to Mr. Payne and Mr. Cave" and to endeavor to "bring the whole affair to succeed" hints that he was operating behind the scenes to promote her early work in the 1750s.[15] He continued his patronage of her until his death.

In the first category of patronage—writing reviews, notices, and advertisements—we know Johnson assisted Charlotte Lennox and others, though no definitive bibliography of these writings can be compiled so long as mysteries of identification and attribution persist, as they do with the notices of Charlotte Lennox's *Harriot Stuart*, *The Female Quixote*, and *Shakespear Illustrated*, all attributed to

---

[14]*The Life of Samuel Johnson, LL.D.*, ed. Bertram H. Davis (New York, 1961), pp. 121–22. For a different view of this celebration, perhaps contributed by Lennox herself, see *The Early Biographies of Samuel Johnson*, ed. O M Brack, Jr., and Robert E. Kelley (Iowa City, 1974), pp. 272–73 and n. 39.

[15]Duncan E. Isles, "The Lennox Collection," *Harvard Library Bulletin*, 18 (1970), 317–44; 19 (1971), 36–60, 165–86, 416–35. This letter appears in 18 (1970), 334 (Item No. 1). Isles assigns the conjectural date as 1750.

Johnson.[16] Review writing was not Johnson's favorite exercise; nevertheless he often brought conviction and moral integrity to the relatively undeveloped genre, as in the review of Soame Jenyns, and he in fact wrote many reviews for the *Literary Magazine* and other publications.[17] Johnson's statement that "a man will more easily write a sheet all his own, than read an octavo volume to get extracts" (*Life*, IV, 214) indicates that reviewing was often merely a chore done for money. But he appreciated that a review had the potential to "influence the public voice, and hasten the popularity of a valuable Work"[18] and so patronized a friend's work with a review so long as the public would not be seriously misled.

Charlotte Lennox probably undertook her well-received translation of the *Memoirs of the Duke of Sully* (1756) at the suggestion of Johnson or his business associates Robert and James Dodsley, who published it. Johnson offers to repay his "debt" to the Sully volumes (perhaps for providing materials for political and historical articles in the *Literary Magazine*) by reviewing them. As the *Memoirs* of Sully approached a second edition Johnson wrote to Mrs. Lennox: "To

[16]See Arthur Sherbo, "Samuel Johnson and the *Gentleman's Magazine*, 1750– 1755," in *Johnsonian Studies*, ed. Magdi Wahba (Cairo, 1962), pp. 139, 140, 145, and G. B. Hill's attribution of the review of *The Female Quixote* in *Boswell's Life of Johnson*, ed. G. B. Hill (Oxford, 1887), I, 367.

[17]See a bibliography of Johnson's journalistic canon, in Edward A. Bloom, *Samuel Johnson in Grub Street* (Providence, 1957), pp. 263–70. See also Donald D. Eddy's *Samuel Johnson: Book Reviewer in the "Literary Magazine: or, Universal Review" (1756–58)* (New York, 1979).

[18]"To the Public," *Literary Magazine*, 1 (1756), iv. Johnson's notion of reviewing was rather advanced, considering most reviews were largely extracts without much critical evaluation or commentary. He told Boswell, "The Critical Reviewers, I believe, often review without reading the books through; but lay hold of a topick, and write chiefly from their own minds. The Monthly Reviewers are duller men, and are glad to read the books through" (*Life*, III, 32). According to Thomas Tyers, Johnson knew the value of his opinion but was reluctant to give it: "He did not always give his opinion unconditionally of the pieces he had even perused, and was competent to decide upon. He did not choose to have his sentiments generally known; for there was a great eagerness, especially in those who had not the pole-star of judgment to direct them, to be taught what to think or to say on literary performances. 'What does Johnson say of such a book?' was the question of every day" (*Early Biographies of Samuel Johnson*, p. 67).

Sully I am in debt. If you can point me out a passage that can be refered to the present times, I will press for a place in the Gentleman's Magazine, and write an Introduction to it, if I can not get it in there I will put it in the new book [*Literary Magazine*], but their readers are, I think, seven to one."[19] His review of the Sully *Memoirs* appeared in the *Literary Magazine* for September–October 1756, declaring for them "the variety of romance with the truth of history" and a style "easy, spritely, and elegant, equally remote from the turgid and the mean" (I, 228).

Johnson offers in the same letter also to press the insertion of "any episode or little story" from her more recent translation, *The Memoirs of the Countess of Berci* (1756), though he tells her honestly that he did "not think it worth your while, our readers are few, and I know not when they will be more." Mrs. Lennox was clearly angry at Johnson for not reviewing the Berci translation earlier. Johnson's defensive tone illustrates the frustration of his attempts to patronize the intemperate and desperate young writer. He had been willing to perform everything possible to please her, including contacting a bookseller: "When Mr. Lennox brought me *Berci* he said you desired me to say something about it, which I promised without hestitation. . . . I conceived that you wanted me to say something to Millar." After explaining further that the *Literary Magazine* usually mentioned only "originals, or books of science or learning," Johnson adds a significant remark that characterizes his patronage of Charlotte Lennox and of others: "This rule, however, I would gladly break to do you either service or pleasure."

Johnson never reviewed *Berci*. But he did assume the role of adviser to Mrs. Lennox in teaching her the art of accepting others' criticism; and in this same letter to her he demonstrates considerable tolerance toward the offending reviewers: "The Letter which you sent me some time ago, was rather too full of wrath for the provocation. I read both the reviews, and though the Critical Reviewers, according to their plan, showed their superiority of knowledge with some ostentation, they mentioned you with great respect, and the other Reviewers though less ceremonious, said

[19]30 July 1756. "The Lennox Collection," 19 (1971), 46 (Item No. 15). No review in the *Gentleman's Magazine* ever appeared.

nothing that can excite or justify much resentment. They both answ[e]red the original rather than the translation. . . . I do not believe that either of the Reviews, intended you any hurt."[20]

Other immediate acquaintances and even friends of friends benefited by Johnson's reviews. A few examples will demonstrate the pattern. In 1756 Johnson wrote several reviews. He also wrote in the *Universal Visiter* of abusive reviewers who, as a result of increased numbers of writers scavenging for praise and meat, "can satisfy their hunger only by devouring their brethren" (I, 164). Johnson's reviews of friends' works in the *Literary Magazine* were occasionally restrained but never abusive. In the first issue he publicized the works of three friends: Thomas Birch, Arthur Murphy, and Joseph Warton, in each case moderating his reservations about some particulars of the work by giving it his general approval.

Birch had come to know Johnson in the early days of the *Gentlemen's Magazine* when they jointly patronized the work of Elizabeth Carter, also on Cave's staff.[21] Although Birch's collection of detail in *History of the Royal Society of London*, Johnson objected, made the work more a diary than a history, he admitted "it is always more safe to admit copiousness than to affect brevity" and followed up with five columns of extracts for the reader to judge independently (I, 30–32). In the next article Johnson reviewed Arthur Murphy's collected edition of *Gray's Inn Journal*, balancing his amusement at Murphy's "sprightliness and humour" with the conviction that an editor's most important task is his successful handling of essays "upon subjects of general and perpetual concern" (I, 32–35).

Another friend, Joseph Warton, invited by Johnson in 1753 to furnish monthly papers for John Hawkesworth's *The Adventurer* (*Letters*, I, 47), also benefited from Johnson's review of *An Essay on the Writings and Genius of Pope*. Aside from his criticism of Warton for passing on second-hand information about a prose version of "Essay on Criticism" and a disagreement with Warton's understanding of the alexandrine, Johnson liberally summarizes and quotes from the work. He praises it as "a very curious and entertaining miscellany

---

[20]"The Lennox Collection," 19 (1971), 44–46 (Item No. 15).
[21]See Edward Ruhe, "Birch, Johnson, and Elizabeth Carter: An Episode of 1738–39," *PMLA*, 73 (1958), 491–500.

of critical remarks and literary history" and claims his intention "to kindle, not to extinguish curiosity, by this slight sketch of a work abounding with curious quotations and pleasing disquisitions" (I, 35–38).

Among others later reviewed by Johnson were Elizabeth Harrison, John Hawkesworth, William Tytler, James Grainger (twice), and Oliver Goldsmith. Elizabeth Harrison's *Miscellanies on Moral and Religious Subjects, in Prose and Verse* is significant in that hers is the only book Johnson is known to have reviewed before its publication. Since he mentions that the volume of pious essays "has been produced by the contribution of many hands, and printed by the encouragement of a numerous subscription," it is reasonably clear he is puffing the book for the modest female author.[22] Hawkesworth was favorably noticed in the *Critical Review* by Johnson's comments on the revised version of Southern's *Oroonoko*. Johnson at once commends Hawkesworth's efforts to reject some comic scenes and effectively preserve the unity of the tragic ones, and excuses what he considers Hawkesworth's modesty in preserving some lines a more severe critic would have "expunged." A generous sampling of the play is offered, with the challenge that "if there be any who looks into this performance, with a desire of finding faults, let him first consider how few opportunities of excellence, the reformation of a play affords."[23]

Johnson's review of William Tytler's vindication of Mary, Queen of Scots, in the *Gentleman's Magazine* for October 1760 (XXX, 453–56) has been called "a voluntary contribution motivated by personal conviction or prejudice."[24] But Thomas Tyers in the *Gentleman's Magazine* for February 1787 (LVII, 87) pointed out, "It was forgot to be told, that twenty years ago he gave an abstract in the Gentleman's Magazine, of Mr. Tytler's book, in vindication of Mary Queen of Scots, at the instigation of an old acquaintance."[25]

[22]*Literary Magazine*, 1 (1756), 282; Donald D. Eddy, "Eighteenth-Century Bibliography: Facts and Opinions," in *Eighteenth-Century English Books* (Chicago, 1976), p. 38.

[23]8 (Dec. 1759), 485. Bloom does not list this review in his bibliography of Johnson's journalistic canon, but it was first attributed in *Biographia Dramatica* (London, 1812), III, 104.

[24]Bloom, p. 183.

[25]*Early Biographies of Samuel Johnson*, p. 88.

Johnson, it seems, was carrying out another favor. He did meet Tytler in Edinburgh nearly fifteen years later, and gave his attention to the younger Mr. Tytler, who "came to shew Dr. Johnson some essays which he had written" (*Life*, V, 387, 402).

On a lighter note, Johnson twice reviewed his friend James Grainger's poem *Sugar Cane*. It was likely Johnson who promoted Grainger, along with some others, to help out Charlotte Lennox with her translation of *The Greek Theatre of Father Brumoy* (1759). Fond of Grainger but amused by a serious poem on sugar, Johnson at first wrote three or four paragraphs prefacing Bishop Percy's excerpts and summaries of the poem in the 1764 *London Chronicle*, then an entire article for the *Critical Review*. The first piece, in playful half-seriousness, rehearses the need for such enlightened visions of America, "well known to be the habitation of uncivilized nations, remarkable only for their rudeness and simplicity."[26] Johnson manages to avoid the issue of poetic merit by dwelling on the curiosity of the subject matter. But in the *Critical Review* Johnson encourages readers "not to be deterred by the title page," for this intriguing new creation—an American poem in loose imitation of Virgil's Georgic—will excite their imaginations. Wherever possible Johnson mentions "a classical regulation," a beautiful description (as of hurricanes and the character of a planter), and presents long sections of the poem for the readers to judge. He justly censures Grainger, however, for forgetting to show "tenderness and humanity" in instructions for buying Negro slaves, and devotes two paragraphs to Grainger's facile rationalization that the Negroes' misery is less on plantations because it would be greater in mines (18 [Oct. 1764], 270–77). But the review is in no way so severe as an unfeeling writer would compose. Johnson patronized the poem with as much grace as possible, considering the laughter it brought to the Club when they heard the line "Now, Muse, let's sing of *rats*" (*Life*, II, 453– 54; IV, 556).

A final example of Johnson's favorably reviewing a friend's work is his review of Goldsmith's *The Traveller* in addition to his contribution of several lines in the poem (*Life*, II, 5–6). The effect of Johnson's conclusions about this poem by a relatively unknown poet was great: "Such is the poem, on which we now congratulate

---

[26] *London Chronicle*, 5 July 1764, p. 12; *Life*, I, 481.

the public, as on a production to which, since the death of Pope, it will not be easy to find any thing equal."[27] Not only did Johnson's review advance the success of the poem but it also assured the later publication of the *Vicar of Wakefield*, sold by Johnson to the hesitant Newbery, who held the novel in manuscript until the poem had succeeded with the public.[28] To Boswell's assertion to Johnson that Goldsmith "is much indebted to you for his getting so high in the public estimation," Johnson replied that Goldsmith only "got *sooner* to it by his intimacy with me" (*Life*, II, 216).

Efforts to collect and analyze book subscription lists in hopes of determining patterns within diversity have verified the significance of subscription publication in the transition of literature from private to public patronage.[29] Charlotte Lennox's failures at subscription, however, despite many attempts and Johnson's patronage, is a reminder of how precarious a literary career could be. Johnson's friends John Hawkesworth and Sir Joshua Reynolds were in one instance recruited to assist in a new illustrated subscription edition of *The Female Quixote* in 1773, a scheme exploded for the larger hopes of a subscription edition of Mrs. Lennox's *Original Works*.[30] Johnson entered in his Diary on 2 Jan. 1775: "Wrote Charlotte's Proposals." The writer hopes, Johnson set down, "that she shall not be considered as too indulgent to vanity, or too studious of interest, if, from that labour which has hitherto been chiefly gainful to others, she endeavours to obtain at last some profit for herself and her children."[31] No doubt Johnson would have written the dedication to the queen had this advertised edition of *The Original Works of Mrs. Charlotte Lennox* come to fruition, for the Proposal announces, "HER MAJESTY has condescended to be the PATRONESS." Although the edition never appeared, Johnson had advanced the

---

[27]*Critical Review*, 18 (Dec. 1764), 462.

[28]*Life*, I, 415. See also *The Collected Works of Oliver Goldsmith*, ed. Arthur Friedman, 5 vols. (Oxford, 1966), IV, 4–7.

[29]See P. J. Wallis, "Book Subscription Lists," *The Library*, 5th ser., 29 (1974), 255–86.

[30]See letter of 16 Oct. 1773 from Hawkesworth to Mrs. Lennox, "The Lennox Collection," 19 (1971), 168–70 (Item No. 28), and letter of 18 Jan. 1775 from Reynolds to Mrs. Lennox, p. 172 (Item No. 30).

[31]*Life*, II, 289–90. A copy of the Proposals is in the Yale University Library.

business details to a considerable level, managing both the arrangements with Strahan for printing the edition and the details of compiling a subscription list.[32]

A most instructive letter Johnson wrote to Charlotte Lennox about the subscription list for *The Original Works* preserves details of the ins and outs of subscription publication in the eighteenth century and portrays Johnson again wearing the patron's garb of professional adviser:

> In soliciting subscriptions, as perhaps in many other cases, too much eagerness defeats itself. We must leave our friends to their own motives and their own opportunities. Your subscription can hardly fail of success, but you must wait its progress. By telling your friends how much you expect from them you discourage them, for they finding themselves unequal to your expectation, will rather do nothing and be quiet, than do their utmost, and yet not please. . . .
>
> You tell me of a numerous acquaintance, and of the vain and the gay, who will be proud of standing in the same list with the Queen. Among these whom I know how many are there to whom I should be welcome if I asked them for a Guinea? With the Vain and the Gay I cannot be supposed to have much conversation, nor indeed with any who will enquire the opinion of the court on the matter.
>
> . . . . .
>
> I therefore venture to tell you again, that in my opinion you will have no reason to fear, but you must be a little patient. The work must be done principally by the great Ladies.[33]

Unfortunately, Charlotte Lennox was out of favor with "the great Ladies."

Many other writers to whose works Johnson was willing to subscribe had already received other types of support or encouragement from him.[34] Concerning Mary Masters's 1755 *Familiar Letters and Poems on Several Occasions*, subscribed to by Johnson, there exists a tradition that Johnson made minor revisions in some poems, though

[32]See letter of 1778 from Mrs. Lennox to Johnson, reprinted in Miriam Rossiter Small, *Charlotte Ramsay Lennox: An Eighteenth Century Lady of Letters* (1935; rpt. Hamden, Conn., 1969), p. 53, from a manuscript in the John Rylands Library.

[33]2 May 1775. "The Lennox Collection," 19 (1971), 173–75, (Item No. 31).

[34]See the list of books in "Johnson as Subscriber," *Johnsonian Newsletter*, 25 (Dec. 1965), 2–3.

it is not clear that he "illuminated [them] here and there with a ray of his own genius," as Boswell reports he did.[35] As noted earlier, in addition to subscribing to Elizabeth Harrison's *Miscellanies* he reviewed the volume. Johnson's subscription to Elizabeth Carter's 1758 translation of Epictetus indicates his continued interest in her career since 1738 when he praised "Eliza" for her poetry in several numbers of the *Gentleman's Magazine*, collaborated with her on translations of Crousaz for Cave, and advised her (without success) "to undertake a translation of *Boethius de Cons.*" (*Life*, I, 139). Versification of the tale of Anningait and Ajut from *Ramblers* 186 and 187 formed one of Anne Penny's *Poems with a Dramatic Entertainment* (1771) to which Johnson also subscribed. We do not know whether Johnson approved of or may even have suggested the versification, but Mrs. Penny's volume of poems is dedicated to him.

These women's works represent but a few subscription lists out of nearly forty known to bear Johnson's name. Others to gain Johnson's support of their works by subscription include Charles Burney (*History of Music*, 1776–89), Thomas Davies (*Dramatic Miscellanies*, 1784, "2 sets"), and John Hoole (Tasso's *Jerusalem Delivered*, 1763 and Ariosto's *Orlando Furioso*, 1783). Herman W. Liebert has pointed out Johnson's "pattern of contribution and subscription" to books by William Woty and his sometimes collaborator Francis Fawkes.[36]

In the history of bookselling, as most literary historians perceive it, subscription gave way to reliance on the trade, as "gradually the system fell into disuse, subscribing, with occasional exceptions, being now left to the publisher."[37] When booksellers gained importance as mediators between the author's works and the public's

---

[35] *Life*, IV, 246; see Arthur Sherbo, "Two Notes on Johnson's Revisions," *Modern Language Review*, 50 (1955), 313–15.

[36] To their joint production, *The Poetical Calendar* (published by Dryden Leach, 1763), Johnson contributed a life of William Collins which he reprinted in his *Lives of the Poets*. He corrected and supplied remarks for Fawkes's translation of the *Idylliums of Theocritus* (Leach, 1767). Johnson is the subject of 14 laudatory lines in Woty's poem *The Graces* (Flexney, 1774). He was also a subscriber for a copy on fine paper of Fawkes's *Original Poems* (Dodsley, Davies, Newbery and others, 1761) and for Woty's *Poetical Works* (Flexney, 1770) ("Summary," *Eighteenth-Century Books*, p. 97 n. 1).

[37] F. A. Mumby and Ian Norrie, *Publishing and Bookselling*, 5th ed. rev. (London, 1974), p. 139.

demands, accessibility to them became essential to writers, as Johnson knew: "A man (said he) who writes a book, thinks himself wiser
or wittier than the rest of mankind; he supposes that he can instruct
or amuse them, and the public to whom he appeals, must, after
all, be the judges of his pretensions" (*Life*, I, 200). As a patron of
both greater and lesser writers, Johnson exerted casual but important influence with the trade on behalf of others.

Throughout the eighteenth century booksellers received their
share of bad press from frustrated writers who, like the poet in
Fielding's *Author's Farce*, complained that when a work is popular
with the public, "authors starve and booksellers grow fat."[38] Charlotte Lennox bitterly complained in a letter to the duchess of Newcastle of her "present slavery to the Booksellers, whom I have the
more mortification to see adding to their heaps by my labours,
which scarce produce me a scanty and precarious subsistence."[39]
But the desperation of struggling writers must be weighed against
the financial success of some others.[40]

The booksellers associated with the *Dictionary* Johnson considered
"generous liberal-minded men," and he called Andrew Millar "the
Mæcenas of the age" (*Life*, I, 304, 287 n.3). Robert Dodsley
("Doddy") Johnson called "my patron" and his doing so makes it
very clear that the word *patron* did not always have a pejorative
meaning for Johnson. Charles Burney was directed to send orders
for the *Dictionary* to Dodsley "because," wrote Johnson, "it was by
his recommendation that I was employed in the work" (*Life*, I,
286). It was on Dodsley's recommendation, ironically, that Johnson
addressed the *Plan* of the *Dictionary* to Lord Chesterfield, and it was
to Dodsley's magazine the *World* that his lordship submitted his ill-
timed remarks on the *Dictionary*. Not only the Dodsleys, but Andrew
Millar, John Newbery, and other booksellers who did business with

[38]Ed. Charles B. Woods, Regents Restoration Drama Series (Lincoln, Neb.,
1966), III. 205.

[39]Newcastle Papers, British Museum Add. MSS. 33067, reprinted in Small,
p. 28.

[40]See Harry Ransom, "The Rewards of Authorship in the Eighteenth Century,"
Univ. of Texas Studies in English (1938), pp. 47–66. Johnson did not himself demand
huge sums for his work. He asked only 200 guineas from the committee of booksellers who approached him with their proposal for *Prefaces, Biographical and Critical,
to the Works of the English Poets* (*Life*, III, 111).

Johnson also found themselves doing business with writers who looked to Johnson for help.

Through Johnson, for example, Charlotte Lennox benefited from associations with booksellers as well as with men influential in publishing, such as Samuel Richardson. Richardson not only read and suggested revisions of the manuscript of *The Female Quixote* (1752) but interceded with Millar to publish the novel (to which the bookseller and his advisers were initially indifferent), then recommended Mrs. Lennox to Dodsley for "a small Thing to translate from the French."[41] When soon afterwards she appealed to Johnson for "some employment in the translating Way,"[42] he promised to seek work for her, though, as he said, translations are "not easy to be had" and he is "much concerned" for her.[43] In his congratulatory letter upon the publication of the first two volumes of *Shakespear Illustrated* (1752–53), Johnson teased her, "When Shakespeare is demolished your wings will be *full summed* and I will fly you at Milton," suggesting he first flew her at Shakespeare and had in mind another source study for her (she never did publish work on Milton).[44] Her most successful translation, *Memoirs of the Duke of Sully*, coincides with Johnson's interest in the political history of France for opening articles in the *Literary Magazine* and was published by Millar and Robert and James Dodsley, all suggesting Johnson's hand in the business.[45] And in March 1757 Johnson wrote to her of other possible employment: "I saw last week at Mr. Dodsly's a Book, called Histoire des Conjurations par P. Tertre which I told him was a good book, as far as could be judged by the title, for

---

[41]"The Lennox Collection," 18 (1970), 334–43 (Item Nos. 1–8).

[42]Manuscript letter of 3 Feb. 1752 in the Library of the Chicago Historical Society.

[43]"The Lennox Collection," 18 (1970), 342 (Item No. 6).

[44]Ibid., 19 (1971), 38–39 (Item No. 11). See Karl Young, *Samuel Johnson on Shakespeare: One Aspect*, Univ. of Wisconsin Studies in Lang. and Lit., No. 18 (Madison, 1924), pp. 147–227.

[45]When James Dodsley and other booksellers violated the copyright law in their intentions to publish a fifth edition of *Memoirs of the Duke of Sully* in 1778, Johnson secured for Mrs. Lennox the services of Arthur Murphy. As a result, the booksellers published her "New Edition" in five volumes as well as their six-volume fifth edition. For the correspondence between Mrs. Lennox and Johnson in this business, see Small, pp. 50–52 and "The Lennox Collection," 19 (1971), 177–78 (Item No. 34).

him to publish, and for you to translate. He seemed not to dislike the proposal."[46] No translation of *The History of Conjurations* appeared, but Johnson's role as liaison between Mrs. Lennox and Dodsley illustrates how influential literary men could serve as a kind of private patron to a struggling writer.

By introducing her to John Boyle, 5th earl of Cork and Orrery, very early in her career, Johnson provided Mrs. Lennox with another enthusiastic patron to supply materials for *Shakespear Illustrated* and to contribute substantially, with Johnson, to her translation of *The Greek Theatre of Father Brumoy* and her short-lived periodical, the *Lady's Museum* (1760–61).[47] Johnson's old friend David Garrick and a member of the Club, George Colman, participated in Mrs. Lennox's career as a playwright; Goldsmith wrote her an epilogue; Sir Joshua Reynolds and John Hawkesworth cooperated in her scheme to publish an illustrated edition of *The Female Quixote* in 1773; and Boswell wrote the 1793 Proposals for "A New and Improved" *Shakespear Illustrated* (which never appeared).[48] Bennet Langton and Lady Frances Chambers, wife of Sir Robert, whom Johnson assisted in writing the Vinerian Law Lectures, shared responsibility for Mrs. Lennox in the last years of her life. Charlotte Lennox lived nearly independently by literature; but she relied on Johnson and his friends to be her patrons, nearly as much as Johnson depended on the booksellers to be his.

Always accessible and on business terms with one or another of the trade, Johnson was in a position to mediate for authors and encourage or recommend their works. Well known are Johnson's efforts to promote Elizabeth Carter's translation of Crousaz's *Examination* of Pope's "Essay on Man" by effectively suggesting to Cave the notice in the *Daily Advertiser* (23 Nov. 1738) and postponing the publication of his own unfinished translation of Crousaz's *Commentary* (*Letters*, I, 13–14). According to the Reverend Mr. Carter, Johnson also gave Miss Carter's work " 'his suffrage free from bias' before it was printed."[49] Johnson's intervention could mean a great deal, as it later did for Goldsmith, whose *Vicar of Wakefield* (1766)

[46]"The Lennox Collection," 19 (1971), 49 (Item No. 17).

[47]*Letters*, I, 44–45; "The Lennox Collection," 19 (1971), 36–37 (Item No. 9).

[48]Ibid., 19 (1971), 183 (Item No. 38) and 421–25 (Item No. 47).

[49]Montagu Pennington, *Memoirs of the Life of Mrs. Elizabeth Carter*, 2 vols. (London, 1808), I, 45.

Johnson sold for 60 guineas (*Life*, I, 415 and n. 1; III, 321). In a much later demonstration of Johnson's reputed powers, it is clear that William Cowper believed Johnson to have "read and recommended my first volume" (published 1782). Although just what influence, if any, Johnson had on the reviewers cannot in this case be documented, Cowper's anxiety about the opinion of the "critical Doctor" was real enough. On the one hand, "one of his pointed sarcasms, if he should happen to be displeased, would soon find its way into all companies, and spoil the sale." On the other hand, "It is possible he may be pleased; and if he should, I shall have engaged on my side one of the best trumpeters in the kingdom."[50]

In the account of 1766 Boswell reports that Johnson "published nothing this year in his own name," then enters a long catalogue of Johnson's writings for others (*Life*, II, 225). Precisely what contributions Johnson made to others' writings are in many cases still not known; but his ready pen in the service of others deserves to be recognized as a form of patronage. He told Murphy and Mrs. Thrale that "he hated to give away literary performances, or even to sell them too cheaply: the next generation shall not accuse me (added he) of beating down the price of literature: one hates, besides, ever to give that which one has been accustomed to sell."[51] But much of his writing was done for free in the form of contributing, revising, and preface and dedication writing.

In the midst of frenzied literary activity between 1755 and 1760 Johnson found himself seriously in debt, obliged to borrow "another Guinea" from Mrs. Lennox's husband, Alexander, and to entreat the assistance of Samuel Richardson in 1756 and Jacob Tonson in 1758.[52] The irony is, as Paul Fussell points out, "if Johnson had

---

[50]*The Correspondence of William Cowper*, ed. Thomas Wright, 4 vols. (London, 1904), II, 373; I, 355–56. See Maurice Quinlan, "An Intermediary between Cowper and Johnson," *Review of English Studies*, 24 (1948), 141–47.

[51]Hester Lynch Piozzi, *Anecdotes of the late Samuel Johnson, LL.D., during the Last Twenty Years of His Life*, ed. Arthur Sherbo (London, 1974), pp. 77. Fanny Burney commented, "I daresay he hardly knows himself what he has written; for he has made numerous prefaces, dedications, odd chapters, and I know not what, for other authors, that he has never owned, and probably never will own" (*Diary and Letters of Madame D'Arblay*, ed. Austin Dobson, 6 vols. [New York, 1904], II, 206).

[52]"The Lennox Collection," 19 (1971), 418 (Item No. 43); *Letters*, I, 89, 105.

charged for this outpouring of free prefaces, dedications, sermons, poetic passages, and law lectures, he could have been, if not rich, at least very comfortable."[53] But when it came to assisting others Johnson was himself the "blockhead" who forgot to write for money. Given his own middle-age financial crisis it is no wonder Johnson found patience and compassion for Charlotte Lennox in her struggle for survival in a profession even more difficult to succeed in as a woman than as a man. The tradition that Johnson wrote chapter xi of Book IX of Mrs. Lennox's *The Female Quixote* has been recently questioned.[54] But it is certain that he wrote the Dedication and translated two essays for *The Greek Theatre of Father Brumoy*.[55] Johnson and the earl of Cork and Orrery contributed to the three volumes and solicited the aid of other translators acknowledged in the Advertisements, including Drs. Sharpe and Grainger.

Plenty of evidence substantiates Boswell's observation that Johnson was "at all times ready to give assistance to his friends, and others, in revising their works, and in writing for them, or greatly improving, their Dedications" (*Life*, II, 1). Among those in addition to Charlotte Lennox to whose work Johnson conspicuously contributed are Robert Shiels, Zachariah Williams, James Bennet, and Robert Chambers. At about the same time Johnson was patronizing Charlotte Lennox's work on Shakespeare's sources, he also allowed generous borrowings from biographical works to assist his Scottish amanuensis, Robert Shiels. In a close study of Shiels's 1753 compilation of *The Lives of the Poets of Great Britain and Ireland, to the Time of Dean Swift* (advertised as the work of Cibber but revealed in Johnson's *Life of Hammond* to be Shiels's work), W. R. Keast has shown that Johnson permitted Shiels to lift huge sections of the

---

[53]*Samuel Johnson and the Life of Writing* (New York, 1971), p. 29.

[54]The attribution was first made by John Mitford in the *Gentleman's Magazine*, N.S. 20 (Aug. 1843), pt. ii, 132 and 21 (Jan. 1844), 41–48. Sherbo in "Samuel Johnson and the *Gentleman's Magazine*, 1750–1755" (p. 140) accepts the chapter as Johnson's; Small (p. 81) accepts the attribution but modifies it slightly. But Duncan Isles has boldly asserted, "There is no convincing external evidence for this claim." See his "Johnson, Richardson, and *The Female Quixote*," in *The Female Quixote*, ed.M. Dalziel (Oxford, 1970), pp. 418–27.

[55]The only Lennox items included in the Sale Catalogue of Johnson's Library are Brumoy's *Greek Theatre* (no. 64) and Sully's *Memoirs* (no. 393).

1744 *Life of Savage*, material from the *Life of Roscommon* in the *Gentleman's Magazine* for May 1748, and the text of the Drury Lane Prologue for the 5 April 1750 benefit performance of Milton's *Comus*. Many years later Johnson used his own material, including some bits of information and commentary he had given Shiels, for the *Lives of the Poets*.[56]

Also in the 1750s Johnson studied the principles of determining longitude and wrote for Zachariah Williams "An Account of an Attempt to ascertain the Longitude by Sea" (1755), enlisted Baretti to make an Italian translation on the opposite pages, helped Williams compose letters to influential men connected with his scientific advances, and penned shortly afterwards Mr. Williams's obituary.[57] Anna Williams, daughter of Zachariah, and Tetty's blind companion, shared Johnson's house from 1766 until her death in 1783 and eventually benefited from his writing Proposals for her poems in 1750. Sixteen years later her *Miscellanies in Prose and Verse* was published, filled out with prose and poetry by Johnson and his acquaintances, Mrs. Thrale, John Hoole, Thomas Percy, and perhaps Francis Reynolds.[58]

Poverty was sufficient to recommend to Johnson one James Bennet, who urged, "I have a large Family and they wholly Unprovided for."[59] Bookseller John Newbery seems to be the moving force behind the edition of *The English Works of Roger Ascham* (1761), planning it perhaps "with the intention of benefiting both Bennet and Johnson," as Hazen suggests.[60] Although Johnson is not credited on the title page, scholars have fairly determined that he wrote the Dedication to the earl of Shaftesbury, the Life of Ascham, and the notes to this imperfect compilation by the poor schoolmaster. Newbery

---

[56]"Johnson and 'Cibber's' *Lives of the Poets*," in *Restoration and Eighteenth-Century Literature: Essays in Honor of Alan Dugald McKillop*, ed. Carroll Camden (Chicago, 1963), pp. 89–101.

[57]*Letters*, I, 433–40; *Life*, I, 301–2.

[58]*Life*, II, 25, 479; Allen T. Hazen, *Samuel Johnson's Prefaces and Dedications* (New Haven, 1937), pp. 213–15. One source claims Mrs. Williams earned £150 by the work ([Lady Phillipina Knight], "Mrs. Anna Williams," *European Magazine*, 36 [Oct. 1799], 226).

[59]Bennet's letter to the Duke of Newcastle, 7 March 1758, quoted in *Life*, I, 551.

[60]Hazen, p. 20.

may be seen acting as Johnson's financial patron, Johnson as Bennet's professional patron, and the earl as Bennet's aristocratic patron. Such dealings point up the complexity of the decline of the old-style system of patronage as the book trade, and then the public, came to command the market for literature.

Not poverty but friendship earned for Robert Chambers substantial contributions by Johnson to the Vinerian Law Lectures between 1766 and 1769 under Mrs. Thrale's suspicion that Johnson "used to visit the University [Oxford] at *Critical Times*, . . . or I thought so."[61] Her further hint that Johnson was extremely liberal with his assistance to others—that "innumerable are the prefaces, sermons, lectures, and dedications which he used to make for people who begged of him"[62]—and her listing of the "Law Lectures for Chambers" in "a Catalogue of such Writings as I *know* to be his" have proved to be fertile.[63] Having met Chambers at least by 1754 on a visit to Oxford, Johnson was in 1766 both responsive to repeated pleas for assistance and attracted to an opportunity to work in law. Bring notes and law books, Johnson hinted, and "I doubt not but Lectures will be produced" (*Letters*, I, 183). Furthermore, Johnson did not permit his help to Chambers, much less the extent of it, to be known.

On one of the 1768 Oxford visits to help Chambers, Johnson wrote also an election address for Henry Thrale—perhaps not for the first time.[64] He wrote several more election addresses for his host at Streatham in 1774 and 1780, as well as other bits of political puff for him. While the law lectures and election addresses required Johnson's expertise in English law, his legal arguments for Boswell required some knowledge of Scots law. Boswell began "this process of picking his brains," as Sir Arnold McNair candidly phrased it,

---

[61]Quoted from the Mainwaring Piozziana, in Arnold McNair, *Dr. Johnson and the Law* (Cambridge, 1948), p. 78.

[62]Piozzi, *Anecdotes*, p. 77; see also *Life*, IV, 344.

[63]*Thraliana*, ed. Katharine C. Balderston, 2d ed., 2 vols. (Oxford, 1951), I, 204. See E. L. McAdam, Jr., *Dr. Johnson and the English Law* (Syracuse, 1951), pp. 65–122. Prof. Thomas M. Curley is presently editing the entire British Library manuscript of the Vinerian Law Lectures.

[64]In his letter to Mrs. Thrale of 29 Feb. 1768 he promises, "I shall yet write another advertisement," suggesting he had written earlier ones (*Letters*, I, 204).

in 1772, and Johnson provided Boswell a final argument in 1781.[65] All together, we know of nine of Boswell's cases that formally received Johnson's attention, while still others Boswell informally tested out on him.

Patronage from Johnson never carried the debt of subservience he condemned in his *Rambler* papers. But his general influence could, and did, extend beyond his contribution to or revision of a specific work. In a rather amusing incident concerning Charlotte Lennox's poetry, Baretti lays at Johnson's door the blame for her new seriousness. Reprinted with the 1752 Proposals for a subscription edition of her 1747 *Poems on Several Occasions* was a slightly revised version of her favorite poem from that collection, "On Reading Hutchinson on the Passions," now more restrained and dignified. Baretti, Mrs. Lennox's Italian tutor, seized upon the revision and her translation work, such as that for *Shakespear Illustrated*, as ill omens for the creative genius for love poetry and pastoral evident in her unperformed *Philander* (1757). In an Italian ode addressed to her, dated 30 May 1754, Baretti complains that some "fatal powers" have caused her to "rebel against Phoebus and Love." That fatal power "and secret cause of all this waywardness" is "Johnson, inflexible Englishman, who thinks a graceful nothing a sin and a vice; who weighs for a month in the balance of his judgment every one of his own lines."[66] The Italian poet understands himself the force of Johnson's mind and its potential influence: "Johnson, Johnson, it is he who has been at you with his terrible words, and I myself feel his austere voice lording it over my own mind and senses." Fortunately, Mrs. Lennox did not follow Baretti's advice to banish "that idle fear which forbids you speaking of love." She continued to translate and to write prose that brought in money for barest survival, but money nonetheless. Baretti, too, survived Johnson's "fatal powers." The "evidence of Baretti's indebtedness to Johnson," Hazen summarizes, "is contained in book after book that he published in English."[67]

---

[65]*Dr. Johnson and the Law*, p. 47. McNair discusses Johnson and the individual cases on Scots law on pp. 47–65. See also McAdam, pp. 123–73.

[66]"Alla Signora Charlotti Lennox" is reprinted in Small, pp. 239–41, and translated into English, pp. 156–60.

[67]Hazen, p. 4.

Although no hope glimmers of ever identifying all the prose and poetry Johnson revised for others, it is useful to be reminded that "authors, long since forgotten, waited on him as their oracle, and he gave responses in the chair of criticism."[68] Among them, the works of Mary Masters and Anna Williams certainly have been forgotten, but Goldsmith's poems *The Traveller* and *The Deserted Village* have not; nor have anthologies omitted the Reverend Mr. Crabbe's *Village*. For this poem, Boswell records, Johnson "had taken the trouble not only to suggest slight corrections and variations, but to furnish some lines, when he thought he could give the writer's meaning better than in the words of the manuscript" (*Life*, IV, 175). In his letter to Reynolds about Crabbe's poem, Johnson shows how solicitous he was to preserve the integrity and the pride of authors whose works he revised: "The alterations which I have made I do not require him to adopt, for my lines are, perhaps, not often better [than] his own; but he may take mine, and his own together, and perhaps between them produce something better than either" (*Letters*, III, 9).

One of the last poets to be honored by Johnson's revisions was young Miss Hannah More from Bristol, lately flattered by lavish praise from Garrick, his peers, and the Bluestocking Ladies. Her 132-stanza ballad "Sir Eldred" was first published and received great acclaim in 1776. On a January evening shortly thereafter, Johnson called on Miss More at the Garricks in a "very communicative" mood. Sometime during the visit, she says, "we then fell upon Sir Eldred: he read both poems through, suggested some little alterations in the first, and did me the honor to write one whole stanza."[69] The "little alterations" in the 1778 edition of "Sir Eldred" were rather extensive, and Herman W. Liebert has shown them to be significant clues to Johnson's principles of revision.[70] Johnson's restraint from the usual "putting out" and "adding," and his simply "correcting" the poem may be, Liebert speculates, "all he felt he could do to a poem which he recited with pleasure, by a poetess he addressed as 'darling' " (p. 243).

---

[68]*Johnsonian Miscellanies*, ed. G. B. Hill, 2 vols. (Oxford, 1897), I, 414.

[69]William Roberts, *Memoirs of the Life and Correspondence of Hannah More*, 2 vols. (New York, 1835), I, 45–46.

[70]" 'We Fell upon Sir Eldred,' " in *New Light on Dr. Johnson*, ed. Frederick W. Hilles (1959; rpt. Hamden, Conn., 1967), pp. 233–45.

What influence Johnson may have had on the prose style of another "darling" late in his life, Fanny Burney, is problematical, as studies of Johnson's influence tend to be. As for Macaulay, he had "not the smallest doubt that [Johnson] revised Cecilia, and that he retouched the style of many passages"—the grave and elevated ones in particular—though Johnson denied seeing even one word of *Cecilia* before it was published.[71] Observing the prose style in all Burney's novels after *Evelina* (1778), Macaulay charges Johnson for causing this "gradual and most pernicious change . . . unexampled in literary history."[72] Madame D'Arblay, of course, in her later novels ruined her own style by inappropriate adaptation and bad imitation of a superior model. The early years when Johnson patronized her formed the basis of a reputation which carried her over an entire career. Between 1778 and Johnson's death in 1784 Fanny Burney walked a precarious line between her craving for Johnson's approbation and her fear of losing it. Austin Dobson's verdict is probably correct: "Decidedly it was good to be praised by Johnson, and one may well forgive Miss Burney for doubting whether she could possibly live up to his laudation."[73] Johnson put her mind at ease by devoting himself to being her unconditional protector, advocate, supporter, and patron.

Dr. Charles Burney received as a favor the last piece Johnson prepared for the press—a Dedication to the king for Burney's *Commemoration of Handel*, published 1 Feb. 1785, shortly after Johnson's death. Patronage in this instance can be seen as still a most uncertain system: Johnson, the proud independent man of letters, penning a Dedication to the king as a kindness to the frantic and frustrated Dr. Burney, who expected compensation for his exceeding difficulties but got none from either the king or the booksellers.[74]

---

[71]"Diary and Letters of Madame D'Arblay," *Critical and Historical Essays*, 3 vols. (New York, 1900), III, 388; *Diary and Letters of Madame D'Arblay*, II, 116.

[72]*Diary and Letters of Madame D'Arblay*, III, 387.

[73]*Fanny Burney (Madame D'Arblay)* (London, 1903), p. 97.

[74]Dr. Burney claimed, "There is not a Bookseller in London who wd not readily give me £100 for a Pamphlet on the subject." But the profits were to go to the Fund for Decayed Musicians, and the dismayed Burney got nothing for his labors, unless some truth survives in the story that Lord Sandwich presented Burney with the £100. See Roger Lonsdale, *Dr. Charles Burney* (Oxford, 1965), pp. 296–314.

Johnson wrote in the Dedication, "By the notice which Your Majesty has been pleased to bestow upon the celebration of HANDEL'S memory, You have condescended to add Your voice to public praise, and give Your sanction to musical emulation."[75] But royal notice brought Burney no royal payment.

It has been observed that "it is somewhat repugnant to our feelings to find a man like Johnson writing compliments to be signed by another" even though "this he does not seem to have felt himself."[76] Johnson was himself stubborn on the point of refusing to make application to a patron after the episode with Lord Chesterfield. But he did not object to authors expecting money from the dedications he wrote for them. The earl of Middlesex, the duke and duchess of Newcastle, and the earl of Orrery could patronize Charlotte Lennox in just the ways Johnson could not—with money, a position for her husband, and housing. The abuse of dedications Johnson strongly condemns in *Rambler* 136 is "to scatter praise or blame without regard to justice." But "to censure all dedications as adulatory and servile," he admits, "would discover rather envy than justice." He concludes: "An author may with great propriety inscribe his work to him by whose encouragement it was undertaken, or by whose liberality he has been enabled to prosecute it, and he may justly rejoice in his own fortitude that dares to rescue merit from obscurity."[77]

[75]Hazen, p. 32.

[76]Henry B. Wheatley, *The Dedication of Books to Patron and Friend* (London, 1887), p. 178.

[77]Speaking of Bishop Burnet's dedication to the *History of his own Time*, Johnson observes, "I do not myself think that a man should say in a dedication what he could not say in a history. However, allowance should be made; for there is a great difference. The known style of a dedication is flattery: it professes to flatter. There is the same difference between what a man says in a dedication, and what he says in a history, as between a lawyer's pleading a cause, and reporting it" (*Life*, V, 285–86). There are limits, however, as Johnson makes clear in the *Life of Dryden*. Although Dryden's dedications are "written with such elegance and luxuriance of praise as neither haughtiness nor avarice could be imagined to resist," Johnson feels that he has made "flattery too cheap. That praise is worth nothing of which the price is known." Later Johnson condemns Dryden because once he undertakes "the task of praise, he no longer retains shame in himself, nor supposes it in his patron." See *Lives of the English Poets*, ed. G. B. Hill, 3 vols. (Oxford, 1905), I, 366, 399, 359.

The excellent collection *Samuel Johnson's Prefaces and Dedications* by Allen T. Hazen tells an extensive story of patronage and rescued merit that need not be repeated here. Some dedications, Hazen notes, such as for Reynolds's *Seven Discourses*, were "little more than a generous act of homage." Others, such as for Bennet's *Ascham* and the six for Mrs. Lennox's works, "were inscribed to patrons with a lively expectation of reward" (p. xx). Booksellers as well as authors solicited Johnson's pen; important London figures such as Dr. Robert James and John Gwynn, and well-meaning amateurs such as Anna Williams and minor literary practitioners such as John Hoole and Thomas Percy, all looked to Johnson's powers. In some instances acquaintances and admirers such as Davies, Goldsmith, and Murphy turned the tables and dedicated books to Johnson.[78]

It should be clear by now that in practice Johnson interpreted *patron* in a broad sense to mean someone who supports and encourages authors' endeavors. When we speak of patronage after the mid-eighteenth century, we should not insist upon the pejorative association of Johnson's first *Dictionary* definition since Johnson certainly did not insist upon it himself. If bitterness lingered from his disappointment in Chesterfield's patronage, it did not seriously disillusion his confidence in the mechanics of survival by authorship. No patron or any other individual alone determined the fate of an author in the late eighteenth century. A neglected author, Johnson reasoned, is one who writes badly and does not answer the demands or tastes of "the world": "A man may hide his head in a hole: he may go into the country, and publish a book now and then, which nobody reads, and then complain he is neglected. There is no reason why any person should exert himself for a man who has written a good book: he has not written it for any individual. . . . When patronage was limited, an authour expected to find a Maecenas, and complained if he did not find one. Why should he complain? This Maecenas has others as good as he, or others who have got the start of him" (*Life*, IV, 172). Johnson did whatever he could to gain for other authors the attraction of aristocrats, booksellers, subscribers, and the public, all potential sources of income in a

[78]See the list in *Johnsonian Newsletter*, 26 (June 1966), 7.

period of transition from court to private patronage to purely commercial publication reliant on mass consumption. His unique middle position as patron and author enabled him at once to be the patron of others and still claim for himself, "No man who ever lived by literature, has lived more independently than I have done" (*Life*, I, 43).

The Language of Reasoned Rhetoric in *The Rambler*

HOYT TROWBRIDGE

I N SPITE OF SEVERAL MORE RECENT STUDIES,[1] THE MOST SEARCH-
ing examinations of Johnson's choice of words are still two well-
known books by the late W. K. Wimsatt, *The Prose Style of Samuel
Johnson* and *Philosophic Words*, both published in the 1940s.[2] These
are solid works of scholarship, very ably argued and documented
within the terms of Wimsatt's particular approach. He was, of
course, one of the leading theorists of the movement called the New
Criticism, and his analyses reflect the aesthetic and linguistic
assumptions, the interpretative methods, and the typical categories
and distinctions of that school of thought. It is true that he does
not search for "ambiguities," "tensions," or "ironies" in Johnson's
prose writings; he says, in fact, that "Johnson's was not the gor-
geously ambiguous poetic gift out of which posterity spins admired
multiplicities of meaning."[3] He does, however, very explicitly and
emphatically deny any relevance or validity, for purposes of literary
interpretation, to the concept of authorial intention.[4] Whatever the
intrinsic merits of that position, its consequence is that he must
describe and explain style by properties of words themselves, taking
no account of the forms a writer seeks to realize or the aims he
hopes to serve.

My purpose here is not to attack Wimsatt's two books on Johnson, but rather to sketch out an alternative approach, based on
other principles. Most fundamentally, it will assume that words,

[1]See, for example, William Vesterman, *The Stylistic Life of Samuel Johnson* (New
Brunswick, 1977) and William Edinger, *Samuel Johnson and Poetic Style* (Chicago,
1977).
[2]New Haven, 1941 and 1946.
[3]Wimsatt, *Philosophic Words*, p. xi.
[4]Ibid., p. ix.

the matter of all writing, have potenialities for many and diverse uses but achieve form and force only through the intentions of their human users. The specific intentions to be considered here are those of rhetoric, the art or faculty of "observing in any given case the available means of persuasion."[5]

Johnson himself seems to think of the *Rambler* essays as rhetorical, designed to persuade his readers of the truth and importance of certain moral and religious observations and conclusions. In his allegory of true and false criticism, he says of all writing, "The task of an author is, either to teach what is not known, or to recommend known truths, by his manner of adorning them."[6] Of *The Rambler* itself he says in the final number that "it has been my principal design to inculcate wisdom or piety," addressing an audience "whose passions left them leisure for abstracted truth, and whom virtue could please by its naked dignity." He hopes to be "numbered among the writers who have given ardour to virtue, and confidence to truth" (No. 208). If these are his stated attitudes and purposes, why should we not use them as guides in the appreciation and interpretation of these short but weighty essays?

According to Aristotle there are three general means of persuasion: the character of the speaker, the emotions aroused in the audience, and the reasoned arguments adduced to support a thesis.[7] All three are at work in the rhetoric of *The Rambler*, and Johnson's choice of words has a role in each.

Discussion of the first means, "ethical" proof, is complicated by two elements in *The Rambler* for which we must make some allowance: the letters from imaginary contributors and the use of a mask. In some of the fictional letters, such as No. 191 from Bellaria, there is a kind of negative persuasion, the extreme silliness of the writer reinforcing our sense of the mindless triviality of the pleasures she so much longs for. This and a few similar letters bring some variety of tone and method to *The Rambler*, but they are a relatively minor element in the whole. The mask Johnson uses, though pervasive,

[5]Aristotle, *Rhetoric*, I.ii.
[6]*Rambler* No. 3. All quotations are from The Yale Edition of the Works of Samuel Johnson, Vols. III–V, ed. W. J. Bate and Albrecht B. Strauss (New Haven, 1969). Volume and page numbers will not be cited.
[7]Aristotle, *Rhetoric*, II.i.

also requires little interpretative adjustment. Since he believes that it is "the duty of an anonymous writer to write, as if he expected to be hereafter known" (No. 208), the difference between the characters of the putative author and the real one is not great. John Wain thinks, as Boswell also did, that Johnson's choice of the Rambler as his fictional mouthpiece is a strangely incongruous one,[8] but in two ways the choice is appropriate and rhetorically effective. The Rambler is a stroller through the infinite variety of human life, observing closely and shrewdly but not actively participating. We trust his observations both because they are founded on wide and thoughtful experience and because they are disinterested, not distorted by personal involvement. Those are important implications, but for the most part we respond to the character of the essayist as if no mask intervened.

The intellectual and ethical qualities of the mind behind the words of the *Rambler* are well stated by Walter Jackson Bate in his fine biography: "The active interplay of qualities—of compassion and anger, of humor and moral profundity, of range of knowledge and specialized focus, of massive moral honesty and specific technical or psychological acumen."[9] We feel throughout the working of a mind of extraordinary mental force, wide and penetrating observation, unillusioned but charitable understanding of human weakness, right feeling about men's virtues and vices, and sympathetic identification with the common human condition. These impressions are less dependent on Johnson's language than on the substance of his statements and arguments, but the dignity, clarity, and vigor of his style undoubtedly contribute to our sense of a speaker to be respected and trusted, so that we are predisposed to believe what he says.

The influence of style in the "pathetic" aspect of Johnson's rhetoric is more specific and more readily documented, but since this essay is no more than a sketch, a few examples will have to suffice. Speaking of modern realistic fiction, he says: "Vice . . . should

[8]John Wain, *Samuel Johnson: A Biography* (New York, 1974), p. 152. See also Johnson, *Works*, III, xxii–iii ("Introduction").

[9]Walter Jackson Bate, *Samuel Johnson* (New York, 1977), pp. 297–98.

[202]

always disgust; nor should the graces of gaiety, or the dignity of courage, be so united with it, as to reconcile it to the mind. Wherever it appears, it should raise hatred by the malignity of its practices, and contempt by the meanness of its stratagems" (No. 4). If disgust, hatred, and contempt are emotions properly raised by fictional depictions of evil, they are surely just as appropriately evoked by the rhetoric of moral admonition. In exposing vices, Johnson chooses language proportional to their magnitude, using words of belittlement for those deserving contempt, of intensification for those that are more destructive and odious.

In his scathing exposure of the malicious detractors of rising talent, he seems less concerned to reform the malefactors than to arouse the scorn of better-hearted people. His choice of words to name the species of detractors—Roarers, Whisperers, and Moderators—is calculated to reinforce our sense of their pettiness and meanness. Although the last class is the most pernicious, because the most plausible, our contempt for them all reaches a climax in Johnson's concluding paragraph. Should we not be ashamed to give credence to the "easy, sordid, and detestable" artifices by which "the envious, the idle, the peevish, and the thoughtless" defeat industry, blast beauty, and depress genius (No. 144)?

In his powerful denunciation of parental cruelty and tyranny, a much more terrible vice than detraction, he seems to attack the offenders themselves, hoping perhaps to persuade them to moderate if not to abandon their behavior toward their children. The enormity of their offenses is heightened throughout by words of magnification: the cruelties exercised in private families are as "dangerous" and "detestable" as the oppressions of bad governments; parental tyranny is "more infamous than cowardice," and the harsh parent "less to be vindicated than any other criminal." In successive paragraphs he describes the natural fondness most men and women feel for their children, then the perverse gratifications by which the unnatural parent "pleases," "delights," and "amuses" himself: "To see helpless infancy stretching out her hands and pouring out her cries in testimony of dependance, without any powers to alarm jealousy, or any guilt to alienate affection, must surely awaken tenderness in every human mind." Contrasted with this touching picture is the devastating analysis of the motives and satisfactions of the tyrannical parent: "He that has extinguished all the sensations of humanity, and has no longer any satisfaction in the reflection that he is loved as the distributor of happiness, may please himself with exciting terror as the inflicter of pain . . . may delight his solitude with contemplating the extent of his power and the force of his commands . . . may amuse himself with new contrivances of detection, multiplications of prohibition, and varieties of punishment; and swell with exultation when he considers how little of the homage he receives he owes to choice." In closing the essay, Johnson remorselessly dissects the state of mind of a parental tyrant in his final hours: the mortifying realization, if he is not "wholly lost in meanness and stupidity," that he is indebted for comfort and support to the undeserved kindness of children whom he has "harrassed by brutality," who have every reason to hate him as their enemy, and whose relief of his miseries is owed "not to gratitude but to mercy" (No. 148).

The language in which vices are exposed may belittle or intensify, according to the degree of evil in the fault, but when his purpose is to strengthen hope and resolution, Johnson's words are firm but gentle. For brief illustration we may consider three separate essays dealing with pain and grief. "It seems determined, by the general suffrage of mankind," he says in No. 47, "that sorrow is to a certain point laudable, as the offspring of love, or at least pardonable as the effect of weakness." We need remedies, however, to soften its pain, for if indulged too long it becomes useless and even culpable. Rejecting the Stoic doctrine of indifference and two other methods proposed by those who lay down rules of intellectual health, Johnson recommends activity and employment as "the safe and general antidote against sorrow." The essay ends with two striking metaphors: "Sorrow is a kind of rust of the soul, which every new idea contributes in its passage to scour away. It is the putrefaction of stagnant life, and is remedied by exercise and motion."

In No. 59, after wishing that Suspirius the screech owl and all his kind might be confined to "some proper receptacle, where they may mingle sighs at leisure, and thicken the gloom of one another," he moves by a sudden turn of thought to a kind of complaining that deserves our sympathy and support, because it "rises from the desire not of giving pain, but of gaining ease." He speaks here not to the sufferer but to those who might comfort him: "It cannot be denied that he who complains acts like a man, like a social being who looks for help from his fellow-creatures. Pity is to many of the unhappy a source of comfort in hopeless distresses, as it contributes to recommend them to themselves, by proving that they have not lost the regard of others; and heaven seems to indicate the duty even of barren compassion, by inclining us to weep for evils which we cannot remedy." In No. 32, as in No. 47, he seeks for means by which our sorrow for real and inescapable evils—pain, poverty, loss of friends, exile, or violent death—may be mitigated and lightened. Here, appealing chiefly to religious arguments, he recommends not employment but patience and submission as the great remedies. He recognizes fully the difficulty of struggling against anguish, especially in "diseases intensely painful, which may indeed suffer such exacerbations as seem to strain the powers of life to their utmost stretch," but he questions whether "the body and mind are not so proportioned, that the one can bear all which can be inflicted on the other, whether virtue cannot stand its ground as long as life, and whether a soul well principled will not be separated sooner than subdued." In words echoing Scripture, the final paragraph commends faith in divine goodness as the best support: "The chief security against the fruitless anguish of impatience, must arise from frequent reflection on the wisdom and goodness of the God of nature, in whose hands are riches and poverty, honour and disgrace, pleasure and pain, and life and death. A settled conviction of the tendency of every thing to our good, and of the possibility of turning miseries into happiness, by receiving them rightly, will incline us to 'bless the name of the Lord, whether he gives or takes away.'" In these simple but noble words he offers the suffering heart relief from its fears and courage to endure whatever may come.

The heart of my subject, because it is also the heart of Johnson's rhetoric, is the third means of persuasion, reasoned argument. The words he chooses as the vehicles of his arguments in *The Rambler* are determined by the kind of reasoning in which he is engaged—most generally by the nature of all rhetorical proof, but more specifically by certain eighteenth-century convictions and attitudes, especially in logic and epistemology. Aristotle observes in the *Ethics* that one mark of an educated man is "to look for precision in each class of things just so far as the nature of the subject admits; it is evidently equally foolish to accept probable reasoning from a mathematician and to demand from a rhetorician scientific proofs." Because he deals with variable things and does not attempt or claim demonstrative certainty and precision, the language of a rhetorician's arguments is that of probability, of a logic which can indicate the truth roughly and in outline, but which reasons from premises that are true only for the most part toward conclusions of the same kind.[10] This vocabulary, common one may say to all rhetoric, is given a distinctive period flavor by theories of knowledge and of proof that Johnson shared with many of his contemporaries.

In recent years, scholars have increasingly recognized that Johnson's way of reasoning is always empirical.[11] It is not for nothing that the general motto of *The Rambler* is the same as that of the Royal Society, *nullius in verbis magistri*, "We judge nothing by authority." Received maxims, principles, and rules are sometimes true, sometimes false; they should never be taken on trust. Johnson supports the saying of Cleobolus the Lindian, "Mediocrity is best," by appealing not to the prestige of that author but to observation: "The experience of every age seems to have given it new confirmation" (No. 38), and when he refutes the "œconomical oracle" that fathers should "marry their daughters lest they should marry themselves," he says that however solemnly it may be transmitted, or however implicitly received, "it can confer no authority which nature has denied" (No. 39). In the search for truth, Bacon says, we must go not to books but to nature, to the things themselves; if we aspire not to guess and divine, but to discover and know, we must "go to facts themselves for everything."[12]

The opening paragraphs of a good many *Rambler* essays, as W. R. Keast suggested in commenting on this paper when it was read at the meeting of the South Central Society for Eighteenth-Century

[10]Aristotle, *Ethics*, I.iii.

[11]See, for example, Donald J. Greene, "Augustinianism and Empiricism," *Eighteenth-Century Studies*, 1 (1967), 33–68, and Richard B. Schwartz, *Samuel Johnson and the New Science* (Madison, Wis., 1971).

[12]Bacon, *Magna Instauratio*, in *The Works of Francis Bacon*, ed. James Spedding 14 vols. (London, 1857–74), VIII, 46.

Studies at the University of Oklahoma in March 1979, give more direct evidence of Johnson's inductive habit of mind. A few of the essays begin with resounding generalizations, apparently unqualified and unproved: "Curiosity is one of the permanent and certain characteristics of a vigorous intellect" (No. 103). "None of the desires dictated by vanity is more general, or less blameable, than that of being distinguished for the arts of conversation" (No. 188). If these sound dogmatic, there are many others that explicitly declare their origin in observation and experience: "It has been observed, by long experience, that late springs produce the greatest plenty" (No. 111). "It is impossible to take a view on any side, or observe any of the various classes that form the great community of the world, without discovering the influence of example; and admitting with new conviction the observation of Aristotle, that "man is an imitative being" (No. 135). "It is impossible to mingle in conversation without observing the difficulty with which a new name makes its way into the world" (No. 144). "The world scarcely affords opportunities of making any observation more frequently, than on false claims to commendation" (No. 189). Some essays begin with a generalization, then immediately follow it with confirmatory examples. Johnson sometimes supplies a transitional "thus" to show the logical relation between the opening proposition and its inductive proofs: "Of the passions with which the mind of man is agitated, it may be observed, that they naturally hasten towards their own extinction by inciting and quickening the attainment of their objects. Thus fear . . . and desire" (No. 47). "Corporal sensation is known to depend so much on novelty, that custom takes away from many things their power of giving pleasure or pain. Thus a new dress . . . and the palate" (No. 78). "Natural historians assert, that whatever is formed for long duration arrives slowly to its maturity. Thus timber . . . and animals" (No. 169). Even without a "thus," the logical structure of such paragraphs is often perfectly clear:

> The first motives of human actions are those appetites which providence has given to man, in common with the rest of the inhabitants of the earth. Immediately after our birth, thirst and hunger incline us to the breast. . . .
>
> . . . . .
>
> It is necessary to the success of flattery, that it be accommodated

to particular circumstances or characters, and enter the heart on that side where the passions stand ready to receive it. A lady . . . a merchant . . . the author . . .

. . . . .

As any action or posture long continued will distort and disfigure the limbs; so the mind likewise is crippled and contracted by perpetual application to the same set of ideas. It is easy to guess the trade of an artizan by his knees, his fingers, or his shoulders; and there are few among men of the more liberal professions, whose minds do not carry the brand of their calling. . . .

. . . . .

There are many vexatious accidents and uneasy situations which raise little compassion for the sufferer, and which no man but those whom they immediately distress, can regard with seriousness. Petty mischiefs . . . a mistake or embarrassment. . . . (Nos. 49, 106, 173, 176)

Among many other signs of Johnson's essentially Baconian outlook are the fairly frequent, always pejorative, references to "speculatists," men "not versed in the living world, but accustomed to judge only by speculative reason" (No. 70). Their "refined speculations" are sometimes specious and pleasing, but too often they fall "under the weight of contrary experience" (Nos. 13 and 14); "every hour will give proofs" that their a priori reasonings are invalid (No. 54). A sensible man must "think for himself," concluding from "his own observations" or from historical evidence, the lessons that "the general story of mankind will evince" (Nos. 45 and 50). In short, if our purpose is to know the living world, "let us look round and see" (No. 58). In these very simple, completely nontechnical words Johnson distills the essence of empiricism, as understood in the seventeenth and eighteenth centuries.

As I have tried to show in some detail elsewhere,[13] Johnson's reasoning as a textual scholar, cultural historian, and literary critic is self-consciously probabilistic, in the manner described by Locke in the fourth book of the *Essay concerning Human Understanding*. His reasoning on ethical questions is of the same kind. The "vicissitudes of life" are perpetual (No. 52), and human affairs are far too mutable

[13]Hoyt Trowbridge, "Scattered Atoms of Probability," *Eighteenth-Century Studies*, 5 (1971), 1–38; also in idem, *From Dryden to Jane Austen* (Albuquerque, 1977), ch. 12.

to admit complete and unquestionable proofs concerning them; among mortals, virtue itself is always uncertain and variable (No. 70). In a pure science, like mathematics, we deal only with ideas, but in moral discussions we are "constrained to submit to the imperfection of matter and the influence of accidents" (No. 14). God has given us reason because He expects us to use it for guidance in the ethical decisions of our lives, but it is as imperfect and fallible as everything else in our mortal nature. As Locke says, the "twilight" of probability, which is all we have both in the natural sciences and in the conduct of life, seems suitable to "that state of mediocrity and probationership he has been pleased to place us in here."[14]

The vocabulary I particularly want to discuss here is not what Wimsatt calls "philosophic words," terms derived from the sciences; rather, it is the language of logic, domesticated for common use. Many of its terms are historically neutral; that is, they would be used in any reasoned discourse in English at any period. From a reader's point of view they are the signs, from a writer's the tools, of systematic argument, whether inductive or deductive, demonstrative or probable. Sometimes a series of such terms, used in a single sentence or paragraph, will sketch out the skeletal structure of an argument: *presume . . . conclude, postulates . . . evidence . . . solution,* or a *position* and its *consequences* (Nos. 4, 154, and 155). Other terms usually occur singly: *premise, axiom, maxim, hypothesis, definition, fallacy, sophism, conjecture, proof, opinion, follow, infer, deduce, confute, support.* Perhaps even more important than these nouns and verbs are the connectives that knit an argument together by designating logical relations among propositions, some stating evidences or proofs, others the conclusions to be drawn from them: *therefore, since, for.* I have not tried to count frequencies for these connectives in all 208 issues of *The Rambler*, but in the first 52, one-fourth of the whole, I find some 56 occurrences of *therefore*, 28 of *since*, and 39 of *for*. *As* and *because* also occur in their logical senses, but less often. *Thus,* already mentioned above, is of course another such connective.

Inductive proofs in *The Rambler*, as in most rhetoric, are by example. The instances may be either individuals, like Catiline, Melancthon, and De Wit (No. 60), or classes of men, such as the warrior,

[14]Locke, *Essay*, IV.xiv. 1–2.

the trader, the lover (No. 53), of activities, such as juvenile pleasures and nobler employments (No. 39), or of motives, as in interest, reputation, or duty (No. 13). They may also be fictional, like Gelidus, Suspirius, or Frolick (Nos. 24, 59, and 61) or the many imaginary female instances, Miss Maypole (No. 55), Melissa (No. 75), Eriphile (No. 112). These too operate as proofs, because readers recognize the likeness of the fictional examples to people and behavior with which they are familiar from their own experience.

A feature of Johnson's style that has been noted and discussed by many readers and critics is the use of terms in pairs, triplets, quadruplets, even quintuplets. These are most often treated as contributing to the rhythms or to the grammatical parallelism of his prose, but I think they can be explained in a more fundamental way as reflecting Johnson's empirical and probabilistic way of reasoning. When he cites the philosopher, the wit, and the beauty to illustrate the dangers following from lack of self-knowledge (No. 24), or the scholar, the merchant, and the priest to show that obscure and undramatic lives may be more appropriate and useful subjects for biography than those distinguished by "striking and wonderful vicissitudes" (No. 60), he does not claim to offer an exhaustive classification of all relevant human types, but he does choose examples sufficiently diverse to imply that if other instances were demanded, they could be given and would support the same conclusion. Johnson reasons in this way, outside *The Rambler*, in the arguments by elimination that provide the simple but powerful structures of *Rasselas* and *The Vanity of Human Wishes*. Bate remarks in discussing the latter that "the structure is open-ended, and the examples could theoretically be continued indefinitely."[15] That is literally true, but I think Bate misses the probative force derived from the range and variety of Johnson's seven examples. If the desires for wealth, power, military glory, learning, beauty, length of life, and even virtue are vain and illusory, surely other conceivable desires must be so too, leaving religious hope as the only solid human wish. Although the examples do not provide a complete induction, they might be described as quasi-exhaustive, a highly probable, though not, of course, a demonstrative, proof.

[15]Bate, *Samuel Johnson*, p. 280.

Many series in *The Rambler* function in a similar way: poverty, sickness, and captivity are not the only human miseries, but they may stand for all the others; if places of urban activity include others than the court, the city, the park, and the exchange, what is true of them is very likely true of the rest; and when Suspirius the screech owl attacks the quiet of a young officer, a genius in the church, a lawyer, and a physician, we easily believe that he could find means of discouraging those pursuing other vocations (Nos. 67, 61, and 59). In all these cases, it would be a mistake both logically and rhetorically to add further examples, for no such list could ever include all conceivable instances, and those cited already constitute as strong a proof as probable reasoning will admit.

Other sets of terms are brought into *The Rambler* by other kinds of argument characteristic of eighteenth-century probable reasoning. In his interesting comparison of fictional with historical narrative in Fielding, Hume, and Gibbon, Leo Braudy coins the useful term *epistemological doublets*. These are pairs of terms, found everywhere in Gibbon's *Decline and Fall*, which designate alternative possible causes of some event, policy, or belief without choosing between them; the pairs are "epistemological" in the sense that they reflect a theory of knowledge in which historical events are not certainly knowable, though effects are more clearly determinable than causes.[16] Braudy's point could be put more technically and precisely by saying that in probable reasoning we must often resort to hypotheses to explain the causes of observed or recorded effects, and that two or several alternative possibilities are sometimes equally plausible.[17]

Johnson's reasoning on ethical questions rests on similar assumptions about the limits of human understanding. In the same essay in which he speaks of "the imperfection of matter and the influence of accidents," he says that it is usually unwise to inquire too closely into the actual behavior of writers whose brilliant moral discourses we admire, because we will often "observe those who seem best able to point the way, loitering below, as either afraid of the labour,

---

[16]Leo Braudy, *Narrative Form in History and Fiction* (Princeton, 1970), pp. 246 ff.
[17]On the frequent necessity, in the human sciences, of conjecturing causes from effects, see *Rambler* No. 13 and cf. Locke, *Essay*, IV.xii and xvi.

or doubtful of the reward" (No. 14). Johnson offers us two possible motives for the conduct of these speculatists; either would explain the discrepancy between their theory and their practice. Later in the same essay he suggests by a more elaborate *either* . . . *or* two reasons why men of letters, though differing in temper, are often socially inept. After years of private study, offering little opportunity for softening or polishing the manners, a writer whose works have been admired may be taken up in society: "When he enters life, if his temper be soft and timorous, he is diffident and bashful, from the knowledge of his defects; or if he was born with spirit and resolution, he is ferocious and arrogant from the consciousness of his merit: he is either dissipated by the awe of company, and unable to recollect his reading, and arrange his arguments; or he is hot, and dogmatical, quick in opposition, and tenacious in defense, disabled by his own violence, and confuted by his haste to triumph" (No. 14). Here we have two contrasted temperaments, operating from contrary motives and behaving in opposite ways. Yet both are successful writers, who deserve esteem for their intellectual achievements but who lose it in society for the same reason, a lack of social experience to teach them the "minuter acts" by which they might have pleased. The alternatives, which again are only quasi-exhaustive, are equally likely, and both confirm the explanation that Johnson advances.

The hypothetical character of this kind of argument is perhaps even clearer in the equally frequent occurrences of terms, phrases, or clauses connected by *whether* . . . *or*. A typical instance is the opening paragraph of *Rambler* No. 20: "Among the numerous stratagems, by which pride endeavours to recommend folly to regard, there is scarcely one that meets with less success than affectation, or a perpetual disguise of the real character, by fictitious appearances; whether it be, that every man hates falsehood, from the natural congruity of truth to his faculties of reason, or that every man is jealous of the honour of his understanding, and thinks his discernment consequentially called in question, whenever any thing is exhibited under a borrowed form." A reader who wants to think well of mankind might prefer to accept the first hypothesis, while one with a more cynical view of human nature might think the second more convincing. In either case, he is likely to accept the conclusion that "this aversion from all kinds of disguise, whatever be its cause, is universally diffused, and incessantly in action." The *Rambler*s are full of such *whether . . . or, either . . . or,* and *neither . . . nor* constructions.

As a final illustration of the influence of Johnson's epistemology on the logic, and hence on the language of *The Rambler,* we may consider a few of the many passages in which he argues from analogy, a procedure as common in probable reasoning as the use of hypotheses.[18] In this kind of argument, an inference is drawn from a simpler, clearer, or better known thing to prove a point about some partially parallel thing that is more obscure and uncertain. If the feature that makes the things parallel is true of both, then another but related feature, validly predicable of the analogue, should also be predicable of the subject. If the common feature is clear and will hold water, the inference is valid even if the resemblance at first seems to be remote and surprising.

At times Johnson will use an analogy without any verbal sign of the logical relation between the propositions. Arguing in No. 25 that vices which exceed the mean are sometimes less culpable than those which fall below it, because "it is more easy to take away superfluities than to supply defects," he clinches the proof with two parallels in animals and plants: "We are certain that the horse may be taught to keep pace with his fellows, whose fault is that he leaves them behind. We know that a few strokes of the axe will lop a cedar; but what arts of cultivation can elevate a shrub?" The common feature is that the speed of horses and the heights of plants admit of excess of defect, as human conduct also does. If it is true in the first two cases that excess is more easily brought by training or cultivation to the desired state, then by analogy it should be true that in moral qualities too much is more easily corrected by admonition or self-discipline than too little.

Occasionally, Johnson will mark the movement of thought from the analogue to the true subject by a phrase or word such as "in like manner" (No. 5) or "likewise" (No. 144). In the first case the transition is from protective coloration in animals to human mental adaptation to changing situations and scenes; in the second he

---

[18]Cf. Locke, *Essay,* IV.xvi.

moves, with comic effect, from the achieved classification of insects, "that torment us with their drones and stings," to a possible division of the persecutors of merit, the Roarers, Whisperers, and Moderators. Elsewhere he can "vary the beaten track of transition" (No. 143) by using a full sentence, as in "The same method may be sometimes pursued in," to mark the turn from certain "natural enquiries" of Bacon to the "moral endeavours" of men struggling toward virtue (No. 14). Similarly, he uses "The same observation may be transferred to" in moving from the claim of Lucretius that only a small part of the earth is suitable for human habitation to the minute fraction of a life that can be spent wholly at our own choice (No. 108). In still another instance the transitional sentence "This remark has sometimes been extended to others" is the pivot of the parallel between the constitution of the human body and man's intellectual faculties. In this case, as we may gather from his dissociation of himself from those who make the extension, the analogy is rejected; he does not deny the proposition about the analogue but does refute its applicability to the subject (No. 43).

Most often, however, Johnson indicates the structure of his arguments from analogy by choosing the clear and familiar *as . . . so* construction. One of the simplest cases is in the opening sentence of No. 184: "As every scheme of life, so every form of writing has its advantages and inconveniencies, though not mingled in the same proportions." This sounds as though schemes of life were the analogue and forms of writing the real subject, but it turns out that his discussion in the first few paragraphs of the problems of writing periodical essays merely lays a groundwork for his much fuller treatment of the difficulties of moral choice. The inference is usually in the opposite direction, the analogue being stated before the subject: "As a glass which magnifies objects by the approach of one end to the eye, lessens them by the application of the other, so vices are extenuated by the inversion of that fallacy, by which virtues are augmented" (No. 28). Here, as often, he reasons from a well-known scientific fact or theory to a less familiar ethical truth—from an optical illusion to a self-commending fallacy of the mind.

Examples of the *as . . . so* construction could be multiplied almost indefinitely, but it would be wiser to be content, as Johnson is, with a quasi-exhaustive induction. We may take as a final instance of the language through which Johnson signals an argument from analogy the last two paragraphs of No. 43, "The inconveniences of precipitation and confidence." In both, the analogue is drawn from the philosophy of Descartes, but in one he treats the doctrine seriously, seeming to grant it at least a measure of truth, while in the other the allusion is ironic. In the penultimate paragraph the transitional phrase is "In like manner": "The student who would build his knowledge on solid foundations, and proceed by just degrees to the pinnacles of truth, is directed by the great philosopher of France to begin by doubting of his own existence. In like manner, whoever would complete any arduous and intricate enterprise, should, as soon as his imagination can cool after the first blaze of hope, place before his own eyes every possible embarrassment that may retard or defeat him."

In the final paragraph he uses *as . . . so*: "As Des Cartes has kindly shown how a man may prove to himself his own existence, if once he can be prevailed upon to question it, so the ardent and adventurous will not be long without finding some plausible extenuation of the greatest difficulties." It is true that human enterprise is more likely to succeed if we are realistically aware of its risks, but since no sensible man doubts his own existence, it seems obvious to Johnsonian common sense that Descartes' proof of it is gratuitous, as much a folly in its own way as the hubristic self-deceptions of precipitate and overconfident men.

The essay ends on a characteristically Johnsonian note, with a logical conclusion that resolves all the issues raised. Because of the uncertainty of all human affairs, opposite extremes are always dangerous: "Security and despair are equal follies, and as it is presumption and arrogance to anticipate triumphs, it is weakness and cowardice to prognosticate miscarriages. The numbers that have been stopped in their career of happiness are sufficient to show the uncertainty of human foresight; but there are not wanting contrary instances of such success obtained against all appearances, as may warrant the boldest flights of genius, if they are supported by unshaken perseverance." Johnson is always trying to bolster our moral resolve, and he never leaves us without hope.

As Johnson makes clear in his allegory of criticism, there is a false as well as a true rhetoric. The fine robes of rhetoric are often

[215]

"sold to falsehood," concealing shallow thought and sophistical reasoning, spreading false colors to cover secret inequalities between the words and the sentiments or between the ideas and the original objects (No. 3). Johnson's is a true rhetoric because all its elements are in harmony. The words and thoughts arise naturally from the intellectual and moral character of the implied speaker, and have added force because of it; the emotions he feels and evokes are those felt by all wise and good men; the language he chooses is proportioned to the real moral worth or worthlessness of the persons and actions he condemns or commends; and his arguments, though no more than probable, are as valid and strong as the conditions of our existence and the imperfections of human understanding will allow. It is by such a rhetoric that Johnson gives ardor to virtue and confidence to truth in his majestic moral discourses.

The Reception of
Rasselas, 1759–1800

GWIN J. KOLB

URING THE TWO CENTURIES SINCE ITS FIRST APPEARANCE, Samuel Johnson's moral tale *Rasselas* has been steadily—probably uninterruptedly—in print in Great Britain, often published in the United States, and translated more frequently into foreign languages than any other of Johnson's works.[1] It has elicited a host of responses, both admiring and censorious, by individual readers, whose identities range from Edmund Burke to the current generation of college students. Over the years it has become a very nearly infallible touchstone of its creator's art and thought. At the present time, having far surpassed the common "test of literary merit,"[2] it seems likely to maintain indefinitely its firm position among the superior achievements in English letters.

Yet a detailed account of the book's critical and publishing fortunes remains unwritten. Some of the pertinent information for such a survey has long been available, and more has been collected by recent investigators primarily concerned with other pursuits. But no one has brought together the results of previous researches, added the requisite facts from hitherto unexplored areas, and produced a complete treatment of the subject. As indicated by its title, the present essay attempts to realize only a very limited part of this ambitious undertaking. It concentrates on not quite the first half century of *Rasselas*'s existence and seeks to disclose the main aspects of the tale's reception during that period. The relevant materials

[1]See James L. Clifford, *Dictionary Johnson: Samuel Johnson's Middle Years* (New York, 1979), p. 213.

[2]"[Shakespeare] has long outlived his century, the term commonly fixed as the test of literary merit" (*Preface to Shakespeare*, in *Johnson on Shakespeare*, Vol. VII of The Yale Edition of the Works of Samuel Johnson, ed. Arthur Sherbo [New Haven, 1969], p. 61).

have been distributed under five headings: (1) formal reviews, (2) partial reprintings in periodicals, (3) editions, including translations, (4) miscellaneous remarks and references, (5) a continuation. After the presentation of the disparate groups of evidence, selected generalizations will be ventured about the youthful life of Johnson's "little book."

1

Rasselas was published—without its author's name—probably on 20 April 1759.[3] By the following January it had been reviewed in at least fourteen different serials. The notices, invariably accompanied by longer extracts from the tale, fall into two groups: six sets of original comments and eight reproductions of observations appearing elsewhere, specifically seven from the *Gentleman's Magazine*, the eighth from the *Monthly Review*.[4] The second group, mentioned again later, is cited here only as a quantitative indicator of the attention accorded the work—attention which, with respect to "the miscellanies," exceeded that given "any previous work of prose fiction, French or English, for at least twenty years" and which makes *Rasselas* "a pivotal novel in the history of magazine fiction."[5] Of the first group, one brief member—in Benjamin Martin's *Miscellaneous Correspondence*—confines its presumably positive reaction to a single not very revealing sentence: "Amidst the Variety of

[3]See Donald D. Eddy, "The Publication Date of the First Edition of *Rasselas*," *Notes & Queries*, January 1962, pp. 21–22.

[4]The seven serials which reprinted the evaluation in the *Gentleman's Magazine* are: *Scots Magazine, Edinburgh Magazine, Lloyd's Evening Post, London Chronicle* (3–5 May 1759, p. 423), *Owen's Weekly Chronicle, Caledonian Mercury* (Edinburgh), and *Universal Magazine of Knowledge and Pleasure* (24 [May 1759], 238). The *Grand Magazine* reprinted part of the assessment in the *Monthly Review*. For more details about all of these reprintings except those in the *London Chronicle* and the *Universal Magazine*, see Helen Louise McGuffie, *Samuel Johnson in the British Press, 1749–1784: A Chronological Checklist* (New York, 1976), pp. 20–21. Pertinent information about various reprintings also appears in Robert D. Mayo, *The English Novel in the Magazines, 1740–1815* (Evanston, Ill., 1962), pp. 240–41, 446, 523–24, 619–20.

[5]Mayo, pp. 408–9. Mayo also notes (pp. 619–20) that "a disguised redaction of . . . *Rasselas*" was published in the "*Weekly Amusement*, II (February 2–March 16, 1765)." And he has kindly informed me that other extracts were printed, still later, in the *Gentleman and Lady's Weekly Magazine* (Edinburgh), 3 (4 February 1744), 41–42; and the *Bristol and Bath Magazine*, 1 (1782), 243–47.

Sentiments exhibited in these Volumes," says the writer, "we shall give our Readers a Specimen of the Language and Genius of the Author, from Vol. 2d, Chap. 29. the Debate on Marriage continued" (3 [1759], 115). The five other reviews plainly state both their authors' opinions of *Rasselas* and, in varying detail, the reasons for their estimates. Three are mostly laudatory; one expresses a mixture of praise and censure; and one, the longest by far, is largely negative. The purpose, matter and plan, style, and author of the tale comprise the chief referents of the reviewers.

The highly favorable notices appear in the *Gentleman's Magazine*, the *London Magazine*, and the *Annual Register*. When assessing the opinions expressed in these three periodicals, we should remember that at least two of them—the first and third—were surely disposed to esteem Johnson's compositions. The writer of the *Gentleman's* estimate was probably Johnson's friend John Hawkesworth,[6] who makes his short remarks at the end of a summary (relying heavily on extracts) of the tale; assessing the work's contents, he notes the abundance of "the most elegant and striking pictures of life and nature, the most acute disquisitions, and the happiest illustrations of the most important truths" (29 [1759], 186). Referring to Johnson himself and his characteristic mode of discourse as well as to the substance of *Rasselas*, the unidentified reviewer for the *London Magazine* informs his audience that "the excellent Author of the *Rambler*, has lately obliged the World with a moral Tale . . . which contain[s] the most important Truths and Instructions, told in an agreeable and enchanting Manner, and in his usual nervous and sententious Stile." "Our Readers," the reviewer adds, "will, no doubt, expect some Account of a Performance which is so much admired, and we shall endeavour to gratify their Expectations" (28 [1759], 258); five pages (258–62) of extracts (linked by an occasional summarizing statement) follow in the May issue, and another eight (324–31) are included in the June number.

The *Annual Register* critic, almost certainly Edmund Burke (who first met Johnson in 1758), prefaces and concludes his descriptive account—consisting mainly of quotations—with a total of three

---

[6]See Clifford, p. 213. Clifford also describes (pp. 213–16) the reviews in the *London Magazine, Annual Register, Critical Review,* and *Monthly Review.*

paragraphs devoted to the intention, narrative, style, and author of *Rasselas*.[7] "In this novel," he asserts, "the moral is the principal object, and the story is a mere vehicle to convey the instruction."

> Accordingly the tale is not near so full of incidents, not so diverting in itself, as the ingenious author, if he had not had higher views, might easily have made it; neither is the distinction of characters sufficiently attended to: but with these defects, perhaps no book ever inculcated a purer and sounder morality; no book ever made a more just estimate of human life, its pursuits, and its enjoyments. The descriptions are rich and luxuriant, and shew a poetic imagination not inferior to our best writers in verse. The style, which is peculiar, and characteristical of the author, is lively, correct, and harmonious. It has, however, in a few places, an air too exact and studied.

Later, ending his notice, Burke says, "There is no doubt that [the author] is the same who has before done so much for the improvement of our taste and our morals, and employed a great part of his life in an astonishing work [the *Dictionary*] for the fixing the language of this nation; whilst this nation, which admires his works, and profits by them, has done nothing for the author" (2 [1759], 477, 479).

Like his fellows in the *London Magazine* and the *Annual Register*, the writer for the *Critical Review*, whose identity remains unknown, makes clear his awareness of Johnson's connection with *Rasselas:* "This little tale," we are told, is "in every respect worthy of the learned and sensible author of the *Rambler*." To "philosophers," the critic declares, the work, which "couche[s] in the method of dialogue the most important truths and profound speculations," may be recommended "as a beautiful epitome of practical Ethics, filled with the most judicious observations upon life" and "the nicest distinctions upon conduct." However, "readers of novels" are likely to find the tale "unintelligible," for, exalting "reflections" and "dissertations" at the expense of "narrative" (which "might have been comprised in ten lines"), it contains "no plot, incident, character, or contrivance . . . to beguile the imagination." After quoting a chapter to illustrate Johnson's "manner," the reviewer again expresses reservations: "Upon the whole, we imagine the talents of

[7]See ibid., p. 216.

the author would appear to more advantage, had he treated his different subjects in the method of essays, or form of dialogue. At present, the title page will, by many readers, be looked upon as a decoy, to deceive them into a kind of knowledge they had no inclination to be acquainted with" (7 [1759], 372–73, 375).

These relatively mild strictures are far exceeded by those of the *Monthly Review* critic, Owen Ruffhead, who, although ostensibly ignorant of the fact, doubtless knew that Johnson had written *Rasselas* and whose negative evaluation probably reflects this knowledge.[8] Ruffhead begins his extended notice (containing numerous extracts) with a tribute to "fiction or romance . . . as the most effectual way of rendering the grave dictates of morality agreeable to mankind in general." "But," he hastily points out,

> to succeed in the romantic way of writing, requires a sprightliness of imagination, with a natural ease and variety of expression, which, perhaps, oftener falls to the lot of middling writers, than to those of more exalted genius: and therefore, we observe, with less regret, of the learned writer of these volumes, that *tale-telling* evidently is not his talent. He wants that graceful ease, which is the ornament of romance; and he stalk[s] in the solemn buskin, when he ought to tread in the light sock. His stile is so tumid and pompous, that he sometimes deals in *sesquipedalia*, such as *excogitation*, *exaggeratory*, &c. with other hard compounds, which it is difficult to pronounce with composed features—as *multifarious, transcendental, indiscerpible, &c.*

Had the writer, Ruffhead continues, "put" "this swelling language" "into the mouth of a pedant only, nothing could be more apt: but unhappily he has so little conception of the propriety of character, that he makes the princess speak in the same lofty strain with the philosopher; and the waiting woman harangue with as much sublimity as her royal mistress."

Turning to the "matter of these little volumes," Ruffhead "cannot discover much intervention in the plan, or utility in the design. The topics . . . are grown threadbare: . . . [the] sentiments are most of them to be found in the Persian and Turkish tales, and other books of the like sort; wherein they are delivered to better purpose, and cloathed in a more agreeable garb. Neither has the end of this work

[8]See ibid., p. 215.

any great tendency to the good of society": we may learn "that discontent prevails among men of all ranks and conditions," Ruffhead asserts, without making a trip "to Ethiopia." Moreover, he maintains for the length of three paragraphs, "the inferences" drawn by Johnson "from this general discontent, are by no means just." Human happiness is more frequent than the theme of *Rasselas* indicates. Then, through a combination of summaries, quotations, and short critical remarks (mostly negative), he outlines the sequence of events in the tale, pausing occasionally to make clear the intellectual context of specific passages. At the end, commenting on the last chapter, he says that, "as nothing is concluded, it would have been prudent in the author to have said nothing. Whoever he is, he is a man of genius and great abilities; but he has evidently misapplied his talents." Ruffhead adds that the "title-page" of the work "will impose upon many" readers, "who, while they expect to frolic along the flowery paths of romance, will find themselves hoisted on metaphysical stilts, and born aloft into the regions of syllogistical subtlety, and philosophical refinement" (20 [1759], 428–29, 437).

2

As has been noted already, all of the reviews discussed above contain numerous passages from *Rasselas*. Ten complete chapters and portions of twenty-three others are reprinted, excluding the extracts that make up parts of the eight notices borrowed from other periodicals.

Additional extracts in the *Grand Magazine of Magazines* produced significant results that should be briefly described. Responding to the action of the *Grand Magazine*, Robert Dodsley, one of the three proprietors of *Rasselas* and representing the other two (William Johnston and William Strahan), brought a suit for infringement of copyright against the *Magazine's* (presumed) owner, Thomas Kinnersley, who, it was asserted, "printed part of the the [tale's] narrative . . . but left out all the reflections."[9] The case was argued in

[9] For evidence of the proprietorships, see Gwin J. Kolb, "*Rasselas:* Purchase Price, Proprietors, and Printings," *Studies in Bibliography*, 15 (1962), 257.

the High Court of Chancery before Sir Thomas Clarke, Master of
the Rolls, on 15 June 1761. During the proceedings

> Mr. [Jacob] *Tonson* [III] and two other booksellers were examined
> for the plaintiffs, who spoke in general, that the sale of the book was
> prejudiced by its being printed in the Magazine; and Mr. *Tonson*
> conjectured, that about two-thirds of the book was printed in the
> Magazine; but it appeared clearly, that he deposed relating to the
> whole work, the second as well as the first volume; whereas only
> part of the first volume was printed in the Magazine when the bill
> was filed (though great part of the second volume was printed after-
> wards); and according to the passages marked, not above one-tenth
> part of it was printed.

For the defendant,

> evidence was read, that it is usual to print extracts of new books in
> Magazines, &c. without asking leave of the authors. That it is often
> done at the request of the author, as being a means to help the sale
> of the book. That the plaintiffs published a larger extract of this very
> book in the *Annual Register*. Also, that the plaintiffs published an
> extract of it in the newspaper called the *Chronicle*, in April, 1759,
> *before the extract was published by the defendant in the Magazine*, of which
> paper the plaintiffs with others are proprietors.

After the presentation of the arguments, Sir Thomas Clarke,
besides making other remarks, called *Rasselas* "a very good, elegant,
and useful book," whose "title may draw in persons to look into it,
which perhaps they would not do if it had a graver title"; observed
that "it does not appear that one-tenth part of the first volume has
been abstracted"; agreed that "a fair abridgment" is "not a piracy";
admitted that "what I materially rely upon is, that [the abstract
in the *Grand Magazine*]," which "may serve the end of an advertisement," "could not tend to prejudice the plaintiffs, when they
had before published an abstract of the work in the *London Chronicle*";
and "dismiss[ed] plaintiffs' bill without costs."[10]

Most (not all) of the factual allegations made for the defendant
in the report on the case of *Dodsley* v. *Kinnersley* can be readily

[10]Charles Ambler, *Reports of Cases Argued and Determined in the High Court of
Chancery*, 2d ed. (London, 1828), pp. 402–5.

verified, and the remainder are almost certainly true too. Specifically, although the portions of *Rasselas* initially reproduced by the *Grand Magazine of Magazines* may come to about 12 rather than 10 percent of the whole text,[11] in 1759 it *was* "usual to print extracts of new books in Magazines, &c. without asking leave of the authors," who very likely "often" encouraged the practice as "a means to help the sale" of their works. Moreover, to say that "the plaintiffs published" an "extract" from *Rasselas* in the *Annual Register* is probably an accurate statement, for Robert Dodsley owned the *Register*, which printed a number of passages (but fewer than the number appearing initially in the *Grand Magazine*) as a part of Burke's review of the tale.[12] Further, the *London Chronicle did* print an extensive extract from *Rasselas* in its issue of 19–21 April (and again in its issues of 28 April–1 May, 3–5 May, and 10–12 May 1759) at the same time the book itself was published and well ahead of the appearance of the *Grand Magazine*'s April number.[13] Last, although by 1759 Dodsley had relinquished his partnership in the *Chronicle*, another of the three proprietors of *Rasselas*, William Strahan, owned a share of the paper (which he also printed);[14] so Kinnersley's representative was correct in asserting that "the plaintiffs published an extract" of the work in the *Chronicle*.

From the disclosure of the opposing parties before Sir Thomas Clarke in 1761, an unsurprising but sometimes forgotten conclusion

[11] I estimate the length of *Rasselas* to be about 38,500 words, that of the first *Grand Magazine* installment (2 [April 1758]: 217–22) to be about 4,700 words, and that of the second installment (2 [May 1759]: 301–4) to be about 3,500 words. At the end of the second installment, we are told (p. 304) that "this well-imagined Tale" will appeal to a wide range of readers. I am indebted to the American Antiquarian Society for photographic reproductions of both installments.

[12] Dodsley's ownership of the *Annual Register* is well known; see, for example, his entry in the *DNB*.

[13] The *London Chronicle* for 28 April–1 May 1759 contains an advertisement announcing the publication of the April number of the *Grand Magazine of Magazines*, which includes, among other pieces, "the story of Rasselas, Prince of Abyssinia."

[14] Patricia Hernlund, who has examined relevant entries in Strahan's ledgers, has kindly informed me that Strahan owned a one-ninth share of the *Chronicle* as early as 12 November 1757. See also J. A. Cochrane, *Dr. Johnson's Printer: The Life of William Strahan* (London, 1964), pp. 103–4.

can be drawn quite firmly: the immediate printed reaction to *Rasselas*, as to countless other books, good and bad, was tinctured by the profit motive, which should not be confused with the disinterested attention and admiration evinced by some excerpting.

3

The same economic element becomes much more prominent, of course, when we turn to editions and translations for evidence of the reception given *Rasselas* during the first forty years, roughly, of its life. Only a blockhead publishes a book for anything besides money, the proprietors of the tale might plausibly declare. But the goal of the literary historian in collecting such information is reader response, however grossly determined, rather than the material gains of the intermediaries between author and audience.

By June 1759—two months after the appearance of *Rasselas*—the 1,500 copies of the first edition had been disposed of, and a second edition (of 1,000 copies) had been issued. The following April saw the publication of the third edition, consisting of another 1,000 copies. Thus, in its initial year of life, the tale reached, from the proprietors' editions alone, the substantial figure of 3,500. During the remainder of the century that number grew steadily with the appearance of the fourth edition (1,000 copies) in 1766, the fifth (1,000) in 1775, the sixth (1,000) in 1783, the seventh (1,000) in 1786, the eighth (1,500) in 1790, the ninth (number apparently unknown but possibly 1,500) in 1793, and the tenth (number apparently unknown) in 1798.[15]

Besides the proprietors' editions, approximately forty other editions (excluding those in the collections of Johnson's works) and translations strongly attest to the increasing scope of *Rasselas*'s popularity, which helped to cause its designation as a "classic tale" early in the nineteenth century. Following the common Irish practice of reproducing English books shortly after their first publication (usually in London), the Dublin booksellers G. and A. Ewing and

[15]For more information about the first ten editions, see Kolb, pp. 257–59; William P. Courtney and David Nichol Smith, *A Bibliography of Samuel Johnson* (Oxford, 1925), pp. 87–88. Patricia Hernlund reports that Strahan's ledgers appear to yield no specific facts concerning the size of the ninth and tenth editions.

H. Bradley brought out in 1759 what may be dubbed the earliest unauthorized edition of the novel. At least four more Dublin editions were published before 1800—in 1777, 1783, 1787, and 1795. Barely honoring the protective period of twenty-eight years afforded the author by the Copyright Act of 1709, alert London booksellers began issuing editions (two) in 1787. Before the end of the century, their total ventures came to at least twelve editions (including the *Novelist's Magazine* version), a number which, when added to the ten authorized, or proprietors', editions, the five Dublin editions, and a single Edinburgh edition (1789), produces a sum of twenty-eight editions printed in the United Kingdom and Ireland between 1759 and 1800.[16]

The extensive diffusion, as Boswell termed it, of *Rasselas* "over Europe" commenced with French and Dutch translations in 1760.[17] Apparently the first edition of the tale to name the author on the title page ("Par M. Jhonnson [*sic*]," we are told, "Auteur du Rambler"), the French translation, published "A Amsterdam, Et se trouve à Paris, chez Prault Fils," was made by Mme Octavie Belot, who included in her preface probably the earliest printed comparison of *Rasselas* and *Candide*. Part of her comment reads:

> Le succès de Candide semble présager celui de son contemporain Rasselas, Prince d'Abissinie. Ces deux ouvrages renferment trop sensiblement les mêmes vues, pour n'avoir pas droit au même accueil. Cependant comme nous préférons quelquefois le coloris au dessein, je sens quel est l'avantage des choses finement dites sur celles qui ne sont que judicieusement pensées,& je m'en allarme [*sic*] pour mon Prince moraliste & voyageur.
>
> L'analogie du fond des idées de Candide & de Rasselas; certains rapports entre Imlac & Martin; entre l'isle d'Aldorado & l'heureuse Vallée, m'avoient fait présumer d'abord que l'Auteur Anglois pouvoit bien n'être qu'un pyrate littéraire. Mais j'ai réfléchi qu'il ne

[16]The information in this paragraph about the nonproprietary editions is drawn from an unpublished checklist of editions of *Rasselas* made available to me by the generosity of David Fleeman (cited hereafter as Fleeman); a part of the Samuel Johnson entry in the *NCBEL* (II, col. 1130); Courtney and Smith, pp. 87–88; and my personal collection of editions of *Rasselas*.

[17]"None of his writings has been so extensively diffused over Europe; for it has been translated into most, if not all, of the modern languages," *Boswell's Life of Johnson*, ed. G. B. Hill and L. F. Powell (Oxford, 1934–64), I, 341.

falloit soupçonner légèrement personne d'un larcin, & que la seule force de la vérité faisoit sans doute penser en Angleterre, comme en France, que le bonheur est une chimère.

Mme Belot then presents her own notions regarding human happiness, paying a lavish tribute to Montesquieu and Voltaire in the course of her discussion.[18] As might possibly have been expected, she also later sent a copy of her work to Voltaire, who thanked her for a book "qui m'a paru d'une philosophie aimable, et très bien écrit."[19]

At about the same time (May 1760), Elie Fréron's *L'Année littéraire* carried an extended review of the translation. The reviewer quotes the opening lines of the tale, states what he takes to be its central theme ("On veut prouver dans ce Roman philosophique & moral que le bonheur n'est attaché à aucun état, à aucun âge, à aucune condition, & qu'il faut perfectionner son esprit & son coeur si l'on veut trouver dans la vie quelques momens heureux"), summarizes the principal events of the story, and finally evaluates both the tale itself and the translation. Seemingly influenced by Mme Belot's preface, his critical remarks first consider the issue of temporal precedence between *Rasselas* and *Candide*. "Si l'auteur de Roman avait prévenue *Candide*," he states, "il auroit beaucoup plus de mérite; ce sont les mêmes vues; vous saisirez les rapports entre *Imlac* & *Martin*, entre l'isle *del Dorado* & l'*Heureuse Vallée*, &c. Si cependant *Candide* n'alloit être qu'une copie, l'Anglois, de son côté, gagneroit infiniment à la comparaison." Then, concentrating on Johnson's work, Fréron rates the first part of *Rasselas* "supérieure de beaucoup" to the second:

> dans cette dernière, l'action est noyée dans des raisonnemens d'une longueur insupportable. L'auteur n'a pas tiré parti de la favorite *Pekuah*; il falloit, pour suivre le fil de la nature, que la Princesse commença se consoler, que l'idée de *Pekuah* devînt moins forte, que le Prince rallentît ses soins pour ses recherches, & qu'après l'avoir

---

[18]*Histoire de Rasselas, Prince d'Abissinie*, pp. iii–iv, xiii. See also L. F. Powell's letter (entitled "*Rasselas*") in the *TLS* for 22 February 1923, p. 124, which describes, and quotes from, Mme Belot's preface; Hill-Powell, II, 500.

[19]*The Complete Works of Voltaire*, ed. Theodore Besterman (Banbury, England, 1968–80), CV, 309; Hill-Powell, II, 500.

retrouvée l'un & l'autre, le frère & la soeur se rendissent compte de leur sentimens, qu'ils s'avouassent tacitement qu'ils avoient manqué à l'amitié, & qu'en rougissant ils convinssent que l'humanité est une source d'imperfections. Cela eût formé alors une situation intéressante, au lieu que cette favorite n'excite aucun attendrissement, & qu'elle n'attache que foiblement. Au reste, il y a très peu d'imagination dans cet ouvrage; c'est un cadre usé; mais que de vérités, que de lumières sur le coeur humain!

These last notes of approval become still louder when Fréron reintroduces *Candide* in his discussion. *Rasselas*, he tells us, "est un miroir moins révoltant que *Candide*; nous nous y voyons cependant avec toutes nos foiblesses & tous nos malheurs. *Candide* fait d'abord rire l'esprit, & laisse ensuite le désespoir dans le coeur; *Rasselas* nous attendrit, nous fait gémir sur les misères de notre nature; *Candide*, en un mot, nous rend en horreur à nous-mêmes, & *Rasselas* nous fait les objets de notre propre compassion; il ne nous désespère pas; il nous invite seulement à nous corriger." Thus, he concludes, "ce livre, avec tous ses défauts, ne peut manquer de réussir, & d'être placé parmi ce petit nombre d'ouvrages dont le but est de nous rendre meilleurs." Fréron goes on to say that "on ne sçauroit trop donner d'éloges à Madame B***. Sa traduction est pure, élégante, quelquefois trop asservie au tour original."[20]

Fréron's laudatory opinion of Mme Belot's translation was evidently shared by a number of other persons, since later editions apparently appeared in 1768 and 1788. To this group of three can be added probably six more editions of French translations of *Rasselas* that were issued in various places (including London) before 1800. And the total of nine obviously excludes the version Joseph Baretti completed in 1764 (of which Johnson contributed the first sentence) that was not published until 1970.[21]

As indicated above, apart from French, Dutch was the earliest foreign language to welcome *Rasselas*. "Published at Amsterdam by Dirk onder de Linden in 1760 and ... entitled *De Historie van*

[20]*L'Année littéraire*, 7 (1760 [Geneva, 1966]), 223, 227–28.

[21]The information in this paragraph about the French translations is drawn from Fleeman; Courtney and Smith, p. 94; *NCBEL*, II, col. 1131; Hill-Powell, II, 208, 499–500; Raffaella Carbonara, ed., *Giuseppe Baretti e la sua traduzione del "Rasselas" di S. Johnson* (Torino, 1970).

Rasselas, Prins van Abissinien. Zynde een verbloemde Shildery van het Menschelyk leven. Door den Autheur van De Hollandsche Wysgeer," the translation, now very rare, "was issued in conjunction with a collective work entitled *De Hollandsche Wysgeer* [*The Dutch Philosopher*] by the same publisher, consisting chiefly of translations from English periodicals and other works; this work appeared in seven deelen, or parts, over the years 1759 to 1763." Unlike Mme Belot's French version, the Dutch translation failed to make clear its derivative character and, of course, to credit Johnson with the authorship of the original. This failure was soon criticized by a reviewer in *De Vaderlandsche Letteroefeningen* (1 [1761], 286), who observed: "This little book, although the title does not say so, is a translation. We make this statement because we trust that a Dutch philosopher does not wish to shine by another man's work, as if it were his own." Without identifying the author (if indeed he knew who it was), "the reviewer then proceeds to give an extensive *résumé* of the story covering ten closely printed pages (286–96)."[22] His summary—and the work he noticed—clearly satisfied Dutch tastes throughout the rest of the century, for the next Dutch translation did not appear until 1824.[23]

Two years (1762) after the publication of the initial French and Dutch versions, Elieser Gottlieb Küster's German translation of *Rasselas* was issued at Frankfurt am Main "bey George Conrad Gsellius." It was joined by three more German versions (1785, 1786, 1787) before 1800. An Italian translation (by Cosimo Mei), which Baretti labeled "a damned one," came out at Padua in 1764, and another at Florence in 1797. Finally, Russian versions appeared in 1764 and 1795, and a Spanish version in 1798.[24] Thus, at about the age of forty, *Rasselas* had been clothed in six foreign languages and at least nineteen editions, which must have numbered, by a conservative guess, several thousand copies.

[22]For information about the first Dutch translation and the review of it, I have relied on the following: L. F. Powell, "For Johnsonian Collectors," *TLS*, 20 September 1963, p. 712; A. J. Barnouw, " 'Rasselas' in Dutch," *TLS*, 11 April 1935, p. 244.

[23]Fleeman; Courtney and Smith, p. 97.

[24]The information about the German, Italian, Russian, and Spanish translations is drawn from *NCBEL*, II, col. 1131; Fleeman; Hill-Powell, II, 499–500.

Five (probably) American editions increased the circulation of the tale among residents of the colonies and fledgling republic. The earliest of these—*Rasselas*, it should be noted, was seemingly the first of Johnson's works to receive an American edition[25]—appeared at Philadelphia in 1768 and was published by Robert Bell. He gave the apologue the formal English title of *The History of Rasselas, Prince of Abissinia. An Asiatic Tale;*[26] omitted, like the publishers of all English editions issued in Johnson's life, the name of the tale's author from the title page (although he revealed it elsewhere); and, observing a practice followed by some of his fellows, patriotically announced on the title page that his version originated in "America" and was "printed for every purchaser." Bell also embellished his production with a frontispiece, a crude engraving labeled "A Perspective View of Grand Cairo,"[27] which started the slow movement, increasingly common in the nineteenth century, toward illustrated editions of the story. Thanks to the thoughtfulness of the young American William White, a copy of Bell's edition made its way to Johnson, who, on 4 March 1773, acknowledged it cordially. "The impression is not magnificent," he wrote, "but it flatters an authour, because the printer seems to have expected that it would be scattered among the people. The little book has been well received, and is translated into Italian, French, German, and Dutch. It has now one honour more by an American edition."[28]

That honor, however, was rather short-lived. For, despite its

[25]I draw this conclusion after an examination of Vols. II–IV (1730–1773) of Charles Evans's *American Bibliography* (rpt.; New York, 1941) and Roger P. Bristol's *Supplement to Charles Evans' "American Bibliography"* (Charlottesville, Va., 1970).

[26]The title pages of all previous English editions read *"The Prince of Abissinia: A Tale"*; however, the heading on the first page of the text is "The History of Rasselas, Prince of Abissinia."

[27]For information about Bell's edition, I am indebted to C. B. Tinker, *"Rasselas in the New World," Yale Review*, 14 (1924), 95–107, esp. pp. 99–101; and Robert F. Metzdorf, "The First American *Rasselas* and Its Imprint," *Papers of the Bibliographical Society of America*, 47 (1953), 374–76. Mary Hyde has also kindly sent me photographic reproductions of the title page of Bell's edition and of what purports to be an extract from "Dodsley's View of Literature" giving the "Character of the History of Rasselas" and, at the end, naming Johnson as the author of the work. In fact, virtually the entire extract is a passage of Burke's review of *Rasselas*, which appeared in the *Annual Register*.

[28]Hill-Powell, II, 207–8, 499.

innovations and democratic tone, Bell's work apparently did not pass beyond a solitary printing, and another American edition did not appear until 1791—again in Philadelphia. Four years later "the little book" and Ellis Cornelia Knight's *Dinarbas* were apparently issued together both in Greenfield, Mass., and New York. And the dawn of the new century saw the publication of what was called the "Second American Edition" at Bridgeport, Conn.[29]

Altogether, then—to summarize—between 1759 and 1800 *Rasselas* was available to readers in six foreign languages and some fifty editions, English and non-English.

4

After the cluster of public responses that greeted its initial publication, the next large body of critical comments on *Rasselas* appeared in the early biographical accounts of the author. The five longest accounts are Mrs. Piozzi's *Anecdotes of Samuel Johnson* (1786), Sir John Hawkins's *Life* (1787), Boswell's *Life* (1791), Arthur Murphy's *Essay on the Life and Genius of Samuel Johnson* (1792), and Robert Anderson's *Life* (1795). Of this group of works, Mrs. Piozzi's alone does not undertake a critique of "that surprising little volume," as she calls the tale. Two of her three brief allusions locate the origin of specific parts in Johnson's experiences and beliefs. "Many of the severe reflections on domestic life," she reports, "took their source from its author's keen recollections of the time passed in his early years"; and the "chapter upon [poetry] . . . is really written from the fulness of his heart" ("very fully was he persuaded of [poetry's] superiority over every other talent") "and quite in his best manner I think." The third mention likens Johnson's conversation to that of "the sage" in Chapter XVIII. Scattered references elsewhere reinforce one's impression that Mrs. Piozzi knew the story well and esteemed it highly.[30]

[29]The information about these editions is drawn from Fleeman; *NCBEL*, II, col. 1130; Evans, X (1795–96), 111; my personal copy of the "Second American Edition."

[30]The passages in Mrs. Piozzi's *Anecdotes* are drawn from G. B. Hill's *Johnsonian Miscellanies* (Oxford, 1897), I, 151, 284–85, 347. For additional references to the tale, see, for example, Mrs. Piozzi's *Letters to and from the Late Samuel Johnson, LL.D.* (London, 1788), II, 129–30, 266, 358, 360. In a note written on the last page of

Sir John Hawkins devotes over six pages of his *Life* to a discussion of *Rasselas*, "numbered," he states, "among the best of [Johnson's] writings." "As none of his compositions have been more applauded than this," Hawkins announces subsequently, "an examen of it . . . may not be improper." The ensuing treatment contains a mixture of praise, causal explanations, summary, quotation (of the passage on pilgrimages in Chapter XI), generic classification, and pointed reservations. "Considered as a specimen of our language," Hawkins begins, "[the tale] is scarcely to be paralleled: it is written in a style refined to a degree of immaculate purity, and displays the whole force of turgid eloquence." But though in form "a general satire, representing mankind as eagerly pursuing what experience should have taught them they can never obtain," and exposing "the weaknesses even of their laudable affections and propensities," the work conveys an excessively bleak appraisal of life, which derived both from the author's habitual pessimism and specifically from his sad condition at the time of creating *Rasselas*, "when the heavy hand of affliction almost bore him down, and the dread of future want haunted him." Hawkins also ascribes to Johnson's personal opinions and psyche several discrete sections of the tale, notably "many conversations on topics . . . known to have been subjects of his meditation," the "dissertation on poetry" (cf. Mrs. Piozzi's similar observation), the "chapter" on "insanity" and the imagination, and "superstitious ideas of the state of departed souls, and belief in supernatural agency." Summing up, the biographer declares "that this elegant work is rendered, by its most obvious moral, of little benefit to the reader." For, he explains, (1) "we would not . . . wish to see the rising generation so unprofitably employed as the prince of Abyssinia"; (2) "it is equally impolitic to repress all hope"; and (3) granted "there is no such thing as worldly felicity . . . it has never been proved, that, therefore we are miserable"; on the contrary, if human beings "bend their attention toward the attainment of" eternal happiness, "they will find no such vacuum as distressed Rasselas." In conclusion, Hawkins remarks that

a copy of *Rasselas* (Sharpe's ed. [1818]), Mrs. Piozzi called the book "unrivalled in Excellency of Intention, in Elegance of Diction: in minute knowledge of human Life—and sublime Expression of Oriental Imagery" (Hilaire Belloc, "Mrs. Piozzi's *Rasselas*," *Saturday Review of Literature*, 2 [15 August 1925], 38).

"Johnson had meditated a second part, in which he meant to marry his hero, and place him in a state of permanent felicity"; unfortunately, however, the continuation was not written because Johnson discovered that "all" earthly "enjoyments are fugacious, and permanent felicity unattainable."[31]

Except for a small qualification, Boswell's well-known assessment, unlike Hawkins's much cooler "examen," expresses uniformly fervent praise for diverse aspects of *Rasselas*, "which," he grandly avows, "though [Johnson] had written nothing else, would have rendered his name immortal in the world of literature." Possessing "all the charms of oriental imagery, and all the force and beauty of which the English language is capable," he elaborates, the book "leads us through the most important scenes of human life, and shews us that this stage of our being is full of 'vanity and vexation of spirit'. . . . they who think justly, and feel with strong sensibility, will listen with eagerness and admiration to its truth and wisdom." Boswell proceeds to compare the tale and *Candide*, concluding that, whereas Voltaire "meant only by wanton profaneness to obtain a sportive victory over religion . . . Johnson meant, by shewing the unsatisfactory nature of things temporal, to direct the hopes of man to things eternal." "The fund of thinking," he says a little later, "which this work contains is such, that almost every sentence . . . may furnish a subject of long meditation. . . . and at every perusal, my admiration of the mind which produced it is so highly raised, that I can scarcely believe that I had the honour of enjoying the intimacy of such a man." After transcribing a short passage (on "apparitions") from Chapter XXXI, he admits a possible connection—presented as a certainty by Hawkins—between Johnson's "melancholy" "constitution" and the dark view of life depicted in *Rasselas*, adding, however, that "there is too much of reality in the gloomy picture." Boswell makes other brief remarks on human life and happiness and then ends his criticism with six lines from John Courtenay's *Poetical Review of the Literary and Moral Character of the Late Samuel Johnson* (1786), which "beautifully illustrate" "the effect of Rasselas [*sic*], and of Johnson's other moral tales." The first four of these lines run:

[31]Vol. I, *The Life of Samuel Johnson, LL.D.*, of *The Works of Samuel Johnson, LL.D.*, ed. Sir John Hawkins (London, 1787), pp. 366, 367, 369–72.

Impressive truth, in splendid fiction drest,
Checks the vain wish, and calms the troubled breast;
O'er the dark mind a light celestial throws,
And soothes the angry passions to repose.[32]

Arthur Murphy begins his one-paragraph, most laudatory evaluation of *Rasselas* with an amused "smile" at the phrases "*immaculate purity*" and "*turgid* eloquence" used by Hawkins to describe the style of the tale. "Both elegant and sublime," the story, Murphy continues, displays a "gloomy" "picture" of human life attributable to "the author's natural melancholy" which his mother's "approaching dissolution" enhanced. The reader's attention is held not by "unexpected incidents" and "adventures" but by "pictures of life," "profound moral reflection," and "a discussion of interesting questions." The parts singled out for mention are "Reflections on Human Life; the History of *Imlac*, the Man of Learning; A Dissertation upon Poetry; the Character of a wise and happy Man. . . . The History of the Mad Astronomer" (which mirrors Johnson's own "apprehensions" about insanity); and "the discourse on the nature of the soul" (which "gives us all that philosophy knows, not without a tincture of superstition"). "It is remarkable," Murphy notes in conclusion, "that the vanity of human pursuits" attracted the pens of "both Johnson and Voltaire" "about the same time"; *Candide* "is the work of a lively imagination, and Rasselas [*sic*], with all its splendor of eloquence, exhibits"—he repeats—"a gloomy picture."[33]

The last of the longer early accounts of Johnson, Robert Anderson's *Life*, relies heavily on its predecessors (eminently, Hawkins, Boswell, and Murphy) for its rather detailed examination of *Rasselas*. The tissue of borrowings is so widespread, in fact, that one may momentarily wonder what Anderson himself really thought of the tale. Nevertheless, his solid admiration seems indisputable, although tempered by criticism of certain features of the narrative and qualifications (echoing those voiced by Hawkins) regarding

---

[32]Hill-Powell, I, 341–44.

[33]The passages from Murphy's *Essay* are drawn from G. B. Hill's *Johnsonian Miscellanies*, II, 471–72.

the book's moral instruction. Examining Johnson's "character" as a "novelist," Anderson states flatly, "There is no doubt that great beauties . . . exist" in *Rasselas.* "The language enchants us with harmony; the arguments are acute and ingenious; the reflections novel, yet just." The work "astonishes with the sublimity of its sentiments, and at the fertility of its illustrations, and delights with the abundance and propriety of its imagery. On the other hand, "the *History* . . . , excellent as it is, is not without its faults. It is barren of interesting incidents, and destitute of originality or distinction of characters. . . . *Nekayah* and *Imlac, Rasselas* and *Pekuah*, are all equally argumentative, abstracted, eloquent, and obstinate." Moreover, the universally "dark catalogue of calamities" embodied in the tale does not depict the human situation either accurately or circumspectly. "The moral" Johnson seeks "to inculcate, that there is no such thing as happiness, is ungrateful to the human heart, and inconsistent with the gratification of our most laudable affections and propensities." Its acceptance "would cripple every incitement to virtue," "paralyse every stimulus to action," and "wrest" "Hope," "the sweet and innocent solace of our frail nature," "from our hands." "The benevolence" of the author's "intentions is indubitable; but in the gloom which his melancholy imagination raised around him, he saw darkly." Therefore, Anderson warns the prospective reader, "to peruse this moral tale with advantage, . . . inexperienced youth" must "guard against the discouraging experience of *Rasselas*, and, . . . keep steadily in view the design of the venerable moralist, by representing the vanity of all earthly pursuits, to elevate our contemplations above this sublunary scene, and to fix our affections on a higher state of existence."[34]

Besides evoking responses in the lengthier works on Johnson's life and writings until 1800 (four of whose authors, Mrs. Piozzi, Hawkins, Boswell, and Murphy, were close friends of the Great Moralist), *Rasselas* figures at least briefly in each of the fourteen, often derivative and repetitious accounts that have recently been collected and edited by O M Brack, Jr., and Robert E. Kelley under the title *The Early Biographies of Samuel Johnson.* Three accounts restrict

---

[34] *The Life of Samuel Johnson, LL.D.*, 3d ed. (Edinburgh, 1815), pp. 491, 533, 535, 536–38.

their notices to the tale's composition or publication. Three others contain short, highly favorable but wholly borrowed critical remarks. The remaining eight present more or less original assessments which range from a single phrase ("immortal work") to a sizable paragraph. The first (1762) of these, by William Rider, describes *Rasselas* as "a Novel in the oriental Way, a Species of Writing . . . in which Mr. *Johnson* [who manifests "through his allegorical and oriental Compositions" a striking "Turn to the sublime"] is allowed to surpass all *English* Authors." The second sketch (1764), by David Erskine Baker, which provided, directly or indirectly, the appraisal found in the three accounts mentioned above, makes a still more sweeping comparison. Johnson, Baker declares, "in his *Eastern* stories in the *Rambler* . . . has not only supported to the utmost the Sublimity of the Eastern manner of Expression, but even greatly excelled any of the Oriental Writers in the Fertility of his Invention, the Conduct of his Plots, and the Justice and Strength of his Sentiments. His capital Work of that Kind . . . is a Novel, entitled *Rasselas* . . . , too well known and universally read to need any Comment here, and in which, as he does at present, so he probably ever will, stand without an equal."[35]

This veritable paean gave way in 1782 to a less exalted encomium when another biographer, possibly William Cooke, placed *Rasselas* among Johnson's "lighter" writings and said merely that the "little work abound[s] with such elegance of sentiment, and moral instructions, as would be in itself sufficient to support the character of *Novel writing* in this country." A little later (1784) two lives—one anonymous in the *Universal Magazine*, the other by Thomas Tyers

[35] *The Early Biographers of Samuel Johnson* (Iowa City, 1974). The first group of three works mentioned includes: Isaac Reed and/or George Steevens, "An Account of the Writings of Dr. Samuel Johnson, Including Some Incidents of His Life" (p. 53); "The Life of Samuel Johnson, LL.D." (p. 236); and James Harrison(?), "The Life of Dr. Samuel Johnson" (p. 279). The second group of three words mentioned includes: James Tytler(?), "An Account of the Life, and Writings of Dr. Samuel Johnson" (p. 11); Isaac Reed (?), "The Impartial Account of the Life, Character, Genius, and Writings, of Dr. Samuel Johnson" (p. 14); and David Erskine Baker (with additions by Isaac Reed), "Samuel Johnson" (p. 21). The phrase "immortal work" occurs in William Shaw's *Memoirs of the Life and Writings of the Late Dr. Samuel Johnson* (p. 170). The quotation from Rider's "Mr. Johnson" appears on p. 2; that from Baker's "Mr. Samuel Johnson, M.A." appears on p. 6.

in the *Gentleman's Magazine*—respectively dubbed the tale an "admirable" and an "excellent" "romance." The anonymous author praises the book for affording a reader "the knowledge how to be happy in what he is" but "suspect[s] that Dr. Johnson does not wholly disbelieve the exploded doctrine of the reality of apparitions." Tyers reports Edward Young's comment "that Rasselas [*sic*] was a lamp of wisdom" and notes Johnson's "uncommon capacity for remark" and "best use of the descriptions of travellers." The next year William Cooke's biography, after sounding the usual round of applause for the "beautiful little novel['s]" "moral sentiments," "design," and "imitation of the Oriental writers," judged the conversation on "Marriage" to be the finest discussion of the topic Cooke had ever read, "and as such must afford no inconsiderable instruction to all married people." Finally, Joseph Towers, whose *Essay on the Life . . . of . . . Johnson* (1786) followed closely behind Cooke's *Life*, also paid tribute to the "disquisition concerning marriage" and, further, to the "character of Imlac" (including "his enumeration of the qualifications of a poet") and of the "Arabian chief" who captured the maid of honor Pekuah. But Towers found "the representations . . . of human life" gloomier "than are warranted by truth or reason," stated that the princess Nekayah "is made too profound a philosopher" on some occasions, and imputed the chapters on madness and the imagination to Johnson's fear of insanity and "morbid melancholy."[36]

Turning from these largely positive evaluations in early biographies, we should note some of the diverse responses to *Rasselas* that additional persons, famous and obscure, both friends and strangers to Johnson, expressed during the period from 1759 to about 1800. The materials offered here are obviously incomplete and can be supplemented by other students of eighteenth-century letters. Negative opinions will be surveyed first, then mixed and favorable reactions.

In her letter of 28 April 1759 to Elizabeth Carter, Hester Mulso (afterwards Mrs. Chapone) directed severe strictures against the work and its author: "Tell me," she asks her correspondent, "whether you do not think [Johnson] ought to be ashamed of publishing such

---

[36]*Early Biographies*, pp. 25, 39, 80, 109, 198.

an ill-contrived, unfinished, unnatural, and uninstructive tale?" She admits that "there is a great deal of good sense, and many fine observations in it." "But," she inquires, "how are these fine sentences brought in? How do they suit the mouths of the speakers? And what moral is to be drawn from the fiction upon the whole?" For Miss Mulso "the only maxim one can deduce from the story is, that human life is a scene of unmixt wretchedness, and that all states and conditions of it are equally miserable: a maxim which," she asserts, anticipating later criticism, "if adopted, would extinguish hope, and consequently industry, make prudence ridiculous, and, in short, dispose men to lie down in sloth and despondency." She goes on to criticize the characterization and the ending of the book and then, returning to Johnson, says that she will not be "taken in to admire what he must know is unworthy of him." Her next letter (dated 15 July 1759), however, contains more temperate opinions. She "allow[s] the justice of every thing [Miss Carter, in an apparently nonextant letter] [has] said relating to Mr. Johnson and his Rasselas [sic]," confesses she "was very angry with him for the conclusion," and "hope[s]" that in the continuation she hears he "proposes," "he will give us antidotes for all the poisonous inferences deducible from the present "story." So far he "has . . . considered the worst side . . . of human nature, and seems . . . but little acquainted with the best and happiest of its affections and sensations." She adds, "Though I am scandalized and grieved at the frightful picture he has drawn of family life, I cannot but admire his truly philosophical manner of placing the advantages and disadvantages of each situation before us."[37]

The poet William Shenstone's first and second impressions of *Rasselas* were seemingly rather more different than were Miss Mulso's. Writing to Richard Graves, author of the *Spiritual Quixote*, on 26 October 1759, Shenstone commented, "Rasselas [sic] has a few refined sentiments thinly scattered, but is upon the whole below Mr. J[ohnson]." By 5 July 1761, however, he had apparently decided, in a letter to Bishop Percy, that "Rasselas [sic] deserves applause, on account of ye many *refined Sentiments* [Johnson] has

---

[37] *The Posthumous Works of Mrs. Chapone*, 2 vols., 2d ed. (London, 1808), I, 108–11. Clifford quotes parts of Miss Mulso's comment on pp. 216–17.

expressed with all possible *elegance* & *Perspicuity*." Shenstone's later appraisal was a response to Percy's comparison of *Rasselas* and John Hawkesworth's recently published Oriental tale *Almoran and Hamet*, "intended," Percy says, "as a rival to Rasselas [*sic*]," which the Bishop rated inferior in "interest" (by virtue of *Almoran and Hamet*'s "very pleasing Love-Story") but superior in "style" and plausibility to Hawkesworth's book.[38]

If Shenstone's real opinion of *Rasselas*, at best hardly enthusiastic, remains ambiguous, no such uncertainty marks the attitude of the Scotsman Archibald Campbell, who in his *Lexiphanes* (1767) roundly assailed Johnson and his works for assorted flaws, especially the frequent use of hard words. Terms from *Rasselas* are cited as examples of its creator's liking for polysyllables, and we are told that whereas "one should naturally expect wit and humour in periodical Essays, Novels, and Romances," the "Ramblers and Rasselas [*sic*]" contain "[nothing] but what [Johnson] calleth, *stern philosophy, dolourous declamation, and dictatorial instruction.*"[39]

Two later critics discerned in the apologue a combination of beauties and faults, the latter being rather more pronounced than the former. William Hayley, whose *Two Dialogues* (1787) includes a *Comparative View of the Lives, Characters, and Writings, of Philip, the Late Earl of Chesterfield*, presents his evaluation through exchanges between two speakers, an Archdeacon (and admirer of Johnson) and a Colonel (and admirer of Chesterfield). For the Archdeacon, *Rasselas*, the "marvellous effort of a great and a tender mind," would have been acclaimed "a noble poem" by the French had it been the production of a Frenchman. "And surely," the cleric maintains, "distinguished as it is by liveliness of description, by dignity of sentiment, by elevation and purity of language, we ought to esteem it as the work of a poetical imagination." The Colonel, on the other hand, declares that "with a total inability to catch or support the proper tone of any assumed character [Johnson] appears to me, among writers, very like what a deformed giant would be

---

[38] *The Letters of William Shenstone*, ed. Marjorie Williams (Oxford, 1939), pp. 528, 583; *The Correspondence of Thomas Percy and William Shenstone*, ed. Cleanth Brooks, Vol. VII of *The Percy Letters*, ed. Cleanth Brooks and A. F. Falconer (New Haven, 1977), pp. 101–2.

[39] *Lexiphanes*, 2d ed. (London, 1767), pp. 24, 30, 32, 55.

in a company of players. . . . An effect of this defective kind (to use the quibble of Polonius) strikes me perpetually in Rasselas [*sic*]. I hardly ever hear a sentence uttered by the Princess, or the Lady Pekuah, but I see the enormous Johnson in petticoats." Moreover, though "there may be minds to whom the pompous and dark fictions of your Moralist are both salutary and pleasant," "to me," the Colonel says, "they are neither; for, instead of quickening my virtues, they only communicate their own gloominess to my spirits."[40]

Like Hayley, William Mudford, who published his *Critical Enquiry into the Writings of Dr. Samuel Johnson* shortly after 1800, also found much to commend but even more to blame in *Rasselas*. "It is entitled to every praise," he asserts with scant originality, "which can be bestowed on language, on sentiment, and on argument; it is the production of a mind abundant in allusion, and capable of sublimity. It . . . is uniformly grand even to a fault; for hence arises a want of discrimination" evident in the unvarying "exalted style" and the energetic reasoning of its characters. Mudford then proceeds to censure the tale's "subject" or theme ("a useless one"), lack of emotional force ("it excites no tumultuous sensations, nor awakens any sympathy"), false portrait of the world and human nature ("the reader finds in it . . . nothing which bears any resemblance to the real events of life"; "man [is] just and equitable, and capable of generous sentiments, and generous actions; and not as Johnson represents him, a mass of fraud, malevolence, and deceit"), and harmful effects on many of its readers ("it is calculated to vitiate the principles of the ignorant, and the young; and as these may be said to compose by far the greater part of society, it is hence calculated to do much injury which can never be repaired").[41]

The penultimate group of miscellaneous responses to *Rasselas* being surveyed is unified by a steady, if varying, note of approval. The first remark comes from outside traditional literary circles. In a letter dated 18 May 1759 to Andrew Mitchell, British ambassador to Berlin, one Robert Symmer informs his correspondent that he has sent him "*the Prince of Abissinia*, a pretty little novel, which happens to be somewhat of a Counterpart to Voltaire's *Candide*"—

---

[40]London, 1787, pp. 48, 107–9.
[41]2d ed. (London, 1803), pp. 82–85, 103–5.

Symmer's comparison of the English and French works is the earliest yet recorded—"and may aford you . . . a few Hours amusement in the Camp."[42]

Although his immense respect for Johnson is widely known, Sir Joshua Reynolds's opinion of *Rasselas* has elicited small attention since F. W. Hilles made it accessible in 1936. Without bothering to date his comment, which, Hilles infers, "indicates that" he "contemplated writing a critique on Johnson's literary ability," Sir Joshua observed:

> The chief advantage that proceeds from young people's reading novels is the habit they acquire of seeking for and finding their amusements in Books. But it gives them very little real knowledge of life. If on the contrary we could suppose Novels writ by an Angel or some superior Being whose comprehensive faculties could develope and lay open the inmost recesses of the human mind, give the result of their experience compressed together in characters and exhibit this in the garb of play or amusement only by being conveyd in some story mixed with interesting events which totally occupy and fix the attention and such Events as might have happend to every reader, supposing his rank whether from being too high or too lower had not exempted him from such accidents, or ever being in such situations, Such a Novel would give in a few hours the experience of ages, such a Novel is Rasilas what is here done whatever part of life it develops the result the moral is undoubted truth.[43]

Reynolds's criteria for judging the "novel"—the "faculties" of the author, "the undoubted truth" of the tale, and its presumed effect on a reader—are neither original nor especially striking. Nevertheless, his comment forms one of the handsomest compliments *Rasselas* has ever received.

Lastly, among Johnson's other contemporaries, James Beattie and Richard Cumberland (both of whom, of course, were acquainted with him) recorded their favorable opinions of *Rasselas* publicly. In his dissertation "On Fable and Romance," Beattie, while calling

---

[42]For this comment, see Robert Halsband, " 'Rasselas': An Early Allusion," *Notes & Queries*, December 1962, p. 459.

[43]Frederick W. Hilles, *The Literary Career of Sir Joshua Reynolds* (Cambridge, 1936), pp. 151–52.

Addison's "Vision of Mirzah" (*Spectator* 159) "the finest" example of "eastern" "fable" "I have ever seen," labels "*Rasselas*, by Johnson, and *Almoran and Hamet*, by Hawkesworth," as "celebrated performances in this way." "The former," he adds, is "admirable in description, and in that exquisite strain of sublime morality by which the writings of this great and good man are so eminently distinguished."[44] For Cumberland, similarly, discussing Johnson's character and compositions in his *Memoirs*, *Rasselas* contains "much to admire, and enough to make us wish for more. It is the work of an illuminated mind, and offers many wise and deep reflections, cloathed in beautiful and harmonious diction." Cumberland concedes that "we are not indeed familiar with such personages as Johnson has imagined for the characters of his fable, but," he goes on, "if we are not exceedingly interested in their story, we are infinitely gratified with their conversation and remarks."[45]

The diversity of the reactions to *Rasselas* may be suggested, finally, by a trio of poems which the book evoked. One, entitled "On Reading *Rasselas*, an Eastern Tale" and obviously, as James L. Clifford has said, the effusion of an "avid" admirer of Johnson, appeared in *Lloyd's Evening Post* (2–4 May 1759, p. 428) soon after *Rasselas* was published. The following lines, chosen from a total of twenty-six, display the adulatory tone and critical emphases of the anonymous author:

> Pictures of such rich colours [Johnson] depaints
> We bend the knee, as Romans to their Saints;
> So pure his diction, and his thoughts so bright,
> His language shines an insula of light;
> A tide of vivid lustre pours along,
> That ev'n his prose is melody and song;
> What depth of sentiment, what height of thought,
> With what sublime, exalted morals fraught![46]

Another set of (twelve, four-line) verses appeared first, apparently, in the *Royal Female Magazine* for May 1760 (1, 230–32) and

---

[44]James Beattie, *Dissertations Moral and Critical*, 2 vols. (Dublin, 1783), II, 241.

[45]*Memoirs of Richard Cumberland*, 2 vols. (London, 1807), I, 363.

[46]I have taken these lines from Clifford, pp. 213–14.

was subsequently reprinted several times elsewhere.[47] Entitled "LIB-
ERTY, *an Elegy*," the poem, ostensibly a lament by "Myra," an
"inhabitant" of the Happy Valley in *Rasselas*, dilates on the theme
that "*the most exquisite pleasures of sense cannot make amends for the want
of liberty.*" An introductory letter signed "Harriet Airy" (presumably
the pseudonym of the real author, Mary Whately)[48] attributes the
inspiration for the verses to the opening chapters of *Rasselas*, described
as an "elegant, eastern tale."

Yet a third poem derived from the same source takes up five
pages (97–101) of the *Miscellanies in Prose and Verse* (1766) officially
assigned to Johnson's blind friend, Anna Williams. Headed "Rasselas to Imlac" and ostensibly written by "Stella" (who may be
Miss Williams herself), the group of quatrains, reminiscent of Mary
Whately's piece, expresses the prince's dissatisfaction with the sensuous pleasures of the Happy Valley and his longing to escape,
with Imlac's aid, into the world outside the prison. The final stanza
reads:

> Methinks already poiz'd, I skim the skies,
> Groves, grots, and lawns, your pleasures I resign;
> New social scenes now meet my ravish'd eyes,
> The wide, the busy world, my friend, is mine.

> [p. 101]

5

Shortly after the publication of *Rasselas*, a rumor circulated, as
Hester Mulso pointed out, that Johnson intended to write a continuation. Much later a similar report, which stated that the process
of composition was actually underway, reached the London newspapers, where it was alternately asserted and denied.[49] Still later
the rumor attained a kind of official authority when Hawkins, as
noted above, recorded it in his *Life of Johnson*. The only other evidence of Johnson's presumed intention is the tale itself, whose conclusion, "in which nothing is concluded," may seem to invite a

---

[47]The verses also appeared, for example, in the *London Chronicle* for 26–
29 December 1761, p. 628, and in the *Royal Magazine* for January 1762, pp. 9–10.

[48]For this identification, see Courtney and Smith, p. 86.

[49]See McGuffie, pp. 255, 269, 275, 277, 278, 282, 298, 302.

sequel. That such a sequel was written and enjoyed considerable popularity again attests to the attraction of the original book for readers of the last decade of the eighteenth century.

The author of the sequel, Ellis Cornelia Knight, who as a young girl was, together with her mother (Mrs. Joseph Knight), a member of Johnson's circle,[50] entitled her work *Dinarbas; A Tale: Being a Continuation of Rasselas, Prince of Abissinia*, which was brought out anonymously, "inscribed" "To the Queen" and published the middle of May 1790.[51] In her short introduction, Miss Knight quickly outlines the "general plan" of Johnson's "inimitable" story, naming as she does so the principal characters—Rasselas, Imlac, Nekayah, Pekuah, and the Astronomer—who reappear in the sequel; admits that Hawkins's report regarding Johnson's presumed intention "suggested" the continuation to her; disavows any "attempt to imitate the energetic style, strong imagery, and profound knowledge of the author of Rasselas"; and expresses her hope that, since Johnson himself did not "delineate" "the fairer prospect" "attendant on humanity," "the narrative of Dinarbas" will "afford" "consolation" "to the wretched traveller, terrified and disheartened at the rugged paths of life."[52]

It is not necessary for our purposes to describe the particular turns of the complicated plot of *Dinarbas*.[53] Picking up the story where *Rasselas* leaves off, Miss Knight introduces Johnson's characters to her own creations, notably the brave young Dinarbas, his sister Zilia, and their father Amalphis; subjects Rasselas and Dinarbas to a succession of (mostly martial) adventures; places the prince on the throne of Abyssinia and marries him to Zilia and Dinarbas

---

[50]See Barbara Luttrell, *The Prim Romantic: A Biography of Ellis Cornelia Knight, 1758–1837* (London, 1965), pp. 25–28. The Rothschild Library includes a copy of the sixth edition (1783) of *Rasselas* which Johnson inscribed "To Miss Cornelia Knight from the Authour. Apr. 19. 1784" (*The Rothschild Library: A Catalogue of the Collection of Eighteenth-Century Printed Books and Manuscripts Formed by Lord Rothschild* [Cambridge, 1954] I, 315).

[51]An announcement of its publication appeared in the 13–15 May 1790 issue of the *London Chronicle*.

[52]*Dinarbas*, 5th ed. (London, 1811), pp. [iii], v–vii.

[53]For modern discussions of the work, see C. J. Rawson, "The Continuation of *Rasselas*," *Bicentenary Essays on "Rasselas*," collected by Magdi Wahba, Supplement to *Cairo Studies in English* (Cairo, 1959), pp. 85–95; Luttrell, pp. 84–86.

to princess Nekayah; and finally makes Rasselas abolish the royal prison which Johnson had ironically called the Happy Valley. During the course of the tale, she also accords the "young men of spirit and gaiety" and the "shepherds" a far more affirmative treatment (pp. 32–35, 37–40) than Johnson had given them (*Rasselas*, Chaps. xvii, xix). In addition, at the end of her work, she causes Rasselas to utter the following assessment of human existence, which contrasts sharply with Johnson's gloomier depiction:

> Let us return thanks to Heaven [says the new monarch], for having inspired us with that active desire of knowledge, and contempt of indolence, that have blessed us with instruction, with friendship, and with love! It is true that we have been singularly favoured by Providence; and few can expect, like us, to have their fondest wishes crowned with success; but even when our prospects were far different, our search after happiness had taught us resignation: let us therefore warn others against viewing the world as a scene of inevitable misery. Much is to be suffered in our journey through life; but conscious virtue, active fortitude, the balm of sympathy, and submission to the Divine Will, can support us through the painful trial. With them every station is the best; without them prosperity is a feverish dream, and pleasure a poisoned cup.

To be sure, he admits:

> youth will vanish, health will decay, beauty fade, and strength sink into imbecility; but if we have enjoyed their advantages, let us not say there is no good, because the good in this world is not permanent: none but the guilty are excluded from at least temporary happiness; and if he whose imagination is lively, and whose heart glows with sensibility, is more subject than others to poignant grief and maddening disappointment, surely he will confess that he has moments of ecstacy and consolatory reflection that repay him for all his sufferings. [pp. 224–25]

The reviewer of *Dinarbas* for the *European Magazine* (18 [July 1790], 39–40) applauded the sequel's "delineation" of "the fairer prospects of humanity" as an "antidote" to the "poison," "render[ing] the mind dissatisfied with the ends of its existence," which *Rasselas*, "perhaps" the gloomiest of Johnson's works, contains;

simultaneously, however, the writer readily admits that the continuation "does not possess the energetic style, strong imagery, and profound knowledge" of the original. A second critic, in the *Analytical Review* (7 [June 1790], 189), begins by saying that "Dr. Johnson's Rasselas [*sic*] . . . is so well known, that any comments on it might appear to be almost impertinent; but it is necessary to inform the public, why the author of Dinarbas [*sic*] attempted . . . to give a happier termination to the story." After quoting part of Miss Knight's introduction and acknowledging "the good sense" and "considerable merit" possessed by the sequel, the reviewer asserts:

> If Rasselas was to have been made happy, without contradicting, or taking all force from the former energetic remarks and inferences, it must have been done by Dr. Johnson himself. The style without the vapid tone of tautology, which renders a servile imitation very wearisome, made us recollect the Rambler; but if this work had not been a professed conclusion of one of that writer's productions, we should simply have remarked that, without the stiff gait of affectation, the writer had let us see that Johnson had been his model.

Lastly, a third notice, prefacing extracts from *Dinarbas* printed in the *Universal Magazine* (87 [July 1790], 21), implies a similar reservation by stating that the tale "certaintly cannot appear with any powerful Prepossessions in its Favour, when considered as the Supplement to a Work of Dr. Johnson's."

Notwithstanding the qualified character of these and possibly other reviews, *Dinarbas*, profiting, one assumes, from its explicit connection to *Rasselas*, fared moderately well at the hands of the reading public. Translated into French and Italian a year after publication, it reached four English editions (1790, 1792, 1793, 1800) by 1800 and apparently at least six more by 1820.[54] Furthermore, usually bound with *Rasselas*, as mentioned above, it attained its first American edition (at Philadelphia) in 1792 and its second (at Greenfield, Mass.) in 1795.[55] Altogether, then, during its initial decade, the sequel appeared in at least eight different printings.

---

[54]Luttrell, p. 87; my personal copies of the first four editions; *CBEL*, II, 549.
[55]Evans, VIII, 165; X, 111.

In conclusion, having indicated the main aspects of the topic, we may venture brief summarizing remarks about the early fortunes of the *Prince of Abyssinia*. These comments focus on two matters, the relative popularity of *Rasselas* and the nature of the critical responses it evoked.

Comparisons, often based on inaccurate and incommensurate data, are not always either valid or illuminating. Neverthless, it may be instructive to place the fifty editions of *Rasselas* (including translations, it should be remembered, but excluding its appearance in collections of Johnson's works) alongside those of several other tales during, roughly, the same period of time, that is, from the middle to the end of the eighteenth century. For obvious reasons, one immediately thinks of the early editions of *Candide*, which was first published in January of 1759,[56] only about three months before the publication of *Rasselas*. Regrettably, a single reasonably comprehensive bibliography of Voltaire's writings has yet to be accomplished; but limited, fragmentary sources of information permit the crude guess, possibly quite wide of the mark, that between 1759 and 1800 the total editions of *Candide* (including translations and its appearance in larger collections of Voltaire's works) *may* have run to between eighty and ninety.[57] Turning to selected English fiction and scrutinizing pertinent lists in the *NCBEL*, one discovers the following figures, which seem to be more or less comparable to that for *Rasselas*: twenty-eight for Smollett's *Peregrine Pickle* (1751), twenty for Richardson's *Sir Charles Grandison* (1754), six for Hawkesworth's *Almoran and Hamet* (1761), seventy-one for Goldsmith's *Vicar*

[56]Clifford, p. 217.

[57]I hazard this tentative figure after consulting the following works: André Morize's edition of *Candide* (Paris, 1957), which lists (pp. lxvi–lxxiv) forty-three "impressions successives que j'ai vues et collationnées"; Theodore Besterman, *Some Eighteenth-Century Voltaire Editions Unknown to Bengesco*, 4th ed. (*Studies on Voltaire and the Eighteenth Century* [cited hereafter as *SVEC*], 111 [1973], 131–52); idem, "Some Eighteenth-Century Voltaire Editions Unknown to Bengesco" (supplement to the 4th ed.), *SVEC*, 143 (1975), 105–12; Mary-Margaret Harrison Barr, *Voltaire in America, 1744–1800* (Baltimore, 1941), pp. 12–13; and the "provisional bibliographies" of editions and translations of Voltaire in these languages: Dutch and Flemish, English, Italian, Portuguese, Scandinavian and Finnish, and Spanish (*SVEC*, 116 [1973], 19–64; 8 [1959], 9–121; 18 [1961], 263–310; 76 [1970], 15–35; 47 [1966], 53–92; 161 [1976], 43–136).

of Wakefield (1766), and sixty-nine for Sterne's *Sentimental Journey* (1768).[58] These numbers, together with my guess regarding the eighteenth-century editions of *Candide*, invite the scarcely startling inference that *Rasselas*, although not at the top of the best-selling fiction of its time (that honor goes to such works as *Candide*, *The Vicar of Wakefield*, and *A Sentimental Journey*), belongs securely in the class of books maintaining a large persistent reading public and hence by 1800, if not previously, would have been deemed eminently worthy of the attention of Johnson the critic.

During its forty years of life, of course, the task of determining the tale's beauties and faults rested on narrower critical shoulders than those of the author. But with no important exceptions, these lesser evaluators—surely to no one's surprise—state or imply a concept of literature which Johnson himself espoused, however much he might have objected to the way specific persons applied that concept to the appraisal of his own writings. As a group, the early critics emphasize the mimetic, the overtly didactic, and the plea-surable functions of verbal art while acknowledging the presence of "expressive" or autobiographical elements in that art. The aspects of a fictional text they discerned and discussed—truthfulness of representation, moral purpose, generic form, plot, characterization, sentiments, style, the sublime, effect on the reader, for example— were commonplaces of the century.

Judged and examined according to these widely accepted prin-ciples and distinctions, *Rasselas* prospered steadily, on the whole, even in the company of its brilliant pendant, *Candide*. To be sure, a succession of commentators pointed to what they deemed serious defects in the book: an inaccurate, excessively dark depiction of human existence (partly attributable to Johnson's melancholy tem-perament); a dismal moral productive of ill effects on the tale's audience (especially young, impressionable readers); a meager, unexciting plot and flat, undifferentiated characters; and a stiff style laden with hard words. A still larger series of critics, however, either praised all features of the work they mentioned or else suggested that its weaknesses were subordinate to what they saw as its primary strengths—the efficacy and variety of pure moral instruction; the

[58]*NCBEL*, II, cols. 963, 918, 836, 1197–98, 951.

remarkably truthful, elegant pictures of life; the wealth of profoundly wise reflections and disquisitions on human affairs; the masterly embodiment of the Eastern tale; an eloquent, harmonious style rising, in unison with other elements, to sublimity.

Thus by the beginning of the nineteenth century it seems safe to conclude, when we consider both its public appeal and critical reception, that Johnson's "little book," possibly written during "the evenings of one week" of 1759,[59] had reached a shining place in the firmament of English literature.

[59]Hill-Powell, I, 341.

From Preface to Practice

Samuel Johnson's
Editorship of Shakespeare

SHIRLEY WHITE JOHNSTON

S AMUEL JOHNSON'S *PREFACE TO SHAKESPEARE* SO BOLSTERS HIS reputation as a literary critic that few Johnsonians have been exercised to examine closely the validity of the depreciation perennially given his editorship of the plays. I have argued elsewhere that Johnson's edition was in fact the first comprehensive achievement of modern Shakespearean scholarship.[1] Its text was a significant, forward-looking improvement over that of any previous edition. Its explicative annotation was far and away superior, both because Johnson selected so judiciously from what had accumulated from earlier editions and because he added more annotation of lasting substance than any previous editor. Johnson's was the first edition to favor the reader's concerns while preserving scholarly quality and utility. Perhaps most important, Johnson's edition deserves to be recognized as the one that established the standards of intellectual fairness and temperateness among editors that characterize responsible modern Shakespeareans. That it is not so recognized seems due mainly to a long-standing disinclination among Johnsonians to look past the *Preface* into the edition itself. Ordinarily, when they do happen to feel such an inclination they naturally reach for Arthur Sherbo's *Johnson on Shakespeare* volumes in the Yale edition. But these volumes, which do not reproduce Johnson's text or all of his annotation and provide only abbreviations of earlier annotation, allow no meaningful comparison of Johnson's

---

[1] "Samuel Johnson's Text of *King Lear*: 'Dull Duty' Reassessed," *Yearbook of English Studies*, 6 (1976), 80–91.

work with that of his predecessors.[2] A credibly supportable assessment of Johnson's relative stature among the many editors of Shakespeare awaits even more tedious collation than Sherbo's many years of effort accomplished.

Meanwhile, some commentators amiably disposed toward Johnson have conserved and embellished old notions of his deficiencies that the edition itself, or at least those portions of it that I have analyzed, simply does not verify. A case in point is Donald T. Siebert's article "The Scholar as Satirist: Johnson's Edition of Shakespeare."[3] It begins with the assertion that when Johnson sat down to write the *Preface* and thus complete his edition, his mood was anxious. Siebert imputes to Johnson at this moment a sense of having "disgraced" himself by his dilatoriness and an equally depressing realization that "the delays have done little toward making the work a model of editorial criticism." He knew also that in notes "emphatically not good-natured" he had treated his predecessors with "contempt," with an "asperity" not far removed from "insolence." Siebert goes on to describe the *Preface* as a "brilliant rhetorical apologia," a kind of mock-heroic satire in which Johnson subtly elevates himself so far above the earlier editors that he tries to stand "close to Shakespeare" himself. The *Preface* is a "prose *Dunciad*" in which Johnson, "like the king of Brobdingnag," looks with "pity, wonder, and horror at the spectacle of man's vicious smallness" personified in the array of "stick-figure" critics of Shakespeare whose work Johnson reviews. Siebert equates the force of Johnson's masked disdain in the *Preface* with that in the "bitingly satiric review of Soame Jenyns." Throughout the annotation itself, Siebert claims, Johnson is openly contemptuous of the previous editors.

Siebert seems to find the *Preface* more admirable for being a satire, archly designed to recoup favor with a public kept too long waiting and to divert its attention from the fact that his edition was not up to the high expectations his reputation had excited. Another way of putting it, if one concurs with Siebert's assessment, is that this

---

[2]Most of the limitations of the Yale edition probably are inevitable, since the only fully useful alternative would be to reprint Johnson's whole edition.

[3]*Studies in English Literature*, 15 (1975), 480–503.

famous *Preface* is in great part a contemptible exercise in cynicism and hypocrisy to which Johnson was driven by the consequences of his sloth and pedestrian editorial achievements. But whether one regards Siebert's reading of the *Preface* with his own apparent benignancy or with all alarm, its credibility rests squarely on the assertion that Johnson's contempt for the early editors is persistently and stridently expressed in his notes. In two plays—*King Lear* and *The Tempest*—that I have analyzed in detail in Johnson's and five other eighteenth-century editions, I find no substantial support for Siebert's thesis. But I find a great deal of evidence with which to dispute it.[4] My reading through Johnson's edition as a whole suggests that his handling of these important plays is representative of his editing throughout, as it is of his demeanor in the *Preface* and other introductory materials for the edition. And I expect, therefore, that when scholarly analysis of Johnson's edition of Shakespeare is more complete, his editorial practice will be deemed appropriate to the motives and objectives expressed in the *Preface* and that his editorship will be seen as not only superior for his time but also germinal.

While time and neglect have obscured Johnson's contributions to Shakespearean scholarship, his first important successor, Edmond Malone, was well aware of them. Both in his notes and preface, Malone frequently cites Johnson as an authority; he adopts editorial

---

[4]The editions whose texts I fully collated are: Charlton Hinman, ed., *The First Folio of Shakespeare: The Norton Facsimile* (New York: Norton, 1968); Lewis Theobald, ed., *The Works of Shakespeare: In Eight Volumes*, 2d ed. (London, 1740); [Thomas Hanmer, ed.] *The Works of Shakespeare: In Six Volumes* (Oxford, 1744); William Warburton, ed., *The Works of Shakespeare: In Eight Volumes* (London, 1747); Sam[uel] Johnson, ed., *The Plays of William Shakespeare: In Eight Volumes* (London, 1768). Johnson's 1768 edition was essentially a reprint of the 1765 first edition, with no changes in the commentary and only minor corrections in the text. In addition, I consulted the Yale *Johnson* frequently. The editions I used for spot textual collation and collation of prefatory materials and annotation, in addition to those texts above, are: Alexander Pope, ed., *The Works of Shakespeare: In Six Volumes* (London, 1725), Edmond Malone, ed., *The Plays and Poems of William Shakespeare: With the Corrections and Illustrations of Various Commentators* (London, 1821). The 1821 edition is a reprint of the Malone edition of 1790. In addition, I consulted Theobald's 1733 Preface (No. 20 in the Augustan Reprint Society), for he abridged his Preface for the 1740 edition.

policies that Johnson formulated and generally followed; he reprints in his own preface the whole of Johnson's *Proposals*, noting that they chart "the true course to be taken by an editor of Shakespeare." Malone's general assessment is this: "At length the task of revising these plays was undertaken by one, whose extraordinary powers of mind, as they rendered him the admiration of his contemporaries, will transmit his name to posterity as the brightest ornament of the eighteenth century. . . . His admirable preface, (perhaps the finest composition in our language) his happy, and in general just characters of these plays, his refutation of the false glosses of Theobald and Warburton, and his numerous explications of involved and difficult passages, . . . and his vigorous and comprehensive understanding threw more light on his author than all his predecessors had done."[5]

More significant than Malone's appreciation of Johnson's edition is, at least for my present purpose, the encomiastic tone. The next great editor after Johnson eschewed the petty, frequently vulgar aggressiveness that marked editors' exchanges in the era of Warburton and Theobald. That "candour" (synonymous, in Johnson's day, with *kindliness*) with which Johnson claimed to have treated other editors, his professed desire to promote editorial objectivity and cooperation and to subordinate editorial reputation to the dramas of Shakespeare are visible virtues in Malone's edition. The proper duty in editing an ancient writer, Johnson says, is "to correct what is corrupt, and to explain what is obscure." Malone echoes: "The two great duties of an editor are, to exhibit the genuine text of his author and to explain his obscurities." Arthur Eastman has said that Johnson's primary editorial goal was "to illuminate the drama's highest pleasure to the untrained reader, to keep his fancy easily and uninterruptibly aloft."[6] Johnson was the first to recognize that, to accomplish this, the editor must keep himself behind the scenes. The second editor of Shakespeare even to try for a responsible text by modern standards, Johnson was the first to make it a fundamental aim to rid the editing of Shakespeare of self-congratulation, pomposity, and acrimony, to arrest the "spontaneous strain

[5]Malone, I, 244–45.
[6]"Johnson's Shakespeare and the Laity: A Textual Study," *PMLA*, 65 (1950), 1121.

of invective and contempt" that had grown since the days of the Pope-Theobald vendetta. Editors' assaults on one another had been "more eager and venomous than is vented by the most furious controvertist in politicks against those whom he is hired to defame."[7] How badly Shakespearean studies stood in need of Johnson's tempering, correcting hand is evident even in a cursory comparison of Johnson's work with that of his predecessors.

Title Pages

The title pages of the editions covered by my comparison immediately suggest that Johnson was pretty much alone in his intention to focus the reader's attention on Shakespeare rather than the work of the editor. Both Pope and Theobald hint on their title pages that the whole job of editing Shakespeare has now been done: Pope says, "The Works of Shakespeare . . . Collated and Corrected from the former Editions"; Theobald echoes, "The Works of Shakespeare . . . Collated with the Oldest Copies, and Corrected." Warburton is blatant: his edition contains "the Genuine Text (collated with all the former editions, and then corrected and emended) . . . Restored from the *Blunders* of the first editors [the Folio editors], and the *Interpolations* of the last two [Theobald and Hanmer]." Pale by comparison, the title page of Johnson's edition reads: "The Plays of William Shakespeare with notes by Sam. Johnson." Siebert might argue that such modesty was calculated to call affirmative attention to itself: Johnson once remarked to Boswell that "all censure of a man's self is oblique praise."[8] Although it is undoubtedly calculated, the low key Johnson chose for the title page was an accurate portent of the tone and content of the prefatory materials, where Shakespeare is kept in the foreground.

Prefatory Materials

Pope included in his edition Rowe's life of Shakespeare and Ben Jonson's memorial poem and provided a preface of some five thousand words. Although the business of a preface, Pope says, is

---

[7] Arthur Sherbo, ed., Vols. VII and VIII of The Yale Edition of the Works of Samuel Johnson (New Haven, 1968), p. 102; hereafter, *Works*. (These volumes are continuously paginated.)

[8] *Boswell's Life of Johnson*, ed. G. B. Hill, rev. L. F. Powell, 6 vols. (Oxford, 1934–64), III, 323.

"to give an account of the fate of his works, and the advantages under which they have been transmitted to us," he launches into an account of Shakespeare's "great defects" as well as his virtues. This critique constitutes about 54 percent of Pope's preface; the tone is positive and admiring, though condescending toward Shakespeare's age and his actor friends. Pope next takes up "the many blunders and illiteracies" of the Folio editors: "In these editions their ignorance shines in almost every page." Pope "lay[s] before the reader some of these almost innumerable errors, which have arisen from one source, the ignorance of the players both as his actors, and as his editors." He knows that the Folio is full of the players' interpolations, for Shakespeare himself could not have written the many "trifling and bombast passages" he found in it; in this vein, Pope "conjectures" that most of *Love's Labour's Lost*, *The Winter's Tale*, *The Comedy of Errors*, and *Titus Andronicus* could not have come from Shakespeare's pen. Accurately, Pope enumerates some of the kinds and sources of textual corruption in the First Folio, but usually· with a superior air, as in the following assertion: "Prose from verse they did not know, and they accordingly printed one for the other throughout the volume." The discussion (amounting to about 31 percent of the preface) closes with this incredible claim: "I have discharged the dull duty of an editor to my best judgement with more labour than I expect thanks, with a religious abhorrence of all innovations, and without any indulgence to my private sense or conjecture."

Theobald's edition does not include Jonson's poem, Rowe's life, or Pope's preface. Theobald's preface—of about nine thousand words—opens with remarks on Shakespeare's greatness, gives an account of his life, a short critical assessment of the plays, a brief discussion of Shakespeare's learning, and concludes with a comparison of Jonson and Shakespeare. As with Pope, critical and biographical material takes up about 54 percent of the whole, and Theobald, too, is positive in tone, admiring of Shakespeare. The rest of his preface has to do with "the mangled condition of Shakespeare," which both Rowe and Pope acknowledged. Theobald notes that Rowe did not help matters at all. As for Pope, he "pretended to have collated the old copies, and yet seldom has corrected the text but to its injury." For "he who tampers with an author, whom he does not understand, must do it at the expense of his subject. I have made it evident throughout my remarks, that he has frequently inflicted a wound where he intended a cure. . . . He has attacked [Shakespeare] like an unhandy slaughterman; and not lopped off the errors, but the poet." Theobald admits bitterness toward his predecessor: "It is not with any secret pleasure that I so frequently animadvert on Mr. Pope as a critick, but there are provocations, which a man can never quite forget. His libels have been thrown out with so much inveteracy, that, not to dispute whether they should come from a Christian, they leave it a question whether they come from a man. . . . I shall willingly devote a part of my life to the honest endeavor of quitting scores." Once he finishes with libeling Pope, Theobald analyzes the causes of the corrruption of the First Folio, noting that subsequent editions were published from the faulty copies "without assistance of any intelligent editor. But where, through all the former editions, a passage has laboured under flat nonsense and invincible darkness, if, by the addition or alteration of a letter or two, or a transposition in the pointing, I have restored to him both sense and sentiment; such corrections, I am persuaded, will need no indulgence." Theobald then expands on his editorial accomplishments before lamenting again (with justification) that he has been the victim of unfair attacks. He is not in the least intimidated: "I may say of [David Mallet], as Falstaff does of Poins: —'Hang him, baboon! his wit is as thick as Tewksbury mustard; there is no more conceit in him, than is in a *Mallet*'."[9]

---

[9]In fairness to Theobald, most modern readers probably need to be reminded that he was, after all, victimized ruthlessly first by the famous poet and then by his erstwhile friend Warburton. Pope's crowning Theobald King of the Dunces in the first *Dunciad* was an attempt by a powerful man of letters to hide his own serious deficiencies as an editor by a vicious and wholly untrue criticism of a lesser-known man and of the whole new field of "verbal criticism." Theobald's *Shakespeare Restored* was a legitimate criticism of Pope's edition and it became the groundwork for his own edition of Shakespeare. Warburton's turning on him after becoming Pope's friend must have embittered Theobald almost unbearably. Still, understanding why Theobald adopted the attitudes he did toward both Pope and Warburton and other critics who took their side does not change the fact that those attitudes marred his edition. He removed from this second edition, for example, nearly all annotation by Warburton that he had used in his first edition, the sections in his preface that Warburton apparently contributed, and the praise of Warburton and others in his first preface that made it clear that Theobald *did* appreciate the efforts of other Shakespeareans. For a good analysis of Theobald's

Hanmer included Rowe's life and Pope's preface in his edition and wrote a quite gentlemanly preface of less than a thousand words. It is complimentary to the editors before him and concerned mainly with what Hanmer thinks was interpolated in the plays (the "low" ribaldry and "trash" that certainly *his* poet didn't write) and with what, preposterously, he claims to have achieved: "What the publick is here to expect is a true and correct edition of Shakespeare's works, cleared from the corruptions with which they have hitherto abounded."

Warburton's edition provides Rowe's life and Pope's preface but not that of his detested competitor, Theobald. Warburton's preface, of about five thousand words, opens with a discussion of the state of the texts, the work of his predecessors, and his own contributions; it concludes with commentary on Shakespeare's greatness and the value of criticism. The section on Shakespeare is only about 15 percent of the preface; Warburton's discussion of his predecessors takes about 31 percent and of his own edition about 46 percent. Warburton argues that Pope, whom he describes as his co-editor, deserves credit for producing "the best foundation for all further improvements" in the text of Shakespeare. But Theobald and even the inoffensive Hanmer get the back of his hand: "Nothing will give the common reader a better idea of the value of Mr. Pope's edition, than the two attempts that have been since made by Mr. Theobald and Sir Thomas Hanmer in opposition to it; who . . . succeeded so very ill in [restoring the text], that they left their author in ten times a worse condition than they found him." Hanmer is thus dismissed. As for Theobald, "What he read he could transcribe; but, as what he thought, if ever he did think, he could but ill express, so he read on: and by that means got a character of learning, without risking, to every observer, the imputation of wanting a better talent. By a punctilious collation of the old books, he corrected what was manifestly wrong in the latter editions, by what was manifestly right in the earlier. And this is his real merit; and the whole of it." After three pages of this kind of abuse, Warburton kills both birds with one stone: "To conclude with them in a word, they separately possessed those two qualities which, more than any other, have

relations with these and other Shakespearean scholars, see R. F. Jones, *Lewis Theobald* (New York, 1919) and also A. W. Evans, *Warburton and the Warburtonians* (London, 1932).

contributed to bring the art of criticism into disrepute, dulness of apprehension, and extravagance of conjecture."

By contrast, Johnson's Shakespeare reprints the Folio dedication and preface, the prefaces by Pope, Theobald, Hanmer, and Warburton: Rowe's life, Shakespeare's will, the award of a coat of arms to John Shakespeare, and Jonson's poem. Johnson's own *Preface*, nearly eighteen thousand words, has four sections: the general critique of Shakespeare (with a long affirmative assessment and a comparatively brief enumeration of his flaws); the famous argument rejecting the unities and defending Shakespeare's disregard of them; a discussion of Elizabethan and Jacobean times and audiences and Shakespeare's originality and classical learning; and last, the discussion of editing and a concluding encomium. The sections on Shakespeare constitute about 60 percent of the *Preface*. Most of the section on editing is devoted to an assessment of previous editions and textual problems; Johnson's discussion of the theories and principles of editing and his elucidation of the dangers of conjectural emendation take up surprisingly little space.

The scholarly part of Johnson's *Preface*, by comparison with the parallel sections in the earlier prefaces, is exceedingly courteous. Siebert, however, is persuaded that "even the 'candid' (i.e., benevolent) acknowledgment of each editor's contributions contains a qualification that effectively negates it. Rowe could not be blamed for what he did not intend to accomplish—that is, to produce a reliable edition. Though a great poet, Pope was untrustworthy and careless as an editor." Johnson makes it "quite clear what [his predecessors'] serious limitations are," Siebert says. It is hard to imagine what else an assessment of previous scholarship would do. In any case, it is clear, I think, that Johnson does not negate or even underestimate the work of others—unless to state a man's limitations is to prove he does nothing valuable. Rather, the evaluations of Rowe, Pope, Theobald, Hanmer, and Warburton are evenly stated and, so far as I can determine, with no ironic intentions; furthermore, by the scholarly standards of the twentieth as well as the eighteenth century, they need little qualification or correction.

Johnson's discussion of Rowe, for example, is not a veiled condemnation but rather a defense, because Rowe has been "clamorously blamed" by others for not concerning himself with "correction and explanation." Johnson compliments some of Rowe's emendations and points out that Rowe did not try for a reliable edition because in Rowe's time (as the context of Johnson's remarks makes clear) the "editor's art was not yet applied to modern languages." (It was not until after Johnson, in fact, that "verbal criticism" won respectability.) Throughout this section of his *Preface*, Johnson is, if anything, too generous. He might legitimately have said that, with respect to their editorial performances, Pope was a fraud and Hanmer was a fool. Instead, although Johnson acknowledges that Pope did "not understand" conjectural or textual criticism and "rejected whatever he disliked, and thought more of amputation than of cure," he nevertheless lavishes praise on Pope's preface and says that he has "retained all his notes, that no fragment of so great a writer may be lost."[10] And of Hanmer: although he "reduce[d] to grammar" what was not grammatical, regularized meter that was not regular, and "made his own edition of little authority" by inserting emendations without notice, still his corrections were "often just"; as "he never writes without careful enquiry and diligent consideration, I have received all his notes, and believe that every reader will wish for more."

Johnson finds Theobald "a man of narrow comprehension and small acquisitions, with no native and intrinsick splendour of genius, with little of the artificial light of learning, but zealous for minute accuracy, and not negligent in pursuing it." He criticizes Theobald for unreliability in "reports of copies and editions," for the "panegyrick[s] in which he celebrated himself," for skill at corrections and explanations, for ostentation and petulance, and especially for not recognizing the sole authority of the First Folio. But he also credits Theobald with collating the old copies, with rectifying "many errors," and with being "commonly right." Johnson retains those notes that Theobald retained himself in his second edition [1740], "except when they were confuted by subsequent annotators, or were too minute to merit preservation." Theobald is the only editor

---

[10]Sherbo points out that Johnson "may have intended to; actually he did not include everything" (*Works*, p. 95).

Johnson probably underrates. He suggests that Theobald achieved a kind of lefthanded fame because he tangled with Pope.

Assessing Warburton was a particularly difficult problem since he was still alive when Johnson was writing his *Preface*; Warburton was, furthermore, a man of considerable learning and a bishop, and yet author of some of the most lunatic emendations, explanations, and conjectures ever made. Johnson manages to be moderate by saying almost nothing about Warburton's text, which was negligible, and by being otherwise respectfully critical. Warburton's "notes exhibit sometimes perverse interpretations and sometimes improbable conjectures; he at one time gives the author more profundity of meaning, than the sentence admits, and at another discovers absurdities, where the sense is plain to every other reader. But his emendations are likewise often happy and just; and his interpretation of obscure passages learned and sagacious." To lose damnation in that faint praise is to lose sight of the true extent of Warburton's deficiencies. Johnson waxes satirical in the *Preface* with respect to "confutation" and the "acrimony of a scholiast," viewed in the abstract. But he evaluates specific Shakespeareans impartially, without testiness, and he creates no petty "stick-figure" critics as Siebert claims.

The Annotation in *Lear* and *The Tempest*

Siebert writes that "without the Preface, the impact of the Notes is undeniably censorious, even in spite of Johnson's occasional attempts to soften the asperity of his remarks by self-depreciation." Well, I deny it. The heart of the edition, of course, is in the text and annotation; Johnson's accomplishments as a textual editor have not been comprehensively studied and, in any case, I will not burden the present discussion with textual technicalities. But my close comparison of Johnson's annotation for *The Tempest* and *King Lear* (the first probably the purest and the latter the most corrupt and difficult of all the received texts) with that in the editions of his predecessors leaves me much at odds with Siebert's judgment. We may be glad that preceding editors did not write more notes than they did, for Johnson had enough to contend with in Theobald and Warburton alone. Rowe printed no notes at all. Pope contributed relatively few, and those mainly textual. Theobald's text was a definite advance over Rowe's and Pope's, in spite of Warburton's complaint to the contrary. But his calumnious rivalry with Pope intruded upon his annotation as it had in his preface. Hanmer marched several giant steps backward in his treatment of the text, and his annotation was negligible. Warburton's text was practically identical to that of Theobald, in spite of his intimation to the contrary. He provided much more annotation than either Theobald or Pope, and much of it, as Johnson says, was useful. But it was infested with his infamous conjectures and sour pugnacity—even scurrility, when one remembers that he was betraying a devoted friend.

Quantitative comparisons also attest to Johnson's sobriety and fairness. Theobald and Warburton of course had fewer predecessors than Johnson; there was nonetheless plenty of published annotation to Shakespeare's plays, which all the early editors from Pope onward used. Yet Theobald, in his 1740 edition of these two plays, reprints without comment only three notes by others, all simple glosses. He is overtly aggressive in 52 percent of the notes in which he responds to earlier annotation, usually Pope's. He explicitly agrees with a predecessor just three times. Except with reference to Pope, however, Theobald blemishes his annotation less with acrimony than with flarings of pride and self-congratulation. Warburton's *Tempest* and *Lear* together provide two brief declarations of agreement with an earlier commentator. He reprints the notes of others much more than Theobald does, but the majority of these are mere glosses. Warburton credits no one else with good strokes or worthwhile insights, and when he criticizes it is with bared teeth. He reprints some predecessors' notes with no apparent motive other than to refute them. Johnson provides far more annotation by others (152 notes in *Lear*, as opposed to 49 in Warburton and 16 in Theobald; 29 in *The Tempest* as opposed to 16 and 7). Furthermore, Johnson generally reprints previous annotation that he regards as informative and valuable, while Theobald and Warburton seem to look for annotation that they can ridicule or make negligible. Johnson reproduces without comment notes by others much more often than not: in *The Tempest*, he adds commentary to only 41 percent of the notes he reproduces; in *Lear*, only 30 percent. The corresponding figures for Warburton are 63 percent and 57 percent; for Theobald 100 percent and 77 percent.

When Johnson does respond to earlier annotation, the great majority of the time he dissents. This is not a departure from the practice of predecessors. But the manner of dissent makes all the difference: in *Lear*, for instance, in 95 percent of the notes in which Johnson comments on earlier commentary he disagrees with it, while the figure for Warburton is only 82 percent. Warburton's annotation for this play is nevertheless far more combative than Johnson's; his outrage at the inferiority of forerunners is uncontained. At the outside, only ten of Johnson's notes for *Lear* could even be said to be critical of others. Theobald seldom and Warburton almost never simply disagree by saying something to the effect that "I think such and such the best reading." Johnson usually disagrees in that way even in *Lear*, a play whose text must wear on the temperament of every editor. Perhaps more telling, the annotation by predecessors that Johnson reproduced, although it naturally contains many simple glosses, is full of historical information, critical insights, important conjectures, and perceptive explications for which the originators are properly credited. In *The Tempest* and *Lear* together, Theobald has not one such note and Warburton has one or two, depending on whether you count a short explication of a line; otherwise, they reprint only glosses and textual notes.

How effectively Johnson moderated and objectified the editing of these plays is most strikingly evident when one examines particular notes. I will cite a few brief examples. One of his most tactful practices was purgatively to compend his precursors' annotation. For example, at I.ii.4 of *King Lear*, where the Folio has Edmund speak of "the *curiosity* of Nations," Theobald emended to *curtesie*, then smote his rival and applauded himself: "*The Nicety of Nations*] This is Mr. Pope's Reading, *ex cathedra*; for it has the Sanction of none of the copies, that I have met with. They all, indeed, give it to us, by a foolish corruption, . . . the *Curiosity of Nations*; but I sometime ago prov'd, that our Author's word was, *Curtesie*. Nor must we forget that Tenure in our Laws, whereby some Lands are held by the *Curtesie of England*." [TLN 338].[11] Johnson, accepting

[11] All citations from *Lear* and *The Tempest* follow the numbering in the Clark-Wright Cambridge edition and the through-line-numbering (TLN) of the Norton Facsimile.

Theobald's emendation, reduced the note thus: "*The Courtesy of Nations*] Mr. Pope reads Nicety. The Copies give—the Curiosity of Nations; but our Author's word was, Courtesy. In our Laws, some Lands are held by the Curtesy of England. Theobald."[12]

Similarly, Johnson silenced editorial audacity when doing so would not eliminate useful information or good insights—a service to his predecessors as well as to readers. When, for example, Warburton conjectures "th'air-vision" to replace "this vision" in Prospero's "our revels now are ended" epilogue, he composed a note of more than 300 words in which he complains of Shakespeare's "wretched autology" and "awkward expression" in the line before arguing circuitously for his silly emendation. Johnson does not reprint the note.

Johnson dealt in the same way with unproductive skirmishes between editors. Antonio tells Sebastian (in II.i.220–21, TLN 905–6 of *The Tempest*) that if he assassinates Alonzo, "to do / *Trebles* thee o'er" (triples his fortunes). First Rowe and then Pope emended to "*troubles* thee o'er"; Hanmer emended to "*Troubles* thee *not*." Theobald scoffed: " 'Troubles thee o'er' is a foolish Reading, which I believe, first got birth in Mr. Pope's two Editions of our Poet; and, I dare say, will lie buried there in a proper Obscurity" (T29). Warburton rightly rejected both emendations; he explicated the line, cited two similar uses of the word *treble* in Fletcher, but then indulged in a jibe at Hanmer—"Yet the Oxford Editor alters it to, *Troubles thee not*" (W37). Neither emendation had any authority, and so Johnson does not perpetuate this quarrel in his edition.[13]

Johnson did not, however, discard combative notes where an authoritative reading did not seem certain. A good example occurs at II.ii.81 (TLN 1148) of *King Lear*. The line reads in the Folio: "which are t'intrince, t'unloose." The other folios read "which art

---

[12]A similar example occurs in the first scene of *The Tempest*, where Johnson abridges Warburton's gloss of *long heath*.

[13]To cite a few more examples, Johnson omitted from his edition of *The Tempest* similar fatuous battles over "pole clipt" (IV.i.67, TLN 1726), over Theobald's attribution of one line to Prospero rather than to Miranda as the Folio had it (I.ii.119, TLN 220), over "Graves . . . have wak'd their sleepers" (V.i.48–49, TLN 1999), and from *Lear*, duels over such things as "stelled fires" (III.vii.61, TLN 2133).

t'intrince"; the quartos read "which are to intrench." Johnson and Warburton followed Theobald's emendation, "Too intrinsicate t' unloose." Johnson reprints Theobald's and Warburton's argumentative notes (amounting to some 250 words), even though Theobald makes such remarks as "thus the first Editors blundered this Passage into unintelligible nonsense. Mr. Pope . . . was not aware of the Poet's fine Meaning." Johnson had nothing to add, but his uncertainty about the genuine text dictated that his readers have the opportunity to review this evidence for themselves. When he had a positive contribution to make to the discussion of a crux, Johnson sometimes added moderating comment to quarrelsome notes that he reprinted. In *Lear* (I.i.282; TLN 305) Goneril is made to part from Cordelia with the obtuse remark: "And [you] well are worth the *want* that you have *wanted*." Hanmer had emended silently to "well are *worthy to want*." Theobald had followed the Folio (there is no Quarto variant), offering this paraphrase: "You well deserve to meet with that *want* of love from your Husband, which you have professed to *want* for our Father." Warburton, emending to "And [you] well are worth the want that you have *vaunted*," carped that Theobald's "nonsense must be corrected [to mean] that dishersion, which you so much glory in, you deserve." Johnson, who like Theobald preserved the Folio reading, ended the dispute on this calm note: "I think the common reading very suitable to the manner of our Author, and well enough explained by Theobald."

Very occasionally, Johnson loses patience with Warburton, as when in *Lear* (II.iv.259–60; TLN 1554–55) he absurdly emended *wicked* to *wrinkled* twice—"Those *wicked* creatures yet do look well-favoured, / When others are more *wicked*." His tortuous justification includes an indictment of those who had failed to achieve his insight. In rejecting the emendation, Johnson printed the whole of Warburton's insipid note, and explained why:

I was unwilling to deny my reader an opportunity of conviction which I have had myself, and which perhaps may operate upon him, though it has been ineffectual to me, who having read this elaborate and ostentatious remark, still think the old reading best. The commentator's only objection to the lines as they now stand, is the discrepancy of the metaphor, the want of opposition between *wicked* and *well favoured*. But he might have remembered what he says in his own preface concerning *mixed modes*. Shakespeare, whose mind was more intent upon notions than words, had in his thoughts the pulchritude of virtue, and the deformity of wickedness; and though he had mentioned *wickedness* made correlative answer to *deformity*.[14]

Familiarity with Warburton's Tom-O'Bedlam-like conjectures and the arguments supporting them raises wonder as to how Johnson could have been as restrained as he was. One of Johnson's impatient notes to *Lear* (III.ii.19; TLN 1674) might indeed seem "testy" or "contemptuous" to Siebert or another reader looking only at the Yale volumes.[15] How harsh the note actually is, is better determined by recalling the situation in the play and reviewing Warburton's editorial tamperings, which number in the dozens. On the heath, whipped by the storm, Lear rages at the elements: "Here I stand, your *slave*." Warburton emends to "brave," concocts a rationale for the purely capricious alteration, and professes not to understand "what led the [other] editors into this blunder"—that is, the blunder of not anticipating his perception. And so Johnson's temper flares: "The meaning is plain enough, he was not their *slave* by right or compact, but by necessity and compulsion. Why should a passage be darkened for the sake of changing it? Besides of *Brave* in that sense I remember no example" [J81]. But that outburst is relatively tame by Theobald-Warburton standards, and it is palpably just. It also is uncharacteristic of Johnson.

If Johnson sometimes could not conceal his irritation with the deficiencies of the former editors, he never used them as opportunities for self-congratulation. His readers were entirely spared such preenings as this by Theobald: "I believe, every accurate Reader, who is acquainted with poetical History, and the distinct Offices

[14]Perhaps a better example, but one too long to cite fully here, occurs at *Lear* III.i.31 (not in Folio), in the dispute over Warburton's foolish emendation of "scatter'd kingdom" to "scathed kingdom." In his footnote, Johnson explains to his readers the source of the confusion—that is, the corruption in the texts; he analyzes Warburton's speculations and chides him mildly: "It is unworthy of a lover of truth . . . to aggravate or extenuate for mere convenience, or for vanity yet less than convenience."

[15]Siebert, pp. 488, 491.

of these two Goddesses [Juno and Ceres], and who then seriously reads over our Author's Lines, will agree with Me, that Ceres' Name ought to have been placed where I have now prefix'd it" [T54]. Or this comment by Warburton on emendations made in *Lear* by Theobald and Hanmer: "All this chopping and changing proceeds from an utter ignorance of a great, a noble, a most expressive phrase" [W61]. Certainly Johnson depreciates such pompous nastiness in his *Preface*, and in a satiric vein, but not at the expense of any individual: "I could have written longer notes, for the art of writing notes is not a difficult attainment: The work is performed, first by railing at the stupidity, negligence, ignorance, and asinine tastelessness of the former editors, and shewing, from all that goes before and all that follows, the inelegance and absurdity of the old reading; then by proposing something, which to superficial readers would seem specious, but which the editor rejects with indignation; then by producing the true reading, with a long paraphrase, and concluding with loud acclamations on the discovery, and a sober wish for the advancement and prosperity of genuine criticism."[16]

As I have shown, Johnson passed up many opportunities to document his complaint: he might have undermined Theobald and Warburton thoroughly by reprinting all of their vacuous exercises in gratuitous emendation and all their venomous attacks. More often than not, he chose to protect them from themselves. When we assess Johnson's editing of *King Lear* and *The Tempest* against that of the previous editors, when we infer his motives and intentions on the basis of what he did not do as well as what he did, we see that his performance was as good as his promise. He did in fact extend that candor to his predecessors "which they [had] not been careful of observing to one another." He was careful to credit other editors and said that if he were ever "found to encroach upon the remark of any other commentator, . . . the honour, be it more or less, should be transferred to the first claimant, for his right, and his alone, stands above dispute." Again and again, Johnson reprinted helpful notes in full, always identifying the author and often paying him a brief compliment. The first note in Johnson's *Tempest*, for example, reprints Warburton's long appreciation of *The Tempest* and

---

[16]*Works*, p. 108.

A Midsummer Night's Dream as "the noblest efforts of that sublime and amazing imagination peculiar to Shakespeare, who soars above the bounds of nature without forsaking sense." Johnson thus presents a confirmation of his own view and at the same time credits Warburton with having said it first.[17]

Johnson's Successors

Johnson warns his readers that although scholarly annotation was necessary, "the mind is refrigerated by interruption." He advises them first to read a play through, with "utter negligence of all . . . commentators," and heedless of obscurities; only when "the pleasures of novelty have ceased let [the reader] attempt exactness, and read the commentators."[18] Johnson's editorial practices are consistent with this advice, helping the reader to become immersed in the drama and to be only dimly aware of the presence of the editor. It is a paradoxical testimonial to the success of Johnson's efforts that much of his influence has worked more or less invisibly on subsequent editions, particularly since the middle of the nineteenth century. The practice of the generation of Shakespeare editors immediately after Johnson bears witness to his impact. Malone and his contemporaries emulate Johnson's methods and maintain his tone. The prolegomenon to Malone's edition, for example, is entirely devoted to prefatory materials—discussions of Shakespeare's learning by several critics, Malone's "Essay on the Phraseology and Metre of Shakespeare and his Contemporaries," and the prefaces by all preceding editors, beginning with Pope. The citation of Elizabethan writers contemporaneous with Shakespeare to substantiate glosses and explications, something which both Theobald and Johnson did a great deal of, is developed by Steevens and Malone and others into a sophisticated art. And these editors adopt an etiquette

---

[17]Johnson could also be modest enough to admit when he was uncertain. All his predecessors had been bothered by the word "plague" in Edmund's line "Wherefore should I / Stand in the *plague* of custom" (I.ii.3; TLN 337 *Lear*). Warburton, finding this "an absurd expression," emends to *plage* (i.e., place). Johnson says: "The word *plague* is in all the old copies. I can scarcely think it right, nor can I reconcile myself to the emendation proposed though I have nothing better to offer" (J19).

[18]*Works*, p. 102.

for dealing with each other, sometimes speaking explicitly of the principle of "candour" they think they should inform their discussions and disputes.

It is true, nonetheless, that squabbles and irritability sometimes appear in editions of Shakespeare produced in the decades following Johnson. Steevens, who worked with Johnson on the succeeding editions of Johnson's Shakespeare to produce the first Johnson-Steevens variorum in 1773, provides an example. After writing a generally polite introduction, he harangues Pope regarding the identity of an archer alluded to in *Troilus and Cressida*: "Had he deigned to consult an old history, called The Destruction of Troy, a book which was to the delight of Shakespeare and of his age, he would have found that this formidable archer was no other than an imaginary beast. . . . If Shakespeare is worth reading, he is worth explaining." But this sort of lapse is more the exception than the rule; Steevens is fairly courteous even when he catches Theobald in the lie that he had read "above 800 of old English plays": "He omitted this assertion, however, on the republication of the same work, and I hope, he did so, through a consciousness of its utter falsehood." Malone expresses irritation with the printers of the Second Folio, occasionally with Steevens for trusting them, and with Steevens's habit of regularizing Shakespeare's verse. Otherwise, Steevens, Reed, Mason, Malone, and the various commentators who contributed notes to their editions write of each other and their predecessors with all the courtesy of Johnson himself. A few samples from Malone:

> Dr. Warburton is not quite accurate. The game was not called *bid the base* but *the base*. To *bid the base* means here, I believe, "to challenge to an encounter."
>
> . . . . .
>
> *Exempt* as defined by Bullokar in his English Expositor, 8vo,1616, "free or privileged from any payment of service"; but this is the forensick, not the colloquial sense of the word: and therefore I think, with Dr. Johnson, that it is used by Shakespeare in the sense of *separated* or *parted*.
>
> . . . . .
>
> It is not without some reluctance that I express my dissent from the

friend [Joshua Reynolds] whose name is subscribed to the preceding note; whose observations on all subjects of criticism and taste are so ingenious and just, that posterity may be at a loss to determine, whether his consummate skill and execution in his own art, or his judgment on that and other kindred arts, were superior.[19]

In Malone's *Lear* and *The Tempest*, this was the closest thing I could find to acrimony: "Dr. Warburton idly objects, that he who leaps upward, must needs fall again on his feet upon the same place from whence he rose. If the commentator had tried such a leap *within a foot* of the edge of a precipice, before he undertook the revision of these plays, the world would, I fear, have been deprived of his labours."[20]

Johnson surely did not civilize Shakespearean editing single-handedly, and immodesty, subjectivity, jealousy, and rancor have not entirely disappeared from Shakespearean scholarship. There were long, bitter disputes among Johnson's immediate successors, the most infamous being incited by Joseph Ritson, who baited Malone and Johnson, among many others. But Bertrand Bronson's 1938 study of Ritson's life and works testifies that Ritson was extravagantly hostile, so much so that other Shakespeareans did not quite know how to respond to his scurrility. Most important, Ritson's extraordinary wars with his contemporaries, like most other contests among Shakespeareans, were kept out of the editions themselves; the scholars of the period after Johnson dueled instead in pamphlets, reviews, and letters. Malone never mentions Ritson by name in his edition, although Ritson had already published high provocations in the *Remarks* (1783) and the *Quip Modest* (1788). One may argue, as Bronson did, that Malone's motives for neglecting Ritson (except sometimes to disagree with the "remarker") were at least partially self-serving—to save himself the embarrassment of having to give Ritson whatever scholarly credit he deserved.[21] The reader remained the beneficiary of an editorial restraint that was little seen before Johnson.

[19]Malone, X, 211, 214.
[20]Malone, X, 219
[21]See Bronson's *Joseph Ritson: Scholar-at-Arms*, 2 vols. (Berkeley and Los Angeles, 1938), especially the chapter entitled "The God of His Idolatry."

The anonymous editors who produced the 1793 edition of Shakespeare, a reprinting of Malone's edition, acknowledged in the Advertisement "that unless in particular instances, where the voice of the publick had decided against the remarks of Dr. Johnson, they have hesitated to displace them; and had rather be charged with a superstitious reverence for his name, then censured for a presumptuous disregard of his opinions." Immediately preceding this remark is the editors' notice that their edition retains a few "manifestly erroneous" notes "to show *how much the tone of Shakespearian criticism is changed.* . . . Nor . . . did we always think it justifiable to shrink our predecessors to pigmies, that we ourselves, by force of comparison, might assume the bulk of giants."[22]

Johnson might seem to be guilty of posturing as a giant among pygmies if, as Siebert would have us do, we read Johnson's Shakespearean scholarship as satire. But when Johnson's edition of Shakespeare is scrutinized in the context of the practice of his predecessors and contemporaries, it is revealed as sound scholarship and exceedingly fair treatment of other editors. Johnson saw not only that enmity among Shakespeareans was futile and counterproductive but also that it intruded upon the reader's attention. His open recognition of the contributions of others, his objective annotation, his concentration on making Shakespeare clear to the common reader—these practices established lasting principles of editing. "Why," Johnson asked Warburton, "should a passage be darkened for the sake of changing it?" Why, we may ask, should Johnson's reputation as an editor be darkened for the sake of a gratuitous reading of his motives? Johnson's motives, if we must judge them, should be assessed by the extent to which his own editorial practice was informed by the precepts he stated in his *Preface.* That done, we should be willing to enlarge his reputation as an editor of Shakespeare in accordance with the valuable improvements that his example induced in the practice of others.

[22]Malone, I, 259; my italics.

Johnson on Psychopathology

GLORIA SYBIL GROSS

W HEN MRS. THRALE PROPOSED RICHARDSON'S CLARISSA AS AN example of a perfect character, she was contradicted by Samuel Johnson on the grounds that "there is always something which [Clarissa] prefers to truth."[1] Johnson's observation is a remarkable psychological inference, considering the cultural milieu of the middle to late eighteenth century. Here was a period of increasing moral pedantry, of sentimentalized heroines immune to sexual feeling, and of burgeoning interest in emotional disturbance—though with no understanding of its origin. In this respect, Johnson's statement seems extraordinarily modern: as Ian Watt has explained, the "truth" for Clarissa is her sexual feeling for Lovelace, which she dares not show.[2] Evidently, Clarissa's constraint was thoroughly endorsed by Mrs. Thrale, who, with many readers of the novel, thought that the moral didacticism of the sins of the flesh and the "perfect" heroine's purification through death were beyond all question.[3] But Samuel Johnson seems to have thought differently. On the deeper level, he appears to have recognized the meaning of repressed motives in Clarissa's tragedy, involving her own complicity, and here and in other places his statements adumbrate some important psychiatric concepts. He describes and accounts for principles of psychological determinism and the unconscious—as well

---

[1] *Johnsonian Miscellanies*, ed. George Birkbeck Hill, 2 vols. (1897; rpt. New York, 1966), I, 297.

[2] *The Rise of the Novel* (1957; rpt. Berkeley and Los Angeles, 1971), p. 228.

[3] On the denial of sexual passion in women and the acceptance of this code by Mrs. Thrale and the general eighteenth-century reading public, see Patricia Meyer Spacks, *The Female Imagination* (New York, 1972), pp. 245–67, and Miriam J. Benkovitz, "Some Observations on Woman's Concept of Self in the Eighteenth Century," in Paul Fritz and Richard Morton, eds., *Woman in the Eighteenth Century and Other Essays* (Toronto and Sarasota, Fla., 1976), pp. 37–54. Mrs. Thrale, of course, repudiated the system with great difficulty in later life.

as possible developments in the realm of psychopathology—in a manner thoroughly advanced for his times.

Johnson's contribution to the history of psychiatry has rarely been acknowledged, chiefly due to his lay status, the preference for some time of Boswell's *Life of Johnson* to Johnson's own writings, and his unflattering stereotype as a morally rigid and severely repressed religious fanatic. The last, in many ways still promulgated, though in a more benign fashion, would particularly disqualify him as a significant precursor of Freud. To whatever religious and moral issues have been of major concern in Johnson studies—and undeniably they are indispensable to the serious student of literary history—perhaps such issues might be alternatively expressed through a more contemporary idiom. The critical literature on Johnson has often been tinged by theological disquisition and ethically uplifting slogans and sentiments. Unfortunately, this means, in many cases, that true interpretative rigor must give way to the rhetoric of Christianity, and Johnson's thought is so pressed into this service. The concepts of Original Sin and the sin of pride, for example, while solid historical ideologies, seem ineffective critical tools, no longer meaningful to a secular-minded, analytically sophisticated twentieth-century audience. To his contemporaries Johnson was a celebrated commentator on what we now call psychiatric problems, and his research was widely read—as well as respectfully cited—by late eighteenth-century physicians, who treated patients suffering a variety of emotional disorders.[4] I sug-

---

[4]For example, Thomas Arnold in *Observations on Insanity* (1782) illustrated cases of megalomaniac patients with Johnson's astronomer in *Rasselas*, praising the accurate description and insight, while Dr. Robert Anderson believed Johnson was a "master of all the recesses of the human mind . . . possessed of a corrosive to eradicate, or a lenitive to assuage the follies and sorrows of the heart." William Perfect, M.D., began his Preface to *Annals of Insanity* (1787) with a quotation from *Rasselas*, and John Haslam, M.D., *Observations on Madness and Melancholy* (1809), bore the same quotation on the title page. For more details on Johnson's recognition by contemporary physicians in the eighteenth century, see Kathleen M. Grange, "Dr. Johnson's Account of a Schizophrenic Illness in *Rasselas*," *Medical History*, 4 (1962), 162–69. Grange's "Samuel Johnson's Account of Certain Psychoanalytic Concepts," *Journal of Nervous and Mental Disease*, 135 (1962), 93–98, also contributes greatly to a psychological view of Johnson's works, as do Walter Jackson Bate, *The Achievement of Samuel Johnson* (Oxford, 1955) and his more recent

gest, therefore, that a medical framework— specifically, a psychoanalytic one—would appropriately modernize the study of Johnson's theories on the fundamental qualities of the mind, qualities that he regards methodically and consistently in his writings.

The medical model defines Johnson's psychological theories for several good reasons, in addition to the advantage of a contemporary idiom. We know from various sources of Johnson's keen interest in medical science, particularly in psychiatric areas. Mrs. Thrale states, "He had studied medicine diligently in all its branches, but had given particular attention to the diseases of the imagination,"[5] and Boswell mentions a case history Johnson wrote of his own melancholy, which Dr. Swinfen, a physician in Lichfield and Johnson's godfather, admired for its "extraordinary acuteness, research, and eloquence."[6] Johnson's library contained a respectable collection of ancient and modern medical volumes, including some on psychiatric subjects,[7] and he himself contributed several biographies of medical men to his friend Dr. Robert James's *Medicinal Dictionary* (1744).[8]

The most striking passages in Johnson's medical biographies, particularly in the *Life of Boerhaave*, advocate empiricism, the belief in direct clinical observation, and experimentation as the bases for reliable knowledge. He vigorously approves the eminent Dutch physician's inquiries into "nature," while he rejects the findings of those who "consult their own imaginations" rather than undertake arduous research.[9] In his own scientific inquiries, Johnson upholds collective human judgment and experience against popular ration-

Samuel Johnson (New York, 1977). See, however, Bernard C. Meyer, "On the Application of Psychoanalysis in W. Jackson Bate's Life of Samuel Johnson," *Journal of the Philadelphia Association for Psychoanalysis*, 6 (1979), 153–61, for a severe criticism of the latter.

[5] *Johnsonian Miscellanies*, I, 199.

[6] James Boswell, *The Life of Samuel Johnson, LL.D.*, ed. G. B. Hill, rev. L. F. Powell, 6 vols. (Oxford, 1934–64), I, 64.

[7] Donald J. Greene, *Samuel Johnson's Library: An Annotated Guide* (Victoria, B.C., 1975), p. 20.

[8] See Allen T. Hazen, "Samuel Johnson and Dr. Robert James," *Bulletin of the Institute of the History of Medicine*, 4 (1936), 455–65, for precise attribution.

[9] *Early Biographical Writings of Dr. Johnson*, ed. J. D. Fleeman (Westmead, 1973), p. 30.

alist and Cartesian beliefs in the powers of the individual mind unaided by experience. He once told Boswell: "Human experience, which is constantly contradicting theory, is the great test of truth. A system, built upon the discoveries of a great many minds, is always of more strength, than what is produced by the mere workings of any one mind."[10] The eighteenth century has often been called the Age of Systems in the history of science and, in particular, psychiatric nosology and rationalist speculation greatly outweighed understanding of the sources of emotional disturbance.[11] Readers of Ernest Jones's biography of Freud will recall the basic distrust of purely speculative reasoning and deep commitment to the empirical method maintained by Freud throughout his career.[12] Not that he denied his imaginative genius or the extraordinary powers of his intuition, but he thoroughly undergirded these with clinical documentation—many times to the discomfiture of his theory-ridden opponents. Johnson's career is likewise exceptional: he combined the empirical faculty with solid intuitive judgment to a degree hardly superseded until the Freudian age itself.

In the *Preface to Shakespeare*, Johnson mentions attempts since the Renaissance "to analyze the human mind, to trace the passions to their sources, to unfold the seminal principles of vice and virtue, or sound the depths of the heart for the motions of action."[13] He seems to think that such efforts have been largely unsuccessful: the study of human nature, he says, is often made with "idle subtilty," apparently the product of the rationalist-doctrinaire methods he repudiated. Although disavowing their influence, Johnson was

[10]Boswell, *Life*, I, 454.

[11]See, for example, the discussions in Franz G. Alexander and Sheldon T. Selesnick, *The History of Psychiatry* (New York, 1966), pp. 89–132, and C. A. Moore, *Backgrounds of English Literature, 1700–1760* (New York, 1969), pp. 179–235.

[12]Jones quotes a letter Freud wrote to his friend Oskar Pfister in which he denies charges of solipsistic reasoning in his work: "If only we could get our opponents to understand that all our conclusions are derived from experience . . . and are not sucked out of our fingers [a German idiom] or put together at a writing table. This is really what they all think, and throws a peculiar light, by way of projection, on their own manner of working" (*The Life and Work of Sigmund Freud*, 3 vols. [New York, 1955], II, 123).

[13]The Yale Edition of the Works of Samuel Johnson (New Haven, 1958–), VIII, 88.

clearly aware of the increasing interest in nervous and mental disorders in the eighteenth century and aware of the prolific literature on the subject. Perhaps these writings are the origin of the modern popular psychology manual, generally a pseudoscientific, commercial venture, replete with rallying mottoes and exalted sentimentality. Like its present-day derivatives, the common eighteenth-century treatise on human nature was of negligible value, while it preyed on a credulous public and advanced schemes of a specious euphoria. Johnson detects the intellectual and—more intolerable to him—emotional fraud. From Shaftesburians to stoics to Soame Jenyns's *A Free Inquiry into the Nature and Origin of Evil* to Pope's *Essay on Man*, Johnson devalues the false paradigms for human behavior and their harmful effects. His disagreement with Pope's belief in the "ruling passion," a popular deist notion, stresses the remarkable progressiveness of his theories, for we see in Johnson's refinement of this rudimentary idea of an "unconscious" a touchstone for modern psychotherapy.

Pope describes the "ruling passion" as inborn determinism, a kind of transitional principle between the theological innate depravity and the psychic determinism of Freudian theory:

> As Man, perhaps, the moment of his breath,
> Receives the lurking principle of death;
> . . . . .
> So, cast and mingled with his very frame,
> The Mind's disease, its ruling Passion came.[11]

With subtle logic, he rationalizes the virtue of this fatalistic instinct and submits to reason and nature as his guiding principles, or, "Whatever is, is Right." Johnson also formulates a deterministic principle in human behavior. He explains in one of the sermons he wrote for his friend John Taylor:

> It is frequently observed in common life, that some favourite notion or inclination, long indulged, takes such entire possession of a man's mind, and so engrosses his faculties, as to mingle thought perhaps he is not himself conscious of, with almost all of his conceptions,

[11]The Twickenham Edition of the Poems of Alexander Pope, 11 vols. (London, 1939–69), III, i, *An Essay on Man*, Epistle II, 11. 133–34, 137–38.

and influence his whole behavior. It will often operate on occasions with which it could scarcely be imagined to have any connection, and will discover itself, however it may lie concealed, either in trifling incidents, or important occurrences, when it is least expected or foreseen. It gives a particular direction to every sentiment and action, and carries a man forward, as by a kind of resistless impulse, or insuperable destiny.[15]

Johnson's supposition of an unconscious mental apparatus seems based more on empirical evidence than on the theory of the ruling passion. Echoes of Lockean psychodynamics—of the mind's receptivity and the association of ideas—and emphasis on vital action and experience are sharply opposed to standards of rationalization and passivity. Moreover, Johnson repudiates the popular theory on empirical grounds in the notes to his translation of Crousaz's commentary on Pope's *Essay on Man* and in the *Life of Pope*, written over forty years later.

In the *Commentary on Mr. Pope's Principles of Morality, or Essay on Man* (1739), Johnson dismisses the ruling passion because it is a product of "reason" instead of "fact and experience." He believes that while the phenomenon may be a real one, its source is not predestined; perhaps, he suggests, it derives from primary impressions received in early childhood: "Men, indeed, appear very frequently to be influenced a long time by a predominant inclination . . . but perhaps if they review their early years, and trace their ideas backwards, they will find that those strong desires were the effects either of example or instruction, the circumstances in which they were placed, the objects which they first received impressions from, the first books they read, or the first company they conversed with."[16] Much later, in the *Life of Pope*, Johnson amplifies his discussion of the ruling passion, or unconcious mental content, which he describes, following Pope, as an "original direction of desire to some particular object, an innate affection which gives all actions a determinate and invariable tendency, and operates upon the whole system of life either openly or more secretly."[17] Again he denies

[15] *The Works of Samuel Johnson*, 9 vols. (Oxford, 1825), IX, 434 (Sermon 16).
[16] London, 1739, p. 109.
[17] *The Lives of the Poets*, ed. George Birkbeck Hill, 3 vols. (Oxford, 1905), III, 173–74.

that the passions or unconscious dictates are "innate or irresistible," and he deliberately refutes superstition and authoritarian dogma: "Men are directed not by an ascendent planet or predominating humour, but by the first book which they read, some early conversation which they heard, or some accident which excited ardour and emulation."[18] Moreover, he remonstrates against those who would encourage the passivity of emotion entailed by the doctrine. Like the maintenance of the status quo to which many neurotic individuals tenaciously cling, the belief in an irresistible, overruling destiny would preclude change. In making the origin of action accessible by understanding—the evoking of primary experience—and by will—the resultant ability to modify retrogressive patterns of behavior—Johnson realizes an essential foundation for modern psychotherapy. His is no attractive rationalization in the service of fatalism or helpless inertia, but he formulates and utilizes a theory of the unconscious as a dynamic principle for change.

Basing his psychodynamic theories on unconscious motivation, Johnson typically conceives of complex and decisive mental operations with causes, but ones often undetected by an individual:

> Whoever shall review his life will generally find, that the whole tenor of his conduct has been determined by some accident of no apparent moment, or by a combination of inconsiderable circumstances, acting when his imagination was unoccupied, and his judgment unsettled; and that his principles and actions have taken their colour from some secret infusion, mingled without design in the current of his ideas. The desires that predominate in our hearts, are instilled by imperceptible communications at the time when we look upon the various scenes of the world, and the different employments of men, with the neutrality of inexperience; and we come forth from the nursery or the school, invariably destined to the pursuit of great acquisitions, or petty accomplishments.[19]

With such details of predetermined behavior, here developed in response to the impression of early childhood, Johnson frequently explains fundamental workings of the mind: the "secret infusions"

[18]Ibid., p. 174.
[19]*Works*, IV, 383–84 (*Rambler* 141).

and "desires" are described in other places as "internal conscious-ness," "tyrannical appetites and wishes," "hidden passions," and the "dangerous prevalence of imagination." In these terms, Johnson demonstrates the causal connection between action in the real world and unconscious mental processes, thus accounting for much nor-mal as well as neurotic and psychotic behavior.

Johnson recognizes the unconscious, with astonishing accuracy, as a repository for repressed ideas. Repression bars unwanted impulses and their derivatives from consciousness, whether they be emotions, desires, or fantasies. The concealment, however, may prove too costly as the repressed material may emerge to create painful neurotic symptoms.[20] "Remember," says Johnson at the end of a *Rambler* essay on a psychiatric theme, "that the pleasures of fancy, and the emotions of desire are more dangerous as they are more hidden, since they escape the awe of observation, and operate equally in every situation, without the concurrence of exter-nal opportunities."[21] His insight is a basic determinant in psycho-pathology: when pleasurable impulses are frustrated in the external world, they influence an individual in opposition to the demands and requirements of reality, thus creating the structure of an emo-tional illness.

Johnson considers the psychopathology of repression as he traces the course of submerged, pleasurably-aimed impulses, which develop into harmful patterns for the individual and for society. Warning in a *Rambler* essay against the ills of nurturing secret yearnings, he writes: "Every desire, however innocent, grows dangerous, as by long indulgence it becomes ascendant in the mind. When we have been much accustomed to consider any thing as capable of giving happiness, it is not easy to restrain our ardour, or to forbear some precipitation in our advances, and irregularity in our pursuits."[22] In a famous reply to a letter of Boswell's, which, he says, "gave me an account so hopeless of the state of your mind," Johnson elaborates on the destructive effect of repressed wishes:

[20]Much of the analytic theory of this paper is standard knowledge, and the reader may be referred to Charles Brenner, *An Elementary Textbook of Psychoanalysis* (New York, 1955).

[21]*Works*, III, 46 (*Rambler* 8).

[22]Ibid., V, 312 (*Rambler* 207).

There lurks, perhaps in every human heart a desire of distinction, which inclines every man first to hope, and then to believe, that Nature has given him something peculiar to himself. This vanity makes one mind nurse aversions, and another actuate desires, till they rise by art much above their original state of power; and as affectation, in time, improves to habit, they at last tyrannise over him who at first encouraged them only for show. Every desire is a viper in the bosom, who, while he was chill, was harmless; but when warmth gave him strength, exerted it in poison.[23]

The operation of repression on the individual, in addition to other, more primitive unconscious mechanisms, is of major clinical interest to Johnson. He investigates the escape from reality against which individuals feel helpless, from mild to more severe disruption, depending on the degree of personality impairment: "The mind of man is never satisfied with the objects immediately before it, but is always breaking away from the present moment. . . . [Such is] the folly of him who lives only in idea, refuses immediate ease for distant pleasures, and, instead of enjoying the blessings of life, lets life glide away in preparations to enjoy them."[24] The "frigid and narcotick infection" that seizes such an individual, Johnson proves "fatal" to mental equilibrium: "This invisible riot of the mind, this secret prodigality of being, is secure from detection, and fearless of reproach. The dreamer retires to his apartments, shuts out the cares and interruptions of mankind, and abandons himself to his own fancy; new worlds rise up before him, one image is followed by another, and a long succession of delights dances round him."[25] Excessive self-absorption coinciding with serious distortion in relationships with others is the essential pathogenic factor, according to Johnson. Such an individual, apart from society, may indulge his wishes to his heart's content—only, however, until reality or the intrusion of other people disturbs him. Thus he is recalled to the world he found so unattractive and unmanageable in the first place: "[He] enters peevish into society, because he cannot model it to his own will. He returns from his idle excursions with the

---

[23]*The Letters of Samuel Johnson*, ed. R. W. Chapman, 3 vols. (Oxford, 1952), Letter 163.
[24]*Works*, III, 10 (*Rambler* 2).
[25]Ibid.

asperity, tho' not with the knowledge, of a student, and hastens again to the same felicity with the eagerness of a man bent upon the advancement of some favourite science. The infatuation strengthens by degrees, and, like the poison of opiates, weakens his powers, without any external symptom of malignity."[26] As with most forms of addiction, the more one indulges, the more destitute and helpless he becomes without his system of support. Thus a vicious circle is formed, typical of many neurotic and psychotic careers.

Johnson closely examines the problem of grandiose fantasies combined with intense feelings of inferiority. Currently termed *pathological narcissism*,[27] the condition is described accurately and with careful clinical detail in many of his writings, particularly in the periodical essays. He shows how the continual search for gratification—in strivings for brilliance, wealth, power, beauty—averts feelings of boredom and emptiness and serious deficiencies in relating to other people. "In the universal conspiracy of mankind against themselves," he explains,

> every age and every condition indulges some darling fallacy; every man amuses himself with projects which he knows to be improbable, and which therefore he resolves to persue without daring to examine them. . . . Such is the general dream in which we all slumber out our time; every man thinks the day is coming, in which he shall be gratified with all his wishes, in which he shall leave all those competitors behind, who are now rejoicing like himself in the expectation of victory; the day is always coming to the servile in which they shall be powerful, to the obscure in which they shall be eminent, and to the deformed in which they shall be beautiful.[28]

Narcissistic disorder, a contemporary idiom for the "vanity of human wishes," presents a shallow emotional life, with little empathy for the thoughts or feelings of others. Individuals with this problem

---

[26]Ibid., IV, 106 (*Rambler* 89).

[27]Two standard references on the subject are Heinz Kohut, *The Analysis of the Self* (New York, 1971) and Otto Kernberg, *Borderline Conditions and Pathological Narcissism* (New York, 1975).

[28]*Works*, II, 390–91 (*Adventurer* 69).

experience little enjoyment from living other than from their grandiose fantasies. The *Rambler* and *Idler* are replete with characters who thus imprison themselves in their own castles in the sky, as Johnson makes clear the underlying pathological structure.

In the history of Cupidus, Johnson illustrates the restless, empty world of the narcissist. Cupidus grew up in a family where "visionary opulence" was the sole occupation. The group met together for years determining schemes of pleasure that depended on the inheritance of a large fortune from relatives who threatened never to die. When finally the relatives did so, they went in protracted succession, to the accompaniment of the family's exasperation and decline, until only Cupidus is left to execute in truth what they all could only imagine. He complains, however, that he is rendered incapable of enjoying the riches, and instead, "I have returned again to my old habit of wishing. Being accustomed to give the future full power over my mind, and to start away from the scene before me to some expected enjoyment, I deliver up myself to the tyranny of every desire which fancy suggests, and long for a thousand things which I am unable to procure."[29] Severely restricted by his fantasy life, Cupidus is estranged from meaningful relationships among people. He is depressed and bored, never having developed constructive channels for self-expression: "I had not enlarged my conceptions either by books or conversation."[30]

Cupidus' problem resembles that of another Johnsonian narcissist, Dick Linger, who languishes and complains: "Burdensome to myself and others, I form many schemes of employment which may make my life useless or agreeable, and exempt me from the ignominy of living by sufferance. This new course I have long designed but have not yet begun. The present moment is never proper for the change, but there is always a time when all obstacles will be removed, and I shall surprize all that know me with a new distribution of my time. Twenty years have past since I resolved a complete amendment, and twenty years have been lost in delays."[31] It is clear from his story that Linger's helplessness is also a result

[29]Ibid., IV, 22 (*Rambler* 73).
[30]Ibid., p. 19.
[31]Ibid., II, 68 (*Idler* 21).

of excessive self-absorption. He confesses a haughty perfectionism, a delight with his own importance, that keeps him from serious involvement in the lives of others. Like Cupidus, he has never learned to diversify his pursuits through productive employment.

Perhaps the most pitiable of narcissists is Johnson's Victoria, a young woman taught only to exult in her beauty,[32] so that when she contracts smallpox, her only means of gratification is snatched from her. She painfully recounts her story: "[A young woman in my condition] is at once deprived of all that gave her eminence or power; of all that elated her pride, or animated her activity; all that filled her days with pleasure and her nights with hope; all that gave gladness to the present hour, or brightened her prospects of futurity."[33] Victoria's life before her illness represents a narcissistic style. She was encouraged by a cold yet overprotective mother—an extraordinary insight concerning the psychogenesis of the disease, confirmed by modern authorities[34]—to luxuriate in her specialness: "I was born a beauty. From the dawn of reason I had my regard turned wholly upon myself, nor can recollect any thing earlier than praise and admiration." Her early development predisposed her to create fantasies of a grandiose self, as she describes her mother's preoccupation: "She contemplated me as an assemblage of all that could raise envy or desire, and predicted with triumphant fondness the extent of my conquests, and the number of my slaves."[35]

Victoria's relationships with others as an adult are characterized by extreme self-centeredness, coldness, aloofness, ruthlessness, envy, exploitation—in short, the cluster of symptoms now associated with pathological narcissism. Clearly, Johnson suggests that the young woman was "diseased" before the onset of smallpox. When the reality does strike, she laments her "helpless destitution" and "dismal inanity," but essentially she is no different from before: the

[32]It is remarkable to compare Johnson's portrait of Victoria in her glory with Freud's comment on the "purest feminine type" in *The Standard Edition of the Complete Psychological Works of Sigmund Freud*, ed. James Strachey, 24 vols. (London, 1953–74), XIV, 88–90 ("On Narcissism").

[33]*Works*, IV, 342 (*Rambler* 133).

[34]Kernberg, p. 276.

[35]*Works*, IV, 326–27 (*Rambler* 130).

emptiness of her social life and her internal emptiness are now merely brought to awareness. Like the other victims of arrested development, she complains: "Every object of pleasing contemplation is at once snatched away, and the soul finds every receptacle of ideas empty, or filled only with the memory of joys that can return no more. All is gloomy privation, or impotent desire; the faculties of anticipation slumber in despondency, or the powers of pleasure mutiny for employment."[36] Victoria's narcissism has allowed her little pleasure other than her imagined omnipotence and the extorted tribute of others. Never having committed herself to another person, she has no source of emotional gratification to turn to. She experiences the world in a frightening way—devoid of meaning, devoid of nourishment, and devoid of love.

If the individual beset by severe emotional problems imagines a primitivist world, Johnson is not reluctant to portray it. With an attitude far from the romantic primitivism of Rousseau's "happy savage" or the "laws of nature," Johnson views infantile man in the tradition of Hobbes, Darwin, and Freud. Moreover, his approach to the problem accords with more recent analyses of contemporary culture that find narcissism—and its symptomatic emptiness, disintegration of the personal meaning of one's environment, unappeasable need, and violence—a fundamental distress of modern life, already at epidemic proportions.[37] In this vein Johnson sees society as a mass of isolated, hostile individuals who inflict suffering on one another in the struggle for the same goals. Civilization and government thus become mere preventive measures, with no magic-giving sanction: "The end of all civil regulations is to secure private happiness from private malignity; to keep individuals from the power of one another."[38] In many of his political statements, Johnson seems intent on unmasking for his starry-eyed adversaries the primitive unmajesty of men, when left to their own devices. Warning sympathizers with the colonists in *Taxation No Tyranny*, for example, he paints a bleak picture of the effects of revoking the governmental

[36]Ibid., p. 342 (*Rambler* 133).

[37]For one of the best recent discussions of this topic, see Christopher Lasch, *The Culture of Narcissism* (New York, 1978).

[38]*Works*, II, 70 (*Idler* 22).

charter: "The society is dissolved into a tumult of individuals, without authority to command, or obligation to obey; without any punishment of wrongs but by personal resentment, or any protection of right but by the hand of the possessor."[39] He believes such suspensions of higher authority would incite acts of chaos and destruction.

Perhaps Johnson's most dramatic example of dangerous, severely regressive behavior is the original *Idler* 22, suppressed when the essays were collected in book form—undoubtedly because Johnson or his printer thought it too shocking for the general public. Here a philosophical mother vulture is instructing her children how to get man's flesh for their diet: " 'Man,' said the mother, 'is the only beast who kills that which he does not devour, and this quality makes him so much a benefactor to our species. . . . Man will, sometimes . . . remain for a long time quiet in his den. The old vultures will tell you when you are to watch his motions. When you see men in great numbers moving close together, like a flight of storks, you may conclude that they are hunting, and that you will soon revel in human blood.' " The reason for this internecine slaughter is attributed by the mother vulture to "some unaccountable power" by which men are "driven one against another, till they lose their motion, that vultures may be fed."[40] Thus Johnson exposes the atrocities of war as archaic forms of oral and sadistic rage. The concept of ravenous animals out to kill, eat, and survive defines man's lowly self-image, pointed by the morbid jest that "higher" evolutionary beings refrain from feeding on what they kill, thus absurdly sustaining the vultures.

Examining many walks of life, Johnson provides abundant examples of primitive aggressiveness. He warns unsuspecting youth about insidious marauding bands "which wealth and beauty draw after them . . . lured only by the scent of prey. . . . There is not one [of the predators] who does not hope for some opportunity to devour or betray them, to glut himself by their destruction, or to share their spoils with a stronger savage."[41] Hostile impulses in the service

[39]Ibid., X, 425.
[40]Ibid., II, 319 (*Idler* 22, original).
[41]Ibid., V, 161 (*Rambler* 175).

of aggression are a social malady, the manifest symptom of which is a lapse in authentic communication with others: "It is apparent that men can be social beings no longer than they believe each other. When speech is employed only as a vehicle of falsehood, every man must disunite himself from others, inhabit his own cave, and seek prey only for himself."[42] The psychopathology underlying such betrayal and alienation is the subject for more character histories in the *Rambler* and *Idler*. The severely impaired individuals in these cases seem prepsychotic, in contrast to the relatively accessible neurotics described earlier. Like modern theorists, Johnson sees the potential psychological growth of an individual on a continuum, ranging from normal to neurotic to borderline to psychotic, depending on the perception of the self and the relationship to the surrounding human world: in general, the more accurate and fulfilling these are, the higher developed is the personality.

The history of Misellus (in Latin, "poor," "little") is a comprehensive account of paranoia. With his solipsistic claims for attention and haughty delusions of grandeur and persecution, he grieves at the end of a delirious tirade: "I live, in consequence of having given too great proofs of a predominant genius, in the solitude of a hermit, with the anxiety of a miser, and the caution of an outlaw; afraid to shew my face, lest it should be copied; afraid to speak, lest I should injure my character, and to write lest my correspondents should steal my papers for the sake of money, or my friends for that of the publick. Thus it is to soar above the rest of mankind."[43] Likewise, Johnson scrupulously details, in the manner of a case history, the grim earnestness and cold rationality of another paranoiac indulging in his favorite obsession:

> With Ned Smuggle all is a secret. He believes himself watched by observation and malignity on every side, and rejoices in the dexterity by which he has escaped snares that never were laid. Ned holds that a man is never deceived if he never trusts, and therefore will not tell the name of his taylor or his hatter; he rides out every morning for the air, and pleases himself with thinking that nobody knows where he has been; when he dines with a friend he never goes to his house

[42]Ibid., II, 62 (*Idler* 20).
[43]Ibid., III, 91 (*Rambler* 16).

the nearest way, but walks up a bye-street to perplex the scent. When he has a coach called he never tells him at the door the true place to which he is going, but stops him in the way that he may give him directions where nobody can hear him. The price of what he buys or sells is always concealed. He often takes lodgings in the country by a wrong name, and thinks that the world is wondering where he can be hid. All these transactions he registers in a book, which, he says, will some time or another amaze posterity.[44]

On the premise that an extreme rupture with one's conception of self in addition to broken relationships with others may lead to insanity, Johnson continues to describe the deteriorating, regressive patterns indicative of major personality impairment. Lady Bustle (who bears an uncanny resemblance to Dora's mother, beset by "housewife psychosis," in Freud's *Analysis of a Case of Hysteria*)[45] lives like an automaton, confining herself solely to domestic chores, with little or no understanding of the existence of other people. She has "contracted her cares into a narrow space, and set herself free from many perplexities with which other minds are disturbed. She has no curiosity after the events of a war, or the fate of heroes in distress; she can hear, without the least emotion, the ravage of a fire, or devastations of a storm; her neighbors grow rich or poor, come into the world or go out of it, without regard."[46] Even more defective is Gelidus (in Latin, "frozen" or "numb"), a natural philosopher who locks himself in the highest room of his house to pursue abstruse research. "He has totally divested himself of all human sensations," Johnson writes, as the great man lives "insensible to every spectacle of distress, and unmoved by the loudest call of social nature, for want of considering that men are designed for succour and comfort of each other . . . and that he may justly be driven out from the commerce of mankind, who has so far abstracted himself from the species, as to partake neither of the joys or griefs of others."[47] Gelidus clearly anticipates the mad astronomer in

[44]Ibid., II, 286 (*Idler* 93).
[45]*Standard Edition*, VIII, 20.
[46]*Works*, III, 278 (*Rambler* 51).
[47]Ibid., p. 133 (*Rambler* 24).

Rasselas. The account of psychotic withdrawal, the delusional reconstruction of a grandiose self, the all-powerful anxieties of persecution, and the cold, nonempathic, nonhumanly evil present the clinical picture of perhaps the most devastating mental illness—paranoid schizophrenia.

Johnson's recommendation for happiness is not dissimilar to Freud's essential directive: "to love and to work." In creative, cooperative ventures, individuals may be yielded the pleasure they so basically crave. The development of a normal or pathological personality depends on the relationships of the individual with himself and with the world of other people. "To receive and to communicate assistance, constitutes the happiness of human life."[48] And perhaps Johnson's best encouragement for mental equilibrium and caveat against the "dangerous prevalence of imagination," which he studies so extensively in his writings, is Imlac's counsel to the mad astronomer in *Rasselas*: "When scruples importune you, which you in your lucid moments know to be vain, do not stand to parley, but fly to business, or to Pekuah; and keep this thought always prevalent, that you are only one atom of the mass of humanity and have neither such virtue nor vice as that you should be singled out for supernatural favors or afflictions."[49]

[48]Ibid., II, 489 (*Adventurer* 137).
[49]Ed. Warren Fleischauer (Great Neck, N.Y., 1962), p. 177. (ch. 46).

"Johnson and . . ."

Conceptions of
Literary Relationship

PAUL J. KORSHIN

1

JOHNSON AND THOMAS BIRCH. JOHNSON AND BOSWELL. JOHNSON
and Burke. Johnson and Charles Burney. Johnson and Fanny
Burney. Johnson and the Young Burneys. Johnson and Chester-
field. Johnson and Benjamin Franklin. Johnson and Garrick. John-
son and Gibbon. Johnson and Goldsmith. Johnson and Gray.
Johnson and Hawkins. Johnson and Hume. Johnson and Mrs.
Knowles. Johnson and Bennet Langton. Johnson and William Lau-
der. Johnson and Charlotte Lennox. Johnson and Macpherson.
Johnson and Malone. Johnson and Matthew Maty. Johnson and
Lord Monboddo. Johnson and Hannah More. Johnson and Orrery.
Johnson and Samuel Parr. Johnson and Thomas Percy. Johnson
and Reynolds. Johnson and Samuel Richardson. Johnson and Adam
Smith. Johnson and Henry Thrale. Johnson and Mrs. Thrale-Piozzi.
Johnson and Horace Walpole. Johnson and Warburton. Johnson
and . . . This list of couplings of Johnson's name with people with
whom he had a personal or literary relationship could be much
longer; I have mentioned only some of the better-known relationships. Such relationships can be very detailed indeed, as the following title suggests: *Dr. Johnson and the Ladies of the Lichfield Amicable
Society.*[1]

---

[1] The essays that deal with Johnson and these people are listed, under various
headings, in *Samuel Johnson: A Survey and Bibliography of Critical Studies*, ed. James L.
Clifford and Donald J. Greene (Minneapolis, 1970). See, in particular, William
Bennett, *Doctor Samuel Johnson and the Ladies of the Lichfield Amicable Society* (Birmingham, 1934).

"Johnson and . . ."

These associations describe an important trend in Johnsonian scholarship, the tendency to study Samuel Johnson in relation to someone else. The trend started early in the nineteenth century and shows no signs of disappearing. It is easy to explain, for there are few authors before the twentieth century about whose life we have so much information available and about whose personal relationships such rich primary sources exist. Practically every man or woman on my list of pairings is someone whom Johnson knew personally; most of them are people whom he knew well and with whom his relationship lasted quite a few years. Many of them have left manuscripts, journals, diaries, correspondence, or personal reminiscences of Johnson; scholars today are fortunate in knowing the location of the majority of such documents or in having them available in printed form. Thus we can readily understand why such a large portion of Johnsonian studies deals with his *personal* relationships. In light of this fact, we can also understand why the obverse is not true, that is, why there have been relatively few studies of Johnson and his *literary* relationships. The great wealth of available biographical materials obviously makes such studies less attractive than they might be for another, less documented author.

Boswell's biographical endeavors are, at least in part, responsible for the depth of the materials relating to Johnson's personal life, for he was remarkably diligent—if not always correct—in "hunting down evidence, especially in the form of reminiscences and anecdotes by acquaintances."[2] It is true, of course, that we have had a small number of "Johnson and" studies dealing with the authors Johnson read as distinct from the people he knew. Among works of this kind are studies of Johnson and William Law, Johnson and the metaphysical poets, Johnson and Milton, Johnson and English writers before 1660 (the subject of a book by W. B. C. Watkins), and Johnson and Swift, but scholarship of this kind is modest in quantity when we compare it with the kind of approach that deals with his relationships.[3] People familiar with Dante, Shakespeare,

[2] Donald Greene makes this point in " 'Tis a Pretty Book, Mr. Boswell, But—," *Georgia Review*, 32 (1978), 23.

[3] See Katherine Balderston, "Doctor Johnson and William Law," *PMLA*, 75 (1960), 382–94; W. R. Keast, "Johnson's Criticism of the Metaphysical Poets," *ELH*, 17 (1950), 59–70; W. B. C. Watkins, *Johnson and English Poetry before 1660*

and Milton scholarship will be aware of the trends in studies of those authors, which include hundreds of books and articles on the relationship of those writers to hundreds, if not thousands, of authors whose works they read (or whose works certain scholars would like us to *believe* they had read) or allude to. One Milton scholar, writing in 1926, remarked casually that Milton, in his writings, mentions, quotes, or alludes to the writings of 2,200 authors;[4] no doubt scholars have discovered others in the ensuing half century.

Students of the eighteenth century have always acknowledged that Johnson's reading and learning were prodigious but, until recently, with Donald Greene's edition of the sale catalogue of Johnson's library, few seemed eager to do anything much about studying these qualities, his *intellectual* biography rather than his life itself.[5] Even so, Johnson's library, or what remained of it at the time of his death, was quite small in comparison to those of many contemporary scholars. Perhaps more representative of the kind of learning that Johnson had is the library of his scholarly contemporary and almost-biographer Samuel Parr, containing more than ten thousand volumes representing about half that many authors.[6] Moreover, unlike Milton, Johnson was not blind for the last twenty-two years of his life, and he lived nine years longer than Milton did. In traditional nineteenth-century *Quellenstudien*, the identification of the books and authors that Johnson read would doubtless be an end in itself. My interest in this essay, however, lies in determining how our awareness of his extensive reading may tell us something about aspects of Johnson's biography that Boswell and the many contemporary biographers and memoirists fail to illuminate. In this context, I should observe that the product of such scrutiny—intellectual biography—is painstaking work. Harris Francis Fletcher only managed to complete the first two volumes of his *Intellectual Development of John Milton* (1954–60), at the conclusion of which Milton was only twenty-four years old! To provide

(Princeton, 1936); and Paul J. Korshin, "Johnson and Swift: A Study in the Genesis of Literary Opinion," *Philological Quarterly*, 48 (1969), 464–78. There are too many essays dealing with Johnson and Milton to list here.

[4] See Martin A. Larson, "Milton and Servetus: A Study in the Sources of Milton's Theology," *PMLA*, 41 (1926), 893, n. 11.

[5] See his *Samuel Johnson's Library: An Annotated Guide* (Victoria, B.C., 1975).

[6] See the catalogue of Parr's library, *Bibliotheca Parriana* (London, 1827).

a test of this kind of study of literary relationship, I will examine two periods in Johnson's life for which we have available considerable evidence of different kinds. The first of these consists of an entire year, the second of a single day.

2

The year that I want to scrutinize is 1751. It is not a year about which Johnson's biographers or the memoirists can tell us a great deal. Boswell devotes less than a page to 1751 in his 1791 quarto of *The Life of Samuel Johnson*, all but two short paragraphs of it comprising a defense of Johnson's position in the affair of William Lauder. Early in 1751 Lauder publicly admitted that he had fabricated his charges that Milton had plagiarized portions of *Paradise Lost* from other modern authors. Johnson, in 1749 and 1750, had at first believed Lauder, and Boswell tries (erroneously) to show that Johnson had never been taken in by the deception. In fact, as Michael Marcuse has shown and as Johnson himself later admitted, Lauder's scholarly fabrications about Milton's Latin sources did at first persuade him that Milton's originality might be open to question.[7] Johnson had been personally acquainted with Lauder and, late in December 1750, helped convince him that he should publish a confession of his Milton forgeries. When the confession appeared, in January 1751, Johnson very likely—as Clifford speculates—found it trivial and unconvincing.[8] The connection between Johnson's literary activities, especially the issues of *The Rambler* that he wrote at about this time, and his biography is fascinating, but students of his life have not explored the matter at all.

Boswell tells us nothing more about Johnson's life and career than this: "In 1751, we are to consider him as carrying on both his Dictionary and Rambler."[9] True, in his account for 1748 Boswell

---

[7] The following essays are relevant: "The Lauder Controversy and the Jacobite Cause," *Studies in Burke and His Time*, 18 (1977), 27–47; "Miltonklastes: The Lauder Affair Reconsidered," *Eighteenth-Century Life*, 4 (1978), 86–91; and " 'The Scourge of Impostors; The Terror of Quacks': John Douglas and the Exposé of William Lauder," *Huntington Library Quarterly*, 42 (1979), 231–61.

[8] See *Dictionary Johnson: Samuel Johnson's Middle Years* (New York, 1979), pp. 68–69.

[9] *The Life of Samuel Johnson, LL.D.*, ed. G. B. Hill, rev. L. F. Powell, 6 vols. (Oxford, 1934–64), I, 228.

had commented on the beginning of Johnson's labors on the *Dictionary* and in his section on 1750 he had included a generous—for Boswell—appraisal of the subject matter and style of *The Rambler*. But in neither place does he say anything that sheds any light whatever on what his subject might have been doing in 1751.[10] Other contemporary writers contribute nothing, and modern biographers like Krutch, Wain, and Bate have said very little more about Johnson in this year. James L. Clifford's *Dictionary Johnson: Samuel Johnson's Middle Years* (1979), in its two chapters on 1750 and 1751, follows Boswell's basic outline of those years, focusing first on the Lauder affair (Chapter IV) and then on the known facts dealing with *The Rambler* (Chapter V). While his account is the best general survey that we have of the period when Johnson wrote *The Rambler*, it does not use the texts of these famous essays as a biographical source or as evidence for what Johnson was reading, thinking, and doing at the time.

Despite the unpromising appearances, we know a great deal more about Johnson in 1751 than we do about many other years, including some after 1763, when Boswell's biographical narrative assumes a personal perspective on him. In 1751 he published 105 issues of *The Rambler*—numbers 83 through 187—of which Elizabeth Carter and Samuel Richardson wrote one apiece, and he wrote 103. Thus on 103 days of 1751, Johnson wrote or prepared for the press an issue of *The Rambler*. In a year for which we have fewer than ten surviving personal letters and no Boswellian table talk at all, this is a memorial of some importance. But what can we make of such a piece of information? Close study of the issues of *The Rambler* for 1751 reveals a good deal about Johnson's biography. Moreover, it is Johnson's longest single work, slightly longer even than *The Lives of the Poets*. Its serial publication made it an occasional work for its original audience which, even with the piratical reprinting of some of the issues in the provincial press, probably did not exceed a few thousand readers. But its considerable sale and wide popularity in many collected editions gave it an extended public, and Johnson's

---

[10]James H. Sledd and Gwin J. Kolb, *Dr. Johnson's Dictionary: Essays in the Biography of a Book* (Chicago, 1955), do not mention Johnson's activities in 1751, but cite Thomas Birch to the effect that, by 20 October 1750, Johnson "had printed off the three first letters of his English Dictionary" (p. 144).

careful revisions to some of the collected editions show how highly he regarded the work. So an understanding of how Johnson wrote those 103 issues may be of particular value in studying his biography in 1751.

We already know that, as he progressed on the periodical, he did not accumulate issues in advance of publication. He later told Boswell that "almost all of his Ramblers were written just as they were wanted for the press; that he sent a certain portion of the copy of an essay, and wrote the remainder, while the former part of it was printing."[11] Boswell had noted, in his account of 1750, almost the same thing: "Posterity will be astonished when they are told, upon the authority of Johnson himself, that many of these discourses, which we should suppose had been laboured with all the slow attention of literary leisure, were written in haste as the moment pressed, without even being read over by him before they were printed."[12] Here Boswell appears to be anticipating Bennet Langton's testimony on the composition of *The Idler*: "Many of these excellent essays were written as hastily as an ordinary letter. Mr. Langton remembers Johnson, when on a visit to Oxford, asking him one evening how long it was until the post went out; and on being told about half an hour, he exclaimed, 'then we shall do very well.' He upon this instantly sat down and finished an Idler, which it was necessary should be in London the next day."[13] This, then, is Boswell's evidence relating to the composition of "many" or "almost all" of his *Rambler* essays. Boswell, as he himself tells us, had read *The Rambler* before he met Johnson, but it is clear that he never studied it closely, for the text of many individual issues contradicts the received notion that Johnson wrote to the moment.

A study of the issues of 1751 produces some evidence that contradicts or is at variance with Boswell's observations. In No. 134 (29 June), Johnson specifically comments on this method of composition. He tells us that he spent the previous morning meditating on the subject for his next issue, "till at last I was awakened from this dream of study by a summons from the press: the time was

[11]*Life*, III, 42.
[12]Ibid., I, 203.
[13]Ibid., I, 331 (ap. 1758); the visit to Oxford took place in July 1759.

come for which I had been thus negligently purposing to provide, and, however dubious or sluggish, I was now necessitated to write."[14] Perhaps Johnson wrote this issue, which is on the subject of procrastination, very hastily, as Mrs. Thrale later alleged, but he also tells us that he spent a good deal of time considering his theme and the proper approach to it. In No. 184 (21 December), he observes that "the writer of essays, escapes many embarrassments to which a large work would have exposed him; he seldom harrasses his reason with long trains of consequence, dims his eyes with the perusal of antiquated volumes, or burthens his memory with great accumulations of preparatory knowledge. A careless glance upon a favourite author, or transient survey of the varieties of life, is sufficient to supply the first hint or seminal idea, which enlarged by the gradual accretion of matter stored in the mind, is by the warmth of fancy easily expanded into flowers, and sometimes into fruit."[15] So Johnson seldom found it necessary to do research to prepare for an issue of *The Rambler*, although he found it useful to start an essay by glancing at a favorite author. We know that this was indeed his method some of the time, for perhaps 20 percent of all *Rambler* essays begin with an allusion to a work that Johnson had either recently consulted or remembered more or less accurately. These opening allusions are almost always to books, works, or authors that Johnson is not quoting; the general tone and vague style of these initial allusions suggests that he usually did not have the book in question open before him. Sometimes it is clear from an introductory allusion that Johnson had not even read the book or author recently.

However, almost half of the *Rambler* essays for 1751, based on the evidence of the text itself, contain additional material that Johnson either quoted carefully or paraphrased roughly from books in his possession. Other issues do not quote or paraphrase, but allude instead with considerable accuracy to books that Johnson must have consulted recently. Clearly, he did not compose essays like these hastily. At least two essays from 1751 do not fall into any of

[14] The Yale Edition of the Works of Samuel Johnson (New Haven, 1958–), IV, 345–46. Hereafter cited as *Works*.

[15] *Works*, V, 201.

the categories I have cited. Numbers 170 and 171 (2 and 5 November), the epistolary history of the prostitute Misella, are the fruits of a sort of investigative journalism. Johnson, according to Malone, interviewed a number of prostitutes about details of their lives before he composed these moving letters. He might have written them rapidly, but the evidence suggests that they were based on rather careful gathering of materials in advance. Thus Johnson's own observations on his methods of writing that he makes in *The Rambler*, coupled with a study of the text for 1751, both correct and largely contradict what our only other "source" for that year, Boswell, reports. Nearly half of the 103 essays for 1751 involve some kind of research, even if it is the only quotation from books. Clearly, then, we must revise our conceptions of Johnson's composing his essays in haste.

The Rambler relates to facts of Johnson's biography in other ways. Scholars have already pointed out two possibilities of relationship. W. K. Wimsatt suggested, over thirty years ago, that the technical and scientific words in *The Rambler* closely parallel his reading of books on natural science and philosophy as sources for quotations in the *Dictionary*.[16] And, more recently, Jacob Leed has noted that many essays contain accounts of or references to aspects of contemporary literary patronage and has suggested that the presence of so many such allusions may have something to do with Johnson's presumed resentment over his treatment by Chesterfield in 1747–48.[17] Both of these possibilities point to general matters—to the known fact that Johnson was at work on the *Dictionary* in 1751 and to the somewhat speculative notion that he had in mind Chesterfield's casual neglect of his needs and later forgetfulness of his promises (whatever they were; we do not know) when he criticized or caricatured patrons. Perhaps Johnson did think of Chesterfield when he wrote some of those essays that deal with or mention patronage in an unfavorable light. However, a close scrutiny of the *Rambler* texts themselves reveals that most of Johnson's thoughts on patronage are actually on poverty or neglected literary merit

---

[16]See *Philosophic Words: A Study of Style and Meaning in the "Rambler" and "Dictionary" of Samuel Johnson* (New Haven, 1948), pp. 70–93.

[17]See his "Patronage in the *Rambler*," *Studies in Burke and His Time*, 14 (1972–73), 5–21.

and not on the sort of brief relationship that he had with Lord Chesterfield.

There is a good deal of further information in the 1751 essays that relates to Johnson's biography. The first essay of the year, No. 83 (which we must read along with the last issue of 1750), provides such evidence. *Rambler* 82 consists of a letter from the collector Quisquilius, and the following issue comments on collections of natural phenomena, archaeological artifacts, and so on. Both essays suggest a firsthand acquaintance with collections of antiquities and natural curiosities. The two most important such collections in England during the early 1750s were the Ashmolean Museum at Oxford and the private collection of Sir Hans Sloane in London. We know that Johnson could not have visited the Ashmolean in the *Rambler* years, for he made his first visit to Oxford since his undergraduate years in 1754.[18] But there is every reason to expect that he could have joined the stream of curious and fashionable visitors who viewed Sloane's collections at his manor house in suburban Chelsea. His reference in No. 83 to "the lanthorn of Guy Faux," an artifact later in the Ashmolean, but during his undergraduate years kept in the Bodleian Library, might suggest that Johnson drew his knowledge of collectors of antiquities from his undergraduate days, but nearly every other particular of Quisquilius's store of rarities is probably drawn either from a visit to Sloane's Museum or from a contemporary account of it.[19] Sloane died in 1753, leaving his 50,000 books, 4,000 manuscripts, and 50,000 other artifacts to the nation "for," as he put it in his will, "the confutation of atheism." These vast holdings form the original nucleus of the British Museum.[20] There is no evidence outside *The Rambler* to hint that Johnson might have visited Sloane's Museum, but such a visit would certainly be consistent with his curiosity

---

[18]See Clifford, *Dictionary Johnson*, p. 129.

[19]Quisquilius's veneration for "the ruff of Elizabeth"—*Rambler* 82; *Works*, III, 69—recalls Young's satire upon Sloane in *Love of Fame* (1728), where he ridicules Sloane's *curiosa* and adds, "He shews, on *holidays*, a sacred pin / That touch'd the ruff, that touch'd queen *Bess's* chin" (Young's *Works*, 4 vols. [London, 1747], I, 108).

[20]See Edward Miller, *That Noble Cabinet: A History of the British Museum* (Athens, Ohio, 1974), pp. 36–41.

about natural phenomena and to his other references to collectors in No. 177 (26 November). *Rambler* 83, then, is important because it presents an example of how Johnson must have gathered the nonliterary information that he used in writing his essays. It is not a satire on Sloane and other collectors of antiquities, but is rather a significant scholarly treatment of the purposes of collections— such as the Harleian Library, which, of course, he had known intimately—as a basis for the studies of learned men.

The fact that Johnson devotes seven essays in 1751 to Milton is, again, closely related to a known incident in his life, his involvement with William Lauder and the controversy that Lauder's false allegations about Milton generated. Five of these essays (Nos. 86, 88, 90, 92, and 94) are on the subject of Milton's versification; they run from 12 January to 9 February, beginning almost on the very day that Lauder published an apology for his forgeries. The other two essays on Milton are Nos. 139 and 140 (16 and 20 July), which are an analysis of the tragic elements in *Samson Agonistes*. The tone of these seven essays, which Johnson definitely did *not* write at the last minute but, rather, carefully researched, using and referring to corroboratory materials, is respectful of Milton's accomplishments; they contain none of the sharply critical tone that we sometimes find in the *Life of Milton*. We must assume that Johnson was aware that people knew his earlier position that tentatively supported Lauder's views on Milton, and that his devoting such a large portion of *The Rambler* in the year of Lauder's disgrace to Milton criticism was his way of making amends for his previous mistake. Less than a fortnight after his two essays on *Samson*, Johnson refers to the Lauder affair once again, in No. 143, in which he deals at length with the associated problems of plagiarism and imitation. Without a single reference to Milton, he shows how literary conventions at a particular time may cause unintentional similarities among various writers and how "not every imitation ought to be stigmatized as plagiarism."[21] No. 143, indeed, is one of Johnson's most carefully researched *Ramblers*, containing two dozen accurate quotations from a wide variety of works both well known and obscure he obviously had gathered together and had available to him as he

---

[21] *Works*, IV, 401.

wrote. So his method of composition here must have been exactly the *opposite* of what Boswell describes as his usual way of writing.

Johnson does not merely employ "philosophic words" from his *Dictionary* sources in *The Rambler*. He mentions his thoughts about his vast compilation in several essays on scholarly works, their harsh treatment by ignorant or malicious critics, and the difficulty of gaining recognition rapidly. By 1751 Johnson was already behind schedule on the *Dictionary* by almost a year, so *Rambler* 169 (29 October), on productions that take a long time to complete, may well represent his answer to the importunities of the *Dictionary* conger. Speaking of "the offspring of the mind," he says, "No vanity can more justly incur contempt and indignation than that which boasts of negligence and hurry." As for prior precedents, "Among the writers of antiquity I remembered none except Statius, who ventures to mention the speedy production of his writings, either as an extenuation of his faults, or as a proof of his facility." Finally, Johnson assures us, "One of the most pernicious effects of haste, is obscurity."[22] He continues to discuss the subject of protracted labor on a single project and the critical reception of an author's major work in two following essays, both of which seem to refer to the difficulties he was having with Volume I of the *Dictionary* in 1751.[23]

The majority of the *Rambler* essays are bookish. If they do not mention particular works and their authors, as most of them do, then they refer to reading or to general categories of literature. A great many of Johnson's literary allusions in 1751 are casual references, like those in his introductory paragraphs to Addison, Bacon, Cicero, Locke, and many others, or scores of different mentions, in the course of the essays, to dozens of classical authors. The references to English authors of the seventeenth and eighteenth centuries often relate to or derive from his reading and quotation gathering for the *Dictionary*, since most of these authors are represented by signed quotations in that work, but some of the contemporary writers that he cites fall outside the scope of this compilation. The classical authors Johnson often—but not always—cites from memory. For

[22]Ibid., V, 130, 132, 134.
[23]See *Rambler* 173 and 176.

example, in an issue like No. 143, where he was writing about plagiarism, he took the trouble to verify his classical quotations, and he certainly took pains to get the classical mottoes for each issue correct (and, with only one exception in the entire *Rambler*, they *were* correct). There is another important category of literary allusion in the 1751 *Ramblers*, one that Johnson almost always cites from the books themselves rather than from his recent or distant recollections. This is the considerable body of references to humanistic authors from the late fifteenth to the late seventeenth century. Johnson alludes to or quotes from such writers as Pontanus, Politian, Scaliger, Erasmus, Sir (now St.) Thomas More, Giles Ménage, Grotius, Vida, Jean Le Clerc, Racine, and La Bruyère. And, of course, he alludes to many other humanistic authors without mentioning their names. We will notice such allusions today if—unlike the editors of *The Rambler* in the Yale Edition of Johnson's Works— we have more than a passing familiarity with the hundreds of Continental and British scholars and humanists whose work Johnson knew. What this category of allusion in *The Rambler* tells us about Johnson's life in 1751 is interesting. First, it points to the fact that his work on the *Dictionary* did not consume all of his time and shows that he worked on quotation gathering in a haphazard manner, taking time frequently to pursue other interests. Second, this body of allusion often shows that Johnson tried to turn his scholarly interests to everyday life as represented in the subjects of his essays. Indeed, a frequent subject in his self-authored letters to *The Rambler* is the unfitness of the scholar for polite conversation and the life of normal society. Johnson appears to have wanted to demonstrate that, whatever he might say about the pendantry or bashfulness of the cloistered scholar, *he* was able to apply his learning to contemporary problems.

A good example of such an application is *Rambler* 114 (20 April). This essay comprises a strong and eloquent criticism of public executions, capital punishment, and the severity of the English common law, with its numerous capital crimes. Early 1751 was a curious year for an English writer to make a powerful statement against capital punishment, for the tide of public opinion at the time was distinctly in favor of the death penalty. Hence Johnson's essay is something of a milestone in English legal and political writing. Boswell ignorantly presents—or rather, caricatures—Johnson in some miscellaneous anecdotes, which he assigns for no good reason to 1783, as supporting public executions and capital punishment.[24] This important oversight shows how little Boswell—and the other early biographers of Johnson—based his study of Johnson's life on his writings, and it casts serious doubt on the authenticity of the anecdotes favoring public hanging that Boswell assigns to Johnson. Birkbeck Hill at least refers in a note at this point in his edition of the *Life* of Johnson's "real opinion" in *Rambler* 114, but he clearly misses the point of that magnificent essay. Johnson does not merely present a strong case against capital punishment; he also gives us, in the final paragraph, his source: "This scheme of invigorating the laws by relaxation, and extirpating wickedness by lenity, is so remote from common practice, that I might reasonably fear to expose it to the publick, could it be supported only by my own observations: I shall, therefore, by ascribing it to its author, Sir Thomas More, endeavour to procure it that attention, which I wish always paid to prudence, to justice, and to mercy."[25]

Johnson's argument is in fact an important statement in itself, for it is not merely borrowed from More, it is a significant reinterpretation of More's appeal for clemency and for a reinstitution of the noncapital punishments prescribed by Greek and Roman law. Although commentators on Johnson's political thought have not noticed his adherence to More's arguments (we should remember that More himself was a lawyer of some eminence), his position on capital punishment was so outstanding for the eighteenth century that Sir Samuel Romilly, at the time of the famous debates on capital punishment in 1818, used *Rambler* 114 as a corroboration for his arguments."[26] Johnson's allusion to More's *Utopia* is not gratuitous or without relevance to events in contemporary English society. Rather, No. 114 is part of a current debate on capital crimes

[24]*Life*, IV, 188–89.

[25]*Works*, IV, 247.

[26]That so thorough a student of Johnson's politics as Donald Greene (*The Politics of Samuel Johnson* [New Haven, 1960]) does not notice Johnson's dependence upon More shows that Johnsonian scholars have not been accustomed to using *The Rambler* as a source of Johnson's political opinions.

and punishment, appearing shortly after Fielding's well known essay *An Enquiry into the Causes of the late Increase of Robbers, etc., with some proposal for remedying this growing evil* (published in January 1751). Crime and punishment were widely discussed topics in 1750 and 1751 and, as the evidence of *Rambler* 114 shows, Johnson used his periodical essay as a vehicle for entering into the controversy over the matter. Fielding's *Enquiry* derives immediately from the case of Bosavern Penlez, who had received a death sentence for his part— a part that was much disputed and highly uncertain—in the celebrated Covent Garden riots of 1749. In his position as a London magistrate, Fielding helped with the administration of a harsh justice, and his *Enquiry* strongly favors capital punishment.[27] Johnson's argument in *Rambler* 114 is quite clearly intended as a refutation of Fielding's position. Central to my purpose here is to suggest that a knowledge of Johnson's reading—in the case of *Rambler* 114 a reading of More's *Utopia*, in many other cases that I cannot discuss in this essay a reading of dozens of other works—enlarges our knowledge of his life in 1751.

I have tried to show how an understanding of Johnson's intellectual development, as we can glean it from close scrutiny of *The Rambler* for 1751, helps to enlarge our knowledge of his life in that year. In many more instances for 1751 than I have been able to mention here, the 103 issues of *The Rambler* he wrote certain relevent evidence to what he was reading, doing, and thinking at a time of his life about which his biographers have had, until now, very little documentation. Of course, 1751 is not the only year in Johnson's life about which we have very little biographical information, but, among such years, it is almost unique in that we have so much collateral evidence, in the form of a long periodical work, to assist us. *Rambler* 114 shows us that Johnson had an admiration for More's *Utopia*—an admiration that he shares with Swift—and the influence raises interesting possibilities about the significance of utopian thought in Johnson's writings, especially *Rasselas*. Further study of *The Rambler* will doubtless reveal more material about Johnson's intellectual habits that scholars have hitherto ignored.

[27]See *An Enquiry into the Causes of the Late Increase of Robbers* . . . (London, 1751), pp. 121–26.

3

The second period in Johnson's life that I want to examine is a single day, Friday, 5 August 1763. It is a day that Boswell documents fully. Boswell presents a number of conversations for this day, on which he was to depart from London for Holland, but I want to consider only one of them. Boswell begins, "On Friday, August 5, we set out early in the morning in the Harwich stage coach. A fat elderly gentlewoman and a young Dutchman, seemed the most inclined among us to conversation." The conversation that ensues is reminiscent of Johnson's famous fictional stage coach journey in *Adventurer* 84, for the real people in the Harwich coach talk on various topics, and Johnson assumes some surprising positions. Boswell continues: "In the afternoon the gentlewoman talked violently against the Roman Catholicks, and of the horrours of the Inquisition. To the utter astonishment of all the passengers but myself, who knew that he could talk upon any side of a question, he defended the Inquisition, and maintained, that 'false doctrine should be checked on its first appearance; that the civil power should unite with the church in punishing those who dared to attack the established religion, and that such only were punished by the Inquisition.' He had in his pocket, *'Pomponius Mela de situ Orbis,'* in which he read occasionally, and seemed very intent upon ancient geography."[28] Then, according to Boswell, Johnson reproved him for overtipping the coachman by sixpence, and the conversation turned to other matters. No other biographer can supersede Boswell in the detailed account he gives of 5 August 1763. Nevertheless, the account deserves some scrutiny. Often in the *Life* Boswell mentions Johnson's ability to argue both sides of a question, but he never again mentions *Pomponius Mela de situ Orbis*. Since Boswell was not a learned man, in eighteenth-century terms, perhaps there is no reason to expect that he should have gone further into Johnson's reading. The very manner in which he cites the work, in italics within quotation marks, suggests that he was unfamiliar with Pomponius Mela.

[28]*Life*, I, 464–65.

Johnson's interest in ancient geography, then, something which his many biographers practically never mention, is obviously remarkable, especially since Pomponius Mela is a *minor* geographer, a figure of far less prominence than the classical geographers like Eratosthenes and Strabo, whom we would have expected him to know well. Boswell ignores the significance of the choice of Johnson's reading matter here; this pattern is usual with him and he repeats it on many other occasions. Neither Boswell nor the other eighteenth-century biographers ever paid any attention to the only unshakeable fact about an occasion with Johnson present—his reading. Witnesses can—and frequently do—misreport conversations; Boswell himself often changes Johnson's conversations to suit what he considered the mood of an occasion. But he never tried to ascertain what accounted for Johnson's interest in a work so curious that he himself, at the age of twenty-three, was most unlikely to have read or even to have heard mentioned before.

Why should Johnson have been reading the small work of a minor first-century Roman geographer or, more properly, cosmographer? As an author and an observer, Pomponius Mela is far inferior to Eratosthenes and Strabo; he has few of the engaging conversational and narrative qualities of Pliny and the Roman historians. Perhaps, as Thomas Curley has suggested, Johnson was merely reading Mela for his amusement.[29] If Boswell had been interested in ancient geography—he was not—he might have been able to say more about Johnson's pocket companion on this memorable journey. Clearly Johnson was not reading Mela's little book because of any relevance that it might have to Boswell's forthcoming journey to Holland—the ancient geographers are weak on northern Europe, and Mela is particularly deficient on the area. Yet it seems most unlikely that he was reading so closely—he "seemed very intent," Boswell says, on the book—Mela's highly inaccurate account of the then known world for his amusement on a long coach ride.

There is, however, a much clearer explanation. Johnson took along a small—undoubtedly duodecimo—copy of Mela to read in the stage coach because the book was decidedly relevant to his

[29]*Samuel Johnson and the Age of Travel* (Athens, Ga., 1976), p. 52.)

edition of Shakespeare, which he was actively preparing in 1763. Shakespeare's Roman plays require a knowledge by their editor of the ancient world's geography, and we know that, by summer 1763, Johnson was coming to an end of his annotation of the Roman plays.[30] We know that Johnson had boldly promised Dr. Burney in March 1758 that he would publish his edition "before summer," but that was the last promise he had dared to make, and we may recall Churchill's taunt—in *The Ghost* (1762)—about his dilatoriness in satisfying his subscribers.[31] Mela is quite a fanciful writer, in the manner of ancient geographers and chroniclers. He has a great deal to say about the lands that abut on the Mediterranean, but he weakens badly the further inland he goes. Hence Mela says that the Scythians have strange customs; curious beasts reside in Asia; Africa is populated inland by anthropophagi, who devour each other, and by griffons, which devour any gold that happens to be around. But Mela, who wrote in Latin rather than in the Greek of his predecessors, is the chief Roman authority on geography about the time that Shakespeare's Roman plays would have taken place, so it must have made sense for Johnson to read him, although he nowhere cites Mela in the notes to the Roman plays in his edition of Shakespeare. The episode in the Harwich coach, then, shows, as do some of the allusions in *The Rambler* to his labors on the *Dictionary*, that Johnson's scholarly, editorial, and other literary concerns were so intimate a part of his life that he carried his work around with him.

4

I have confined myself to a single example from Boswell but, although he seldom cites the subject of Johnson's reading in such specific terms as he does in his account of 5 August 1763, other such references would serve equally well to illustrate my point that we can learn much that is new about Johnson's life from a closer study of

[30]See *Works*, VII, xxiii. Arthur Sherbo notes that evidence about the stages of Johnson's progress on his edition is "scarce and indecisive," but we do know that Johnson worked on the last plays in his edition, which include the Roman plays, in the late spring and summer of 1763, at the very time of his journey to Harwich.

[31]Boswell quotes from Churchill's *The Ghost* (1762)—see *Life*, I, 319–20—but assigns this anecdote to 1756.

his reading. Boswell seldom, if ever, follows up such hints, and most of Johnson's biographers have followed his example. Think of the opportunity Boswell had on the first occasion that he visited Johnson at Bolt Court (24 May 1763), when Johnson recommends "to every man whose faith is yet unsettled" the works of Grotius, John Pearson, and Samuel Clarke.[32] We now know, thanks to James Gray's study of Johnson's sermons, how important Samuel Clarke was to the development of Johnson's religious thought, but, from Boswell forward, nobody has bothered to ascertain why Johnson should praise Grotius and Pearson so extravagantly and should bracket them with Clarke.[33] A twentieth-century biographer—someone of the stature of Richard Ellmann on Yeats or Joyce or Martin Gilbert on Churchill—would doubtless pursue such important evidence, but Boswell, curious about Johnson's opinions rather than about the *formation* of those opinions, does not. We must not censure Boswell too severely for such oversights, since in the context of emerging eighteenth-century biography, they are not so much oversights as they are expected characteristics of the genre as it then existed.

In *The Rambler*, examples of untraced allusions to authors Johnson read are numerous and, as we study them further, we will no doubt arrive at a better idea of his intellectual biography in the early 1750s. *The Rambler* is also a work of the 1730s and '40s, for it relates closely to Johnson's early years in London, to his journalistic activities, to the wide and curious reading that he undertook in relation both to them and to such chores as library cataloguing, lexicography, and editing, and to his early circle of friends and acquaintances. Hence the focus on Johnson's life that we may obtain from *The Rambler* is not, after all, limited just to the years of its composition. For instance, his many references to the ephemera of learning (Nos. 106, 145, and 177) must look back at least a decade to the period when he was cataloguing the vast collection of printed ephemera in the Harleian Library. Some of the characters he recalls in his feigned letters to *The Rambler* also must recall his many acquaintances over nearly fifteen years of London life. The portrait

---

[32]*Life*, I, 398.
[33]See James Gray, *Johnson's Sermons: A Study* (Oxford, 1972), pp. 65–92.

of Hirsutus, the indefatigable collector of incunabula and books in black letter in *Rambler* 177, seems to be modeled on Michael Maittaire, the historian of early printing (*Annales Typographici* [1717]) with whom he worked on the Harleian catalogue, and the characters of certain antiquarians are probably modeled on Gerard Langbaine and William Oldys, whom he also knew from his first years in London.

It should now be possible to consider reversing the familiar trend in Johnsonian studies that I discussed at the beginning of this essay. We need not study Johnson principally in terms of his personal relationships. So to conclude, let me recapitulate my beginning in somewhat different terms. Johnson and Bacon. Johnson and Boileau. Johnson and Clarendon. Johnson and Crashaw. Johnson and Erasmus. Johnson and Grotius. Johnson and Richard Knolles. Johnson and Langbaine. Johnson and Le Clerc. Johnson and Locke. Johnson and Maittaire. Johnson and More. Johnson and Politian. Johnson and Pomponius Mela. Johnson and Pontanus. Johnson and Sir Walter Raleigh. Johnson and Vida. Johnson and . . .

The Biographer as Advocate

Boswell and the
"Supper of Larks" Case

JOHN RIELY

B OSWELL'S "ANIMADVERSIONS" ON MRS. PIOZZI TOWARD THE END
of the *Life of Johnson* are the climax of his attempts to impugn
her authority as a rival biographer.[1] From a purely artistic stand-
point the "animadversions" were a mistake, for they conspicuously
interrupt Boswell's narrative of Johnson's last months. Many
admirers of the *Life* have regretted that he felt "obliged" to attack
Mrs. Piozzi's *Anecdotes of Johnson* at such length. But the "animadversions" do provide the opportunity for a revealing look at certain
aspects of Boswell's practice as a biographer. A few years ago, in
an illuminating analysis of Boswell's revisions of the "animadversions" in the manuscript of the *Life*, Irma Lustig convincingly demonstrated his "prime responsibility for the final text" even though
he made use of information and advice from his friends John Courtenay and Edmond Malone.[2] I wish to examine in greater detail
the concluding anecdote that Boswell held up for censure and to
provide new evidence concerning its circumstances and the reporting of those circumstances by Boswell and others. Here as elsewhere
in the "animadversions" we see Boswell's professional training as
a Scots advocate dictating his procedure and shaping his case against
his literary rival.

I should like to thank Irma S. Lustig, Marshall Waingrow, and Peter S. Baker,
of the Yale Editions of the Private Papers of James Boswell, for generous advice
and assistance in the preparation of this essay.

[1] *Boswell's Life of Johnson*, ed. G. B. Hill, rev. L. F. Powell, 6 vols. (Oxford, 1934–
64), IV, 339–47.

[2] "Boswell at Work: The 'Animadversions' on Mrs. Piozzi," *Modern Language
Review*, 67 (1972), 11–30.

After Mrs. Piozzi published her *Letters to and from the late Samuel Johnson* in 1788, Boswell had a personal grievance to redress, for the letters contained slighting references to him. But the ostensible reason for his attack on her in the *Life* was the alleged inaccuracy of various stories of Johnson related in her *Anecdotes*. Her frequent "incorrectness . . . as to particulars," he feared, was likely to produce a "mistaken notion of Dr. Johnson's character." He therefore considered it his "duty, as a faithful biographer," to expose her inaccuracies.[3] Boswell's own attention to "minute particulars," which he "spared no pains to ascertain with a scrupulous authenticity," is familiar to every reader of the *Life*.[4] In his concern to get at the truth, whether it was a matter of fixing a date or of determining the exact circumstances of an event, Boswell the biographer may be said to have assumed the role of a judge. When he could not speak from his own knowledge of an event, he listened to the testimony of all available witnesses, tested their credibility, weighed any other evidence that had come to light, and only then arrived at a decision as to what had actually been said or done. Such is Boswell's usual modus operandi in the *Life*. But in the "animadversions" it is otherwise: Boswell abandoned his role as a judge and renewed his vocation as an advocate.

Mrs. Piozzi's *Anecdotes* was published on 25 March 1786. Boswell was away from London at the time, having gone on the Northern Circuit to try his mettle as a new member of the English bar. He received a copy of the book, forwarded to him by Malone, at Lancaster on the thirtieth and immediately "devoured" it. His first reactions were set down in a letter written to Malone the next day. The book, he admitted, "has a great deal of valuable memorabilia, which prove themselves genuine. But there is seldom the true *zest*. She puts cherries in the brandy." And he mentioned several anecdotes whose accuracy he had reason to doubt, among them an instance of Johnson's "roughness" in conversation. "The story of spitting her relations is I suppose exagerated" he told Malone, "or she must have provoked him confoundedly by *affectation* of grief."[5]

[3]*Life*, IV, 343, 340, 347.
[4]Ibid., I, 6–7 (Advertisement to the first edition of the *Life*).
[5]Boswell to Malone, 31 March 1786, Boswell Papers L 934, Yale University Library; quoted in *The Correspondence and Other Papers of James Boswell Relating to the Making of the Life of Johnson*, ed. Marshall Waingrow (New York, 1969), p. 143.

Here is the story as Boswell read it in the *Anecdotes:* "When I one day lamented the loss of a first cousin killed in America— 'Prithee, my dear (said he), have done with canting: how would the world be worse for it, I may ask, if all your relations were at once spitted like larks, and roasted for Presto's supper?' Presto was the dog that lay under the table while we talked."[6] In the *Life*, published five years later in May 1791, Boswell pointed out that "the evident tendency of the . . . anecdote is to represent Dr. Johnson as extremely deficient in affection, tenderness, or even common civility." He suspected Mrs. Piozzi's version of "exaggeration and distortion. I allow that he made her an angry speech; but let the circumstances fairly appear, as told by Mr. Baretti, who was present: "Mrs. Thrale, while supping very heartily upon larks, laid down her knife and fork, and abruptly exclaimed, 'O, my dear Mr. Johnson, do you know what has happened? The last letters from abroad have brought us an account that our poor cousin's head was taken off by a cannon-ball.' Johnson, who was shocked both at the fact, and her light unfeeling manner of mentioning it, replied, 'Madam, it would give *you* very little concern if all your relations were spitted like those larks, and drest for Presto's supper.' "[7] How did Boswell manage to obtain this account from Giuseppe Baretti, with whom he was never on friendly terms? Clearly he had no such information in March 1786 when writing to Malone—a letter that shows his annoyance at Mrs. Piozzi's book.

Malone felt more strongly than Boswell about the distortions and inaccuracies in the *Anecdotes*, as his letters to Boswell of 25 and 27 March 1786 reveal.[8] At this time, or possibly at a later date, he wrote in his copy of the book next to the "supper of larks" anecdote: "This story basely misrepresented for the purpose of calumniating Johnson and throwing a gloss on her own insensibility."[9] Referring

[6]*Anecdotes of the late Samuel Johnson, LL.D.* (London, 1786), p. 63; reprinted in *Johnsonian Miscellanies*, ed. G. B. Hill (Oxford, 1897), I, 189–90.

[7]*Life*, IV, 347.

[8]Boswell Papers C 1906, C 1907. See Waingrow, pp. 140–41.

[9]Malone's copy of the *Anecdotes* (formerly owned by F. F. Urquhart of Balliol College, Oxford; present whereabouts unknown) is filled with marginal comments that attest to the virulence of his dislike for Mrs. Piozzi. I am indebted to the late James M. Osborn for making available to me a transcript of Malone's marginalia. Some of his annotations were apparently made after the publication of Boswell's *Life* in 1791.

to another passage in the book, Malone made the following comment in his own collection of anecdotes (later published as *Maloniana*): "Mrs. Thrale has caught something of this story and marred it in the telling, as she has many other of her anecdotes of the Doctor just now published. On the whole, however, the publick is indebted to her for her lively, though very inaccurate and artful, account of Dr. Johnson."[10] Writing again to Boswell on 7 April, Malone said that he was thinking of sending some "strictures" on her book to the *Gentleman's Magazine* for its next number.[11]

No "strictures" by Malone appeared in the *Gentleman's Magazine* for April 1786 (published on 1 May). But the newspapers were filled with notices concerning Johnson's biographers, including three items (two anonymous) contributed by Boswell himself.[12] As he was in London at the time, he could not have failed to see an unsigned letter that was printed in the *St. James's Chronicle* of 6–9 May 1786:

Mr. Baldwin.

How much Injury the Character of Dr. Johnson has sustained through imperfect Recollection, and unfair Separation of his Sayings from their Context (I mean the Circumstances that gave Birth to them) the following Instance may serve to show.

Mrs. Piozzi tells us (Page 63) "When I one Day lamented the Loss of a first Cousin killed in America—Prithee, my dear, said the Doctor, have done with canting: How would the World be worse for it, I may ask, if all your Relations were at once spitted like Larks,

---

[10]Sir James Prior, *Life of Edmond Malone . . . With Selections from his Manuscript Anecdotes* (London, 1860), p. 364. Malone grew more violent on the subject of Mrs. Piozzi in following years. A later entry in *Maloniana*, *sub* 9 August [1791], refers to her as "that despicable woman Mrs. Piozzi" and concludes: "She was careless about truth, and therefore not to be trusted" (pp. 412–13). But the roots of Malone's enmity towards Mrs. Piozzi surely go deeper than this. He probably felt that she had selfishly rejected Johnson during his last years, and his reverence for Johnson would not tolerate any such disloyalty on her part.

[11]Malone to Boswell 7 April 1786, Boswell Papers C 1908.

[12]For details of these pieces see Mary Hyde, *The Impossible Friendship: Boswell and Mrs. Thrale* (Cambridge, Mass., 1972), pp. 111–13. Boswell's own file of marked cuttings from newspapers and periodicals is preserved with his papers at Yale; it enables us to identify with certainty most of his anonymous contributions.

and roasted for Presto's Supper? Presto was the Dog that lay under the Table while we talked."

Mrs. Piozzi, however, should have registered the Words of Johnson with greater Exactness. She should also have informed her Readers, that this seemingly rude Reply was made while she was at Dinner, eating Larks; and that she had uttered her lamentable News with such a Smile on her Face, as evidently proved the Loss of her Relation was an Object of no real Grief to her. As the Doctor observed this Contradiction between her Looks and her Tongue, his Answer was a proper one, and characteristic of his blunt Sincerity.—"Prithee, my dear, have done with canting: *you would not care* if all your Relations were at once spitted, like *these* Larks, and roasted &c."— Dr. Johnson meant a Satire on one who relates a tragic Incident with such a cheerful Look, as proves her Story to have made no serious Impression on her own Mind.

———*Si vis me flere, dolendum est*
Primum ipsi tibi.

I received my Narrative, Mr. Baldwin, from a Person of undoubted Veracity and tenacious Memory, who was at Table when Dr. Johnson produced the Remark which our very accomplished Authoress has not exhibited with her usual Accuracy and Candour.

I may probably, Sir, trespass further on the St. James's Chronicle, by requesting Room in it for Strictures on such other Portions of Mrs. Piozzi's Book, as seem liable to similar Animadversion.

I am, Sir,
Your very obedient Servant &c.

Who was the *Chronicle*'s anonymous correspondent? Unfortunately, there is no conclusive evidence. The eyewitness described as "a Person of undoubted Veracity and tenacious Memory" was surely Baretti. Mrs. Piozzi, as we shall see, never denied that he was present on this occasion. But it does not seem possible that Baretti wrote the letter: its style and tone are not in the least characteristic, and he would not have felt the need to adopt a disguise. A more likely candidate is Malone, who respected Baretti's abilities as a scholar and probably believed him to be "a Person of undoubted Veracity and tenacious Memory." The precise yet animated phrasing of the letter is not un-Malonian. But could Malone have allowed himself to refer to Mrs. Piozzi as a "very accomplished Authoress" noted for "her usual Accuracy and Candour"? Probably not, unless he was being sarcastic, and in context the statement does not seem intended to be sarcastic. Another possible candidate is John Courtenay, the witty member of Parliament who only a month before had published his *Poetical Review* of Johnson.[13] An intimate friend of Boswell and Malone, Courtenay was acquainted with Baretti and might have recently heard the story from him. The correspondent need not, of course, have had any connection with Boswell or his friends. Whoever it was that wrote the letter, he confirmed Boswell's suspicion that Mrs. Piozzi had provoked Johnson by her "*affectation* of grief." Her version of the story had omitted this as well as other material circumstances.

Some of the circumstances of the incident can be verified with reasonable certainty. To begin with, it is possible to identify Mrs. Piozzi's "first cousin killed in America." He was not, as Arthur Sherbo has speculated, Thomas Cotton but rather his brother Richard.[14] Thomas and Richard Cotton were younger sons of Sir Lynch Salusbury Cotton, 4th Bt., Mrs. Piozzi's uncle. Richard Cotton, a captain in the 33rd Regiment of Foot (Cornwallis's regiment), died from the wounds he suffered in the Battle of Camden, which took place on 16 August 1780.[15] I have been unable to discover the exact date of his death, but more important for our purpose is Mrs. Thrale's announcement, in her letter to Fanny Burney of 3 February 1781, that "poor Richard Cotton is dead of the Wounds he got in

[13]Courtenay's *A Poetical Review of the Literary and Moral Character of the late Samuel Johnson, LL.D. with Notes* was published on 6 April 1786 (*Morning Herald* 6 April 1786).

[14]Sherbo, in his edition of Mrs. Piozzi's *Anecdotes* (London, 1974), p. 179, identifies the cousin as "probably Thomas Cotton, but I cannot discover how he died." Thomas Cotton, the fourth son of Sir Lynch Salusbury Cotton, died in 1820.

[15]The *Daily Advertiser*, 11 Oct. 1780, prints the official "Return of the Killed, Wounded, and Missing, of the Troops under the Command of Lieutenant-General Earl Cornwallis, in the Battle fought near Camden, South Carolina, on the 16th of August, 1780," enclosed in Cornwallis's letter of 21 August to Lord George Germain. Capt. Richard Cotton of the 33rd Regiment is listed as "wounded." On 3 Jan. 1781 Cornwallis wrote to General Clinton, the commander in chief in North America, "recommending to vacancies occasioned by the death of Capt. Cotton of the 33d Regt." (Historical Manuscripts Commission, *Report on American Manuscripts in the Royal Institution of Great Britain* [London, 1904–9], II, 232).

the battle of Cambden about two or three Months ago."[16] It is clear from the letter that she had just learned the news. The "supper of larks" incident must have occurred not long after 3 February, while the news was still fresh, and almost certainly before Henry Thrale's death on 4 April of that year. The Thrales were then occupying a house in Grosvenor Square that they had rented for the winter season. Baretti was by no means a frequent guest in Grosvenor Square, having given up his regular employment in the Thrale household (as a language teacher to their eldest daughter) nearly five years earlier. Thus the fact that he came to dinner at the Thrales' with Johnson and Sir Philip Jennings Clerke on 2 April may be significant. Mrs. Thrale mentioned the dinner in her diary, *Thraliana*, but the only conversation that she recorded concerned Thrale's dangerous overeating.[17] This may well have been the occasion of Johnson's outburst, although we cannot prove it.

According to Baretti's account, as quoted by Boswell, Mrs. Thrale was "supping very heartily upon larks." These were circumstances that Mrs. Piozzi vigorously denied. Two copies of the *Life of Johnson* formerly owned by her—one a copy of the fifth edition (1807), the other a copy of the eighth edition (1816)—have survived and are filled with her marginal annotations.[18] In her 1807 copy she wrote: "Mrs. Thrale never *saw* a Supper in those Days, never eat a Lark for Supper in England." And in her 1816 copy she repeated the denial: "I never did eat any Supper: —&there were no Larks to eat. . . . nor was ever a *hot dish* seen on the Table after Dinner at

---

[16]Unpublished MS in the James Marshall and Marie-Louise Osborn Collection, Yale University Library, quoted by kind permission of the Curator, Dr. Stephen Parks. Richard Cotton was only one of many first cousins of Mrs. Thrale in the Cotton family; she is not known to have had any special fondness for him.

[17]"On Monday [2 April 1781] . . . Sir Phillip and Dr Johnson [came] to Dinner—so did Baretti: Mr Thrale eat voraciously . . . Baretti and them two spent the Evening with me" (*Thraliana: The Diary of Mrs. Hester Lynch Thrale (Later Mrs. Piozzi) 1776–1809*, ed. Katharine C. Balderston, 2d ed. [Oxford, 1951], I, 488). The "supper of larks" episode is nowhere mentioned in *Thraliana*.

[18]The marginalia have been published in a special edition of the *Life*, ed. Edward G. Fletcher, 3 vols. (London, 1938; rpt. New York, 1963). Mrs. Piozzi's copy of the 1807 edition is in the Hyde Collection, Somerville, New Jersey; her copy of the 1816 edition is in the Houghton Library at Harvard. She owned a copy of the first edition, but it has not been traced.

Streatham Park." In the latter annotation Mrs. Piozzi implies that the incident took place at Streatham, the Thrales' country estate in Surrey. Writing some thirty-five years after the event, she could easily have forgotten at which of her houses the episode occurred. But the domestic routine of "those days" (that is, before Henry Thrale's death) was fixed in her memory. Moreover, her recollection is corroborated by Boswell's own observation. He noted in his journal entry for 28 March 1775: "Mr. Thrale [meaning the Thrale family] has no supper, as he dines at five."[19]

In view of Mrs. Piozzi's disclaimers, it is worthwhile investigating how Boswell secured the testimony of Baretti. The manuscript of the *Life*, which exhibits all the stages of Boswell's composition from rough draft to printer's copy, contains some complex but extremely interesting evidence. The rough draft of the "animadversions," including the "supper of larks" anecdote, was written in December 1788 or January 1789.[20] After quoting the passage from Mrs. Piozzi's *Anecdotes*, Boswell said he did not deny that Johnson had made her an angry speech. "But let the circumstances fairly appear as related by a gentleman who was present. She it seems was whining and pretending to great concern about the death of a cousin ⟨of Mr Thrales *inserted above the line*⟩ with whom it does not appear that she had any freindship. There were a dozen of larks for supper, and while she was talking of her great sensibility on this melancholy occasion she continued devouring the larks. When she was got to the seventh or eigth, Dr. Johnson was so provoked with her affectation, that in his haste he called out it would be no great matter ⟨meaning no doubt to *her*⟩ if all her relations were spitted like *those* larks she was eating and given to Presto for his supper."[21] Boswell

[19]*Boswell: The Ominous Years 1774–1776*, ed. Charles Ryskamp and Frederick A. Pottle (New York, 1963), p. 106.

[20]Writing to Sir William Forbes on 12 Dec. 1788, Boswell reports that he has reached June 1784 in the *Life* (the "animadversions" immediately follow a paragraph dealing with events of 1 July 1784). His letter to W. J. Temple of 10 Jan. 1789 mentions that he is "very near the conclusion of my rough draught of Johnson's *Life*" (Waingrow, pp. 282, 285).

[21]Boswell Papers, MS of the *Life of Johnson*, p. 997. This unpublished passage from the MS and that cited in n. 27 below are quoted by kind permission of Yale University and the McGraw-Hill Book Company.

went on to relate, without a break in the paragraph, a similar anecdote that his friend John Wilkes had told him after hearing the "supper of larks" story.

As Lustig has pointed out, the version of the story in Boswell's rough draft is rather flatly presented in indirect discourse. Although it strains for ironic contrast, the effect is unclimactic. It is clearly intended to bias: Mrs. Thrale is described as "whining and pretending to great concern"; Johnson is "provoked with her affectation."[22] Boswell gives the impression of having detailed knowledge ("a cousin of Mr Thrales," "a dozen of larks for supper") while at the same time he is noticeably vague ("it seems," "it does not appear that"). One feels that he is retelling the story from memory rather than from any written account. He must have known about the letter in the *St. James's Chronicle*, but it could not have been his only source of information, for the draft version contains details not mentioned in the letter. On the other hand, there are important similarities. In both the letter and the draft the informant remains anonymous ("a Person . . . who was at Table" vs. "a gentleman who was present"); and Johnson's retort is essentially the same in both ("*you would not care* if all your Relations were at once spitted, like *these* Larks" vs. "it would be no great matter (meaning no doubt to *her*) if all her relations were spitted like *those* larks").

So the story stood in the rough draft of the *Life* until after 5 April 1789. On that date, exactly a month before he died, Baretti dined at Courtenay's. Malone was also there and heard Baretti tell a number of stories of Johnson.[23] He recorded some of Baretti's stories in *Maloniana*, and there we find the following account of the "supper of larks":

> Mrs. Thrale has grossly misrepresented the story which she has told of Dr. Johnson's saying a harsh thing to her at table (*see* her *Anecdotes*). The fact was this. A Mr. Thrale, related to Mr. Thrale, Johnson's friend, for whom they both had a great regard, had gone some time before to the East or West Indies. Dr. Johnson had not yet heard

[22]Lustig, pp. 17, 22.
[23]See Lacy Collison-Morley, *Giuseppe Baretti. With an Account of his Literary Friendships and Feuds in Italy and in England in the Days of Dr. Johnson* (London, 1909), p. 349. At least one of the stories of Johnson told by Baretti at Courtenay's is demonstrably inaccurate (ibid., p. 87).

of his fate; and Mrs. Thrale very abruptly while she was eating some larks most ravenously, laid down her knife and fork—"Oh dear, Dr. Johnson, do you know what has happened? The last letters from abroad have brought us an account that poor Tom Thrale's head was taken off by a cannon ball in the action of———." Johnson, who was shocked both at the fact and at her gross manner of telling it, replied—"Madam, it would give you very little concern if all your relations were spitted like those larks, and dressed for Presto's supper." Presto was the dog which lay under the table, and which Mrs. Thrale was feeding just as she mentioned the death of Mr. Thrale's cousin.[24]

Here the story is told dramatically using action, dialogue, and background details.

Malone evidently passed on his *written* account to Boswell sometime before leaving for Ireland in mid-November of 1790. Although Boswell had long disliked and distrusted Baretti, he accepted Baretti's testimony—coming as it did by way of Malone, whose judgment he regularly relied on. Boswell then canceled what he had written in his rough draft and substituted a new version that closely follows the *Maloniana* account. The substitution may not have been made until 22 February 1791, when Courtenay (in Malone's absence) assisted Boswell in "lightening" the "animadversions" on Mrs. Piozzi for his own credit.[25] But since Boswell could have made this particular revision easily enough without Courtenay's help, it is possible that he did so by himself soon after receiving the written account from Malone.[26] Still keeping his informant anonymous, Boswell wrote:

[24]Prior's *Life of Malone*, p. 398. Although Malone does not name Baretti as his source, the next entry in *Maloniana* records another anecdote of Johnson that Baretti told Malone "as I walked home with him from Mr. Courtenay's" (ibid., p. 399). The entry immediately preceding the "supper of larks" is dated 2 June 1789.

[25]*Private Papers of James Boswell from Malahide Castle in the Collection of Lt-Colonel Ralph Heyward Isham*, ed. Geoffrey Scott and Frederick A. Pottle (New York, 1928–34), XVIII, 109.

[26]Lustig (pp. 21–22) suggests that the "supper of larks" anecdote was revised in Courtenay's presence, but she now thinks (as she informs me) that this and other revisions in pp. 987–99 of the "animadversions" may have been accomplished by Boswell alone. Once the "radical surgery" on the first five pages (982–86) had been performed with Courtenay's help, the pattern and tone of the

A relation not of hers but of Mr. Thrales, for whom both Thrale and Johnson had a regard had been ordered with his regiment to America where he had been killed in battel. Dr. Johnson had not yet heard of his fate and Mrs. Thrale while she was supping very heartily upon larks, laid down her knife & fork and abruptly exclaimed "O dear Mr. Johnson do you know what has happened. The last letters from abroad have brought us an account that our poor cousin's head was taken off by a cannon ball." Johnson who was shocked both at the fact & her unfeeling manner of telling it replied "Madam it would give *you* very little concern if all ⟨those *deleted*⟩ your relations were spitted like those larks, and drest for Presto's supper."[27]

Wilkes's parallel anecdote, which had immediately followed in the text, was relegated to a footnote. It was this new version of the "supper of larks," along with the rest of the heavily revised "animadversions," that went to the printer.

If we compare Boswell's revised version with the *Maloniana* account from which it was derived, we do find some variations. According to *Maloniana*, Thrale's relation "had gone some time before to the East or West Indies" and was killed "in the action of ———," but Boswell says that he "had been ordered with his regiment to America where he had been killed in battel." Boswell never refers to "Tom Thrale" by name. In *Maloniana* Mrs. Thrale is actually feeding the dog, Presto. And whereas the *St. James's Chronicle* letter stated that Mrs. Thrale was "at Dinner" and *Maloniana* simply mentions "eating," Boswell (in both his rough draft and the revised version) has her "supping."[28]

Boswell's reasons for departing from the written account that Malone gave him cannot be fully known. But his final revision, made when correcting the proofs of this section in late February 1791, suggests that all along he lacked confirmation of certain

revisions were set and Boswell could have proceeded on his own with the rest. He had in fact undertaken some "intermediate revision" before having the session with Courtenay (ibid., pp. 18–19).

[27]MS of the *Life of Johnson*, p. 996v.

[28]Lustig comments on this last discrepancy: " 'Supping' was Boswell's own inference from Johnson's angry reference to Presto's supper. It was a very natural inference, but on Boswell's own principles inadmissable unless he could assure himself that it was circumstantially accurate. It probably did not occur to him, however, that his change was more than stylistic" (p. 22, n. 2).

points.[29] There he struck out the entire first sentence, in which the unfortunate cousin, identified (incorrectly) as a "relation not of hers but of Mr. Thrales," was said (correctly) to have been "ordered with his regiment to America." Boswell apparently did not know for certain who the relation was; he probably deleted the sentence because he could not verify its accuracy. Another change involved Mrs. Thrale's manner of addressing Johnson. Boswell's manuscript reads "O dear Mr. Johnson" (*Maloniana* had "Oh dear, Dr. Johnson"), but the revise has "O, my dear Mr. Johnson." Boswell must have inserted "my" in proof, and he allowed it to stand. This drew another protest from Mrs. Piozzi. "I never address'd him so familiarly *in my Life*," she insisted in her 1816 copy of the biography, and her 1807 copy contains a similar disavowal.

The only other significant change made in proof was the naming of Baretti as the "gentleman who was present." By identifying his informant here, Boswell offset a loss of documentation earlier in the "animadversions," where he had suppressed the fact that Malone was the "eminent critick" who furnished him with two other "instances of [Mrs. Piozzi's] inaccuracy." As a lawyer, Boswell knew that a named source was more likely to be credited than an anonymous one. Lustig has observed that "he sought to speak with citable authority."[30] But his authority in this case was certainly a dubious one: a man who was not noted for truthfulness and whose violent hatred of Mrs. Piozzi had been vented publicly in three long articles printed in the *European Magazine* in 1788.[31] Baretti's abusive

---

[29]The first proofs of the "animadversions" have not been recovered, but Boswell's corrections can be deduced by comparing the manuscript (i.e., printer's copy) with the revises, which are now in the Hyde Collection. I am grateful to Mrs. Donald F. Hyde for providing me with a microfilm of the revises.

[30]Lustig, p. 25.

[31]"On Signora Piozzi's Publication of Dr. Johnson's Letters," *European Magazine*, 13 (1788), 313–17, 393–99; 14 (1788), 89–99. In his third "Stricture" Baretti wrote (p. 90): "So numerous are the cunning misrepresentations and the downright falsehoods disgraceful to Dr. Johnson in that book of Anecdotes, that no small quantity of paper and patience will be required to rectify and confute them all." But, interestingly enough, Baretti raised no objection to the "supper of larks" anecdote. Malone's satisfaction with Baretti's diatribes on Mrs. Piozzi is expressed in a letter to Boswell of 17 June 1788: "Baretti's *Strictures* in the European on the 1st of this month were very good; more temperate than usual; and prove decisively that Esther Lynch is a sad jade" (Boswell Papers C 1914).

"Strictures" were filled with false charges and fabrications. As Mrs. Piozzi herself expressed it in her 1816 copy of the *Life*, "Boswell appealing to Baretti for a Testimony of the *Truth* is comical enough." Boswell never revealed the fact that Baretti's account came to him at third hand via Malone: it was hearsay evidence, and Boswell's legal training had taught him that such evidence must be avoided. By concealing Malone's role as an intermediary, he could in effect produce Baretti as a witness and ask that he be allowed to tell his story. Baretti's testimony as printed in the *Life* is entirely enclosed within quotation marks (omitted here). The reader has no way of knowing that the testimony is hearsay evidence that was edited and revised by Boswell on more than one occasion.

Boswell's handling of the "supper of larks" case is consistent with his strategy in the rest of the "animadversions," but in one important respect it runs contrary to his usual practice as a biographer. I have already characterized the difference as a shift from a judicial to an advocatory role that occurs when Boswell begins to plead this cause "in behalf of [his] illustrious friend." He argued that Mrs. Piozzi's *Anecdotes* "must not be held as good evidence against [Johnson]," but at the same time he was willing to present evidence against her that, by his own standard of "perfect authenticity," should have been rejected as untrustworthy.[32] As one scholar has concluded, "Boswell thus erred in accepting such a story from a known enemy of the lady. Although usually he checked carefully, this time his own desire to get back at Mrs. Piozzi led him to accept dubious evidence."[33] Or to put it another way, Boswell was for once less interested in getting at the truth than in demolishing his rival. This is not to say that he had ceased to be concerned about circumstantial accuracy or "minute particulars," but only that as a biographer he was human.

[32]*Life*, IV, 346.
[33]James L. Clifford, *From Puzzles to Portraits: Problems of a Literary Biographer* (Chapel Hill, N.C., 1970), p. 78. It remains to be said that some of the disputed circumstances of the episode can probably never be verified, and here we have only Baretti's word against Mrs. Piozzi's.

Disaffection of the
Dissenters under George III

DONALD DAVIE

THE LAST FORTY YEARS OF THE EIGHTEENTH CENTURY HAVE through recent decades attracted disproportionate attention from political historians—disproportionate, yet very natural. For this was the period that saw the political severance of most of the English speakers of North America from Great Britain, and there is every reason why Americans and Britons alike should continue to ask themselves why and how this momentous and drastic surgery came about, to ask even if it could have been avoided. Moreover, this period saw some crucial stages in that amorphous but even more momentous development that we call the Industrial Revolution; a social transformation the strain of which, experienced by the British sooner than by any other nation, more than once brought Britain to the brink of a political revolution that nevertheless never quite happened. For these reasons, not to mention others that might be cited, changes in the historical understanding of these decades inevitably and properly continue to inflame passions in the here and now. An American's sense of his own national identity or of the rectitude of his citizenship is in some degree at risk in any retelling of the War of Independence, in any attempt for instance to correct the long-established view of the part played at that time by the king of England. As Edmund S. Morgan remarked more than twenty years ago, "The righteousness of the Americans is somewhat diminished through the loss of the principal villain of the piece [George III] . . . no longer the foe of liberty seeking to subvert the British constitution, but an earnest and responsible monarch."[1] And, on the other hand, a British patriot of today, if

---

[1] See Edmund S. Morgan, *William and Mary Quarterly*, 3d ser., 14 (1957), 3–15. Quoted by Ian R. Christie, *Myth and Reality in Late Eighteenth-Century British Politics* (Berkeley and Los Angeles, 1970), p. 23.

he thinks of himself as in some sort a radical, cannot examine without emotion the course of events by which the British Revolution that ought to have happened mysteriously didn't. It cannot be a coincidence that this stretch of British history, this bit of the past that may be dead but clearly won't lie down, should have been chosen by Sir Lewis Namier as the test case on which to push through a revolution in the methods of historical research.

When a period has come in for such intense professional attention, the inevitable consequence is that in the interests of rigor studies are narrowed down to specific problems that reveal their complexity only when considered thus minutely. And there is already a formidable body of scholarship of this kind, much of it very impressive. There remain, however, larger, more general questions, and these tend not to get asked because they call for an altogether looser, more sweeping and foolhardy treatment. One such question concerns the role played in this period by the people called at some times Dissenters, at other times Nonconformists, and nowadays for the most part Free Churchmen. That the Dissenters played a crucial role in politics under George III is what nobody denies; yet who they were, these people called Dissenters, is a question at once too large and too rudimentary to get very much attention from those whose analytical skills have been developed to deal with knottier and more sophisticated problems. This broad and obvious question is the one I am concerned with: who *were* the Dissenters under George III? And are we right to lump them together so confidently as we commonly do?

To begin with, the fluctuating nomenclature is itself significant: it causes difficulties, and it raises questions—of which the most troubling and unwelcome to an English Free Churchman of the present day is whether he is, in any more than a formal sense, the heir to the Nonconformists of yesterday and the Dissenters of two hundred years ago; whether in fact his tradition has not in the past suffered breaches and discontinuities papered over by generous sentiment but become really irreparable, so that today's Free Churchman is a wholly different animal from such as Joseph Priestley and Thomas Hollis. To such as Hollis in the 1750s and 1760s this was already a burning question that presented itself in the form of whether he and those who felt like him were truly, in more than a formal sense, the heirs of Milton and Cromwell; and further, if he was such an heir, what actions and sentiments that inheritance compelled him to, in political situations different from those that Milton and Cromwell had contended with. The answer that such as Hollis found, which made them a significant political force in the 1760s and 1770s, is pointed to in the very title of Caroline Robbins's justly well regarded study *The Eighteenth Century Commonwealthman.*[2] That is to say, they decided that their situation under George III and Lord North was not after all significantly different from the situation of their ancestors under Charles I and Strafford. For making this decision they were applauded by some (mostly) Americans in their own day, and have been applauded ever since by those who think, or else expediently affect to think, that the decision was a correct one because grounded in a correct historical analysis. But this is precisely what twentieth-century historians have challenged and may be thought to have disproved: George III was *not* Charles I, neither in private life nor as a politician, despite what Tom Paine pretended; Lord North was *not* Strafford; and accordingly (it may seem to follow) Cromwellian republicanism was *not* a responsible or apposite political position in the England of the 1770s. Indeed, it may be thought that this was proved by events long before twentieth-century historians addressed themselves to the question; as J. H. Plumb has pointed out,[3] the out-and-out republicanism of an Algernon Sidney, as espoused and promulgated by Hollis's protégés such as the Dissenting minister Richard Baron,[4] merely withered away as soon as the differences with the American colonies became a state of war, and more particularly when the American colonists became the allies of Britain's old enemy, France. And this development casts a shadow backwards so as to raise the question whether the republicanism of Hollis or Baron or the diarist Sylas Neville was ever, even in the 1760s, practical politics.[5] Was it ever more than the irresponsible speculation of persons far from the centers where political decisions

[2]Caroline Robbins, *The Eighteenth Century Commonwealthman* (New York, 1959).

[3]J. H. Plumb, "British Attitudes to the American Revolution" (1964), in Plumb, *In the Light of History* (Boston, 1973), pp. 70–87.

[4]For Baron, see *Memoirs of Thomas Hollis* (1780).

[5]*The Diary of Sylas Neville, 1767–1788*, ed. Basil Cozens-Hardy (London, 1950).

were taken? And did the majority of English Dissenters ever regard these republicans as anything more than a lunatic fringe? This question is still debated;[6] but we may certainly suspect that Robbins's "commonwealthmen" have an interest and an importance in the history of political ideas such as they never had in the history of politics. This is to say that very few English Dissenters at any time under George III harbored sentiments and designs that were positively treasonable; few can be said to have been at any time disloyal, though at certain times many of them can be properly described as "disaffected."

And yet even this may be questioned. For who were these people that we are speaking of? James E. Bradley, in an important article,[7] has accused Whig historiographers of "a preoccupation with the dissenting elite," at the expense of the rank-and-file of English Dissenters up and down the country. And this is surely a true bill; historians of all sorts, and especially those of a literary turn, inevitably pay too much attention to the articulate and self-appointed leaders of opinion, without sufficiently considering that their "lead" may not have been followed by the relatively inarticulate fellow citizens whom they addressed. Just here indeed we see one of the entering wedges of the Namierite method of political historiography; and Bradley, by applying that method, has no difficulty proving that in one English borough after another Dissenters were no less "corrupt" than other Englishmen; that the votes of the Dissenting interest were up for sale in a way that was not just time-honored but essential if the eighteenth-century political machine in England was to function at all. Indeed, while still shirking the laborious Namierite discipline of scrutinizing the electoral returns and division lists on crucial votes, in the municipalities as well as at Westminster, we can cite a case where the "country" Dissenters

[6]See Ian R. Christie, *Wilkes, Wyvill and Reform* (London, 1962), p. 15: "Attacks of a fairly traditional and arid kind came from a little group of *soi-disant* republicans: Thomas Hollis of Lincoln's Inn, his cousin, Timothy, Richard Baron, Thomas Brand, and a few others. Their republicanism, based on a high and dry whiggism drawn directly from later seventeenth-century tradition, had little popular appeal." But contrast Plumb, pp. 70–87.

[7]James E. Bradley, "Whigs and Nonconformists: 'Slumbering Radicalism' in English Politics, 1739–89," *Eighteenth-Century Studies*, 9 (1975), 1–27.

quite plainly refused to follow the lead of their metropolitan spokesmen. This was the application to Parliament in 1772 to relieve Church of England clergy from having to subscribe to all the Thirty-Nine Articles and, as regards such subscription, to secure for Dissenters more than the two or three exemptions they enjoyed already. Henry F. May believes that the failure of the initiative "caused some English dissenters to believe in a new conspiracy against Protestant liberty." And no doubt he is right; but he fails to remark that the initiative was ultimately defeated, when it was launched again in 1773, *by the country Dissenters*, for these, still mostly Trinitarian Calvinists, rightly saw that those who sought relief were Dissenters of a Socinian or Arian or Unitarian cast.[8] Dissent was not monolithic; and the most taciturn Calvinist Dissenters would on occasion strike down the liberties sought by their more vociferous brethren, Socinians and Arians.

It may be that on other issues besides this one, for instance on the broad issue of loyalty to the Crown, there was at any time a substantial minority of English Dissenters, if not indeed a majority at times, who go unremarked because they were relatively inarticulate. They did indeed sometimes find articulate spokesmen. But these are hard to discern, perhaps because there were disproportionately few of them, more certainly because it has been in nobody's partisan interest, from their day to ours, to have them remembered. One of them, hardly a spokesman at all except in his immediate circle, seems to have been John Merivale of Exeter, described as "a sturdy conscientious Dissenter of the old school; combining with his dissent an absolute horror of Radicalism and disloyalty."[9] In 1792, when Timothy Kenrick, avowedly Unitarian minister of the Presbyterian George's Meeting in Exeter, had prayed extempore "for the success of people struggling for their liberty" (having in mind specifically, as he admitted, the French), Merivale expostulated in a letter: "It is so utterly repugnant to my Conception of what is right to join in prayers offer'd up to the God of Mercy for the further success of a wretched Faction which has already involv'd a country in a most deplorable state of Anarchy & Distress,—that

[8]Henry F. May, *The Enlightenment in America* (New York, 1976), p. 157.
[9]Anna W. Merivale, *Family Memorials* (Exeter, 1884), p. 129.

I feel myself obliged to seek some other Place of Worship."[10] And Merivale was as good as his word, signally absenting himself and his family thereafter from Kenrick's ministrations. It is not clear, however, whether he carried out his threat "to seek some other Place of Worship." For Kenrick shared the pastorate there with two others, and in his reply to Merivale he explained, "Mr. Tozer, Mr. Manning and myself may publickly pray for the spread of Christianity, altho' we each of us affix different ideas to the phrase— the first meaning by it Trinitarianism, the second Arianism, and the last Unitarianism." This arrangement by which, if he chose, Merivale could still profit by the devotions of Mr. Tozer or Mr. Manning is of a liberalism so thorough-going that one might suppose it invented only in the present century; but in fact such blithe inclusiveness, like the eager ardor of a Timothy Kenrick who could take pride in it, is as common among nominal Presbyterians in George III's England as among leftward-leaning clerics and confident laymen of our own times. And it had, then as now, the effect of fostering, and absolving in advance, every sort of irresponsible pulpit eloquence, whether in politics or theology.

It may well be asked whether John Merivale belonged, in James E. Bradley's sense of the term, to the dissenting elite. From one point of view, as the son and pupil at the Exeter Dissenting Academy of Samuel Merivale, himself a pupil of the great Doddridge, John Merivale may be thought to belong with the bluest blood of West Country Dissent. And this certainly weighed with Kenrick, may even have dismayed him. But since Merivale published nothing and was a leader of opinion only in his own congregation, I think he does not fall into the category of "dissenting elite" as Bradley conceives of it. And so the question arises, quite pressingly: How many John Merivales were there, up and down the country, their very existence perpetuated only in the records, where they survive, of long disbanded and extinct Dissenting churches?

It is not clear how that question can be answered. And that no doubt is one reason why it is never or seldom asked. But there are other more prejudiced reasons why the mere existence of the John

[10]See Alan Brockett, *Nonconformity in Exeter, 1650–1875* (Manchester, 1962), pp. 142–43.

Merivales, of loyalist and nonradical yet principled Dissenters, should be passed over in silence. These reasons become clearer if we shift our attention from the 1790s back to the 1770s, from the French Revolution to the American; and if we attend particularly to Free Churchmen of the present day, concerned to celebrate with a proper pride the tradition they inherit.

In 1976 the bicentenary of the Declaration of Independence was noticed in Britain by Free Churchmen as by others; and there were obvious and proper reasons why on such occasions radical Dissenters, those who sympathized with the colonists, should be remembered, and loyalist Dissenters like John Merivale should be driven still further into the shadows. An example is the lecture "Nonconformists and the American Revolution," by the distinguished historian of the English Baptists, Ernest A. Payne.[11] Given the occasion, and deciding sensibly that the Methodists (though not strictly Nonconformists) could hardly be left out of account, Dr. Payne had to do something about the vehement and intransigent loyalism of the Wesley brothers. Taking note of Charles Wesley's anguished poem that castigates General Howe for mismanaging the American campaigns, and Lord Shelburne for making peace in 1783 ("That smooth, perfidious perjur'd Shelburne sold / His King his country and his God for gold"), he commented: "Poor Charles Wesley! This is not the right note to end on, not really fair to the Methodists of that day, certainly not fair to the Colonists and their supporters in this country. The rebels and their friends should not be idealized, but the future was with them." This is compassionate. And of course that "the future was with them" is what none of us, two centuries later, can deny. But Charles Wesley's concern in that poem and others was not with which of the opposing bodies of opinion in Britain had the future in its keeping, but with which of them had felt and acted constitutionally; and he was sure that the winning side had been the one that mocked and flouted the British Constitution. The same is true of the other anti-Whig document that Dr. Payne takes note of: Johnson's *Taxation No Tyranny*. Johnson was, he says, "unfortunately prejudiced against Americans," and

[11]Published in *The Journal of the United Reformed Church History Society*, 1, No. 8 (October 1976), 210–27.

"he could not see how people who practised and upheld the slave system could protest against ill-treatment and the denial of rights." Johnson does indeed gibe at libertarian slaveholders, and who will say that the gibe was unwarranted? But such an argument ad hominem is nowhere near the center of Johnson's powerful pamphlet, which on the contrary turns upon the strictly constitutional questions of what "sovereignty" means, and what "representation" means. And it is not clear that Johnson's argument on these properly dry and philosophical grounds has ever been controverted.[12] For Dr. Payne, however, it is a case of "poor Sam Johnson," no less than poor Charles Wesley—to whom we may add poor John Wesley also, who was persuaded by Johnson's pamphlet and thereafter agreed with his brother. Of all three of them it seems we must say that they were left behind by history or, if we agree to think that way, "proved wrong in the event." To extend to three such massive and formidable figures the charity of our faintly amused compassion appears somewhat hazardous, but from Payne's point of view it is the best we can do. Certainly among those, Dissenters and others, who took the opposite view, we find no men of comparable stature. And for that matter, if among the Dissenters there were any who made the same mistake as Johnson and the Wesleys did, Dr. Payne—understandably enough, considering the occasion—chose not to identify them.

His account in fact is only a little more cautious than that of a Nonconformist spokesman eighty years ago, C. Silvester Horne, in his *Popular History of the Free Churches* (1903):

> If the voice of the Free Churches had been listened to, the American Colonies would have been saved for England. It was natural, doubtless, that English Nonconformists should sympathize with those who represented their own ideals. Across the thousands of miles of sea they united themselves in sympathy with the brave children of the Puritans who were defying British tyranny and dying in thousands for their independence. . . . Only John Wesley's political instinct failed him; and his attack on the colonists was unworthy of his shrewd intelligence and generous heart. English Nonconformity was not

[12]See The Yale Edition of the Works of Samuel Johnson, Vol. X, *Political Writings*, ed. Donald Greene (New Haven, 1977), pp. 402–9.

represented in Parliament, but when Burke and Chatham and Fox pleaded the cause of the Americans, the Free Churchmen at home had no need to be ashamed of the men who defended their opinions in the Legislature.[13]

These ringing tones (Horne in his day was a famous pulpit orator)[14] are not what we are used to. But the substance of what Horne asserts appears still to be the received opinion, and not only among Free Churchmen like Ernest A. Payne. British and American historians alike still assume or assert that the English Dissenters were unanimously on the side of the colonists, though it is sometimes conceded that their enthusiasm cooled rather precipitately soon after the war started. James E. Bradley in some entertaining pages has shown that for Whig historiographers like Lecky and Trevelyan what particularly recommended the Dissenters was precisely that they were, as Horne says, "not represented in Parliament." For, once the First Reform Bill had acknowledged how corrupt the parliamentary system had been while it sustained the Whig hegemony, Whig virtue could be saved for the nineteenth century only by vesting it in those Whigs who had been outside the system—which is to say, the Dissenters.[15] Silvester Horne, however, had no such sophisticated ends in view when he roundly declared that under George III "Nonconformity was winning its soul, and coming to see and to declare the beauty of the ideal of a Free church in a Free State." At this point Horne has in mind not so much his Dissenters' opposition to coercion of the colonists as, in domestic policy, their agitation for parliamentary reform. But the two issues can hardly be kept apart, if only because the pro-Americans were almost always active for parliamentary reform also. Horne identifies as heroes of this Dissenting thrust not just Joseph Priestley but also "the eloquent and impassioned Baptist minister, Robert Robinson."[16]

Readers of Herbert Butterfield[17] will know Robinson already, as instigator of a notorious meeting for parliamentary reform on

[13]Horne, p. 323.

[14]For Horne, see Clyde Binfield, *So Down to Prayers* (London, 1977), pp. 199–213.

[15]Of course they were *not* outside the system (as Bradley points out).

[16]Horne, p. 326.

[17]See Butterfield, *George III, Lord North and the People* (London, 1949), pp. 284–88.

25 March 1780, in Cambridge. This is described by a contemporary as "a mob of Dissenters of all Hues, Colours & Denominations in every part of the Country, called together . . . in order to draw up a Petition of œconomy, Alterations in the Method of Parliament, and other wild and republican Schemes, first engendred at Mr. Robinson's conventicle, & then recommended to the notice of the Corporation by a modest Republican, if that is compatible, Alderman Burleigh." And at the end of a turbulent day, we are told, "Robinson, the Anabaptist Teacher, who lives at Chesterton, set the Bells a Ringing in that Church as soon as he got Home, and made a great Supper at night for all his Party, where strong Liquors, good Cheer, and Zeal for the Cause, so far got the better of their discretion, that many of the Ebenezers were laid flat on their Back, & had Assistance to convey them to their several Habitations." There is much other evidence to bear out this image of what Robinson was like. Joseph Ivimey, historian of the Baptists in the next generation, was prepared to think that by the time Robinson died a Socinian and Unitarian, he must have been insane. Is this, we may ask mildly, the sort of figure whom we should find, with the advantage of hindsight, politically more admirable and enlightened than John Wesley or Dr. Johnson?

At any rate, Lecky and Payne and Horne notwithstanding, there were in the 1770s English Dissenters who rightly or wrongly found themselves of one mind with Johnson and the Wesleys. One of them was the already venerable Job Orton of Shrewsbury, friend and literary executor of the great Philip Doddridge. On 29 September 1775 we find him already resenting, on behalf of the provincial Dissenters, the politicizing of dissent by the ministers of the metropolis: "Whatever 'the principle of the *Americans*' may be, the spirit they shew is malignant, rebellious, and wicked. My Bible teaches me 'not to speak evil of dignities' &—I wish the London ministers would leave Politics to Statesmen, and give themselves wholly to their ministry."[18] By 1778 his tone has sharpened, and by a pregnant allusion to Northampton Academy under Doddridge he by implication invokes the authority of that most famous and influential of all Hanoverian Dissenters:

[18]Job Orton, *Letters to Dissenting Ministers*, ed. S. Palmer, 2 vols. (1806), I, 167.

I have been looking over Sallust's *History of Cataline's Conspiracy*; in which I think you will find some things suitable to your purpose, particularly in his speech to the conspirators; which you will meet with towards the beginning of the history; where he pleads Liberty, as a ground for his undertaking; but mentions honour, power, wealth, &c. as also in their plan, and throws out some bitter reflections against the ministers and placemen of those days. . . . There is a great deal to the same purpose in *Cataline's* speech, and in other parts of the history; but it is near forty years ago since I last read it, which was with the pupils at *Northampton*, in 1739. I have long thought there are many passages in the account of that conspiracy very parallel to the present case of our nation, between loyal men, and those who are called patriots, and who choose by a figure of speech to call themselves Whigs, just as they call me a Tory. Many are angry with me, because I discountenance their disloyalty; but I despise their anger, as much as I dislike their principles and conduct. I would willingly be doing some good while I am here; and to promote loyalty, subjection, and peace, is doing good. I think I have already softened some sharp spirits amongst us, at least brought them to hold their tongues, or to be less confident.[19]

And in the next year Orton can afford to be contemptuously sarcastic: "I know nothing of Mr. —— but by report. It is very well to be 'valiant for *liberty*,' if the courageous man has a proper idea of it; but I should have rejoiced more to have heard that he had been *valiant for truth*, holiness, and peace, and remarkably alive for the conversion and salvation of souls. We have some ministers who are zealous for liberty, but the souls of their flocks are neglected, and our interest is sinking under them."[20]

Some may read out of these comments only a pusillanimous quietism. But Orton is addressing ministers of religion; and his contention, which can hardly be denied, is that however ardent a minister's political convictions and however he may interpret his political duties as a perhaps prominent and certainly influential citizen, all such matters must have for him a lower priority than the performing of his pastoral and priestly duties. These comments

---

[19]*Letters to a Young Clergyman from the late Reverend Mr. Job Orton* (Shrewsbury, 1791), p. 133.

[20]*Letters to Dissenting Ministers*, II, 4.

therefore are of a piece with Orton's sacramentalism: "I cannot agree with you, that administering the Sacraments is the easiest and least important part of our office. I always considered them as most important, and found it more difficult to administer them, as they should be, than to preach."[21] To those who when they consider late-Hanoverian dissent think first of Priestley and Richard Price, not to speak of Richard Baron and Robert Robinson, it will come as a surprise that sacramentalism has any part at all in the Dissenting tradition. But the proper administering of the sacraments had a central place in the Dissent of Doddridge, with whom in this emphasis also Orton is keeping faith. Moreover, Orton could, if he chose, appeal behind Doddridge to John Flavel in 1691 declaring, "When God puts a crown upon the head, and a sceptre into the hand of a man, he engraves upon that man (in a qualified sense) both his name, and the lively characters of his Majesty and authority." And behind Flavel there is the patriarch Richard Baxter telling the Lord Protector Cromwell that "we took our ancient monarchy to a blessing, and not an evil to the land; and humbly craved his patience that I might ask him how England had ever forfeited that blessing, and to whom that forfeiture was made." In short, Orton's submissive, monarchical, and loyalist Dissent has rather better credentials than the republican Dissent of Hollis and Baron, who can establish their lineage from Milton and Cromwell only by way of the infidel Algernon Sidney.

In 1780 Orton is recommending "Public and Domestic Devotion, written by one *Martin*, a Baptist minister in London . . . very sensible, serious, and useful." This is John Martin (1741–1800) who, far from advancing his loyalist sentiments only in private communications, rushed into print impetuously and often, as he acknowledges in *Some Account of the Life and Writings of the Revd. John Martin* (1797). This autobiography is a charming sturdy brief narrative in epistolary form, which could well bear reprinting, both for its intrinsic virtues and for the light it casts on a little-noticed element in the society and ideology of late Hanoverian England. Martin's justification for writing it is explicitly Johnsonian—the famous judgment that "there has perhaps rarely passed a life, of

[21]Ibid., I, 131.

which a judicious and faithful narrative would not be useful." The
son of a publican and grazier in Lincolnshire, Martin, largely self-
educated, abandoned a family tradition of Anglicanism to join the
Baptist ministry, and after ministering to various congregations in
the East Midlands came to a metropolitan church in Grafton Street
only in 1773. His interests and his publications were not in any
blatant or invidious sense "politicized"; yet he published his views
on each of the vexing constitutional issues that arose in his lifetime,
and always on the loyalist side. Himself aware of this bias in his
political sentiments, Martin explains in a very interesting way how
he thinks it originated:

> As I was born at Spalding, in the year 1741, at the close of the
> rebellion in favor of the Pretender I was about five years of age. At
> that time, and for some years afterwards, the story of him, and of
> those that countenanced his cause, was often sounded in my ears;
> and as the inhabitants of Spalding were well affected to Government,
> this story made so deep an impression on my mind, that before I
> was fifteen, I could not see without alarm the shadow of civil dis-
> turbance; and Sir, let me add that at fifty-five rebellious positions,
> on whatever pretence they are brought forward, strongly excite my
> indignation; above all, when they seem to be sanctioned by religious
> frenzy.

Accordingly, it comes as no surprise that in 1775, inflamed by
talk on behalf of the American colonists, Martin should have published a polemic on the loyalist side, of which he was to say: "In
this paper, called the Monitor, I attempted to shew, that rebellion
first commenced in heaven; that by the suggestions of a ruined
rebel, our adversary, it gained admittance into Paradise; and that
since the fall of our first parents, the rebellious of all ages, in all
conditions of life, have always had an illicit love for dominion; so
that, from the first generation to the present, were they to meet
together in one body, they might say to each other, Walked we not
in the same spirit? Walked we not in the same steps?" When we
consider John Rippon telling John Manning in 1784, "I believe
that all our Baptist ministers in town except two, and most of our
brethren in the country, were on the side of the Americans in the

late dispute,"[22] we cannot doubt that one of the recalcitrant pair was John Martin, who had the year before reasserted his position in *Queries and Remarks on Human Liberty.* (And it is interesting to note that Rippon concedes there were more John Martins in the country than in the town.) Morever, in 1776 Martin had published *Familiar Dialogues between Americus and Britannicus* in which, he says, he "attempted to explain . . . some things that had given offence in the Monitor," but "daring, in this performance, to censure some things advanced by Dr. Price, his partizans were exasperated at my supposed temerity." From that point to the end of his life Martin was always aware of speaking for an unpopular minority among the articulate Dissenters and, reading between the lines, we recognize in him the sort of personality that relishes such an isolated position, exults in it, and seeks it.

Richard Price can still attract partisans, as do his contemporaries Wilkes and Paine and preeminently Burke. But whereas those men were furiously partisan themselves, and in different ways turbulent and passionate, what distinguishes Price is on the contrary a sort of glacial serenity. And so his pro-American *Observations on the Nature of Civil Liberty . . . and the Justice and Policy of the War with America* (1776) should be considered in the light of his later *Discourse on the Love of our Country* (1789) where he asks, of such love, "What has it been but a love of domination; a desire of conquest, and a thirst for grandeur and glory, by extending territory and enslaving surrounding countries?" When patriotism is thus dismissed as an unworthy prejudice, the rights and wrongs of any political situation are wonderfully simplified. But the undoubtedly irrational yet time-honored promptings of pietas toward kindred and native land cannot be set aside by most people so serenely; and such promptings are felt by Dissenters sometimes, even by Dissenters of Price's own Arian and rationalistic kind. Thus the Presbyterian John Bowring showed that his rationality fell short of Price's when he wrote to a cousin in 1778: "After the most deliberate consideration of the nature of the quarrel between us, I freely own it appears to me that they are right and we wrong, nor is there anything I more ardently

[22]Cited by Payne, p. 210.

wish for relative to our national concerns than a thorough change both of men and manners in the British Cabinet. *Yet, as an Englishman, I by no means wish to see my country vanquished by the arms of France.*"[23] More remarkably the pioneer industrialist Joseph Wedgwood, Unitarian and friend of Benjamin Franklin, is found in 1779 expostulating: "Methinks I would defend the land of my nativity, my family and friends against a foreign foe, where conquest and slavery were inseparable, under any leaders—the best I could get for the moment, and wait for better times to displace an obnoxious minister, and settle domestic affairs, rather than rigidly say, I'll be saved in my own way and by people of my own choice, or perish and perish my country with me."[24] To men like Bowring and Wedgwood, thus touchingly embroiled in the consequences of their own unargued patriotism, Richard Price's coolly dispassionate statement of the case could offer no help at all. As the war went on, *in particular as it went worse and worse for British arms*, the political conduct and sentiments of a Bowring or a Wedgwood inevitably became for all practical purposes indistinguishable from those of a Job Orton or John Martin. For when the Crown finally admitted defeat it was not under pressure from any body of persistent pro-American sentiment but, as J. H. Plumb valuably points out, because "the country interest, the independent members who sat in Parliament as Knights of the Shire, who never spoke in debates and usually voted with the government, finally rebelled."

Robert E. Schofield's comment on Wedgwood's changing sentiments seems unimaginative as well as inaccurate: "How long his 'my country, right or wrong' attitude lasted is hard to say; probably not much longer than it took to discover that the military alliance between America and France was not going to result in an invasion of Britain."[25] The tone and implication of this remark by a scrupulous American historian are probably inescapable whenever an American observes the sentiments of Britons during the War of the Revolution. And yet what it overlooks is obvious: once the colonists had declared their independence, Americans constituted for the

---

[23]*Autobiographical Recollections of Sir John Bowring* (London, 1877), pp. 2–3 (my italics).

[24]Quoted by J. H. Plumb.

[25]Robert E. Schofield, *The Lunar Society of Birmingham* (Oxford, 1963), p. 138.

British "a foreign foe," just as the French did. A parallel case is when C. H. Guttridge reports on the American correspondence of Richard Champion, no Dissenter but one of Edmund Burke's powerful constituents in Bristol. Guttridge observes that "Champion remained loyal to the cause of his American friends, even to the extent of conduct which could with some reason be termed unpatriotic." But, of course, when Champion in December 1775 conveyed to America information about "where the government intended to concentrate armaments, what the numbers of the reinforced army at Boston would be, and what disposition of troops would be made between New York, Virginia, and South Carolina,"[26] the name for such conduct may be thought to be not "unpatriotic" but "treasonable." Burgess and Maclean and Rosenberg, Hiss and Pontecorvo and Philby are names from our own century that suggest how hard it is for intellectuals to acknowledge that treason is a matter not of opinion but of legal *fact*. Everyone knows that when treason is successful "none dare call it treason"; but this does not excuse one literary historian after another making delicate comedy out of police agents sent by Pitt's government to eavesdrop on Blake and Coleridge and Wordsworth—without at any point reminding their readers that French agents *were* active in the England of that time, and *did* suborn some Englishmen. This underlining of the obvious seems called for if we are to recognize that when Orton and Martin and Wesley advance submission to the civic power as a religious duty, this is not necessarily a maneuver of the ruling class, nor yet an anachronistic survival of feudal sentiments into an enlightened age, but one possible solution to a conflict of loyalties that may entangle us, just as it entangled Josiah Wedgwood in 1779.

What no proponent of the Whig version of events under George III can be brought to admit at all readily is that very few of the zealots for "civil and religious liberty" had any intention of extending those liberties to Roman Catholics. Thus of Thomas Hollis we are told that he was "persuaded . . . as every sensible and impartial

---

[26]C. H. Guttridge, *The American Correspondence of a Bristol Merchant, 1766–1776* (Berkeley, 1934), pp. 4–5.

man must be, that the civil and religious liberties of Englishmen will ever be endangered in proportion as popery increases, and is not discouraged"; and that he felt "the clergy of the established church had been too remiss in their opposition to it."[27] This we have on the authority of one who was himself a clergyman of the established church, though of a rather peculiar kind. He was Francis Blackburne, archdeacon of Cleveland, author of *Considerations of the present state of the controversy between the protestants and papists of Great Britain and Ireland* (1768), of which Hollis, as was his habit with books he approved of, bought and distributed 110 copies. Blackburne with much self-congratulation recounts this himself in his *Memoirs of Hollis* (1780). It was Blackburne who issued the invitations to a meeting at the Feathers Tavern in the Strand on 17 July 1771, at which was first mooted a petition to Parliament for the abolition of compulsory subscription to the Thirty-nine Articles, this for the benefit of Anglican ministers who were in fact Unitarians, as Blackburne was. This measure, framed so as to relieve also the Dissenting ministers (mostly Presbyterians) who were Unitarians no less, was as we have seen defeated, largely at the instigation of the Dissenting Calvinists. To regularize their position, some half-dozen Anglican clergy resigned their livings, following Theophilus Lindsey who, like his fellow Cambridge don Jebb, thereby sacrificed also his academic career. Blackburne had no such scruples, or none that he could not swallow; and this sufficiently explains his special interest in applauding libertarian (though of course antipapist) Dissenters such as Hollis. Blackburne is the first of several Anglicans in the period who show unwonted tenderness to the Dissenting interest; their motives for doing so, while not often so impudent as Blackburne's, can in most cases be discerned without too much trouble. The truth is that the rapid growth of Unitarianism in this period, alike among parsons and Dissenting ministers, and in either case mostly masked (however perfunctorily) as something else, blurs the borderline between Establishment and Dissent as perhaps at no other period before or since.

The only Dissenter I have found at this time who was in any way prepared to accept papists as fellow Christians was, to give

[27] *Memoirs of Thomas Hollis* (London, 1780), p. 251.

him his due, Richard Price, who seems to have been ready to contemplate Catholic emancipation, at any rate in Ireland. Perhaps not all Dissenters were quite so ferociously antipapist as some of the Establishment would have wished them to be. Such seems to have been the view of Horace Walpole who was during the war with the colonies an extreme Whig, presumably out of filial piety; who accordingly grumbled into his diary in 1776, "In all this contest with America, the Presbyterians and other Dissenters, who could not but see the designs of the Court, and its notorious partiality to Roman Catholics, were entirely passive in England, being bribed or sold by their leaders."[28] It is not clear what Walpole could have pointed to as evidence of "notorious partiality to Roman Catholics." It was not until the Catholic Relief Act of 1778 that some of the disabilities imposed on the English papists in 1701 were lifted: officiating Roman Catholic clergy were thereafter no longer liable to life imprisonment; and the requirement was abolished by which land in England and Wales must pass over any papist heir in favor of the next Protestant in line. These reliefs, though conditional on an oath of allegiance being taken before a Court of Record or Quarter Sessions, were protested in a series of petitions which, orchestrated by Lord George Gordon, precipitated the Gordon Riots of 1780; and these, according to Peter Brown,[29] "combined with the excesses of the French Revolution, delayed parliamentary reform in Britain for forty years." This casts a sardonic light on Silvester Horne's claim for the Protestant bigots, that they were the pioneering heroes of parliamentary reform. As for Walpole, he can have had in mind only the leave extended to the citizens of vanquished Quebec to practice their Roman Catholicism with impunity. And of this Johnson, who to this day figures in radical and dissenting mythology as a fulminating Blimp if not indeed a court-pensioner, had written nobly in *The Patriot* (1774): "Persecution is not more virtuous in a Protestant than a Papist; and . . . while we blame Lewis the Fourteenth, for his dragoons and his gallies, we ought, when power comes into our hands, to use it with greater equity." Johnson said also that "in an age, where every mouth is open for

---

[28]Quoted by Bradley, p. 23.
[29]Peter Brown, *The Chathamites* (London, 1967).

liberty of conscience, it is equitable to shew some regard to the conscience of a Papist, who may be supposed, like other men, to think himself safest in his own religion"; and finally, irrefutably, "if liberty of conscience be a natural right, we have no power to withhold it; if it be an indulgence it may be allowed to Papists, while it is not denied to other sects."[30] Alas, far more typical was the platform on which the youthful Lord Mahon stood in 1774 as a candidate for Westminster; a platform in which promises to destroy or diminish bribery in elections, to strive for the repeal of the Septennial Act, and for the expunging of the vote of the Commons which had unseated Wilkes, stood alongside a pledge to seek the repeal of the Quebec Act.[31] So happily, under George III, did measures that we are eager to consider "liberal" or "enlightened" or "democratic" go along with antipapist bigotry! And while it is no doubt too much to hope for that any Dissenter should have declared himself on the issue as fearlessly as Johnson did, it is a pity to have to say so, of people who were "coming to see and to declare the beauty of the ideal of a Free Church in a free State."

After Francis Blackburne the next prominent Anglican to take up the cudgels for the Dissenters, or for some of them, was Christopher Wyvill in his *Defence of Dr. Price, and the Reformers of England* (1792). Wyvill's motives were more altruistic than Blackburne's, and more responsible. In the 1780s his Yorkshire Association had been the best organized and most level-headed of the movements for parliamentary reform, and the one that came nearest effecting some real change. He had got some support, though it is not clear how much, from the Dissenting interest in Yorkshire. And it looks as if, by springing to Price's defense in the wake of Burke's fierce attack on him in the *Reflections on the French Revolution*, Wyvill was trying to defend the Dissenting interest from Burke's accusations of disloyalty, against the day when he, Wyvill, might need to call on the Dissenters once more in the service of what was genuinely a reformist rather than revolutionary objective. Accordingly, Wyvill's

[30]J. P. Hardy, ed., *The Political Writings of Dr. Johnson* (London, 1968), pp. 93, 94.
[31]See Butterfield, p. 383.

pamphlet, though predictably vituperative about Edmund Burke, is on the whole meant to be conciliatory. In particular it marks the disowning, by English liberal reformers, of Tom Paine—and not on religious grounds (Paine's *Age of Reason* was not to appear until 1795), but on the very sensible grounds that "his avowed purpose is, not to reform or amend the System of our Government, but to overturn and destroy it." Of the author of *The Rights of Man*, Wyvill writes judiciously and severely:

> He supports the doctrine of Republicanism, with an enthusiastic zeal, with an imposing confidence, and with reasoning often specious, and always daring; some truths are interspersed among many fallacies and misrepresentations, and a vein of coarse, but strongly sarcastic wit runs through and clumsily enlivens the whole. His Counsel, to break up and destroy the noble fabric of our Constitution, and rebuild a new political edifice on the plans of America, seems to be conveyed in the most dangerous shape, and far more likely to make an impression on those, to whom it is chiefly addressed, than if it had been delivered in a more classical composition.

It may well be thought that Wyvill should in logic have disowned Price no less than Paine. For Price undoubtedly advocated a unicameral legislature, and to effect that would certainly have been "to break up and destroy" the Constitution, as that was understood by Montesquieu and John Adams no less than Burke. There are signs in fact that Wyvill was uneasy about some of the positions that Price had taken up, but he was committed to exonerating this alarming and prominent Whig Dissenter if he was to clear Dissenting whiggery in general from any taint of disloyalty. And his protestations to this effect are rather too vehement to carry conviction. Thus he asserts that "during the miseries of the American war no symptom of dissatisfaction to the Constitution appeared." But only a few years before that war people in the group around Thomas Hollis were to be heard declaring that "no person is a true friend of Liberty who is not a Republican"; and during the war many in Britain as well as America were reading with enthusiasm Catherine Macaulay's *History of England from the accession of James I*, that "imaginative work in praise of republican principles." It may be that Caroline Robbins and J. H. Plumb have overestimated the influence of Dissenting republicanism, but it can hardly be pooh-poohed so blandly as by Wyvill or his modern biographer Ian Christie. Though it is doubtless true that the views of "the Commonwealthmen" had little popular appeal when promulgated by themselves in editions of Algernon Sidney and Marchamont Nedham, they could have such appeal when cautiously and partially enunciated by charismatic or demagogic figures like Chatham and Wilkes (who both had connections with the Hollis group) or by an energetic popularizer like Mrs. Macaulay. Thus it seems that there must have been, in the 1790s as in the 1760s and 1770s, Dissenters who were also Jacobins whose reading of their Dissenting heritage pushed them well beyond constitutional reform, however radical. And this means surely that when Burke in his *Reflections* imputed disaffection or disloyalty to the Dissenters generally, his alarm was not so groundless and chimerical as is commonly supposed. Indeed, Wyvill himself in 1792, while seeming to reassure, is really threatening:

> The Proselytes to republican notions are few at present, and inconsiderable: They probably would be increased in number by prosecution; but by impunity a wise forbearance will effectually prevent any eventual danger from their speculations, provided the condition of the People be rendered more easy by the farther diminution of their burthens, and their wishes be gratified by a timely correction of those abuses in the Constitution, which have been so justly complained of. By these means, and by these means alone, the possible growth of a great Republican Party in this Country may be prevented.

There is a clear threat in that last sentence. Was it a real threat? Did not Wyvill, no less than Burke, think that it was?

The Dissenters meanwhile had failed in their agitation for a repeal of parts of the Test and Corporation Acts. John Martin, inflexible as ever, had once again espoused an immovably conservative position, and was so much in a minority that by his own account he was not permitted to speak at the meeting of the London Dissenting ministers in Red Cross Street in December 1789. He therefore published his contribution to the debate as a pamphlet, *A Speech on the Repeal of such parts of the Test and Corporation Acts as affect Conscientious Dissenters* . . . (1790). But this is an unhappy and disingenuous performance; and a bitter anonymous rejoinder by "no Reverend Dissenter" is scurrilous and intemperate, but convincing. There is, however, one passage in Martin's pamphlet that is of interest because it shows that the idea of "oppressive toleration," brandished as a novelty by radicals of the 1960s, was already part of the dissenters' armory in 1790:

> We are repeatedly told, "That the pretended *toleration* of Dissenters is a real *persecution*." Such language is as impolitic as it is unjust. Toleration and persecution may exist at the same time; but can they be considered as the same thing? All legal persecutions, in this country, have been the offspring either of *Statute* law or of *Canon* law; nevertheless, that Act which repeals the oppressive power of preceding Acts, and prevents the wasps and hornets in low life from darting out their stings, should ever be mentioned with becoming temper.

What Martin has in mind is the Act of Toleration passed under William III; and he proceeds to a panegyric, in thoroughly Burkean vein, on the wisdom of that monarch and his ministers.

There appeared a new spokesman for loyalist Dissent when the Independent minister John Clayton (1754–1843) took advantage of the Birmingham riots against Joseph Priestley by publishing a sermon in which he argued in effect that Priestley had asked for what he got. This provoked many rejoinders, among them Robert Hall's *Christianity Consistent with a Love of Freedom* (1791). A more curious loyalist document appeared in Adam Callender's *Thoughts on the Peaceable . . . Nature of Christ's Kingdom* (1794):

> Let us remember therefore, that it is in heaven where our interest chiefly is. There is our citizenship; and in the view of possessing it shortly will the main of our conversation be directed. We are called upon to set our affections on things above, and not on things on the earth; and our Lord lays it down as a maxim, that if we are laying up treasures above, our hearts will be there also; in the same way as they who heap up treasures here have their hearts on earth. If then heaven be our chief banking house, our conversation will be much taken up about the security of our property there, and we shall find, to our comfort, that if once laid up in the sacred mansions

[341]

above, they will remain inviolable from thieves and unhurt by the moth.

We are pilgrims in this world, as all our forefathers were, and we, like them, seek a country above. It does not suit well with the idea of a pilgrim, when passing through a strange country, to retard his journey by stopping to dispute and settle the manners of a country, to which he means not to return.

Perhaps not many present-day Christians are sufficiently devout and evangelical to accept this obviously extreme case for political quietism. Yet the argument takes on force when it is seen to rest on the grounds that the church is indeed catholic and universal:

We ought rather to admire the more excellent way which Jesus has taught us, which leaves no room for doubt, by making it our positive duty to obey every kind of government, without exceptions to the characters of those who rule. Here perplexity is at an end, and we are led to admire the wisdom of Christ in establishing a rule of obedience, so suitable to christians in every age, and in every country where they may dwell on the earth: so that we may conceive of christians in various nations, all harmoniously sending up their petitions to God for their Kings and governors, and for the good of their respective countries, though the governments . . . may be totally different to each other.

One wonders if this evangelical Protestant would follow through the implications of this position so far as to endorse the sentiment in Burke that has infuriated so many from his day to ours—Burke's sympathy with the ejected and persecuted Roman Catholic clergy of France.

This writer must interest us in any case. For in 1795, when his contribution to Adam Callender's volume was reprinted separately under the title *Scriptural Subjection to Civil Government*, the author was revealed as Thomas Sheraton. Yes, the great cabinetmaker—who was also, we discover with surprise, a Baptist minister. Sheraton, though a household name in an unusually literal sense, is a very shadowy figure. If he at any time fulfilled his ministerial function, it seems to have been in his native northeast, not in the London to which he migrated. (And he therefore figures, it is interesting to note, as a *provincial* Dissenter, though domiciled in London.) More-over, in case it should be thought that Sheraton as purveyor to the luxury trade needed to flatter the prejudices of the nobility and gentry, it should be noted that in his own lifetime his furniture designs seem to have brought him no patronage and no profit; he died unknown, and in penury.

In 1794 Sheraton was not content to keep a lordly and scriptural distance from particular disputed issues in the politics of his time. He goes out of his way, for instance, to emphasize that an English Christian's submission to the civil power involves loyalty to a bica-meral legislature: "But, by honouring the King, according to our present form of government, it implies the two houses of parliament. There are two branches of the legislative authority in this kingdom, without which there is not a supreme power; and therefore we must honour these with our prayers in connection with the King. And if these three are to us the reigning powers, we know then to whom subjection is due." This passage was shortened and softened in the 1795 reprint, for reasons that we can only guess at, though they may be in the background of what Sheraton says in his Preface to that reissue:

> Should the writer's motives for publishing on this subject be inquired into—he has to say, that at a time when the loyalty of Dissenters in general was doubted, he accepted an invitation and opportunity of announcing openly that he was not amongst that class of non-con-formists, who scruple not to revile the good constitution under which Divine Providence has happily placed them; *reserving at the same time the important distinction between a good constitution, and those corruptions that may exist in its administration*, to point out which he conceives would be as much beyond his ability as foreign to his duty to attempt it (my italics).

(Sheraton, it will be observed, was not so nimble a craftsman with the English language as he was in rosewood and mahogany.)

Doubtless what is most striking about this Preface is its use of the past tense. As the news came in from France, so the attitudes of observers changed week by week, or month by month; and so it is that in 1795 Sheraton can look back upon public opinion of a

[343]

year earlier as belonging to a past era. And so it is that by 1797 John Martin, looking back to the 1770s but with sly allusions to the 1790s, can manage a wry urbanity:

> Some of my friends, (for I have had friends of various complexions,) affected to wonder, that I, who had so much trouble and sorrow at Grafton Street, should meddle, as they pleased to call it, with political subjects. This, Sir, is the way of some gentlemen in Town, and I suppose it is so with some in the country. They can meet together, form associations, and corresponding societies, to propagate indecent, and unfounded reports of the powers that are, and aggravate, with pleasure, the inadvertence of our rulers, whatever may be the condition of their own affairs; whereas, if others attempt to make the best of that which is, by pleading for order, and legitimate subordination, these gentlemen are sure to censure their proceedings, and to speak of them in very harsh and disrespectful terms.

In 1799 the tide of opinion had changed so markedly and was so hostile to any who might seem to be pro-French radicals that the alleged though unproven unanimity of the English Dissenters, which before had counted unto them for virtue and has been so taken through many generations since, could be and was turned around so as to validate a comprehensive indictment. This seems to be the significance of *Observations on the Political Conduct of the Protestant Dissenters; . . . in Five Letters to a Friend*, by the Reverend David Rivers, who identifies himself on his title page as "Late Preacher to a Congregation of Dissenters at Highgate." The line of argument open to a prosecuting counsel like Rivers should be obvious. A few excerpts will give the flavor of it:

> But were not the Dissenters strenuously active in serving the interest of the disaffected Colonies at home? Was not the courage and vigour of the enemy much heightened by the repeated assurances they had of cordial assistance from their brethren on this side of the Atlantic? Did not the Dissenters use their utmost endeavors to blacken the measures of Government, and to weaken and destroy the confidence of the nation in its rulers? and were not their endeavours crowned with too much success? So much so, that I attribute the loss of America to the Protestant Dissenters. Dr. Price, that firebrand of sedition, did the most essential service, by his inflammatory publications, to animate and invigorate the Colonies to persevere in their

revolt. His exertions were seconded by the whole phalanx of the Dissenters, headed by the members of the senate in opposition to government; thus, powerfully supported by a rank and discontented party here, they carried on the contest till they gained their independence.

. . . . .

But, I limit not myself to the conduct of Price and Priestley: it may be justly retorted, that the Dissenters as a body, were not to be censured for the imprudent conduct of two of their teachers. I will take a wider range; I will prove to you, Sir, that the Dissenters as a body tacitly approved of the conduct of their leaders. . . . If they had been that loyal body of men, which they are sometimes arrogant enough to stile themselves, why did they not pass a vote of censure upon Dr. Price and Dr. Priestley for their political conduct? Why did not they disavow their principles? These queries are easily replied to: because, they secretly *approved of them.* Secretly, did I say, they openly approved of them.

. . . . .

As to calling the *King* a *fool* and a *blockhead;* refusing to pray for him in their public worship; drinking success to the French; adorning their parlours with portraits of Buonaparte, Tom Paine, Horn Tooke, and others; and, *perhaps,* a *little ivory Guillotine* in some sly corner; I pass over such circumstances as these; what I limit myself to, is their *plotting Treason.*

. . . . .

. . . Godwin, the author of Political Justice, was a Dissenting Minister at Beaconsfield; Gilbert Wakefield is a Dissenter; Frend, who was expelled the University of Cambridge, now associates with Dissenters. . . . And among those persons who have been convicted of high treason . . . we shall find them altogether Dissenters. Thomas Muir, Fysche Palmer, Gerald, and Skirving, all Presbyterians.

. . . . .

I hope, Sir, that you will acquit me of a want of candour, in what has been stated in these letters; if I have erred, it is in favour of that sect among whom I first drew my breath; but from whom, from motives of the purest integrity, I have now separated.

Rivers's attack has topical point because of the Irish rising of '98 in which, as he does not fail to note, Ulster Presbyterians made common cause with Wexford papists. But his tone is too intemperate, and his polemic falls in too pat with what his public wanted

[345]

to hear, for us to take him very seriously. Yet he makes a case that needs to be answered. And his judgment—"I attribute the loss of America to the Protestant Dissenters"—is at least as plausible as Silvester Horne's directly opposite verdict, "If the voice of the Free Churches had been listened to, the American Colonies could have been saved for England." No doubt both are equally wide of the truth, which is more nearly caught in the sour retrospect of one of Washington's officers:

> The disappointment of a few smugglers in New England worked upon by the ancient Oliverian spirit, that panted to suffer once more for the "good old cause," the idle opulence of the Southern provinces, where something was wanted to employ the heavy hours of life, the stupidity of two or three British Governors, & the cruel impolitic behavior of their government, brought on & kept up the war, which was conducted on both sides, & terminated in a manner that has convinced me, that there are certain extensive operations determined upon by providence, which are not to be foreseen, aided, or obviated by human means.[32]

It is to be hoped, and expected, that scholarship will uncover other loyalist dissenters than those we have taken note of. Those few—Job Orton and John Martin, Clayton and Sheraton, Merivale and Rivers—obviously constitute too small a sample to generalize from. Yet it is worth saying that in surveying them we find nothing to contradict a generalization that has been risked by the distinguished historian of Methodism, Bernard Semmel. Semmel suggests that if we ask what the loyalist Dissenters had in common, one plausible and surprising answer might be: John Calvin. For certainly it seems to be the Calvinists among the Dissenters who are conspicuous by their absence from pro-American and later pro-French demonstrations and writings. And John Martin for one was a fiercely old-style Calvinist, who lived long enough to attack Andrew Fuller of his own church for attempting to moderate the high Calvinism traditional among Particular Baptists. (Martin's account of his own conversion to high Calvinist principles is affecting and impressive.) Thus the church-and-king rhymester in Manchester who wrote a loyalist squib against the Anglican Thomas Walker

---

[32]Francis Kinloch of South Carolina, in 1785. Quoted by May, p. 146.

and his radical friends may have been shrewd and accurate when
he accused them of being disloyal to Calvin as well as to the
Establishment:

> Next Tommy Tax, that Lad of Wax,
> If Charly Fox said Yea, Sirs,
> Would souse the Church and Calvin lurch,
> And after that, Huzza, Sirs.

In this instance, as time and again, the use of the blanket term
Dissenter, which darkened counsel at the time, continues to do so
today. For the Manchester loyalists wrote of "Legions of Dissenting
Congregations, headed by their respective Pastors" invading a loyalist meeting in 1789;[33] but in another of their publications on the
same topic, when an inquirer asks, "What caused so so much turbulence at the Meeting?" the answer he gets is: "The *Presbyterians'*
obtrusion" (my italics). And by 1789, if not indeed ten years earlier,
Presbyterian nearly always means *Unitarian*—which is to say, the
Calvinists' bitterest opponents.

This may explain why, though Presbyterians and many Baptists
are to be found at various times in the radical ranks, Congregationalists (the old Independents) are hard to find there. Ernest
Payne finds one, Samuel Wilton, of whom we read: "If in anything
he discovered what approached to an enthusiastic zeal, it was for
the success of America in her struggle for independence." Caleb
Fleming may have been another. But Fleming, doctrinally liberal
like Philip Furneaux of Clapham and Hugh Farmer of Waltham-
stow, was very far from typical of the Independents' ministry in
the 1770s. In the previous decade Independent congregations, like
John Hammer's in Plymouth or John Burnett's in Hull, had shown
themselves ready to dismiss ministers who did not dispense the
pure milk of Calvinism.[34] As Leighton Pullan pointed out long ago
in his Bampton Lectures, already in 1761 "Methodism and the
general Evangelical movement were not only stemming the whole

[33]See Frida Knight, *The Strange Case of Thomas Walker* (London, 1957), pp. 40–
42.

[34]See Jeremy Goring, "The Break-up of the Old Dissent," in C. G. Bolam et
al., eds., *English Presbyterians: From Elizabethan Puritanism to Modern Unitarianism*
(London, 1968), pp. 209–10.

tide of Arian and Socinian opinions, but were ousting them from the meeting-houses of the Independents," though "the English Presbyterians showed less power of recovery."[35] Accordingly, the late Basil Willey seems to have been wrong when he explicitly included the Independents along with Presbyterians and Baptists in his in any case rash judgment that "Priestley in his development from Calvinism to Unitarianism merely illustrates in epitome what was going on widely amongst the dissenting congregations in the eighteenth century."[36] In the 1760s and 1770s Calvinism was, on the contrary, regaining lost ground. And by 1780 Calvinists and anti-Calvinists had largely sorted themselves out between the two denominations, the Calvinists deserting Presbyterianism for Independency, in which long-established theological "liberals" like Furneaux and Farmer were anachronistic survivors. It is thus somewhat disingenuous of Ernest Payne to wonder that historians of Congregationalism like R. W. Dale and Tudur Jones should "give so little, indeed virtually no attention to the American War and Revolution"; the suspicion is irresistible that Dale and Jones kept silence because otherwise they would have had to concede that most Congregationalists of the 1770s were not, in the matter of America, "on the side of the future."

The natural affinity between Calvinism and loyalism has been obscured by John Wesley. For Wesley, even as he wrote his vehemently loyalist tracts at the time of the war with the Americans, at the same time persisted in, and stepped up, his polemic against what he called "antinomianism" among his own Methodists; that is to say, against the Calvinistic Methodism of those who followed George Whitefield. Hence Wesley, and those who supported him, like John Fletcher of Madeley, identified the Calvinism of New England with that of old England, and so accused their opponents, the Calvinistic Baptist Caleb Evans of Bristol and the Establishment Calvinist Augustus Toplady, of being disloyal revolutionaries and levelers. But as Bernard Semmel points out, the English Calvinists were in important ways quite different from their American fellows, and there is no reason to doubt that both Evans and Toplady

---

[35]Leighton Pullan, *Religion since the Reformation* (Oxford, 1923), p. 141; and cf. Michael R. Watts, *The Dissenters* (Oxford, 1978), pp. 468–69.

[36]Basil Willey, *The Eighteenth Century Background* (London, 1946), pp. 181–82.

were, though Whigs, entirely loyal. When Evans spoke of the "superb, I had almost said, the divine edifice" which was the British Constitution, there is no reason to think he was insincere or panicked into hypocrisy; and he made a fair point when he invoked the name of Blackstone, and asked if Blackstone was "a *Calvinist, an Anabaptist, an Antinomian* patriot" for enunciating the constitutional principles that Evans also held. Similarly that unamiable character Toplady had a point when he invited readers to compare "the loyalty of the Calvinistic archbishop Usher, with that of the Arminian ranter and fifth monarchy man John Goodwin." Wesley had mistaken his enemies; or rather he had rashly confounded his theological with his political adversaries. As Semmel implies, the truly disaffected Dissenters were Unitarian or Quaker, not Calvinist.[37] And so it seems to be high time that, in studies of this period, we stopped taking the Dissenters as a homogeneous and self-explanatory political entity or pressure group.

But we may fairly go a little further, and take a wider range. Nonconformist, Dissenter—the old names announce, proudly and exultantly on the part of those who so describe themselves, a condition of *alienation* from the consensus, and from (though also within) the societies of which thinkers about politics have made great play, ever since the youthful Karl Marx. Gerhart Niemeyer, for instance, has distinguished three types of alienation: first, that of the ancient Gnostics; then, that oldest alienation which "stems from sorrow at being separated from God, the source of truth, order, and peace"; and then again, "modern ideological alienation," that of the man who "becomes alienated by his own act of accepting an idea structure that implies a declaration of war by some men on the historical existence of all men." Of this last, Niemeyer writes: "The ideological system bears the stamp of an imperious pretension in rebellion against that which exists. The symbol of Prometheus, perverted into a modern hero of rebellion, is present in all modern thinking. Thus modern alienation is based not on faith but on choice. . . . The alienation is intentionally entered and its maintenance deliberately cultivated. Its character is willful rather than experiential."[38]

[37]Bernard Semmel, *The Methodist Revolution* (New York, 1973), pp. 61–71.
[38]Gerhart Niemeyer, "Loss of Reality: Gnosticism and Modern Nihilism," *Modern Age*, 22 (1978), 341.

Those who assert that the eighteenth-century English Dissenter was—or *had to be*, if he thought his position through—a political revolutionary (pro-American in 1780, pro-French in 1790), are contending that the alienation which the Dissenter by that very title confessed or proclaimed was alienation of the modern, ideological variety. But when John Martin contends "that rebellion first commenced in heaven; that by the suggestion of a ruined rebel, our adversary, it gained admittance into Paradise; and that . . . the rebellious of all ages . . . have always had an illicit love for dominion," he is asserting that *his* alienation, confessed and embraced, and imposed on him by history, is *not* alienation of the modern, ideological kind. In particular, by identifying Prometheus with the other superhuman rebel Lucifer, Martin rejects the Promethean myth that Niemeyer sees as crucial to the alienation that is "modern" and "ideological." It is in this way, and at this deep mythological level, that Martin refuses to have "religious Dissenter" mean "political dissident." It would be rash to suppose that in John Martin's generation, and in subsequent generations, others have not reached the same position by the same reasoning.

Enlightenment Studies

The Last Ten Years

LESTER G. CROCKER

THE FOUNDING OF THE AMERICAN SOCIETY FOR EIGHTEENTH-Century Studies seems in the present perspective a response to the intensification of scholarly investigation into the Enlightenment in the preceding generation. At the time of the Society's founding it had become a veritable explosion. It follows that the task before me is *une tâche ingrate,* if not *une tâche impossible.* Even if I had read all that has been printed, and even if I could discover a way to synthesize limitless heterogeneity, the account would far surpass reasonable limits of space. Hence, *une tâche ingrate.*

Most of the scholarship has been devoted to individual writers. Yet this aspect of eighteenth-century studies is precisely the one that defies the kind of account I give here. My concern is mainly with studies of a general nature. Nevertheless, I shall comment on a sample of four writers, two British and two French.

It is a current cliché to speak of "the Johnson industry." To be sure, we know far more and ever more about the man, his work, his charmed circle of literati. What matters is not this enlargement but the qualitative revision that has put them in a truer and brighter light. Among the several scholars who began the work of completing Boswell's portrait, we count two of the distinguished members of this society, the late James L. Clifford and Donald Greene. Then, within a period of three years, we have had two momentous biographies. That of John Wain (1975) (who apparently used Clifford without giving him credit) was hailed as a great and possibly definitive account of the man and his work. That of Walter Jackson Bate (1977) (who does not mention Wain) was hailed as great and definitive—which it may well be. Both recognized the need to apply modern psychological analysis to fathom the murky depths of this complex and contradictory personality. Bate is more prudent, but

[351]

I think too consistently apologetic, a bit too eulogistic and abounding in superlatives from the opening sentence. His book is more thoroughly researched, more complete in its analysis, much fuller in detail, and beautifully orchestrated. Wain's is livelier and has the quality of keeping us conscious of John Wain knowing and reading Johnson, of Wain's being intrigued and perplexed by him. I confess my fondness for his biography, though Bate's surpasses it, because it has its own literary quality. It is interesting to compare, as a sample, the two authors' treatment of *The Vanity of Human Wishes*. Wain's two pages neatly catch the poetic qualities of that work. Bate, in a ten-page explication de texte, tells us far more of its place in literary history, its themes, its expression of Johnson's mind and attitudes. The difference is between a poet's appreciation of poetry and a scholar's analysis. Then there is the famous question of Johnson's supposed masochistic tendencies. While Bate dismisses this idea angrily, the fact is that no final statement can be made—according to psychiatrists I have consulted. Bate explains away rather than explains ("infantilism," self-punishment excludes punishment, etc.), and Bate makes light of the modes of expression, which he elsewhere considers significant. He omits a phrase from Mrs. Thrale's letter ("tempts you to . . . brood upon an idea hateful in itself, but which your kind partiality to me has unhappily rendered pleasing"), and he quotes another phrase "do not quarrel with your Governess for not using the Rod enough," apparently without realizing that *Governess* in England may suggest punitive qualities. My point is, then, that the question cannot be answered decisively.

Johnson's place as related to the Enlightenment is still problematic. As Greene and Richard B. Schwartz have shown, he had a skeptical turn of mind; he was an empiricist, an iconoclastic searcher who was interested in new ideas in politics and science. He was involved in the problems of the age—happiness, for instance, in regard to which he represented what may be called the "darker side" of the Enlightenment, which some Anglo-Saxon historians mistakenly minimize, or exclude, as not belonging to it. Like Voltaire, he thought that evil is inscribed in the order of things and that it is metaphysically unsolvable, but that we should do what we can to alleviate it. For both men, action, experience, and human responsibility are the risks and the hopes we should assume. Unlike Voltaire (although he asked Why?), he does not utter Zadig's rebellious *but* in human protest against the divine order, not as a challenge to God's wisdom, but as a demurrer to its incomprehensibility and unjustifiability to us humans over whom he rules. The question remains, whether he partook in what I conceive to be the heart of the Enlightenment attitude—the search for new ways of thinking about the world and man himself. This meant more than open-mindedness to scientific advances; it was a commitment to such a search, to questioning all assumptions and authorities, and to entertaining new expectations, especially in regard to the social environment. Johnson did write,

> Still raise for good the supplicating voice,
> But leave to heaven the measure and the choice.

For Burke the notable book is also by a member of the American Society for Eighteenth-Century Studies. I refer to Isaac Kramnick's *The Rage of Edmund Burke* (1977). In it we see for the first time the psychological depths of another complex, tormented, ambivalent man, and the translations of these depths into his thought. Like Wain and Bate with Johnson, Kramnick has undertaken to rescue Burke from a stereotype, that of American neoconservatives who have taken him as their mascot. With powerful documentation Kramnick shows us Burke the conservative struggling and alternating with Burke the rebel. I have long thought that Burke's place in intellectual history has not always been seen in its true light. However conservative his parliamentary politics, his commitment to tradition, and his aversion to reform, he was, in relation to the utopian strains in the French Enlightenment and to the French Revolution, truly a liberal who fought for the open society against plans for closed, monolithic, authoritarian societies that would efface history and impose millenarian, ready-made, abstractly rational schemes of redemption. Like others of his time whom we today call "liberals," he favored a minimal intrusion of government in the nation's economic life. As a result of the historical reversal, this is what endears him to present-day conservatives. He opposed the Jacobins and their English supporters on the grounds of personal rights and a pluralist society, as well as on the ground of the value of tradition. Yet, like the same French utopians, he stressed the evil in human nature and the role of government in its control. This contradictory fact further complicates the disconcerting problem of Burke. Kramnick does not bring out all these historical complexities as clearly as he opens up the complexities of Burke himself.[1] His aim is to paint the "real" Burke as he studies the psychological conflicts that divided his personality between the public man and his alter ego. To be sure, this poses a historical problem. The real Burke may well be the Burke that Kramnick has revealed. But is he the "historical" Burke, the Burke of history? His dominating philosophy, in his published writings that have influenced Western thought, is indeed that of the Burke of the conservatives. In a sense it may be idle to speak of the "real" Burke.

Among the French writers of the Enlightenment, Diderot and Rousseau, more than any other philosophes, have engrossed scholarly minds and energies. Clearly, they still speak to us today. Clearly, they puzzle us and tantalize us more than ever, as we leave the surface of the depths. After a hundred years, we have not one, but two new editions of Diderot's *Oeuvres complètes*. Arthur Wilson has completed his monumental biography. Attention has been divided. On the one hand, intellectual historians have given us fresh insights into Diderot's febrile, heaving thought. Paolo Casini's overview (*Diderot "philosophe"* [1962]) is a brilliant achievement, far too neglected. Chouillet's *thèse doctorale* (*La Formation des idées esthétiques de Diderot* [1973]) is another example of an academic philosopher's devoting himself to a philosophe, this time in the field of aesthetics. I am sure that if Diderot could read it, he would learn much about his own thinking. Yves Benot (*Diderot, de l'athéisme à l'anticolonialisme* [1970]) has painted a too revolutionary Diderot, in a somewhat disjointed but spirited work. I have tried to make my own contribution in *Diderot's Chaotic Order*. On the other hand, Diderot the writer has attracted even more scholars. It is fascinating to read in sequence Herbert Josephs and Carol Sherman on Diderot's art of

[1]He identifies the English Dissenters and reformers with the French utopian rationalists. However, in regard to economics, at least, and the role of government in that sphere, they were actually more akin to French conservative reformers like the Physiocrats.

the dialogue and gesture (Josephs, *Diderot's Dialogue of Gesture and Language* [1969]; Sherman, *Diderot and the Art of the Dialogue* [1976]). *Le Neveu de Rameau, Jacques le fataliste,* and the other novels have been subjected both to ideological and aesthetic analyses, in numerous books and articles, and even to the hermetic schematizations of structuralists—all with discordant but ever-stimulating results.

But Rousseau, a musician, would surely hold his hands over his ears on listening to the cacophony he has evoked. Again, his meaning and his art—but also his personality—continue to arouse his readers and provoke them to clamorous controversy. Because I am heavily involved, and because space does not allow me to describe and to debate, I shall not attempt to give an account of the plethora of publications, throughout Europe and the Americas, but go on to the core of my presentation, to general studies of the Enlightenment.

Two works, by Georges Gusdorf and Ira Wade, summon our attention by their imposing mass. There are doubtless some yahoos who might consider studies of such monstrous length as these to be intellectual obscenities. But if dogged scholars grit their teeth, grind through 1,675 pages of Gusdorf and wade through nearly 1,100 pages of Wade, what will they find? Aside from two qualities they share, length and turgidity, all else is different.

Gusdorf's thinking, in its main lines and interpretations, is personal and radical, and the ordering of his materials is rigorous. To put it briefly, the Enlightenment for him must be considered as an essentially scientific enterprise. Somewhat in the fashion of Comte, he sees a progression from the stage of philosophy and theology to a panoply of positivistic sciences, each intensely preoccupied with defining its new "mental space" and methodology. Taken globally, they brought about for mankind a new way of being in the world. Thus Gusdorf (as I had done in my own way) makes the human condition—man as he sees himself in relation to God, cosmos, and nature—the prime directive of attitudes toward the problems of life and thought. When man became self-centered, and his own master, all else had to change.

In the first of three massive volumes, *Les Principes de la pensée au siècle des lumières* (1971), Gusdorf paints a general picture of the

[355]

Enlightenment's key ideas, stressing its pan-European extension, bringing out its different national characteristics, and positing Galilean-Newtonian science as the paradigm of Enlightenment thought in all domains. It led to the reign of empirical truth, although thinkers could not be faithful to their ideal. With man placed at the center, such notions as rights, humanitarianism, reform, progress, pacifism, anticolonialism flowed from the scientific outlook. Gusdorf properly emphasizes the elitist attitude of Enlightenment thinkers. With equal discernment he brings out the "dark side" of the Enlightenment, the polarity to its impersonal scientific utilitarianism, which expressed itself in antirational phases, occultism, the demonic, and climaxed in *Werther* and in the writings of Sade.

The second volume, *Dieu, la nature, l'homme au siècle des lumières* (1972), has two divisions. The first treats what Gusdorf calls "the religious sciences." His major points are that the conscience of the Enlightenment remained largely Christian—with the French anomaly—and that the attitudes toward religion became at the same time more critical or scientific, and more tolerant. He considers the Protestant countries to be most typical, for there the aim was to reconcile reason and faith and to study religion as a fundamental psychological and cultural phenomenon. Gusdorf's viewpoint is original and is not to be found in other interpretations. It follows from the Newtonian paradigm whose usefulness, though great, is limited. The refusal of transcendent finalism derived from Descartes, not Newton. In the second division of the volume, "les sciences de la vie," which include natural history, anthropology, and medicine, Gusdorf highlights a new attitude of respect or reverence toward the body and towards life itself as the ultimate outcome and value of the advances in these fields.

The final volume of the trilogy, *L'Avènement des sciences humaines au siècle des lumières* (1973), describes first the various tendencies in the nascent "science" of psychology. We are taken next into the realm of pedagogy and shown how the importance that the Enlightenment inevitably attributed to education generated new goals (nationalistic, utilitarian, sometimes utopian) and, consequently, new methods. Gusdorf describes the schools and universities of the time, reserving his approval for the German universities, especially Halle and Göttingen. Linguistics also entered into the domain of scientific inquiry, and Gusdorf gives a good account (if not always a good explanation, for he is stuck in his Newtonian model) of the gropings toward a science of language and toward an answer to the problem that particularly intrigued the age, the origin of language.

Gusdorf next tackles history, political theory, and economics. The same quest for intelligible law manifested itself in historiography; but history itself frustrated that quest. Empirical inquiry faded into distortions as history was forced into the Enlightenment's conceptual framework. Again the exception is made for Germany, where modern historical research was born. It is much the same for political science, since *droit naturel* theories flourished in countries free from Catholic dogmatism. Gusdorf correctly remarks that Enlightenment politics was largely reformist and monarchical, rather than revolutionary or republican. And finally, the autonomous laws of the economic sphere of life became the object of still another search, based on the conviction that these, too, would harmonize with Enlightenment ideas of progress and rationality.

As we look back over these wide-ranging pages, two features are self-evident: the scope of the inquiry, and the emphasis on the Enlightenment's international repercussions. Most striking, however, and most controversial, is Gusdorf's revision of historical perspective. Germany, in his account, becomes the main hearth for the flames of light. France, at best, must share the *avant-scène*, and often comes off second-best. While some interpreters have gone too far in excluding Christianity from Enlightenment thought and in defining it as secularization, it nevertheless remains difficult for us to accept Gusdorf's extreme reversal, one which makes the philosophes' *écrasez l'infâme* a petty provincial affair. Quite the contrary, it was inseparable from a process of demythologizing to which the philosophes themselves tried to put a limit, because they were only halfheartedly committed to it. Without understanding this process, I do not see how it is possible to understand the Enlightenment. The great French philosophes did not belong to the "second team." The accomplishments of the Germans were manifold and solid. Yet how trivial they appear in comparison to the French giants! From these the *rayonnement* of Enlightenment ideas spread throughout the world, into the nineteenth century and our own. Gusdorf's view of

[357]

the French and American revolutions follows the same *optique*. Whereas Wade considers the former to be inscribed in the Enlightenment and tries, however ineffectually, to relate the latter to it, Gusdorf sees them both as lying outside of the Enlightenment, and German cameralism, conservatism, and authoritarianism as its more authentic expressions.

Ira Wade's *The Structure and Form of the French Enlightenment* (1977), despite the rather pretentious title, scarcely deals with structure or form, and has none of its own. Moreover, it is poorly written.[2] It consists almost entirely of lengthy summaries of eighteenth-century works (some well known, others minor and platitudinous), and of works on eighteenth-century works, with a modicum of rambling discussion. This is not an interpretation of the Enlightenment. But even a straightforward history of ideas cannot evade the reality of interpretation that is required by each element of the total history. Wade avoids interpretations as much as he can. When he does interpret isolated works, it is usually in an isolated way that does not establish a relation with the whole. Wade was an eminent scholar, but work on the Enlightenment has progressed to a plane of philosophical and historical sophistication that seems to be alien to his style of scholarship. Reading him, one has the odd feeling of being carried back to the scholarly world of the 1920s, with its emphasis on sources and influences. For instance, we are given a long analysis of the composition of Voltaire's *Traité de métaphysique*, but nothing significant about the philosophical problems it raises or the character of its thought. With the notable exception of aesthetics, Wade more often than not misses the underlying problems

---

[2] A few random solecisms from a long list will document my criticism. "The poetic reality of these . . . beings are guaranteed" (I, 307); "this phenomena" (I, 309); "the phenomena as it is" (I, 522); "Morals had not been flaunted" (for "flouted," II, 353). Many sentences or paragraphs are clumsy or obscure in their sequence of ideas. Just one example: "The travel of important people from one country to another changes the 'moeurs' of the country, which do not vary" (I, 454). There are careless errors, too. Wade apparently cannot decide whether Diderot's title is *Lettre sur les aveugles* or *Essai sur les aveugles*, and at one point he seems to attribute the work to Voltaire (I, 237). Some articles in the *Encyclopédie* that were probably—or certainly—not Diderot's are attributed to him.

and the ultimate inferences.[3] Nor does he inquire into the meaning his authors attached to words, such as *nature*. In brief, he fails in the essential task of providing clear lines with which to conceptualize the Enlightenment—despite his title, "structure and form."

To be sure, he does refer to a vague framework, which divides the Enlightenment into three steps of development. The "philosophic spirit" (of the seventeenth century) became in time the "esprit encyclopédique" or "esprit philosophique," which in turn was transformed into the "esprit révolutionnaire" (II, 399). The divisions of his book and the method of presentation leave the procession from one step to another in limbo. These three "esprits," as he calls them, are at best formal categories, at worst platitudes. They are in any case too weak, too loose, too general, to serve as an adequate framework for interpreting the intricacies of eighteenth-century intellectual history. Their vague and amorphous character does not allow him to achieve his desired result, which is to demonstrate the "coherence," the "organic unity" of the Enlightenment.[4]

In a study containing such a mass of facts, embodying Wade's erudition, even the mature *dix-huitiémiste* is bound to learn some that are new to him and to be refreshed on others. There are some excellent pages: on aesthetics, Fontenelle's ideas about history, the transmission of English literature and thought into France, the theories of the abbé de Saint Pierre, and others. The summary of economic ideas is useful despite the usual lack of evaluation, critical

---

[3]For instance, in the two major areas of ethics and politics, we should like to see a thorough discussion of the theoretical problems, a clear-cut view of their forms and development, instead of long and largely uncritical summaries in series. Many enduring problems were raised during the century. How can self-interest and social interest be brought to coincide? Can they, should they? Shall we convince or constrain the naturally egoistic man in us? How can collective right have validity in itself? If social rules are agreed on by individuals, can they be valid outside of individual moral experience? Or does ethics flow from the collectivity, in which case there are no inherent rights?

[4]Wade seems to be aware of his failure. He has appended to the 1100 pages a so-called Index of Ideas, which he introduces as follows: "I would like to organize in some useful way the contents which can be found in this lengthy presentation. It is the problem with which I have been faced during the last twenty-five years."

delving, or confrontation. Nevertheless, one is dismayed by the frequency of well-worn or retreaded ideas: Diderot used philosophy to discredit religion; the church has played an enormous role in life since the Middle Ages, and so on.

Wade is obsessed by the idea of organic unity. The Enlightenment itself, and everyone in it—with the exception of Diderot—must be "coherent" and unified. He never explains why this should be a necessity, why, for instance, the Enlightenment cannot be apprehended as an organic duality, polarity, or multiplicity, or how unity (even if it were to be found in more significant terms than what he gives us) would account for diversity, or be more meaningful than it. Aside from such an approach being naive and unhistorical, Wade's own method cannot lead to his goal: one cannot derive unity from a process of addition. When one reads the chapters in the section that takes up the "organic unity" of some separate parts of the supposed "organic unity" of the whole (Voltaire, Diderot, Rousseau, the *Encyclopédie*), the outcome is baffling, and we come out with no clear idea of what their unity is.

In the third part of the postulated (but undemonstrated) progression, Wade credits certain writers with forming an "esprit révolutionnaire," but it is difficult to see what was "revolutionary" about them. Beyond this, the essential question is whether the impact of such abstract, hypothetical tracts was sufficient to form an "espirt révolutionnaire" in France. This I do not believe. Indeed, if Mornet stopped short at 1787, it was doubtless because he, too, was unable to justify such a transition, even though the scope of his material was much broader. If in fact there was such an *esprit*, one would have to search elsewhere for its causative factors—social, economic, and political. One would have to look at the group of frustrated intellectuals arising in the 1780s, men who made the Revolution, whose role Robert Darnton has so well clarified in writings we must add to those Wade ignores.

I have sincere admiration for Wade's erudition. Alas, I must add that this impressive erudition falls short. First, in regard to the eighteenth century itself, for much that is essential is omitted.[5] But

[5]I cannot agree that it is possible to give an estimate of d'Alembert while virtually ignoring his *Elémens de philosophie*; of Condillac, when limiting oneself to the *Essai sur l'origine des connaissances humaines*; of Rousseau, when excluding *La*

there is something more surprising. While it would be inaccurate to say that Wade's bibliography stops short at 1960, there are large gaps in the 1960–65 period, relatively few works between 1965 and 1970, and scarcely any after 1970. For Wade, the scholarly world stopped spinning sometime in the 1960s, whereas it has been spinning since ever faster. I am compelled to say that his study was hopelessly out of date at the moment of its birth.[6]

I turn with relief to books of more modest length and pretensions. In the writing of history as in architecture, less is often more. The piling up of facts frequently obscures more than it reveals. The goals should be to combine vital ideas with measured doses of significant information. To some degree, Franco Venturi's *Utopia e Riforma nell'Illuminismo* (1970, English trans. 1971) does this. A rich but disconcerting book, it falls somewhat short, in my opinion, of the praise that has been lavished on it.

Beginning with methodology, Venturi asserts that the history of ideas is irrelevant, inasmuch as the philosophes opposed philosophic systems. This statement, in addition to its apparent *saut de logique*, overlooks the philosophes' predilection for constructing

Nouvelle Héloïse and the later political tracts. Nor can I guess that a true picture is presented when such figures as Sade, Restif, Dom Deschamps, Mercier go unmentioned, and La Mettrie's important place in ethical thought goes by the board. We are told that we know practically nothing about Morelly, a statement that apparently rests on ignorance of R. N. Coe's two articles published in 1957. Wade speaks of the malleability of man without reference to Hartley or to John Passmore's recent study of the subject.

"To cite just a few examples of the gross inadequacies in the case of Diderot and Rousseau, Wade uses Keim (1907) and Grossman (1926) on Helvétius, but not D. W. Smith. We have a d'Alembert without Grimsley or Hankins, a Condorcet without Keith Baker, a utopianism without Frank Manuel, Franco Venturi, Raymond Trousson, et al. Other works are honored only by mention. Scholarly works such as those of Vyverberg, Darnton, Chouillet, Leith, and many others, as well as collective works, are missing. Also striking is the complete exclusion of scholarly work in the Italian language, which has become of tremendous importance to eighteenth-century studies. Thus we have a Mably without the illumination of Maffey's two books; and many of Wade's pages on the Physiocrats, taxation, economics, and political reform, and the relation between England and France would have profited greatly from the work of Furio Diaz. The important contributions of distinguished scholars like Casini, Moravia, Alatri, Tonelli and others are nowhere to be found.

[361]

political systems. Becker and Gay are scored for interpreting the eighteenth century in terms of what came before it (the pagan world was only an ornament, not a presence), instead of in terms of political realities and praxis. But is it not true that the philosophes' "involvement" was quite limited because of their inability to insert themselves into the realities of the political process, and so it was easily sublimated into speculation? I wonder how we are to understand Rousseau and, one might add, Diderot's *Le Rêve de d'Alembert*, if we eliminate philosophy. I should think that the major conquest of recent historiography has been precisely that of justifying the study of Enlightenment thought as authentic philosophy. Venturi's conception of the Enlightenment, insofar as we can guess at it (for he never tells us) seems to concentrate on politics, the rest being ancillary.

He goes on to criticize the new method of studying social groups, which uses techniques of economics and sociology, "schemes, tables and diagrams." Sociological methods cannot solve political or historical problems, he warns; they only use new methods to tell us what was already known (e.g., the Alphonse Dupront group and the *Livre et Société* enterprise). The class struggle, quantification, structuralism—these are all varieties of the Procrustean bed. Practitioners of these methods are mostly Marxists, Venturi declares, who apply Marxist schemes to interpret the Enlightenment instead of looking into the Enlightenment for the origins of Marxism. Unfortunately, the last remark, however just in itself, seems to contradict his initial censure of interpreters of the Enlightenment who have looked at *its* origins.

His own method, he explains, is economic and sociological, but without any interpretative key. In this way, he promises to show us the philosophes as men who changed the reality around them. It is puzzling that Venturi gives Furio Diaz's study as a model. Diaz's theme is that the philosophes remained largely in the realm of theory and failed to alter reality.

Venturi's theme, more precisely, is the "impact of the republican tradition on the Enlightenment"; this will lead him to the question of utopia and reform, which he will study in the restricted paradigmatic problem of the right to punish, centered in turn on the figure of Beccaria. As one can see, his method involves a progressive reduction of scope, which, however, will open up in the last chapter.

Following this plan, then, Venturi first shows that the republican image was a mythical model related to the modern republics which, having deviated from it, were no longer models. The significance of the republican tradition was now to be found only in the English monarchy. (I note in passing that Venturi does not pay heed to disenchantment with the English model after 1763.) The middle years of the century witnessed a "republican" ferment in France.[7] Next Venturi studies modifications of the republican tradition in the philosophes' reactions to the problems of Geneva, Corsica, Poland, and Holland. The picture he gives us, historically accurate, is of a confusion of disparate ideas.[8]

The chapter on punishment seeks to confront utopianism with reformism. Venturi takes us over the familiar ground of utopian schemes. He refers to "this typical Enlightenment determination to create paradise on this earth, to create a completely human society which was egalitarian and free"—a conclusion that is historically inaccurate—unless by "typical" he means typical of utopians. In fact, the Enlightenment was by and large elitist and antiutopian. Even in the utopias we find freedom only in the few that were primitivist or anarchic. Communism and the abolition of property were, Venturi says, utopianism's lasting bequest to the future. How strange that some scholars are ready to find the roots of modern liberalism and communism in Enlightenment thought but object if one also finds the roots of modern totalitarian and nihilist thought! As for Beccaria, Venturi explains that he turned away from his deeply felt utopianism toward the goal of a society of free and equal men. I suggest that nothing could be more utopian,

---

[7]On Rousseau's republicanism, Venturi writes, "Civil society and government would be indistinguishable from one another, and . . . the governed and the governors . . . the same." This statement is followed by a quotation: "le peuple et le souverain serait une seule personne." Venturi seems not to be aware that the two statements say quite different things, and he apparently misunderstands Rousseau's theory by failing to take into account his essential distinction between sovereignty and government.

[8]The American Revolution, Venturi remarks, belongs to "a completely different historical cycle." He does not explain what he means by this. Despite their native roots and coloration, the American founders belonged to what Venturi would call the British republican tradition, and he acknowledges that their universe of discourse was that of the European Enlightenment.

and that the proper conclusion from Venturi's presentation of Beccaria is that a man could be a utopian *and* a reformer, somewhat as Diderot could be an immoralist and a moralist, with private speculation and a public face. Moreover, some "reforms" may verge on the utopian.

The conviction finally prevailed among the philosophes that only a complete transformation of society would make possible the improvements advocated by Beccaria. I am not sure how this conclusion fits in with the ones that follow: that the prevailing utilitarian mood led to the proposals for social exploitation of criminals, and that some writers held that reforms could improve society. Venturi maintains, however, that there was a general disenchantment with reform and that revolution was being prepared in the minds of men.

The last chapter takes a different track and traces the chronological and geographical diffusion of Enlightenment ideas in the various countries of Europe. The place of honor is given to the *Encyclopédie* and the economists. We are somewhat surprised to learn, in light of the general tenor of the book, that it was the abstract quality of the philosophes' thought that "enabled the new ideas to penetrate and spread beyond national frontiers"; and also that in France an atheistic society "had come into being and was very much alive." No less surprising is the asseveration that the *Contrat social* was the "great model of a democratic society." I fail to see which countries in the democratic tradition of the West have followed it. France, Venturi concludes, was utopian and revolutionary, but also reformist. He next takes us back to England, where the essential economic changes took place in the eighteenth century yet produced no "parti des philosophes." This, he declares, disproves the Marxist interpretation of the Enlightenment as the ideology of the bourgeoisie. To find an Enlightenment in Britain, Venturi asserts, we must go to Scotland; its antithesis is Samuel Johnson. The denial of an English Enlightenment on the grounds that no political group was trying to replace the inherited organism is debatable in its restrictiveness. Insofar as England was taken as a model by the French, was it not because Enlightenment objectives were thought to be already there? Is it not puzzling to suggest, in effect, that England had no Enlightenment, but was enlightened?

Some reviews of Venturi have found his book "difficult." If this is so, it is a result of the looseness of its organization and theoretical underpinning. The argument lacks simplicity and cogency in its wandering development. Venturi concludes that "the tension between utopia and reform increased everywhere." It is not easy to see how he has adhered to this theme. Political theory was not limited to republicanism, as his readers might think. It is not certain that religious and moral questions faded in importance in the last decades, that d'Holbach's atheistic campaign was important only for its political implications. Venturi is apparently not aware that Methodism may have saved England from revolution in the turbulence and misery attending the Industrial Revolution. This omission is the more troubling because he attaches great importance to economic developments. Indeed, in view of the importance attributed to economics and to Montesquieu's model of England ("a republic disguised as a monarchy"), one would have expected more to be made of the latter's conception of a republic, which in this respect resembles Hume's ("Of Civil Liberty"), as a manifestation of a commercial objective. How different from Rousseau's model of heroic virtue!

More serious, as is obvious from the foregoing, the theoretical basis or model of the republican image is never clearly delineated. When Holland, Sweden, Poland, Venice, Geneva, Genoa, and even Great Britain are lumped together under the masthead of republicanism, we wonder how there could be a "republican idea." When the American example is shrugged off, we wonder further.[9]

The reformers, though Venturi does not give that impression, did not desire to upset the monarchic institution, either in France

[9]Admittedly, the notion was a variable one at the time and was undergoing redefinition. The *Dictionnaire de l'Académie Française* (1762) defines a republic as an "Etat gouverné par plusieurs," meaning, I suppose, that the final authority is not invested in one person, while Jaucourt's article in the *Encyclopédie*, repeating Montesquieu, places the essence not in the form of government, but in the locus of sovereignty. A republic, Jancourt says, may give its citizens less freedom than a monarchy. He goes on to discuss the theory of the republic. None of this interests Venturi. Apparently, then, republicanism is to be taken to mean anything except despotism; but enlightened despotism is not excluded. Discontent with absolute monarchy appears to be equated with "republicanism." We are told that it was no longer a question of sovereignty; however, for Rousseau it was that.

or in England. In wanting a distribution or redistribution of power, they were thinking, if I follow Venturi's own thinking, in republican terms. Here is where the American Revolution was important, in a way that escapes him. For the first time a republic was founded not in response to utopianism (in contrast to Robespierre's republic), but on realities that *included* Enlightenment ideas and ideals. It rejected all models except the liberal British tradition, and it did not depend on that. It was free of the repressive oligarchic corruption that made it impossible to take European republics as a model, free of the monarchy and hereditary nobility that prevented Britain from being a truly republican model despite its republican spirit. That is why French writers from Mably to Tocqueville worried about the danger of corruption in the new republic.

Venturi's knowledge of the European eighteenth century is perhaps unmatched by any living scholar. From the dazzling documentation he brings to bear, one would expect a dazzling result. What we have is a deeper exploration that does not change in any important way what we knew before. Yet the picture he paints is both unique and valuable. He has given us a book one must read.

John Redwood's *Reason, Ridicule and Religion: The Age of Enlightenment in England 1660–1750* (1976) provides a contrast to Venturi's treatment of the English scene. It locates the drive of the new thinking in the second half of the seventeenth century and the first quarter of the eighteenth. Not only was there an Enlightenment in England, but it antedated the flowering of the French Enlightenment, to which it gave an impetus. Indeed, just before the period studied by Redwood, Milton and Harrington had voiced ideas that would be heard in France a century later. Redwood's book is a work of synthesis, the first devoted to the English Enlightenment as a movement. He shows that debates over politics, natural philosophy, theology, and social structures were all parts of a greater debate about Christianity and its world view. Religion, then, was the focus, to which all else was ancillary, but necessarily joined. The tension was between theological and philosophical modes of explanation. The new natural philosophy had led to fundamental revisions in what Gusdorf would call the "mental space," and believers sought to define and defend a new conception of a religious world order. After mid-century, the fuss subsided. England settled down, according to Redwood, to the conformity of natural religion. Perhaps; but other kinds of dissent and unrest were to arise, we know, as a result of the changes wrought by a new industrial way of life. Redwood's study shows that we must accept the English Enlightenment as a reality, but accept it as a quite different pattern from the French.

Another contrast is provided by Martin Battestin's *The Providence of Wit* (1974). Battestin, taking an opposing tack, shows that a man like Pope, generally considered an Enlightenment figure with an extensive influence on early Enlightenment thought, expressed the Christian humanist tradition and the fear of its dissolution into a menacing chaos. This fear among the defenders of religion is a part of Redwood's theme. Redwood, however, does not dissect the intellectual scene in such a way as to excise Christian humanism from the Enlightenment or to leave it unaffected by it, but rather presents a picture of tensions and struggles. Battestin's book raises, but does not address, the important and troubling question of the role of Christian-oriented deism or liberal Christian thought within the Enlightenment. (Peter Gay, of course, would call the latter anti-Enlightenment, or the "treason of the clerks.")

Battestin's theme is that Augustan literature, art, music, and gardening were informed by the belief that art should imitate nature, and that nature is the ordered plan of the Creator. It follows that art is an imitation of the divine creation, with its qualities of order, symmetry, harmony, and variety; and that life, in turn, should be an imitation of art, order being expressed in restraint and prudence and reflecting belief in Divine Providence. For Battestin, Newton, not Locke is the tutelary figure. It will be objected that there were other aspects of the period, which Battestin excludes, in which Locke played an important role, and that he slights Bacon's influence as well—indeed, that he does not always interpret these men correctly. It may also be objected that Battestin's telescope shrinks the multivalent facts of an age to its field of view. Yet there is much of value in this distinctly original book.

In Eric Voegelin's *From Enlightenment to Revolution* (1975) we come upon Joseph de Maistre redivivus. This new scourge of the Enlightenment calls it "a spiritual disease" that dehumanized man. (A curious reversal!) Progressivism is a plague, and every "advance" a regression. The absurd dream turned into the nightmare of Marxist and fascist societies, into an effort to change the substance of man by means of the "pragmatically planning will." And all this because of "self-divinization," the "atrophy of Christian transcendental experiences," the loss of our sense of our "creaturely nothingness" and of *"contemptus mundi."* Man, emptied of moral substance, was conceived of as a pleasure-pain mechanism to be manipulated, instead of being ordered toward a transcendental aim. This argument is expressed with frequent use of invective and with uncontrolled rage.

Reading Voegelin evokes some personal comment. In my own work I have emphasized (perhaps overemphasized) the historical fact that the first, paradigmatic expressions of totalitarian and nihilistic thinking, in modern form, germinated within the Enlightenment. I maintained that the attempt to "define them out"—as Cobban, Ford, Gay, and some others have done—is a gross imposition of personal preferences on history. The preferences of these scholars largely coincide with my own; but preferences are irrelevant to our proper concern: to illuminate the Enlightenment as a critical period of change and to bring out its rich deposit within the flow of history. Because Voegelin discerns some of the same phenomena as I have, I consider it necessary to dissociate myself completely from him. Voegelin writes from the viewpoint of an a priori revealed truth, which history has violated and which is a standard of judgment. I do not share his idea of the truth, which belongs to the Platonic-Christian tradition, or his method of attributing responsibility to any age for what happened in later periods. Voegelin condemns the Enlightenment for bringing into question ultimate certainties that should have remained certainties. I see the Enlightenment as a stage in mankind's growing up—an inevitable stage within the forms of thought of Western civilization.

Our last subject brings us back to homegrounds. The Enlightenment in America has recently been explored in four books of major importance. Donald H. Meyer's *The Democratic Enlightenment* (1976) is a model of enlightened historiography. Its judicious assessment of evidence, its lucid interpretations, its achievement of synthesis are impressive. Meyer's theme is the application and transformation of the critical, "experimental" reason of the Enlightenment on these shores, in the realms of religion, ethics, politics, and education, resulting in the consensus of the nineteenth century—the great tradition of our country. While the French philosophes dreamed and spun their systems but were largely unable (as Furio Diaz has shown) to insert their ideas into their world, the Americans institutionalized their forms of Enlightened thinking, before reacting against them and modifying them drastically.

Meyer's extremely broad use of *Enlightenment* to include Jonathan Edwards, Witherspoon, and Channing is open to question. The portrait of Edwards shows us not a man of the Enlightenment but a paradigm of the anti-Enlightenment mind—sin, corruption, enthusiasm, humility, virtue as holiness—"the life of faith." In Witherspoon and Channing we see not the Enlightenment but the deposit or legacy that was absorbed into a new and different synthesis. "The democratization of the Enlightenment," Meyer writes, "changed it from a critical to an apologetic instrument," whose purpose was "to defend the faith." I do not recognize the Enlightenment in this description, for it was preeminently critical doubting, even when, as with the Scottish realists, it supported basic traditional beliefs.[10] It would also have been desirable to emphasize that the philosophes were not faithful to their ideal of the experimental method of reasoning, which, by Meyer's own definition, "assumes nothing" and rejects what is beyond verification.

Rather than insisting on the essential unity of the Enlightenment, as some historians have done, Meyer holds that "there was not one Enlightenment but many." The question is important, and both positions are arguable. He is right in asserting that for many thoughtful persons it was possible to accept the new ways of thinking and still remain attached to traditional (though not unmodified) beliefs and authorities. They "wanted to remain at once Christian and Enlightened. . . . to be Enlightened was not necessarily to be modern." Meyer also defends "reading history backwards"—the observation of root ideas of the eighteenth century that had their "logical flowering" in the nineteenth and twentieth.

[10]In ascribing to the democratic context the purpose of "moving public opinion," Meyer is apparently unaware of the increasing demands in France, during the last decades of the century, to use art and theatre for similar purposes.

Meyer's study is concentrated, schematic, intensively analytic. The tone of Henry Steele Commager's *The Empire of Reason* (1977) is primarily descriptive and enthusiastic, though when he tackles the analysis of difficult notions, such as federalism, prescription, separation of powers, and balance of interests, he is acute and illuminating, and there are many insightful gems. But Commager's outstanding virtue is to make the period live for us, by precision of detail and wealth of color. He treats us to a grand tour, of Europe as well as America, and of their interrelations. Where he does not go deeply into ideas, he illuminates them in the light of reality. Meyer's book is in the best tradition of history of ideas; Commager's is history. Finally, Commager's emphasis is on the contrast between what happened here and the European scene, on the originality and wisdom of our founders. In a real sense, it is a celebration. He, too, shows that it was in America that philosophes were men of action and politically realistic and effective. Whereas Venturi slights the American experience as belonging to a different tradition, Commager, while constantly illuminating the differences as well as the filiations, shows that the fundamental revolution of republicanism—that of society limiting goverment through charters of power—took place here (pp. 212, 217–28). Only in America did the paradoxical notion of majoritarianism with limits on the majority arise and become a reality.

Henry F. May's *The Enlightenment in America* (1976) does not have Meyer's lapidary incisiveness or Commager's wit and verve. But it is a thoughtful book, one that gives a more detailed, more complete account. May also takes a broad view of the Enlightenment. Like Meyer, he emphasizes its relation to Protestant Christianity, the basic American outlook and ethos. Like Meyer again, he sees the clash and amalgam of the two in the early nineteenth century, but lays greater stress on the termination of the Enlightenment's vital force as a movement (compare the two on William Ellery Channing), rather than on its sublimated continuation. Yet he does point out its persistence in institutions and as an "essence" (hope for the future, rational solutions). May also makes useful distinctions. The Enlightenment succumbed not only to its archenemy, popular revivalism, but to popular democracy (which he wisely states was not an Enlightenment philosophy), and to romantic antirationalism. He further distinguishes four aspects or moments of the Enlightenment and clearly traces their influence and the limits of their influence. The four are what he calls the Moderate, the Skeptical, the Revolutionary, and the Didactic—the last being already essentially counter-Enlightenment. About the European Enlightenment, he tells us nothing new; but his views are sound and thoughtful, and superbly integrated with the American scene.[11] May has been criticized for treating ideas outside their social context, especially because he admits that the Enlightenment was rejected by large sections of the people. The charge is somewhat exaggerated, and at all events leads only to another question of larger historical import: what was the role of the leaders, who were the intellectuals, what was the role of the people, and how did these evolve?

Meyer's study best helps the reader to conceptualize the period. Commager's brings it to life. May's shows it to us most thoroughly. If we add to these three Garry Wills's more focused, more controversial and daring but brilliantly original *The Inventing of America*, we can only conclude that one of the major accomplishments of the last ten years of scholarship is to have clarified the problem and the picture of the American Enlightenment as has never been done before.

Limits prevent me from giving a critical account of a number of important books. These include Donald Greene's succinct and sometimes iconoclastic *The Age of Exuberance* (1970) and Lionel Gossman's original *French Society and Culture* (1972). Italy has given us Sergio Moravia's fine account of the sunset years of the Enlightenment, *Il tramonto dell' illuminismo* (1968), and Paolo Casini's marxist-oriented survey, *Introduzione all' illuminismo, da Newton a Rousseau* (1973), in which he labels those who discern the totalitarian character of Rousseau's community "bourgeois liberals." (There I am, classified.)[12] In England, Robert Niklaus's *The Eighteenth Century 1715–1789* (1970, a volume of the series "A Literary History of

---

[11]May's presentation of the American dissenters is an excellent example of his lucid expositions. But the acceptance of judicial review, which appears to May as a puzzle (pp. 359–60) is clearly explained by Commager (pp. 227–32).

[12]Casini's book is not as slanted or overtly propagandist as J. M. Goulemot and M. Launay's *Le siècle des lumières* (1968).

France") and J. H. Brumfitt's *The French Enlightenment* (1972) cannot be too highly recommended. (What a pity that the latter is marred by the decision to omit Rousseau, on the grounds that he is covered by another volume in the series.) To these I add Australia's contribution of Colm Kiernan's *The Enlightenment and Science in Eighteenth Century France* (2d ed., 1973). The woman philosopher Simone Goyard-Fabre has given us a philosophical if not very original *La philosophie des lumières* (1972). She recognizes Rousseau's political theory as one of an organic society, and maintains (contrary to Venturi) that the thought of the age was, politically, less revolutionary than is sometimes argued. "La Révolution en France est moins la conséquence de la diffusion des lumières . . . que de forces opposées à la diffusion des lumières." The German Enlightenment has been studied in Peter H. Reill's erudite but somewhat dry volume *The German Enlightenment and the Rise of Historicism* (1975), and the Spanish-American scene in the arresting and vital collection of papers edited by A. Owen Aldridge, *The Ibero-American Enlightenment* (1973).

Although the books I have discussed may well constitute the major contributions of the last ten years, they fall far short of giving an adequate picture of the work accomplished. Let me first call attention (as if that were needed) to the proliferation of articles. These appear in journals, *Festschriften*, collections of articles by individual scholars or by research groups associated with universities, the published transactions of international and national societies and their regional divisions, and of special colloquia or congresses of which there are presently about a dozen each year. Each and every one of these categories has increased in number during the last decade. Theodore Besterman's *Studies on Voltaire and the Eighteenth Century* alone has given us more than 175 volumes during that period.

In searching library shelves, I could not help noticing the increasing volume of work relating to the role and position of women, women writers, and female characters.[13] I was also impressed by the fact that few of the hundreds of articles I looked at dealt with

[13]See, for instance, the McMaster University symposium, *Woman in the Eighteenth Century and Other Essays*, ed. Paul Fritz and Richard Morton (Toronto, 1976).

general problems and issues of interpretation. Some that do are Arthur Wilson's "The Philosophes in the Light of Present-Day Theories of Modernization," Aram Vartanian's "Intertextures of Science and Humanism," David Ginsberg's "David Hume versus the Enlightenment," James Leith's "Nationalism and the Fine Arts in France," "The Concept of Modernization and the French Enlightenment" by Harriet Branson Applewhite and Darline Gay Levy (an article I should recommend in counterpoint to Venturi's book and to Gay's), Durand Echeverria's "The Emergence of American Libertarianism into French thought and Literature before 1776" (also a corrective to Venturi), and Margaret Jacob's stimulating "Newtonianism and the Origin of the Enlightenment"—all these by members of our Society. Franklin Ford's "The Enlightenment: Towards a Useful Re-definition," has the effect of convincing us, contrary to the author's intentions, that the definitional method of history is not useful. *In partibus infidelium*, I recommend Pierre Chartier's "Le XVIIIe siècle existe-t-il?" Norman Suckling's "The Unfulfilled Renaissance" throws down a gauntlet to enthusiasts. Kay Wilkins's "Some Aspects of the Irrational in Eighteenth Century France" sharpens our perceptions of that aspect of the age, too often passed by. John Windsor's "The Enlightenment: Towards a Synthesis" relates art and literature in a suggestive way, concluding that "the final dissolution of objects into color and light reflects the collapse of the philosophers' moral systems and the feeling of moral nihilism they at all times experienced." I could cite perhaps a dozen others, no more, along with the notable addition of two volumes of our companion French society's *Dix-huitième siècle*, No. 6, "Lumières et Révolution" and No. 9, "Le Sain et le malsain au XVIIIe siècle."[14]

We must not fail to pay due notice to the application of new methods of research and explanation. The proselytes of Derrida,

[14]Vartanian, *Studies in Eighteenth-Century Culture*, 1 (1971), 77–126; Leith, *Studies on Voltaire and the Eighteenth Century*, 89 (1972), 919–37; Applewhite and Gay, ibid., 84 (1971), 53–98; Echeverria, ibid., 152 (1976), 647–62; Jacob, *Eighteenth-Century Studies*, 11 (1977), 1–25; Ford, *Studies in the Eighteenth Century*, ed. R. F. Brissenden (Toronto, 1968), pp. 17–29; Chartier, *Dix-huitième siècle*, 5 (1973), 41–47; Suckling, *Studies on Voltaire and the Eighteenth Century*, 86 (1971), 25–136; Wilkins, ibid., 140 (1975), 107–21; Windsor, *Journal of European Studies*, 1 (1971), 259–67.

Foucault, Kristeva, Hillis Miller, et al., have not failed to apply their several methodologies to the eighteenth century. So far the results have been meager, sometimes trivial. Whether this scantiness is inherent in the ingredients, or whether the votaries are too faithful to their scriptures, like Marxists to theirs—citing them as authorities who have set the rules and laws and language of the game—I cannot say. The catechumens participating in a recent MLA seminar imparted a distressing impression of smugness, of being the in-group that possessed the esoteric vocabulary and the keys of the chapel, taking their exegetical exercises with solemnity and reciprocal self-congratulation. The literary text, it seemed, was the excuse for the game. Some structuralists have been commendably more ambitious. They have undertaken to rewrite works of Diderot and Rousseau, and doubtless others, transposing them into their own scales and modes, and of course, language. Novel methods are always to be encouraged. "New forms arise, and diff'rent views engage, / Superfluous lags the vet'ran on the stage." So far, however, these have served largely to confirm the initiates' own faith and (to quote Johnson again), we should be cautious in committing ourselves to "chase the new-blown bubbles of the day."

A far more productive method of research has been pursued by what may be loosely called the historians of the *Annales* school. They have helped to complete our picture of an age by going beyond or behind literature and philosophy to general social phenomena and to the particular social functions and involvement of writers. That ideas are molded by cultural context—economic, social, institutional—is a commonplace too often neglected, except by Marxists, but it is by no means limited to their doctrinal approach. On the other hand, there is the danger of forgetting that ideas have an internal dynamics and a life of their own. While some of the work resulting from the sociological approach is of limited and antiquarian interest, the best of it unites the social and the intellectual, enriches our knowledge of the period and vivifies it. Robert Darnton, who won the first article prize offered by this Society, represents the best in the new methodology. His *Mesmerism and the End of the Enlightenment in France* (1968) and his many articles on the book trade are major contributions. I recommend, too, his article "In Search of the Enlightenment."

Alan Kors's *D'Holbach's Coterie* (1976) also successfully combines sociological and intellectual history. I shall not try to summarize this thoroughly researched, judicious, and insightful study, but limit myself to one or two comments. Kors discharges the coterie from the obvious accusation that they did not live according to their precepts by showing that they despised *le peuple*, feared disorder, and opposed upheavals. (We might say that there was no Jefferson among them.) Their role as they saw it was to work within the regime to enlighten its rulers and induce them to make the reforms that would prevent upheaval. Their privileges and emoluments were rewards for their merit. All this is true; but I should put it somewhat differently: while aspiring to a better reality, they accepted the reality that was theirs and did the best for themselves within it. When their interests, inevitably involved with the Ancien Régime, were jeopardized, they reacted according to the same pattern of self-interest that they had stipulated as the law of human behavior. This ambivalence may have been one reason among others for their limited influence on political realities. If the men of 1789 did indeed reflect their abstract thought, they themselves were not prepared to see changes brought about in their own time that could compromise their interests, any more than were other sectors of the Establishment. Again we see a stark contrast with the American situation, which alone was truly republican. To this I should add that the men of the coterie, relatively radical, were not the most radical thinkers of their time. They were demythologizers, but not radical demythologizers, except (in the case of some of them) in the realm of religion. Whether for reasons of social position or commitment, or because of ideological conviction (Marxists would argue that the two are inextricable), they wanted to call a halt on this side of what they perceived as danger to social stability.

Still another striking work of this kind is Pierre Chaunu's *La civilisation de l'Europe des lumières* (1971). Chaunu may be something of an anomaly, for he belongs to the political Right. Distortions analogous to those we see in writers on the other side ensue from his perspective.[15] If his account of ideas is inadequate, ideas are

[15]For instance, those he associates with empiricism and progress toward nineteenth-century liberalism, even *parlementaires*, are favored over utopians and materialists (deemed anti-empirical). Chardin is praised, the rococo disparaged.

for him only part of a larger picture, which includes demography, health, the book trade, and social customs. In his study, he uses quantification—abhorred by the French of an earlier generation as "American" methodology—as far as possible. Other productions of merit, such as Robert Favre's *La Mort au siècle des Lumières* (1978) and the collective volume *Images du peuple au XVIII° siècle* (1973), could be cited.

From all I have said, it is evident that eighteenth-century studies are in a state of turmoil and almost unmanageable proliferation. This fact testifies to the intrinsic importance of the period. Publications have multiplied with the self-increasing force of an avalanche as research has become a cottage industry. One could misquote Johnson and speak of "the academical conspiracy for the destruction of paper." This is both fortunate and unfortunate. We cannot ignore the danger of ever-inflating hyperspecialization in a field that is already specialized. Have we reached—or are we approaching—a point where a scholar can no longer control the period as a whole?

One other conclusion imposes itself. As I reviewed the great amount of material, it became clear that the American Society for Eighteenth-Century Studies, born a decade and a half ago, has fulfilled the high hopes and justified the excitement that attended its founding. By our publications and other activities we have made our full share of contribution to the treasury of knowledge about the eighteenth century, and we shall continue to do so.

The Encyclopaedic Spirit

ROBERT SHACKLETON

WHEN HE WAS ILL IN LATE SUMMER OF 1755, DIDEROT WROTE one of the longest and most remarkable articles in the *Encyclopédie*. This was the article entitled "Encyclopédie" and it constituted Diderot's profession of faith. He was to draw on it ten years later when writing the preface, in Volume VIII, to the concluding ten volumes, which appeared simultaneously in 1765. It contains a prophecy. One day there may come a revolution, and this revolution will be followed by a period of calm. It will be then that the *Encyclopédie* will be justly appreciated, and will give its name to the reign of the monarch under whom it was published, to the great who encouraged it, and to the authors who contributed to it. This forecast was indeed true in its essentials (though Louis XV was never called an *encyclopédiste*): the word *encyclopaedist* summarizes the spirit of the age.

The earlier history of the word is full of interest. *Encyclopaedia* means the circle of knowledge. It exists neither in ancient Greek nor in classical Latin, save that Pliny the Elder and Quintilian both record it as a word used by the Greeks, but this is believed to be a false reading, in each case. Du Cange notes it in medieval Latin in a life of the Spanish Saint Ildefonso. The Italian equivalent,

This paper was originally read at the April 1979 Annual Meeting of the American Society for Eighteenth-Century Studies in Atlanta, where I had the great pleasure of being introduced by Donald Greene. My attention was subsequently drawn to an invaluable work which treats part of the same theme: C. Vasoli, *L'Enciclopedismo del Seicento* (Naples, 1978). I have made some revisions in the light of this book. The same author's *Profezia e Ragione* (Naples, 1974, pp. 821–916) refers at length to Giacinto Gimma's *Nova Encyclopaedia*, an unpublished manuscript at Bari which I have not yet been able to see. Most interestingly for our present concern, Gimma compiled (and Vasoli reproduced) a list of writers who have written encyclopaedias (*Auctorum Catalogus, qui Encyclopaedia nomine inscripserunt volumina*). This lists adds a great deal to my own, but I have not been able to take account of it.

enciclopedia, is not known to the Accademia della Crusca as late as 1746. In French the dictionary of Furetière in 1701 records *encyclopédie* as meaning "science universelle, recueil, ou enchaînement de toutes les sciences ensemble." He adds, however, that the word is archaic and used only in humorous writing ("n'est plus en usage que dans le burlesque"). The word was certainly used facetiously from time to time. A man with learned pretensions might be mocked as thinking that he possessed "toute l'encyclopédie"; Rousseau, gently mocking himself in the *Confessions*, relates how as a young man he tried to teach himself "l'encyclopédie." A thoroughly facetious use, in Italian, is found in a work entitled *Fior di virtù*, published at Venice in 1725. The author, who calls himself Nioanto Inizuch (surely an anagram of Antonio Zuchini), explains the word *enciclopedia* to his puzzled readers, and laughingly treats it as etymologically cognate with the Cyclops.

When was the word, in whatever language, first used as the title of a book? I have made an attempt to list those books, before Diderot's *Encyclopédie*, in whose title the word *Encyclopaedia* (or *Cyclopaedia*) occurs, in any language. The list is drawn up on the basis of a variety of sources: the *Bibliotheca Britannica* of George Watts; the article "Enciclopedia" in the *Enciclopedia Italiana*; Robert Collison's *Encyclopaedias: Their History throughout the Ages* (New York and London, 1964), which is a mine of information; and chance encounters in reading, in libraries and bookshops, and in booksellers' catalogues. I am sure that the list is not complete. It is already much longer than in the first draft, and I should welcome additions. It shows how far the concept and the name of an encyclopaedia extends back in time. In principle it shows the first edition, and that only, of each book. I have personally inspected all the books and manuscripts listed, with the exception of one or two recently added.

1536   Alanus de Insulis, *anti-Claudiani singulari festivitate lepore et elegantia poetae libri IX, non credibili doctrina, ordine et brevitate complectens* την κυκλοπαιδειαν *universam.* Basle, 1536.

Alan of Lille was a twelfth-century theologian and philosopher. Dr. Nigel Palmer (to whom I am indebted for knowledge of this work) tells me that none of the thirty manuscripts of Alanus which are in Great Britain has in its title the word *cyclopaedia*, which must therefore be attributed to the sixteenth-century editor.

1541   Joachim Fortius Sterck van Ringelberg, *Lucubrationes vel potius absolutissima* κυκλοπαιδια. Basle, 1541.

A Flemish humanist (c. 1499–c. 1536) who was a friend of Erasmus.

1559   Paulus Scalichius de Lika, *Encyclopaedia, seu orbis disciplinarum, tam sacrarum quam prophanarum, epistemon.* Basle, 1559.

A learned adventurer (1534–75) of Slavic origin, who pretentiously assumed the name Scaliger. He lived in Prussia and died at Danzig.

1565   Ramondus Lullius, *Artificium, sive ars brevis . . . ad absolvendam omnium artium encyclopaediam.* Barcelona, 1565.

Catalan philosopher (c. 1235–1315) and polymath; the "doctor illuminatus."

1605   Matthias Martinius, *Encyclopaedia philosophica.* MS in Stadtbücherei, Erfurt, dated 1605; microfilm in Columbia University Library.

German Protestant theologian (1572–1630); student and later professor at Herborn.

1606   Matthias Martinius, *Encyclopaedia brevis, seu idea methodica, vel adumbratio universitatis de principiis naturalibus.* Herborn, 1606.

Possibly an abridgment of the manuscript preceding.

1610   Joannes Henricus Alstedius, *Panacea philosophica, id est, facilis, nova et accurata methodus docendi et discendi universam encyclopaediam.* Herborn, 1610.

A Protestant theologian, philosopher, and eminent polymath (1588–1638); professor at Herborn and then at Alba Julia in Transylvania. His name was seen as an anagram of *sedulitas.*

1621   Joannes Irlen, *Specimen bibliothecae theologicae, sive encyclopaediae sacrae.* Frankfurt, 1621.

Protestant theologian (1597–1653); professor and later rector (1628–34) at Herborn.

1630   Joannes Henricus Alstedius, *Encyclopaedia septem tomis distincta.* Herborn, 1630; 7 vols.

Alstedius was inspired by Lullius. This was the principal encyclopaedia of the age.

1632   Ramondus Lullius, *Le Fondement de l'artifice universel sur lequel on peut appuyer le moyen de parvenir à l'encyclopédie ou universalité des sciences par un ordre méthodique. . . . Le tout traduit . . . de latin en françois . . . et mis en lumière par R. L. Sieur de Vassi.* Paris, 1632; 2 pts.

The word *encyclopédie* here is descriptive not of the book but of the state of possessing knowledge.

1635 Jean Macé, *Fratris Leonis Encyclopaediae praemissum, seu delineatio sapientiae universalis.* Paris, 1635.

A reformed Carmelite (ob. 1671), who was a theologian and ecclesiastical historian. "Fratris Leonis" may refer to Fray Luís de León.

1642 Helfricus Ulricus Hunnius, *Encyclopaedia Hunniana juris universi.* Cologne, 1642.

A celebrated German professor of law (1583–1636) whose works were posthumously published under this title.

1646 Pierre Morestel, *Encyclopaedia, sive artificiosa ratio et via circularis ad Artem Magnam Raymundi Lullii.* [La Saussaye], 1646.

A priest and cabbalistic writer (ob. 1648), tutor to Charles d'Elboeuf, duc de Lorraine.

1648 Christianus Gueinzius, *Encyclopaediae pars prior.* Halle, 1648.

A well-known college rector (1592–1650) who wrote on legal, historical, and theological topics.

s.d. *Encyclopaedia, seu orbis disciplinarum complectens liberalium artium et scientarium ideae.* Lyon, Bibliothèque Municipale, MS. 236. No date but clearly seventeenth century.

An anonymous manuscript which draws heavily on Aristotle.

1652 Abraham Calovius, *Encyclopaedias disciplinarum realium ideae.* Lübeck, 1652.

A polemical Lutheran controversialist (1612–86) and an opponent of Grotius.

1653 Apátzai Tsere János, *Magyar Encyclopaedia.* Utrecht, 1653.

A Hungarian philosopher from Transylvania (1625–59) who suffered for his acceptance of Cartesianism. His work is written in Hungarian and is the first with the title *Encyclopaedia* to be written in a vernacular language.

1656 *Encyclopédie de l'âme en forme de dialogue contre les libertins de ce tems.* MS. Loches 35. 1656.

A polemical work in the tradition of Garasse, *La Doctrine curieuse de beaux-esprits de ce temps* (1624).

1657   Francisco Macedo, *Encyclopaedia in agonem litterarium producta.* Rome, 1657.

     A Portuguese Franciscan (1596–1681) whose twenty-four-page encyclopaedia was based on his three-day Roman thesis *de omni re scibili.*

1658   Giuseppe Artale, *Dell'Enciclopedia poetica.* Perugia, 1658.

     A Sicilian poet (1628–79); this collection of his lyrics was completed by second and third parts in 1660 and 1672.

1659   Sebastian Izquierdo, *Pharus Scientiarum . . ., quo verae Encyclopaediae orbis facile a cunctis circumvolvendus.* Lyon, 1659.

     A Spanish Jesuit (1601–81) who claimed to follow Lull. His work is dedicated to Jesus Christ.

1684   Joannes Dolaeus, *Encyclopaedia medicinae theoretico-practicae.* Frankfurt, 1684.

     A German doctor (1651–1707) whose medical encyclopaedia was followed in 1690 by one of surgery.

1692   Giacinto Gimma, *Nova encyclopaedia, sive novus doctrinarum orbis.* MS in 7 volumes in Biblioteca Consorziale, Bari. Dated 1692.

     An Apulian *abbé* (1668–1735) who compiled his encyclopaedia under the influence of Alstedius and Charles Sorel.

1699   Joannes Jacobus Brusaschi, *Encyclopaedia aphoristica.* Rome, 1699.

     A little-known Piedmontese doctor of the late seventeenth century.

1708   Joannes Laurentius Lucchesini, *Encyclopaedia panegyrici et satyrae.* Rome, 1708.

     A Jesuit theologian and man of letters (1638–1716) whose *Encyclopaedia* is a collection of Latin poems imitating different classical authors.

1721   Martin de Torrecilla, *Enciclopedia canonica, civil, regular y orthodoxa.* Madrid, 1721; 2 vols.

     A Spanish Carmelite (ob. 1709), a moral theologian, philosopher and canonist.

1728   Ephraim Chambers, *Cyclopaedia: or, an universal dictionary of arts and sciences.* London, 1728; 2 vols.

     The first great modern encyclopaedist (c. 1680–1740); F.R.S.

The relationship of these works would be an intricate subject for research. It is not perhaps by accident that the first three emanate from Basle. A more certain connection links some of the German titles. At the small town of Herborn, near Marburg, a Protestant college was founded in 1584. Matthias Martini was both student and professor there, the matriculation roll bearing against his name the annotation "ad miraculum doctus." His encyclopaedia was published at Herborn in 1609. Alsted and Irlen were professors there, each in turn becoming rector. In 1629 Alsted left Herborn to teach at the new college at Alba Julia (Weissesburg) in Transylvania. The Protestant theologian Bisterfeld was Alsted's disciple and son-in-law, and regularly recommended the reading of his *Encyclopaedia* to his pupils. The latter included Apátzai, whose *Magyar Encyclopaedia* was dedicated to Bisterfeld. The Latin preface of Apátzai establishes the link through Bisterfeld to Alsted. I am indebted to Dr. Robert Evans for help in tracing out this connection.

The publication in 1728 of the great work of Ephraim Chambers was an event of European significance: more than European, indeed, for the list of subscribers includes Cadwallader Colden, M.D., of New York, and James Logan of Pennsylvania. In spite of the entry it contains for "Cyclopaedia," which reads, "The circle, or compass of Arts and Sciences; more ordinarily call'd Encyclopaedia," these are the first of the ninety-nine words which make up the title in *Cyclopaedia*. The dedication to George II begins with the proud words, "The Arts and Sciences humbly crave audience of Your Majesty." The preface claims the French Academy as a predecessor, and places the *Cyclopaedia* in a rich tradition of writing on the practical arts.

The work received great success. Chambers was promptly elected to the Royal Society, and on his death in 1740 was buried in Westminster Abbey. Several new editions appeared. The *Cyclopaedia* was seen as a pioneering work, based on a new approach to the sciences and making them accessible to the nonspecialist. It became widely known on the Continent. The article *Plague* was translated into Italian and prefaced to a translation of Richard Mead's *Short Discourse concerning pestilential contagion* in 1744. The translator described the philosophical lexicon of Chambers as "opera insigne per la rarità ed universalità di cognizioni." At least three complete Italian translations of the *Cyclopaedia* were executed. One was published at Naples in 1747 and republished at Genoa in 1770. Another appeared at

Venice in 1749. A third, executed by Carlo Gagliardo in 1754, was recorded by the general inventory of Italian manuscripts in 1896 as being in the Biblioteca Comunale at Sulmona in the Abruzzi, but it has been mislaid for decades. During the pontificate of Clement XIII both published versions were condemned by the Congregation of the Index. If credence is to be given to a monk of Bologna, whose manuscript notebook, itself entitled *Encyclopaedia*, is at Arezzo,[1] the reasons for the condemnation were that accents were incorrectly shown, and that the work encouraged criticism of the clergy. "In somma è inglese," writes the monk, "*Fuge tanquam a facie colubri, cave, cave.*"

The influence of Chambers was still more far-reaching in France. A young man called Lambert, born in 1726 or 1727 of the Protestant banking family and later himself connected with Rousseau, began to make a translation in Paris, and claims to be the first to have had this idea.[2]

Then came the *Encyclopédie* itself. It is unnecessary to rehearse the eventful history of its preparation and publication, from the original project by the *libraire* Lebreton to publish a translation of Chambers and the early association of Diderot and d'Alembert, through the periodic crises and two suppressions, to the completion of the publication of the text in 1765. It is enough to say that this gave a great impetus—and its name—to the Encyclopaedic movement, in which the greatest subsequent event was the beginning of the *Encyclopaedia Britannica* in 1768.

The full title of the work is always to be remembered: *Encyclopédie, ou Dictionnaire raisonné des sciences, des arts, et des métiers*. Alphabetical order, by no means then a requisite of the encyclopaedia, was imposed by the word *dictionnaire*. As a dictionary the work was expected to give an account of the present state of the arts and sciences, and in this respect it had, as well as Chambers, other precursors that did not have a specific encyclopaedic aim. Such were, most notably, the *Dictionnaire des Arts et des Sciences*, published by the Académie Française in 1694 and edited by Thomas Corneille, and the *Lexicon technicum* of the Englishman John Harris.

[1] MS. Arezzo 316.
[2] *Précis de la vie du citoyen Lambert* (N.p., n.d.) (Bibliothèque Nationale: Ln^{27} 11217). I am indebted to Professor R. A. Leigh for this reference.

Strictly as an encyclopaedia, however, Diderot's work had another role, and this is outlined in the Prospectus: "Il s'agissait . . . de faire sentir les secours mutuels que [les sciences et les arts] se prêtent; d'user de ces secours pour en rendre les principes plus sûrs et leurs conséquences plus claires; d'indiquer les liaisons éloignées ou prochaines des êtres qui composent la Nature, et qui ont occupé les hommes; de montrer par l'entrelacement des racines et par celui des branches, l'impossibilité de bien connaître quelques parties de ce tout, sans remonter ou descendre à beaucoup d'autres." The encyclopaedia was indeed the circle of knowledge, embracing all and uniting the parts into a perfect whole. These parts were to be analyzed and understood in their relation to one another and to the whole; and if the parts are to be defined they must be classified.

The classification of knowledge was a task by which many earlier writers had been tempted, and the numerous compendiums of knowledge drawn up in the Middle Ages often contained graphical arrangements of the different branches of knowledge, often with a unifying astrological base. This tradition was continued in many of the encylopedias listed above. In 1559 Scalich includes in his volume a complicated folding diagram with a series of concentric circles. Six of the outer circles are given to the earth, the sun, the moon, two forms of light called *lux* and *lumen*, splendor, heat, and generation. To these correspond the qualities of unity, kindness, mind, soul, nature, and body (if indeed the four last can be called qualities). This is matched by Fortius, whose *Lucubrationes* contains a drawing of the human hand, with its different parts marked by the signs of the zodiac.

Mention must be made of one of the most splendid examples of the French book production in the sixteenth century. The author of this work is Christophle de Savigny, and its short title is *Tableaux accomplis de tous les arts libéraux* (Paris, 1587). This folio volume contains twenty magnificent plates showing the divisions of the sciences. The first plate is the most striking of all, since it has the heading, *Encyclopédie, ou la suite et liaison de tous des arts et sciences*. It shows an oval figure, bordered by a chain whose links are named, in French, with names of the sciences. Within is a division into general and special branches, with subdivisions into speech and reason, quality and quantity, corporal and incorporal, human and divine. It shows a remarkable degree of maturity both in typographic skill and analytic thought.

In the century following, the Lyons manuscript contains an elaborate circular drawing in which the signs of the zodiac are made to correspond to different subjects. Thus the ram is allied to grammar, the virgin to music, and Sagittarius to ethics. How far is this scheme removed from the *esprit encyclopédique* of the eighteenth century! And yet the one historically begets the other.

These early encyclopaedists began to move from fanciful iconography to more sober tabulation, usually in the form of a horizontal genealogical tree. Fortius, the first of them, gives a series of tables. In one of them relationship (*relatio*) is divided between simple (*simplex*) and mixed (*mixta*). Simple relationship provides substance, quality and quantity. Mixed relationships give the subheadings action, passion, place, time, position, and dress. A complicated table drawn by Alstedius divides philosophy into precepts and prolegomena, and divides each into a curious systematic pattern. The work of Calovius consists entirely of such tables, drawn in a much more modern spirit. The first table, for example, starting on the left with the "real disciplines" as a general category, by successive subdivision arrives at individual subjects such as metaphysics, artithmetic, geometry, cosmography, optics, and finally the subjects of the higher faculties of the universities, theology, law, and medicine. A greater man than Calovius had meanwhile drawn up a similar table. This is Hobbes, whose *Leviathan* of 1651 contains an ingenious tabular analysis of science, which he defines as knowledge of consequences, "which is called also philosophy." A first subdivision into natural and civil philosophy leads ultimately, on the far right of the page, to individual subjects from geometry to the "science of just and unjust."[3]

In the preface to his *Cyclopaedia*, Chambers likewise produces an analysis which, by five stages of subdivision, proceeds to the individual subjects, his initial differentiation being between the two parts of knowledge, the one "natural and scientifical," the other "artificial and technical."

[3]Hobbes, *Leviathan*, ed. M. Oakshott (Oxford, 1946), pp. 54–55.

Diderot and d'Alembert, though essentially modern and innovative in outlook, accepted the tradition of a tabular classification of the sciences. But whereas Calovius and Hobbes, the most sophisticated of the early writers mentioned, were guided in their plan by ingenious applications of logic, the method chosen in the *Encyclopédie* was different, deriving its framework from the human faculties used in the study of each subject.

This faculty basis of division was of some antiquity. Its genesis can be found in a succinct statement made by St. Augustine, "Quod scimus, debemus rationi, quod credimus, auctoritati."[4] Jansenius in his *Augustinus* had developed on this base a formula that assigned philosophy to the control of reason and theology to memory alone.[5] Pascal, writing in 1651, produced in his *Préface sur le Traité du Vide* a more complete classification. History, geography, jurisprudence, languages fall under the domain of authority, while in mathematics (including music), physics, medicine, architecture, and the other sciences, reason should be man's guide.[6] The importance for a man of Pascal's outlook of the exclusion of reason from theology, and the exclusion of all but reason from science, is evident. Pascal's *Préface* was unknown until its publication in 1779, but similar ideas were expressed, much more elaborately, by a philosopher whose works Pascal could have known.

Francis Bacon was described by d'Alembert as "l'immortel chancelier d'Angleterre," and his influence in eighteenth-century France was far-reaching. In the second book of his *De dignitate et augmentiis scientarium* Bacon makes his division of sciences—tripartite, unlike Pascal's. The first chapter of this second book (I quote from the English translation) begins with the words "That is the truest partition of humane learning, which hath reference to the *three faculties* of Man's Soul, which is the seat of learning. History is referred to Memory, poesie to the imagination, philosophy to reason."[7] From this initial division Bacon elaborates a full and completed system.

---

[4]St. Augustine, *De utilitate credendi*, Ch. XI (ed. Migne, XLII, p. 83; cited in *La Logique, ou l'art de penser*, Part IV, Ch. 12).

[5]Jansenius, *Augustinus*, II, preliminary book, Ch. IV.

[6]Pascal, *Oeuvres complètes*, ed. J. Mesnard (Brussels, 1970), II, 777–81.

[7]*Of the Advancement and Proficiencies of Learning*, trans. Gilbert Watts (London, 1674), pp. 49–50 (first published, 1640).

He does not himself produce a schematic diagram; but his English translator of 1640 prefaces to the text a series of tables that summarize the arguments of the work. The first of these, entitled "The Emanation of Sciences," represents the division by faculties and carries them through to the individual subjects.

Of the *Encyclopédie*'s debt to Bacon there is no doubt. It is openly avowed: "Nous déclarons ici que nous devons principalement au Chancelier Bacon l'arbre encyclopédique dont nous avons déjà parlé . . . et que l'on trouvera à la fin de ce Discours."[8] A folding sheet, 20 by 15½ inches, bearing the title *Système figuré des connaissances humaines*, is inserted immediately before the first article of the *Encyclopédie*. At the end of the work and prefaced to the first volume of the *Table des matières*, published in 1780 when Diderot had long ceased to be associated, is an immense folding sheet 39 by 24 inches. This bears the portrayal—natural, not schematic—of a tree. The main trunk is labeled "Raison," a large branch to the left is called "Mémoire," and a smaller branch "Imagination" is to the right. The trunk and the main branches have small branches issuing from them, and from these spring twigs. All these carry innumerable ovals of print resembling fruit, which enumerate and describe the various subjects, and the whole forms a remarkable representation of human knowledge and its constituent elements. This giant plate was engraved by Robert Benard, an artist who had been one of the two principal engravers of the *Encyclopédie* since 1754, and designed by Chrétien Frédéric Guillaume Roth, a person unknown to history. The colophon describes the plate as having been issued at Weimar in 1769.

The plate and the diagram sum up what the *Encyclopédie* owes to ancient tradition: the urge to classify all knowledge, and the feeling that the classification should be expressed in a visual representation. In the substance of the classification there is individual originality. The smallness of the share attributed to imagination is less surprising in an age in which imaginative literature was on the whole defective in quality, than it is from the person of Diderot, whose imagination is fecund. Under memory come all forms of history, including natural history, and all the manual arts and

---

[8]*Discours préliminaire* (*Encyclopédie*, I, p. xxv).

crafts. In the age of Montesquieu, Buffon, and Diderot himself the exclusion of reason from these realms seems an unthinking reversion to the standards of another age. But innovating vigor is shown in the history of disciplines made subject to reason: not only the science of nature and the science of man but also the science of God; and within this last not only natural religion, whose instrument is indeed reason, but also revealed religion. The assertion that revealed religion was subject to rational criteria, and to rational criteria alone, would have provoked angry reaction, *lettres de cachet*, arrest, the Bastille and perhaps exile if it had been spelled out with plain clarity. Advanced, however, in the archaic form of a diagram or symbolic plate, it was received by the public with calm and by authority with equanimity.

Calm and equanimity did not characterize the reception of the work as a whole. Uncontroversial as the great majority of the articles were, being largely factual and expository, the minority of articles which were new and audacious in character provoked conflict and official hostility—that same hostility which Voltaire and Helvétius knew. The encyclopaedists faced first the professional jealousy of the Jesuit authors of the *Dictionnaire de Trévaux*, who sought to have the privilege of the *Encyclopédie* withdrawn; yet one of their publishers, Laurent Durand, was one of the four who published the *Encyclopédie*. The government was hostile, yet the work was dedicated to the comte d'Argenson, minister for war, and the chancellor's son, Malesherbes, was a sympathizing protector as *directeur de la librairie*, while the royal mistress, Mme de Pompadour, favored the *philosophes* in general and the *Encyclopédie* in particular. But struggle characterized the *Encyclopédie*. Without a struggle, it would have been a less famous and less influential work. Its supplement, and its rearrangement, the *Encyclopédie méthodique*, published in quieter days, lack the fire and the inspiration of the enterprise of Diderot and d'Alembert.

The name and the example of the *Encyclopédie*, however, continued vigorous. As early in 1751 the Englishman George Barrow prefaced to his *New and Universal Dictionary of Arts and Sciences* a long essay on the history of civilization which was taken, without acknowledgment, from the *Discours préliminaire* of d'Alembert. A projected London translation of the *Encyclopédie* never materialized.

In 1772 a London publisher produced a volume of *Select Essays from the Encyclopedy*, and of course in 1768 the first volume of the *Encyclopaedia Britannica* appeared.

New editions of the *Encyclopédie* appeared in Switzerland, along with a rival work, the *Encyclopédie d'Yverdon*, directed by an exiled Italian, then called De Félice, previously De Felíce. In Italy the *Encyclopédie* itself was twice reprinted in the original French, at Lucca and at Livorno. The press which printed it in the latter city came to be known as the *Stampa Enciclopedica*, and had a by no means inglorious career in Enlightenment publishing. At Pistoia, as Eric Cochrane has pointed out, there was an Accademia Enciclopedica; it was founded in 1763.[9] Twenty-five years later the Grand Orient of France approved the constitution, at Toulouse, of a lodge of freemasons with the title Loge Encyclopédique.[10] In another medium and another country, the two Portuguese university libraries at Evora and Coïmbra each have painted ceilings that proudly carry the inscription *Encyclopaedia*.[11]

In spite of the seriousness of the Encyclopaedic movement, sometimes the early burlesque sense remained. The Cambridge scholar and royal librarian Thomas James Mathias, in the fourth dialogue of his satirical *Pursuits of Literature*, first published in 1797, invented the character of Dr. Morosophus the pedant, whose attainments are sardonically summed up thus:

> Chambers abridg'd! in sooth 'twas all he read
> From fruitful A to unproductive Z.[12]

A discussion of the "encyclopaedic spirit," taken in the broadest sense, could have been concerned with almost the whole of French, and much of European, eighteenth-century thought. I have preferred to take it in a restricted and more literal sense, avoiding wide

[9] E. W. Cochrane, *Tradition and Enlightenment in the Tuscan Academies* (Rome, 1961), p. 36. For the date, see *Relazione del principio, progresso, e stato presente dell'Accademia enciclopedica erretta nella Città di Pistoja* (Livorno, 1764).

[10] A. Le Bihan, *Loges et chapitres de la Grande Loge et du Grand Orient de France* (Paris, 1967), p. 239.

[11] A. Masson, *Le Décor des bibliothèques du Moyen-Age à la Révolution* (Geneva, 1972), p. 120.

[12] T. J. Mathias, *Pursuits of Literature* (London, 1805), p. 363.

generalization. As a result I have spoken a good deal about an earlier age. We have seen that the most massive publication of the French Enlightenment—and one of the major elements in the modernity of the eighteenth century—has its roots and its analogies in the remote past. But this genealogy in no way diminishes the essential achievement of Diderot. He, and those inner members of his team who shared the common purpose, sought to use an instrument with a long tradition behind it to achieve new ends: to educate the people, to spread enlightenment, to change the common mode of thought. They used this instrument with skill and perseverance, and attained their end.

Thomas Pinckney's London Mission, 1792–1794

A Reappraisal

CHARLES R. RITCHESON

M AJ. THOMAS PINCKNEY OF SOUTH CAROLINA, HIS COUNTRY'S second minister plenipotentiary to the Court of St. James's, has not fared well at the hands of the historians. Ignored or quickly dismissed, John Adams's successor has been allowed, in the unfortunate phrase of a recent writer, "to wallow in obscurity."[1]

The basic facts are not in dispute. Pinckney's appointment to London, in November 1791, came at President Washington's own initiative and caused great surprise—to Treasury Secretary Hamilton, the president's closest adviser; to Secretary of State Jefferson, Hamilton's enemy and chief political rival; and to Thomas Pinckney himself, sometime lawyer, major in the Revolutionary army, and governor of South Carolina. The shock was undoubtedly greatest for Jefferson, however, who found himself unexpectedly presented with a senior but unknown and unwelcome diplomatic subordinate. The secretary of state's last-minute effort to divert Pinckney from London to Paris, his own old post still vacant, was thwarted by the president himself. Washington preferred London, he wrote with almost curt brevity, for "reasons mentioned to you yesterday."[2]

[1] Jack L. Cross, *London Mission: The First Critical Years* (East Lansing, Mich., 1968), p. 3.

[2] See Washington to Jefferson, 9 November 1791, *Writings of George Washington*, ed. John C. Fitzpatrick (1939), XXXI, 413; Charles Cotesworth Pinckney, *Life of General Thomas Pinckney* (Boston, 1895), p. 98. See, further, Thomas Jefferson to William Short, chargé d'affaires at Paris, 9 November 1791 (cipher), *Writings of Thomas Jefferson*, ed. Paul L. Ford, 10 vols. (New York, 1892–99), VI, 324: "There was never a symptom by which I could form a guess on this subject till 3 days ago."

More information about those reasons would be welcome. What-ever the inference, Jefferson acquiesced gracefully, sending the same day to Pinckney in South Carolina a warm and friendly message covering the presidential offer. It arrived on 23 November, and the recipient honored the request for a speedy response. After two hours' consideration, he accepted the appointment. Misgivings and even anguish accompanied the decision, however. "Almost every private consideration," Pinckney confessed to a close friend, "appears to me to be against this determination, but every public one (my inability excepted) in favor of it." He withheld news of "this unfor-tunate appointment" for a time from his wife, who was just recover-ing from illness, fearing it might interfere with her convalescence.[3]

Confirmed by the Senate as minister plenipotentiary on 12 January 1792 (after a debate on the wisdom of establishing permanent diplomatic missions anywhere), Pinckney, with his wife and six children, left Charleston by ship on 20 April. They stopped in Philadelphia, where the minister conferred with Washington and Jefferson and received the latter's instructions. Sailing from New York for London on 18 June, the party arrived on 3 August, and Pinckney quickly established his legation at 1 Great Cumberland Place. His sizable domestic ménage was housed in Hertford Street, Mayfair.

The new minister's instructions issued from Secretary Jefferson. They were brief and general.[4] In addition to the conventional admo-nitions to show friendship to Britain, to conciliate its government,

[3] Pinckney, *Life*, pp. 98–100. See, further, Samuel Flagg Bemis, "The London Mission of Thomas Pinckney, 1792–1796," *American Historical Review*, 28 (1922–23), 228–47. The close friend was Edward Rutledge, to whom Pinckney wrote on 24 November 1791. John Adams's spiteful charge, made in a private letter of 1792 and published with malice aforethought by Tench Coxe during the presidential campaign of 1800, that Pinckney and his brother intrigued to win the post, was altogether without foundation. Adams cleared the brothers of the accusation at the expense, perhaps, of a little of his own dignity. See Bemis, "Mission," p. 229, n. 4. Mrs. Pinckney was grief-stricken when she learned of her husband's appoint-ment. She had a "too great fondness for retirement and an exclusive attachment to domestic life," under the right circumstances beyond price but scarcely helpful to a minister at the Court of St. James's. The unhappy lady died in London in 1794. See Judge Iredell to Mrs. Iredell, Charleston, 19 April 1792, Pinckney, pp. 101–2.

[4] Jefferson's Instructions to Pinckney are found in *Jefferson's Writings*, VI, 74–77.

and to avoid meddling in its domestic affairs, Pinckney was assigned the "patronage" of American commerce with specific reference to American trade to the British West Indies. Further, his "most active exertions and protection" were bidden for American seamen pressed into the Royal Navy. Indeed, he was to seek a settlement of the entire issue. These two major tasks were accompanied by some subordinate but not unimportant ones: the supervision and coordination of the American consular system in Britain and Ireland; regular reports to Jefferson on British and continental affairs; the recruitment of artisans and artists for the United States mint; and facilitating negotiations with the piratical Algerian authorities.

The outbreak of war between France and Britain early in 1793 necessarily enlarged Pinckney's responsibilities, especially as they touched the twin issues of impressment and spoliation of American maritime commerce under Orders-in-Council. John Jay arrived on his special mission to London in June 1794 to deal with a burgeoning crisis arising in large measure from events in North America unknown to Thomas Pinckney. Despite a certain awkwardness in his situation, the South Carolinian assisted the envoy extraordinary to the best of his ability; and at the end of the year, with Jay's Treaty signed, he was dispatched to Madrid, himself envoy extraordinary and sole commissioner plenipotentiary. Having negotiated the Treaty of San Lorenzo with Spain, Pinckney returned to the London post for a few months in 1795, to wind up his affairs there before resigning as minister and returning home.

For well over a century past, wisdom of the conventional sort has given Thomas Pinckney short shrift. William Henry Trescot wrote a brief passage in 1859 on Pinckney's contribution to the diplomatic history of the Washington administration. In a few words, he set out the first statement of the traditional judgment: from 1792 to 1796, Anglo-American diplomatic relations were in the hands, first, of Secretary Jefferson and British minister George Hammond in Philadelphia; and, secondly, of John Jay and Secretary Grenville in London.[5] Pinckney's own role was negligible and confined to minor and routine business, as, for example, the purchase of copper for the United States mint, the hiring of European technicians to

---

[5] William Henry Trescot, *Diplomatic History of the Administrations of Washington and Adams, 1789–1801* (Boston, 1857), p. 88.

superintend the coinage, assisting President Washington's private efforts to win freedom for the marquis de Lafayette from his Prussian-Austrian imprisonment, and acting in support of his government's attempts to negotiate with the Algerines.[6]

Writing at the end of the nineteenth century, Charles Cotesworth Pinckney showed more familial piety in his *Life of General Thomas Pinckney* than historical acumen and did little to retrieve his grandfather's reputation as American minister to London. Thirty years later the English diplomatic historian Robert Balmain Mowat, surveying Anglo-American relations, dismissed Pinckney with scarcely a nod; and in 1955, his fellow countryman H. C. Allen dealt with the American almost en passant: respectable and amiable, he lacked driving power. In 1928, Beckles Wilson, chatty and superficial, delivered ad hominem criticism. Pinckney, he wrote, was "too heavily handicapped . . . by his English education, his American combatant record, and his former pro-French sentiments to have produced the right impressions" in London. Exactly three decades later Alexander DeConde treated Pinckney in a single sentence. "President Washington reciprocated [Britain's appointment of George Hammond to Philadelphia] by sending to London as American Minister Thomas Pinckney of South Carolina, a man satisfying to the British government, and one described by Hammond as belonging to the party of the British interest."[7]

Ten years ago, Jack L. Cross undertook to provide a reassessment and a more extended treatment of the Pinckney mission "in the light of full documentary background." Unfortunately, his work is so seriously flawed by methodological and stylistic shortcomings that it fails of the purpose. The interpretation harmonizes—a minor

[6]See Washington to Hamilton, No. 29, 1792, *Papers of Alexander Hamilton*, ed. Harold L. Syrett (New York, 1972), XIII, 2–5.

[7]Charles Cotesworth Pinckney's *Life* is cited in n. 3 above. See, too, Robert Balmain Mowat, *Diplomatic Relations of Great Britain and the United States* (London, 1925), pp. 21–22; Harry C. Allen, *Great Britain and the United States* (New York, 1955), pp. 268–99; Beckles Wilson, *America's Ambassadors to England, 1785–1928* (London, 1928), p. 55; Alexander DeConde, *Entangling Alliance* (Durham, 1958), p. 79; and Frances Leigh Williams, *A Founding Family: The Pinckneys of South Carolina* (New York, 1978). Thomas A. Bailey, *A Diplomatic History of the American People*, 9th ed. (Englewood Cliffs, N.J., 1974), makes no mention of Pinckney's mission to London.

dissonance here and there excepted—with the magisterial pronouncement made in the early 1920s by Samuel Flagg Bemis.[8]

Most recently, Frances Leigh Williams has written a useful and
well-researched book, *A Founding Family* (1978), about the Pinckneys of South Carolina. In dealing with Thomas, she adds much
information about the appointment, Jefferson's effort to divert
Pinckney to Paris (to make room at London for his old friend and
confidant William Short, whom he had left as chargé d'affaires at
the French capital), Thomas's systematic preparation for the
assignment by extensive readings in international and English law,
and the establishment of his legation in London. His mission, however, was marked by "frustration" and "failures." Pinckney was no
more successful in his negotiations with Foreign Secretary Grenville
than Jefferson in his efforts with George Hammond. The dependence on Samuel Flagg Bemis is obvious and is duly acknowledged.[9]

Bemis, then, is the standard authority upon whom all contemporary historians depend. His work must therefore be read closely
and his interpretation analyzed carefully. Pinckney's London mission figures briefly and in general terms both in *Jay's Treaty: A Study*

[8]The quotation is found in Cross, p. 3. At the best, Cross only softens a little
the interpretation presented earlier by Bemis (who gave *London Mission* a critical
reading before publication). Further, the voluminous British manuscript sources
have been left unconsulted; and there is a seriously misplaced faith in newspaper
evidence. A single organ, *The Times* (London), is frequently cited to demonstrate
British public opinion of the day, although *The Times* was not a major newspaper
of the period. Newspapers are among the most questionable sources short of overt
forgery available to students of eighteenth-century Anglo-American history. Cross's
use of them is uncritical to the point of naiveté. He quotes anonymous letters from
Britain printed in American newspapers, for example, as authoritative statements
about high British policy.

There is also a regrettable unfamiliarity with the ways the British government
made its policy, and, indeed, with the structure of the British Government itself.
For instance, Cross places Foreign Secretary Grenville at the head of the Pitt
ministry.

In his conclusion, Cross writes that Pinckney and Grenville "preserved peace
with honor and introduced to the family of nations a young Republic on an equal
footing with its parent, Great Britain, inaugurating one of the great alliances of
modern history—one which would survive even the crisis of the War of 1812"
(p. 132). This assertion is extravagant.

[9]See pp. 301–2, n. 72, and p. 307.

in Commerce and Diplomacy (1923) and in *Pinckney's Treaty, America's Advantage from Europe's Distress* (1926). The authoritative treatment, "The London Mission of Thomas Pinckney," appeared a little earlier in the *American Historical Review* of 1922–23.[10] All these assessments have passed virtually unquestioned into the mainstream of American historiography. Yet there are important reasons why the Bemis treatment must be judged unsatisfactory.

Pinckney's appointment, for example, Bemis argues, was "largely a matter of form." Utterly devoid of diplomatic experience, the new minister was assigned a "paucity of specific duties." Jefferson's communications with him were so meager that none could doubt the insignificance of the mission. Rare praise is bestowed with condescension: when Pinckney reported in August 1792 that Britain might become involved in the French Revolutionary War, he showed "unusual discernment for a man of his limited European experience."[11]

When the war gave Pinckney's mission an unforeseen importance, Pinckney's response to the challenge was ineffectual and clumsy. Dealing with the impressment of American seamen, he simply acquiesced in British Admiralty Court procedures and sought only to hasten that body's decisions, not controvert its outrageous violation of international law and the rights of neutrals. Similarly, when Britain impeded his country's maritime trade with the high-handed and indefensible Order-in-Council of 8 June 1793, Pinckney's protest was "perfunctory," and he weakly advised Philadelphia to limit any countermeasure to mere commercial retaliation. In the great controversy that developed over neutral rights, Pinckney served as reporter, not a principal.[12]

On the single occasion when Pinckney took a major initiative, he committed an unfortunate indiscretion. Clearly exceeding his instructions, he raised with Foreign Secretary Grenville the question of the Northwestern American posts the British had retained in violation of the Treaty of Peace of 1783. By seeming to admit in

[10]Publication data for the article are found in n. 3 above. *Jay's Treaty* was published first in 1923, and, subsequently, in a slightly revised edition, by Yale University Press in 1962. *Pinckney's Treaty* was first published by the John Hopkins Press in 1926; and Yale University Press brought out the revised edition in 1960.

[11]Bemis, "Mission," pp. 228, 231–32, 234.

[12]Ibid., pp. 238, 241–42.

the course of the conference that his own country had yet to fulfill some of its treaty obligations, Pinckney gave Grenville an opening (hitherto denied by a masterful Jefferson) to cite American infractions as justification for Britain's own. Then, inferring that Britain intended a permanent retention of the posts, the "impressionable" Pinckney concluded that war was inevitable and began to talk about moving his family to France. Little wonder that the United States administration did not bestow full confidence on its minister.[13]

Pinckney escapes deserved obscurity, Bemis believes, only because of his triumphant performance as special envoy to Spain in 1795. The Treaty of San Lorenzo notwithstanding, however, the stark verdict on the London mission stands: a brief and negligible passage, marked by mediocrity and ineptitude, in the history of Anglo-American relations.[14]

In the face of a case so powerfully stated and widely accepted, it may seem bold indeed to confess certain doubts about the Bemis thesis. Still, at least mild encouragement is provided by two venerable if not magisterial voices from the past. Early in the present century, Andrew McLaughlin, reporting on the diplomatic archives of the State Department, observed rather cryptically that Pinckney's diplomatic experiences were "far from being unimportant or lacking in interest." They were, in fact, "scarcely less trying though not quite so dramatic" as those of John Adams,[15] his country's first minister to the Court of St. James's. Henry Cabot Lodge, in his *Life of George Washington* (1917), said of Pinckney that he was a man "who really did something, who did work worth doing and without many words." Consigned to oblivion, he was ignored while "many of his contemporaries, who simply made a noise, are freshly remembered in the pages of history."[16] The senator had in mind Pinckney's

---

[13]Ibid., pp. 243–44. In stating that Pinckney "did not share the confidence of his government," Bemis was referring specifically to the celebrated "Abortive Armed Neutrality." Beckles Wilson, *American Ambassadors*, p. 41, also speaks of Pinckney as an outsider and ignorant of "what was in the mind of the administration."

[14]Bemis, "Mission," p. 247.

[15]Andrew C. McLaughlin, *Report on the Diplomatic Archives of the Department of State, 1789–1840* (Washington, D.C., 1906), p. 11.

[16]Henry Cabot Lodge, *Life of George Washington*, 2 vols. (Boston and New York, 1917), II, 168.

Spanish mission, but his remarks, as McLaughlin's before him, apply to Thomas Pinckney's diplomatic career as a whole, whether in London or Madrid; and they suggest a view of the man and his mission very different from Bemis's. Whether they are right or wrong, they help to lift Bemis's thesis out of the context of traditional authority and open it—and the Pinckney mission—to fresh examination. This is the first of two major purposes of the present essay.

Bemis alleges that Pinckney was appointed minister pro forma, that he was given few specific duties, and that Jefferson's subsequent communication was meager—all indication of Pinckney's personal and diplomatic insignificance. Reserving for the moment the circumstances of Pinckney's appointment, let me consider first the matter of Pinckney's duties.

While impressment and the "patronage" of American commerce were certainly not trivial or unimportant, Jefferson's instructions to Pinckney were admittedly brief and general, the more so when compared with those carried by John Jay (and signed by Jefferson's successor, Edmund Randolph) in 1794. Obviously, Jefferson wished to keep negotiations firmly in his own hands and, hence, to minimize Pinckney's responsibilities in London. The secretary of state's intentions and actions, however, should not be used to disparage a man virtually unknown to Jefferson at the time the instructions were drawn. The initiative was Jefferson's, and the burden of explanation and justification should lie with him. Further, a comparison of Pinckney's terms of reference and powers with those carried by John Jay, envoy extraordinary and plenipotentiary in 1794, is manifestly unjust to the South Carolinian. Jay, after all, was dispatched to Britain to deal with a dangerous crisis in Anglo-American relations arising from numerous sources—events along the Canadian frontier, for example, and fresh spoliation of American commerce under a new and secret Order-in-Council—unknown to and beyond the control of Minister Pinckney.

Similarly, if Jefferson's dispatches were meager, should Pinckney be faulted? In addition to the secretary's effort to preserve Philadelphia as the prime locus of Anglo-American negotiations, other, admittedly less important contributing factors are evident. Trans-Atlantic communication of the day was slow and insecure, the more so after the outbreak of war in Europe. The yellow fever epidemic disrupted the workings of the American government and forced its abandonment of the capital in the summer and autumn of 1793. The United States government faced other problems of great magnitude. All these factors must have affected the quality and quantity of Jefferson's communications with Pinckney. None constitute the slightest ground for criticism, implicit or explicit, of Thomas Pinckney.

Exception may be taken, too, to the patronizing praise of the minister's "unusual discernment" in foretelling, in August 1792, Britain's possible involvement in the continental war then underway. The traditional enemy, France, wracked by a revolution of unprecedented proportions, was a chief belligerent. British allies of long-standing were in the lists. British interests in every point of the compass were in question. How much "discernment" was required to make Pinckney's prediction? If praise is offered on such questionable grounds, might not criticisms be treated with at least a measure of skepticism? As for the minister's "limited European experience," at the age of forty, Pinckney could look back on almost half his life spent abroad—eighteen years in England and a year in France.

A more fundamental question concerns the circumstances and nature of the appointment itself. Was it "largely a matter of form;" or did it serve more important purposes? The initiative came from President Washington himself, not Secretary Jefferson. Moving without consulting his cabinet advisers, a rare occurrence, Washington appointed Pinckney and insisted on London as his post contrary to the manifest wishes of Secretary Jefferson. Both John Adams as minister in the mid-1780s, and Gouverneur Morris as Washington's unofficial envoy a few years later had urged reciprocal appointments by London and Philadelphia; and American leaders generally, Jefferson excepted, believed that both national pride and sound policy called for full diplomatic relations with the former mother country. American standing on the international stage would be enhanced; and serious issues arising chiefly from differences over American trade to the British West Indies and unfulfilled portions of the Treaty of Peace of 1783 would be put in the way of negotiation. After much delay—it was difficult to find a British diplomat to accept the distant and minor post—and wounded American amour propre, George III's first minister plenipotentiary to the United States, the youthful but experienced George Hammond, arrived at Philadelphia in October 1791. Both governments understood that the British initiative, delayed as it was, required an American response in kind; and Hammond specifically established the point before formally presenting his credentials. The surprise is not Washington's immediate move to name a minister to London but Jefferson's opposition to any such appointment and his unsuccessful last-minute effort to divert Pinckney to Paris.[17]

Why did Washington choose Pinckney? The evidence, not always full or explicit, is sufficient to show that the president intended more than a pro forma appointment. Political debt-paying, so large a consideration in modern ambassadorial selections, played no part in the decision. Washington and Pinckney had met once, perhaps twice, before the spring of 1791; and the circumstances were both public and brief. The president knew Pinckney by reputation, of course, as a member of a prominent South Carolina planter family, a soldier of the Revolution honorably wounded on the field of battle, an officer of the Cincinnati, a champion of the Constitution, moderate Federalist, and successful governor of his state. In 1789, indeed, Washington offered Pinckney a federal judgeship which he declined for family reasons. His list of bona fides included, too, the soundest legal education of the time and personal qualities that the president must have found highly compatible.

Washington reached beyond his immediate circle of friends and associates, beyond, indeed, the principal figures of American political life, to a man who was in many important respects much like himself. Both were southern planters of solid English stock, imbued with the same sense of personal honor and public duty. Lacking intellectual brilliance, they possessed sound intelligence and disciplined minds, and a dignity that at its best became quiet charm.

---

[17]Jefferson was convinced that it was useless, possibly worse, to send an American minister to London so long as George III lived. When rumors of Hammond's appointment began to circulate, he expressed skepticism, but added that even if the fact were true, it did not mean Britain intended serious negotiation or performing its commitments under the Treaty of Peace. See Jefferson to Edward Rutledge, 29 August 1791, *Jefferson's Writings*, VI, 309.

Political moderates, they held to the new Federal Constitution but disdained the vituperation and turbulence swirling around Jefferson and Hamilton. In appointing Pinckney, Washington chose a gentleman who could represent in Britain the best of American life as the president knew it.

Washington knew, too (as Bemis recognizes), that Pinckney's appointment was also a conciliatory gesture to the British. As governor of South Carolina, Pinckney had shown himself a strict constructionist on Article IV of the Treaty of Peace prescribing humane and equitable treatment of the loyalists. Further, he knew Britain well. Taken there as a three-year-old boy by his father, agent for the then colony of South Carolina, Pinckney, educated successively at Westminster School, Christ Church, Oxford, and the Inner Temple, did not return home until the eve of the American Revolution.[18] English education and friendships, however, did nothing to undermine a staunch support for the colonial cause. As the quarrel developed, he won the nickname "Little Rebel," and one of his last activities before leaving London for Charleston was to join other resident Americans in a protest against the Coercive Acts.

By 1791 wartime animosities had been largely forgotten in Britain;[19] and in official circles Pinckney's appointment elicited widespread expressions of approbation. George Hammond wrote to Grenville that the American possessed "mild and liberal manners" and was "perfectly untinctured with any sort of prejudice." James Bland Burges, undersecretary for foreign affairs, told Lord Auckland (erstwhile William Eden), upon Pinckney's arrival in London, that he was "an old friend and brother-Westminster of mine, whose

[18]Williams, *A Founding Family*, supersedes all other works in the treatment of Pinckney's life before his mission to London. Commenting on Pinckney's love of Greek which he acquired at Westminster School, Bemis writes rather grumpily: "If his intellectual training and eighteen years in England did not leave him with a pleasing style, it endowed him with an appreciation of literary merit and a devotion to the classical culture which the best English minds of that day were so content to indulge." On Pinckney's appointment, he writes further: "As much as any American patriot could be who had nearly died of his wounds received on the field of battle against the troops of George III, Pinckney was a friend of England" ("Mission," p. 230).

[19]See my "London Press and the First Decade of American Independence," *Journal of British Studies*, 2 (1963), 88–109.

manners and temper exactly qualify him for the place he has taken. I have known him for about thirty years, and I do not know a more worthy and excellent man." A few days later, Home Secretary Henry Dundas, acting for Grenville, who was away from London, presented the new Minister at a royal levee. He was, Dundas told his collegue in manner characteristically laconic, "rather a gentlemanlike man."[20] President Washington had in London, the chief focus of American foreign policy, then, no pro forma minister but a representative with whom he felt a personal affinity, who was a proven patriot but no partisan zealot, and who by education and temperament was reasonable and conciliatory, qualities of great merit to a president troubled at home by rancorous quarrels between Federalists and Republicans, and abroad by a war of great ferocity. In the face of manifest need and wide consensus supporting the appointment of Pinckney, the burden of making a case rests with those who assert the new minister went to London as a mere matter of form. It has yet to be made to the satisfaction of the objective observer.

Another reason for faulting Bemis's work is his paradox of the two Pinckneys—one in London, the central figure in the "Mission" article, the other in Madrid, who dominates the climax of *Pinckney's*

---

[20]Hammond to Grenville, private, 9 January 1792, *Royal Historical Manuscripts Commission Report, Fortescue Papers*, 10 vols. (London, 1892), II, 250; and same to the same, 8 June 1792, quoted by Bemis, "Mission," p. 231. Hammond said further that all Americans favoring a good understanding with Britain supported the appointment, since they considered "the circumstances of his education . . . and of his having passed a great part of his life in England, as having a natural tendency to inspire him with a predilection for the country, and a desire of rendering his conduct satisfactory."

Under the courteous and conciliatory exterior, however, much of the "Little Rebel" remained. See Pinckney to Jefferson, December 1792, Pinckney, *Life*, pp. 103–4, for his tart response to George III's reference to American disunion. See, too, p. 104, for the minister's early impressions of coldness at Court.

It took several more decades for American ministers to London to rid themselves of hypersensitivity in the royal presence and to disabuse themselves of an idée fixe that royal small talk was an important though usually delphic clue to British intentions and policy toward the United States.

See, further, Burges to Auckland, Pinckney, *Life*, pp. 102–3; and Dundas to Grenville, 8 August 1792, *Fortescue Papers*, II, 299.

Treaty. The first, a rather pedestrian functionary, busied himself with routine matters in a routine way, speaking, when occasion required, from a script written by Thomas Jefferson. The second, acting virtually alone, achieved a brilliant triumph, "one of the greatest successes in American diplomacy," the treaty with Spain of 1795, which still bears his name.[21] The treatment of the London Pinckney in the 1926 book is significantly more favorable than in the earlier book and article. He was sent to London, Bemis writes, because he was "a distinguished and representative southerner," and he served there "in a distinguished if not a highly important capacity." Pinckney possessed "a cogency of reasoning and some perspicuity of argument," urbanity, dignity, and social grace. He was a man of culture, at home in the world, showing good judgment and elegance as he moved "easily and nobly through a distinguished life, doing well the tasks he was called on to perform, making no great mistake and encountering no measurable public misfortune." The friendlier and mellower tone extends even to Pinckney's shortcomings. There was a certain deficiency of literary style, intellectual alacrity, and energy, to be sure, in notable contrast to Jefferson and Madison. His character continues "somewhat impressionable." In London he "handled no great issue," but performed "the routine business of the day." Hamilton declined to admit him to the "inside" of his own "pro-British foreign policy"; and he was "not one of the half-dozen great leaders in the United States of his time," although Bemis finds no fault in not ranking him among the immortals. Pinckney achieves the level of Jefferson's friend William Short (who would have gone to London in Pinckney's place if Jefferson's wishes had prevailed), shunted aside in his turn by Washington as his country's representative in Madrid when the South Carolinian was appointed to his own special mission. Short "equalled Pinckney in ability if not in urbanity and poise"; and he had "a closer grip on the complicated European diplomacy of the French Revolution."[22] Still, Pinckney produced "one of the greatest successes in American diplomacy." How does Bemis explain the paradox?

[21]Bemis, *Pinckney's Treaty* (1960 ed.), pp. 284, 312.
[22]Ibid., pp. 246–50.

Pinckney's success in Madrid, Bemis contends, contained a very strong element of good luck. The Spanish principal in the negotiation of the Treaty of San Lorenzo was Manuel de Godoy, duke of Alcuida, a "court adventurer" and lover of the queen who used his "princely parts and comely person" to win dominance in the government itself. Lacking moral stamina, maturity, and judgment, Godoy was not a statesman of even second-rank stature.[23] It was fortunate, indeed, that Pinckney did not have to face an Aranda or a Floridablanca.

Fortune favored the American minister in another way. The terms of Jay's treaty with Britain remained unknown during the Spanish negotiations. Godoy was seized of an overriding and logical (though groundless) fear: that the Anglo-American accord might contain an alliance against Spanish interests in North America. Further, on the eve of deserting Britain in the war against France, Godoy desperately wanted an understanding with the United States to help ward off anticipated British reprisals.

Even the final moment of high drama does not redound in the first instance to the credit of Thomas Pinckney. With Godoy refusing the right of deposit for American goods at New Orleans, Pinckney requested his passports, a critical show of determination to rupture the negotiation. Godoy capitulated, and the treaty was concluded. The inspiration for Pinckney's bold and highly successful démarche, however, came from William Short.[24]

Was the Madrid Pinckney simply more fortunate than the London Pinckney? Diplomatic triumphs of the magnitude of the Treaty of San Lorenzo rarely occur as strokes of good fortune. More commonly, they are hard-fought victories won by diplomats of skill, initiative, judgment, and insight, qualities not very apparent in Bemis's pro forma London minister. The very magnitude of Pinckney's success in Spain indicates far more than luck.

Pinckney possessed a tremendous advantage in Madrid denied him in London: the character and powers of envoy extraordinary and sole commissioner plenipotentiary. Kept on a close rein by Jefferson at his first post, Minister Pinckney received from Edmund

[23]Ibid., pp. 170–71.
[24]Ibid., pp. 279–80.

Randolph, who succeeded to the State Department in 1794, a broad freedom of action in Madrid not unlike Jay's in London in 1794. Empowered to negotiate and sign a treaty subject only to presidential and Senate approval, Pinckney effected a definitive settlement of outstanding differences with the Spanish court. In the process William Short's advice and assistance were doubtless useful and supportive, much as his own had assisted Jay in London; but the Treaty of San Lorenzo remains to this day "Pinckney's Treaty." What might Pinckney have accomplished in London had Jefferson allowed him broader powers? Quite possibly, even probably, the impressment issue at the least would have been defused by the acceptance of a system of citizenship certificates. Conceivably, then, with Jay's Treaty extinguishing other important Anglo-American differences, the future might not have held a new and senseless war. Speculation aside, however, the irrefutable fact remains that there was but a single Pinckney; and the triumph he won in Madrid must be taken into account in judging his diplomatic *sagesse* and performance in London.

Two reservations of a more general nature remain. Bemis's treatment of Thomas Pinckney is too brief and the exploitation of the evidence too cursory. The result is a telescoped, even fragmentary impression which does less than justice to the subject. Bemis's principal interest during the time of Pinckney's mission to London concerned, of course, John Jay's special mission; and he held it in sharp focus. Pinckney's career, by contrast, is perceived in the peripheral vision. Had the minister been more assertive and self-seeking, had he "simply made a noise," Bemis and his successors might have paid him more attention. Possibly, their verdict would still have been one of dismissal, but it would have been at least more firmly grounded.

Secondly, Bemis's frame of reference requires brief comment. Following World War I, perhaps because of it, the preoccupations of American historians generally underwent a notable change from colonial to national history. An important dimension of the new development was the appearance of diplomatic history, and, considering the scope and nature of the Anglo-American past, it is not surprising that relations between the two powers claimed early attention. Bemis himself led the way, blazing a trail and setting an

[405]

interpretation influential until the present day. Sharing the general disillusionment with Europe after the 1914–18 war, Bemis wrote in an America disgusted with "the 'corrupt' statescraft of the European powers,"[25] a view in striking harmony with Jefferson's own assumptions a century and a half earlier, particularly as they related to the former mother country. In the eighteenth-century context, Britain, for both men, was unquestionably the aggressor; America, by contrast, the bastion of a purer political life and liberty itself. From these general attitudes each developed certain specific assumptions. In the early years of the Republic, Americans who sought cooperation, compromise, and a community of interests with Britain were, at best, misguided, at worst, devious and inimical to their country's true principles. Alexander Hamilton must take pride of place. Pinckney "handled no great issue" in London, Bemis writes in *Pinckney's Treaty* (thus overlooking the minister's work on both impressment and the Orders-in-Council), because Jefferson was speaking to Hammond, "always remembering in this connection that Alexander Hamilton's informal and intimate contact with the British Government was the determining factor in Anglo-American affairs during Washington's Administration."[26] Thus, with an aside, he clears Jefferson of responsibility for the collapse of his own negotiations with Hammond, and his criticism is reserved for the Federalists who accepted Hamilton's pro-British policies. John Jay was an instrument, and so, rather down the ladder of eminence, was Thomas Pinckney.

Bemis's disposition to accept Thomas Jefferson's view uncritically has a double meaning. Gratitude to and admiration for France combined with suspicion of Britain formed the underlying principles of wise foreign policy during the Washington administration; and second, efforts at conciliation and compromise with the former mother country, personified by Hamilton, Jay, and Pinckney, were supping with the devil with a very short spoon. The result is a post hoc ergo propter hoc: Jefferson's dispatches were meager; hence Pinckney merited short shrift. Jefferson intended the Pinckney mission to be a matter of form and of negligible importance, and so

[25]John Higham (with Leonard Krieger and Felix Gilbert), *History* (Englewood Cliffs, N.J., 1965), p. 188.
[26]Ibid., p. 247.

Bemis judged it. This is to allow the thought and action of Thomas Jefferson too great a measure of self-validation. More objectivity is required.

The second major purpose of this essay, then, is to identify an important problem that arose during Pinckney's mission and to examine it free of the usual a priori Jeffersonian assumptions. Consider, for example, Pinckney's diplomacy in dealing with Britain's spoliation of American maritime commerce under the Orders-in-Council of June and November 1793, after the outbreak of war with revolutionary France.

It should be noted immediately that as a diplomat, Pinckney was in London not to make policy but to execute it. The diplomat's views and assessments may—ideally, should—contribute to the formation of policy by his principals; but his prime functions are faithfully to execute the instructions of his government and to procure and transmit to responsible officials at home timely and accurate information and intelligent surmises about the domestic and foreign policies of the country where he is accredited, particularly as they bear on the interests of his own. In dealing with unforeseen matters about which he is inadequately instructed, a problem in the eighteenth century that scarcely exists today, he must use initiative and sound judgment in extrapolating from known principles of his nation's foreign policy to an appropriate course of action; and he must carefully distinguish between personal sentiment and public interest, his sole guiding star. Finally, he must simultaneously secure both the ear—as sympathetic as he can contrive—of the host government, and maximum freedom of action for his own until new positions are defined and instructions formulated, dispatched, and received. By these criteria Thomas Pinckney proved himself an able and effective representative of the United States and guardian of its interests as he dealt with the dangerous issue of Britain's treatment of American shipping early in the war with France.

By the Order-in-Counil of 8 June 1793, Britain interdicted (under certain conditions) neutral nations' grain (except rice) and flour bound for France. It was grounded on three reasons. In order of ascending importance, there were France's earlier wartime experimentation along the same lines; the unprecedented mobilization of the French nation, the *levée en masse*, which vitiated the distinction between civilian and military; and, finally, a dearth of grain, the result of several years' bad weather, which offered, British leaders believed, a prospect for starving the French into peace. Fundamental interests of the United States, a chief source of foodstuffs for needy Europe, were immediately and directly involved.

In January 1793, on the eve of war, Prime Minister Pitt, Hawkesbury, president of the Committee of Trade, and Home Secretary Dundas met as the Committee of Trade. They decided to prohibit shipment by British subjects of foodstuffs to France; to forbid the supply of war materials to that nation; and to inform masters of foreign vessels in British ports with grain and flour bound for France that the government was prepared to purchase their cargoes and to allow reasonable profit and charges.[27]

Through some channel that can only be guessed at—perhaps it was Pinckney's old friend, the British undersecretary for foreign affairs James Bland Burges—Pinckney quickly learned at least the general nature of the committee's decisions. Only ten days after the meeting he dispatched a warning to Secretary of State Jefferson. Expecting interdiction of (instead of an offer to purchase) all American foodstuffs bound for France, he urgently requested instructions. In the meantime, he said, he intended to remonstrate against the presumed measure, as soon as it was officially announced, as an infringement of neutral rights.[28] Pinckney's information was timely and accurate enough. He had secured maximum freedom of action for his government, and he had laid the groundwork for defense of American private interests affected by the British measure.

In the event, the British Ministry, hoping to cajole neturals with favorable prices, not coerce them with harsh regulations, moved more cautiously than Pinckney anticipated. At the end of February, American wheat was fetching 7 shillings the bushel compared with 5 shillings ten pence for the domestic produce; and weeks later, with the war a month old, Pinckney had still to hear that American grain vessels had been restrained from proceeding to whatever destination they chose. He was prudent enough, however, to renew

[27]British Library, Add MSS. 38352, fols. 130–32. The purpose was obviously to deprive France of foodstuffs, not to supplement domestic British supply as Cross, p. 56, asserts.

[28]Pinckney to Jefferson, 30 January 1793, quoted by Cross, p. 47.

his urgent request for instructions covering what he believed was bound to become a more forceful British policy. In the meantime, he assured Philadelphia he intended to "contend for the amplest freedom of neutral bottoms."[29]

Pinckney's efforts were not confined to the officialdom. With discreet energy, he helped organize mercantile opposition to the Traitorous Correspondence Bill forbidding British merchants from dealing with any foreign vessels carrying forage, provisions, military stores, and precious metals, and intending to proceed from British ports to France.[30] War was bringing rapid changes, however. The bill became law; and Foreign Secretary Grenville's assurances in March that American grain vessels would not be stopped en route to France gave way, first, to detention, then, seizure to search for suspected French property. Pinckney, still uninstructed, immediately engaged proctors—lawyers specializing in such matters—to assist Americans before the Admiralty Court.

In June the American Neutrality Proclamation was published in London; but British relief was mixed with a certain skepticism: let the United States Government speak as it would, careful watch would have to be kept on individual merchants and shippers. Already, in late April, a British naval cutter had brought into Guernsey the American brig *Sally*, bound for LeHavre with 2,109 barrels of flour. Asserted by the master to be American, the foodstuff was quickly proved to be French property; and aside from the prevarication and collusion, a second major point of contention had arisen: the question of "free ships, free goods." Cajolery was useless. Official regulation was required. It came in the Order-in-Council of 8 June 1793.[31] Without mentioning French property found aboard neutral vessels, the order declared the ships laden wholly or in part

---

[29]See Robert Crew to Jefferson, London, 22 February 1793, Jefferson MSS., Library of Congress, Vol. 81, fol. 14184, for grain prices. See also Pinckney to Jefferson, 13 March 1793, quoted by Cross, pp. 54–55. Jefferson subsequently sent instructions on 7 May 1793. They are cited below.

[30]Cross, p. 56.

[31]See my *Aftermath of Revolution* (Dallas, 1969), pp. 278–79. The order and appropriate additional instructions for British commanders in American waters were forwarded to Hammond, the British Minister in Philadelphia, in a dispatch of 5 July. It contained, too, Britain's official justification of the order, a guide for Hammond in his dealings with the American authorities, and, in substance, the position already developed by Grenville to Pinckney.

CHARLES R. RITCHESON

with wheat, flour, or meal bound for ports of Britain's enemies were to be intercepted and detained. Neutral cargoes would not be treated as out-and-out contraband but would be purchased at a fair price, with reasonable freight and other charges allowed. Upon security, a master might choose to sell his cargo in the port of a power in amity with Great Britain.

The Admirality did not receive the order until 28 June. Pinckney knew of it about the middle of the month, however, and he immediately lodged a protest with Grenville. Using "every argument that suggested itself to me," he told the foreign secretary that the new system was a violation of neutral rights—presumably "free ships, free goods—and the cause of great inconvenience for his countrymen. Further, in a rebuttal of a cardinal point in the British justification of the measure, Pinckney denied that there was any reasonable hope of starving France into peace, since provisions in French ports were actually cheaper than in English.

Bemis terms Pinckney's protest "perfunctory," and his "best efforts" limited to winning freight and demurrage for American ships whose cargoes had been preempted for purchase.[32] This judgment is too harsh. Certainly the American minister spoke of general principles, but without word from Philadelphia he could have done nothing else. As it was, in his representations to Grenville, he succeeded in establishing that the United States regarded the order as "infringements of neutral rights," that it was detrimental to American commerce, and that it would excite ill-will against Britain. He had done this, too, without sacrificing the Washington administration's freedom of action: "As I cannot speak from authority on the subject," he wrote home, "I have not said what measures we shall adopt in consequence."

In his response Grenville made two points. No loss was involved for the owners, who would always receive a liberal price; and Britain's policy had the support of her allies, particularly Spain and Russia. Retreating not a whit, Pinckney took the only reasonable course open to him: he would, he said, transmit both the Order and the British justification to Philadelphia. He succeeded in extracting from Grenville assurances, however, that neutrals would

[32]Bemis, "Mission," pp. 241–42.

be treated as gently as the necessities of war would allow, and that the law officers of the Crown would bring to book Britons who injured American shipping contrary to the law.[33]

Pinckney's major difficulty arose not at the Foreign Office but at the Court of Admiralty. When Grenville and his subordinates were punctilious in their discussions with Pinckney, American vessels detained under the order were in the toils of a branch of the British judiciary notoriously slow in performing its duties.

By mid-August, Pinckney had reached two major conclusions: that both the government and people of Great Britain desired good relations with the United States; but secondly, that British conduct toward neutrals was fixed and would continue to cause dissatisfaction to his countrymen. He did not, however, see the issue as a crisis, let alone as a casus belli. American economic interests, he reasoned, could still be served. So long as Britain paid a good price for American grain, he wrote privately to Jefferson, the restrictive policy, despite inconveniences, could still benefit American commerce. Writing officially (but in cipher), he advised moderation in responding to the order. "I may, perhaps, estimate too highly the blessings of peace in general, and the advantages of our neutral situation," he stated, "not withstanding all the deductions to be made on account of the conduct of this country. But it appears to me that, if the United States should deem it necessary to go beyond the line of remonstrance on this occasion, prudence will dictate, that our opposition should be confirmed to commercial regulations."[34] As events were to show, Pinckney's view coincided exactly with Madison's and the Republicans', who early in 1794 tried to

[33]Pinckney to Jefferson, 5 July 1793, *American State Papers, Foreign Affairs* (Washington, D.C., 1832), I, 241. See also Bemis's "Mission," pp. 228–47.

Precedents for the 8 June Order are to be found during the War of the Spanish Succession. Copies of those dated 28 April and 19 May 1709 are to be found, significantly enough, in Lord Hawkesbury's papers, British Library Add. MSS. 38353, fols. 196–97. See, too, Pinckney to Jefferson, 15 August 1793, *American State Papers, Foreign Affairs*, I, 241. This follows Pinckney's 5 July dispatch, his first report of efforts to counter the 8 June Order by diplomatic protest. In the dispatch of 28 August, cited below, Pinckney stated that he had handed Grenville a protest in writing based on Jefferson's instructions on 7 May.

[34]Pinckney to Grenville, 22 July 1793, and Grenville's response, 31 July 1793, *A.S.P.,F.A.*, I, 242; and Pinckney to Jefferson, 12 August 1793, cited below.

pass discriminatory regulations against British trade to the United States.

Suddenly, the eagerly awaited instructions arrived in Jefferson's dispatch of 7 May. Composed in response to Pinckney's first warning that a total interdiction of neutral trade to France was in the offing, Jefferson's arguments (and many of his words) were immediately incorporated into a written memorial "that the evidence of our opposition to the measures pursued here, should not rest merely on official conversations."[35] Jefferson, through Pinckney, charged that Britain violated neutral rights in two ways. The first, a generalization, perhaps, arising from the case of the *Sally*, was her action contrary to the principle, dear to American hearts, of "free ships, free goods." The second was the effective prohibition of American provisions trade to the unblockaded ports of France.

The principle, Jefferson argued, rested on the consensus of "a considerable majority of the Maritime Powers of Europe," which had emerged in the previous twenty years—reaching back to the American Revolution and including Britain's own commercial treaty with France in 1786. Practice was also supported by reason. Why should a neutral suffer the loss of innocent trade with any belligerent in a war? Further, it was certainly reasonable that a belligerent should take and destroy enemy property, but the right did not extend to neutral territory; and, by extension, neutral territory reached to neutral *vessels*: "the distinction . . . does not appear to form a difference sufficiently substantial to preclude the application of the same principle to both."

The second principle—the neutral right of innocent trade to unblockaded ports of a belligerent—was so ancient a prescription of international law and practice that little elaboration was needed. It was particularly applicable at the present juncture since (the American insisted) there existed no well-grounded hope of starving France, "where there is by no means any scarcity," into submission.

In addition to the outright infringement of neutral rights, the American statement continued, Britain gave Americans serious

---

[35]Jefferson to Pinckney, 7 May 1793, *Jefferson's's Writings*, VII, 312–15. Pinckney's memorial to Grenville, 9 August 1793, is in Foreign Office 5/3, fols. 159–61, and is printed (without date) in *A.S.P.,F.A.*, I, 242–43. See, also, Pinckney to Jefferson, 28 August 1793, ibid., p. 241.

inconveniences. It interrupted established forms of remittance in Franco-American trade; and the similarity of language shared by British and American seamen opened the latter to "contumelious treatment" by their captors and to "offers of bribery, to commit unworthy actions." In general terms, the chief evil arising from British policy was inevitable animosity between the powers and the undermining of Anglo-American friendship.

The memorial is not vintage Jefferson. There is the characteristic argument from and appeal to reason, and the familiar tendency to state abstract principles as dogmatic truth. The assertion that national jurisdiction covered a merchant vessel at sea as thoroughly as if it were national territory was highly disputable. More important, at least in the immediate sense, the absence of detailed information about specific injuries to American vessels meant that the protest was essentially an academic and theoretical exercise. It merited and received an answer in kind.

Grenville was polite but utterly firm: the British government guaranteed complete and impartial justice to any person suffering in body or property from illegal acts. It completely disapproved of violence and severity against innocent parties. In the course of a worldwide naval war, however, occasional inconvenience to neutrals was unfortunately unavoidable. Every effort would be made to keep these to a minimum, and if "irregularities" occurred, he would wish full communication of the facts. When that was done, the law officers of the Crown would act. The same statement of the British position had already been transmitted to Hammond in Grenville's dispatch of 5 July, and Pinckney informed Jefferson at the end of August that a full representation was to be expected from the British minister in Philadelphia. A particular concern, he predicted, would be enemy property found aboard netural vessels, that is, the question of "free ships, free goods."[36]

---

[36]Grenville to George Hammond, 5 July 1793, *Instructions to British Ministers to the United States*, ed. Bernard Mayo (Washington, D.C., 1941), pp. 40–42. See, also, Pinckney to Jefferson, 12 August 1793, *A.S.P.,F.A.*, I, 315. The editor doubts the date, but it is probably correct. President Washington sent the dispatch to Congress on 22 January 1794. See, also, the 28 August dispatch cited above.

The memorial's references to Britain's 1786 Treaty of Commerce with France and its acceptance of "free ships, free goods" requires comment. According to

With the debate over general principle and international law relegated, Pinckney and Grenville assumed, to Philadelphia, the American minister, whose original instructions gave him the "patronage" of his countrymen's commerce, turned to urgent business of a practical kind. Numerous American vessels carrying grain, contraband, or suspected enemy property were detained in British ports, their cases duly entered in the rolls of the Admiralty Court. There, proceedings took a most leisurely course. With a fine sense of the division between executive and judicial functions, Admiralty judges kept their own counsel, jealous of any hint of interference even by His Majesty's secretary of state for foreign affairs. As representatives of a foreign government, neither Pinckney nor his consuls had direct access to British courts. The prescribed channel of communication ran from the minister to the foreign secretary; and aside from the employment of proctors to guide bewildered American skippers through the maze of unfamiliar legal terms and technicalities, Pinckney could only exercise whatever leverage he possessed with Grenville to hasten the deliberations of the Admiralty Court.

The Briton was as helpful as the circumstances permitted. Upon one occasion, when Pinckney complained of "irregularities" committed by British privateers upon American vessels, Grenville immediately invited him to cite specific examples and to provide clear evidence for criminal prosecution of the offenders. Pinckney at once handed in information about three ships, "a small part of the American vessels brought into different ports of Great Britain," only to be told by Grenville that his examples were in the course of Admiralty adjudication and hence beyond the interference of the Executive.[37] Pinckney, nonetheless, continued to bombard the Foreign

William Eden (future Lord Auckland), Britain's chief negotiator of the treaty, the principle was accepted because it was deemed a trivial concession under the circumstances. In any major war, it was assumed, France would be an enemy, hence unable to benefit from this exception to long-standing British policy. See my *Aftermath*, Appendix H, pp. 376–77.

[37] In addition to Pinckney's dispatches already cited, see his to Jefferson (cipher), 15 August 1793, *A.S.P.,F.A.*, I, 241. Cipher was used because of the "frequent interruptions our vessels experience, especially in navigating the European seas." Washington sent the dispatch, along with much other material on relations with France and with Britain, to Congress on 5 December 1793.

Office with protests in behalf of American seamen awaiting judgment and of skippers unable to proceed to sea because compensation for preempted cargoes was as slow in coming as the verdict itself. On 28 August, Pinckney, noting again the slight likelihood of a change in British policy toward neutrals, complained to Jefferson about the tedious and costly delays in judicial proceedings. British measures, he wrote, "are attended for the present, with greater inconvenience, and consequent irritation to our citizens on account of the court of admiralty having, as yet, given no decision on the freight, demurrage, &c. to be allowed to the vessels brought in." The judiciary in every country deserved respect, of course, and he could but make "repeated applications" to the Foreign Office. In that quarter he had made it clear that justice delayed was justice denied; and it was particularly irksome that the Admiralty Court, recently adjourned to 4 September, continued silent on freight and demurrage. His most recent representation to Grenville elicited an appearance of surprise at the continued procrastination, from which Pinckney concluded "that he will endeavor to accelerate this business, at the time to which the court stands adjourned."[38]

The precise degree of Grenville's—or Pinckney's—influence on the course of events at this point is unclear; but the Admiralty Court's decision, dated the day before it met again for public business, must have been extremely gratifying to the American. In an Order of 3 September, freight, demurrage, and reasonable expenses were awarded neutral carriers under detention. A condition, plainly directed at all-too-common efforts to disguise French property as American, stated there should be no evidence of bad faith or prevarication. Arbitration of disputed settlements was also stipulated.[39]

There is no evidence to support Cross's assertion, p. 68, that Pinckney independently approached the Danish and Swedish envoys at this time (or any other time) to ask about the possibility of their joining the United States in strong and concerted measures to counter British policy.

[38]Pinckney to Jefferson, 28 August 1793, cited above. Pinckney was referring, of course, to his 9 August memorial.

[39]Pinckney transmitted the order to Philadelphia. It is printed in *A.S.P.,F.A.*, I, 315. There is no evidence to support Cross's picture, pp. 75–76, of a Pinckney depressed to the lowest depths of despair before the 8 January Order, and exulting in a personal victory of the first magnitude thereafter.

Appeals to higher courts against Admiralty verdicts were possible, of course, but Pinckney reported "our seafaring people, in general, rather inclined to submit to the first inconvenience than risk the event of a lawsuit."[40]

Pinckney's choice of words is significant. He saw quite correctly that the Order of 8 June 1793 constituted an "inconvenience" to American merchants and seamen, not the naked aggression some writers Bemis among them, have assumed. The British rule was purchase and allowance of expenses, not confiscation, unless, of course, French property or contraband—implements of war—were involved. Further, the American's relations with Grenville remained cordial. The former's complaints about tardy justice found the Foreign Office sympathetic and responsive. When Pinckney told Grenville, in July 1794, that fourteen American merchantmen were in British ports, cargoes purchased and expenses awarded, but unable to proceed to sea because they had not been paid, Grenville immediately arranged for an advance of funds even though the Admiralty Court decrees were not yet final.[41] Mutual courtesy and consideration characterized Pinckney's business with Grenville, but Bemis criticizes Pinckney not only for his perfunctory opposition to the 8 June Order, but also for a de facto acquiescence in Britain's offensive and injurious policy. Instead of pursuing mere commercial advantage for his countrymen, the minister should have contended, apparently, for the total overthrow of the newest example of British aggression.

How would "our sea-faring people" have regarded a great and legalistic controversy over abstract principle? While Pinckney and Grenville argued subtleties and ancient precedents relating to the contraband status of provisions in time of war, they would have watched idly from the sidelines, ships detained, the Admiralty Court grinding slowly, expenses mounting, neglected in their extremity by an American diplomat busy interpreting passages from Vattel instead of facilitating the passage of their vessels down the Thames. Speculative genius would have ill-served detained American skippers.

[40]Pinckney to Jefferson, 25 September 1793, *A.S.P.,F.A.*, I, 243. Washington transmitted the dispatch to Congress on 5 December 1793.
[41]Pinckney to Grenville, 5 July 1794, F.O. 5/7, fols. 161–62.

They required a practical man of affairs, and Thomas Pinckney was this man in full measure. He acted to relieve the suffering, but did not sacrifice a whit his country's freedom of action in formulating a response to the 8 June Order.

Sometime in late summer and early autumn 1793, authentic news of the Order reached Philadelphia. Yellow fever had made its sinister appearance in the American capital and was soon to reach epidemic proportions. With the government on the eve of fleeing the stricken city, Secretary Jefferson prepared fresh instructions for Pinckney.[42] The Order (not so far-reaching as Pinckney had first feared) was of a "very exceptional nature." The British government owed explanations. The restraints on American trade were "so manifestly contrary to the law of nations, that nothing more could seem necessary than to observe that it is so." Neutrals possessed a "natural right," based on established usage and reason, to trade freely as if the war did not exist. The United States, except for customary prohibitions against contraband (which in the American view certainly did not extend to wheat, flour, or meal) and against trading to blockaded places, could dispose of its innocent produce and purchase what it wanted wherever it chose.

Neutrality itself, Jefferson continued to Pinckney (and through him to Grenville), required the United States to permit its grain to go impartially to Britain and to France. A contrary behavior might bring an American war with France, since restraining its own trade to that country and permitting others to restrain it amounted to the same thing. If provisions were withheld from France, it followed, American neutrality required that the United States withhold them from all belligerents. Hinting thus broadly at embargo, Jefferson told Pinckney to enter into immediate explanations with the British government. His language was to be friendly and temperate, but he was to be explicit about his country's sense

[42]Jefferson to Pinckney, 7 September 1793, *A.S.P.,F.A.*, I, 239, Jefferson's initial reaction to the Order of 8 June 1793 was to consider it a casus belli. See his letter to Madison, March 1793, *Jefferson's Writings*, VII, 250–52.

The dispatch of 7 September also took exception to mildly favorable treatment (required by existing treaties) the British gave Swedish and Danish vessels attempting to enter ports under British blockade: a first attempt was to draw a warning; seizure was reserved for subsequent violations.

of injury, its earnest desire for a revocation of the Order; and its expectation of indemnification for its victims. No ultimatum was intended; but if Britain's habitual silence to American representations prevailed—a reference to Jefferson's own stalled negotiations with Hammond—the Minister was to report by 1 December to permit Congress to take appropriate action during the existing session.

A few days later, Hammond acted on Grenville's earlier instructions, sending Jefferson an official copy of the Order and setting out the defense supplied (and made earlier to Pinckney) by Grenville. The reply was crisp: the Order struck at the root of American agriculture; it had already been seen by the president; Pinckney had been instructed to take up the matter in London; and Jefferson would forbear its further discussion with Hammond.

Pinckney acknowledged the new instructions in his dispatch of 25 November; and a formal memorial was delivered in January of the new year. Making only occasional changes, Pinckney drew verbatim from Jefferson.[43] Grenville's response, however, was to order Hammond to reply to the memorial in Philadelphia. This was no discourtesy to the American minister in London. Hammond had already taken up the 8 June Order with Jefferson, it was assumed; and Grenville concluded, perhaps unfortunately in view of Hammond's deteriorating relations with the American government, that the Briton could answer American complaints more quickly than the foreign secretary himself and Pinckney could contrive in London.

Jefferson's dispatch was firm, to be sure, but its language, argumentative as it was, showed no sense of impending crisis. Indeed, until about the middle of March 1794, there was evidence in the United States of an understanding and acceptance—grudging and grumbling, to be sure—of the British system. Agitation among the

[43] *A.S.P.,F.A.*, I, 448–50. Pinckney's few changes achieved a certain moderating of Jefferson's tone. For example, he deleted the phrase calling the loss of market for American grain producers "a tax too serious for us to acquiesce in." See, also, *Jefferson's Writings*, VIII, 27. Grenville directed Hammond to answer Pinckney's memorial, a maneuver much criticized by Bemis, "Mission," pp. 241–42, who sees here a clever strategem by which "the matter was kept in a train of innocuous legal argument while the work of the cruisers went on unmolested."

public and in Congress was pronounced in December 1793 and January 1794, but it arose from more sources than Britain's Order-in-Council and was succeeded by some months of uneasy calm. A disgruntled Jefferson left office with the New Year; and his successor as secretary of state, Edmund Randolph, another Virginian, lacked the stature, both intellectual and political, of his predecessor. Congress stood on the verge of delivering what a Federalist member called "a decided Sentiment in favor of those measures which could insure Peace; and were disposed even to conform to the present state of things."[44] Secretary of the Treasury Hamilton, mulling over a draft letter on the 8 June Order that Secretary of State Randolph proposed to send George Hammond, wanted no asperity and urged that, aside from a general statement to the British minister, he be told the matter had been assigned to John Jay, recently appointed envoy extraordinary to Britain. Hamilton was uneasy, frankly admitting to this colleague that "from some latter lights I have received" more justification for the 8 June Order to be found in international practice "than I was originally aware of."[45] The 8 June Order, in short, was not—and in itself, never

[44]The letter, dated 2 March 1794, is anonymous, and is in F.O. 5/6, fols. 32–35. A second copy is in the Melville (Dundas) Papers, Clements Library. Several others in similar vein are there as well.

[45]To Randolph, 27 April 1794, *Papers of Alexander Hamilton*, XVI, 346–47. See also Randolph to Washington, 28 April 1794, ibid., p. 348 n. 6. The president approved Randolph's draft of a "particular" answer and implicitly rejected Hamilton's suggestion of a general response. Washington did, however, endorse Hamilton's advice to avoid asperity. Randolph's reply to Hammond is printed here, too.

Hammond's response, 11 April 1794, is printed in *A.S.P.,F.A.*, I, 449–50. It is an elaborate argument, replete with citations from ancient and modern authorities on international law, in behalf of the doctrine that a belligerent had the right to seize provisions en route to the enemy. Treaties setting aside the principle were specific exceptions to the rule and bilateral modifications by the signatories for the life of the treaty.

William Eden stated the British doctrine more succinctly still: "It would be little purpose to undertake or to prosecute a maritime War, if the Conveyance of the Enemies' property might be secured from Molestation under the Banner of Neutrality and of Friendship." Lord Hawkesbury provided a blunter and more general principle: "In time of War," he told Pitt, "the conduct of belligerent, as well as of neutral Powers, has been governed in these Respects, and probably will

became—the cause of a crisis in Anglo-American relations, even though the two governments expressed to each other official positions diametrically and sharply opposed.

The point-by-point rebuttal of Pinckney's memorial based on Jefferson's dispatch was duly presented to Secretary of State Randolph by Minister Hammond. It is important in developing Britain's rationalization of the 8 June Order, but it is of little relevance to a treatment of Thomas Pinckney's diplomacy. Randolph's long and angry response (against the advice of Treasury Secretary Hamilton) is important, too, not because it won a debate but because it showed that the 8 June Order had become subordinate to more serious matters. Its prime importance lay in the fact that it contained, Secretary Randolph wrote, "the germ of subsequent harsher measures."[46] The American disposition "to conform to the present state of things" was destroyed by a grave British miscalculation.

The "harsher measures" Randolph had in mind flowed from a new Order-in-Council dated 6 November 1793, and consequent savage spoliations of American shipping in West Indian waters; but the measure was merely one of a series of grievances, old and new, which, taken together, very nearly carried the United States into war with Britain in 1794.

Before the new Order was known on the western side of the Atlantic, Washington transmitted to Congress two voluminous sets of correspondence between Secretary Jefferson and the disastrous French envoy Genêt, and between the secretary and George Hammond. Thomas Pinckney's dispatches to 25 September also provided part of the presidential communication of 5 December 1793. From Jefferson it was learned that while both belligerents had

always, be, by the Occasions and Circumstances, which the Necessities of War produce." See Eden's memorandum on "free ships free goods," British Library, Add. MSS. 34421, fols. 287–88; and Hawkesbury to Pitt, 12 Oct. 1791, Add. MS. 38351, fols. 3–93. As plain Charles Jenkinson years earlier, Hawkesbury laid down the classical definition of the Rule of '56, forbidding to a neutral trade with an enemy's colonies not enjoyed in time of peace. His pamphlet is *Discourse on the Conduct of Great Britain in Respect to Neutral Nations* (London, 1757), and stated British policy in the French Revolutionary Wars as authoritatively as he had done in the days of the Seven Years' War.

[46]*Instructions to British Ministers*, pp. 45–47. See, also, Hammond to Randolph, 11 April 1794, and Randolph's response, 1 May 1794, *A.S.P.,F.A.*, I, 449–54. Both were sent to Congress on 12 May.

abused American shipping, Britain, by clear inference, was the prime culprit. Further, the negotiations with the British minister at Philadelphia had proved fruitless. Britain obviously refused to fulfill the Treaty of Peace of 1783 by surrendering the northwestern posts, or to negotiate a commercial accord with the United States. Her intransigence meant negotiations had ended, and her ill-will was attested by the Indian war raging with her encouragement along the American frontier.

The 5 December message was the opening shot in a triple salvo. On the sixteenth following, Jefferson sent Congress his long-depending report on privileges and restrictions extended by foreign powers to American trade. It was, in effect, a call for commercial retaliation against an unfriendly Britain who excluded American shipping from its West Indian ports. On the same date another message from the president informed Congress that Britain had engineered a truce in favor of its ally Portugal with the Algerine pirates, widely interpreted as a vile maneuver to incite piratical attacks upon shipping of the United States. Jefferson himself wrote of war: "Tho' not wished for, it seems not to be feared."[47]

On New Year's Day 1794 the House of Representatives took up Jefferson's commercial report. Two days later James Madison moved resolutions placing an extraordinary tax on British vessels trading between the West Indies and the United States. Throughout the month and much of February, bitter debates swirled around embattled Federalists and Jeffersonian Republicans, the former arguing eloquently that an interruption of trade with Britain would cost the United States more than it would the object of its wrath; the latter insisting that British behavior and the national dignity made some mark of American resentment absolutely necessary. For several weeks Madison and his friends seemed in command of the House and discrimination against Britain inevitable; but, then, slowly, the Federalists began to prevail, and, as stated earlier, a drift away from retaliatory measures developed. Notable speeches in the House by William C. Smith of South Carolina (mouthpiece for Hamilton himself) and Fisher Ames of Massachusetts engendered cool common sense and calm second thought: "Trade flourishes on our wharves," Ames told the Representatives, "although

---

[47]To Martha Randolph, *Jefferson's Writings*, VIII, 124–25.

it droops in speeches."[48] Powerful support came, too, from Hamilton, whose two "Pacificus" essays were published on 31 January and 7 February 1794.[49]

Into the cauldron near the boil there suddenly fell another cooling draught: Thomas Pinckney's dispatch of 25 November 1793, which Washington transmitted to Congress on 24 February 1794.[50] Acknowledging his instructions of 7 September and promising the written memorial on the 8 June Order discussed above, he wrote without awaiting the result of any representation—he was "tolerably certain what the purport of the answer will be"—to report a far-reaching and important conference with Lord Grenville. The Portuguese truce with the Algerines procured by the British consul at Algiers and the most recent failure of the United States to negotiate peace with the Northwestern Indians seemed so portentous to him that he had sought explanations on these vital subjects. In the meeting with Grenville, the foreign secretary began with polite expressions of his satisfaction that the yellow fever epidemic at Philadelphia was abating. Pinckney seized the opportunity to express gratitude for this interest in American welfare and assured him his countrymen hoped that friendship between the two countries should continue and grow. It was, however, "unfortunate," he continued, "that the circumstances which occasioned any material diminution of the prosperity of the United States, apparently originated from the measures of this country; that I had a well grounded hope, that

---

[48]Ames's speech is in *The Works of Fisher Ames*, ed. J. T. Kirkland (Boston, 1809), pp. 26–57.

[49]*Hamilton Papers*, XVI, 12–19.

[50]*A.S.P.,F.A.*, I, 327–28. Bemis states, "Mission," p. 243, that Pinckney's dispatch made "a painful impression" which added to the growing crisis of March 1794. Cross, p. 85, 90, follows Bemis, terming the letter "explosive" and seeing it as a great support for those demanding retaliatory measures against Britain. (He also incorrectly states that it reached Randolph only on 8 March 1794.) Neither Bemis nor Cross recognizes the brief but important relaxation of tensions in the United States—a disposition "even to conform to the present state of things"—which occurred in the weeks before arrival of news about the spoliations under the Order of 6 November 1793. Neither Bemis nor Cross documents the "painful" and "explosive" nature of Pinckney's dispatch; and, indeed, both finally dismiss its importance in the rising crisis. Painful and explosive or unimportant? In terms of strict logic, the dispatch cannot be both. In fact, it was neither.

it was not the intention of administration to do us injury; that I was certain it was not their interest so to do; but that people who felt grievances, who imagined they knew the parties had it in their power to remove them, could scarcely view, with that eye of cordiality we mutually wished to promote, those who were the willing causes of their misfortunes." He spoke of the Indian war, which he attributed to Britain's retention of the northwestern posts; of "the letting loose Algerines upon us"; and of the interruption to American commerce by the 8 June Order. (Its successor of 6 November remained a profound secret.) As he was particularly instructed on the latter, he promised a written memorial. On all three, however, he "enlarged severally . . . with such arguments as suggested themselves to me," and concluded by expressing the conviction "that this administration would not hestitate to relieve us from the inconvenience we felt in consequence of their measures."

Grenville's response could not have been more conciliatory. The truce for the Portuguese held "not the least intention or a thought of injuring us thereby." No more than friendship for any ally required, it also served to free the Portuguese fleet for action against France. If, as Pinckney informed him, the Portuguese offered American vessels within their harbors convoy protection, Britain certainly had no objection.

Turning to the posts, Grenville observed that this particular negotiation was relegated to Philadelphia, and both men agreed that "for obvious reasons" it should remain there. Grenville then stated explicitly and categorically that "this negotiation was not terminated." Indeed, a major British interest required its continuation, since he constantly received "pressing applications from the commercial subjects of his Majesty, on account of the non-execution of the treaty on our part," a reference to the massive unpaid pre-Revolution debts still owed by Americans to British creditors. In addition to that consideration, moreover, if Britain relinquished the posts under existing circumstances, its North American frontiers would suffer the same ravages, and its government the same expense and disadvantages which Pinckney found so onerous for the United States. For these reasons, Grenville thought, the "administration would not be justified in relinquishing the posts at this time; and expressed his regret, that Mr. Hammond had not been permitted by us, to enter into a negotiation for some arrangements relating particularly to the posts, and (as I apprehended him) Indian affairs, which, he had no doubt, would have terminated in our common advantage and mutual satisfaction; but that, when Mr. Hammond wished to open that business, he was given to understand (though in the most civil terms) that the less that was said on that subject the better."[51]

Pinckney's critics have made much of this letter. In the face of Grenville's "uncompromising tone," the American gratuitously took up the matter of the posts, "a subject not delegated to him as one of his duties." The indiscretion was followed by a bêtise. By asking Grenville outright whether Britain would evacuate the posts if the United States fulfilled the Treaty of Peace, he gave an opening previously withheld by Jefferson's masterly denial that the United States had ever violated the Treaty except as retaliation by some states for previous British infractions. Grenville immediately exploited the gaffe, telling Pinckney that where one party to a treaty had deferred fulfillment of its obligations for nine years, making complete execution impossible, nether reason nor the law of nations could expect strict compliance from the other party.[52] The British

---

[51]Pinckney's dispatch contained three passages in cipher, two innocuous, the third of considerable interest. In the last the minister wrote that he induced Grenville to enlarge upon the "hint" about the posts, and asked explicitly whether "in case we should comply with what they conceived to be the full execution of the treaty on our part, they would relinquish the posts to us?" Grenville responded "that in case one party to a treaty had deferred the accomplishment of their part of the obligation for nine years, whereby the complete execution could not afterwards be had, neither reason nor the law of nations would exact a strict compliance from the other party." Bemis sees Pinckney as committing an unfortunate indiscretion, providing Grenville with an "opening." My own and very different reading of the dispatch is fully set out in the essay. Cross, p. 90, suggests that the ciphered passages were not sent to Congress. If this is true, it follows that they could not have affected congressional opinion in February and March 1794. Pinckney's remark that the British "meditate fresh embarrassments" to American maritime commerce is also in cipher.

[52]See Bemis, *Jay's Treaty*, pp. 205–6; and "Mission," p. 243. Cross, pp. 80–81, is even harsher in his criticism of Pinckney, although in the process, he puts words into Pinckney's mouth. Both Bemis and Cross interpret Grenville's remarks as an intention not to give up the occupied posts. Bemis interprets Grenville's reference to the disadvantages Britain would suffer in the event of a cession to refer to the

government thus cleverly shifted the onus of prior infraction of the peace to American shoulders and revealed an intention to hold the posts indefinitely.

The truth is very different. Pinckney, troubled by the Algerine truce and the continuing Indian warfare along the American frontier, clearly apprehended some fundamental change in British policy toward his country. He was duty-bound, therefore, to seek out Grenville, not to make pompous and high-flown declarations, but to discover whatever he could about British intentions. Since his question went to Britain's American policy as a whole, he naturally engaged in a tour of the horizon, examining with Grenville the whole range of problems besetting Anglo-American relations. At any event, Jefferson himself had specifically suggested months earlier that he take some such action. To have omitted talking about the posts, long a major concern to both countries and specifically linked to Indian warfare and prewar debts, would have been an imbecility: a description of the *Berneroberland* without the Jungfrau.[53]

But Pinckney did not make the northwestern posts a principal—or secondary, or even tertiary—topic of negotiation with Grenville. Both the American and the Briton agreed quite explicitly to exclude it. The issue, they said, was reserved to the on-going *pourparlers* in Philadelphia. Here was no "opening" granted by a diplomatic tyro to a skillful antagonist. If there was an "opening" at all, it had been supplied long since by Secretary Jefferson himself when, at the outset of his abortive negotiations with Hammond, he asked the Briton (naturally enough), to state specifically the American acts the British Government considered breaches of the Treaty of Peace. In subsequent exchanges between the two, the issue over "prior infraction" was well and truly joined. Pinckney's conference

loss of the frontier fur trade. This ignores the Briton's clear and explicit connection of posts and prewar debts, and also potential Indian hostility toward unfaithful friends.

[53]See Cross, p. 65, citing Jefferson's dispatch to Pinckney, 14 June 1793, enclosing several protests from Hammond about French violations of American neutrality. Jefferson told Pinckney that when he saw Grenville for a review of American developments, he should seize the opportunity to introduce all questions at issue. Hammond, Jefferson continued, had been relentless in the pursuit of British rights. Pinckney should be the same, even threatening reprisals if he judged it necessary.

with Grenville was altogether irrelevant to the issue except as a reaffirmation of a fact long known to the government of the United States: that the posts were ineluctably connected with the prewar debts. Pinckney's dispatch revealed, in fact, that he himself was more concerned about another matter altogether: information he had received that the British "meditate fresh embarrassments to our trade."

Read dispassionately and in toto, Pinckney's dispatch told Congress and the American people that, problems notwithstanding, Anglo-American relations were at the moment essentially friendly, and the British Government conciliatory. British measures caused inconvenience and concern; but the American minister made it abundantly clear that, to his knowledge, there was no existing difference, posts included, not amenable to the diplomatic process. Pinckney thus provided a most valuable corrective to the several bitterly anti-British communications to Congress in December 1793. He gave, too, a reassurance of special importance in the heated political struggle in America during the spring of 1794: the courtesy and friendliness manifested in the Pinckney-Grenville conference were more characteristic of the true state of Anglo-American relations than were the ill-tempered and acerbic exchanges between the secretary of state and George Hammond.

The crisis of early 1794, however, arose many thousands of miles from London. In the United States old quarrels over the unfulfilled conditions of the Peace of 1783 and commercial differences joined with newer causes of discord—impressment, the preemption of American grain cargoes, the seizure of French property aboard neutral carriers—to intensify a rising resentment in the United States. It remained to three other new developments to bring the crisis to the breaking point. The first was a bellicose and provocative speech made by Canadian governor Lord Dorchester to the Indians of the Old Northwest in February 1794, predicting war with America and, in that event, inviting the red men to draw a new boundary with their tomahawks. The second was a move by Simcoe, governor of Upper Canada, southward from Toronto with a small force to reoccupy a post at the foot of the Maumee River rapids, indisputably well within American territory. Actions by both men were profoundly defensive, motivated by a frantic fear that the American Anthony Wayne, known to be advancing into the Old Northwest, aimed at British-occupied Detroit. To Americans, however, the speech portended war, and the thrust to the south was actual invasion. Although they figured prominently in Randolph's negotiations, if the word may be used, with Hammond, and in John Jay's special mission to Britain, these two matters did not enter directly into Pinckney's own work in London. But a third measure became his last major problem there. It was the Order-in-Council of 6 November 1793.

In the autumn of 1793 the French West Indies, particularly the island of Santo Domingo, seemed to dissolve into a grisly shambles as black slaves, intoxicated with the heady doctrines of the French Revolution, rose in bloody rebellion. Terrified whites gathered what property they could readily transport and fled to Europe, to the United States, or to whatever refuge they could find. Britain, seeing in the chaos and anarchy an opportunity to seize valuable French possessions, quickly assembled a military expedition for an attack and in the process ordered the seizure of "all ships laden with goods the produce of any colony belonging to France or carrying provisions or other supplies for the use of any such colony." Violating a fundamental precept of its own Rule of '56—allowing a neutral's peacetime trade to the colonies of an enemy during war—Britain thus severed an important artery of trade between the United States and the French West Indies. It operated with special brutality because of the large number of American vessels attracted to the area by the desperate needs of white refugees. Of the 250 American vessels seized by British crusiers, 150 were subsequently condemned, many by irregularly constituted courts of admiralty in the islands presided over by judges who made little distinction between neutral Americans and enemy French. When the Order became known in the United States sometime about the middle of March, a bitter Federalist, long a supporter of Anglo-American friendship, lamented that an open declaration of war by Britain would have been more magnanimous.[54] At the end of March, Congress passed

[54]See n. 44 above.

and the president proclaimed an embargo on all foreign trade. Hammond believed it was the prelude to hostilities.[55]

For this sorry state of affairs, British leaders had only themselves to thank. In executing their plan they made three grave miscalculations which very nearly destroyed peace with the United States. Intended from its inception as a temporary measure—to deal with the extraordinary outflow of French property from the islands and to assist British military operations there—the November order was to have been published to the world simultaneously with its revocation by the Order of 8 January 1794. For this reason, every effort was made to keep the November measure a profound secret. Success in doing so constituted an almost unique event in eighteenth-century British political history. On this occasion, Pinckney received no early warning. A copy of the additional instructions implementing the Order reached him only on Christmas Day 1793, and, in great alarm, he immediately prepared a dispatch for Philadelphia.[56] With a few days before the sailing of the North American packet, he called at the Foreign Office for some word of official explanation. Grenville was out of town, but he saw Burges, who subsequently described the visit in the Foreign Office Journal for his chief's benefit: "Mr. Pinckney called, much agitated in consequence of the new instruction . . .—very anxious to know whether it would be rigorously enforced—insisted strongly on the injustice of such a measure, and on the destructive consequence it must entail on his country, which now would be deprived of every means of exporting its produce, as the Act of Navigation [sic] shut them out from those of France; so that nothing but a few inconsiderable markets would be left to them."[57]

[55]Hammond to Grenville, 12 March 1794, F.O. 5/4, fols. 136–37. For a full discussion of the 6 November 1793 and 8 January 1794 Orders-in-Council, see my *Aftermath*, pp. 299 ff.

[56]Pinckney to the secretary of state, 2 January 1794, containing a copy of additional instructions to British naval commanders based on the Order-in-Council of 6 November 1793, *A.S.P.,F.A.* I, 430. Pinckney also stated here that his appointment with Grenville on the same day had been cancelled and, since the packet was about to sail, he had to send his dispatch without any explanation from the British Goverment.

[57]*Fortescue Papers*, II, 488.

In the emergency Pinckney had acted as forcibly as circumstances allowed; refusing to leave his protest with a subordiate, he fixed a conference with Grenville for 2 January. Bad fortune continued to dog the Briton. At the last minute Grenville, heavily engaged with other duties, canceled the appointment. It was another major miscalculation. With the sailing of the packet imminent, Pinckney could but transmit to Philadelphia the bare news of the November Order, bereft of official explanations and of British intentions to revoke the measure. He did add the news that the Swedish minister also appeared alarmed at the new policy and that a committee of merchants interested in the American trade had protested to Pitt himself. The vital fact remained, however, that official news of the November Order reached the United States without the ameliorating effect of the cancellation.

Pinckney finally met with Grenville on 9 January. The day before, a new Order-in-Council, laying down the "Rule of '56," and the dictum that free ships did *not* make free goods, authorized the capture of French West Indian produce found aboard whatever vessel en route from the islands to Europe. If it was French property, it could be seized regardless of destination. The usual rules prohibiting trade in military and naval stores and to blockaded places were also prescribed. The Americans were confirmed in their prewar right to trade to the French islands except, of course, in the restricted categories of contraband. (The original Order of 8 June 1793 was not revoked; and the preemption of American grain and flour bound for France remained in force.)

Pinckney receives rare praise for his "firmness" in bringing these changes about and for "important victories" in winning the revocation of the November Order. It has also been asserted that the 8 January Order resulted from British fears of the "dangerous hostility" roused in the United States by the November measure.[58]

---

[58]Pinckney's dispatch of 9 January 1794 covered additional instructions to British naval commanders based on the new Order-in-Council of 8 January 1794 (revoking the 6 November 1793 Order). It is printed in *A.S.P.,F.A.*, I, 430–31. President Washington sent both the November and January orders to Congress on 4 April 1794.

For the allegation that the revocation of the November order was caused by British concern for a dangerous hostility rising in the United States, see Bemis,

Pinckney certainly never claimed a triumph in this regard; and, indeed, the revocation came the day before his conference with Grenville. It was months later, too, before the nature of the American reaction to the November Order was known in London. The truth is that both November and January Orders were integral elements of the same plan. That they did not burst upon the world simultaneously was due to bad luck, worse timing, and the sailing of the packet for North America shortly before the revoking Order was issued. Worse still—a third miscalculation—the revocation did not work with the surgical precision the British Ministry anticipated. Seizure, adjudication, and condemnation, often accompanied by physical abuse of American seamen by tars of the Royal Navy, continued for many months. Distribution of the January order to British cruisers at sea proved difficult and time-consuming; and until the arrival on board of authentic instructions to the contrary, British commanders pursued their predatory work at American expense with zeal and gusto. There was thus ample opportunity for American outrage to grow during the first half of 1794.

In these difficult circumstances, Pinckney made one of his most effective representations in asserting the American position to the British government. In his interview with Grenville on 9 January, the foreign secretary was clearly at a disadvantage; and Pinckney kept him there. The British plan had misfired; and Grenville labored mightily to conciliate, to reassure, and to explain. Attempting to seize the intiative, the Briton sought to focus on the January Order, not its predecessor. It was, he said, "a manifestation of the good will of this Government towards the United States." Pinckney responded dryly that "it was certainly much less injurious to us than the instruction which it revoked, and might be as favorable as the principles upon which this Government acts would admit." The real issue, however, was the material difference between the two powers over neutral rights; the American position was simply

"Mission," pp. 241–42. For Pinckney's "important victories," see Cross, p. 84. In a particularly opaque passage, Cross states that the 8 June Order "set in motion the divisive developments leading to the rupture between the two powers." Several important "divisive developments" in Anglo-American relations at the time derived their origin and impetus from causes far removed from the 8 June Order; and there was no rupture between the powers.

stated: a belligerent had no right to interfere with neutral trade beyond preventing articles commonly accepted as contraband from reaching the enemy, or trading to blockaded places. Here was an unqualified rejection of the Rule of '56, and a reassertion that free ships made free goods.

Again, Grenville hedged, avoiding a direct confrontation and introducing further extraneous matter. The January revoking order testified to Britain's desire "to maintain the best understanding and harmony with the United States," but more, it showed the wish— the subject was so delicate Grenville could not mention it officially and hence expected no answer from Pinckney—"to take away every pretext from evil disposed persons" in the United States, those turbulent spirits who seemed to desire hostility with Britain, an end to neutrality, and a reduction of their country to "the present situation of France," a misfortune Britain deprecated, "as well for our sakes as for the common welfare of mankind." Third, America merited such special consideration because of its generally scrupulous regard for its duties as a neutral and Britain's consequent conviction that the United States desired to persevere in that policy.

Pinckney brushed aside the sweet words. What, he asked, was the effect of the November Order on American vessels actually seized by British cruisers? The Briton's desire to conciliate sacrificed candor. There was, Grenville replied, a distinction to be made between vessels merely brought in for "adjudication" and those ordered condemned. It was a flimsy answer. Both knew that a fuller reckoning was reserved for a future date. For the moment, lacking specific information from his government and from the West Indies, Pinckney could go no further until Philadelphia spoke.

When Anglo-American relations almost reached the breaking point in the spring of 1794, President Washington and his Federalist advisers made a last desperate effort to save the peace. Chief Justice John Jay was dispatched to London as special envoy to ascertain, Hammond reported to Grenville, "the real views of his majesty's government toward this country."[59] Some saw the appointment as an affront to the resident minister, none more so than Jefferson,

---

[59]Hammond to Grenville, 12 March 1794, F.O. 5/4, fols. 136–37; and the same to the same, 23 March 1794, F.O. 116/2, pp. 259–66.

the former secretary of state, embittered and suspicious of Britain and what he believed to be the Anglophile proclivities of his Federalist enemies. Writing savagely from his Monticello retreat to Monroe, he declared that a "more degrading measure could not have been proposed." Why was Pinckney to be recalled? It was impossible for him to remain in London "after such a testimony that he is not confided in." He supposed his former colleagues "think him not thorough fraud enough." Pinckney's own response to Jay's appointment possessed a finer balance. Admitting privately to "unpleasant feelings" despite reassurances from both the president and the secretary of state, he quickly put out of sight considerations of a personal nature. It was not the least testimonial to Pinckney's patriotism, innate decency, and personal modesty that, despite initial chagrin, he accepted the Jay mission as the best means to deal with a crisis arising from many causes, some altogether unconnected with his own negotiations in London.[60] He was cooperative and helpful to Jay, briefing him thoroughly upon his arrival in London in June 1794 and providing advice and opinions that gave Jay "light and advantage" during the negotiations which followed. In due course, when Jay's Treaty was concluded, Pinckney expressed his approbation, much to the delight of the American negotiator, "not merely because his opinion corresponds with my own, but also from the sentiments I entertain of his judgement and candor."[61]

The comprehensive settlement Jay achieved reached, of course, to compensation for despoiled American shipowners and merchants suffering under the November Order. The broader issues of neutral rights and definition of contraband were put aside to a more tranquil future date; but the questions of "free ships, free goods" and grain as contraband remained—quite explicitly in Jay's Treaty— open. The special envoy's success in defusing the explosive issues was built upon the bases provided earlier by the diplomacy of Thomas Pinckney. Indeed, the preservation of the peace between

[60]Jefferson to Monroe, 24 April 1794, quoted by Cross, p. 95. The chief value of Cross's work lies in the discussion of Pinckney's mission after the arrival of John Jay in June 1794.

[61]Jay to Randolph, 19 November 1794, *A.S.P.,F.A.*, I, 503–4; and Pinckney to Randolph, 10 November 1794, quoted by Cross, p. 111.

Britain and America owed much to the conscientiousness, pragmatism, courtesy, and commonsense of the South Carolinian.

What more might Pinckney have accomplished in Britain had Jefferson's instructions been less restrictive? His later triumph in Spain with the Treaty of San Lorenzo is suggestive. Whatever answer may be adduced, however, it is clear beyond question that old dogmas do not gain validity by mere repetition; and Thomas Pinckney seen through Jeffersonian eyes is a very different being from the second minister of the United States at the Court of St. James's.

Pictures to the Heart

The Psychological Picturesque in Ann Radcliffe's
The Mysteries of Udolpho

JEAN H. HAGSTRUM

THE TERM *PICTORIAL* IS OFTEN USED AS A SYNONYM FOR GRAPHIC, visual, scenic, or sensuous. In his analysis of renditions of reality in Western literature, Erich Auerbach is concerned with the pictorial in this sense, making it the source of important literary value. Failure for him is to be "dry and unvisualized," while success lies in being sensory and pictorial. To write with circumstantial detail is to write "plastically"; the graphic manner floods a work with "a clear and equal light," leaving nothing mysterious in the background.[1] What Auerbach praises is the ancient rhetorical value called *enargeia*—that is, clarity, palpability, a living daylight freshness and fullness of vivid detail.[2]

For many works in the Western tradition the term *pictorial* as defined is not adequate to the visual richness and variety that one finds; and one must have resort to the ungainly but useful word *pictorialist*, which evokes the tradition of literary pictorialism and such specific conventions as the description of an art object real or imaginary; the "quotation" of particular works of graphic art or the reflection of easily identifiable schools of art; ways of seeing trained by visual models in tapestry, sculpture, painting, or the

[1] *Mimesis* (Princeton, 1968), pp. 26, 27, 46.
[2] Jean H. Hagstrum, *The Sister Arts* (Chicago, 1958), Index, s.v. *Enargeia*.

cinema; methods of proceeding and ordering that suggest spatial rather than temporal art. For almost two millennia now—from Homer to Yeats—these Sister Arts conventions have persisted in poetry, providing even within the visual matrix abundant opportunity for imitation and adaptation, convention and revolt.[3]

Pictorialist novels also exist. These have not been much studied, except in notable isolated instances, and little has been said about the tradition, if one in fact exists apart from that associated with the ancient admonition *ut pictura poesis*. The *Pilgrim's Progress* of antiquity, the *Tablet* (or *Tabula*) of Cebes of Thebes, is pictorialist in the sense that it begins by introducing the reader to an allegorical picture and proceeds by describing its every section and detail.[4] Similarly, Longus' *Daphnis and Chloe* presents at the outset a large landscape painting from which the action of the novel seems to derive.[5] In the *New Arcadia* Sidney's vision of persons and scenes is stylized into picture and statue, and the action often proceeds in a series of tableaux. In the prose of Laurence Sterne the "attitude" of an individual character is likewise often statuesque or pictorial, sometimes suggesting a specific source in the visual arts: "My father instantly exchanged the attitude he was in, for that in which *Socrates* is so finely painted by Raffael in his school of *Athens*."[6] In *The Marble Faun* Hawthorne loads every rift with iconic ore: the faun itself by Praxiteles, the statue of the pope in Perugia, and paintings by Guido Reni—all of them symbolic equivalents of human characters or the chief purveyors of meaning and value.[7] George Eliot's novels form a tissue of traditional pictorialist conventions as these had been modified by Hazlitt and the Romantics—traditions that she in her turn adapted to her needs as a Victorian author.[8] Henry James

[3]See ibid. in general.

[4]Ibid., pp. 33–34.

[5]See Preface, anon. trans. (London, 1719).

[6]*Tristram Shandy*, IV.vii. See William V. Holtz, *Image and Immortality* (Providence, 1970), a study of Sterne and painting.

[7]See Judith Kaufman Budz, "Nathaniel Hawthorne and the Visual Arts," Diss., Northwestern, 1973.

[8]See Hugh Witemeyer, *George Eliot and the Visual Arts* (New Haven, 1979) and my review in *Nineteenth-Century Fiction*, 34(1979), 217–20.

[435]

often disposes his scenes like pictures in a gallery or tapestries on a wall, and in Chapter xxx of the *Ambassadors* Strether, on an excursion into the French countryside, enters, as it were, a canvas of Lambinet; and the ensuing scene is composed as a series of impressionist paintings.[9] Some of the outdoor scenes of *Women in Love* suggest, as Lawrence says, the picnics of Watteau and also, as he does not say, the ferns, fronds, and petals on water of Claude Monet. Finally, Nathanael West makes a painting by one of his characters, Tod's apocalyptic *Burning of Los Angeles*, central to the meaning and movement of *The Day of the Locust*. The painting appears at the Day-of-Wrath climax as well as at the beginning, and not only frames the action but insinuates it.[10]

To this partial list of pictorialist novels must be added Mrs. Anne Radcliffe's *The Mysteries of Udolpho* (1794), a work which marked the apogee of the romantic gothic novel and which held the throbbing attention of more than one generation of young readers.[11] About the picture making in this novel two essential points need to be made. The first is that to Radcliffe's pictorialism the then fashionable contemporary term *picturesque* can be applied. The other is that, by subtle but persistent metaphorical substitutions, Radcliffe extends her pictures into the heart and spirit of man—an extension that Longus, other writers of Greek romance, Sidney, and writers in the tradition of emblematic and allegorical visualization were unable to make. Hence the phrase of the title of this paper: "the psychological picturesque."

The picturesque anticipated Ann Radcliffe by only a few years; but when it came into her hands, it bore the weighty sanctions of Edmund Burke, of some of the greatest landscapists of Western culture, of exciting novelistic experiments, and of a contemporary set of enthusiastic aestheticians. The story has often been told of how various ingredients came together to form the pre-Romantic

[9]Viola H. Winner, *Henry James and the Visual Arts* (Charlottesville, 1970), pp. 74–77.

[10]Donald T. Torchiana, "*The Day of the Locust*: The Painter's Eye," in *Nathanael West: The Cheaters and the Cheated*, ed. David Madden (De Land, Fla., 1973), pp. 249–82.

[11]James R. Foster, *History of the Pre-Romantic Novel in England* (New York, 1949), p. 263.

[436]

picturesque: the grand sublime of terror that Burke had distinguished from the soft beauty of tenderness, the savage and irregular landscapes of Salvator that contrasted with the delicate landscapes of Claude, the obsessive love of Alpine scenery, and a quickened appreciation of Oriental and Hebrew imagery.[12] Radcliffe's rendition of the historical picturesque is precise and nuanced. She understands both the sublime of religious awe and the sublime of natural fear in the presence of physical danger. And her beauty has all the largeness of Claude's vistas in tender lights and the intimacies of cottage and fishing hut expressed by contemporary water colorists—a beauty that soothes the mind and ministers to the affectionate sensibilities. To the Salvatorian sublime and Claudian beauty only a few more pictorial strains need to be added for a full understanding of Radcliffe's picturesque: the fluttering and exotic beauty of Guardi's and Canaletto's Venice; the Magnasco-like chiaroscuro of the gypsy scenes; the disturbing effect of Piranesi's grotesquely imagined interiors in the dark corridors, grating gates, and blood-stained steps of French and Italian castles; and the traces of the "dark pencil" of Domenichino, whom the author invokes by name, on the dark, torch-lit chapel interior where the mild face of a venerable monk, his features revealed by his pulled-back cowl, contrasts with the fierce features and wild dress of the condottieri.

These are the colors of Mrs. Radcliffe's pictorial palette, which brought her the rewards of immediate fame. This "great impresario of beauty, wonder, and terror"[13] riveted the attention of her own and succeeding generations of readers. Sir Walter Scott reports that "the volumes flew, and were sometimes torn from hand to hand,"[14] and Joseph Warton was surely not the only one whom the *Mysteries of Udolpho* kept from sleep.[15] How shall one explain the spell of this "enchantress"?[16] Surely it was not only the imagined danger of distant places that thrilled her readers. Nor, it seems, would the pictorialist skill alone—what Cazamian praises as the variety, the

[12]Christopher Hussey, *The Picturesque* (London, 1927).

[13]Foster, p. 262.

[14]Quoted by Devendra Varma, *The Gothic Flame* (London, 1957) p. 94.

[15]Ibid., p. 94.

[16]De Quincey's word, quoted by Bonamy Dobrée, ed., *The Mysteries of Udolpho* (London, 1966), p. x.

wealth of coloring, and the charm of her pictures, a talent hitherto unequaled in the English novel[17]—have fastened the reader to those many pages of extended description that our own age finds languid. Nor could it have been the supernatural, which the author almost always in the course of the novel explains in natural terms once an educated character has had time to get in all the facts and refute the ignorant servants. The appeal must have lain in the immediate and intimate suggestiveness, for Mrs. Radcliffe was one of the most richly nuanced authors ever to have unfolded a slow-moving plot through several volumes.

Many critics have made hints about the hints of Mrs. Radcliffe, implying that her many-layered suggestiveness has its roots deep in our nature and arouses resonances of feeling much deeper than superficial titillation. Catherine Morland turns from immediate concerns in Bath to "the luxury of a raised, restless, and frightened imagination over the pages of Udolpho,"[18] and these strong and weighty adjectives of Jane Austen should give pause to those who think that *Northanger Abbey* merely makes fun of Mrs. Radcliffe's melodrama. Others have noted that Mrs. Radcliffe's heroines have an almost morbid craving for fear and that her adventures have a dreamlike quality that reveals a mind tremblingly alive to imaginative fear.[19] Even within the novel there is some awareness that an emotional life quickened by the picturesque can be dangerous. Emily's father warns her that excessive sensibility is to be feared, and Mrs. Radcliffe, who believed that terror can be wholesome and "expand the soul and awaken the faculties," was careful, like Coleridge after her, to keep terror from becoming an annihilating, freezing horror.[20]

Where shall we locate the fear and terror of her novel, emotions which can, as Hazlitt says, make "the nerves thrill with fond hopes and fears" and which witness to a power of evocation greater than

[17]Emile Legouis and Louis Cazamian, *A History of English Literature* (New York, 1935), p. 970.

[18]*Northanger Abbey*, Ch. vii.

[19]Foster, p. 265; Varma, p. 86.

[20]Dobrée, p. xi.

that of any of her countrymen?[21] It should be located in that part of the civilized psyche where sexual love and sexual encounters are anticipated but never formulated in direct and unequivocal terms or images. To accept this view one must be sympathetic to the notion that profoundly suggestive pictures can be socially or morally acceptable substitutes for forbidden feelings or wishes. Literature of course abounds in examples of pictures as substitutes for real people or for real experience. In Sidney's *New Arcadia* they often take the place of a person, of a loved and lost husband or friend,[22] as is also true in Chekhov's "The Bear," in which a grieving Russian lady caresses her late husband's portrait.

Mrs. Radcliffe's substitutions are less for what is loved and lost than for what is loved and hoped for. Her heroines usually dally with larger pictures than miniatures, but the suggestions are insistent that the sublime-beautiful landscapes are an anticipation of the rewards that came to Pygmalion, who embraced his statue. The bedchambers, often in an older and isolated part of the castle, with secret entrances, sliding panels, steps leading to deep unexplored recesses, have overtones of sexual danger which, had these been totally displeasing, would have made all life and motion cease. "To the warm imagination, the forms," to quote Mrs. Radcliffe's own language, "which float half-veiled in darkness afford a higher delight than the most distinct scenery the Sun can show."[23] Such a statement, taken alone, reformulates one quality in the Burkean sublime. But, placed in a Radcliffian context of "warm imagination," that "half-veiled delight" may sometimes be viewed as being as impatient of the "Busie old foole, unruly Sunne" as ever Jack Donne was—and for Donne's reasons.

Mrs. Radcliffe was much more than a formulary novelist illustrating Burke's distinction between the sublime and the beautiful[24] and merely alternating between Salvatorian danger and Claudian

---

[21]Varma, p. 128.

[22]See *New Arcadia*, Vol. I, Bk. II, passim.

[23]Varma, p. 103.

[24]Malcolm Ware, *Sublimity in the Novels of Ann Radcliffe* (Upsala, 1963). For a sensitive discussion of Radcliffe and the Sublime, see Samuel H. Monk, *The Sublime* (Ann Arbor, 1960), pp. 217–20.

repose.[25] Although she does provide these fashionable alternations, she essentially unites what Burke and his followers had put asunder. Extremes do not always meet, of course, and it would do the melodrama disservice if on one level we did not keep the black villainous Italians, the Montonis and the Orsinos, worlds apart from the good white French, the St. Auberts and the Villerois. But the really interesting zone in the *Mysteries of Udolpho* is that protoerogenous zone where terror and delectation meet, namely, the heart of the heroine. *Sensibility* is the historical word for the inward psychological response to the external picturesque of interreacting terror and beauty—a word that Jane Austen uses unmistakably for sexual love.[26]

Radcliffe almost, in fact, makes explicit the association of pictorialized landscape and love-experience. Valancourt, Emily's lover, first flits unseen but not unnoticed (as poet, lute player, and harmless thief) in a favorite setting near the family home on the edge of the Pyrenees. On the first journey he materializes mysteriously on the road and accompanies the party, it now being perfectly clear that the taste for wild sublimity is a shared one. Even in the sinister abode of the evil Montoni in the Apennines the love-feelings are by no means dissipated, since that formidable pile possesses the "gothic greatness" of a "gloomy and sublime object" and produces "melancholy awe" in Emily—precisely the emotion that Emily shares with her lover, a sure sign that they belong together.[27] After the return to France, Valancourt appears in a delicious southern French vintage; and again, near the climax at the place of first meeting,

<hr>

[25]See Elizabeth Manwaring, *Italian Landscape in Eighteenth Century England* (New York, 1925), pp. 212–18. Manwaring perceives that Mrs. Radcliffe's "most characteristic scenes are composed of a union of the savage and the soft, Salvator and Claude" (p. 217).

[26]Catherine Morland "had reached the age of seventeen, without having seen one amiable youth who could call forth her sensibility; without having inspired one real passion." (*Northanger Abbey*, Chap. i). See also my *Sex and Sensibility: Ideal and Erotic Love from Milton to Mozart* (Chicago, 1980), pp. 268–74.

[27]*Mysteries* (London, 1794), II, 170–71. The passages most clearly illustrating the union of expectant love with picture or landscape occur on the following pages of the first edition, cited here: I, 26, 89, 277; II, 10 (love is banished by mountains here), 170, 189 f, 210, 212, 220, 230; III, 101–2, 336–38, 350, 358; IV, passim, but esp. 189 ff., 226 ff., 409 ff.

his mysterious presence is felt and stirs deep chords of fear as well as trembling anticipation. (For one thing his identity is not at once known: is he a robber or the lover or possibly, in a psychophysical sense, both?) It is the cumulative effect of just such juxtapositions as these that make one feel that the sensuous in Mrs. Radcliffe is also the sensual, or at least anticipates the sensual. The sublime-beautiful, dangerous-safe, savage-mild, wild-cultivated alternations and fusions of the pictures suggest love-play and love-experience—an earnest of the full physical and sexual inheritance that physical union will bring.

Prose fiction has often, to use Johnson's phrase, created "pictures to the mind."[28] The ethical and moral emblems of Mrs. Radcliffe are conventional and superficial, but those of Sidney, Richardson, and others are weighty and impressive, whether they are the ideal representations of *la belle nature* or the grotesque of evil and distorted nature. Verbal pictures have also been—particularly in the romances—supernatural or magical or superstitious, but Radcliffe tends to explain them away. Even deeper than either the ethical or the religious, the moral or the mysterious, are the psychological pictures, pictures to the heart, dreamlike pictures that arise from the inner man and either disturb or animate the conventions. The nerve of Mrs. Radcliffe's literary eye extends deep within her being, with the result that the mountain ways of Gascony and the winding corridors of a castle in the Apennines carry their suggestions to the untrodden passes of the human heart and body.

[28]Donald Greene, "Pictures to the Mind," in *Johnson, Boswell, and Their Circle: Essays Presented to L.F. Powell* (Oxford, 1965), pp. 137–58.

The Task of Telling Lies

Candor and Deception in Sense and Sensibility

R. F. BRISSENDEN

NO ONE WOULD WISH TO ARGUE THAT *SENSE AND SENSIBILITY* IS Jane Austen's greatest novel. The title, however, is one of her most brilliant touches. Titles of this sort, in which two related, often antinomous, qualities or concepts are set together, were of course, popular at the time.[1] No other, I think, crystallizes so lightly and precisely such a large and significant subject. The debate concerning the relative merits of the head and the heart, the reason and the feelings, had been pursued widely and vigorously during the eighteenth century—to such a degree, indeed, that by the time Jane Austen put her novel into its final shape one could have been forgiven for assuming that the subject was exhausted. The freshness, vivacity, and openness with which she explores it, however, prove that in her hands at least it was not. Indeed, one of the strongest impressions which the novel leaves us with is the sense that the question is ultimately irresolvable and inexhaustible. Among the most surprising and admirable features of what in some ways is very much a "first" book is the air of ambiguity and mystery with which in the end it is pervaded.

At one level it purports to resolve the question posed by the title in a simple and final way—and it is possible that Jane Austen thought that this was what she was doing. If we believe this we shall no doubt read *Sense and Sensibility* as little more than a *roman à thèse* and find it, as Marilyn Butler does, "the most obviously

---

[1] See Kenneth L. Moler, *Jane Austen's Art of Allusion* (Lincoln, Neb., 1968), pp. 46–58.

tendentious of Jane Austen's novels and the least attractive."[2] In this view the work is relatively uncomplicated, and what complexities do exist have arisen incidentally to what the author saw as her primary objective: "Marianne, and to some extent Elinor, are drawn with strong feelings which the reader is accustomed to sympathise with, and actually to value for their own sake. But it is the argument of the novel that such feelings, like the individuals who experience them, are not innately good. Unfortunately, in flat opposition to the author's obvious intentions, we tend to approach Marianne subjectively. Right or wrong, she has our sympathy: she, and our responses to her, are outside Jane Austen's control."[3] Quite apart from the very large assumptions made about the author's aims and purposes, such a reading of the novel strikes me as limited and unsatisfactory. It sets up a moral paradigm to which Jane Austen would no doubt have been happy to acknowledge allegiance—but it does not take adequately into account the extent to which as a human being and specifically as a creative writer she was aware of the incongruities—often painful, often amusing—that arise when one attempts to fit the lives of ordinary, fallible people to preordained moral patterns. It may well be that her consciousness of these incongruities grew as she was writing the book: like most first novels *Sense and Sensibility* is a work of self-discovery. As a result there is a degree of untidiness about the action which leaves us at the conclusion with some dissatisfaction: the neatness with which the two sisters, Marianne and Elinor, are disposed of does not fully accord with our sense of them as living, individual,and to a degree unpredictable people—a sense that has been able to develop only through the imaginative insight and vitality with which Jane Austen has envisaged them, and the dramatic freedom with which she has allowed them to move and grow. But this does not mean that they are out of her control or that, specifically, she does not appreciate the degree to which Marianne has engaged our sympathies. What it does suggest, I think, is that she came to realize in the course of writing and rewriting the novel that the questions it raised were incapable of any final solution—at least within the

[2] *Jane Austen and the War of Ideas* (Oxford, 1975), p. 195.
[3] Ibid., p. 196.

context of the situation with which she originally set herself to work. But the questions themselves have not been evaded. As Ian Watt observes, "Clearly no very simple verdicts are being invited in this early novel,"[4] and "there is every evidence that Jane Austen intended a complex and not a complacent response."[5] Although *Sense and Sensibility* may be a minor piece, it is the work of a major writer; and among its most striking qualities are the creative flexibility, imaginative insight, and human sympathy with which the author renders and reanimates a stereotyped situation.

Her originality displays itself most powerfully and also most subtly in her treatment of the "sensible" sister, Elinor. According to a well-established fictive convention, stories in which "sense" and "sensibility" characters were set against each other were designed to demonstrate the dangers of trusting entirely to the feelings and the merits of being reasonable, conventionally moral, and to a degree hard-headed. Although *Sense and Sensibility* in general conforms to this pattern, the triumph of sense is by no means clear-cut: Elinor and Marianne act not only as foils to but as moderating influences upon each other.[6] By the end of the novel Elinor has learned to acknowledge and respect the power and value of spontaneous feeling just as much as Marianne has learned the necessity of prudence and self-control. But there is more to her spontaneity than this. The freshness, honesty, and strength of Marianne's feelings and the depth of her suffering (it almost brings about her death) arouse in us an unavoidable sense of loss: the price that is paid not merely by Marianne but by society in order to acquire

---

[4]"Sense Triumphant Introduced to Sensibility," in *Jane Austen*: Sense and Sensibility, Pride and Prejudice *and* Mansfield Park: *A Casebook*, ed. B. C. Southam (London, 1976), p. 139.

[5]Ibid., p. 145.

[6]Andrew Wright puts it well: "Marianne . . . does gradually acquire sense; but it is also true that Elinor becomes increasingly sensitive as the book progresses" (*Jane Austen's Novels*, [London, 1954], p. 86). More recently Joseph Wiesenfarth makes the more general point that the novel "is . . . about the reality of sense and sensibility being integral to every life that is meaningfully human, and it is about the necessity of sense and sensibility, blending harmoniously to make life meaningful" (*The Errand of Form* [New York, 1967], p. 53). A. Walton Litz argues interestingly that while this may be the intention of the novel, it is not always achieved (*Jane Austen* [London, 1965], pp. 78–79).

prudence, restraint, and conventional wisdom is substantial. And it is a mistake to assume that Jane Austen is neither aware of nor troubled by this sacrifice. The felt and acknowledged complexity of her attitude is borne out not merely through the power with which Marianne's passion is delineated—to a degree this is what the formula demands—but also and more interestingly by the sympathetic yet at the same time ironic and probing manner in which Elinor's character and the moral and social attitudes she stands for are presented and examined.

In the end it is Elinor who engages most deeply not only our attention but also our feelings. Stuart M. Tave puts it well: "*Sense and Sensibility* is the story of Elinor Dashwood. The action of the novel is hers; it is not Marianne's and it is not equally divided between the sisters; it is Elinor's."[7] Although Marianne's grief and anguish are moving, in the process of the novel they eventually become significant not so much in themselves as in the effect they have on Elinor. The incident in London in which Willoughby publicly rejects Marianne provides a significant instance. Ostensibly, the main focus of our regard is directed toward Marianne: she has been deeply wounded, and it soon becomes clear from the intensity of her grief that hers is no merely sentimental or hysterical reaction. What guarantees the authenticity of her suffering, however, is Elinor's behavior: she also—but uncharacteristically—gives way "to a burst of tears . . . scarcely less violent than Marianne's."[8] And when she reads the letter in which Willoughby brutally breaks off the relationship her response in its own way is almost more angry and shocked than Marianne's:

> She [could not] have supposed Willoughby capable of departing so far from the appearance of every honourable and delicate feeling— so far from the common decorum of a gentleman, as to send a letter so impudently cruel: a letter which, instead of bringing with his desire of a release of any profession of regret, acknowledged no breach of faith, denied all particular affection whatever—a letter of which every line was an insult, and which proclaimed its writer to be deep in hardened villany.

[7]*Some Words of Jane Austen* (Chicago, 1973), p. 96.
[8]*Sense and Sensibility*, ed. Claire Lamont (London, 1970), pp. 157–58. Subsequent references are to this edition and appear in text.

> She paused over it for some time with indignant astonishment; then read it again and again; but every perusal only served to increase her abhorrence of the man, and so bitter were her feelings against him, that she dared not trust herself to speak. [p. 159]

On the evidence Elinor's attitude would not appear to be unreasonable, and her sister's loyalty to the Willoughby she thinks she knows seems sentimental and self-delusory. "'Elinor, I have been cruelly used, but not by Willoughby.' 'Dearest Marianne, who but himself? By whom can he have been instigated?' 'By all the world rather than by his own heart. I could rather believe every creature of my acquaintance leagued together to ruin me in his opinion, than believe his nature capable of such cruelty'" (p. 164). Later in the same conversation Marianne swings over to Elinor's position— "It is too much! Oh! Willoughby, Willoughby, could this be yours! Cruel, cruel—nothing can acquit you. Elinor, nothing can" (p. 165). But her first response is not completely unjustified: Willoughby's heart has not been entirely corrupted, and he has indeed been used. But we are not to learn this fact until later. The revelation comes in what is unquestionably the most powerful scene in the novel— a scene that for all its theatricality is one of the most powerful in the corpus of Jane Austen's fiction—the final confrontation between Elinor and Willoughby. The meeting, be it noted, is with Elinor not Marianne—although Marianne's near fatal illness is what has brought it about. But it is to say the least interesting that Elinor's relationship with Willoughby should in the end be the most significant in the novel—more significant than the relationship between Marianne and Willoughby and more significant than the relationship between Elinor and her own lover, the colorless Edward Ferrars.

The quality of the scene in which Elinor hears Willoughby's confession has been commented on by a number of critics—and this is not surprising.[9] What has not been brought out, however, is the extent to which its effectiveness and force derive from what

---

[9]See in particular Moler, *Austen's Art of Allusion*, pp. 70–71. Litz maintains that "this fine scene is ultimately negated by the reversion to literary stereotypes in the final chapter" (*Jane Austen*, p. 82), and while this may be true it does not detract from the power of the episode in itself.

has gone before, especially from what occurs in Volume I. The way in which the situation, the developing action, and above all the character of Elinor are here presented to the reader is of the greatest importance. The presentation is, one need hardly say, ironical—but the full range and subtlety of the irony are not perhaps immediately apparent, particularly in the case of Elinor. Probably the main reason for this is that the primary objects of Jane Austen's wit and satire stand out so clearly. Marianne's sentimental self-indulgence and her determination to see everything in romantic and literary terms are obvious targets; so too are the insensitive heartiness and oppressive sociability of the Middleton family and the sly hypocrisy of the Steele sisters. Jane Austen's touch in this first volume of her first novel is as delicate and assured as it is anywhere in her later work. She evokes a world which is full of noise, bustle, and people—Sir John Middleton's "prevailing anxiety was the dread of being alone" (p. 136)[10]—but which is, or at least appears to be, essentially empty. It is a world in which privacy seems to be impossible; and the incessant gossip and boisterous teasing, the unrelenting succession of hints, digs, and queries about beaux and lovers, soon induce an atmosphere of mounting claustrophobia. Austen gives this claustrophobia a disturbingly physical dimension in scenes such as the one in which the Middletons, Mrs. Jennings, and the Palmers practically burst in upon Elinor as she sits alone for a few moments in the cottage enjoying the luxury of being able to think about Edward. Sir John doesn't bother to knock at the door but steps across the turf, obliging her "to open the casement to speak to him, though the space was so short between the door and the window as to make it hardly possible to speak at one without being heard at the other" (p. 90); Mrs. Jennings also comes "hallooing to the window"; Lady Middleton and the two strangers walk in through the door; and Mrs. Dashwood and Margaret come down the stairs—everybody talking at once. One is left with the enduring impression that Barton Cottage is rather small and constricted while Barton Hall is excessively noisy.

[10]Sir John cannot understand why, once they are thrown into each other's company, the Misses Steele and Dashwood should not immediately become friends: "to be together was, in his opinion, to be intimate" (p. 107).

Against this background Marianne's genuine (as distinct from her conventional) spontaneity of feeling, Willoughby's apparent directness and lack of stuffiness, and Elinor's sensitive and tactful awareness of other people stand out with refreshing sharpness and clarity. Willoughby, like the Dashwood sisters, brings a breath of clear air and good humor into the artificially polite and strenuously sociable world of Barton; and from his first conventionally gallant entrance onto the scene the aspect of his character that most impresses everybody—including the reader—is its pleasant candor. He is open and direct in his response to people while at the same time preserving an air of tact and friendliness. When he brings Marianne into the cottage after her fall we are told that "he apologized for his intrusion . . . in a manner so frank and so graceful, that his person, which was uncommonly handsome, received additional charms from his voice and expression" (p. 36). The next day, when he calls to inquire after her health, Marianne soon loses her shyness when she sees "that to the perfect good-breeding of the gentleman, he united frankness and vivacity" (p. 39). He has "good abilities, quick imagination, lively spirits, and open, affectionate manners"; and the only fault that Elinor can find in him is a propensity to say what he thinks "without attention to persons or circumstances." But in a world of Middletons, Palmers, Steeles, and John Dashwoods it seems a positive virtue rather than a fault to slight in this way "the forms of worldly propriety" (p. 41). Elinor's reservations about his social recklessness cannot in the end withstand his charm—or his genuine candor. The whole force of their final interview for Elinor lies in the reassurance it gives her that, at least in his feelings for Marianne, he had been honest and sincere—he had not been deliberately deceptive. His "disposition," she is able to tell herself, was "naturally open and honest," and he had "a feeling, affectionate temper." It was "the world [that] had made him extravagant and vain" (p. 290).[11]

[11] Elinor, of course, cannot completely exonerate Willoughby—but the extent to which she now pities him and sympathizes with him is surprising even to her: "Willoughby, in spite of all his faults, excited a degree of commiseration for the sufferings produced by them, which made her think of him as now separated for ever from her family with a tenderness, a regret, rather in proportion, as she soon acknowledged within herself—to his wishes than his merits" (p. 292).

Willoughby may be more of a fool than a knave, but it cannot be denied that he has acted badly. Nonetheless, the genuineness and spontaneity of his feelings set him apart from the cold, self-deluding, and hypocritical villains of the piece, John Dashwood and Robert Ferrars. These are damned completely because they have almost no feelings, no sensibility at all. Willoughby has feelings and, even though he eventually acts against them, he suffers for it. And it is because of this quality that he not only appears to be but is more interesting, a richer character than Edward. From the beginning Edward is set in contrast to Willoughby. Edward suffers from a "want of spirits, of openness, of consistency" (p. 87), and although he takes a much tougher line with Marianne's sentimental enthusiasms than anyone else does, he is not sufficiently confident of the validity of his *own* feelings to be emotionally honest with either Lucy or Elinor. Edward's coolly deflating comments on landscape and the picturesque somehow don't carry as much weight as Willoughby's frank avowal of his affection. And even though he behaves irresponsibly and eventually very cruelly, Willoughby does not in the end deny either his love for Marianne or the weakness and selfishness that have led him into his marriage. He may be a deceiver but he is not a hypocrite. And it is this honesty of feeling to which Elinor responds—almost like a thirsty woman reaching for a glass of water—in their final conversation. Willoughby may have been corrupted by "the world," but not without some sort of fight nor without some understanding of the cost. Edward Ferrars never openly says what he really thinks about his mother or his brother—Willoughby, on the other hand, is prepared to confess to Elinor that his wife's death would give him a "blessed chance at liberty," (p. 291), a chance to think of Marianne again. The thought is reprehensible, the dream is impossible—but the candor is refreshing; and even though Elinor reproves Willoughby for the thought, she cannot prevent herself from entertaining it, if only briefly, in the days after their meeting. "Willoughby, 'poor Willoughby' as she now allowed herself to call him, was constantly in her thoughts . . . She . . . doubted whether . . . [Marianne] could ever be happy with another; and for a moment wished Willoughby a widower. Then, remembering Colonel Brandon, reproved herself . . . and wished any thing rather than Mrs. Willoughby's death" (pp. 293–94). To admit openly to such feelings is not what "the world" would advise; and, despite all his faults, Willoughby, though defeated and corrupted by it, never belongs entirely to "the world." Indeed, in the opening sequences of the novel Willoughby's frankness and lack of cant serve as a means of criticizing the society of which he is a member. In this respect he shows most clearly his lineal connection to Richardson's Lovelace. Lovelace, of course, is a genuine and deliberate villain—but he is also a shrewd exposer of the hypocrisies and vanities of the world.

It is against "the world" that Jane Austen's irony is most obviously directed, especially in the first volume. And the contrast between those who clearly belong to the world and those who do not is so marked and so dramatically effective that our attention is drawn away from another level at which Jane Austen's irony is operating, and operating in a much more gentle and subtle manner. Because the Dashwood family—and to all appearances, Willoughby—are so different from the majority of the people with whom they have to mix, and because we see things for the most part from Elinor's point of view, we do not immediately realize that Elinor herself is also an object—indeed the most important object—of Jane Austen's ironic vision. *Vision* is the operative word: while the way in which Elinor sees herself and the world often coincides with the way in which Jane Austen sees these things and presents them—and thus with the "truth" or "reality" of the fictive world of the novel—there are occasions on which this coincidence is lacking. These occasions, as one would imagine, are of considerable significance; and one of the central elements in the process of the novel is the gradual clarification and realignment of Elinor's vision of herself and the world. By the end of the novel she has, like Emma, learned, though not so painfully, "to understand, thoroughly understand her own heart."[12]

---

[12]*Emma*, ed. Stephen M. Parrish (New York, 1972), p. 283. The parallels between Emma and Elinor are worth exploring: Elinor's false assessment of Mrs. Jennings, for instance, is similar in some ways to Emma's treatment of Miss Bates; and Emma, to much greater and more dangerous degree, is like Elinor "a victim of moral-emotional blindness." (The phrase is Moler's; see *Austen's Art of Allusion*, p. 46.)

The question of how people in general—not merely Elinor—see themselves is of central importance. Equally if not more important is the question of how people wish to be seen by the world, and consequently of how they present themselves to others. The contrast between appearance and reality and the fact that things are not always what they seem, that our eyes and ears can deceive us, is continually emphasized. Mistaken interpretations of character and situation function as one of the primary motive forces of the novel. And they range from things as complex as the assessment of Willoughby by the Dashwoods to things as simple and as broadly theatrical as Marianne's mistaking Edward Ferrars for Willoughby, Elinor's assumption that the lock of hair Edward wears in his ring is from her own head, Mrs. Jennings's mistaking Colonel Brandon's conversation with Elinor for a proposal, and the conclusion that Lucy had married Edward and not Robert Ferrars—a conclusion drawn by the Dashwood's servant who, significantly, does not see Lucy's husband clearly nor hear him speak: "I just see him leaning back in [the carriage], but he did not look up;—he never was a gentleman much for talking" (p. 311). It is indicative of the fundamental unity and coherence of *Sense and Sensibility* that this incident, the most blatant piece of stage machinery in the novel, should be so completely in harmony with its essential thematic preoccupations.

Jane Austen is, of course, concerned throughout her fiction with the conflict between illusion or appearance and reality. But the emphasis given to this theme in *Sense and Sensibility*, particularly in Volume I, seems to be unusually pronounced. As new characters are brought on to the scene we are repeatedly shown how they "appear," what they "seem" to be, how their "address" or "manner" strikes people on first acquaintance. We are then invited—often within the space of a few sentences—to consider whether the "appearance" accurately reflects or expresses the reality. Thus when Sir John Middleton calls on his cousins in their new home we are told that "his countenance was thoroughly good-humoured; and his manners were as friendly as the style of his letter." Then the qualification is added: "Their arrival *seemed* to afford him *real* satisfaction, and their comfort to be an object of *real* solicitude to him

(p. 25; my italics). With Lady Middleton the contrast is made even more sharply. After sending the Dashwoods a "very civil message" and receiving "an invitation equally polite," she calls at the cottage. "They were of course very anxious to see a person on whom so much of their comfort at Barton must depend; and the elegance of her appearance was favourable to their wishes. . . . her face was handsome, her figure tall and striking, and her address graceful. . . . But . . . her visit was long enough to detract something from their first admiration, by shewing that though perfectly well-bred, she was reserved, cold and had nothing to say for herself beyond the most common-place inquiry or remark" (pp. 25–26).

Throughout Volume I the theme is developed and explored. The Dashwood family, for instance, in their response to their acquaintance—and especially, in the end, to Willoughby—come back always to the question of genuineness and integrity. "You must think wretchedly indeed of Willoughby," says Mrs. Dashwood to Elinor, "if after all that has openly passed between them, you can doubt the nature of the terms on which they are together." The key word is "openly"—Willoughby *must be* what he has *appeared* to be. Then she goes on to ask (in expectation of being refuted) the basic question: "Has he been acting a part in his behaviour to your sister all this time?" Elinor's reply, of course, is "No, I cannot think that" (p. 69). But later, in a theoretical discussion of the whole business of assessing people she confesses that she sometimes makes mistakes: "I have frequently detected in myself . . . a total misapprehension of character . . . fancying people so much more gay and grave, or ingenious or stupid than they really are, and I can hardly tell why, or in what the deception originated" (p. 80). The reductio ad absurdum is reached when Elinor asks Mrs. Palmer whether they saw much of Willoughby at Cleveland and "whether they were intimately acquainted with him." "Oh! dear, yes," she replies, "I know him extremely well. . . . Not that I ever spoke to him indeed; but I have seen him for ever in town" (p. 98).

The climactic touch is achieved with the arrival of the Miss Steeles. Sir John enthusiastically commends them as "the sweetest girls in the world, and they are so "doatingly fond" of Lady Middleton's spoiled children that she declares them "to be very agreeable girls" (p. 102). "Agreeable" appears more than once in the account given of the Steele sisters—but Elinor's response is cool: "Their manners were particularly civil, and Elinor soon allowed them credit for some kind of sense, when she saw with what constant and judicious attentions they were making themselves agreeable to Lady Middleton" (p. 103). The way in which Lucy Steele and her sister sweetly suffer the Middleton brats is the occasion of some of the happiest comedy in the novel. But they serve as more than a mere source of amusement. They act, in a fairly obvious way, as foils to the two Dashwood sisters; and less obviously, perhaps, they provide a means by which the moral and social sensibilities of the two girls may be tested and compared.

Marianne's response is quick and positive to the point of rudeness. She "had never much toleration for anything like impertinence, vulgarity, inferiority of parts, or even difference of taste from herself"; and "the invariable coldness of her behaviour towards them" cannot be disguised (p. 109). Elinor, however, allows them "some kind of sense"—a significant allowance, surely, in view of the title and the theme of the novel—and although she has no illusions about the real nature of the Steele sisters, particularly Lucy, she is prepared to play the social game with them. She allows Lucy to involve her in long—and, ultimately, very painful—heart-to-heart discussions, even while admitting to herself that "she could have no lasting satisfaction in the company of a person who joined insincerity with ignorance, and who suffered from "a thorough want of delicacy, of rectitude, and integrity of mind" (p. 110). And when Marianne, who finds it "impossible . . . to say what she did not feel, however trivial the occasion," becomes so disgusted that she cannot even bring herself to take part in social small talk with the sisters, we are told that "upon Elinor therefore the whole task of telling lies when politeness required it, always fell" (p. 105).

"Telling lies"—the phrase is used lightly; and Jane Austen's wry insistence that absolute honesty in conversation would make ordinary social intercourse impossible is amusing rather than horrifying. But, as always, she is perfectly aware of what the words she is using mean. In order to be tactful and prudent Elinor has to tell lies—and the degree of her prevarication is heightened by the very falsity and hypocrisy of the society in which she moves. To compromise with people like Lucy Steele and Lady Middleton is to be corrupted: despite her own toughness and honesty Elinor is seduced into playing the game of polite lying to some degree on their terms. And she does it, of course, very well: in the two "confidential discourses" she has with Lucy about Edward, the honors may appear to be even, but there is no doubt as to who has the real mastery of the situation or the better understanding of it.

And yet it is Elinor's understanding—her "sense"—that at crucial points in the action, lets her down or leads her astray, even though in the end it may be her salvation. This is most obvious in her commitment to decorum. She assumes that, provided one knows what one is doing, provided one is prepared to call a lie a lie, it is often better to preserve the social priorities than to embarrass others through excessive frankness. This is a view that we may safely assume Jane Austen would have endorsed. Commenting on the passage, Tony Tanner observes that "the astringent realism of Jane Austen's vision is [here] clearly in evidence . . . for society is indeed maintained by necessary lies."[13] But it is maintained at a cost—and the way in which the limitations in Elinor's position are exposed and explored suggest very clearly what the cost may be. It is not that she undervalues candor—on the contrary. And her unwillingness to follow Marianne's example and attempt to speak the truth at all times no matter what the penalty may be is understandable and indeed commendable. But to begin with at least she is rather too ready to follow the apparently easier and wiser paths of polite prevarication. And at certain crucial points in the action this has a disproportionately significant effect. There are moments at which if Elinor had been prepared to say what she really thought and felt the outcome of events may have been rather different.

This is demonstrated most clearly in her response to the relationship between Marianne and Willoughby. Her intuitive assessment of the situation is basically sound. As she says to her mother, "I want no proof of their affections . . . but of their engagement I do" (p. 40). And she sensibly points out that the whole problem could be settled very simply: "Why do you not ask Marianne at once whether she is or is not engaged to Willoughby?" (p. 72). But

[13]"Secrecy and Sickness in *Sense and Sensibility*," in *Jane Austen:* Sense and Sensibility, Pride and Prejudice *and* Mansfield Park: *A Casebook*, p. 137.

when her mother refuses to do this for fear of hurting Marianne's feelings, Elinor allows herself to be persuaded against her better judgment to remain silent: "[She] urged the matter farther but in vain; common sense, common care, common prudence, were all sunk in Mrs. Dashwood's romantic delicacy" (p. 73). In one way this is a triumph of "sensibility" over "sense." But in another it is not. To begin with, Mrs. Dashwood's "delicacy" is a false delicacy: it is "romantic." And then Elinor's acquiescence exhibits "some kind of sense"—though not the highest kind. She refuses to commit the impropriety of going against the wishes of her mother. Thus decorum is preserved—as it is when Elinor sustains polite conversation with the Steeles—and Marianne's feelings are, for the moment, spared. And the convenient fiction—the lie—of Willoughby's engagement to Marianne remains unchallenged.

Elinor's greatest error—and it is one that Marianne to begin with, but only briefly, also falls into—occurs in her assessment of Mrs. Jennings. Although at first sight merely a comic buttress to the main action, Mrs. Jennings plays a most significant role in the novel—a role that is similar to and almost as important as that of Miss Bates in *Emma*. Elinor initially is repelled by Mrs. Jennings's apparent vulgarity, her insensitivity to the demands of decorum and propriety, and repelled to such a degree that when the old lady asks them to stay with her in London Elinor at first rejects the invitation not only on her own behalf but also—assuming a right she does not possess—on Marianne's. "Though I think very well of Mrs. Jennings' heart" she tells her mother primly, "she is not a woman whose society can afford us pleasure, or whose protection will give us consequence" (p. 134). She makes a similar and potentially much more disastrous mistake in her initial refusal to take Marianne's illness seriously. Mrs. Jennings, even though she enjoys the morbid drama of the situation, is the one who acts with real sense and prudence: it is she who insists that the apothecary be sent for, that Mrs. Palmer and the baby be got out of the house, and that she stay to help look after the patient—displaying in all this "a kindness of heart that made Elinor really love her" (p. 269). Kindness and common sense—these are what she invariably shows when the chips are down. When Marianne collapses after receiving Willoughby's dismissal, Mrs. Jennings shows "real concern" and "great compassion"—and a healthy feminine contempt for the perfidy of men: "a good-for-nothing fellow! I have no patience with him. . . . I wish with all my soul his wife may plague his heart out . . . if I ever meet him again, I'll give him such a dressing as he has not had this many a day" (p. 166). And once Willoughby is out of the way she immediately starts thinking of how this will improve Colonel Brandon's chances:

> Lord how he'll chuckle over this news! I hope he will come tonight. It will be all to one a better match for your sister. Two thousand a year without debt or drawback—except the little love-child, indeed; aye, I had forgot her; but she may be 'prenticed out at a small cost, and then what does it signify? Delaford is a nice place, I can tell you; exactly what I call a nice old fashioned place, full of comforts and conveniences; quite shut in with great garden walls that are covered with the best fruit-trees in the country: and such a mulberry tree in one corner! Lord, how Charlotte and I did stuff the one time we were there! Then, there is a dove-cote, some delightful stewponds, and a very pretty canal; and everything, in short, that one could wish for. [pp. 170–71]

No nonsense concerning flannel waistcoats and middle age here—this is the real world that Mrs. Jenning is talking about, and doing so with a warmth and concreteness that bring it vividly to life and give the whole novel a solidity and vitality that it would otherwise lack.

This is the world with which Elinor and Marianne and through them the reader have to come to terms. It is also true that they are forced by both social and literary conventions to come to terms with something less—with the accepted priorities and niceties of civilized behavior as the world in Jane Austen's day understood it. The concluding chapters of *Sense and Sensibility* are neat, banal, and to a degree unsatisfying—the characters are reduced to ciphers, and the whole task of telling lies that politeness demands is here deftly picked up by the author herself. But in a real sense this does not matter—we can easily accept the conclusion as a mere conventional formality that cannot and does not destroy the authenticity of what has preceded it. And we can do so because both Elinor and Marianne in the course of the action have had to acknowledge and bear witness to the truth about themselves and their society. In coming to terms with the reality of the world in which they live, a world embodied so substantially in Mrs. Jennings and all she stands for, they also come to terms with, learn to understand, their own natures. In the beginning, if Elinor had possessed more confidence in her feelings and less in her judgment and if Marianne had been more sensible, had acted with prudence, the affair with Willoughby would never have been allowed to develop. But for this to have occurred they would have had to be already the mature women they are to become by the end of the novel—and there would have been no story for Jane Austen to tell. And the reader would have been denied a unique chance of learning something not only about sense and sensibility but also about the human capacity both for deception and for simple honesty of feeling.

A List of
The Published Writings of
Donald Greene

PAUL J. KORSHIN

Journal titles are abbreviated as follows:

ECCB	*The Eighteenth-Century: A Current Bibliography*
ECS	*Eighteenth-Century Studies*
JEGP	*Journal of English and Germanic Philology*
MLN	*Modern Language Notes*
MP	*Modern Philology*
N&Q	*Notes & Queries*
PQ	*Philological Quarterly*
RES	*Review of English Studies*
SBHT	*Studies in Burke and His Time*
TLS	*Times Literary Supplement*
UTQ	*University of Toronto Quarterly*

1949

1 "Johnson's Definition of 'Network.' " *N&Q*, 194 (1949), 538–39.

1950

2 "The Johnsonian Canon: A Neglected Attribution." *PMLA*, 65 (1950), 427–34.

3 " 'Sooth' in Keats, Milton, Shakespeare, and Johnson." *MLN*, 65 (1950), 513–17.

1951

4 "The Adjutant" [a short story], *Atlantic Monthly*, 188 (November 1951), 67–72.

1952

5 "Was Johnson Theatrical Critic of the *Gentleman's Magazine?*" *RES*, N.S. 3 (1952), 158–61.

6 "Logical Structure in Eighteenth-Century Poetry." *PQ*, 21 (1952), 315–36.

1953

7   "Smart, Berkeley, the Scientists, and the Poets. A Note on Eighteenth-Century Anti-Newtonianism." *Journal of the History of Ideas,*
14 (1953), 427–52.

8   "With Sinclair Lewis in Darkest Saskatchewan," *Saskatchewan History,* 6 (1953), 47–52.

9   "Jane Austen and the Peerage." *PMLA,* 68 (1953), 1017–31. Reprinted
in *Jane Austen: A Collection of Critical Essays,* ed. Ian Watt (Twentieth-
Century Views.) (Englewood Cliffs, N.J.: Prentice-Hall, 1962),
pp. 154–65.

10 "Comment and Criticism," pp. 239–313 of Hilda Neatby, *So Little
for the Mind* [a critique of public education in Canada] (Toronto:
Clarke, Irwin & Company, Ltd., 1953). The author cites Donald
Greene in her Preface as "D. M. Greene," credits him with "the
original draft of Chapter VII, and certain passages in other chapters" (p. xi), of which the most easily recognizable is Chapter III,
note 7 (pp. 345–46), a long comment on eighteenth-century English
literature.

1954

11 "Yeats's Byzantium and Johnson's Lichfield." *PQ,* 33 (1954), 433–
35.

12 "Johnson on Garrick." *Johnsonian News Letter,* 14 (September 1954),
10–12. [This is the first of Donald Greene's many similar notes in
JNL from the early 1950s to 1982; the others are not included in
this "List."]

13 Review of: Jean H. Hagstrum, *Samuel Johnson's Literary Criticism*
(Minneapolis, 1952) in *RES,* N.S. 5 (1954), 200–203.

14 Review of: R. W. Chapman, *Johnsonian and Other Essays and Reviews*
(Oxford, 1953), in *RES,* N.S. 5 (1954), 332.

1956

15 "Johnson's Contributions to the Literary Magazine." *RES,* N.S. 7
(1956), 367–92.

16 Review of: James H. Sledd and Gwin J. Kolb, *Dr. Johnson's Dictionary:
Essays in the Biography of a Book* (Chicago, 1955) in *JEGP,* 55 (1956),
331–34.

1957

17 "Dr. Johnson and *An Authentic Account of the Present State of Lisbon.*"
N&Q, 202 (1957), 351.

1958

18 "Johnson and the Harleian Miscellany." *N&Q*, 203 (1958), 304–306.

1959

19 Edited, with George Knox: *Treaty Trip: An Abridgment of Dr. Claude Lewis's Journal of an Expedition Made by Him and His Brother Sinclair Lewis to Northern Saskatchewan and Manitoba in 1924.* Minneapolis: University of Minnesota Press, 1959.

20 "Some Notes on Johnson and the *Gentleman's Magazine.*" *PMLA*, 74 (1959), 75–84.

21 Review of: Edward A. Bloom, *Samuel Johnson in Grub Street* (Providence, 1957) in *MLN*, 74 (1959), 169–72.

1960

22 *The Politics of Samuel Johnson.* New Haven: Yale University Press, 1960. Reprinted: Port Washington, N.Y.: Kennikat Press, 1973.

23 "*The False Alarm* and *Taxation No Tyranny*: Some Further Observations." *Studies in Bibliography*, 13 (1960), 223–31.

24 "Johnsonian Critics." *Essays in Criticism*, 10 (1960), 476–80. There is a continuation of this discussion, ibid., 14 (1964), 427–28.

1961

25 "Becky Sharp and Lord Steyne—Thackeray or Disraeli?" *Nineteenth-Century Fiction*, 16 (1961), 157–64.

26 Review article: "Recent Studies in the Restoration and Eighteenth Century." *Studies in English Literature*, 1 (1961), 115–41 [a survey covering "1959 and most of 1960"].

27 Review of: W. S. Lewis, *Horace Walpole* (New York, 1961) in *New Mexico Quarterly*, 31 (1961), 67–70.

1962

28 "Dr. Johnson's 'Late Conversion': A Reconsideration." In *Johnsonian Studies*, ed. Magdi Wahba (Cairo: distributed by Oxford University Press, 1962), pp. 61–92.

29 Compiled, with James L. Clifford: "A Bibliography of Johnsonian Studies, 1950–1960, With Additions and Corrections, 1887–1950 [and a survey of Johnsonian studies, 1950–1960]." Ibid., pp. 263–350.

30 "Is there a 'Tory' Prose Style?" *Bulletin of the New York Public Library*, 66 (1962), 449–54.

31 Review of: Bertrand A. Goldgar, *The Curse of Party: Swift's Relations with Addison and Steele* (Lincoln, Neb., 1961) in *PQ*, 41 (1962), 629–30.

32 Review of: Sir John Hawkins, *The Life of Samuel Johnson*, ed. Bertram H. Davis (New Haven, 1960) in *New Mexico Quarterly*, 32 (1962), 65–69.

1963

33 "The Development of the Johnson Canon." In *Restoration and Eighteenth-Century Literature: Essays in Honor of Alan Dugald McKillop*, ed. Carroll Camden (Chicago: University of Chicago Press, 1963), pp. 407–27.

34 "Reflections on a Literary Anniversary." *Queen's Quarterly*, 70 (1963), 193–208. Reprinted (abridged) in *Twentieth-Century Interpretations of Boswell's Life of Johnson*, ed. James L. Clifford (Twentieth-Century Views.) (Englewood Cliffs, N.J.: Prentice-Hall, 1970), pp. 97–103.

35 "Samuel Johnson and 'Natural Law.' " *Journal of British Studies*, 2, No. 2 (1963), 59–75 [see also ibid., 84–87, Donald Greene's reply to comment by Peter J. Stanlis and ibid., 3, No. 1 (1963–64), 164–67, further reply to other comments].

1964

36 " 'Dramatic Texture' in Pope." In *From Sensibility to Romanticism: Essays in Honor of F. A. Pottle*, ed. Frederick W. Hilles and Harold Bloom (New Haven: Yale University Press, 1964), pp. 31–54.

37 "The Sin of Pride: A Sketch for a Literary Exploration." *New Mexico Quarterly*, 34 (1964), 9–30.

38 Review of: *The Poetical Works of Richard Savage*, ed. Clarence Tracy (Cambridge, 1962) in *UTQ*, 32 (1964), 411–13.

1965

39 Edited: *Samuel Johnson: A Collection of Critical Essays* (Twentieth-Century Views.). Englewood Cliffs, N.J.: Prentice-Hall, 1965.

40 " 'Pictures to the Mind': Johnson and Imagery." In *Johnson, Boswell, and Their Circle: Essays Presented to Lawrence Fitzroy Powell*, ed. Mary Lascelles et al. (Oxford: Clarendon Press, 1965), pp. 137–58.

41 Review essay: "Theology and the Literary Scholar." *Canadian Journal of Theology*, 11 (1965), 207–16 [review of: Maurice J. Quinlan, *Samuel Johnson: A Layman's Religion* (Madison, Wis., 1964)].

1966

42 Review of: Frank Brady, *Boswell's Political Career* (New Haven, 1965) in *JEGP*, 65 (1966), 198–99.

1967

43   "Augustinianism and Empiricism: A Note on Eighteenth-Century Intellectual History." *ECS*, 1 (1967–68), 33–68 [see also the response by Vivian de Sola Pinto, "Augustan or Augustinian? More Demythologizing Needed?" Ibid., 2 (1968–69), 286–93, and Donald Greene's reply, Ibid., 2 (1968–69), 293–300].

44   "On Swift's Scatological Poems." *Sewanee Review*, 75 (1967), 672–89.

45   "Johnsonian Attributions by Alexander Chalmers." *N&Q*, N.S. 14 (1967), 180–81.

46   Review of: John N. Morris, *Versions of the Self: Studies in English Autobiography from John Bunyan to John Stuart Mill* (New York, 1966), in *PQ*, 46 (1967), 320–21.

1968

47   "No Dull Duty: The Yale Edition of the Works of Samuel Johnson." In *Editing Eighteenth-Century Texts*, ed. D. I. B. Smith (Toronto: University of Toronto Press, 1968), pp. 92–123.

48   "The Uses of Autobiography in the Eighteenth Century." In *Essays in Eighteenth-Century Biography*, ed. Philip B. Daghlian (Bloomington: Indiana University Press, 1968), pp. 43–66.

49   "A Reading Course in Autobiography." Ibid., pp. 111–17.

50   "Western Canadian Literature." *Western American Literature*, 2 (1968), 257–80.

51   Review essay: "Man versus Society." *SBHT*, 10 (1968–69), 1049–60 [review of *Man versus Society in Eighteenth-Century Britain*, ed. James L. Clifford (Cambridge, 1968)].

52   Review of: Arieh Sachs, *Passionate Intelligence: Imagination and Reason in the Work of Samuel Johnson* (Baltimore, 1967) in *SBHT*, 9 (1968), 877–82.

53   Review of: John M. Beattie, *The English Court in the Reign of George I* (London, 1967) in *PQ*, 47 (1968), 297.

54   Review of: Geoffrey Holmes, *English Politics in the Age of Anne* (London, 1967) in *PQ*, 47 (1968), 303–304.

55   Review of: J. H. Plumb, *The Growth of Political Stability in England, 1675–1725* (London, 1967), in *PQ*, 47 (1968), 308–10.

56   Review of: Robert Donald Spector, *English Literary Periodicals and the Climate of Public Opinion during the Seven Years War* (The Hague, 1966) in *PQ*, 47 (1968), 345–46.

1969

57 Review of: Peter Brown, *The Chathamites: A Study in the Relationship between Personalities and Ideas in the Second Half of the Eighteenth Century* (London, 1967) in *SBHT*, 10 (1969), 1170–75.

58 "Johnson on Shakespeare." Correspondence in the *TLS* relating to its (anonymous) review of *Johnson on Shakespeare* (The Yale Edition of the Works of Samuel Johnson, Volumes VII and VIII), 17 July 1969, p. 779; 4 September, p. 979; 6 November, p. 1288; 27 November, p. 1362.

59 Review of: Phillip Harth, *Contexts of Dryden's Thought* (Chicago, 1968) in *ECS*, 2 (1968–69), 478–83.

50 Review of: R. J. White, *The Age of George III* (New York, 1968) in *ECS*, 2 (1968–69), 486–89.

1970

61 *The Age of Exuberance: Backgrounds of Eighteenth-Century English Literature.* New York: Random House, 1970.

62 Compiled, with James L. Clifford: *Samuel Johnson: A Survey and Bibliography of Critical Studies.* Minneapolis: University of Minnesota Press, 1970.

63 *Samuel Johnson.* (Twayne's English Authors Series.) New York: Twayne Publishers, 1970.

64 "What Indeed Was Neoclassicism?" *Journal of British Studies*, 10 (1970), 69–79.

65 Review of: Chester F. Chapin, *The Religious Thought of Samuel Johnson* (Ann Arbor, 1968) in *SBHT*, 11 (1969–70), 1388–95.

66 "Comment on Patrick O'Flaherty, 'Johnson as Rhetorician: The Political Pamphlets of the 1770s.' " *SBHT,* 11 (1969–70), 1585–88 [see also Donald Greene's "Comment on Patrick O'Flaherty's Reply." ibid., 12 (1970–71), 1695–99].

67 Review of: John Harley, *Music in Purcell's London: The Social Background* (London, 1968) in *ECS*, 4 (1970–71), 115–20.

1971

68 Edited, with Clauston Jenkins (textual editor): Jonathan Swift, *Gulliver's Travels.* New York: Bantam Books, 1971 [Donald Greene's contributions include an introduction, notes, and a critical appendix].

69 "Smollett the Historian: A Reappraisal." In *Tobias Smollett: Bicentennial Essays Presented to Lewis M. Knapp*, ed. G. S. Rousseau and Paul Boucé (New York: Oxford University Press, 1971), pp. 25–56.

70 "Samuel Johnson and the Great War for Empire." In *English Writers of the Eighteenth Century: Essays Presented to James L. Clifford by His Students*, ed. John H. Middendorf et al. (New York: Columbia University Press, 1971), pp. 37–65.

71 "The Education of Lemuel Gulliver." In *The Varied Pattern: Studies in the Eighteenth Century*, ed. Peter Hughes and David Williams (Toronto: A. M. Hakkert, 1971), pp. 3–20.

72 "The *Via Media* in an Age of Revolution." Ibid., pp. 297–320.

73 Review essay: "The Making of Boswell's *Life of Johnson*." *SBHT*, 12 (1971), 1812–20 [review of *The Correspondence and Other Papers of James Boswell Relating to the Making of the Life of Johnson*, ed. Marshall Waingrow (New York, 1969)].

74 Review of: Robert H. Hopkins, *The True Genius of Oliver Goldsmith* (Baltimore, 1969) in *SBHT*, 12 (1971), 1933–36.

1972

75 "Augustinianism, Authoritarianism, and Anthropolatry." *ECS*, 5 (1971–72), 456–63 [a reply to Paul C. Davies, "The Debate on Eternal Punishment in Late Seventeenth- and Eighteenth-Century England," ibid., 4 (1970–71), 257–76].

76 Review essay: "The Burdensome Past." *SBHT*, 14 (1972–73), 81–90 [review of W. J. Bate, *The Burden of the Past and the English Poet* (Cambridge, Mass., 1970)].

77 Review of: Richard B. Schwartz, *Samuel Johnson and the New Science* (Madison, Wis., 1971) in *South Atlantic Quarterly*, 71 (1972), 269–71.

78 Review of: *Johnson's Life of Savage*, ed. Clarence Tracy (Oxford, 1971) in *UTQ*, 42 (1972), 82–83.

79 Review of: William L. Sachse, *Restoration England, 1660–1689* (Cambridge, 1971) in *PQ*, 51 (1972), 515–16.

1973

80 "Swift: Some Caveats." In *Studies in the Eighteenth Century. II: Papers Presented at the Second David Nichol Smith Memorial Seminar, Canberra, 1970*, ed. R. F. Brissenden (Canberra: Australian National University Press, 1973), pp. 341–58.

81 "The Wicked Marquess: Disraeli to Thackeray to Waugh." *Evelyn Waugh Newsletter*, 7 (1973), 1–5.

82 Review essay: "A Breakthrough into Spaciousness: *The Collected Poems of Donald Davie*," *Queen's Quarterly*, 80 (1973), 601–15 [review of Donald Davie, *Collected Poems, 1950–1970* (New York, 1972)].

1974

83 "The Proper Language of Poetry: Gray, Johnson, and Others." In *Fearful Joy: Papers from the Conference on Thomas Gray and Humanism at Carleton University*, ed. James Downey and Ben Jones (Montreal: McGill-Queen's University Press, 1974), pp. 85–102.

84 "The Study of Eighteenth-Century Literature: Past, Present, and Future." In *New Approaches to Eighteenth-Century Literature: Papers from the English Institute*, ed. Phillip Harth (New York: Columbia University Press, 1974), pp. 1–32.

85 Review of: Leopold Damrosch, Jr., *Samuel Johnson and the Tragic Sense* (Princeton, 1972) in *MP*, 71 (1973–74), 443–48.

86 Review essay: "Johnson without Boswell," *TLS*, 22 November 1974, pp. 1315–16 [review of John Wain, *Samuel Johnson* (London, 1974)].

1975

87 *Samuel Johnson's Library: An Annotated Guide.* (English Literary Studies, Monograph Series, 1.) Victoria, British Columbia: University of Victoria, 1975.

88 "Jane Austen's Monsters." In *Jane Austen: Bicentenary Essays*, ed. John Halperin (Cambridge: Cambridge University Press, 1975), pp. 262–78.

89 "Jane Austen: The Myth of Limitation." In *Jane Austen Today*, ed. Joel Weinsheimer (Athens, Georgia: University of Georgia Press, 1975), pp. 142–57.

90 Review of: *The Early Biographies of Samuel Johnson*, ed. O M Brack, Jr., and Robert E. Kelley (Iowa City, 1974) in *PQ*, 54 (1975), 966–68.

91 "On Misreading Eighteenth-Century Literature: A Rejoinder," *ECS*, 9 (1975–76), 108–18 [a reply to Leopold Damrosch, Jr., "On Misreading Eighteenth-Century Literature: A Defense," ibid., 8 (1974–75), 202–206; cf. No. 85, above].

92 Review essay: "The Newgate Pastoralist," *TLS*, 6 June 1975, pp. 614–15 [review of *The Poems of John Gay*, ed. Vinton Dearing and Charles E. Beckwith, 2 vols. (Oxford, 1974)].

93 "New Verse by Jane Austen." *Nineteenth-Century Fiction*, 30 (1975), 257–60.

94 Review of: Pat Rogers, *The Augustan Vision* (London, 1974) in *ECS*, 9 (1975–76), 128–33.

1976

95 " 'More than a Necessary Chore': *The Eighteenth Century: A Current*

Bibliography in Retrospect and Prospect." *ECS*, 10 (1976–77), 94–110.

96 Review of: Leon Guilhamet, *The Sincere Ideal: Studies in Sincerity in Eighteenth-Century English Literature* (Montreal, 1974) in *Yearbook of English Studies*, 6 (1976), 273–75.

97 Review of: Joseph Spence, *Letters from the Grand Tour*, ed. Slava Klima (Montreal, 1975) in *Queen's Quarterly*, 83 (1976), 146–47.

98 "Swift's Scatological Poems." *PMLA*, 91 (1976), 464–65 [a "Forum" reply to Thomas B. Gilmore, Jr., "The Comedy of Swift's Scatological Poems," ibid., 91 (1976), 33–43].

99 "Samuel Johnson, Journalist." *Humanities Association Review*, 27 (1976), 441–57 [a memorial issue for Roy M. Wiles]. Reprinted in *Newsletters to Newspapers: Eighteenth-Century Journalism*, ed. Donovan H. Bond and W. Reynolds McLeod (Morgantown: West Virginia University School of Journalism, 1977), pp. 87–101.

1977

100 Edited: Samuel Johnson, *Political Writings*. (The Yale Edition of the Works of Samuel Johnson, X.) New Haven: Yale University Press, 1977.

101 "From Accidie to Neurosis: *The Castle of Indolence* Revisited." In *English Literature in the Age of Disguise*, ed. Maximillian E. Novak (Publications from the Clark Library Professorship, UCLA, 4.) (Berkeley and Los Angeles: University of California Press, 1977), pp. 131–56.

102 "Latitudinarianism and Sensibility: The Genealogy of the 'Man of Feeling' Reconsidered." *MP*, 75 (1977–78), 159–83.

103 Review of: Howard Erskine-Hill, *The Social Milieu of Alexander Pope* (New Haven, 1975) in *Clio*, 7 (1977), 218–20.

104 Review essay: "A Bear by the Tail: The Genesis of the Boswell Industry." *SBHT*, 18 (1977), 114–27 [review of David Buchanan, *The Treasure of Auchinleck* (New York, 1975)].

105 Review of: Bertrand A. Goldgar, *Walpole and the Wits: The Relation of Politics to Literature, 1722–1742* (Lincoln, Neb., 1976) in *TLS*, 24 June 1977, p. 752.

106 Review of: Richard B. Schwartz, *Samuel Johnson and the Problem of Evil* (Madison, Wis., 1975) in *Modern Language Review*, 72 (1977), 664–66.

107 "Who Was Father Rothschild?" *Evelyn Waugh Newsletter*, 11 (1977), 7–9.

1978

108 " 'Tis a Pretty Book, Mr. Boswell, But—." *Georgia Review*, 32 (1978), 17–43.

109 "On *The Pilgrim's Progress*." *Christianity and Literature*, 28, No. 1 (1978), 11–13.

110 Introduction to *The Renaissance Man in the Eighteenth Century* (Los Angeles: William Andrews Clark Memorial Library, 1978), pp. v–xi.

111 Review of: Walter Jackson Bate, *Samuel Johnson* (New York, 1977) in *The American Scholar*, 47 (1978), 277–81.

112 Review of: William Edinger, *Samuel Johnson and Poetic Style* (Chicago, 1977) in *TLS*, 28 July 1978, p. 858.

113 Review of: Helen Louise McGuffie, *Samuel Johnson in the British Press, 1749–1784: A Chronological Checklist* (New York, 1976) in *SBHT*, 19 (1978), 235–38.

114 Review of: Jack Lindsay, *Hogarth: His Art and His World* (London, 1977) in *Queen's Quarterly*, 85 (1978–79), 692–94.

115 Review of: Robin Furneaux, *William Wilberforce* (London, 1974) in *ECCB*, N.S. 1 (1975; published 1978), 125–26.

116 Review of: Victor D. Sutch, *Gilbert Sheldon: Architect of Anglican Survival, 1640–1675* (The Hague, 1973) in *ECCB*, N.S. 1 (1975; published 1978), 150–52.

117 Review of: *The Oxford Book of Literary Anecdotes*, ed. James Sutherland (Oxford, 1975) in *ECCB*, N.S. 1 (1975; published 1978), 240–41.

1979

118 "The Term 'Conceit' in Johnson's Literary Criticism." In *Evidence in Literary Scholarship: Essays in Memory of James Marshall Osborn*, ed. René Wellek and Alvaro Ribeiro (Oxford: Clarendon Press, 1979), pp. 337–51.

119 "Voltaire and Johnson." In *Enlightenment Essays in Honor of Lester G. Crocker*, ed. Virgil Topazio and Alfred J. Bingham (Oxford: Voltaire Foundation, 1979), pp. 111–31.

120 "Do We Need a Biography of Johnson's 'Boswell' Years?" *Modern Language Studies*, 9 (1979), 128–36.

121 "The Great Long Beach Waugh Memorial." *Evelyn Waugh Newsletter*, 13, No. 1 (1979), 1–4.

122 "Two Small Notes." *Evelyn Waugh Newsletter*, 13, No. 3 (1979), 6–7.

123 "Periodical Publications in Post-Restoration and Eighteenth-Century Studies." *Scriblerian*, 11 (1979), 87–91.

124 Review of: *Johnson on Johnson; A Selection of the Personal and Autobiographical Writings of Samuel Johnson*, Introd. John Wain (London, 1976) in *ECCB*, N.S. 2 (1976; published 1979), 310–11.

1980

125 "James Lowry Clifford, 1901–1978." *The New Rambler*, Serial C, No. 19 (1978; published 1980), 3–14.

126 "William Cowper." *N&Q*, N.S. 27 (1980), 421–22 ["Replies"].

127 Review of: John Butt, *The Mid-Eighteenth Century*, ed. and completed by Geoffrey Carnall (Oxford History of English Literature, VIII.) (Oxford, 1979) in *English Language Notes*, 18 (1980), 58–65.

1981

128 "Alexander Pope and the Constant Muse." *Forum: A Journal of the Humanities and Fine Arts*, 17, No. 1 (Winter 1979; published 1981), 21–28.

129 Review of: Brian McCrea, *Henry Fielding and the Politics of Mid Eighteenth-Century England* (Athens, Georgia, 1981) in *TLS*, 11 September 1981, p. 1028.

130 Review of: Jonathan Swift, *Gulliver's Travels: A Facsimile Reproduction of a Large-Paper Copy of the First Edition . . .*, Introd. by Colin McKelvie (Delmar, N.Y., 1976) in *ECCB*, N.S. 3 (1977; published 1981), 283–85.

131 Review of: Johnson, *Selected Poetry and Prose*, ed. Frank Brady and W. K. Wimsatt, Jr. (Berkeley and Los Angeles, 1977) in *ECCB*, N.S. 4 (1978; published 1981), 354–55.

1982

132 "Evelyn Waugh's Hollywood." *Evelyn Waugh Newsletter*, 16, no. 3 (1982), 1–4.

133 "Eighteenth-Century Poetry." *PMLA*, 97 (1982), 871–72 [a "Forum" contribution].

1983

134 "Johnson, Stoicism, and the Good Life." In *The Unknown Samuel Johnson*, ed. John T. Burke and Robert Kay (Madison: University of Wisconsin Press, 1983), pp. 16–37.

135 Review of: Linda Colley, *In Defence of Oligarchy: The Tory Party 1714–60* (Cambridge, 1982) in *The American Scholar*, 52 (1983), 422–27.

136 Review of: Roger L. Emerson, Gilles Girard, and Roseann Runte, eds., *Man and Nature*. Proceedings of the Canadian Society for Eighteenth-Century Studies, Vol. I (London, Ontario, 1982) in *UTQ*, 52 (1983), 416–19.

1984

137 Edited: *Samuel Johnson* (The Oxford Authors.) Oxford: Oxford University Press, 1984 [an anthology of Johnson's writings].

Miscellaneous Early Writing

DONALD GREENE

The Editors asked Donald Greene for assistance in locating and preparing a list of his juvenilia, and in response he provided us with the following account.

Like others who came to academia late—thanks, in my case, to the Great Depression and drought of the 1930s, and then World War II—I did a fair amount of pre- and nonacademic writing, chiefly in the hope of earning a few much-needed bucks. Most of it is pretty forgettable, but the Editors have asked me to write a note about it, and this is the result.

I can't boast anything so striking as the first entry in the late James L. Clifford's bibliography, *Experiments in Atomic Science for Amateurs*, incorporating articles contributed in his teens to popular scientific journals, or as the seven-year-old Evelyn Waugh's uncompleted first novel, a hair-raising adventure story entitled *The Curse of the Horse Race*. But, like Waugh, I came from a family infected with the *cacoethes scribendi*. A female cousin of my father was for decades the chief agricultural reporter of the Montreal *Family Herald and Weekly Star*, staple reading for farmers throughout Canada. My mother contributed short stories and articles to the weekly Literary Supplement of the *Winnipeg Free Press*, which were praised by her fellow contributor, the then unknown Frederick Philip Grove. My father was an incurable writer of violent letters to the editors of western Canadian newspapers on controversial issues in current party politics. One of my uncles, among much else, published (in monthly installments, in a short-lived western magazine) a tedious novel based on his experiences as a young Anglican missionary in the pioneering days of the Canadian prairies. Still another uncle composed a lyric poem tenderly descriptive of the beauties of my native city of Moose Jaw, Saskatchewan, which he persuaded a friend to set to music, and which for many years he vainly urged the city fathers to adopt as its official anthem. I was not immune from the family disease.

I still have a copy of my first "publication," at the age of seven—the first, and only, issue of a newspaper reporting the current events of the tiny Saskatchewan village where we then lived. A business associate of my father's had his secretary transcribe it in neat typing, with small illustrations beside the news items, many of which had to do with the pregnancies and other vicissitudes of the matriarchal village cat, Lady McTavish, and her offspring, Princess, Duchess, and Countess McTavish. From about nine to fourteen, I indefatigably contributed prose and poetry to the weekly "children's supplement" of the Regina, Saskatchewan, *Leader Post*—the "Torchbearers' Magazine" a rather remarkable publication, all written by pre-teens and early teenagers, some of whom became nationally-known Canadian writers. I was once even runner-up in the annual election for its post of "Poet Laureate."

In my early teens I used to pick up a few dollars contributing social items about local doings to the provincial newspapers. When I was seventeen I struck a blow for the freedom of the press by volunteering to furnish the *Leader Post*, at space rates, regular accounts of social and athletic doings at the Regina Normal School, which I had just entered. When my first column appeared, I was called into the office of the principal, and given a royal dressing down: he, the principal, had always appointed the student reporter, and would continue to do so; I was to cease and desist from my activity forthwith. I reported this to the city editor (Chester Bloom, later a distinguished name in Canadian journalism), and told him that it looked like a choice between giving up my budding journalistic career and expulsion from the Normal School. Bloom picked up his telephone, got hold of the principal, and read him a powerful lecture on the independence of the press: the newspaper would decide whom it wanted to do its reporting, not some outside jack-in-office. For a long time after that, when I passed the principal in the hall, I was greeted with a scowl, and shivered in my shoes. But I was allowed to go on writing up the school's activities, and gratefully collected my pittance during the rest of the year.

After graduation from the one-year Normal program, I earned my living teaching in one-roomed rural elementary schools. So did my mother. One of our recurring problems was the organization of the annual Christmas concert by the pupils. This was the cultural event of the year in backwoods farming communities, and there was considerable competition among the various schools as to which could produce the most successful one. One of our main difficulties was the lack of short plays (or "dialogues" as they were called) for youthful performers; the available repertoire in print was decades old and not very funny. We decided to write our own—situation comedies they would now be called—on topical themes; for instance, a burlesque of the "hype" about the birth of the Dionne quintuplets. My mother in particular was unscrupulous in laying on the slapstick. A small publishing firm heard of them and paid us $10 outright for each of the two dozen they published—a great windfall in the 1930s. We should have held out for a royalty arrangement, for they proved immensely popular; I wouldn't be surprised if some of them are still making the rounds of western Canadian rural school systems.

For a year I contributed a monthly column to the *Saskatchewan Teacher* of advice on teaching elementary English grammar and usage, with practical exercises. Some of this I later incorporated into a systematic elementary textbook in grammar, which I used, in mimeographed form, not only in my precollege teaching, but in later university "bonehead English" courses. Occasionally I still take it out and think it pedagogically sound; perhaps some day, when I've finished with Johnson and his contemporaries, I'll revise it and offer it to a national publisher. When I finally made it to college, I flooded the student magazine with fiction, nonfiction, and drama. As a junior instructor I reviewed current novels for the local newspaper and published in it fulminations about the abominable preparation of our freshmen, which got me into trouble with the university administration. I even published "poetry" in Canadian "little magazines."

The location of this last, in particular, I have no intention of disclosing, and, on the whole, the editors do well to limit their formal listing to things published after I received my Master of Arts degree.

Index

Godoy, Manuel de, 404
Goethe, Johann Wolfgang von, *Werther*, 356
Goldsmith, Oliver, 21, 139, 178, 182, 183, 184, 189, 288; *The Deserted Village*, 195; *The Traveller*, 183, 189, 195, 198; *The Vicar of Wakefield*, 184, 189–90, 247–48
Goldstein, Malcolm, 126
Gordon, George, Lord, 337
Goring, Jeremy, 347 n.34
Gossman, Lionel, 371; *French Society and Culture*, 371
Goudsmit, Samuel A., 156 n.38
Gould, Rupert T., 154 n.35
Goulemot, J. M., 371 n.12
Goyard-Fabre, Simone, 372; *La philosophie des lumières*, 372
Grainger, James, 182, 183; *Sugar Cane*, 183, 191
Graves, Richard, 238; *The Spiritual Quixote*, 238
Gray, James, 305 n.33
Gray, Thomas, 288
Gray's Inn Journal, 181
Greene, Donald, xi–xx, 36 n.26, 146 n.12, 165 n.57, 206 n.11, 273 n.7, 289 n.2, 290, 300 n.26, 351, 352, 377n, 441 n.28; "The Adjutant," xx; *The Age of Exuberance*, 371; "Augustinianism and Empiricism," xviii, 75 n.6; "From Accidie to Neurosis," xx; "Logical Structure in Eighteenth-Century Poetry," xiii; *The Politics of Samuel Johnson*, xiv; "The Sin of Pride," xx; "Smart, Berkeley, the Scientists, and the Poets," 61 n.8; "With Sinclair Lewis in Darkest Saskatchewan," xx
Greene, Edward Burnaby, 94, 99, 100, 103
Gregory, Francis, 4
Grenville, William Wyndham, 393, 396, 397, 401, 402, 409, 410, 411, 412 n.35, 413–18, 422–26, 428–31
Grimsley, Ronald, 361 n.6
Grossman, Mordecai, 361 n.6
Grotius, Hugo, 299, 305, 306, 380
Gsellius, George Conrad, 229

Guardi, Francesco, 437
Gueinzius, Christianus, 380
Gusdorf, Georges, 355–58, 360; *L'Avènement des sciences humaines . . .*, 356–57; *Dieu, la nature, l'homme . . .*, 356; *Les Principes de la pensée . . .*, 355–56
Guttridge, C. H., 335
Gwynn, John, 198

Hagstrum, Jean H., 434 n.2, 435 n.8, 440 n.26
Hall, Robert, *Christianity Consistent with a Love of Freedom*, 341
Haller, William, 75 n.8, 78 n.10
Halley, Edmund, 44
Halsband, Robert, 106 n.27, 241 n.42
Hamilton, Alexander, 391, 394, 406, 419
Hammer, John, 347
Hammond, George, 393–95, 400, 401, 406, 409 n.31, 413, 418–20, 423–26, 428, 431 n.59
Hankins, Thomas L., 361 n.6
Hanmer, Thomas, 252 n.4, 254, 257, 258–68
Hanzo, Thomas, 67 n.13
Hardy, John P., 338 n.30
Hardy, Thomas, 59
Hare, Francis, 75 n.6
Harley, Robert, 1st earl of Oxford, 177 n.13
Harrington, John, 366
Harris, John, 383; *Lexicon Technicum*, 383
Harrison, Elizabeth, 182; *Miscellanies*, 182, 186
Harrison, John, 153
Harth, Phillip, 25 n.6, 39 n.19
Hartley, David, 41, 42–43, 47, 49, 50, 53, 55, 56, 361 n.5
Haslam, John, 272 n.4
Hawkesbury, Charles Jenkinson, Lord, 408, 411 n.33, 419, 420 n.45
Hawkesworth, John, 181, 182, 184, 189, 219; *Almoran and Hamet*, 239, 242, 247